critical globalization studies

critical globalization studies

edited by

richard p. appelbaum
william i. robinson

Routledge
Taylor & Francis Group

NEW YORK AND LONDON

Published in 2005 by
Routledge
Taylor & Francis Group
270 Madison Avenue
New York, NY 10016
www.routledge-ny.com

Published in Great Britain by
Routledge
Taylor & Francis Group
2 Park Square
Milton Park, Abingdon
Oxon OX14 4RN
www.routledge.co.uk

10 9 8 7 6 5 4 3 2 1

Library of Congress Cataloging-in-Publication Data
    Critical globalization studies / edited by Richard P. Appelbaum and William I. Robinson.
        p. cm.
    Includes bibliographical references and index.
    ISBN 0-415-94961-0 (hc : alk. paper) -- ISBN 0-415-94962-9 (pb : alk. paper) 1. Anti-globalization movement. 2. Globalization. 3. Social justice. 4. Human rights. 5. Power (Social sciences) 6. Social conflict. I. Appelbaum, Richard P. II. Robinson, William I.

    HN17.5.C75 2004
    303.48'4--dc22

2004010709

Acknowledgments

It would be utterly impossible to acknowledge all of those people whose time and effort have gone into seeing this book come to fruition. Above all, we want to express a very special gratitude to an extraordinary group of young scholar-activists who assisted us in organizing a four-day conference held at the University of California at Santa Barbara to debate the future of globalization. The conference, held May 1–4, 2003, under the title "Towards a Critical Globalization Studies: Continued Debates, New Directions, Neglected Topics," was the original inspiration for this book. It brought together some 100 leading social science and humanities scholars, key public intellectuals, and global justice activists from around the world, a number of whom have contributed to the present volume. The conference would not have been possible without the assistance of our graduate student, Jessica Taft, who worked nearly round-the-clock, week on end, with great cheer, intelligence, and remarkable skill. We are also grateful for the selfless commitment of our conference staff and team of student volunteers, among them (in alphabetical order): Ryan Alaniz; Aidee Bugarin; Nick George; Joy Hylton; Edwin Lopez; Adriana Mcelwain; Erin Middleton; Rebecca Oloh; Amandeep Sandhu; Hugo Santos; and Matthew Tompkins. Edwin Lopez subsequently worked with remarkable diligence and efficiency as an editorial assistant in the preparation of the volume. The members of this marvelous team, with their unbounded enthusiasm and commitment to combining academic pursuits with the struggle for social justice, are a shining example of a new generation of scholar-activists. It is to them, and the hope that we place in their generation for a better world, that we dedicate this volume.

We also want to acknowledge the financial assistance provided by a number of offices at UC–Santa Barbara for the conference and for subsequent editorial work on this volume. In particular, we are grateful to: Chancellor Henry Yang; the offices of the Executive Vice-Chancellor, the Vice-Chancellor for Research, the Provost of the College of Letters and Sciences, and the Deans of Social Science and Humanities and Fine Arts; the Global and International Studies Program; the Graduate Division; the Interdisciplinary Humanities Center; the Institute for Social, Behavioral, and Economic Research, including its Centers for Global Studies and Middle East Studies; the Walter H. Capps Center for the Study of Religion, the Multicultural Center; the Hull Chair of Women's Studies; the Academic Senate; the Office of Instructional Development; and the Departments of Anthropology, Asian-American Studies, Chicano Studies, Law and Society, History, Political Science, and Sociology. We also thank UC-Riverside's Institute for Research on World-Systems for its financial support.

Many thanks as well to our editor at Routledge Press, David McBride, and to our project editor, Elise Oranges.

Finally, we owe very special and affectionate thanks to our wives, Marielle Robinson and Karen Shapiro, for their support and patience, and to Karen for her excellent graphic design of the poster and conference materials.

William I. Robinson
Richard P. Appelbaum

Contents

New Directions in Globalization Research and Implications of Globalization for Scholarship in the Academy

Linking Globalization Studies to Global Resistance Movements: Marginalized Voices and Neglected Topics

Introduction: Toward a Critical Globalization Studies — Continued Debates, New Directions, Neglected Topics

Richard P. Appelbaum and William I. Robinson

How many times have we heard the refrain, "Globalization has become a buzzword"? What originated as an arcane term of the corporate world of the 1960s had by the late 1980s become established in academia, and by the 1990s was no less than a catchphrase of public discourse. Yet, how we come to grips with the concept of globalization is by no means clear. It has generated raging debate among academics, no less intense than the political conflicts that the process has generated. About all that scholars and political actors across the board are likely to agree upon is that the world has become more interconnected in recent years, and that our awareness of these interconnections has heightened. There is also an apparent sense that the troubled state of humanity in the new century — escalating political military conflict, unprecedented social inequalities, cultural clashes, the disintegration of old dogmas, environmental disasters, and a crisis-ridden global economy — is somehow bound up with globalization. It has become abundantly clear that behind the multiple fates of peoples and nations is the fate of a humanity internally divided — yet a single humanity. If we are to attempt to understand the world in the new century, we cannot but come to grips with the concept of globalization.

The academic field of global studies emerged in the last decade of the twentieth century in response to the impact of new economic, social, technical, and cultural globalizing forces around the world. It is related to the older, more established field of international studies, which emerged in the 1950s in response to the establishment of new nation-states and a new world-system of nationalities. But global studies has a substantially different emphasis than its predecessor. Global studies views the world as a single interactive system, rather than as the interplay of discrete nation-states. Its focus is on transnational processes, interactions, and flows, rather than international relations, and on new sets of theoretical, historical, epistemological, and even philosophical questions posed by emergent transnational realities. Moreover, its analytic perspectives in studying this phenomenon are not rooted in the single field of political science, but are based on theoretical literature from a variety of disciplines in both the social sciences and the humanities.

In the 1990s the field of global studies expanded exponentially with an explosion of interest in studies of various aspects of globalization. This interest has fostered the development of numerous book series and journals that deal exclusively with global studies and globalization, not to mention special issues of major academic journals that have been dedicated to the topic, and a veritable boom in books on the subject (Our quick search on Amazon.com in November 2003 of *globalization* came up with an incredible 11,102 titles!). Scholars in England established in 2000 a professional organization, the Global Studies Association, with offices in Manchester, England, and branch chapters established or planned in Europe, North America, Asia, and elsewhere.

It is clear that a new globalization studies is emerging. The process of globalization, and the raging debates on what this process is all about, are transforming every discipline in the social sciences and the humanities. Globalization is reshaping how we have traditionally gone about studying the social world and human culture. It has major implications for all areas, from ethnic studies to area studies, from literature and the arts to language and cultural studies, from economics and sociology to history, anthropology, law, business administration, race and ethnic studies, and women's studies. And as globalization studies has grown, it has become increasingly institutionalized in the academy. Research institutes on global studies were established in the 1990s at numerous universities around the world. Indeed, it is rare these days to find a single major center of higher education that does not boast of a global studies center, program, or research unit. The typical university curriculum now offers dozens, and even hundreds, of courses on the subject. At the University of California at Santa Barbara, our home institution, a Program in Global and International Studies was created in 1995 to house various area studies programs and majors, including (in 1998) a global studies major, one of the first at a major research university. By 2003 there were 750 students at the University of California at Santa Barbara majoring in global studies, and plans to launch the first-ever master's degree program in global studies.

But is it enough to *study* globalization? Most people around the world do not have the privilege of studying the deep-seated structural processes that shape their lives. And those that have developed an awareness of the potential or actual devastating effects of the process are not scholars, but leaders of diverse communities around the world. Indeed, parallel to the appearance of globalization studies in the academy, a powerful global justice movement has taken shape out of countless resistance struggles. A new transnational social activism is increasingly a potent political force in the global equation.

What is the relevance of globalization studies to the global justice movement? As academics at the University of California at Santa Barbara, whose scholarly work has been deeply informed by our political activism (and, indeed, vice versa), we have been engaged in building a program in globalization studies that is centrally concerned with issues of social justice. This volume is a natural offshoot of the effort to develop a globalization studies centrally concerned with global justice. To be successful, such an effort would have to seek dual objectives. One would be to scrutinize and recast the emerging field of globalization studies; the other, to build bridges between this field and the global justice movement. It is clear that in order for a globalization studies to have any meaning, it needs to be linked to an exploration of the relationship between global studies in the academy and the actual process of globalization. More specifically, we believe it important to build bridges between the academic study of globalization and the policymakers, social justice activists, and advocacy movements that are directly engaged with the processes of globalization. Any attempt to understand the world, and to act in the world as social agents, must contemplate globalization both as a concept and as a process.

We believe that the dual objectives of understanding globalization and engaging in global social activism can best be expressed in the idea of a critical globalization studies. We believe that as scholars it is incumbent upon us to explore the relevance of academic research to the burning political issues and social struggles of our epoch, and to the many conflicts, hardships, and hopes bound up with globalization. More directly stated, we are not indifferent observers studying globalization as a sort of detached academic exercise. Rather, we are passionately concerned with the adverse impact of globalization on billions of people as well as on our increasingly stressed planetary ecology. Moreover, we believe that it is our obligation as scholars to place an understanding of the multifaceted processes of globalization in the service of those individuals and organizations that are dedicated to fighting its harsh edges. We are not antiglobalists, but we are staunchly opposed to the highly predatory forms that globalization has assumed throughout history, and particularly during the past quarter century.[1]

This volume brings together some of the leading scholars and activists concerned with these matters. The objective of this collection of essays is to take a systematic look at what academics and activists have been debating regarding globalization, to identify the novel types of inquiry and activism that both communities are — or should be — concerned with. The volume examines topics that too often have been kept at the margins, or even fallen by the wayside, and seeks to shed light on a number of broad questions. In the discussion below, we group these under five broad headings, which correspond to the five sections in this collection:

1. What is a critical globalization studies?
2. The debate on globalization — competing approaches and perspectives.
3. What is the nature of power and conflict in the world today?
4. New directions in globalization research and implications of globalization for scholarship in the academy.
5. Linking the study of globalization to global resistance movements — marginalized voices and neglected topics.

Globalization has provided not just a time of change and turbulence but also enormous opportunities — and risks — for scholars and scholar-activists. This is truly an exciting time to be creating a new field of study and action — an excitement we believe is reflected in the chapters of this book.

What Is a Critical Globalization Studies?

The very notion of globalization is problematic. There are a multitude of partial, divergent, and often contradictory claims surrounding the concept. Considering the political implications of these claims, it is clear that, at the least, globalization has become what we refer to as an essentially contested concept (Robinson, 2004: 1). This means that because there is no consensus on what the term refers to, there are competing definitions, each of which gives us a distinct interpretation of social reality. Does globalization, for instance, refer to a process or to a condition? How novel is the current wave of globalization? Is the core of the process economic, political, or cultural? Is it best to see globalization as the continuation of earlier historical processes, as quantitative changes? Or should we see it as a discontinuity, as a qualitative change, as an entirely new epoch?

Debate over the meaning of essentially contested concepts such as globalization goes beyond mere semantics. The contending battleground of such concepts is a leading edge of political conflict. Their meanings are closely related to the problems they seek to discuss and what kind of social action people will engage in. In our view, there are two questions with regard to globalization that stand out most. First, are these changes helpful for most people in the world or are they harmful? And second, is the process intractable, or can it be altered? Scholars who study globalization do not agree on these matters. Most scholars and commentators would agree, however, that the pace of social change and transformation worldwide seems to have quickened dramatically in the latter decades of the twentieth century, and that this social change is related to deepening connections among peoples and countries around the world. Most of the contributors to the present volume would go further, agreeing that the dominant version of globalization imposedfrom above constitutes an assault on the world's people, that there is nothing inevitable and foregone about the current course of history, and that human agency makes the whole process contested and open-ended. Perhaps the contributors would agree as well that these premises would form part of the conception of a critical globalization studies. But beyond these premises debate begins.

The first part of this volume therefore brings together three contributions that attempt to define a critical globalization studies. Susan George, a prominent leader of the global justice movement and herself an accomplished scholar, appropriately opens the collection (chapter 1) asking, "What should be the role and the responsibilities of academia and intellectuals in the global justice movement?" Academics, she observes, "are mostly called upon to transmit the received wisdom" and tend to "acquire a vested interest in mainstream interpretations of a given reality." The responsibility of the progressive academic, she argues, is to "make explicit these presuppositions and make visible this ideological framework [of mainstream interpretations], particularly for their students." She goes on to give three pieces of advice to academics who wish to make a relevant contribution to progressive social change. First, they should be more concerned with studying the rich and powerful than the poor and powerless. "The poor and powerless," in her words, "already know what is wrong with their lives and those who want to help them should analyze the forces that keep them poor and powerless. Better a sociology of the Pentagon or the Houston country club than of single mothers or L.A. gangs." Second, they should use whatever methods seem to yield results or a fresh perspective, not necessarily the standard methodology of the discipline. And third, intellectuals whose goal is to contribute to social movements have to be more rigorous than their mainstream colleagues.

Robinson and Mittelman (chapter 2 and chapter 3) carry forward these themes by attempting to identify what distinguishes a critical globalization studies. For Robinson, two features stand out: (1) the subversive nature of its thought in relation to the status quo, and (2) the linkage (actual or attempted) of theory to practice, or the grounding of a critical globalization studies in praxis, in a theoretically informed practice. For his part, Mittelman asks "precisely what kind of knowledge about globalization is and should be summoned" by a critical globalization studies? The components of a critical globalization studies, he argues, are reflexivity, historicism, decentering, crossovers between social inquiry and other streams of knowledge, and transformative practices. And similar to Robinson, he suggests that a critical orientation "calls for not only deconstructing extant knowledge and practice but also constructing new knowledge about what exists and what ought to exist on the basis of transformed relations of power."

The Debate on Globalization: Competing Approaches and Perspectives

If it is true that globalization is one of the key concepts of the twenty-first century, it is also true that it is one of the most hotly debated and contested. One principal point of contention that surely gets to the heart of the underlying ontological issue is the temporal dimension of globalization. Is it a very old or a relatively new process? How we answer this question will shape what we understand when we speak of globalization, or if we even feel that the term is worthwhile, or simply superfluous and misleading. We can identify three approaches in the debate (Robertson, 1992. In the first, globalization has been underway since the dawn of history, with a sudden recent acceleration. In this version, the process dates back at least 5,000 years, with the rise of exchange across societies, the spread of religious systems, world-cultural diffusion, and so forth. In the second approach, globalization is coterminous with the spread and development of capitalism and modernity, an approach closely associated with much (but not all) of the scholarship in world-system theory, and theories of the modern. In the third, globalization is a more recent phenomenon associated with social changes of the late twentieth and early twenty-first centuries. Behind the temporal question are significant epistemological issues that frame the assumptions we make about the social world, what cognitive lenses we peer through, and therefore, what conclusions about the contemporary social world we are likely to draw. Sooner or later we will need to ask, is there something new going on in the world that cannot be adequately explained by extant theories?

Although the popular literature portrays the world as experiencing a degree of global economic and political interdependency unprecedented in human history, there is much debate among scholars over the degree to which global integration is in fact unprecedented. In perhaps the most oft-cited study, Hirst and Thompson (1999), for example, argued that global trade and other measures of economic integration were at comparable levels in the late nineteenth century, and that most of the current global increase in trade and direct foreign investment has been among the core advanced economies, rather than incorporating the world's periphery. This thesis, which emphasizes continuity with the past rather than a radical rupture, is advanced in a somewhat different form by Chase-Dunn, Kawano, and Brewer (2000), whose analysis of the relationship between imports and gross domestic product in a broad range of countries suggests that the current wave of globalization actually began as early as 1830, with peaks of ever-increasing amplitude in the 1880s, 1920s, and today.

This line of thinking, consistent with world-systems theory's emphasis on long waves or cycles in the world economy, contrasts with the arguments of Robinson (2001, 2003, 2004) and Sklair (1999, 2000, 2001), who view the current wave of globalization as fundamentally transforming the nature of global economics and politics, giving rise to a truly global society of transnational businesses, institutions of governance, social classes, and cultural practices. According to this line of reasoning, the explosive rise of transnational corporations has led to the parallel rise of a transnational capitalist class, one that lacks national loyalty and indeed sometimes operates against the apparent interests of powerful states such as the United States, and increasingly exerts its power through such transnational governing bodies such as the World Trade Organization (WTO). In this view, the rise of such transnational actors and institutions calls for a paradigm shift away from "nation-state centric" thinking, and towards a more global framework. National, political, and economic institutions are seen as being transformed by globalization, as they become increasingly articulated in the emerging transnational institutions of the world economy.

A parallel set of challenging issues can be raised with regard to other actors and institutions, from states to social movement organizations. Globalization poses a particular challenge to legal institutions, for example, since laws historically are national in origin and enforced in national courts (Appelbaum, Felstiner, and Gessner, 2001). To what extent are transnational legal frameworks and institutions reinforcing — or even supplanting — national ones? From the enforcement of global neoliberal trade practices through the Dispute Resolution Mechanism of the WTO, to the trial of accused war criminals in the International Criminal Court, national legal sovereignty is being challenged by transnational juridical and quasi-juridical bodies (Falk et al., 2002). Moreover, a range of informal mechanisms is emerging to provide predictability in transnational business relations, including the increasing privatization of regulation and enforcement (Appelbaum, 1998, 2004 [this volume]; O'Rourke, 2003).

The second set of contributions takes up a range of these debates. Two of the five contributions in this section examine the relationship between world-system theory and recent variants of globalization theory. Arrighi (chapter 4) observes that world-systems scholars "were not shy in claiming that the explosion [of globalization discourse] vindicated their often frowned-upon insistence on the transnational interconnectedness of national communities and developments." Focusing on what, for him, are the two main substantive contentions of world-systems theorists that globalization scholars have questioned — the persistence of the core-periphery structure of the global political economy, and the long-term, large-scale nature of the processes that have culminated in contemporary globalization — Arrighi reasserts the validity of these contentions by drawing on research by himself and others within and outside the world-systems perspective. The core-periphery structure, he argues, shows few signs of being superseded by other forms of stratification. Yet he goes on to make the provocative and intriguing claim that such a supersession may well become one of the most important tendencies of the twenty-first century. Finally, Arrighi concludes that a critical globalization studies can benefit from an engagement with some of the findings of world-systems analysis, among them, the persistence of the North–South divide.

Along similar lines, Chase-Dunn and Gills (chapter 5) provide a conceptualization of globalization that sees recent waves of international and transnational integration in the modern world-system as a continuation of the "pulsations of intersocietal interaction networks" that have been occurring in world-systems for millennia. They distinguish between "structural globalization" — the expansion and intensification of large-scale interaction networks relative to more local interactions — and the "globalization project" — a specific political ideology that glorifies the efficiency of markets and privately held firms in order to attack labor unions, entitlements, and other institutions that have protected the incomes of workers. The latter, a basic theme in the globalization literature, they suggest, can be explained in terms of the former. Thus, "The so-called information age, the 'New Economy,' global cities, the transnational capitalist class, and other hypothetically radical departures did not create a huge chasm between recent decades and earlier world history." They concede, however, that the world-system has now reached a point at which both the old interstate system based on separate national capitalist classes, and the new institutions representing the global interests of capital, are simultaneously powerful. In this sense, the old interstate system now coexists with a more globalized or "transnationalized" world economic system brought about by the past two decades of neoliberal economic globalization.

In the chapter that follows (chapter 6), Sklair identifies three types of units of analysis that different competing groups of globalization theorists and researchers take to define their field of inquiry. First is the internationalist (state-centrist) approach, which takes as its unit of analysis the state and sees globalization "as something that powerful states do to less powerful states, and something that is done to less powerful groups of people in all states." This approach, he suggests, is sometimes difficult to distinguish from older theories of imperialism and colonialism and more recent theories of dependency, and leads to the currently popular theme that globalization is the new imperialism. Second is the globalist approach as "the antithesis to the state-centrist thesis," in which the state has all but disappeared, a borderless world is before us, globalization is an accomplished fact, and the global economy is driven by nameless and faceless market forces. Finally, the transnational is "the synthesis of the collision of the flawed state-centrist thesis and the flawed globalist antithesis." This he views as "the most fruitful approach, facilitating theory and research on the struggle between the dominant but as yet incomplete project of capitalist globalization and its alternatives." He argues that the debate on globalization could be elucidated by distinguishing globalization in a generic sense from its dominant type, namely capitalist globalization.

Roudometof (chapter 7) is concerned with distinguishing between related concepts — transnationalism and cosmopolitanism — that are central motifs in the globalization literature. Whereas cosmopolitanism is an expansive attitude and orientation towards the global, captured in such diverse notions as cosmopolitan nation, cosmo-politan democracy, cosmopolitan citizenship, cosmopolitan society, and cosmopoli-tan perspective, transnationalism refers to the experience of distinct groups across and beyond national spaces (such as transnational migrants) in transnational social spaces created through diverse global cultural and material flows. The creation of such transnational spaces leads to a bifurcation of attitudes, expressed in terms of a continuum with cosmopolitanism at the one end and localism at the other end. The relationship between transnationalism and cosmopolitanism is not a linear one whereby greater transnationalization leads to greater cosmopolitanization. On the contrary, the extension of transnational social spaces into the global cultural milieu is responsible for producing both cosmopolitan and local attitudes. For a critical globalization studies, he concludes, making a choice between the two is a matter of ethics and moral judgment, but this judgment should stand independently from our ability to describe the conceptual alternatives.

For his part, O'Byrne (chapter 8) argues for a Habermasian approach to a critical theory of globalization. He distinguishes three approaches: (1) process accounts — globalization as a process, usually a historical and long-term one, which is either synonymous with or simultaneous to "modernization"; (2) transformative accounts — globalization as a significant (and quite recent) transformation within the logic of modernity; and (3) dialectical accounts — globalization as the interplay between conflicting historical processes reflecting the contradictions within modernity. What has been seen as an era of intensified globalization can be better described as the conflict between competing projects that equate to Habermas' distinction between competing forms of rationality — an instrumental or systemic rationality and an abstract or subjective form, or lifeworld rationality. Globality, he suggests, has impacted upon the dominance of systemic rationality by fracturing the relationship between its two principal forces — capitalism and the nation-state. Globality has opened up to capitalism new opportunities for expansion, but itsimpact on the nation-state has been to reveal the latter's fragile and unpredictable nature. Through globality, hitherto abstract concerns with rights such as emancipation, self-discovery, and so on have been transformed into political action in a direct, unmediated, pragmatic way. The global lifeworld is developed through the recognition of the unmediated relationship between the individual and the globe as an arena for her or his action.

What Is the Nature of Power and Conflict in the World Today?

Although the Cold War carried with it the threat of global annihilation by the world's two superpowers, the very threat of nuclear Armageddon contributed to a degree of global political and military stability, in which "hot wars" were often fought in proxy states (Korea, Vietnam), and religious and nationalist sentiments were to a degree contained. Today's global map was largely drawn by European powers, reflecting the colonial legacies in the Americas, interests of nineteenth century colonialism in Africa and Asia, the carved-up remnants of the Ottoman Empire after the First World War, and the Soviet sphere of influence in Eastern and Central Europe during the Cold

War. That map today is rapidly dissolving, as old colonial boundaries give way to precolonial tribal, ethnic, and religious identities. From Indonesia to Rwanda, from the former Yugoslavia to the Middle East, nation-states increasingly appear to be inadequate to the task of providing legitimate governance in the modern world. As the historian Paul Kennedy (1993) observed more than a decade ago, most nation-states today are both too small and too large for the challenges they confront — too small in the face of transnational social forces such as global capital and global religious movements and too large for their constituent peoples to cohere into functioning states (see also Tilly 1992; Arrighi, 1996).

Since September 11, 2001, a "new Cold War" (Juergensmeyer, 1993, 2001) has come to dominate global politics — a war seemingly between secular modernism and religious fundamentalism, but clearly rooted in the diverse material, social, and cultural conflicts bound up with globalization. Although this war did not began with the horrific images of hijacked jetliners crashing into the World Trade Center and the Pentagon, those events opened the way for the Bush administration to declare a global war against terrorism and to pursue a policy of aggressive military intervention justified on the grounds of national security (Falk, 2002).These developments seem to have given new meaning to earlier conflicts and unleashed a host of new ones around the world, raising major questions for a critical globalization studies about the nature of power and conflict in the twenty-first century.

Yet the U.S. invasion and occupation of Iraq, initiated over the strong opposition of leading U.S. allies and without UN support, was envisioned by key Bush strategists long before September 11 provided a publicly acceptable rationale. Its most recent roots can be found in the Project for a New American Century's September 2000 report, *Rebuilding America's Defenses: Strategy, Forces, and Resources for a New Century*, which opens with the statement: "At present the United States faces no global rival. America's grand strategy should aim to preserve and extend this advantageous position as far into the future as possible." *Rebuilding America's Defenses* calls for a permanent U.S. military presence in the oil-rich Persian Gulf — as well as a strong military presence anywhere in the world where, the document claimed, vital U.S. interests were at stake.

The events in Iraq loomed large behind the deliberations among contributors as they discussed the preparation of this volume. The claim that we are witnessing the establishment of an American empire intended to secure U.S. global economic dominance through any means, including, if necessary, military force, came up time and again. Bush's willingness to act unilaterally — not only in Iraq, but with reference to numerous treaties and agreements, some long-standing — provided critics with evidence for this empire thesis. In the perspective of many international relations and world-order paradigms, an empire, unlike a hegemonic power, rules through force rather than consent. But empire itself is a contested concept. It contrasts, for instance, with the account of world-system theory, according to which the history of capitalism is the history of successive hegemonic powers — dominant core countries whose capitalist classes shape an ever-expanding world economy to serve their interests (Arrighi, 1994). In this view, the present conflicts are seen as transitional to yet another hegemonic arrangement in a succession of such arrangements, rather than presaging the emergence of something novel — be it empire or the emergence of a truly global capitalism, characterized by a transnational capitalist class (TCC), a transnational state apparatus, and the eventual decline in power of national hegemonic powers altogether. What is clear amid these debates is that a central contradiction of globalization is the transnationalization of the economy through a nation-state based political system. The contributions in this section examine diverse dimensions of power and conflict in the world today (more local and intimate dimensions of power relations are taken up in subsequent sections), yet all grapple with the theme of U.S. domination and the prospects of empire as well.

"If the United States is no longer sufficiently large and resourceful to manage the considerably expanded world economy of the twenty-first century," asks Harvey (chapter 9), "then what kind of accumulation of political power under what kind of political arrangement will be capable of taking its place, given that the world is heavily committed still to capital accumulation without limit?" Harvey argues that the new "capitalist imperialism" can best be analyzed as a contradictory fusion of a "territorial logic" derived from the use of state power and a "capitalistic logic" derived from market-driven processes of capital accumulation in space and time. The former stresses the political, diplomatic, and military strategies used by a state to secure its goals in the world at large, whereas the latter focuses on the ways in which economic power flows across and through space, toward or away from territories through the daily practices of production, trade, capital flows, labor migration, cultural impulses, and the like. In broad strokes, territorial logic and capitalist logic have come together in the new U.S. imperialism, which involves a new wave of "accumulation through dispossession." This new round began in the 1980s and 1990s with neoliberalism and its dual mantras of privatization and commodification. But the failure of neoliberalism to deliver on its promises produced a crisis within globalization that led to the shift towards neoconservative imperialism, a drive to "convert the low-level global warfare largely orchestrated by neoliberal state apparatuses around the world into a frontal military assault to gain command over a primary global resource."

Bello (chapter 10) also sees unilateralism in U.S. foreign policy as the result of the crisis of the globalization project. This crisis has experienced "three moments." The first was the Asian financial crisis of 1997 (the "Stalingrad of the IMF"). The second was the collapse of the Third Ministerial of the WTO in Seattle in December 1999, and the third was the collapse of the stock market and the end of the Clinton boom, which signaled the reassertion of the classical capitalist crisis of overproduction, and suggested that the global economy appeared to be headed for a prolonged period of Schumpeterian "creative destruction." The Bush regime represented the rise to power of less globalist and more nationalist fractions among the ruling elites in the United States, more tied for their survival and prosperity to the state and to the military-industrial complex (MIC). But the great problem for unilateralism is overextension. This is evidenced by the ongoing crises in Iraq, Afghanistan, Israel and Palestine, the collapse of the Cold War Atlantic Alliance, the rise of a powerful global civil society movement against U.S. domination, and the increasingly negative impact of militarism on the U.S. economy. "We have," in Bello's somber conclusion, "entered a historical maelstrom marked by prolonged economic crisis, the spread of global resistance, the reappearance of the balance of power among center states, and the reemergence of acute interimperialist contradictions."

Approaching the matter from a related lens, McMichael (chapter 11) suggests that the "development project" which was implemented after the Second World War and the "globalization project" that replaced it from the 1970s and on were two sides of the same coin, essentially euphemisms for capitalism in different guises at different times. But the development–globalization project has entered into crisis, giving way, suggests McMichael, to an apparent "imperial project," captured by the Project for the New American Century mentioned earlier. The imperial project entails a more explicit use of force to protect U.S. dominance where market rule (the globalization project) falls short. We now see, through the emerging imperial project, a realignment of market rule, where the iron fist of imperialism and its geopolitical imperatives, is ungloved. Arguably, from development through globalization projects to an emerging imperial project, the universal appeal of development has shrunk to a crystallization of its core power relation: that of securing resources and markets to sustain a dominant consumer-state. Certainly state-centric analysis alone cannot help comprehend such changes, but neither can a transnational perspective unrooted in analysis of the changing coordinates of state sovereignty, in the context of the contradictory machinations of an imperial state.

Shifting the spotlight to the racial dimensions of global conflict, Winant (chapter 12) argues that "the new imperialism is a racist policy not only globally but locally, not only abroad but at home as well." The second Gulf War was the opening salvo of a renewed U.S. imperialism. "With imperialism comes colonialism," and "with colonialism comes racism." The new imperialism is not a Huntingtonian "clash of civilizations" but principally a geopolitical one, in Winant's view, centering on issues of race and class. But this attempt to generate a global hegemonic project for the twenty-first century is deeply threatened by demands for global redistribution of resources and wealth. This emerging global democratic project, an effort to reclaim the traditions of participatory democracy and sociopolitical pluralism in the postcolonial and postsocialist era, links conditions in the global South and East to those in the metropole. The parallel between post–Second World War antiimperialmovements and antiracist ones continues, as the new imperialism confronts an ongoing demand for greater democracy in the global South and East, while post–civil rights racial hegemony confronts an ongoing demand for greater democracy in the U.S. "homeland." It may be somewhat surprising, he concludes, "to hear that 'the clash of civilizations' is occurring no less in Washington than in the Middle East!"

McLaren and Jaramillo (chapter 13), both critical education scholars, identify another site where global conflict and power relations are manifest: the classroom, which has been invaded by neoliberalism, "colonized by the corporate logic of privatization and the imperial ideology of the militarized state." But this global capitalist onslaught has also domesticated much of critical pedagogy, which earlier served as "a trenchant challenge to capital and U.S. economic and military hegemony." They call for a *critical globalization pedagogy* to "challenge current attempts to corporatize, businessify, and moralize the process of schooling and to resist the endless subordination of life in the social factory so many students call home." A critical globalization studies should examine education as a social process embedded within global social relations of production. This pedagogical encounter must contribute to developing the "revolutionary potential of a transnational, gender-balanced, multiracial, antiimperialist struggle."

Harris (chapter 14) argues that TCC theory has concentrated on economic and political forces while ignoring the role of the MIC. But because coercive power is fundamental for class rule "the nature of the U.S. MIC must be examined because of its special role in maintaining security for global capitalism." The MIC is split among a number of different influential fractions, the most important being the division between transnational globalists and international hegemonists. The former support strategic coordination with global allies in the North and South and industrial and technological mergers with allied defense manufacturers. In contrast, international hegemonists promote unilateral world leadership and military preeminence, a protected industrial base, and often elevate national security interests above globalist economics. The globalist strategy was strongly promoted during the Clinton years but 9/11 provided a new worldwide threat that let the hegemonists out of their antiglobalist box and created the long-sought post–Cold War enemy. The hegemonists' strategy, he concludes, became articulated through the neoconservatives and operationalized by the Bush coalition.

New Directions in Globalization Research and Implications of Globalization for Scholarship in the Academy

Globalization has had an enormous impact on academic scholarship. We have already alluded to many of these changes: the growing acceptance of global studies as a legitimate field of research and teaching, the emergence of global studies programs in the United States and elsewhere, and a host of books and academic journals devoted to the topic. If the nation-state has not yet been fully decentered as the central analytic unit for social scientists, it has certainly been strongly challenged. The very notion of "area studies," which defined both scholarship and funding during the Cold War period, is being challenged. A recent conference at the University of Chicago, whose area studies programs have been among the strongest in the United States, raised such challenges as:

> Isn't it passé ... to specialize in an "area" — living there, learning its language and customs — while vast numbers of the world's populations migrate and meld? What, for that matter, counts as an "area" amid globalization: a sovereign nation-state or region comprising several nations, or a strip of curry and kebab houses springing up in a white working-class London suburb? .... And, perhaps most difficult of all: If area specialists do persist, where will the funding for their cost-heavy research and fieldwork come from now that grant-making agencies have transferred their allegiances and grants to the hot research topics of the past decade: globalization and transnational studies? (Stewart, 2003)

At least since Edward Said deconstructed Western neocolonial notions of the Islamic Near East a quarter century ago in *Orientalism*, the more culturally oriented disciplines — particularly history, comparative literature, the arts, ethnic studies, anthropology — have experienced revolutions within, and fundamental questionings of their subject matter, approaches to research, and indeed their basic epistemologies. How is ethnography to be conducted at a global level? What epistemological stand-point is to be adopted when studying cultures other than one's own — particularly those that have historically had a subaltern relationship with the West?

Globalization has had a similar impact on important theoretical traditions within the social sciences. Two of these have already been mentioned: the challenges to international relations (a major subfield of political science, and one that remains hostile to the very notion of global studies), and to area studies. Within sociology, world-system theory emerged in large part as a challenge to the insularity of 1960s development studies, which failed to take into account relations of unequal exchange between nation-states in explaining the failure of so-called modernization in the "Third World" (So, 1990; McMichael 2003). Today, world-system theory itself is under attack for continuing to privilege the nation-state over truly transnational actors and social forces. At the same time, development studies is experiencing a resurgence, although in a vastly different form: one that emphasizes the central role of subaltern groups, particularly Third World women, focusing on their lifeworlds and cultural understanding in fostering social change in the face of global forces (Bhavnani et al., 2003). This new approach to development studies views develop-ment less in terms of discrete territories and nation-states, and more in terms of distinct social groups in a transnational setting (Robinson, 2003).

The study of globalization itself long ago moved beyond a simple macro focus on global economic and political structures. Academics and scholar-activists have taken up with increasing vigor a wide range of issues and processes that are seen to engage the dynamics of globalization. Although there is no one set of conditions or processes that can accurately sum up these diverse topics, one that stands out is the unprece-dented migrationand wide geographic dispersion of populations since 1945. Such migratory movements, particularly since the mid-1980s, together with their potential as a force for local and global social transformation, have led Castles and Miller to dub the closing years of the twentieth century and the beginning of the twenty-first "an age of migration" (Castles and Miller, 1998: 3). Scholars working within the framework of transnationalism, as Chinchilla notes (in this volume), generally see transnational links, activities, and spaces both as an effect of globalization and as a force that helps to shape, strengthen, and fuel it. Scholars are increasingly concerned with "deterritorialization," which in the broadest sense refers to the disembedding of sets of social relations, phenomena, and processes from territorial space (more spe-cifically, from nation-state space). Some have even floated the controversial idea of a global culture (see, e.g., Featherstone, 1990; Tomlinson 1999). This sectionexplores some of these cutting-edge topics that critical globalization studies have taken up in recent years, such as global cities, transnational migration, border regions, global class formation, new global cultural trends, and the transnationalization of civil society and law.

In chapter 15, Sassen argues that focusing on such subnational settings as global cities — a concept that she pioneered — allows us to move beyond the typical focus on "imperial spatialities" by situating complex global processes in specific places and "making legible not only the upper but also the lower circuits of globalization." Such a recovery of place is central to a critical globalization studies because it allows us to better understand the concrete, localized processes through which much of globalization operates "Countergeographies of globalization" are spaces where we can find resistance to global power, "and as yet undetected forms of participation by actors typically represented as powerless, as victims, or as uninvolved with global conditions," such as informalized and devalued immigrant and feminized labor pools. Much of the multiculturalism in large cities, she concludes, is as constitutive of globalization as is international finance, though in ways that differ sharply from the latter, and allows us to see an interesting correspondence between great concentrations of corporate power and large concentrations of "others."

Chinchilla (chapter 16) takes up this call for a critical mapping of subnational spaces and actors of globalization, an enterprise that uncovers the global not so much — in Sassen's words — through the "cosmopolitan route" but through the "knowing multiplication of local practices." She observes that in the field of immigration studies, scholars interested in understanding the effects of transnationalism have called for a paradigm shift that recognizes the importance of globalization. This shift also requires a critical reexamination of traditional bipolar dichotomies, such as assimilation vs. ethnic solidarity, sojourner vs. settler, citizen vs. noncitizen, and sending vs. receiving countries. She then explores Central American migrants to the Los Angeles area and their constitution there as a dynamic transnational community involving not only remittances, but also the growth of a transnational infrastructure that includes couriers; travel agents; airline, telephone, express mail, and import–export companies that cater to the Central American market; and immigrant political-organizing activities across borders. Such processes allow transnational Central American communities in the United States to live simultaneously in two or more worlds or to create and live in "transnational spaces" to a degree not previously known. She finds, moreover, that these processes have the contradictory and ambiguous effects of both undermining and supporting existing power relations: "Just as grassroots oppositional groups can take advantage of globalization for counterhegemonic activities … nonmigrant transnational activities may contest, resist, and negotiate as well as reinforce the hegemonic order."

Although scholars have emphasized the creation of a TCC, Derne (chapter 17) notes that they have given less attention to how globalization is shaping other classes. However, by inciting consumption, the TCC generates a transnational middle class that is oriented to cosmopolitan consumption and that provides the primary consumers fueling the capitalist system.Looking at India, which opened up to the global economy in the early 1990s, he finds that a transnational middle class has emerged whose members define their status by cosmopolitan consumption and gender arrangements. Drawing on new high-paying jobs oriented to the global market and the availability of international products, these affluent Indians see themselves as a middle class on a global stage, between the Indian poor and the consuming classes of the rich countries. But this class contrasts with a locally oriented middle class whose members, lacking the English-language skills and global connections that would allow them to take off with the global economy, are still limited by local markets for consumption and employment and who find status on a local field. These two groups have divergent gender practices reflecting divergent structural locations within the global economy. The transnational middle class advertises its cosmopolitan orientation by easing restrictions on women's movements outside the home, experimenting with love marriages (marriages outside the traditional arranged-marriage framework, and emulating transnational standards of fashion and beauty. Their locally oriented counterparts advertise a local orientation by embracing what they regard as distinctively Indian gender arrangements, limiting women's movements outside the home, and rejecting dating and love marriages.

Axford (chapter 18) turns his attention to networks as key to understanding the impact of globalization on civil society. He argues that virtual networks, such as those developed by the Internet, can foster communities across space, providing "support and opportunities for friendship for a host of people ill served by the public services in the 'real' civic spaces where they live out their lives." These transnational identities do not simply reproduce national identities; rather, they represent a "cultural shift" with implications for identity formation and social movements. Such networks do not occur in a vacuum; they must be understood with reference to existing institutions, including the state institutions that often promote and regulate them. Yet global networks are not merely local networks writ large; they are unique, "networks of networks where individuals and groups are drawn into a more globalized existence." This is where a network perspective can be helpful in understanding globalization, because "it captures the openness of social relationships," portraying "a looseness and diversity, which go some way to capture the inchoate character of contemporary globalization."

Cutler (chapter 19), Hajjar (chapter 20), and Falk (chapter 21) take up some of the challenging legal aspects of globalization. Cutler begins with a seeming paradox: despite "the growing ubiquity and plurality of legal orders involving a multiplicity of different actors and geographical and territorial spaces, law 'still seems inherently national.'" Although law enforcement remains "a prerogative of the state," creating an international rule of law increasingly involves "private, nonstate actors and private, nonstate law," thanks to the growing importance of transnational economic forces and the declining power of the state. As a consequence of the tension between transnational forces and national law, Cutler argues that "critical globalization studies in law means the development of a critical understanding of the dialectical relationship between the deterritorialization and reterritorialization of law." Her chapter examines some of the challenges to the foundations of international law (notably *lex mercatoria*), and considers some of the institutions that have arisen to provide a transnational legal framework, along with their limitations. All of these pose a challenge to "the state-centric foundations of international law."

Hajjar continues this theme, with a focus on human rights. She argues that "states are both the makers and the subjects of international laws." She notes that between 1948 (when the Universal Declaration of Human Rights was created) and 1993 (when the UN Ad Hoc Tribunal for the former Yugoslavia was established), "international politics was 'realist': shaped, guided and governed by states' interests rather than laws." This has begun to change, she argues — both through international criminal law and enforcement (which remains largely beholden to states), but, more significantly, through what she terms "legal entrepreneurialism" involving "universal" international law enforcement. The watershed example of this is the Belgian "universal jurisdiction" (antiatrocity) law, which permitted that country to prosecute people accused of gross violations elsewhere (most famously, the former Chilean dictator Augusto Pinochet).

Law and human rights also concern Falk, given the enormous impact of 9/11 on both global conflict and the search for new forms of international regulatory authority. Falk examines the implications of the U.S. war against Iraq, a war that was launched "without international or regional backing in a context in which there was no credible past, present, or future threat." This, he argues, represented a fundamental alteration of the post-Westphalian world legal order, in which state sovereignty is challenged (indeed, ignored) in the name of antiterrorism. It also indicates a significant change in the nature of globalization, elevating war and force to a central role in world politics, "while dimming the lights that had been illuminating the rise of markets and the primacy of *corporate* globalization." Falk fills out his argument with an examination of five "overlapping approaches to governance" that arguably will shape globalization in this century: corporate globalization, civic globalization, imperial globalization, apocalyptic globalization, and regional globalization.

Henderson (chapter 22) takes up a different challenge for globalization research: understanding the differing impacts of globalization on state policy, with special reference to the relationship between economic policy and inequality. After citing research supporting the argument that a state's "competence for economic governance" is positively associated with the reduction of poverty, he goes on to show that in both South Korea and Malaysia, poverty reduction was not the result of progrowth governmental policies alone, but of "a state-orchestrated form of capitalism" that resulted in high value-added forms of growth whose benefits were relatively widespread throughout society. (Governmental welfare programs also played a role.) In South Korea, however, the move towards greater market economics in the 1990s left the country vulnerable to global economic forces, with the consequence that poverty increased sharply following the Asian economic crisis of 1997–1998. This was not the case for Malaysia, which was the only nonsocialist developing country "to have explicitly pursued antipoverty and redistributional policies as a central component of its development project," and which weathered the economic crisis far better as a consequence (although poverty reduction in that country was mitigated somewhat by governmental corruption).

Parreñas (chapter 23) and Pyle (chapter 24) turn our attention to more localized research on the impacts of globalization. Parreñas examines the impact of globalization on paid domestic work, typically performed by female immigrants (she notes that there are some sixty million women living outside their country of origin, a highly vulnerable, economically significant, and little-studied population). She argues that "the global economy of caring work" can serve "as a critical platform from which to view unequal relations between men and women, and poor and rich nations in globalization." Using the Philippines as a case study, Parreñas shows how there is a "three-tier transfer of care," under which upper-class women entrust family care to migrant domestic workers, who in turn leave their own family care to relatives back home — or sometimes even to hired domestics who are yet more impoverished.

Migrant domestic workers thus "ease the entrance of other women into the paid labor force," thereby contributing to economic growth in their adoptive countries. The feminization of labor in industrialized countries has placed a special burden on working women, who usually face a "second shift" at home. This burden is partly alleviated by immigrant workers who staff daycare centers and provide low-cost domestic labor, ranging from housekeeping to caring for children and the elderly. Immigrant status turns these workers into second-class citizens at best, vulnerable to abuse and permanently segmented into low-wage status.

Pyle is also concerned with the effects of globalization on gender. She focuses on the impact of globalization on women's work, including the creation of gendered global networks, particularly in the informal sector. Globalization, in its contemporary neoliberal form, has been especially harsh on women workers: they provide much of the low-wage workforce for multinational corporations (MNCs), occupy bottom-rung jobs in subcontracting networks, and are ultimately often pushed out entirely into the informal sector in order to survive. They are among the principal victims of structural adjustment policies that shred governmental services for the poor. Pyle looks at three highly gendered sectors to understand how globalization impacts female labor — export-oriented production, sex work, and domestic labor. These are all growing industries, exploitative of women, and often fostered by governmental policies such as export-oriented industrialization, tourism, and the export of surplus labor to other countries. Pyle ends with a discussion of what can be done to counter these trends, and foster a degree of social justice for women workers.

Daniel (chapter 25) turns our attention to racism, examining the "racial projects" that originated with Eurocentrism, focusing on the postcolonial discursive frameworks that have both decentered the West and deconstructed race as a binary category Drawing on the notion of hybridity, he argues that "postcolonial discourse not only challenges any notion of racial purity but also interrogates the concept of race." This is not to say that race has somehow been transcended — something that "would be unthinkable until the struggle to achieve equality of racial difference has been won." But it is to argue that racial categories are best understood nonbiologically as "unstable and decentered complexes of sociocultural meanings that are constantly being created, inhabited, contested, destroyed, and transformed by political struggle," within systems of neocolonialism that effectively maintain racial hierarchy. Daniel then turns to a consideration of Afrocentrism, arguing that while the "fostering of group pride, solidarity, and self-respect among African-descent individuals" is undeniably important on the one hand, it also runs the risk of essentializing notions of black identity, rearticulating nineteenth-century notions of racial purity. Daniel concludes by arguing that "if Afrocentrists wish to dismantle Eurocentrism they must also move beyond the 'either/or' thinking that underpins both Eurocentric and radical Afrocentric discourse. The goal should be to embrace a moderate Afrocentrism based on a 'both/neither' mentation that is compatible with the postcolonial concept of critical hybridity."

Finally, Langman and Halnon (chapter 26) takes globalization research in still another direction — an examination of what they term "the universalization of consumerism as an ideology and a set of practices that articulate identities and lifestyles that 'willingly assent' to domination." Lost, they argue, is culture as a "contested terrain," a site of protest and alternative identities that challenge the dominant ideologies. In its place we find the "carnivalization of the world," a series of "grotesque" subcultures and practices that — although superficially oppositional — in fact reproduce hegemonic global capitalism. Whereas medieval carnivals (or their more contemporary Brazilian form) traditionally served as a liminal mass culture that challenged that of the elites, today they have been thoroughly co-opted and commodified into "touristscapes," from Mardi Gras to Spring Break. Langman and Halnon examine a number of subcultures of the grotesque — body modification, punks, Goths, professional wrestling, shock music, shock television, "freak shows" (Jerry Springer et al.), and reality television. This ever-expanding "carnivalization of culture" may seem to critique the dominant system, but it serves as a vehicle for "letting off steam," blunting dissent and reproducing the very system it seems to challenge.

Linking Globalization Studies to Global Resistance Movements — Marginalized Voices and Neglected Topics

Within the field of global studies, there is a growing emphasis on the importance of understanding globalization from the situated viewpoint of oppression and resistance among peoples that are marginalized on the basis of race, class, and gender. This understanding often requires a shift in the focus of research, from asking broad questions about global social processes to studying their local instantiation in everyday life and intimate realms. There is a growing body of research that focuses on the family, sexuality, and the nuances of gendered and other power relations at the most local level. This research calls for the translation of scholarly understanding into social action — a praxis that conveys the assurance of the relevance of scholarly knowledge to those individuals and organizations that are fighting for economic and social justice. As we came to realize at the conference, this is one of the most vexing challenges facing academic scholars who align themselves with progressive social movements. What is the appropriate balance between a research agenda that is driven by legitimate scholarly concerns, and one that is shaped by the immediate and pressing needs of social movement activists? The reward system of most academic disciplines undervalues practical- or policy-oriented research at best — and, more commonly, punishes those who engage in such research, according their preferred journals lower status and making it difficult for them to progress through the academic ranks. Moreover, scholars who carry their passions into the classroom may encounter strong resistance — sometimes (although decreasingly, we believe), by students who are challenged by what they are hearing; more often by colleagues and administrators who regard the dominant scholarly discourse within a discipline as canonical "truth," and challenges to that discourse as "biased." How does the engaged teacher present his or her ideas in a balanced fashion, giving adequate voice to other viewpoints?

These, of course, are hardly new issues: during times of rapid social change, established fields and scholars are frequently challenged with calls for changes in underlying paradigms, often by younger (and frequently nontenured) scholars. The contributions in this final section reflect a number of those challenges. They are concerned with the global fight for social justice. These range from resistance struggles on the part of traditionally oppositional groups, such as labor, to new forms of social movements being generated by women and other marginalized groups.

Grosfoguel (chapter 27), Smith (chapter 28), and Silver (chapter 29) all examine broad conditions and trends that have implications for resistance movements. Grosfoguel argues that an "epistemic perspective" derived from ethnic studies — one that challenges universalist ways of thinking by showing how all knowledge is situated — contributes centrally to a critical globalization studies. He argues that Western philosophy and science produced an ideology of universalism in keeping with its "coloniality of power," "an entanglement of multiple and heterogeneous hierarchies of sexual, political, epistemic, economic, spiritual, and racial forms of domination and exploitation." Grosfoguel then argues that a number of canonical ideas are challenged by the decentering of Western thought, among them evolutionary notions of national development, Marxist notions of base and superstructure (replaced now by a "colonial power matrix" that encompasses different forms of domination, including gender and race), the division between culture and political economy, the belief that the end of formal colonialism meant an end to coloniality, and reductionist views of social change. He concludes by arguing that "critical border thinking ... redefines modernity from the cosmologies and epistemologies of the subaltern, located in the oppressed and exploited side of the colonial difference"; only with such a perspective can we have "a redefinition of citizenship, democracy, human rights, and humanity, beyond the narrow definitions imposed by European modernity."

If Grosfoguel raises epistemological challenges to mainstream knowledge, Smith challenges the popular learning derived from the East Asian economic crisis of 1997–1998, examining that crisis for the lessons it provides about the limits of neoliberal economic policies. After a review of the history and depth of the crisis — which falsely was seen as heralding the end of talk of the "Asian miracle" among neoliberal thinkers — Smith turns to the ideological implications of the crisis. Drawing on a world-systems perspective, Smith explains East Asia's rapid development prior to the economic downturn, as well as its downturn in 1997–1998. This approach reveals the limits of state-led dependent development; an understanding of global capital and of institutions such as the IMF are key to an adequate explanation of the region's fortunes and misfortunes. Smith also shows how the crisis provided opportunities for resistance movements from economic elites, including some corporate leaders in South Korea, as well as popular movements, exemplified by the popular overthrow of the Suharto dictatorship in Indonesia and a day-long general strike among 130,000 workers in South Korea.

Silver provides an important historical perspective on resistance movements today. Drawing on the world-systems perspective — which looks to past hegemonic transitions to provide insights into present ones — she examines "the central role played by war and world politics in the dynamics of global social protest." Escalating war and social unrest, she argues, feed off one another during times of hegemonic transition. Moreover, she demonstrates, "the time it has taken for war to trigger massive social unrest has decreased from one hegemonic transition to the next." Support for these theses is provided by various sources, including an empirical analysis of labor unrest from 1870 to the present as reported in *The New York Times* and *The Times* (of London), and an historical analysis of parallels between the contemporary period and the transition to British hegemony in the late eighteenth and early nineteenth centuries. Silver concludes with some historically based conjectures about social unrest in the coming years, predicting that "the crisis and breakdown of U.S. world hegemony" will be characterized by increasing speed and intensity of the dynamics of war and unrest. For example, whereas in the past cycles of unrest tended to lag behind the outbreak of war, today the movement opposed to the war in Iraq — the largest global protest movement in history — began before a single shot was fired. It remains uncertain whether global protests, along with resistance from within the U.S. military, will "facilitate a relatively smooth transition from the decaying hegemonic order to a more peaceful and equitable world order."

Thai (chapter 30) explores the dynamics of globalization as they shape and are shaped by gender and sexuality. He addresses the key questions of how social status is converted across transnational social fields and how this convertibility becomes gendered across transnational space. In an attempt to understand why and how some immigrant men of color, particularly those in low-wage work, use globalization as a gender strategy to "achieve" masculinity, he narrates the story of two migrants living in heavily populated Vietnamese metropolitan areas in California who both chose to pursue marriage with women of Vietnamese origin through arrangements of family and kin throughout the Vietnamese diaspora The convertibility of such masculinity into social status allows these men, located "at the intersection and interstices of vast systems of power: patriarchy, racism, colonialism, and capitalism," to feel, if not become, more "marriageable" in the global hierarchy of marriage markets and to construct their own sense of respectability.

Bhavnani, Foran, and Talcott (chapter 31), McGovern (chapter 32), and Moghadam (chapter 33) all look at the role played by women in resisting capitalist globalization. Bhavnani et al. review examples throughout the world of women's efforts to "slow the apparent 'juggernaut of globalization' in favor of visions of development as planned social transformation and redistribution." In opposition to conventional, purely economic notions of development, they offer the "Women, Culture, and Development" (WCD) paradigm, with its emphasis on the interplay of economic, cultural, feminist, and developmental forces, and calling for "a politics based on a socialist, green, antiracist, and feminist vision of social justice" (these are the four aspects of politics that are captured in the title of their chapter, "the Red, the Green, the Black, and the Purple"). The need for this new politics is illustrated with reference to the expansion of private property into biology, as seen in the WTO's Trade Related Aspects of Intellectual Property (TRIPS) regulations. The threat of patenting traditional medicinal plants poses a direct challenge to age-old traditional "women's knowledges," and as a consequence has spurred resistance movements based on feminist principles and notions of sustainable development. The Zapatista movement in Chiapas — whose core values call for "love of life, love of people, love of justice" — is seen as offering some hopeful examples.

McGovern calls for a transnational feminist scholarship that "gives voice to Third World women" in active support of their resistance to globalization. A transnational feminist scholarship would question some ideas from traditional feminism — for example, the notion that women's equality means that women should serve in the military. On the contrary, McGovern argues, transnational feminists question whether women should serve at all in "the imperial army"; women should instead be integrated into the global peace movement. The very category "Third World women" should be contested because the experience of globalization differs greatly according to one's class, race, and work experience. Whereas some Third World women may experience oppression transnationally (e.g., as migrant domestic workers or as prostitutes in sex tourism), others experience oppression in their home countries (e.g., as landless peasants, workers in multinational assembly lines, service workers, workers in the informal sector, slum dwellers, street vendors, or as members of discriminated indigenous peoples). The ways in which the state "represses, divides, and rules to contain women's activism and other forms of resistance" must also be considered. Transnational feminists have much to learn from feminist epistemology's methodological emphasis on standpoint, reflexivity, positionality, and immersion.

Moghadam's chapter focuses on the transnational networks that have emerged around women's social movement organizations, in such diverse areas as women's rights, reproductive health, violence against women, peace and antimilitarism, and feminist economics. She argues that this "globalization-from-below" is rapidly growing, providing an increasingly effective counterweight to "globalization-from-above." In fact, these emerging transnational women's networks are a direct result of the impact of neoliberalism on women throughout the world, and the threat that neoliberal economic policies pose for women's rights. Third World women are, in Moghadam's apt phrase, "riled." After briefly tracing the rise and impact of neoliberal economic thinking and religious fundamentalism (two of the ideologies that have especially "riled the world's women"), Moghadam discusses the rise of transnational feminist networks (TFNs) in response to these ideologies. These networks emerged throughout the 1990s, and have three sets of activities and goals: they "create, activate, or join global networks to mobilize pressure outside states"; they "participate in multilateral and intergovernmental political arenas"; and they "act and agitate within states to enhance public awareness and participation."

Bonacich (chapter 34), Appelbaum (chapter 35), and Tran (chapter 36) focus their contributions on the prospects for workers' struggles in the new global age. Bonacich analyzes a little-studied yet strategically pivotal sector of the global economy: logistics. However far-flung and opaque may be the rapidly expanding global network of factories that produce the world's goods, ultimately the goods must get to market — and such markets are necessarily local. The United States, for example, accounts for nearly a third of the world's economy, yet almost all imports enter the country through a relatively small number of ports. Bonacich's chapter focuses on the port complex of Los Angeles–Long Beach, the United State's largest port (and the world's third largest, behind Hong Kong and Singapore), and its ancillary distributional networks. She shows how the "logistics revolution" has impacted the distribution of goods, offering a fascinating account of an integrated system of container ships, ports and their off-loading facilities, warehouses, railway and trucking networks, and giant retailers such as Wal-Mart that increasingly drive the entire system. The scale described is vast — but so are the opportunities for disruption. Although there are factors that weaken workers' capacity for militant coordinated action (outsourcing, the use of contingent labor, the employment of immigrants and people of color who are especially vulnerable to job loss), there are factors that strengthen it as well. These include the interconnectedness of the system, which renders it potentially fragile: "the incredible strategic importance of the ports and surrounding logistics systems in terms of globalization and world trade," which has become dependent on just-in-time delivery and is therefore extremely vulnerable to any interruptions in the supply chain.

Appelbaum turns to the problem of sweatshops in the global economy, asking the question: How can the rights of low-wage workers, such as those in the apparel industry, be secured under conditions of capital hypermobility? Unlike the distribution networks studied by Bonacich — which are inherently local and thus relatively vulnerable to work stoppages — low-wage production (such as apparel) can be easily moved from one factory to another at the first signs of labor unrest. Appelbaum develops a framework for advancing labor's interests in light of trends in the organization of the global economy (global subcontracting, the rising power of giant retailers, etc.), focusing on the privatization of enforcement of labor laws — the shift from state-centered enforcement at the factory levelto corporate self-enforcement focused on branded labels He argues that, at least within the United States, state-centered enforcement has declined, while globally, there are no internationally binding labor laws. Although some corporate self-monitoring schemes are better than others, all suffer from the absence of workable enforcement mechanisms that apply throughout the supply chain. Nonetheless, efforts to form independent unions — although still limited in much of the developing world — have shown some surprising successes in recent years, especially when coupled with consumer activism.

Tran focuses on a country with one of the lowest wages in the global apparel-supply chain — Vietnam — examining the impact of flexible modes of production on pay and working conditions, and how workers have responded to fight for their own interests. After chronicling the low wages and poor working conditions in the industry, she argues that competition among workers is fostered by a labor surplus and job scarcity, contributing to labor exploitation. The role of unions has been undermined by flexible production, as union representatives are themselves workers and thus beholden to the multinationals where they work. The fees paid by unions to their representatives are low, and state subsidies nonexistent; union work is thus at best part-time, and generally ineffective. Power increasingly shifts from the party-state to the MNCs; workers face "self-exploitation triggered by the piece-rate system; and labor unions are weakened. Nonetheless, a recent surge in labor disputes and strikes shows that Vietnamese workers are far from quiescent. Worker resistance proved successful in a number of instances, especially in firms with some form of union. Even under extremely adverse conditions, she finds that "workers remain faithful to their historical legacy of self-organization to fight for their legitimate economic interests, with or without labor union assistance," showing "evidence of class and union consciousness."

Finally, Roddick (chapter 37) and Njehu (chapter 38), prominent antiglobalization activists, discuss the prospects for progressive social change and celebrate the new forms of global solidarity. Njehu observes that, given the billions of dollars spent to sell the globalization project, "it is surprising that most people are, in fact, suspicious, skeptical, and concerned about the many promises and few deliverables from the process." The campaigns undertaken by the global justice movement, however, "are not just about opposition, but also about global solidarity, a valued and positive aspect of globalization." Global justice activists "are not trying to turn back the clock. Rather, we are fighting for a just world." Such global solidarity is manifest in the World Social Forum process, in the international debt cancellation campaigns under the Jubilee banner; in the World March of Women, in the antiprivatization "Our World Is Not for Sale" coalition, in the international farmers network *Via Campesina*, and in many other ways. Campaigners and activists under these and other banners are demanding equality; sustainability and environmental protection; a globalization that puts people before profits; peace; debt cancellation; universal access to treatment, especially for HIV or AIDS affected people; respect for and defense of human and labor rights; and more.

For her part, Roddick insists that change will not come about by governments or businesses but by "moral dissenters and by the persistence of small committed groups of people willing to fail over long periods of time until that rare wonderful moment when the dam of oppression, indifference, and greed finally cracks and those in power finally accept what the world's people have been saying all along: that there now has to be a revolution in kindness." Perhaps the real threat to corporate globalization, opines Roddick, "is the irresistible appeal of carnival as a tactic of resistance and dissent. Spontaneity and pleasure are the order of the day. If resistance and rebellion are not fun and do not reflect the world we wish to create, then we will have lost that joyous abandonment and lust for life." The millions of grassroots initiatives around the world point to "the most creative explosion of social initiatives and solidarity our history has ever seen."

Note

1. It is with these convictions that we convened a 4-day conference to debate the future of globalization at the University of California at Santa Barbara. The conference, held from May 1–4, 2003, under the title *Towards a Critical Globalization Studies*, involved the participation of some one hundred leading social science and humanities scholars, key public intellectuals, and global justice activists from around the world. The conference's rich mixture of plenary presentations and paper panels attracted more than a thousand students, academics, and activists from universities and social justice organizations across the state of California and well beyond. It was out of that conference that the idea for the present volume emerged.

What Is a Critical
Globalization Studies?

1

If You Want To Be Relevant:
Advice to the Academic from a Scholar–Activist

Susan George

What should be the role and the responsibilities of academia and intellectuals in the global justice movement? Can we, together, create a body of work relevant to the theme of a critical globalization studies? Can we help this movement attain its goals through the tools of scholarship? Can we help it to analyze the present structures of injustice, formulate workable proposals for change, devise the best strategies to convince ordinary people and decision-makers of their relevance, and change the *rapport de forces?* I think we can, and the brief history of the global justice movement supports this view. This movement has no leaders, fortunately, in the sense of a cadre who give orders, but it does have individual moral and intellectual authorities who have symbolic status and who are looked up to. The question of their relevance seems a foregone conclusion. The fact remains that the road ahead is full of potholes, not to mention bomb craters. So while I believe firmly in the positive role of academia and intellectuals in this movement, I intend to concentrate more on the risks and the mistakes we should try to avoid.

The area that can now be called "critical globalization studies" used to be called "critical development studies." I have been a practitioner of the latter for a long time and hope to be forgiven if I offer a personal answer to the question about academia and intellectuals before trying to formulate a more general one.

My first attempt at critical development studies, though I did not know the term at the time, was my first book, *How the Other Half Dies* (George, 1976). Its subtitle was *The Real Reasons for World Hunger,* because it had gradually dawned on me that few were attempting to explain what those reasons were. The gap in research and analysis seemed due less to dissimulation, although there was some of that, than to subservience to a dominant ideology. The categories and concepts needed for dealing with the "real reasons" were simply unavailable, not part of the mental equipment of most people considered experts on the subject.

The above statements must sound insufferably smug: "All the seasoned scholars were blind, mistaken, idiots, or all three; only the rank newcomer Susan George saw things clearly." Point taken, but I cannot approach the question of academia and intellectuals without showing my cards. Allow me to recapitulate before explaining why I believe my judgment is not unduly harsh. From 1973 to 1974 the world went through yet another food crisis. Famine and malnutrition were taking their usual toll

3

in Africa and Asia, and the press as well as the scholarly literature overwhelmingly offered only variations on the standard themes of drought, population pressures, low-grade technology, and poor crop yields. The more adventurous might have alluded to government corruption, but they were not interested in the paradox that most hungry people lived in rural areas, and if they mentioned poverty it was mostly to affirm that the poor needed mechanization, Green Revolution seeds, and all that went with these. There was virtually nothing about agribusiness or cash crops, the role of food aid in changing local food habits, the Green Revolution as a negative factor, land concentration and inequalities, share-cropping and exploitative tenure arrangements, and migration from rural areas to cities. The agricultural production and policies of rich countries rarely appeared on the academic hunger horizon because, doubtlessly, such aspects of the food picture were assumed to be positive. A statement as simple and obvious as the one I made in my book — "If you want to eat, you must either have enough land to grow your own food or enough money to buy it" — was exotic in the extreme.

Who was I to say the proponents of climate-population-low-tech explanations of hunger were wrong or biased? I was nobody. I had no credentials in the field. Not only were my academic degrees unrelated to the subject but my only, extremely marginal experience was my participation in a team set up by the Institute for Policy Studies in Washington to write a report for the World Food Conference held at the Food and Agricultural Organization (FAO) of the United Nations in Rome in 1974. And even there, my role was mostly that of dogsbody. The featured writers of the report were the recently exiled ministers of agriculture and of land reform in Allende's Chile with a supporting cast of three smart, experienced Brazilians. It was my privilege to listen to them and my job to recast the report in readable English, get it printed, get it publicized, and get it there. When my luggage laden with reports and I finally made it to Rome, it was to discover that: 1) the largest delegation at the World Food Conference came from from agribusiness (a.k.a. the FAO's "Industry Cooperative Programme"), immediately followed by the Americans, and: 2) no one was talking the way the people on our team had talked. Once home, not knowing any better, I decided to take the topic as far as I could and in the fullness of time, a courageous editor at Penguin took a chance on the resulting book. Everyone should have a right to one enormous, flukey stroke of luck, and this was mine.

It was unlikely that an academic would write such a book because it approached the subject in an unconventional way guaranteed to attract abuse and cause damage to a professorial reputation. It was even more unlikely that it be published by pres-tigious house in London rather than by a small, out-of-the-way imprint with no capacity for distribution in, say, Cheltenham. This project had oblivion written all over it.

Along with Joe Collins' and Frances Moore-Lappe's *Food First* (Joe had, like me, been part of the World Food Conference report team), neither of them academics, *How the Other Half Dies* did initiate a new way of looking at an age-old but very modern problem. Widely translated, selling briskly and much appreciated by the general public (and even by the critic for the FAO magazine *CERES*) it was icily received by most of academia. I later got a doctorate from the Sorbonne with a thesis concerning the transfer of the U.S food system to the rest of the planet because, as I continued in the field, I got sick of hearing pompous, usually male professors proclaiming that "this woman has no credentials for saying all the terrible things she's saying." Now I get myself announced as "Dr." when I fear a hostile environment.

I hope a few lessons may be drawn from this story, which I have inflicted upon the reader at some length. The first is that this book got around because it was clear and straightforward; it eschewed a false "balance" and cautious hedging. To reach people beyond their own disciplines, academics must throw jargon to the winds, take a genuine stand and write simple (not simplistic) prose. Next we must deal with a basic Marxist, infrastructural, crassly materialist question: Can critical scholars survive? Progressive intellectuals rarely can unless they are either, like me, extraordinarily lucky (my late husband supported my initial efforts) or hold down an academic job. Some so-called Third World scholars may get support from Northern funders but North or South, the great majority of critical, progressive intellectuals will teach and they will have a tough job.

Whatever their field, they are mostly called upon to transmit the received wisdom, are discouraged from crossing disciplinary boundaries, must frequently please their departments before pleasing themselves, and for the increasingly large percentage without tenure, can't take too many risks or they will never benefit from job security. The best argument for tenure is that it creates space for critical enquiry, which is, of course, also the principle reason not to grant it. So the choice for most progressive intellectuals lies between taking a vow of poverty or academia. Fortunately, many still do get tenure with their creative faculties intact and their willingness to take unconventional approaches unsmothered.

In any case, risk-taking is brave and I salute all those academics willing to take them, especially our American colleagues who are fighting day by day against odious policies at a particularly difficult time in American history when conformity is more than ever demanded. For academics, freedom to speak out is hedged about on all sides and this is surely one reason that few social-science practioners contribute to the global justice movement. Another reason is that most academics gradually acquire a vested interest in mainstream interpretations of a given reality. It is emotionally, professionally and often materially impossible to give up such interpretations: emotionally because the development of a world-view often coincides with a period of youth, energy and discipleship; professionally because the mainstream insures membership in the club and consequent self-esteem; materially because, aside from one's salary, lucrative contracts may depend on telling the contractor what he wants to hear. A social science expert is, after all, an expert in repackaging the conventional wisdom so as to make the fewest possible enemies.

Thomas Kuhn (1962) shows masterfully how the tenacious defense of the reigning paradigm rules the hard sciences. He quotes Max Planck to the effect that paradigms don't change only because they are proved to be inadequate or wrong but because their defenders eventually weaken (and sometimes eventually die), and a new paradigm can at last rise to replace the outmoded one. What Kuhn never thought of exploring when he wrote *The Structure of Scientific Revolutions* was the concerted and successful effort of right-wing forces in the United States and Britain to buy and pay for the development and popularization of their own neo-liberal ideology. After the Second World War, virtually all thoughtful Americans and Europeans were Keynesians, Social or Christian Democrats or some stripe of Marxist. But from the early 1950s onwards, a small covey of foresighted, far-right forces realized that *"ideas have consequences"* (the title of a 1948 book by conservative guru Richard Weaver) and set out to fund scholars and writers, endow university chairs and research centers, pay for conferences and colloquia, serious journals and campus newspapers and generally create a closely-knit intellectual cadre to propagate their ideas. Unlike more progressive, left-leaning foundations which would fund "projects" but never the production of ideas; conservative foundations based on entrepreneurial fortunes like Olin, Scaife-Mellon or Bradley funded think tanks like the American Enterprise Institute or the Heritage Foundation in Washington or the Adam Smith Institute in London. I call them "right-wing Gramscians" because the neo-liberals, unlike progressives or Marxists, truly believed in the power of ideas and the concept of cultural hegemony. We now live with the consequences (see George, 1997).

Despite the overwhelming evidence that one can, by spending tens of millions of dollars, effectively buy an intellectual climate sympathetic to the most reactionary policies, the social sciences still tend to claim for themselves the supposed neutrality of the hard sciences. I'm not competent to judge whether a truly detached, neutral stance can exist even in mathematics, but I'm quite sure it can't in economics, sociology or political science. In the name of "neutrality" or "objectivity," one usually gets the pre-suppositions and the ideological framework of the reigning paradigm. In our case, in the current moment, this will be the neo-liberal worldview.

The responsibility of critical intellectuals is to make explicit these pre-suppositions and visible this ideological framework, particularly for their students. They should also have the honesty to make their own stance clear. This can normally be done by stating one's social goals and one's notion of citizenship. Unfortunately, in most lecture halls and most scholarly publications, the academic is not supposed to have goals or to act as a citizen. These categories (like religion) are supposed to be reserved for private life.

How the academic initially frames and defines an issue is critically important. What, for example, is the point of "economics"? One's definition determines one's goals. In Karl Polanyi's (1957) sense, is the economy at the service of society or—as in an advanced capitalist economy—is society supposed to sit back and let the market get on with it? I assume most of us would define the object of economic science as the satisfaction of basic human needs for all members of a given society. The task of the economist is therefore to discover and to propose the most efficient methods for the collection, production, and distribution of scarce resources so as to meet those needs, which will include but may not be limited to adequate food, clean water, clothing, shelter, energy and access to transport, health care, education and culture. This definition, like any other, implies value judgments. It is the starting point for the global justice movement and Adam Smith, not to mention Karl Marx, would sympathize with it.

Many institutions, however, would not. Human needs may even be completely absent from their worldviews although they would be unwilling to admit it. The

World Bank rhetorically claims to uphold the "satisfaction of needs" but rarely follows through in practice, whereas the International Monetary Fund would say, if pressed, that these needs are more likely to be satisfied by free market and "Washington Consensus"–type, macro-economic measures. The World Trade Organization is even more caricatural since for the WTO, all human activities, including food, water, health, education, culture, etc., are potentially profitable commodities, tradable in the world market. The Bank, the Fund and the WTO all nonetheless profess to be concerned with "development" (e.g., the Doha Development Round).

These institutions employ huge numbers of academically trained social scientists, particularly economists, yet they consistently refuse to test their hypotheses against objective criteria (or even agree on what those criteria should be). Under such circumstances, it is impossible to claim the status of a "hard science" for economics. We know, for example, that measured against the satisfaction of human needs, the structural adjustment policies imposed by the World Bank and the IMF are resounding failures. Dozens, perhaps hundreds of studies have documented the devastating impact of structural adjustment on the poor, the deterioration of health care and education in indebted countries, the increasing scarcity of adequate food and clean water, the mounting income inequalities. We know also that the "export or perish" policies of these same institutions have contributed hugely to drastic drops in world primary commodity prices (and therefore in living standards) since so many countries are simultaneously trying to export the same limited range of products.

This is not the place to elaborate on such well-known themes. The point is rather that the "science" of economics is concerned with matters of life and death yet provides no mechanism, no method, no check or balance which could oblige powerful economic institutions to recognise policy failure. Scientists whose experiments produce consistently negative results must eventually reject their hypotheses and change course. Not so international economic and financial institutions. Several years devoted to studying and writing about Third World debt and structural adjustment taught me the hard lesson that no level of human suffering in and of itself would cause their policies to change. They would, instead, insist that these policies were not in themselves faulty but had not been applied forcefully enough or long enough and they would blame the governments (whence the new universal emphasis on "governance"). In this regard, the book by former World Bank chief economist Joseph Stiglitz, *Globalization and Its Discontents* (2002), showing how the IMF caused one disaster after another, although somewhat self-serving, is a breath of fresh air.

Either one must conclude that economics as practiced by major global institutions is not concerned with human needs or, if the satisfaction of such needs is indeed the goal, then the economists who people these institutions are hopeless at their trade. Either way, the global justice movement and critical intellectuals are devoted to combating major global institutions, their devastating impact on innocent human bystanders, and the harmful social science they represent. As someone who spent a couple of decades fighting such institutions with a comparatively tiny band of brothers and sisters, I'm joyfully overwhelmed that thousands should now turn up in Seattle, Prague, Washington and other venues to voice their opposition to the Bank, the Fund, the WTO and the G7.

Finally, I'd like to deal rapidly and in no particular order with three other aspects of the role and responsibilities of academics and intellectuals in the global justice movement.

First, let's consider the choice of subjects. Those who genuinely want to help the movement should study the rich and powerful, not the poor and powerless. This point is much better understood now than when I first wrote the same thing in *"How the Other Half Dies."* Although wealth and power are in a better position to hide their activities and are therefore more difficult to study, any knowledge about them will be valuable to the movement. The poor and powerless already know what is wrong with their lives and those who want to help them should analyse the forces that keep them poor and powerless. Better a sociology of the Pentagon or the Houston country club than of single mothers or L.A. gangs.

Second, one should use whatever methods seem to yield results or a fresh perspective, not necessarily the standard methodology of the discipline. One should also take as a given that, just as rules are made to be broken, disciplinary boundaries are made to be crossed. This is how Fabrizio Sabelli, an anthropologist, and I approached the World Bank in *Faith and Credit* (George and Sabelli, 1995), by treating the Bank as a religious institution. The fit was surprisingly close (not to mention more fun for the authors) and I hope revealing to readers.

Third, intellectuals whose goal is to contribute to social movements have to be more rigorous than their mainstream colleagues. This is a simple rule of survival. If you're in the academic minority, you must assume that the majority will be out to get you and you'll need high-quality body-armor to be unassailable. One way to do this is to use the adversary's own words. The Internet has made this technique easier than it used to be. Our adversaries all have sites and they are often unconscious of how their documents may sound to "normal" people. The corollary is unfortunately that the most informative documents may not be on the net. A good rule of thumb is: the smaller the intended audience of a document, the franker and more revealing the content. Leaks are best of all. I tried to illustrate this point by inventing a fake, leaked document. "The Lugano Report" (George, 1999) was a "factual fiction" I wrote from start to finish but which purported to be the report of an expert group to unnamed commissioners whose question was how best to preserve capitalism in the 21st century. The answer is not a pretty one but only fictional form allowed me to explore the full horror of the future if the present system prevails. I wouldn't be surprised if a genuine report of this kind existed, but if it does, it hasn't been leaked so far.

In conclusion, it's clear that if they can avoid the pitfalls and observe a few simple rules, academics and intellectuals have much to contribute to the global justice movement. Let's remember, however, that the opposite is also true. The growing strength and visibility of this movement is itself a rebuttal of the famous TINA doctrine ("There Is No Alternative") which the neo-liberals so desperately want people to believe. Why else would they spend so much blood and treasure constructing and disseminating their ideology? The presence of a hundred thousand people at the World Social Forum in Porto Alegre proclaiming that "another world is possible" is surely as effective in unmasking and demolishing neo-liberalism as the critiques of a hundred intellectuals. As we analyze, criticize, propose and strategize, let's never forget that we are all part of a vast mutual liberation society, that as we work to free others, they are also working to free us.

2

What Is a Critical Globalization Studies?
Intellectual Labor and Global Society

William I. Robinson

Who would deny we are living in troubled times? Some would even argue that the very fate of humanity has never been so uncertain as it is in the early twenty-first century. It is clear, regardless of what conclusions we reach, that these troubled times are fundamentally shaped by transnational processes. Academics cannot hope to understand the social world of the twenty-first century without taking into account these processes. But I am primarily concerned here with a related problematic; the role and responsibility of intellectuals in the face of these processes. Those who attempt to understand our world cannot avoid addressing a set of challenging questions. What is the relevance of our research to the burning political issues and social struggles of our epoch, to the proliferation of conflicts bound up with globalization? How does our study of globalization help us to understand the urgent and vital matters facing humanity in the twenty-first century, the matters of war and peace, social justice, democracy, cultural pluralism, and ecologically sustainable development?

I want in this chapter to call for the development of a critical globalization studies. What does it mean to talk of a *critical globalization studies?* What do we mean by *critical?* What do we mean by *globalization?* It is by no means obvious what we want to convey when we employ these concepts. And, in fact, it is not necessarily even obvious what we mean by *studies,* insofar as we would agree that we cannot separate study from practice and that all intellectual labor constitutes a social practice. Although we may disagree on the meaning of these three concepts, I put forward as an initial point of reference the affirmation by one well-known nineteenth-century social thinker, that critical theory is "the self-clarification of the struggles and wishes of the age" (Marx, as cited in Fraser, 1987: 31). With this affirmation as the backdrop, let us focus on the following two observations.

First, a *critical* studies is one that is concerned with *reflexivity,* and that must acknowledge the historical specificity of existing social arrangements. That is, we must acknowledge that the society in which we live is only one possible form of society. And if we acknowledge the historic specificity of these arrangements, then we must recognize the centrality to our understanding of the world of social struggles as well. Such struggles, in analytical abstraction, can be seen as divided into two diametrically opposed categories, namely, struggles to reorganize and reconstruct on new bases these arrangements, that is to say, struggles for social emancipation, and at the same time struggles to defend or sustain these arrangements. We could say, in other words, that we must acknowledge struggles from below and struggles from above, and the interplay between them.

Second, social arrangements in the early twenty-first century must increasingly be understood — indeed, can only be understood — in the context of global-level structures and processes, that is to say, in the context of globalization. The perceived problematics of the local and of the nation-state must be located within a broader web of interconnected histories that in the current era are converging in new ways. Any critical studies in the twenty-first century must be, of necessity, also a globalization studies.

Problems, however, arise when we fail to recognize that while global-level thinking may be a necessary condition for a critical understanding of the world, it is not sufficient. "Indeed, one need only think back to early attempts to come to terms with the phenomenon of multinational corporations as harbingers of what is now called globalization to see that a global perspective has long marked the thinking and practice of transnational elites themselves," observes Neufeld. "The obvious point is that global thinking is not inherently critical. Accordingly, care must be taken to identify what kinds of global-level thinking are critical — that is, promote emancipatory change — and which do not" (Neufeld, 2002: 2).

In other words, if we can conceptualize a critical globalization studies, then we must be also able to conceive of its opposite, a noncritical globalization studies. How may we distinguish between the two? Here is where debate heats up, and where it becomes clear that the intellectual exercise is, as well, a political one. If a critical studies is one that acknowledges the historical specificity of existing social arrangements, then its noncritical opposite is one that takes the existing world as it is. It is a studies that denies that the world we live in — in this case, twenty-first century global society — is only one particular historical form, one that has a beginning and an end, as do all historical forms and institutions. In contradistinction, a critical approach is one which acknowledges that *history*, whether spelled with a lower-case *h* or an upper-case *H*, has no end.

Free-Floating Academics or Organic Intellectuals?

I want to foreground here the social and the historical character of intellectual labor. The distinction between critical and noncritical ways of thinking is what Max Horkheimer (1972) first called "traditional" vs. "critical" thinking, and what Robert Cox (1995), more recently has referred to as "problem-solving" vs. "critical" thinking. The critical tradition in the social sciences, not to be confused with the related but distinct *critical theory* as first developed by the Frankfurt School in Western Marxist thought, refers in the broadest sense to those approaches that take a critical view of the prevailing status quo and explicitly seek to replace the predominant power structures and social hierarchies with what are seen as more just and equitable social arrangements.

Let us say, then, that a critical studies is distinguished from a noncritical or mainstream studies by the fact that it does not take for granted the prevailing power structure, the existing arrangements, and established institutions. A critical studies can only mean that we do not accept the world as we find it as being in any sense natural. Hence, the first step in any critical globalization studies is to *problematize* the social reality that we study and in which we exist. And once we ask, what is the beginning — and how may we imagine the end — of the existing order of things, then the next question a critical studies must ask is, *what are the collective agents at work?* What are the real and potential human agencies involved in social change? What is their relationship to the prevailing order and to one another?

The exercise of studying the world, of trying to know the world, is itself a social act, committed by agents with a definite relationship to the social order. Intellectual production is always a collective process, and knowledge, a social product. By *collective* I do not just mean collaborative projects among scholars or ongoing research programs. The raw material of intellectual production are the hopes and struggles for survival of communities and peoples around the world, the contending social forces, the conflicts, the ideological clashes, the alternative visions, and the raging political battles that characterize our epoch. It is the daily labor of billions of people in global society, at the cost of much sweat, not to mention blood, grief, and pain, that makes it materially possible, among other things, for us to engage in intellectual labor. For the critical intellectual, along with the privilege of being able to engage in intellectual labor comes the social responsibility to use that labor in the service of the many who enjoy no such privileges yet make ours possible. In my view, all those who engage in intellectual labor or make knowledge claims are *organic* intellectuals, in the sense that all such labor is social labor and its practitioners, social actors.

Many mainstream academics, shielded by the assumptions of positivist epistemologies, would no doubt, take issue with my characterization of intellectual labor as, by definition, a social act by organic social agents. There are those who would posit a free-floating academic, a neutral generator of knowledge and ideas. What can we make of such an argument? Certainly, scholars and intellectuals are knowledge producers, and few would disagree that with the assertion that "knowledge is power." And once we agree on this, it is incumbent on us to ask, *power for whom?* Power exercised by whom? Power to what ends? Academics who believe they can remain aloof in the face of the conflicts that are swirling about us and the ever-higher stakes involved are engaged in a self-deception that is itself a political act, and we very often find these mainstream academics performing legitimating functions for dominant groups.

We know from the philosophy and the sociology of knowledge that knowledge is never neutral or divorced from the historic context of its production, including from competing social interests (see, inter alia, Therborn, 1985; Fray, 1987; Chalmers, 2000; Robinson, 1996). Intellectual production always parallels, and can be functionally associated with, movement and change in human society. There is no such thing as an intellectual or an academic divorced from social aims that drive research — not in the hard sciences, and much less in the social sciences and humanities. The mainstream scholar may "well believe in an independent, 'suprasocial,' detached knowledge as in the social importance of his expertise," observes Horkheimer. "The dualism of thought and being, understanding and perception is second nature to the scientist … [such mainstream scholars] believe they are acting according to personal determinations, whereas, in fact, even in their most complicated calculations they but exemplify the working of an incalculable social mechanism" (1972: 196–197).

If we are to speak of a critical globalization studies, then we must address the matter of the responsibility of intellectuals. This is to ask, what is the relationship between our intellectual work and power? What is the relationship between our research into globalization, and power in global society? What ends and whose interests does our intellectual production serve? For whom do we speak (or claim to speak)? In short, as academics and researchers examining globalization, we must ask ourselves, whose mandarins are we?

Exercising a "Preferential Option" for the Subordinate Majority of Global Society

Let me deepen the polemic (taking up polemics is in the spirit and the very marrow of a critical studies) and return to the earlier citation, "the self-clarification of the struggles and wishes of the age." If this is at the heart of critical thought, and if our undertaking is predicated on acknowledging the historical specificity of existing social arrangements, then we cannot engage in a critical studies without identifying and foregrounding the nature of the particular historical society in which we live. That society is *a* capitalist society — *a* global capitalist society.

The prevailing global order has its share of intellectual defenders, academics, pundits, and ideologues, who in the end serve to mystify the real inner workings of the emerging order and the social interests embedded therein (see Robinson, 1996). These intellectuals are central cogs in the system of global capitalism, performing not only legitimating functions but also providing technical solutions in response to the problems and contradictions of the system. In short, they exercise a "preferential option" for a minority of the privileged and the powerful in global capitalist society. In opposition to such defenders of the dominant order, a critical globalization studies needs to exercise in its intellectual labor a "preferential option" for the subordinate majorities of emergent global society, and for the future that is latent within them.

But, what does it mean to exercise a preferential option for the majority in global society? In my view, what is required in global society — seen from the needs and aspirations of the poor majority of humanity for whom global capitalism is nothing short of alienation, savagery, and dehumanization — are organic intellectuals capable of theorizing the changes that have taken place in the system of capitalism in this epoch of globalization. They would be capable of assisting popular majorities in their efforts to arrive at these theoretical insights as inputs for their real-world struggles to develop alternative social relationships and an alternative social logic — the logic of majorities — to that of the market and of transnational capital. In other words, a critical globalization studies has to be capable of inspiring emancipatory action, of contributing to the development of a program that integrates theory and practice.

A critical globalization studies means:

- Challenging the dominant mythologies of our age, such as that ecologically sustainable development is possible under capitalism or that "democracy" exists when tiny minorities control wealth and power

- Exposing the ideological content of theories and knowledge claims often put forward as "objective" social scientific discourse
- Applying our training and experience to elucidating the real inner workings of the social order and the contradictions therein, which includes putting forward a cogent and systematic critique of global capitalism
- Questioning everything, deconstructing everything, interrogating every claim to knowledge
- Reconstructing what we have deconstructed, contributing to the construction of an alternative future.

We must ask ourselves, how, as organic intellectuals, do we assume our responsibilities in our institutions, such as our universities, and the mass media, as scholars, as journalists, as opinion makers, as organizers, and as cultural agents? Notwithstanding the contradictory nature of much intellectual production, our intellectual labor can legitimate the prevailing social order and provide technical solutions to the problems that arise in its maintenance, or it can expose contradictions and reveal how they may be resolved by transcending the existing order.

Doing a Critical Globalization Studies

With the apparent triumph of global capitalism in the 1990s, following the collapse of the old Soviet bloc, the defeat of Third World nationalist and revolutionary projects, and the withdrawal of the left into postmodern identity politics and other forms of accommodation with the prevailing social order, many intellectuals who previously identified with resistance movements and emancipatory projects seemed to cede a certain defeatism before global capitalism (Robinson, 2003). Such defeatism has no place in a critical globalization studies. It could only have come about as a result of intellectuals' distancing themselves from grassroots resistance movements that remained robust, despite the defeat of organized left projects, and that were experiencing an exhilarating upsurge by the turn of the century. The decline of the left and socialist movements worldwide was a result, among other factors, of the chronic gap between theory and practice, thought and action, and led to a degeneration of intellectual criticism as well. An embrace of the End of History thesis (Fukuyama, 1992) is the end not of history but of critical thought.

A critical globalization studies, in my view, should be broad enough to house a diversity of approaches and epistemologies, from Marxist to radical variants of institutional, Weberian, feminist, poststructural, and other critical thought, and should, as well, emphasize questions of contingency, culture, and subjectivity. But what distinguishes (or must distinguish) a critical globalization studies are (1) the subversive nature of its thought in relation to the status quo, and (2) the linkage (actual or attempted) of theory to practice, or the grounding of a critical globalization studies in praxis, in a theoretically-informed practice. We cannot really know the world without participating in efforts to change it, which is the same as to say that it is when we engage in collective efforts to change the world that we only truly come to know the world. A critical globalization studies must not only link intellectual production and knowledge claims to emancipatory projects. It must also enjoin discursive with material struggles, lest the former become reduced to irrelevant word games. These, I would say, are essential epistemological "ground rules" of a critical globalization studies.

A critical globalization studies is, by definition, interdisciplinary — or more accurately, *transdisciplinary*. It is holistic in conception and epistemology, which is not to say, as a matter of course, that particular studies must necessarily take the "whole" as the object of inquiry. As Palan has noted, "The broadly critical tradition in the social sciences is naturally attracted to holistic interpretations of social relations. ... The assumption being that there are totalizing processes driven by a predominant logic that we call capitalism, and that such totalizing processes manifest themselves in all aspects of social life" (Palan, 2000: 16). The critical tradition maintains, therefore, that there is no point in studying each facet of social life as an independent system of relationships, for the simple reason that they are not independent but interdependent, as internally related elements of a more encompassing totality. Consequently, the critical tradition does not accept the analytical legitimacy of formal academic divisions.

This does not mean that there is any single "right" way to engage in a critical globalization studies. I would insist, nonetheless, that it is not possible to understand global society in the absence of a political economy analysis. Political economy historically has concentrated on the analytical as well as prescriptive questions of how order and change come about. The history of the breakup in the nineteenth and twentieth centuries of political economy into artificial and compartmentalized "disciplines" is well known (Blackburn, 1972; Therborn, 1985; Wallerstein, 2001). We need to recapture the critical essence of political economy, which takes as its basis the production and reproduction of our material existence, and on that basis seeks to ask how change can be brought about, by whom, and for whom.

Yet it is equally true that the manifold dimensions of the social totality cannot be reduced to epiphenomena of the material bases of global society. Such an approach would not be dialectical — that is, holistic — but mechanical and misleading. The opposition of political economy to cultural analysis, for instance, is a false dualism that obscures rather than elucidates the complex reality of global society, insofar as our material existence as humans is always, of necessity, only possible through the construction of a symbolic order and systems of meaning. Both are, themselves, the products of historically situated social forces and have an ongoing recursive effect on material reality. Indeed, culture is itself a material force (on culture as an indispensable underpinning of resistance movements; see Reed and Foran, 2000).

A critical globalization studies, therefore, requires dialectical thought at the level of epistemology as a way of knowing. In epistemological terms, dialectics means a dialogue seeking truth through exploration of contradictions and through identifying the internal relations that bind together diverse and multifaceted dimensions of social reality into a totality. In the dialectical approach the different dimensions of our social reality do not have an "independent" status insofar as each aspect of reality is constituted by, and is constitutive of, a larger whole of which it is an internal element. An internal relation is one in which each part is constituted in its relation to the other, so that one cannot exist without the other and only has meaning when seen within the relation, whereas an external relation is one in which each part has an existence independent of its relation to the other (Ollman, 1976). Viewing things as externally related to each other inevitably leads to dualist constructs and false dichotomies (e.g., political economy vs. culture). The distinct levels of social structure — in this case, global social structure — cannot be understood independent of each other, but neither are these levels reducible to any one category. They are internally related, meaning that they can only be understood in their relation to each other and to the larger social whole.

Critical thought, in this regard, means applying a dialectical as opposed to a formal logic, one that focuses not on things in themselves but on the interrelations among them (that is, on systemic connections). A dialectical logic involves identifying how distinct dimensions of social reality may be analytically distinct (such as the three most salient axes of social inequality: race, class, and gender) yet are mutually constitutive of each other as internal elements of a more encompassing process. Our task is to uncover internal linkages among distinct sets of historical relationships and their grounding in an underlying (that is, more primary) historic process, which in my view are material relations of production and reproduction, and the historical ordering principle those relations put forth. This is to argue that historical processes of production and reproduction are causal processes. To take the case of race and class, it is not that racialization processes occurring around the world in the twenty-first century can be explained in terms of class but that class itself became racialized in the formative years of the world capitalist system because of the particular history of that system. I will not draw out the point further here. Suffice it to note that ultimately we are concerned here with the dialectical relationship between consciousness and being.

Twenty-first century global society is characterized by a far greater complexity and much faster change and interaction than at any time in human history. It is only possible to grasp both the complexity of these structures and processes, and the dynamics of change, through a dialectical approach. For Ollman, the dialectic method involves six successive moments. The *ontological moment* has to do with the infinite number of mutually dependent processes that make up the totality, or structured whole, of social life. The *epistemological moment* deals with how to organize thinking in order to understand such a world, abstracting out the main patterns of change and interaction. The *moment of inquiry* appropriates the patterns of these internal relationships in order to further the project of investigation. The *moment of intellectual reconstruction* or *self-clarification* puts together the results of such an investigation for oneself. The *moment of exposition* entails describing to a particular audience the dialectical grasp of the facts by taking into account how others think. Finally, the *moment of praxis* uses the clarification of the facts of social life to act consciously in and on the world, changing it while simultaneously deepening one's understanding of it (Ollman, 1998: 342). Applied to the matter before us, we could say that a critical globalization studies becomes self-knowledge of global society through active theorizing and political work.

To engage in a critical globalization studies means to maintain contact with everyday concerns. Whether they acknowledge so or not, all intellectuals are engaged in active participation in everyday life, acting as agents or organizers, or in Gramsci's words, as "permanent persuaders" in the construction of hegemonic social orders (Gramsci, 1971: 9–10). The intellectual in this case contributes to the active construction of hegemony by particular social forces that construct and maintain a social order on an ongoing basis. But such intellectual labor can also entail a connection with opposing initiatives, with forces from below and their attempts to forge a counterhegemony by drawing out the connections, through theoretical reflection, that link the distinct lived realities, everyday spontaneous and organized forms of struggle. By propagating certain ideas, intellectuals play an essential mediating function in the struggle for hegemony, Gramsci reminds us, by acting as "deputies" or instruments of hegemony, or by performing a valuable supporting role to subordinate groups engaged in promoting social change (Gramsci, 1971: 5–23, 52–55).

We would do well, in conclusion, to recall that in times of great social transformation established social theories are called into question and new ones proliferate to give explanation. And at times of social crisis, such as the one we appear to face in early twenty-first century global society, sound theoretical understandings are crucial if we hope to intervene effectively in the resolution of such crises. The current epoch is a time of rapidly growing global social polarization between a shrinking minority of haves and an expanding majority of have-nots. It is a time of escalating political and military conflict as contending social forces face each other in innumerable yet interwoven struggles around the world. The global capitalist system faced by the turn of the century a structural crisis of overaccumulation and also an expanding crisis of legitimacy (Robinson, 2004) in the face of the "irresistible" rise of a global justice movement (Notes from Nowhere, 2003). There was certainly no wanting of mass mobilization and political protagonism from below, before which a critical globalization studies could, and must, make a major contribution. The task of a critical globalization studies is certainly daunting, given such a vast and complex theoretical object as emergent global society, and the character of the current situation as transitional and not accomplished. The gauntlet, nonetheless, is before us.

Acknowledgment

I would like to thank John Foran and Richard Appelbaum for providing critical suggestions on early drafts of this chapter.

3

What Is a Critical Globalization Studies?

James H. Mittelman

In the burgeoning of globalization studies, different kinds of knowledge have emerged. These overlap and are variously described as historical, empirical, formal, intuitive, theoretical, and critical knowledge sets. The levels of abstraction range from basic to applied, with room for both theoretical and fire-brigade research. At all levels, there is no dichotomous split between theory and praxis. Both professional and lay theorists, intellectuals who prefer the contemplative life and scholar-activists alike, have contributed importantly to globalization studies.

In the genre of knowledge under consideration here, *critical* globalization studies scholars are not wedded to any single worldview. There is no universal agreement on how the critical conception should be understood or what characterizes it.

Not surprisingly, critical thinkers' different backgrounds and interests have produced varied emphases. These are linkages between globalization and specific themes, such as cities (Sassen, 2001), class structures (Overbeek, 2001; Abdul Rahman Embong, 2002; Sklair, 2002), culture (Robertson, 1992; Friedman, 1994; Tomlinson, 1999; Nederveen Pieterse, 2004), development (McMichael, 2004; Benería, 2003), the environment (Wapner, 2002), ethical life and religion (Held, 1995; Falk, 1999), gender (Tickner, 2001; Peterson, 2003), governance (Hettne and Odén, 2002; Rosenau, 2003), hegemony (Arrighi and Silver, 1999; Hardt and Negri, 2000), human rights (Cheru, 2002), ideology (Rupert, 2000; Steger, 2002), markets (Dicken, 2003; Peck and Yeung, 2003), regions (Olds et al., 1999; Zeleza, 2003), regionalism (Hettne, 2002b; Väyrynen, 2003), resistance (Gills, 2000; Smith and Johnson, 2002; Amoore, forthcoming), the state (Panitch, 1996; Robinson, 2001), and war and peace (Kaldor, 1999). In addition, critical globalization studies offers engaging and insightful textbooks (Scholte, 2000; Steger, 2003) and samplers of readings (Held and McGrew, 2003; Robertson and White, 2003). Public intellectuals outside academe have also produced major statements, partly based on participant-observation, which are integral to critical globalization studies (Bové and Dufour, 2000; Wallach and Sforza, 2000; Barlow and Clarke, 2001; Danaher, 2001; Bello, 2003; Klein, 2002).[1]

Without detailing individual authors' work or tracing the tributaries of critical globalization theory, it is worth identifying the broad commonalities among them. Most important, from a critical perspective, precisely what kind of knowledge about globalization is and should be summoned? What do critical globalization scholars really want to find out? What is the desired knowledge? This article is an attempt to answer these guiding questions, at least in a preliminary way.

A Critical Perspective

For critically minded scholars, globalization encompasses a historical transformation in the interactions among market forces, political authority, and the life ways embodied in society, as they encounter and join with local conditions. On the critical flank, scholars persistently question the positivist faith in empiricism — the distinction between facts and values, the separability of variables, and hypothesis-testing as a means to discover objective "truth" — and, rather, examine how facts are constructed and whose interests they serve. In the tug of war with positivist knowledge, critical conceptions do not necessarily mean opposition; some scholars and activists, especially the ones mindful of postmodern sensibilities, strive for a multiplicity of conditions that makes room for numerous dominant and subaltern positions. A critical perspective can have elements of both conventional and heterodox fields, but does not confuse them and is aware of how they are formed.

At minimum, a critical approach is suspicious, troubling, and open-ended in its search for knowledge. It seeks to reconstruct what Antonio Gramsci (1971, 2000) called "common-sense" propositions, which are the product of historical processes that leave the individual in a particular relationship with social groups. For Gramsci, common-sense meanings are multiple, changing, and fragmented among strata. These "chaotic" conceptions absorb the sediment of folklore, contradict one another, and form an incoherent whole. Some elements of common sense are consistent with hegemonic stability, whereas others run counter to it. Critical intellectuals attempt to sharpen the tensions, gain leverage from them, and go against meanings established by institutions such as the mass media, incorporated in cultural goods, and apparent in imaginary realms (e.g., films, television, and magazines). These products can diminish the capacity to think independently and make individuals more susceptible to the language of competitive market relations. For Gramsci, critical thinking should not merely oppose but become part of people's understanding of their own conditions, bringing about a new common sense.

To delimit meaningful knowledge, critical scholarship thus seeks to do more than unmask normal knowledge. A critical orientation calls for not only deconstructing extant knowledge and practice but also constructing new knowledge about what exists and what ought to exist on the basis of transformed relations of power.

Preconceptions

In this vein, international studies may be construed as an impediment to understanding the discourses of globalization. We know that the main actors are not nations, as the term "international" suggests, or, arguably, even states, for emergent interactions, as tragically exemplified on 9/11, are now between the state-centric and multi-centric worlds (Ferguson and Rosenau, 2003).

There is not, however, a bifurcation of two worlds. The state-centric system, like the multi-centric form of world order, harbors diverse forms of state–nonstate modes of governance, and different sources of social solidarity. Just as the state-centric world actively exists within the multi-centric world, so does the multi-centric world operate in the interstices of the state-centric world. To the extent that there is not a complete cleavage between these worlds, one might speak of a *polymorphous world* — orders with many forms that pass through one another. Surely common-sense knowledge does not sufficiently grasp the interpenetration of myriad worlds, perhaps because of the complexity and, postmodernists would add, the impossibility, of delineating a master pattern. In fact, globalization blurs categories of analysis and outruns traditional explanations that fail to capture the interplay of market dynamics, power relations, and social forces that slice across borders.

In the reconstruction of knowledge, it is useful to consider "standpoint epistemology." The main claims here are that knowledge must be situated in the material lives of actors and, in arriving at a standpoint, actors' social locations are crucial, for as Max Weber had emphasized, a perspective is never total but always partial (Weber, 1949; Harding, 1991; Hekman, 1997). Before contemporary feminists elaborated this thesis about the need for divergent standpoints in knowledge seeking, Fernand Braudel (1990) grappled with the importance of viewing phenomena from multiple observation points: different stations in social hierarchies, diverse axes in ordering human affairs, various zones in the global political economy, and distinct speeds of time. In his own research, including a prescient book on civilizations (prepared for the secondary-school syllabus in France but rejected by the intellectual establishment there), Braudel preferred the *longue durée* — the long view of origins and gradual, slow-moving transformations. Although the long perspective requires patience, it is in no way incompatible with other time frames: what Braudel called the span of the conjuncture (10, 20, or even 50 years) or the immediate history of events (Braudel, 1980, 1994). Putting together standpoint epistemology and Braudelian interactions, then, the task is to comprehend multiple orientations within multiple time frames.

Cognizant of the dimensions of hierarchical power relations, time, and space, intellectuals embarked on reconstructing knowledge face the difficult challenge of constructing grounded utopias. I use the term *grounded utopia* to mean an imagined alternative that has never existed, yet with a future or futures rooted in real historical tendencies and embodied practices. In Weber's sense, the challenge is to achieve "an ethical *imperative* ... of what ought to exist" (1949: 91–92; emphasis in original). Without adopting a positivist separation of "is" and "ought," globalization critics can usefully work toward a grounded utopia by reconciling Gramsci and Weber, such that common sense is reconstituted and its historical contradictions and potentials drawn out, in an attempt to enact the ethics of a desired order.

For his part, Gramsci disavowed a value-free, ahistorical knowledge, exemplified in the pernicious tendencies of both scientism and utopian Marxism. Similarly, while emphasizing that ideal types are methodological constructs, not goals to be realized, Weber cautioned against utopianism, in that it underestimates the coercive components of authority and hierarchical social relations — for example, efforts to eliminate increasingly bureaucratic organizations in the functioning of capitalism (1971: 229). For both Gramsci and Weber, history is powered by structural forces, yet open-ended and free to continuously evolve a new order, not imprisoned by a foreordained or closed schema. So, too, Gramsci and Weber, albeit somewhat differently, emphasized the role of authority and hierarchical institutions in the elevation toward utopias.

Mindful of this intellectual legacy, other theorists pushed the notion of utopia. Just as Polanyi (1957) criticized the "stark utopia" of a self-regulating market for being ahistorical and then projected a preferred scenario of reembedding the market in society as a means to increasing freedom, E. H. Carr (1964; also Cox, M., 2000, and Hettne, 2002a), often regarded as the father of realism, held that utopian thinking can cloak interests, yet he ultimately came down in favor of a balance between an appreciation of power relations and utopian approaches to peace:

> We can describe as utopian in the right sense (i.e., performing the proper function of a utopia in proclaiming an ideal to be aimed at, though not wholly attainable) the desire to eliminate the element of power and to base the bargaining process of peaceful change on a common feeling of what is just and reasonable. (Carr, 1964: 222)

In other words, peaceful change requires both utopian visions and critical realist analysis. A common ground among the often divergent perspectives of these thinkers is that grounded utopias can be a valuable heuristic if anchored in history, adjusted for interests of material power, and attuned to possible means to achieve social justice.

For these theorists, there are hidden aspects of life that lie beneath the visible problems that one encounters. Why? Perhaps the holders of power want them concealed. For example, when a ruling coalition goes to war, it may reveal some reasons, but others remain undisclosed. Also, certain issues may be uncomfortable to talk about (e.g., self-interest, genocide, ethnic animosity, gendered power structures, and disappearances). To be sure, some contemporary conflicts, as in South Asia, are partly about historical memory, which involves matters of cultural dignity, and others, perhaps in parts of the Middle East today, are partially about humiliation. It may be difficult to forthrightly express these experiences, although in some cases, they have come out in truth commissions.

Even if one would not expect classical theorists to have programmatic answers for the problems of contemporary globalization, it was their insight that something was terribly wrong: for Marx, alienation; for Weber, the iron cage of bureaucratic rationality; and for Durkheim, anomie. Their critical thinking — precursor theories for knowing today's vexed world — emerged in the context of turmoil in Europe: from Marx's perspective, the revolutions of 1848; from Weber's, the social conflicts accompanying Germany's shift from the age of Bismarck to an industrial era; and from Durkheim's, the *bouleversements* of France's transition from the Third Republic and long revolution to a modern social order. These reflections brought to light the dark side of historical transformations, including the havoc visited on ordinary people (Lemert, 1993: 9, 15). The master critical theorists of the nineteenth and early twentieth centuries were suspicious of the common-sense propositions of their day and deeply skeptical about received wisdom. Furthermore, they imagined alternative orders that would alleviate the basic problems of their times.

Traps and Confusions

The dawn of the twenty-first century is also a period racked by social turmoil — the disruptions caused by globalizing capitalism, new wars, and a renewed search for meaning in life. What is more, the means of producing knowledge have changed. Today, knowledge is not primarily the work of lone thinkers, but conditioned by powerful material infrastructures — traveling paradigms, funding agencies, think tanks, publishers and journals, professional associations, technologies and networks, and vast research parks. In addition, there are mechanisms for policing knowledge production, such as intellectual property rights, as well as efforts to subvert discursive power.

One way in which these mechanisms operate is through narrative entrapment. There is a danger of entrapping ourselves in worlds of our own making. These worlds can be constructed as language, mental pictures that represent social phenomena, and paradigms that filter ideas inside and keep others outside a knowledge structure (Shotter, 1993: 26–31). The risk of falling into this trap is acute for academic educators — for example, assigning a paper and formulating a research question, thereby telling students what to look for. To the extent that a preconceived conceptual filter is employed, it can block intuitive knowledge, silence tetchy questions, and thereby deny the discovery of newly critical knowledge.

The fall into this trap can come about through the use of words. They, of course, convey meanings. Consider the iconography of the term "antiglobalization move-ment." Indeed, if resistance to globalization manifests at diverse sites, including in people's heads and in cultural expressions (novels, plays, cartoons, etc.), why should resistance be put into a social-movement filter? If resistance is an integral part of globalization itself, it cannot be antiglobalization. Resistance is clearly inherent in global restructuring, which produces new winners and a multitude of losers, some of whose counteractions coalesce into social movements while others do not. In short, antiglobalization is the wrong way to conceptualize resistance. Now, in the teeth of military globalization, resistance to globalization dovetails with peace marches that have used the networks and technologies mounted by global justice movements protesting globalization; these, in turn, were built on the antiapartheid movement, IMF riots, the student revolts and the black-power movement of earlier decades, black and Third World feminisms, and Zapatista support structures.

In the context of militarized globalization, the term "terrorism" has gained cur-rency. The appropriation of this vocabulary varies according to the standpoints of the strong and the weak and along the spectrum of state-sponsored to nonstate terrorism. It is worth recalling that the insurrectionists who took lives and property and attacked the state during the American Revolution are known in the United States for their heroism and not decried as terrorists. During the anticolonial, armed strug-gle in Southern Rhodesia (today, Zimbabwe), the white minority regime and its supporters made frequent references to the "terr war," but after the coming to power of a postcolonial state in 1980, the labeling of violence was reversed. Also, during the apartheid era, South Africa's white redoubt and President Ronald Reagan alike called the imprisoned Nelson Mandela a terrorist, but he later received the Nobel Peace Prize. Putting aside these discrepancies and exercising discursive power, President George W. Bush's wordsmiths invoked the terrorism trope to pigeonhole quite diverse responses to domination, including elements of resistance to globalization.

To set the matter right, the intellectual resistance is in good part an ethical move. Whose words and voices are represented? Some neorealists and neoliberals paint pictures of globalization crises that touch down in Africa, Asia, and Latin America, and do so from the standpoint of the West or even just Washington, D.C. For example, Robert Gilpin, a senior scholar whose work on the changing nature of global capitalism offers deep insights, derives his information on the Asian financial crisis mainly from Western sources, such as the Washington-based Institute for International Economics. Asian scholars, especially critical thinkers, are barely represented in Gilpin's chapter on "Asian Regionalism" in *The Challenge of Global Capitalism* (2000), a basic text that has been widely adopted. The discussion of migration (Gilpin, 2000: 295, 310) excludes the voices of migrants themselves, which could easily be tapped through interviews and other methodologies. In this case, one influential book among many, the subalterns are not permitted to speak.[2]

Whose voices, then, should be represented? By making this choice, the analyst necessarily integrates normative aspects of reflection in the account. There is no getting around it. The dilemma is that with multiple objects of study — a shifting and complex ontology — there must be a conceptual imposition. But who authorizes the interlocutor? What is the role of the interpreter? Is there a means to escape this dilemma?

The best way to cope is to make observations from the standpoints along the range of the powerful to the powerless. The globalization critic must be self-monitoring. The critic must listen, remain open, and make ample room for a wide range of voices from various zones, in a vertical and horizontal sense, in the globalization matrix. Epistemologically, the task is to elicit beliefs embedded in the agents' own consciousness about their conditions of existence and their notions of the good life. One must find out if the agents are actually suffering and frustrated, and explore what causes or explains the pain. In presenting evidence and plausible theorems, the globalization critic is not just observing what is out there but in part constructing propositions about hidden or subsurface phenomena, some of which may belie common sense (Geuss, 1981).

The Components of Critical Globalization Studies

Building on the foregoing, a robust conceptualization of critical globalization studies would include the following complex of interacting components:

1. *Reflexivity* is an awareness of the relationship between knowledge and specific material and political conditions. To be reflexive is to probe historical beginnings and interests underpinning, or embedded in, a perspective or theory (Cox, 1986). A critical conceptualization of globalization warrants a searching consciousness of a series of transformations that constitute this set of processes.

2. *Historicism* incorporates the time dimension in globalization studies (Cox, 2002). It corrects the ahistorical approaches to globalization. For example, the commonsense notion that globalization is an inevitable force presupposes that it is a timeless essence without a beginning and an end. Rather, proceeding from definite historical locations, globalization is a distinctive configuration, with its own social power relations and whose future is open-ended. Thus, it is wrong to either engage in only presentism or collapse globalization into the vicissitudes of all world history. If globalization is historically constructed, then critical globalization studies requires rigorous historical thinking.

3. *Decentering* involves myriad perspectives on globalization from both its epicenters and the margins. Inasmuch as most globalization studies is produced in the West, local knowledge elsewhere has the potential to generate distinctive discourses — on, say, Islamic globalization — and fresh questions. Indeed, aerial views of globalization require grounding. With its own specificity and contingencies, Africa offers a particularly auspicious standpoint for entering the intricate dialectics of globalization and marginalization. This lens provides peripheral vision in that it enables the critic to see globalization from the outside in.

4. *Crossovers* between the social sciences and complementary branches of knowledge are key to a critical understanding of globalization. Two types of crossovers are most pertinent: to other strands of critical theory, such as critical legal studies and critical cartography, and to real world problems, understood in a holistic manner. For example, to come to grips with the global HIV–AIDS pandemic and SARS (severe acute respiratory syndrome), and the obstacles to mitigating these diseases, one must break disciplinary barriers. This entails a combination of medical, social, cultural, economic, and political research. Similarly, ecological renewal requires bridging social inquiry, humanistic studies, and the natural sciences.

5. *Strategic transformations* are about establishing counterhegemony: how to engage hegemonic power, upend it, and offer an emancipatory vision.[3] The goal is to inculcate a new moral order in lieu of the dominant ethics — currently, an ethos of efficiency, competition, individualism, and consumption inscribed in neoliberalism. At issue, among other objectives, is democratic globalization, including accountability and self-determination. The means would be countervailing power. At the end of the day, transformative action must have practical purposes.

The challenge is to excavate the above components of critical knowledge, examine their reciprocal interactions, and pull them together in a coherent whole. In other words, to cultivate critical globalization studies, conceptual interconnections must be strengthened so that they can account for global shifts.

A Post–9/11 Transformative Agenda of Studies

By any standard, September 11 was a cataclysmic event, but it did not herald the end of globalization, as some pundits hastily proclaimed (Gray, 2001). Rather, 9/11 marked a restructuring of the processes that constitute globalization. Monumental violence, understood as an instrument of causes and interests, came to the fore. The political and military dimensions of globalization gained ascendance relative to its economic forces, often seen as the main root.

Post–9/11, there is a reconfiguration of global politics, with an opening of space. This is not necessarily a democratic opening, unless one thinks that free-market democracy is tantamount to substantive democracy. Rather, political space is increasingly occupied by nonstate actors, some of which are networks, such as Al Qaeda, with potential access to weapons of mass destruction. Perpetrated by transnational networks, hegemonic power, and "rogue states," *militarized globalization* is a historical force defining our times. The corollaries are an enhanced role for police surveillance, as well as a "we-ness" and an "othering" promoted by the hegemonic power structure.

Presently, a transformative agenda of study would seek to explain the geostrategic side of globalization and link it to the geoeconomic side as well as the biosphere.[4] It would explore the material structure of power that constitutes globalization. It would also examine resistances to globalization: not only the macrovariants, like the battles of Seattle, but the microencounters, which manifest in the cultural sphere, and the several ways in which the macro and micro are mediated (Mittelman, 2000, 2004).

How are these critical studies to be executed? The place to begin is thinking through the genesis of the contemporary order and then identifying the fault lines of power that would open up the possibilities for a transformation. A conspicuous fault line today is the contradiction between globalization and unilateralism, which goes far beyond the historical pattern in U.S. foreign policy of oscillation between engagement with and isolation from external forces. On the one hand, the United States is the chief beneficiary of globalization. On the other hand, its political authorities are undermining globalization by imposing the ideas of an ensemble of neoconservative organic intellectuals, the Christian right, and militarists.

Leading up to the 2003 Iraq war, the G.W. Bush administration refused to go along with its European allies and endorse the Kyoto Protocol on the environment, withdrew from the Antiballistic Missile Treaty with Russia, and challenged the accord banning landmines. The Bush team also flouted the International Criminal Court, refused to cooperate with Mexico on immigration, applied tariffs on steel in violation of international trade rules, approved an increase in subsidies to U.S. farmers despite its lip service to lowering barriers to free trade, and told developing countries that it would not approve reducing the cost for life-saving drugs through exemptions from trade rules. In fact, with the backing of the American pharmaceutical industry, the United States vetoed an agreement in the World Trade Organization, supported by the Europeans, that would have saved millions of lives. Meanwhile, when its allies in the Security Council threatened to veto U.S. policy on Iraq, Washington criticized the use of the veto power and announced that it was prepared to go it alone. President Bush's decision to wage war also prompted a series of consumer boycotts of U.S. icons such as Disney, McDonald's, and Coca-Cola, and aroused anti-American sentiment.

After the removal of Saddam, the Bush administration had to return to the UN Security Council to seek legitimacy, troops, and money, demonstrating that unilateralism does not preclude multilateral initiatives. U.S. unilateralist policies contain elements of multilateralism partly because unilateralism is not in the interest of either American or global capital. Unilateralism is self-centered and adopts a short-run perspective, whereas the dominant fractions of capital are extroverted and take a longer view. Unilateralism, including the 2003 war in Iraq, is a retreat from the professed ideal of self-regulating globalization. To maintain a neoliberal world economy, multilateral political cooperation, at least among the principal actors, is needed. Overall, the trend suggests that a series of trade wars *and* military wars based on preemptive policies and, following Afghanistan and Iraq, "regime change" may well constitute the next phase of globalization. In this sense, *unilateral globalization*, especially when militarized, is a quagmire if not an oxymoron. The two strands of *the new globalization* — unilateralism and free markets — are incommensurate.

In seeking out such contradictions, critical globalization studies requires research that probes embodied practices. This research can be carried out by networks of scholars and activists. Multisited and comparative research may provide diverse perspectives. Interregional and intraregional work illuminates the myriad ways in which globalization touches down and articulates with local conditions. Critical inquiry, including its pedagogy, is a means to a new common sense, and priority must be given to etching alternatives to the current order.

Desired Knowledge

To sum up as concisely as possible, globalization studies is a highly contested domain, and there are no absolute lines for demarcating it. Within this broad compass, however, the distinctive province of a critical orientation is coming to be defined by a set of interrelated features: reflexivity, historicism, decentering, crossovers between social inquiry and other streams of knowledge, and transformative practices.

One advantage of a critical approach is that it offers a broad scope of knowledge. Although the institutions of organized power are major loci of globalization, it is also appropriate to consider informal and intersubjective processes (Cox, 2002).

Furthermore, critical globalization studies is a departure from other perspectives on globalization. Unlike economism, it does not underestimate agency, gender, mental frameworks, culture, and the environment. Unlike realism, it is not silent about social forces and the normative aspects of world order. Unlike neoliberal approaches to globalization, it does not focus on cross-border flows, interdependence, or technological advances as managerial problems and without linking them to hierarchic power relations and the structure of global hegemony.

It is one thing to distinguish critical globalization studies from related approaches, but does this mode of inquiry help to explain the transformations of our era? Critical globalization studies points to an interregnum that maintains elements of the old order, identifies continuities and discontinuities with the contemporary order, and permits glimmers of a transition to a new order. I will call the old world order, *multilateral globalization*; the contemporary structure, *militarized globalization*; and the potential constellation, *democratic globalization*. These three tendencies are not discrete and mutually exclusive alternatives. Their elements may coexist as parts of a contradictory whole that embody varying aspects of globalization and different mixes of consent and coercion. Whereas the first two tendencies are driven by the United States, the third is a counter to hegemonic globalization.

From the 1970s until 9/11, world order was based on a predominance of consensus, especially among dominant classes, along with the periodic application of brute force. Built on a Westphalian model of formal equality among sovereign states, multilateral globalization embraced the principle of territoriality and the material capabilities of globalizing capitalism. The interstate system thus interacted with transnational processes, especially in the economic and cultural spheres. Not only has there been enormous structural inequality among the states themselves, but also globalizing markets produced increasing polarization among the rich and the poor, in some cases leading to heightened state repression, as in certain Middle Eastern countries. Accompanying these problems in the run-up to 2001 was a rapid rise in global environmental harms, including global warming, the hole in the ozone layer, and the loss of biodiversity.

Post-9/11, the pendulum in global hegemony swung from the side of consent toward coercion. Following the Asian financial crisis, the shock of market reforms in Russia and elsewhere, the Argentine debacle, and diminishing confidence in international economic institutions, the "Washington consensus" needed refreshing, as evidenced by sharp criticism from even some erstwhile proglobalizers (Soros, 2002) and neoclassical economists themselves (Rodrik, 1997, and insiders such as Stiglitz, 2002). Clearly, a more coercive, less consensual framework became ascendant. Washington increasingly relied on military power, covert agencies, and police force relative to more subtle forms of domination. Militarized globalization is characterized by both interstate war, notably in Iraq, and an erosion of the Westphalian system, with the territorial state facing increasing pressure from above — particularly the disciplinary power of markets and regionalizing processes — and from below in the form of civil society (Falk, 2003). The attempt to universalize American-led globalization has stimulated a surge in macro- and microresistance.

The resistance offers alternative futures, but they are more of a potential than a set of lived practices. There are many voices, sometimes at odds with one another; different visions; and no lack of concrete proposals (Sandbrook, 2003). The centerpiece is a new normative architecture — an ethics based on concerns about social justice and equity. There are also calls to relax the Westphalian system without at all diminishing state capacity to regulate capital and strengthen social policies. Democratic globalization would, in Polanyian terms, reembed the economy in society. And in a Gramscian sense, it is about building a counterhegemony: an order that is tolerant of differences, seeks new ways to reconcile them in an open and participatory manner, and embraces a dispersion of power.

Currently, the three world orders intersect and compete, their different logics colliding with one another. The motor of transformation is not only countervailing power, but also alternative knowledge. It is neither metatheory nor a recipe for action. Rather, critical knowledge feeds on both contesting ideas and putting them into practice. The desired knowledge would provide conceptual tools to effect practical results. This should not be intellectually tortuous, but demystifying and empowering. Critical globalization studies thus imagines and may be used to achieve a civilized future.

Acknowledgment

I am indebted to Priya Dixit for superior research assistance; Patrick Jackson, for sharing sources; and Paul Wapner, Linda Yarr, and *International Studies Perspective's* anonymous reviewers and its editors, especially Robert Denemark, for comments on an earlier draft of this chapter.

Notes

Author's Note: Whereas I have sought to map the overall features of globalization studies elsewhere (2002), this work explores the *critical* genre.

1. There are infrastructures as well, such as the San Francisco–based International Forum on Globalization. In addition, since 2001, the World Social Forum, which has been meeting in Porto Alegre, Brazil, and then in Mumbai, India, has been thinking about ways to enact alternatives to neoliberal globalization.
2. "Can the subaltern speak?" is a theme elaborated by Gayatri Chakravorty Spivak (1990) and other postcolonial critics.
3. Compared to the Frankfurt School thinkers, who studied capitalism and mass society and sought critical distance in order to develop insight before translating theory into political interventions, the globalization critic is less apt to make the initial maneuver of political disengagement.
4. This emphasis is a corrective to an earlier generation of globalization studies that underemphasized the military factor as a motor of contemporary globalization.

*The Debate on Globalization:
Competing Approaches and
Perspectives*

4

Globalization in World-Systems Perspective

Giovanni Arrighi

World-systems analysis as a distinctive sociological paradigm emerged at least 15 years before the use of globalization as a signifier that blazed across the headlines and exploded as a subject of academic research and publication. Understandably, world-systems scholars were not shy in claiming that the explosion vindicated their often frowned-upon insistence on the transnational interconnectedness of national communities and developments. "Not only did [world-systemists] perceive the global nature of economic networks 20 years before such networks entered popular discourse, but they also saw that many of these networks extend back at least 500 years" (Chase-Dunn and Grimes, 1995: 387–8; see also Friedmann, 1996: 319).

Not all world-systemists agreed on the affinity or even compatibility between their research program and the emerging globalization studies (see e.g., Wallerstein, 1998), which typically departed from what had been the two main substantive contentions of world-systems scholars: the persistence of the core-periphery structure of the global political economy (with or without "semi-periphery"), and the long-term, large-scale nature of the processes that have culminated in contemporary globalization. Many of the contributors to this volume, for example, challenge these two fundamental tenets of world-systems theory, emphasizing the near absolute novelty of contemporary globalization (and hence the irrelevance of the multicentury time frames deployed by world-systemists in analyzing the contemporary dynamics), as well as the increasing irrelevance of the core-periphery structure of the global political economy.[1] Indeed, as in other representations of the contemporary global political economy (see, among others, Harris, 1986: 200–2; Hoogvelt, 1997: xii, 145; Held et al., 1999: 8, 177, 186–7; Burbach and Robinson, 1999; Robinson and Harris, 2000; Hardt and Negri, 2000), the decreasing relevance of the core-periphery structure is presented as one of the main novelties of contemporary globalization.

The purpose of this chapter is to question the validity of these contentions by drawing on research by myself and others within and outside the world-systems perspective. In the first section, I will argue that the core-periphery structure of the global political economy shows few signs of being superseded by other forms of stratification. In the second section, I will go on to argue that such a supersession may well become one of the most important tendencies of the twenty-first century. In order to understand which forces are promoting this tendency and which are holding it back, however, we need to adopt precisely the kind of multicentury time frame that globalization scholars find irrelevant to an understanding of contemporary globalization. In the third and final section, I will draw some conclusions concerning the place of world-systems analysis in critical globalization studies.

Globalization and the Persistence of the North–South Income Divide

The contention of globalization scholars that the North–South or core-periphery divide[2] is being superseded by the formation of a transnational capitalist class and a world proletariat, both of which cut across core-periphery relations, has been advanced on the basis of rather cursory observations, without paying much attention to the available empirical evidence on global inequality and to the conceptual problems involved in interpreting this evidence. The main empirical basis of the contention seems to be the widely observed dispersal of manufacturing activities across the North–South divide. The "new world" that has emerged from this dispersal no longer lends itself, in Nigel Harris' words, "to the simple identification of First and Third, haves and have-nots, rich and poor, industrialized and nonindustrialized" (1986: 200–2).[3]

The dispersal of manufacturing across the North–South divide is indisputable. Suffice to mention that between 1960 and 1998 the manufacturing share of gross domestic product (GDP) in the North (i.e., the former First World) decreased from 28.9 percent to 19.7 percent, whereas in the South (i.e., the former Third World) it rose from 21.6 percent to 23.3 percent. Nevertheless, this industrial convergence between North and South has not resulted in any reduction of the income gap between the two formations, the gross national product (GNP) per capita of the South as a proportion of that of the North being 4.5 percent in 1960 and 4.6 percent in 1999.[4] This North–South industrial convergence without income convergence is not the spurious result of heterogeneous national experiences — that is, of countries that experienced a narrowing of both the industrialization and income gaps and countries that did not. Rather, it is the result of the absence of any positive correlation between industrial and income performance (Arrighi, Silver, and Brewer, 2003a: 11–12, 15–16).

The decreasing effectiveness of industrialization as a means in the pursuit of national wealth was an early finding of world-systems analysis (see Arrighi and Drangel, 1986: 53–57). Although this finding was incorporated in some later reconceptualizations of national development (e.g., Gereffi, 1994: 44–45), development continued to be identified with industrialization across theoretical (and ideological) divides.[5] And so did globalization scholars thereby mistake the waning distinction between an industrialized and a nonindustrialized world for a waning distinction between a wealthy North and a poor South. What is generally missed is the "composition" or "adding up" effect that has characterized the association between industrialization and development. As long as industrialized countries accounted for a small proportion of world population, the association between industrialization and national wealth was positive. But as soon as countries accounting for a growing proportion of world population industrialized in an attempt to increase their national wealth, the association weakened or turned negative.

This composition effect can be conceptualized in terms of Joseph Schumpeter's theory of competition under capitalism and Raymond Vernon's closely related theory of the "product cycle."[6] In Schumpeter's theory, the main determinant of the intensity of competition across space and time under capitalism is the process of "creative destruction" driven by major clusters of profit-oriented innovations, defined broadly to include the introduction, not just of new methods of production, but also of new commodities, new sources of supply, new trade routes and markets, and new forms of organization (Schumpeter, 1954: 83). These major clusters of innovations throw "to a small minority of winners" spectacular "prizes much greater than would have been necessary to call forth [their] particular effort." These spectacular prizes, in turn, propel "the activity of that large majority of businessmen who receive in return very modest compensation, nothing, or less than nothing, and yet do their utmost because they have the big prizes before their eyes and overrate their chances of doing equally well" (Schumpeter, 1954: 73–74).

A similar logic is at work in Vernon's product cycle model (1966, 1971: chapter 3). In this model, the diffusion of innovations is a spatially structured process. Innovations originate in the more "developed" (that is, wealthier) countries and gradually diffuse to poorer, less "developed" countries. At the same time, however, the spatial diffusion of innovations goes hand in hand with their routinization — that is, with their ceasing to be innovations in the wider global context. We may infer from this that, by the time the "new" products and techniques are adopted by the poorer countries, they tend to be subject to intense competition and no longer bring the high returns they did in the wealthier countries.

It follows that opportunities for economic advancement through industrialization, as they present themselves successively to one country after another, do not constitute equivalent opportunities for all countries. As countries accounting for a growing proportion of world population attempt to catch up with Northern standards of wealth through industrialization, competitive pressures in the procurement of industrial inputs and disposal of industrial outputs in world markets intensify. In the process, Southern countries, like Schumpeter's "majority of businessmen," tend to underrate their chances of becoming the losers in the intense competitive struggle engendered by their very success in industrializing. To be sure, some Southern countries did succeed in climbing up the global value-added hierarchy through industrialization, South Korea and Taiwan being the most conspicuous examples. Nevertheless, the virtual absence of any positive correlation between income performance and industrialization noted above suggests that, for most countries, industrialization turned out to be an ineffectual means of economic advancement.

The growing "financialization" of Northern economies has been an integral aspect of the process that has reproduced the North–South income divide in spite of North–South industrial convergence. As Greta Krippner (2002) has shown for the United States, heightened international competition (especially in trade-intensive activities like manufacturing) induced corporations to divert a growing proportion of their incoming cash flows from investment in fixed capital and commodities to liquidity and accumulation through financial channels. In a sense, this diversion is a continuation of the logic of the product cycle by other means. The logic of the product cycle for the leading capitalist organizations of a given epoch is to ceaselessly shift resources through one kind or another of "innovation" from market niches that are becoming overcrowded (and therefore less profitable) to market niches that are less crowded (and therefore more profitable). When escalating competition reduces drastically the actual and potential availability of relatively empty and highly profitable niches in the commodity markets, the leading capitalist organizations have one last refuge for retreat and from where to shift competitive pressures onto others. This last refuge is the world's money market — the market that, in Schumpeter's words, "is always, as it were, the headquarters of the capitalist system, from which orders go out to its individual divisions" (1961: 126).

The fact that Northern deindustrialization along with financialization has been a mechanism of reproduction of the North–South income divide does not mean that it has not been also a mechanism of class and other kinds of economic polarization within both North and South. What it does mean is that inequality between countries remains a far more important component of total global inequality than inequality within countries. Thus, recent studies of world income inequality have shown the percentage of total world inequality accounted for by intercountry inequality in the 1990s to be somewhere between a high of 86 percent (Korzeniewicz and Moran, 1997: 1017) and a low of 68 percent (Goesling, 2001: 752). These and other estimates (based on the decomposition of the Theil index) all find that intercountry income inequality in the 1990s accounted for at least two-thirds of total world income inequality (see also Milanovic, 1999: 34; Firebaugh, 1999: 1597–8; Firebaugh, 2001; Bourguignon and Morrison, 2002; Galbraith, 2002).[7]

There is also a broad consensus that today's enormous between-country income inequality is the outcome of the "great divergence" in national incomes that began in the late eighteenth century and that this gap continued to widen through at least the mid-twentieth century.[8] Disagreements concern the trend in recent decades. Using FX-based data, Roberto P. Korzeniewicz and Timothy Moran (1997) find that the between-country component of the Theil index increased from 79 percent in 1965 to 86 percent in 1992. Using PPP-based data and focusing on the period from 1988 to 1993, Branko Milanovic (1999: 34, 51) found that the same component remained roughly constant — that is, 75 percent in 1988 and 74 percent in 1993. Also using PPP-based data but extending the analysis another couple of years, Brian Goesling (2001: 752) finds a rather sharp decline in the percentage from 74 percent in 1992 to 68 percent in 1995. Nevertheless, as Goesling points out, if China is excluded from the analysis the declining trend in between-nation inequality "flattens out" (2001: 756) — a crucial point to which we shall return presently.

In light of the available evidence, the contention of a supersession of core-periphery by other kinds of polarization thus seems to be only half rather than entirely false. There is indeed some evidence that lately intracountry inequality has increased even more than intercountry inequality. The latter kind of polarization, however, shows few signs of diminishing and remains by far the predominant source of inequality.

Stable as the core-periphery structure of the global economy may appear to be, we can nonetheless detect at least two major signs of an impending destabilization, one concerning China and the other financialization. The China factor has been widely noted in statistical studies of past trends in world income inequality, because whether intercountry inequality over the last 20 years has risen or declined depends entirely on whether we include in the calculations China's huge demographic size and exceptionally rapid economic growth. Were China to experience for another 20 years the same kind of growth as in the past 20, the entire core-periphery structure of the global economy would be subverted, not just statistically, but in all likelihood politically and culturally as well. But under what kind of historical circumstances can we expect China to sustain its extraordinary economic performance for another 20 years?

As for financialization, the bursting of the Japanese speculative bubble (1990 to 1992) and of the U.S. "new economy" bubble 10 years later show how unreliable a mechanism of empowerment and enrichment financialization can be in the longer run. But if this mechanism of the reproduction of the North–South divide is running out of steam, what will take its place? In order to address meaningfully this question, or the question of how sustainable the Chinese ascent can be, the time frame of our analysis must be much longer than is usual in globalization studies. For both questions raise issues of systemic transformation, in the analysis of which — to paraphrase Schumpeter (1954: 163) — a century is truly a "short run."

Globalization and Systemic Transformations

The contention that the absolute novelty of contemporary globalization makes the multicentury time frames deployed by world-systems analysis irrelevant has induced Chris Chase-Dunn (1999) to draw a distinction between "structural" and "ideological" globalization — the former referring to the growth of intensive, large-scale networks relative to more localized ones, the latter referring to neoliberal political ideology, the so-called "Washington consensus" (see also Chase-Dunn and Gills elsewhere in this volume; cf., McMichael, 2003 and Tilly, 1995). In this account, ideological globalization appears to be a new phenomenon, whereas structural globalization is a long-term process, the ups and downs of which can be identified only by deploying a multicentury time frame. Moreover, whereas structural globalization denotes processes that *at any given time* have a dynamic of their own, which conditions and constrains human action, ideological globalization denotes attempts by particular social groups and political communities to turn those processes to their own advantage. The distinction is undoubtedly useful as an antidote against widespread confusion about the novelty and reversibility of globalization. Nevertheless, it can easily lead to the unwarranted conclusion that contemporary structural globalization is the unstoppable continuation of trends that have been going on for centuries (even millennia, according to some accounts), whereas only ideological globalization is a truly novel and, through struggle, stoppable or even reversible development.

In reality, there is much in structural globalization that is new or that can be reversed, and there is much déjà vu in ideological globalization. The main reason for deploying a multicentury framework in the analysis of globalization, therefore, is not to distinguish between structural and ideological globalization. Rather, it is to identify the true peculiarities, both structural and ideological, of present tendencies towards globalization and of present struggles to turn those tendencies to the advantage of particular political communities and social groups.

It follows from the rules of the comparative method that in order to identify the true peculiarities of contemporary globalization, we must preliminarily identify what is recurrent and therefore not new. Which particular recurrent process is chosen as the foundation of the comparison varies with the problem at hand and the theoretical framework that informs the analysis. But a historical analysis of recurrence is essential to the identification of present novelties.

One such analysis has shown that lengthy periods of systemwide "financialization" — like the one to which we have attributed a key role in the reproduction of the North–South income divide over the last 30 years — is no novelty of the late twentieth century. Rather, it is the most conspicuous form of recurrence of the world capitalist system from its earliest beginnings in early modern Europe right up to the present. In all such periods, financial expansions have been symptomatic of an underlying and unresolved crisis of overaccumulation, which transformed the capitalist game on a world scale from a positive-sum into a negative-sum game. Moreover, they have also been an integral aspect of hegemonic crises, and of the eventual transformation of these crises into hegemonic breakdowns.[9]

This is what happened in past hegemonic transitions. In the present transition, the bursting of the "new economy" bubble and September 11 may well be signs of an approaching breakdown of U.S. hegemony. But whether or not they are such a sign, the financialization of U.S. capital of the last 30 years or so presents striking similarities, not just with the financialization of British capital of the late nineteenth and early twentieth centuries as many observers have noted, but also with the finan-cialization of Dutch capital of the mid-eighteenth century. These similarities make the financialization of U.S. capital and the attendant reflation of U.S. power of the 1980s and 1990s the sign of a hegemonic crisis comparable to those of 100 and 250 years ago. Comparability does not, of course, mean identity. Indeed, as soon as we compare the three financial expansions and the underlying hegemonic crises, we can detect major novelties in the present expansion/crisis. Three novelties are particularly germane to our present concerns.

Geopolitically, the most important novelty of present transformations is a bifur-cation of military and financial capabilities that has no precedent in earlier hegemonic transitions. In all past transitions, financial expansions were characterized by the interstitial emergence of governmental-business complexes that were (or could be plausibly expected to become) more powerful both militarily and financially than the still dominant governmental–business complex — as the U.S. complex was relative to the British in the early twentieth century, and the British complex was relative to the Dutch in the early eighteenth century. In the present transition, in contrast, no such emergence can be detected. As in past transitions, the declining but still dom-inant (U.S.) complex has been transformed from the world's leading creditor into the world's leading debtor nation. Unlike in past transitions, however, military resources of global significance have become more than ever concentrated in the hands of the still dominant complex. The declining hegemon is thus left in the anomalous situation that it faces no credible military challenge — a circumstance that makes war among the system's great powers less likely than in past transitions — but it does not have the financial means needed to solve system-level problems that require system-level solutions. The latter is a circumstance that may very well lead to a hegemonic breakdown even in the absence of world wars among the system's great powers (Arrighi and Silver, 1999: 88–96, 263–70, 275–8, 286–89).

Equally important is the social novelty of present transformations. In past hegemonic transitions, systemwide financial expansions contributed to an escalation of social conflict. The massive redistribution of resources and the even greater social dislocations entailed by financial expansions provoked movements of resistance and rebellion by subordinate groups and communities whose established ways of life were coming under attack. Interacting with interstate power struggles, these movements eventually forced the dominant groups to form a new hegemonic social bloc that selectively included previously excluded groups and communities. In the transition from Dutch to British hegemony, the aspirations of the European propertied classes for greater political representation and the aspirations of the settler bourgeoisies of the Americas for self-determination were accommodated in a new dominant social bloc. With the transition from British to U.S. hegemony — under the joint impact of the revolt against the West and working-class rebellions — the hegemonic social bloc was further expanded through the promise of security of employment and high mass consumption for the working classes of the wealthier countries of the West, and of rights to national self-determination and "development" for the elites of the non-Western world. It soon became clear, however, that this package of promises could not be delivered. Moreover, it engendered expectations in the world's subordinate strata that seriously threatened the stability and eventually precipitated the crisis of U.S. hegemony (Arrighi and Silver, 1999: 153–216; Silver, 2003: 149–167).

Here lies the peculiar social character of this crisis in comparison with earlier hegemonic crises. The crisis of Dutch hegemony was a long drawn-out process in which a systemwide financial expansion came late and systemwide social conflict later still. The crisis of British hegemony unfolded more rapidly but the systemwide financial expansion still preceded systemwide social conflict. In the crisis of U.S. hegemony, in contrast, the systemwide explosion of social conflict of the late 1960s and early 1970s preceded and thoroughly shaped the subsequent financial expansion. Indeed, in a very real sense, the present financial expansion has been primarily an instrument of the containment of the combined demands of the peoples of the non-Western world and of the Western working classes. Financialization and the associated restructuring of the global political economy have undoubtedly succeeded in disorganizing the social forces that were the bearers of these demands in the upheavals of the late 1960s and 1970s. At the same time, however, the underlying contradiction of a world capitalist system that promotes the formation of a world proletariat but cannot accommodate a generalized living wage (that is, the most basic of reproduction costs), far from being solved, is a constant source of tensions and conflicts within, between, and across political communities (Arrighi and Silver, 1999: 282–6; Silver, 2003: 20–25, 177–179).

These tensions and conflicts are unfolding not just in the context of the bifurcation of military and financial power noted above but also of a third major novelty in terms of the present transformations. This is the shift of the epicenter of the global economy to East Asia — a region that unlike all previous organizing centers of world capitalism lies outside the historical boundaries of Western civilization.[10] Suffice it to mention that between 1960 and 1999, the East Asian share of world gross national product (a good measure of the share of the world market controlled by the residents of the region) increased from 13 percent to 25 percent, while the North American share decreased from 35.2 percent to 29.8 percent, and the Western European share decreased from 45.5 percent to 32.3 percent. Even more pronounced was the shift in the shares of world value added in manufacturing, with the East Asian share increasing in the same period from 16.4 percent to 35.2 percent, against a decrease in the North American share from 42.2 percent to 29.9 percent and of the Western European share from 32.4 percent to 23.4 percent. The shift, however, is even more significant than these figures imply as persistent current account surpluses in the balance of payments of Japan and the "China Circle" (mainland China, Singapore, Hong Kong, and Taiwan) on the one side, and large and growing U.S. current account deficits on the other, have completely reversed the positions of East Asia and the United States in the international credit system. Indeed, the obverse side of the transformation of the United States into the world's leading debtor nation, noted above, has been the emergence in the 1990s of Japan and the China Circle as the world's leading creditor nations (Fingleton, 2001; Arrighi, Hui, Hung, and Selden, 2003: 307–8).

True, the inability of the Japanese economy to recover from the crash of 1990 to 1992, followed by the regionwide financial crisis of 1997 to 1998, has led many to question the real extent of East Asian financial and economic power. Nevertheless, the economic and financial crises in East Asia in the 1990s do not in themselves support the conclusion that the "rise of East Asia" is a mirage. In past transitions, it was the newly emerging centers of world-scale processes of capital accumulation that experienced the deepest financial crises, as their financial prowess outstripped their institutional capacity to regulate the massive amounts of mobile capital flowing in and out of their jurisdictions. This was true of London and England in the late eighteenth century and even more true of New York and the United States in the 1930s. We would not use the Wall Street crash of 1929 to 1931 and the subsequent U.S. Great Depression to argue that the epicenter of global processes of capital accumulation had not been shifting from the United Kingdom to the United States in the first half of the twentieth century. Nor should we draw any analogous conclusion from the East Asian financial crises of the 1990s (Arrighi and Silver, 1999: especially chapter 1 and conclusion).

Be that as it may, the most important tendency for understanding the present and future of the global hierarchy of wealth may be the continuing economic expansion of China. Given the demographic size and historical centrality of China in the region, this continuing expansion is far more significant for the subversion of the global hierarchy of wealth than all the previous East Asian economic "miracles" put together. For all these miracles (the Japanese included) were instances of upward mobility within a fundamentally stable global hierarchy of wealth. The hierarchy could and did accommodate the upward mobility of a handful of East Asian states (two of them city-states) accounting for about one twentieth of the world population. However, accommodating the upward mobility of a state that by itself accounts for about one fifth of the world population is an altogether different affair. Statistically, the very pyramidal structure of the hierarchy would be subverted. Indeed, as pointed out in the first section of the paper, to the extent that recent research on world income inequality has detected a statistical trend towards declining intercountry inequality in the 1990s, this is due *entirely* to the rapid economic growth of China.

As shown elsewhere (Arrighi, Hamashita, and Selden, 2003), China's rapid economic growth over the last 20 years has deep roots, not just in its social and political reconstitution in the Cold War era, but also in its achievements in state- and national-economy-making prior to the subordinate incorporation of the East Asian region within the European-centered world-system. As such, it can be expected to be a more stable tendency than the sudden and eventually unsustainable spurts of economic growth typical of lower-income countries. Nevertheless, by Northern standards, China is still a low-income country subject to the polarizing tendencies of the global economy discussed in the first section of the paper. And even if China's rapid growth continues for another 20 years, the chances are that it will be punctuated by crises because, as just noted, crises are integral aspects of emerging economic centers. These crises may well lead to a reversal of the Chinese expansion and to an exacerbation of the geopolitical and social contradictions of the global political economy. But they may also lead to the resolution of these contradictions through the construction of a more equitable and less wasteful world order than the one that has characterized U.S. hegemony. Which outcome will actually materialize depends not just on how Chinese elites will manage the crises but also on the evolution of the global context — an issue to which we shall return in the chapter's concluding section.

World-Systems Analysis and Critical Globalization Studies

To conclude, the emerging field of critical globalization studies can only benefit from an engagement with some of the findings of world-systems analysis. One such finding is the persistence of the North–South divide in spite (or because) of Northern deindustrialization and Southern industrialization. The finding runs counter not just to mainstream and Marxist modernization theories but dependency and globalization theories as well. More important, it runs counter to the view widely held by Northern labor and "antiglobalization" activists that the dispersal of manufacturing across the North–South divide is responsible for a "race to the bottom," which drives the life-chances of Northern labor down toward Southern standards. Although some sectors of Northern labor have indeed been hit hard by the dispersal, there is no evidence of any significant *overall* convergence between the life-chances of Northern and Southern peoples, workers included.

There is, nonetheless, considerable evidence of growing social inequality within both North and South. This tendency is due primarily not to North–South industrial convergence, but to U.S.-led financialization — that is, to the widespread disposition of capitalist enterprise to respond to intensifying competition by diverting incoming cash flows from investment in fixed capital and commodities (including labor) to liquidity and accumulation through financial channels. Another important contribution of world-systems analysis is to have shown that this tendency, and the intense interstate competition for increasingly mobile capital with which it has been associated, are not as new and unstoppable as the promoters of ideological globalization implicitly or explicitly claim. Rather, they are recurrent tendencies, which in the past have invariably ended in escalating systemic chaos and a fundamental reorganization of world society. It follows that the most fundamental question that critical globalization studies and the global social justice movement face is not how to stop the hypermobility of capital. It is, instead, how to anticipate and act upon the reorganization of world society of which financialization and the hypermobility of capital are premonitory signs.

Also in this respect, world-systems analysis has some insights to offer on the likely trajectories of such reorganization. Thus, the peculiar social character of the present hegemonic crisis, in comparison to previous ones, makes us expect that conflicts over means of livelihood (including cultural identities) will remain the main engine of the struggle for social justice within, between, and across political communities and jurisdictions. These conflicts will nonetheless be embedded in a global context thoroughly shaped by the geopolitical and civilizational peculiarities of the present hegemonic transition — that is, the bifurcation of military and financial power, and the shift of the epicenter of world-scale processes of capital accumulation to East Asia. Needless to say, it is impossible to foresee the eventual outcome of this new combination of systemic circumstances. But the range of historically possible outcomes appears to be delimited by two main vectors of systemic transformation.

One vector is the consolidation of the East Asian expansion now centered on China, and its transformation into a model of world development capable of superseding the global hierarchy of wealth that emerged under British hegemony and has been consolidated under U.S. hegemony. As mentioned in the preceding section, possibilities of success along this vector are limited not just by the capacity of the region's ruling groups — China's in particular — to provide "right" answers to the multiple crises that they are likely to face. They are limited also by the strength of the forces that are simultaneously pushing world development in other directions.

The most important of these forces is U.S. unwillingness to adjust to a less exalted position. Integral to this unwillingness is the attempt to use the unprecedented and unparalleled military power of the United States to transform into outright tribute, or "protection payment," what the United States needs to balance its equally unparalleled and unprecedented current account deficit with the rest of the world. Nothing short of a new, and for the first time in history, truly universal world empire can make the exaction of such a tribute possible. Unrealistic as such a project may seem and probably is, U.S. responses to September 11 show that its pursuit is real enough, and will continue to influence the ongoing transition to a yet unknown destination.

This yet unknown destination will probably lie somewhere between the East Asian and the U.S. vectors. But it is also possible that U.S. resistance to adjustment and accommodation will plunge the world into a new period of systemic chaos with no light at the end of the tunnel. Either way, I see no more important task for critical globalization studies than to monitor closely the evolving situation, and to provide the global social justice movement with as reliable a map as possible of the vectors that lead to a more equitable and just world as opposed to those that lead to an exploitative empire or endless chaos.

Notes

1. See, for example, the contributions by Sassen, Sklair, and Robinson.
2. The dichotomies *core-periphery* and *North–South* are often used interchangeably, even though conceptually they refer to different kinds of relationships. As I understand them, the core-periphery dichotomy refers primarily to relationships between high- and low-value added activities carried out in different geographical locations, whereas the North–South dichotomy refers primarily to relationships between geohistorical formations, one of which (the North) encompasses predominantly core activities, and the other (the South) encompasses predominantly peripheral activities. For the purposes of this paper the distinction between the two dichotomies is not essential. I will therefore follow the common practice of using them interchangeably.
3. Michael Hardt and Antonio Negri go further and claim that the dispersal involves not just manufacturing but banking and finance as well. In their representation, while the Third World "enters into the First … as the ghetto, shanty town, *favela*," the First World "is transferred to the Third in the form of stock exchanges and banks, transnational corporations and icy skyscrapers of money and command." As a result, "center and periphery, North and South no longer define an international order but rather have moved closer to one another" (2000: xiii, 253–4, 334–7).
4. The percentages have been calculated from the World Bank (1984 and 2001). The North consists of North America, Western Europe, Australasia, and Japan. The South consists of Latin America, Africa, and Asia (including China). The aggregates include only countries for which data are available for both 1960 and 1998–1999. In calculating the manufacturing share of GDP we have weighted countries by their total GDP and in calculating GNP per capita we have weighted countries by their population. The particular indicator used for industrialization and the use of income data at actual exchange rates (FX-based data) rather than at purchasing power parity (PPP-based data) exaggerates the contrast between industrial convergence and income non-convergence. Nevertheless, the contrast persists regardless of which particular indicator and data we use.
5. This has been as true of dependency and Marxist theories as of mainstream modernization theories. See especially Cardoso and Faletto (1979) for dependency theory and Warren (1980) for Marxist theories. In both texts, industrialization and development are treated as equivalent terms. In the late 1980s and early 1990s, the postmodernist critique of modernization and development theories (see especially Escobar, 1995 and the contributions to Sachs, 1992) became an important corrective of the acritical acceptance across the ideological spectrum of development and industrialization as a generally beneficial pursuit. Nevertheless, in rejecting the alleged benefits of development and industrialization, postmodernist critics have tended to treat the two terms as equivalent, just like those whom they criticized. For a recent exchange on this issue, see Amsden (2003) and Arrighi, Silver, and Brewer (2003b).
6. For an early conceptualization of this kind, see Arrighi and Drangel (1986). For a later conceptualization, which incorporates Vernon's theory of the product cycle, as well as Pierre Bourdieu's concept of *illusio* (Bourdieu, 1984), see Arrighi, Silver, and Brewer (2003a: 16–23).
7. The differences among the estimates are almost entirely due to whether income data are converted into U.S. dollars at actual exchange rates without adjustment for differences in costs of living (FX-based data) or they are adjusted for "purchasing power parity" (PPP-based income data) (Firebaugh, 1999: 1601 and table 3). Korzeniewicz and Moran measure income in different countries at actual exchange rates, whereas Milanovic and Goesling use purchasing power parities. Korzeniewicz and Moran's finding are based on data for 1992, Milanovic's for 1993, and Goesling's for 1995. Goesling's findings for 1992 (74 percent) are the same as Milanovic's for 1993.
8. For reviews of the evidence, see O'Rourke (2001), Firebaugh (2001), and Bourguignon and Morrison (2002). Since this was a period of simultaneous Western industrial and territorial expansion, there is little agreement in the relevant literatures on whether present inequality is primarily the legacy of Western industrialism or Western colonial imperialism.
9. See especially Arrighi (1994: 214–238) and Arrighi and Silver (1999: 258–264). As argued in these texts, the impact of financial expansions on the tendency of crises to turn into breakdowns is not linear because initially they inflate the power of the declining hegemonic state. To paraphrase Fernand Braudel (1984: 246), they are

the "autumn," not just of major capitalist developments, but also of the hegemonic regimes in which these developments are embedded. Thanks to its continuing centrality in networks of high finance, the declining hegemon can turn the competition for mobile capital typical of financial expansions to its advantage and thereby contain, at least for a time, the forces that challenge its continuing dominance. Over time, however, financial expansions strengthen these same forces by widening and deepening the scope of interstate and interenterprise competition and social conflict, and by reallocating capital to emergent structures that promise greater security or higher returns than the dominant structure. Sooner or later, even a small disturbance can tilt the balance in favor of the forces that wittingly or unwittingly are undermining the already precarious stability of existing structures, thereby provoking a breakdown of systemic organization.

10.   This shift above all else prompted Samuel Huntington (1993) to advance his highly influential and controversial thesis of a coming "clash of civilizations." In reality, a clash between Western and non-Western civilizations has been a constant of the historical process whereby the world capitalist system was transformed from a European into a global system. The transition from Dutch to British hegemony was marked by the violent conquest or destabilization of the indigenous world-systems of Asia. The transition from British to U.S. hegemony was marked, first, by a further extension of Western territorial empires in Asia and Africa, and then by a general revolt against Western domination. Under U.S. hegemony, the map of the world was redrawn to accommodate the demands of this general revolt for national self-determination. Except in East Asia, this new map reflected the legacy of Western colonialism and imperialism, including the cultural hegemony that led non-Western elites to claim for themselves more or less viable "nation-states" in the image of the metropolitan political organizations of their former imperial masters. In East Asia, in contrast, apart from some states on its southern fringes (most notably Indonesia, Malaysia, the Philippines, and the city-states of Hong Kong and Singapore), all the region's most important national states — from Japan, Korea, and China to Vietnam, Laos, Kampuchea, and Thailand — had all been nations long before the European arrival. What is more, they had all been nations linked to one another, directly or through the Chinese center, by diplomatic and trade relations and held together by a shared understanding of the principles, norms, and rules that regulated their mutual interactions as a world among other worlds. On the importance of this peculiar regional legacy for the East Asian economic renaissance of the late twentieth century, see Arrighi, Hamashita, and Selden (2003).

5

Waves of Globalization and Resistance in the Capitalist World-System: Social Movements and Critical Global Studies

Christopher Chase-Dunn and Barry Gills

The world-systems perspective provides a useful framework for discerning the continuities and discontinuities (emergent properties) of long historical waves of globalization and social resistance to domination. The study of world-historical systems (including comparative analyses of different world-systems) uses whole world-systems (i.e., intersocietal interaction networks) as the unit of analysis to describe and explain social change. All world-systems, large and small, experience oscillations in which interaction networks expand and larger-scale interactions become denser, and then the networks contract spatially and large-scale interactions decrease in intensity. These historical oscillations, which we term "pulsations," have been found in all world-systems, small and large. In this chapter we will provide a conceptualization of globalization that sees recent waves of international and transnational integration in the modern world-system as a continuation of the pulsations of intersocietal interaction networks that have been occurring in world-systems for millennia. We will seek to comprehend both the continuities and the discontinuities or newly emergent properties that have occurred in the long waves of globalization and resistance.

The scientific study of globalization should begin with the recognition that globalization is a contested concept (Gills, 2000). One reason why there is so much confusion and contention about the meaning of globalization is that it is both a political ideology and a long-term structural process of spatial integration of formerly unconnected or only loosely connected peoples. In order to sort this out we distinguish between what we call structural globalization — the expansion and intensification of large-scale interaction networks relative to more local interactions (Tilly, 1995), and the "globalization project" (McMichael, 2003b) — a specific political ideology that glorifies the efficiency of markets and privately held firms in order to attack labor unions, entitlements, and other institutions that have protected the incomes of workers.

We will study both structural globalization as integration and the globalization project in order to make sense out of contemporary world history. We find it useful to distinguish between two types of economic globalization (trade and investment) and to conceptualize political and cultural globalization in terms of interaction networks that are analogous to economic globalization (Chase-Dunn, 1999). The latest

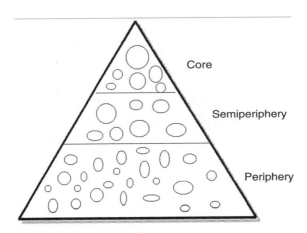

Figure 5.1. A core-periphery hierarchy: the blobs are societies.

wave of post–Second World War structural economic globalization was preceded by an earlier great wave of expanded international trade and investment in the second half of the nineteenth century (Chase-Dunn, Kawano, and Brewer, 2000; O'Rourke and Williamson, 2000). These waves of global economic integration were separated by a troubled trough of deglobalization and globalization backlash that included the decline of British hegemony, the Great Depression of 1873 to 1896, the Mexican, Russian and Chinese revolutions, the worldwide depression of the 1930s, the rise of fascism, and the Second World War.

The modern world-system can be understood structurally as a stratification system composed of economically and politically dominant core societies (themselves in competition with one another) and dependent peripheral and semiperipheral regions, a few of which have been successful in improving their positions in the larger core-periphery hierarchy, although most have simply maintained their relative positions as the whole system develops (see figure 5.1).

This structural perspective on world history allows us to analyze the cyclical features of social change and the long-term trends of development in historical and comparative perspective. We can see the development of the modern world-system as driven primarily by capitalist accumulation and geopolitics in which businesses and states have competed with one another for power and wealth. Competition among states and capitals is conditioned by the dynamics of struggle among classes and by the resistance of peripheral and semiperipheral peoples to domination and exploitation from the core. It is not possible to understand the history of social change in the system as a whole without taking into account both the strategies of the winners and the strategies and organizational actions of those who have resisted domination and exploitation.

It is also difficult to understand why and where innovative social change emerges without a conceptualization of the world-system as a whole. New organizational forms that transform institutions and that lead to upward mobility most often emerge from societies in semiperipheral locations. Thus, all the countries that became hegemonic core states in the modern system had formerly been semiperipheral (the Dutch, the British, and the United States). This is a continuation of a long-term pattern of social evolution that Chase-Dunn and Hall (1997) have called "semiperipheral development." The largest empires were formed by semiperipheral states that conquered older core states, and semiperipheral capitalist city-states acted as the agents of commercialization for millennia. This phenomenon arguably also includes organizational innovations in contemporary semiperipheral countries (e.g., Mexico, India, South Korea, and Brazil) that may transform the now-global system.

In this perspective, many of the phenomena that have been called "globalization" correspond to recently expanded international trade, financial flows, and foreign investment by transnational corporations and banks. Conventional globalization discourse generally assumes that until recently there were separate national societies and economies, and that these have now been largely superseded by an intensification of international integration driven by information and transportation technologies. However, rather than a wholly unique and new phenomenon, globalization, understood primarily as international integration, is a historical feature of world-systems, a feature that has oscillated as well as increased for many centuries.

The so-called "information age," the "New Economy," global cities, the transnational capitalist class, and other hypothetically radical departures did not create a huge chasm between recent decades and earlier world history. What is truly new as well as the true continuities can only be known by comparing recent decades with the past.

The "New" Imperialism

U.S. unilateralism and especially the use of preemptive military force by the hawks of the George W. Bush presidency have caused critical analysts to theorize anew about empire and a "new imperialism." The theorists of a global stage of capitalism organized by an integrated global capitalist class have elaborated their distinction between national and international capital in order to deal with what seems to be a renewed round of interimperial rivalry among the core states. Those who have been saying all along that neoliberalism is mainly an "Anglo-American thing" rather than the permanent emergence of a global "new economy" based on finance capital seem to be vindicated. And the assumption that military power has been permanently transcended by economic power is also now debated.

Critics of the world-systems perspective as well as apologists for global capitalism have long downplayed the importance of the core-periphery hierarchy. Some claimed that core/periphery inequality ended with decolonization. Dependency theory was declared a dead letter by "poststructuralists" just at the time that many Third World countries were being subjected to the structural adjustment programs of the International Monetary Fund. Others claimed that the categories of core and periphery, or First World and Third World, were no longer valid because countries in Africa, Asia, and Latin America have different histories. But no one ever claimed that all peripheral countries were the same. Core and periphery are relational concepts, and the nature of the power-dependence relations changes over time, but the core-periphery hierarchy has not evaporated. The industrialization of some noncore countries and the nearly complete marginalization of many other countries (in what some have called the Fourth World) did not eliminate the core-periphery hierarchy. Neither did the formal decolonization of the Third World eliminate neocolonial forms of domination by which core countries and international financial institutions came to exercise power over Third World countries. Imperialism in the sense of unequal power among countries has not been eliminated by the organizational changes in the world division of labor that have taken place since the Second World War. So the discovery of a "new imperialism" needs to be clarified as to how what is allegedly new differs from what went before.

David Harvey (2003) contends that U.S. unilateralism constitutes a renewal of capitalist primitive accumulation based on military geopolitical power. The world-systems perspective on capitalism (Chase-Dunn, 1998) has long argued that primitive accumulation was not a stage in the creation of capitalist world economy, but has rather been a constant and necessary feature of capitalism all along. Peripheral capitalism has used political coercion in mobilizing labor since the expansion of slavery in the New World and the development of "capitalist serfdom" in the peripheralized economies of Eastern Europe. After the abolition of capitalist slavery and serfdom Third World working conditions have continued to be conditioned by political coercion in the form of state-organized and core-supported suppression of labor unions and peasant movements. So primitive accumulation has been an important component of the capitalist world economy all along.

The rediscovery of the importance of military power in the structuring of the capitalist world economy is another instance in which even the critics of global capitalism have been bamboozled by the rhetoric of the free market. Military Keynesianism, in which the U.S. federal government has spent over half of its total discretionary budget on "defense," began in earnest during the Korean War, and these huge expenditures have continued despite the demise of the "Soviet threat" that was the main justification for this massive use of public monies to pump up the U.S. economy. But is there not something new in the willingness of the Bush administration to ignore the will of French, German, and Russian allies in the conquest of Iraq? What is new and frightening is what appears to be the beginning of a breach in the core-wide multilateral foreign policies of the post–Second World War period. Certainly the Bush administration has pursued a more open and pronounced unilateralism and disdain for multilateral solutions than previous U.S. administrations. But why has the Bush regime done this? We contend that this is similar in many respects to the British use of its comparative advantage in military power during its decline of economic comparative advantage. The United States has a massive advantage in military technology because of the huge investments that military Keynesianism have provided. The development and production of military technology is not an ideal industry from the point of view of profit-making in the world market, but direct conquest can provide important geopolitical returns, especially where the control of significant scarce raw materials (oil) is concerned. So the declining hegemon plays one of the only cards it has left — the military card.

The other U.S. advantage has been its centrality in global financial transactions and the importance of the U.S. dollar in international financial and trade transactions.

The world market for oil is denominated in U.S. dollars. And the U.S. trade imbalance has been counteracted by a huge inflow of foreign lending for the last decade. Money from Europe and East Asia has flown into U.S. stock and bond markets, making the United States extremely dependent on these inflows of foreign moneys to finance its growing trade imbalance.

Recent declines of the U.S. dollar relative to the Euro could foreshadow a new kind of structural adjustment. Foreign investors believed in U.S. superiority in information technology and biotechnology, but the dot-com collapse and the Enron scandal have shaken the confidence of these foreign investors to some extent. The very size of the U.S. market and its ability to generate prodigious new forms of financial "security" (e.g., derivatives) mean that the alternatives for receiving some return on the huge amounts of "fictitious capital" that are now flowing in the world financial markets are few. At the current exchange rate the GDP of the European Union (EU) is now larger than the U.S. GDP. But the EU does not have the capacity to absorb the vast financial capital that is now invested in the United States. What this means is that there will probably not be a rapid exodus of finance capital from the United States unless the whole system collapses.

Globalization and Social Movements of Resistance

Because of alleged overemphasis on large-scale social structures like the core-periphery hierarchy, some critics have asserted that the world-systems perspective denies the possibility of agency. On the contrary, the focus is on both how successful power-holders concoct new strategies of domination and exploitation, and how dominated and exploited peoples struggle to protect themselves and build new institutions for social justice. The structuralist aspects of the world-systems perspective make it more possible to understand where social forces are more likely to be successful, and perhaps where not.

Phillip McMichael (2000) has studied the "globalization project" — the abandoning of Keynesian models of national development and a new (or renewed) emphasis on deregulation and opening national commodity and financial markets to foreign trade and investment. This approach focuses on the ideological aspects of the recent wave of international economic integration, so-called neoliberalism, Reaganism–Thatcherism, or the Washington Consensus. Samir Amin (1997) convincingly argues that, whereas the Keynesian development project that was the main model for reconstruction and national industrialization between the Second World War and the 1970s was truly a global political project, a global New Deal, the neoliberal policies of Reaganism–Thatcherism are better understood as crisis management than as a coherent political project.

It has been argued that the main structural basis of the rise of the globalization project is the new level of integration reached by the global capitalist class (Robinson, 1996; Sklair, 2001). Some of the analysts of global capitalism contend that the transformations that have occurred in recent decades are so radical that it is unnecessary to know anything about the world before 1960. Surely this is to fall into the trap of breathless globalization promoted by those who tout the wonders of information technology. The real task is to know both the present and the past so that we may intelligently designate both the continuities and the important changes.

The internationalization of capital has long been an important part of the trend toward economic globalization. There have been many previous claims to represent the general interests of "business" (i.e., capital). Indeed, every modern hegemon (the Dutch, the British, and the Americans) has made this claim. But the real integration of the interests of capitalists all over the world has very likely reached a level greater than at the peak of the nineteenth-century wave of globalization. This is the part of the theory of a global stage of capitalism that must be taken most seriously, though it can certainly be overstated.

The world-system has now reached a point at which both the old interstate system based on separate national capitalist classes and new institutions representing the global interests of capital exist and are powerful simultaneously. In this sense, the old interstate system now coexists with a more globalized or "transnationalized" world economic system brought about by the past two decades of neoliberal economic globalization. In this light each country can be seen to have an important ruling class fraction that is allied with the transnational capitalist class (Robinson and Harris, 2000). A central question is whether or not this (new) level of transnational class integration will be strong enough to prevent competition among states for world hegemony from turning into warfare, as it has always done in the past, during a period in which a reigning hegemon (i.e., the United States) is entering its declining phase (Chase-Dunn and Podobnik, 1995).

The insight that capitalist globalization has occurred in waves, and that these waves of integration are followed by periods of resistance to capitalist globalization, has important implications for the future. Figure 5.2 shows the two-and-a-half waves of trade globalization that the world economy has experienced since 1830.

Capitalist globalization increased both intranational and international inequalities in the nineteenth century (O'Rourke and Williamson, 2000), and it did the same thing in the late twentieth century. Those countries and groups that are left out of the *belle époque* either mobilize to challenge the hegemony of the powerful or they retreat into self-reliance, or both.

Decolonization of the colonies of the European core states occurred in waves beginning in the eighteenth century (see Figure 5.3). These waves of antiimperialism show that the capitalist world-system has been marked by a dynamic struggle between core and periphery for centuries. Figure 5.3 shows the decolonizations that occurred in the colonial empires of Britain, Italy, Japan, the Netherlands, Portugal, Spain, and France.

The most recent wave of globalization protests emerged in the noncore with the anti-IMF riots of the 1980s. The numerous transnational social movements that participated in the 1999 protest in Seattle surrounding the World Trade Organization (WTO) meetings brought globalization protest to the attention of observers in the core, and this resistance to capitalist globalization has continued and grown despite the setback that occurred in response to the terrorist attacks on New York and Washington in 2001 (Podobnik, 2003). The recent global antiwar demonstrations in

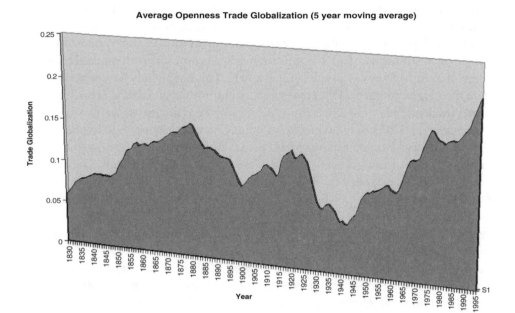

Figure 5.2. Waves of trade globalization, 1830–1995. From Chase-Dunn, Christopher, Yukio Kawano, and Benjamin D. Brewer. 2000. "Trade Globalization Since 1795: Waves of Integration in the World-system." *American Sociological Review* 65 (1): 77–95.

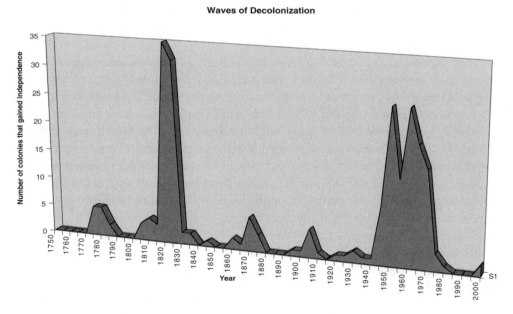

Figure 5.3. Waves of decolonization, 1750–2000. From Henige, David P. 1970. *Colonial Governors from the Fifteenth Century to the Present*. Madison, WI: University of Wisconsin Press.

February 2003 against the Bush administration's "preventative" war on Iraq have involved many of the same movements as well as some new recruits. The transnational social movements face difficult problems of forming alliances and sustaining cooperative action. The idea of semiperipheral development implies that support for more democratic institutions of global governance will come from democratic socialist regimes that come to power in the semiperiphery. This has already happened in Brazil, where the new labor party (PT) government supports the global social justice movement. President Lula's current support for fiscal austerity in order to woo global finance capital is likely to fade once it becomes clear that not enough finance capital will flow in to make much difference. If Lula is not willing to confront global capital, some other leader from his party or from a new party is likely to do it. The Brazilian working class does not need foreign capital to construct a national economy that can provide a good living for all Brazilians. And a Brazilian democratic socialism will support, and be supported by, friendly regimes in other Latin American countries. Friends of socialism in the United States may need to prevent the bond traders from mobilizing an intervention.

There is an apparent tension between those who advocate deglobalization and delinking from the global capitalist economy and the building of stronger, more cooperative and self-reliant social relations in the periphery and semiperiphery (e.g., Bello, 2003; Amin, 1997; McMichael, 2003a), on the one hand, and those who seek to mobilize support for new, or reformed institutions of democratic global governance (George and Sabelli, 1994; Boswell and Chase-Dunn, 2000). In fact, these strategies can be complementary, and each can benefit by supporting the other. Defensive self-reliance by itself, though an understandable reaction to exploitation, is not likely to solve the problems of humanity in the long run. The great challenge of the twenty-first century will be the building of a democratic and collectively rational global commonwealth. World-systems theory can be an important contributor to this effort.

The intensification of transborder or transnational economic interaction, including global financial flows, requires a corresponding transnational social and political response and elicits precisely this response from social forces. The primary questions are how a new global political architecture will be built and whose interests will it represent — the global elite or the global popular majority? Although many governments and political parties seem captured by neoliberal dogma, the new social movements appear to have more maneuverability and better potential to bridge the gap between national and global political spheres. It is precisely because neoliberal elites and governments are constraining the ability of governments and traditional political parties to pursue substantive democracy and social justice that neoliberal globalization can be understood to be activating new social movements across the globe.

It is not a coincidence that the new global social movements of resistance are led primarily from the South, that is, from the global periphery and semiperiphery. This composition of social forces of resistance reflects the fact that much of the gains of neoliberal economic globalization have been at the expense of the South and among its poor or working majority. The advent of better global communications has served not only the expansion of global capital but also the expansion of global solidarity among resistance forces. We can call this "the globalization of resistance." With such a broad array of social forces coming into action and able to communicate with one another, even to meet physically, it is natural that global solidarity movements pursue a politics that is not only more participatory and direct but also more inclusive than in the past. This is useful in order to mobilize the maximum strength of global social forces in opposition to corporate-led neoliberal globalization, and in the post-9/11 era, in opposition to imperialism and war. Opposition to corporate control of the global economy and globalization is the overarching theme unifying the social movements of resistance (Broad, 2002: 3) However, positive values also characterize these movements, which are ultimately about reinvigorating a politics based on grassroots motivation, participation, democracy, decentralization and autonomy, while at the same time striving to build bridges and solidarities.

The core values of the new global social movements of resistance include nonviolent struggle, democratic practice, social justice, inclusiveness, secularism (as opposed to religious fundamentalism), peace (in opposition to the use of force in international affairs), solidarity (in opposition to localism, parochialism, and narrow nationalism or chauvinism) and equality (including opposition to patriarchal forms of oppression against women as well as class, caste, and ethnic-based discrimination).

The new movements differ in important ways from those that characterized the earlier wave of resistance to colonialism and imperialism in the last two centuries. Unlike the traditional armed revolutionary movements with their focus on taking state power, and the traditional left parties with their hierarchical discipline and rigid ideologies, the new movements do not seek violent revolution or the capture of state power to this end. There is now a much more diffuse pattern of ideas and organization that characterizes many of the new social movements, and there is a higher participation by women and other previously marginalized groups, especially by indigenous peoples (particularly in Latin America, e.g., in Ecuador, Peru, Bolivia, and Guatemala).

The diverse and often ad hoc nature of these new social movements and their spontaneity and autonomy can make them appear somewhat disorganized. The movements themselves recognize this situation but are not prepared to attempt to unify all the movements under a single ideology (even a general one such as "anti-capitalist"), a single organization, or a single political party. Rather, their primary goal today appears to be to create a new political space at national, regional, and global levels in which the many movements can meet together and share experiences of action and resistance, and sometimes plan or take common actions based on areas of agreement. The World Social Forum, which met for its third annual gathering in Porto Alegre, Brazil, in January 2003, continues to argue for this approach and for an open and plural process that works with a great diversity of resistances, organizations, and proposals (WSF International Council, 2003). The world social movements that convene at the WSF reflect an extremely broad agenda of the new social movements of resistance.

However, there is a growing self-criticism and concern among the movements that a new stage is needed if the movements are to be successful in the long term. Critics of the new movements argue that there is a lack of specific goals and coherent platform, and that tactics and strategy remain unclear. Weaknesses of the new form of resistance point to a lack of coherent ideology, a lack of formal organizational structure, and the lack of a common political platform and strategy to achieve its goals. However, the great diversity of the new movements may explain the lack of coherence and the prudent choice to avoid a premature effort to unify all the movements in this way, but it does not relieve the anxiety that such a diffuse set of movements will suffer from inherent weaknesses or limitations on action.

The most important theoretical and practical political question facing the new social movements of global resistance is whether they are capable of acting as a counterhegemonic bloc in global politics and achieving significant transformation of the global system. Can they overcome the political weakness inherent in such a broad and inclusive movement and work towards achieving more coherence in organization, program, and action? Can they move beyond the initial phase of protest, education, and networking and develop a more structured organizational form that allows them to enter into a position of political negotiation with the neoliberal power structure, forcing it to make concessions to popular demands? The real challenge in this new wave of resistance to capitalist globalization is to maintain the impetus to action and to global solidarity and achieve more concrete political results. It is the diversity of the movements and their insistence on participation, inclusiveness, and autonomy that give the new movements their real strength. However, these same qualities now challenge the global movement to solve the problem of political representation and organization in the new global politics of resistance.

Stephen Gill (2000, 2002) has advocated the building of a world party, a peoples' international party, that could help to coordinate the several antisystemic movements emerging in resistance to global corporate capitalist and neoliberal policies. Gill invokes Gramci's characterization of the Italian Communist Party as the "modern prince," a network of organic intellectuals and workers who would challenge the hegemony of capital. Gill is careful to distance his idea from the putative errors of the left parties of old — hierarchy, dogmatism, and so on. He says, "… the multiple and diverse political forces that form the postmodern Prince combine both defensive and forward-looking strategies." This is an appropriate stance, especially in light of what happened to the New Left in the 1970s. A period of broad encompassing social movement activism morphed into a bevy of small sectarian parties yelling slogans at potential recruits and at each other. The sectarian model is obviously not one to emulate, and Gill is careful in this regard.

Warren Wagar (1992, 1996) has also had the temerity to suggest that an organized group of political actors making use of and further developing the world-systems perspective might come together in what he calls the World Party (1999). The angle here would be the use of a world-historical and comparative perspective on the development of capitalism to help the family of antisystemic movements see the big picture and to cooperate with one another on feasible projects. The risks of Napoleonic hubris and accusations of Stalinism are probably worth taking because of the great strategic and tactical importance of theoretical perspective for constructing a democratic and collectively ration global commonwealth.

6

Generic Globalization, Capitalist Globalization, and Beyond: A Framework for Critical Globalization Studies

Leslie Sklair

Introduction

Theory and research on globalization appear to have reached a mature phase in a relatively short period of time.[1] Most attempts to survey the field, while differing radically on their interpretations of the literature, agree that globalization represents a serious challenge to the state-centrist assumptions of most previous social science. Nevertheless, those qualities that are generally considered to be the natural qualities of societies bounded by their nation-states, the difficulty of generating and working with data that cross national boundaries, and the lack of specificity in most theories of the global, all conspire to undermine the critique of state-centrism. Thus, before the idea of globalization has become firmly established, the skeptics are announcing the limits and, in some extreme cases, the myth of globalization. Globalization, in the words of some populists, is nothing but globaloney!

Many globalization theorists and researchers, including myself, have a good deal of sympathy with the skeptics. However, I shall argue that globalization is more than an ideology, though various versions of globalization can be, and have been, promoted as ideologies. Globalization in a generic sense needs to be distinguished from its dominant type, namely, capitalist globalization, and both of these have to be confronted in theory and research if we are to have any grasp of the contemporary world and, in particular, the prospects for alternative forms of globalization. This can be done in the context of what I have termed *global system theory*. To illustrate its central themes, I argue that the global system can best be analyzed in terms of transnational practices and, in this way, alternatives to capitalist globalization can be conceptualized. In order to reach this stage in the argument, it is necessary to distinguish three competing approaches to globalization, namely, internationalist (state-centrist), transnationalist (globalization as a contested world-historical project with capitalist and other variants), and globalist (capitalist globalization as a more or less completed and irreversible neoliberal capitalist project).

Capitalist globalization cannot succeed in the long term because it cannot resolve two central crises, those of class polarization and ecological unsustainability on a global scale. This lays the transnational capitalist class and its institutions open to the attacks of an ever-widening antiglobalization (and increasingly anticapitalist) movement, and makes the search for alternatives to capitalist globalization urgent. I introduce the idea that the best prospect for ending capitalist globalization in the long run is to be found in the globalization of economic and social human rights, and that this is attainable through the spread of genuine democracy. Thus, the focus of critical globalization studies is clearly such alternative, genuinely democratic forms of globalization, but we have little chance of successfully articulating such forms unless we understand what generic globalization is and how capitalist globalization really works.

Competing Approaches to Globalization

By competing approaches I mean ideas about the fundamental unit of analysis used when we discuss globalization.[2] This is basic to all scientific inquiry, and argument about the scientific method and paradigms of science revolve around agreements and disagreements over these basic units of analysis. In this context, there are three types of units of analysis that different (competing) groups of globalization theorists and researchers take to define their field of inquiry. First, and most common, the internationalist (state-centrist) approach to globalization takes as its unit of analysis the state (often confused with the much more contentious idea of the nation-state). In this approach, globalization is seen as something that powerful states do to less powerful states, and something that is done to less powerful groups of people in all states. It is sometimes difficult to see where this line of argument differs from older theories of imperialism and colonialism, and more recent theories of dependency. The theme that globalization is the new imperialism is thus quite common among radical critics of globalization, by which they often mean (but do not always say) *capitalist globalization*. I reject this view on the grounds of theoretical redundancy and empirical inadequacy. It is theoretically redundant because if globalization is just another name for internationalization or imperialism, or more of the same, then the term is redundant at best and confusing at worst. State-centrist approaches to globalization offer no qualitatively new criteria for globalization and, paradoxically, appear to offer at least nominal support to those who argue that globalization is a myth.

The globalist approach is the antithesis to the state-centrist thesis, for example, in the work of Kenichie Ohmae (formerly McKinsey chief in Japan) and other management gurus (but very few actual researchers). Globalists argue that the state has all but disappeared, that we have already entered a borderless world, and that globalization is a done deal. The global economy is driven by nameless and faceless market forces — the globalist unit of analysis, often referred to as neoliberal globalization. I also reject this approach for its failure to theorize correctly the role of the state and the interstate system. Globalists (like state-centrists) are unable to analyze adequately the changing role of state actors and agencies in sustaining the hegemony of those who drive capitalist globalization, that is, the transnational capitalist class. In my formulation, it is the globalizing politicians and bureaucrats who are responsible for mobilizing the parts of the state that they control in the interests of the transnational capitalist class.

The transnational approach to globalization is the synthesis of the collision of the flawed state-centrist thesis and the flawed globalist antithesis. I consider this to be the most fruitful approach, facilitating theory and research on the struggle between the dominant but as yet incomplete project of capitalist globalization and its alternatives. My own version of this synthesis proposes transnational practices (TNPs) as the most conceptually coherent and most empirically useful unit of analysis. Within the familiar political economy categories — economy, politics, and (somewhat less familiar) culture-ideology — we can construct the categories of economic, political, and culture-ideology TNPs and conduct empirical research to discover their characteristic institutional forms in the dominant global system (manifestation of globalization). However, despite their fundamental differences, these three approaches stem from a real phenomenon, generic globalization.

Generic Globalization

The central feature of all the approaches to globalization current in the social sciences is that many important contemporary problems cannot be adequately studied at the level of nation-states (i.e., in terms of national societies or international relations), but need to be theorized, more or less, in terms of globalizing (transnational) processes, beyond the level of the nation-state. For state-centrists, remember, it is the state (or usually the most powerful states) that drives globalization. The dominant form of globalization in the world today is clearly capitalist globalization, and I argue that much of the confusion in the literature is due to the inability of most theorists and researchers to distinguish adequately between generic globalization and its historical forms, actual and potential.

I define generic globalization in terms of two new phenomena that have become significant in the last few decades:

1. The electronic revolution, notably transformations in the technological base and global scope of the electronic mass media and in most of the material infrastructure of the world today.[3]
2. The subsequent creation of transnational social spaces in which qualitatively new forms of cosmopolitanism flourish.[4]

I take these two new phenomena — the electronic revolution and transnational social spaces generating cosmopolitanism — to be the defining characteristics of globalization, in a generic sense. They are both irreversible in the long run (absent global catastrophe) because the vast majority of the people in the world, rich or poor, men or women, black or white, young or old, able or disabled, educated or uneducated, gay or straight, secular or religious, see that generic globalization could serve their own best interests, even if it is not necessarily serving their best interests at present. This is the world most people live in — big landlords as well as subsistence farmers in villages, corporate executives as well as laborers in sweatshops in major cities, well-paid professionals as well as informal workers in tourist sites, and comfortable manual workers as well as desperate migrants in transit in the hope of better lives.

But, of course, these polarities point to the inescapable fact that we live both in a world of generic globalization and in a world of actually existing capitalist globalization. So, the dominant global system at the start of the twenty-first century is the capitalist global system, and I argue that the most fruitful way to analyze and research it is in terms of its transnational practices.

Global System Theory

Global system theory is based on the concept of transnational practices, practices that cross state boundaries but do not originate with state agencies or actors (although they are often involved). This conceptual choice offers, as it were, a working hypothesis for one of the most keenly contested disagreements between globalization theorists and their opponents — that the nation-state is in decline.[5] The concept of transnational practices is an attempt to make more concrete the issues raised by such questions in the debate over globalization. Analytically, transnational practices operate in three spheres: the economic, the political, and the cultural-ideological. The whole is what I mean by the global system. The global system at the beginning of the twenty-first century is not synonymous with global capitalism, but the dominant forces of global capitalism are the dominant forces in the global system. To put it simply, individuals, groups, institutions, and even whole communities (local, national, or transnational) can exist, perhaps even thrive, as they have always done outside the orbit of the global capitalist system. However, this is becoming increasingly more difficult as capitalist globalization penetrates ever more widely and deeply. The building blocks of global system theory are the transnational corporation, the characteristic institutional form of economic transnational practices, a still-evolving transnational capitalist class in the political sphere, and, in the culture-ideology sphere, the culture-ideology of consumerism.

In the economic sphere, the global capitalist system offers a limited place to the wage-earning masses in most countries. The workers, the direct producers of goods and services, have occupational choices that are generally free within the range offered by prevailing class structures. The inclusion of the subordinate classes in the political sphere is very partial. The global capitalist system has very little need of the subordinate classes in this sphere. In parliamentary democracies, successful parties must be able to mobilize the masses to vote every so often, but in most countries voting is not compulsory and mass political participation is usually discouraged. In nondemocratic or quasi-democratic capitalist polities even these minimal conditions are absent.

The culture-ideology sphere is, however, entirely different. Here, the aim of global capitalists is total inclusion of all classes and, especially, the subordinate classes insofar as the bourgeoisie can be considered already included. The cultural-ideological project of global capitalism is to persuade people to consume above their biological needs in order to perpetuate the accumulation of capital for private profit; in other words, to ensure that the global capitalist system goes on forever. The culture-ideology of consumerism proclaims, literally, that the meaning of life is to be found in the things that we possess. To consume, therefore, is to be fully alive, and to remain fully alive we must continuously consume. The notions of men and women as economic or political beings are discarded by global capitalism, quite logically, as the system does not even pretend to satisfy everyone in the economic or political spheres. People are primarily consumers. The point of economic activity for ordinary members of the global capitalist system is to provide the resources for consumption, and the point of political activity is to ensure that the conditions for consuming are maintained. The importance of the transnational corporations and of consumerism are now widely recognized by proponents, opponents, and those who claim to be neutral about globalization, but the idea of the transnational capitalist class is less familiar and much more controversial.

The Transnational Capitalist Class[6]

The transnational capitalist class (TCC) is transnational in the double sense that its members have globalizing rather than, or in addition to, localizing perspectives, and it typically contains people from many countries who operate transnationally as a normal part of their working lives. The transnational capitalist class can be conceptualized in terms of the following four fractions:

1. Those who own and control major transnational corporations (TNCs) and their local affiliates (corporate fraction)
2. Globalizing state and interstate bureaucrats and politicians (state fraction)
3. Globalizing professionals (technical fraction)
4. Merchants and media (consumerist fraction)

This class sees its mission as organizing the conditions under which its interests and the interests of the system can be furthered in the global and local contexts. The concept of the TCC implies that there is one central transnational capitalist class that makes systemwide decisions and that it connects with the TCC in each locality, region, and country. Although the four fractions are distinguishable analytic categories with different functions for the global capitalist system, the people in them often move from one category to another (sometimes described as the revolving door between government and business, *pantouflage* in French).[7]

Together, these groups constitute a global power elite, ruling class, or inner circle in the sense that these terms have been used to characterize the class structures of specific countries.[8] The transnational capitalist class is opposed not only by those who reject capitalism as a way of life and an economic system but also by those capitalists who reject globalization. Some localized, domestically oriented businesses can share the interests of the global corporations and prosper, but many cannot and perish. Influential business strategists and management theorists commonly argue that to survive, local businesses must globalize. Though most national and local state managers fight for the interests of their constituents, as they define these interests, government bureaucrats, politicians, and professionals who entirely reject globalization and espouse extreme nationalist ideologies are comparatively rare, despite the recent rash of civil wars in economically marginal parts of the world. And although there are anticonsumerist elements in most societies, there are few cases of a serious anticonsumerist party winning political power anywhere in the world.

The TCC is transnational in the following respects:

1. The economic interests of its members are increasingly globally linked rather than exclusively local and national in origin. Their property and shares, and the corporations they own and control are becoming more globalized. As ideologues, their intellectual products serve the interests of globalizing rather than localizing capital. This follows directly from the shareholder-driven growth imperative that lies behind the globalization of the world economy and the increasing difficulty of enhancing shareholder value in purely domestic firms. Although for some practical purposes the world is still organized in terms of discrete national economies, the TCC increasingly conceptualizes its interests in terms of markets, which may or may not coincide with a specific nation-state, and the global market, which clearly does not. I define domestic firms as those serving an exclusively sovereign state market, employing only local conationals, and whose products consist entirely of domestic services, components, and materials. If you think that this is a ridiculously narrow definition for the realities of contemporary economies, then you are more than halfway to accepting my concept of globalization.

2. The TCC seeks to exert economic control in the workplace, political control in domestic and international politics, and culture-ideology control in everyday life through specific forms of global competitive and consumerist rhetoric and practice. The focus of workplace control is the threat that jobs will be lost and, in the extreme, the economy will collapse unless workers are prepared to work longer and for less in order to meet foreign competition. This is reflected in local electoral politics in most countries, where the major parties have few substantial strategic (even if many rhetorical and tactical) differences, and also in the sphere of culture-ideology, where consumerism is rarely challenged.

3. Members of the TCC have outward-oriented globalizing rather than inward-oriented localizing perspectives on most economic, political, and culture-ideology issues. The growing TNC and international institutional emphasis on free trade, and the shift from import substitution to export promotion strategies in most developing countries since the 1980s have been driven by alliances of consultancies of various types: indigenous and foreign members of the TCC working through TNCs, government agencies, elite opinion organizations, and the media. Some of the credit for this apparent transformation in the way in which big business works around the world is attached to the tremendous growth in business education since the 1960s, particularly in the United States and Europe, but increasingly all over the world.

4. Members of the TCC tend to share similar lifestyles, particularly patterns of higher education (increasingly in business schools) and consumption of luxury goods and services. Integral to this process are exclusive clubs and restaurants, ultraexpensive resorts in all continents, private as opposed to mass forms of travel and entertainment and, ominously, increasing residential segregation of the very rich, secured by armed guards and electronic surveillance, all over the world — from Los Angeles to Moscow and from Manila to Beijing.

5. Finally, members of the TCC seek to project images of themselves as citizens of the world as well as of their places of birth. Leading exemplars of this phenomenon include Jacques Maisonrouge, French-born, who became, in the 1960s, the chief executive of IBM World Trade; the Swede Percy Barnevik who created Asea Brown Boverei, often portrayed as spending most of his life in his corporate jet; the German

Helmut Maucher, CEO of Nestle's far-flung global empire; David Rockefeller, said to be one of the most powerful men in the United States; the legendary Akio Morita, the founder of Sony; and Rupert Murdoch, who actually changed his nationality to pursue his global media interests. Today, major corporate philanthropists, notably Bill Gates and George Soros, embody the new globalizing TCC.

The inner circle of the TCC gives a unity to the diverse economic interests, political organizations, and cultural and ideological formations of those who make up the class as a whole. As in any social class, fundamental long-term unity of interests and purpose does not preclude shorter-term and local conflicts of interests and purpose, both within each of the four fractions and between them. The culture-ideology of consumerism is the fundamental value system that keeps the system intact, but it permits a relatively wide variety of choices, for example, what I term *emergent global nationalisms*, as a way of satisfying the needs of the different actors and their constituencies within the global system.

The four fractions of the TCC in any region, country, city, society, or community perform complementary functions to integrate the whole. The achievement of these goals is facilitated by the activities of local and national agents, and organizations connected in a complex network of global interlocks. A crucial component of this integration of the TCC as a global class is that virtually all senior members of the TCC will occupy a variety of interlocking positions, not only the interlocking directorates that have been the subject of detailed studies for some time in a variety of countries but also connections outside the direct ambit of the corporate sector, the civil society as it were, servicing the state-like structures of the corporations. Leading corporate executives serve on and chair the boards of think tanks, charities, scientific, sports, arts and culture bodies, universities, medical foundations, and similar organizations. It is in this sense that the claims that the business of society is business and the business of our society is global business, become legitimated in the global capitalist system. Business, particularly in the TNC sector, then begins to monopolize symbols of modernity and postmodernity such as free enterprise, international competitiveness, and the good life, and to transform most, if not all, social spheres in its own image.

The End of Capitalist Globalization

The literature on globalization is suffused with a good deal of fatalism. Even some progressive academics, popular writers, and political and cultural leaders seem to accept that there is no alternative to capitalist globalization and that all we can do is to try to work for a better world around it.[9] Although I cannot fully develop the counterargument to this fatalism here, it seems to me to be both morally indefensible and theoretically shortsighted. Capitalist globalization is failing on two counts fundamental to the future of most of the people in the world and, indeed, to the future of our planet itself. These are the class polarization crisis and the crisis of ecological unsustainability. There is, further, evidence to suggest that capitalist globalization may be intensifying both crises.[10] Nevertheless, generic globalization should not be identified with capitalism, though capitalist globalization is its dominant form in the present era. This makes it necessary to think through other forms of globalization, forms that might retain some of the positive consequences of capitalism (insofar as they can exist outside capitalism) while transcending it as a socioeconomic system in the transition to a new stage of world history.[11]

One path out of capitalism that is clear to some, but quite unclear to most, takes us from capitalist globalization (where we are) through what can be termed *cooperative democracy* (a transitional form of society) to socialist globalization (a convenient label for a form of globalization that ends class polarization and the ecological crisis). One strategy to achieve such a transformation involves the gradual elimination of the culture-ideology of consumerism and its replacement with a culture-ideology of human rights. This means, briefly, that instead of our possessions being the main focus of our cultures and the basis of our values, our lives should be lived with regard to a universally agreed system of human rights and the responsibilities to others that these rights entail. This does not imply that we should stop consuming. What it implies is that we should evaluate our consumption in terms of our rights and responsibilities, and that this should become a series of interlocking and mutually supportive globalizing transnational practices.

By genuinely expanding the culture-ideology of human rights from the civil and political spheres, in which capitalist globalization has often had a relatively positive influence, to the economic and social spheres, which represent a profound challenge to capitalist globalization, we can begin seriously to tackle the crises of class polarization and ecological unsustainability. But political realism dictates that this change cannot be accomplished directly; it must proceed via a transitional stage. Capitalism and socialism, as can be seen in the case of market socialism in China, are not watertight categories. Capitalist practices can and do occur in socialist societies (for example, making workers redundant to increase profits) just as socialist practices can exist in capitalist societies (for example, trying to ensure that everyone in a community enjoys a basic decent standard of living). The issue is hegemony — whose interests prevail, who defends the status quo (even by reforming it), who is pushing for fundamental change, and how this is organized into effective social movements for change globally.

The transition to socialist globalization will eventually create new forms of transnational practices. Transnational economic units will tend to be on a smaller and more sustainable scale than the major TNCs of today; transnational political practices will be democratic coalitions of self-governing and cooperative communities, not the unaccountable, unelected, and individualistic TCC. Also, cultures and ideologies will reflect the finer qualities of human life, and not the desperate variety of the culture-ideology of consumerism. These sentiments might appear utopian, indeed they are, and other alternatives are also possible. However, in the long term, muddling through with capitalist globalization is not a viable option if the planet and all those who live in it are to survive.

Thus, although the discourse and practice of capitalist globalization would seem to suggest that it is a force for convergence, the inability of capitalist globalization to solve the crises of class polarization and ecological unsustainability makes it both necessary and urgent to think through alternatives to it. This implies that capitalist globalization contains the seeds of divergence. The globalization of economic and social human rights leading to what can (but need not necessarily) be termed socialist globalization is certainly one, if presently rather remote, alternative, and there are many others. Communities, cities, subnational regions, whole countries, multicountry unions, and even transnational cooperative associations could all, in principle, try to make their own arrangements for checking and reversing class polarization and ecological unsustainability. It is likely that the twenty-first century will bring many new patterns of divergence before a global convergence on full human rights for all is established. This is unlikely to occur in a world dominated by transnational corporations, run by the TCC, and inspired by the culture-ideology of consumerism. Thus, the focus of critical globalization studies is clearly such alternative, genuinely democratic forms of globalization, but we have little chance of successfully articulating such forms unless we understand what generic globalization is and how capitalist globalization really works.

Notes

1. There are a few ideas in the social sciences that have spawned textbooks of several hundred pages, a decade after they have been announced. See, for example, J. A. Scholte, *Globalization: A Critical Introduction* (London: Macmillan, 2000) and dozens of collections, notably, F. Lechner and J. Boli, eds., *The Globalization Reader*, 2nd edition (Oxford: Blackwell, 2003). There is a useful account of the origin of the term in the social sciences in the first, short textbook, M. Waters, *Globalization* (London: Routledge, 1995), chapter 1. The present paper borrows from my own contributions in *The Transnational Capitalist Class* (Oxford: Blackwell, 2001) and *Globalization: Capitalism and Its Alternatives* (Oxford: Oxford University Press, 2002), the third and much revised edition of a book originally published in 1991.

2. In *Globalization* (Sklair, 2002), chapter 3, I distinguish four competing conceptions of globalization that focus on who or what is driving the processes. The approaches discussed here are at a higher level of generality, and units of analysis operate at the level of metatheory rather than theoretical concepts, in this instance.

3. See, for example, M. Castells, *The Rise of the Network Society* (London: Blackwell, 2000); E. Herman and R. McChesney, *The Global Media: The New Missionaries of Corporate Capitalism* (London: Cassell, 1997).

4. Worked out in different ways in T. Faist, *The Volume and Dynamics of International Migration and Transnational Social Spaces* (Oxford: Oxford University Press, 2000); U. Beck, *World Risk Society* (Cambridge: Polity Press, 1999); P. Smith and L. Guarnizo, eds., *Transnationalism from Below* (Brunswick, NJ: Transaction Books, 1998).

5. For good critical discussions of these issues, see R. Holton, *Globalization and the Nation-State* (London: Macmillan, 1998) and S. Strange, *The Retreat of the State* (Cambridge: Cambridge University Press, 1996).

6. For a useful survey of the literature on this concept, introduced in the first edition of my *Sociology of the Global System* in 1991, see W. Carroll and C. Carson, The network of global corporations and elite policy groups: a structure for transnational capitalist class formation. *Global Networks*, January 3, 2003: 29–58.

7. For a constructive critique of this apparent inflation of the class concept, see A. R. Embong, Globalization and transnational class relations: some problems of conceptualization. *Third World Quarterly*, June 21, 2000: 989–1000.

8. Preglobalization capitalist class theory, for which, see J. Scott, *Corporate Business and Capitalist Class* (Oxford: Oxford University Press, 1997), does not necessarily exclude the globalizing extension proposed here.

9. The most politically important example is the Third Way thesis, for which, see A. Giddens, *The Third Way and Its Critics* (Cambridge: Polity Press, 2000).

10. These two crises of capitalist globalization are elaborated in Sklair, Globalization, pp. 47–58 and *passim*.

11. The following paragraphs are based on *Globalization* (Sklair, 2002), chapter 11.

7

Transnationalism and Cosmopolitanism: Errors of Globalism

Victor Roudometof

The neoliberal ideology of globalism (Beck, 2000a: 9) asserts the worldwide dominance of so-called free markets, suggesting that greater connectivity inevitably leads to a more open, democratic, and prosperous public sphere. Accordingly, globalism presents a highly distorted image of globalization, an image at odds with the very reality of social life in most underdeveloped regions of the globe but, significantly, also within the boundaries of the West itself (for an insightful discussion, see Brennan, 2003). To differentiate between *globalism* and *globalization* is an important task of critical social science and critical globalization studies. Such an engagement necessitates the theoretical and empirical critique of taken-for-granted assumptions in the social–scientific literature.

In order to expose the errors of globalism, then, it is necessary to interrogate the proclaimed correlation of transnationalism and cosmopolitanism, as well as the assumption that a sheer increase in social connectivity is going to lead to greater levels of cosmopolitanism. Indeed, in contemporary discourse, cosmopolitanism is evoked in a two-fold manner: it is either a methodological and, to some degree, moral and ethical standpoint or, as an existing reality, a lived experience. In this respect, it is tempting to think of transnationalism as intimately involved in the global production of cosmopolitanism — with localism opposed to both of them. Transnationalism is typically connected to recent (and poorer) immigrant cohorts, whereas cosmopolitanism is evoked as an expression of the transnational mobility of more affluent groups. Class and racial boundaries are also intimately involved in this labeling process.

This chapter is a contribution toward gaining conceptual clarity with regard to the task of clearly conceptualizing (and distinguishing between) transnationalism and cosmopolitanism. My central argument is that the transnational experience should be conceived as involving several layers ranging from the construction of transnational social spaces to the formation of transnational communities. In turn, transnationalism's relationship to cosmopolitanism is less straightforward than what it might seem at first glance. In itself, the creation of transnational social spaces leads to a bifurcation of attitudes. This bifurcation is expressed in terms of a continuum with cosmopolitanism at the one end and localism at the other end. Overall, the relationship between transnationalism and the cosmopolitan-local continuum cannot be predetermined in theoretical terms.

Globalist Images of Transnationalism and Cosmopolitanism

There is a disjuncture between image and reality that lies underneath our judgment about who appears to be a "cosmopolitan" vs. who looks like a "transnational" or "transmigrant." It is in the space between stereotype and reality, between our theorization of transnationalism and our images of cosmopolitanism that one finds an unwanted yet all too apparent complexity — and it is this complexity I wish to explore here. It is also this complexity that is rendered invisible in globalist readings of these terms, whereby the concepts are assumed to be unproblematic and self-evident. Contemporary discourse on transnationalism and cosmopolitanism suffers from spatially and culturally specific stereotypes that color our imagination and limit our grasp of these terms. These concepts are applied and decoded with reference to specific groups of people, thereby signifying not just a social reality, but also an association between class, status, race or ethnicity, on the one hand, and linguistic use, on the other.

It is not accidental in this respect that transnationalism emerged in the 1990s as a new concept aiming to describe the situation of relatively recent immigrant cohorts entering into the labor force and the social fabric of advanced industrial societies in North America and Western Europe (see Basch et al., 1994; Smith and Guarnizo, 1998; Schiller and Fourton, 2001; Dominguez, 1998). In this context, transnationalism emerged as new powerful metaphor capable of capturing many of the processes previously subsumed under the rubric of globalization. Indeed, as globalization has become a bitterly contested buzzword, invoked by ideological camps with radically opposed viewpoints, social scientists appear to employ transnationalism as a term that captures the reality (as opposed to the rhetoric) of contemporary social life.

Indeed, the concept's original application was restricted to the experiences of recent U.S. immigrants — with the potential of extending the term's application to other groups that occupy a similar position. In this respect, contemporary research remains bound by traditional stereotypes. By and large, contemporary discourse does not take fully into account an entire range of other groups such as tourists, musicians, actors, doctors, professors, corporate managers, and so on. Neither does it take into account the existence of transnational communities that are not necessarily constituted by immigrants — such as the communities of taste constructed by members of musical and youth subcultures or those built and maintained by followers of sports teams, or even those communities constructed by members of professional and nongovernmental associations. Conceptualizing transnationalism in a less restricted sense allows us to incorporate these less permanent or visible, yet not less real, communities (for examples, see the essays in Kennedy and Roudometof, 2002; see also Kennedy, 2003).

In contrast to transnationalism, cosmopolitanism is being discussed simultaneously as a moral or ethical standpoint and as a real experience. The boundary between the descriptive and the prescriptive aspects of cosmopolitanism is hazy at best. Theorists such as Held (1995), Beck (1999, 2000b, 2001), Delanty (2000: 51–67), or Giddens (1998) use terms such as "cosmopolitan nation," "cosmopolitan democracy," and cosmopolitan citizenship, or "cosmopolitan society" and "cosmopolitan perspective" both as descriptive terms (i.e., terms that describe current reality) and as prescriptive terms (i.e., terms that denote public policy strategies that they consider suitable for twenty-first century global realities). In their conceptualizations, these theorists engage in the process of simultaneously assessing a pervasive feature of modern life and proposing ways policymakers (and sociologists) should deal with this reality. It is clear that the social theorists' attempts to provide a prescription for modern social problems can only benefit from a sound analysis of *existing* reality. This issue is particularly thorny because the intellectuals' own social position is one that allows them to simultaneously experience both transnationalism and cosmopolitanism — albeit under conditions that are certainly not typical of most social groups and classes worldwide (for a discussion, see Pels, 1999).

In numerous contemporary analyses, the sheer movement of peoples across borders is often taken to signify the presence (or at least the potential) of a cosmopolitan orientation. This has become the entrenched conventional wisdom of our time. Even Beck (2000b: 96–7) considers many features of contemporary transnationalism — such as dual citizenship, transnational criminal activity, transnational ways of life, transnational news coverage and mobility — as indicators of *cosmopolitanization*. Cosmopolitanization then leads Beck (2000b: 100) to propose an ideal type of a cosmopolitan society — a deterritorialized society, defined by the processes of cosmopolitanization as well as by its own reflexive cosmopolitanism, and "a society in which cosmopolitan values rate more highly than national values." Beck moves back and forth between sociological description and prescriptive moral argument, and this does not allow for an effective conceptual separation between cosmopolitanism as a moral or ethical standpoint and cosmopolitanism as a real, empirical variable. To put it differently, a society of cosmopolitan values is an ethical or moral goal, whereas cosmopolitan attitudes should be measurable, observable phenomena.

If I dwelled upon the specifics of Beck's argument, it is simply to show how contemporary discourse blends the lines between description and prescription. I should point out that the association between transnationalization and cosmopolitan attitudes is not inevitable: on the contrary, other groups that move across national borders — such as refugees, transmigrants, illegal immigrants, and international students — are not necessarily cosmopolitan in orientation. "A true cosmopolitan," Iyer (2000: 210) reminds us, "is not someone who has traveled a lot so much as someone who can appreciate what it feels like to be the Other." Some of the September 11th hijackers were, after all, "international students." Of course, Beck (2000b: 100) acknowledges that a "cosmopolitan society means cosmopolitan society *and its enemies*" (emphasis in the original). Still, Beck's intertwining between transnationalization and cosmopolitanization lacks sufficient conceptual clarity — and in many respects contributes to the slippery slope whereby the theorists' prescriptive statements are interwoven with sociological description.

Transnational Social Spaces and the Cosmopolitan-Local Continuum

In its broader interpretation, transnationalism might be understood as a form of experience that cannot be restricted to immigrant groups. Beck (2000a) speaks of "transnational social spaces" — spaces that, by definition, cannot be restricted to transnational labor markets. On the contrary, they can extend into other spaces, including spaces of transnational sexuality, popular music, and journalism, as well as a multitude of other identities (ranging from those based on gender to those based on race, religion, or ethnicity). Hence, the notion of transnational social space is considerably broader than the concept of transnational communities.

Transnational social spaces are constructed through the accelerated pace of transnational practices that become routine practices in social life. Such practices do not necessarily involve international migration. On the contrary, transnational interactions involve such routines like international calls, faxes, e-mails, satellite television broadcasting, simultaneous media access through Internet sources and television stations, international conferences, the different varieties of international tourism (ranging from recreational tourism to sex tourism or ecotourism), as well as the everlasting formalized agreements and ongoing negotiations of a wide array of international organizations and nongovernmental groups. The above list is far from exhaustive but it clearly shows that the range of transnational practices involves a rich tapestry encompassing a bewildering array of activities. Not all these activities are formalized. Some of them might be fleeting or relatively inconsequential to the parties involved, whereas others might be of paramount importance to all (or some of the) parties.

Let me illustrate the differences between the fleeting or short-lived interactions and more sustained or structured patterns of transnational practices by using the example of transnational sexuality. Fueled by the travel and leisure industry, sexual relations between hosts and guests have been a recurrent phenomenon in numerous societies that play host to large numbers of tourists. The carnal hunt and late-night escapades of tourists and locals particularly in Mexico, Italy, Greece, and the Middle East are fairly well-known byproducts of international tourism. Although these interactions are recurrent and certainly form a part of the social fabric of life in these places, they remain less formalized insofar as romantic relations remain fleeting. Obviously, given the threat of sexually transmitted diseases, it is not that such relations are unimportant. However, the order of magnitude of romantic liaisons changes dramatically in case we are dealing with long-term relationships that involve people who come from different countries, might be of different ethnic or racial backgrounds, and might even speak different languages.

In such cases, relations and transnational interactions become part of larger and more enduring structures — and hence, the necessity for states worldwide to institute provisions governing the status of spouses who are not members of a specific nation-state. In cases of cross-national marriages, the individuals involved, the state agencies that have jurisdiction (and hence power) over them, nonstate agents (such as attorneys or priests), and international agencies (such as different UN-sponsored organizations) are all involved in a web of interactions and relations. Such relations are far from egalitarian because state agencies have power over their own nationals and sometimes they might even favor their own nationals over other parties. For example, German courts have often privileged the rights of German parents over the rights of U.S. parents in custody disputes involving mixed German–U.S. couples. In these (and numerous other) instances, the recurrent and formally organized transnational practices are not simply interactions within transnational spaces. These practices involve power relations and hence they might be conceptualized as *transnational social fields*. Although transnational social fields pertain to the relations among individuals, organizations, and agencies, the people who are thus connected are not necessarily themselves transnational. For example, attorneys involved in a child custody case between U.S. and German parents are part of a transnational field but they might not have to even step outside the borders of their respective states.

Finally, there is the conventional interpretation of transnationalism with respect to the transnational networks formed by immigrants. In this case, the transnational networks are constructed by groups of people who live across state borders. As I have already alluded to, these transnational networks encompass areas of activity that might include transnational entrepreneurs and managers (Portes, 2000), but they might also include musical subcultures, publishing or academic activities, or other forms of international organizations that operate across borders (McNeely, 1995; Meyer et al., 1997; Kennedy and Roudometof, 2002).

Transnational social fields are considerably broader than transnational networks of immigrants or other groups of transnational people. Groups of immigrants in conflict with each other might be located within the same transnational social field — but this does not imply that the transnational field is by any means identical to the transnational networks of these immigrants. For example, Macedonian and Greek immigrants in Australia and Canada have formed transnational social networks that connect them to the Macedonian and Greek nation-states. However, both groups are locked into a conflict with each other over the monopolization of the label "Macedonian" on behalf of each group (Danforth, 1995, 2000; Roudometof, 2002). Their transnational struggle takes place within a transnational social field that extends beyond Australia's boundaries and includes the Greek, Macedonian, and Bulgarian nation-states as well as international human rights organizations and conferences. But none of this means that these immigrants form a *single* transnational network; on the contrary, each national group is connected with its own nation-state through churches, associations, and other forms of social activism.

The growth of transnational social spaces is borne out of the increasing volumes of cross-cultural interaction. In turn, this increased volume of interaction leads individuals to adopt an open, encompassing attitude or a closed, defensive posture. In the first case, individuals are labeled *cosmopolitans*, whereas in the second case they are labeled *locals* (Hannerz, 1990, 1996). In a world that becomes increasingly interconnected, these attitudes can be extremely influential in a whole array of topics, ranging from terms of trade to support for fundamentalist organizations to attitudes about religion or culture to expressions of tolerance or hostility toward immigrants (Reich, 1992; Beyer, 1994; Robertson, 1992; Tomlinson, 1999; Beck, 2001; Barber, 1995; Giddens, 2000).

In other words, the presence of a cosmopolitan outlook (or its conceptual opposite, a local outlook) is conceptually distinct from the transnational experience. It is conceivable that large numbers of people around the globe are exposed to other cultures on a daily basis without crossing borders on a regular basis, simply through the variety of communication media (including satellite broadcasting, radio, and other forms of communication). Furthermore, they might encounter immigrants, refugees, or tourists in their own locality. They might also encounter cultural artifacts and commercial establishments that bring other cultures into close proximity to their own — a process referred to in contemporary debates as "McDonaldization" or "Americanization" or, more broadly, as "cultural imperialism" (Ritzer, 2000; Barber, 1995; Watson, 1997; Epitropoulos and Roudometof, 1998; Tomlinson, 1999; Karim, 1998).

I would therefore suggest that the degree to which cosmopolitanism is related to the presence or absence of transnational experience is a relationship that can be (and should be) considered in empirical terms—and the link between the two is not theoretical (see Beck, 2000b) but, rather, empirical. The two concepts need to be conceptualized in a manner that preserves clarity of definition. They should not be blended, and the one should not be confused with or reduced to the other.

In addition to the cosmopolitan-transnational relation discussed above, it is necessary to clarify the relationship between cosmopolitanism and the nation-state. Once again, the conventional wisdom is that cosmopolitanism is antithetical to nationalism (see Nussbaum, 1996, for an overview). This interpretation is not substantiated from the historical record. On the contrary, over the eighteenth and early to middle nineteenth centuries, cosmopolitanism was concomitant with the reorganization of the world into a cultural universe of nation-states. For the French philosophers of the Enlightenment, a cosmopolitan was a citizen of the world, a universal humanist who transcended particularistic distinctions based on territory, language, or culture (Schlereth, 1977).[1] In this historical era, the cosmopolitan outlook was not antithetical to the emergence of the "nation" as category of classification. Philosophers, historians, and social and political theorists have pointed out that cosmopolitanism was closely tied with the assumption that people are divided into different nationalities.[2] During the nineteenth century, then, nation-states required the existence of a cosmopolitan attitude for their own processes of legitimization.

It was only during the post-1870 period, the golden period of nation-state building in Europe (cf. Hobsbawm, 1990), that nation-state building reconfigured the meaning of cosmopolitanism in a manner inconsistent with nationalism. This reinterpretation rested on the principle that a person's loyalty should be connected primarily to the soil of the nation. But this connection has been largely destabilized in the post-1945 period, as the anthropological accounts of long-distance or transnational nationalism indicate (Danforth, 1995; Basch et al., 1994; Glick Schiller, and Fourton, 2001; Anderson, 1993). On the contrary, the movement of peoples has strengthened the tendency of individuals living outside the borders of their national homeland to maintain their ties with their nation and to participate in national projects connected to their nation.

Therefore, it should be clear that cosmopolitanism should not be confused with the negation of national identity — and vice versa: Localism is different from nationalism. Of course, there is a specific dimension of the cosmopolitan-local relation that is linked to nationalism. That is, ethnocentrism is a quality that should be conceptually linked to locals, who are expected to adopt the viewpoint of unconditional support for one's country, putting one's country first, and protecting national interest irrespective of whether their own position is morally superior or not. On the contrary, cosmopolitans are unlikely to support such attitudes.

In this respect, Beck's (2000b: 100) call for a reopening of the intellectual debate on the relationship between cosmopolitanism and nationalism is a fruitful contribution to the dilemmas of contemporary nation-states. His advocacy of "cosmopolitan society" or "cosmopolitan nation" where the ideals of cosmopolitanism gain the upper hand against local ethnocentrism is indeed consistent (and not antithetical) with older, civic, and more democratically orientated conceptualizations of nationalism. Reviving such notions does provide an alternative political solution to waves of antiimmigrant ethnocentric protests sweeping European Union states. But this moral standpoint should not be confused with the reality of cosmopolitanism; indeed, the only way to accurately measure the success (or failure) of cosmopolitan values is to clearly separate our moral advocacy of them from cosmopolitan (and local) attitudes as observable phenomena.

Although moral entrepreneurs and policymakers might wish to represent cosmopolitans and locals as discontinuous variables, as an "either/or" choice, reality is far more complex than such a caricature. It is more appropriate to look upon the two terms as opposite ends of a continuum. To conceptualize the *cosmopolitan-local continuum*, then, it is necessary to specify those dimensions where it would be reasonable to expect that these two groups would display conflicting visions and priorities. These visions and priorities take the form of different degrees of attachment to specific locales, countries, local cultures and communities and, finally, to the "national economy." Specifically, the continuum between locals and cosmopolitans might vary with respect to the dimensions that will now be discussed.

First, cosmopolitans and locals diverge with respect to the *degree of attachment to a locality* (neighborhood or city). Cosmopolitans have a low degree of such attachment, and locals have a high degree of such attachment. Contemporary cultural theorists (Appadurai, 1995, 1996; Hannerz, 1996; Basch et al., 1994) have pointed out the extent to which locality is becoming differentiated from a physical place. Although transmigrants or transnational peoples provide the paradigmatic case of individuals who experience such a separation between "homeland" and the place where they live, this experience is not necessarily restricted to these groups. Nor is there any reason to assume that it is only those who cross state borders who are susceptible to such a rift.

Second, cosmopolitans and locals diverge with respect to the *degree of attachment to a state or country*. Locals are likely to value being a native of their country, having the country's citizenship, and having a sense of belonging to the country's dominant national group. Cosmopolitans are likely not to value these attributes. This dimension highlights the degree to which cosmopolitans and locals adopt different postures when it comes to reconfiguration of state sovereignty (Sassen, 1996). Citizenship has been traditionally interpreted as closely connected to formal membership in a state, and in most cases, such membership is justified through inclusion to the dominant national or ethnic group or by birth. The decoupling of citizenship from its traditional association with the nation-state is a feature observed in numerous analyses, whereby theorists detect a trend toward "post-national" membership to the state (Soysal, 1994; Jacobson, 1996; Delanty, 2000; Ong, 1999).

Third, cosmopolitans and locals diverge with respect to the *degree of attachment to, and support of, local culture*. Obviously, such an attachment and support for local culture is likely to take a variety of different forms depending upon the specifics of different national cultures around the globe. Religion, language, and other cultural characteristics would be invariably relevant as indicators of attachment and support to a local culture. Also, such indicators are likely to fluctuate, depending upon the regional and national differences of particular nation-states. For example, religion serves as an important marker for national identity in several European states — ranging from Poland to Greece and Ireland. This association is absent from other national cultures — such as the United States, for example — where the separation between church and state is constitutionally guaranteed and the subject of never-ending debates. Irrespective of such cases of national variation, however, locals should value cultural membership to the nation and cosmopolitans oppose it since, by definition, such a membership excludes people on the basis of ascribed criteria. By and large, locals are more ethnocentric than cosmopolitans.

Fourth, cosmopolitans and locals diverge with respect to the *degree of economic, cultural, and institutional protectionism*. Support for such protectionism varies widely depending upon the specific problems faced by nation-states worldwide. For example, antiglobalization rhetoric in the United States leads to arguments in favor of institutional protectionism in a variety of fields, whereas in Europe similar rhetoric identifies globalization with Americanization. Going beyond the rhetoric, however, locals and cosmopolitans display different attitudes when in comes to pragmatic issues such as support for tariffs, prohibition of land ownership by foreigners, opposition to or support of international interventions, and willingness to move for reasons of work or for obtaining more favorable living conditions.

Conclusions

In this discussion, I have tried to clarify the relationship between transnationalism and cosmopolitanism. Both terms are frequently evoked in sociological description and even everyday speech. It is important to note that these terms are not exclusively sociological concepts, but also commonsense concepts. Hence, our understanding of these terms is colored by considerations of status, national origin, ethnicity, race, and gender. Whereas contemporary discourse has been focusing attention on the extent to which transnationalism is a phenomenon closely connected to international migration, I argue that this interpretation is unduly restrictive.

Transnationalism involves three different layers of activities, each of which entails different degrees of structuration with regard to the permanence of the transnational practices performed by actors. First, there are the *transnational social spaces*, which are constructed through the recurrent transnational interactions and practices of actors worldwide. Such spaces involve a wide range of activities, but these activities might range from the trivial to the deadly serious. Second, the more structured and permanent interactions and practices that take place in transnational social space involve the exercise of power relations by a multitude of agents and actors. These more structured practices take place within *transnational social fields*, fields that connect people and institutions from different countries across the globe. Transnational mobility is not a prerequisite for participating in such a field. Third, there are *transnational communities*, communities constructed by new immigrants in advanced industrialized countries, but also communities constructed by other professional or managerial groups that routinely cross the globe.

The proliferation of transnational social spaces as a permanent feature of global life leads to a bifurcation of attitudes among the public. Faced with the reality of transnational experience, members of the public might opt for an open attitude welcoming the new experiences or they might opt for a defensive closed attitude seeking to limit the extent to which transnational social spaces penetrate their cultural milieu. In the first instance, we speak of cosmopolitans, whereas in the second instance we speak of locals. However, instead of thinking of these two categories as discontinuous variables, I suggest that most people are likely to develop highly complex attitudes with regard to the two alternatives, and, therefore, it is better to conceptualize the two categories as forming a single continuum.

Keeping this analysis in mind, we can look upon the formation of transnational communities as attempts to ground cosmopolitanism in something more stable than the cracks of the nation-state system. Transnational communities come in different varieties, including those formed by new immigrant groups migrating to First World countries, as well as those older diasporic populations whose status and attitude is continuously influenced by the accelerating pace of economic, cultural, and institutional globalization. In addition to these two categories, members of cultural communities who live in different countries but remain connected to each other through their cultural tastes or pastimes also construct transnational communities. Finally, managerial, professional, and nongovernmental organizations also contribute to the formation of groups with their own ethos and practices (for example, Kennedy, 2003). Consequently, although some of these transnational communities might be predisposed toward cosmopolitanism, it is equally possible to argue that some of them would be predisposed toward localism. The relationship between transnationalism and cosmopolitanism is not a linear one whereby greater transnationalization leads to greater cosmopolitanization. On the contrary, the extension of transnational social spaces into the global cultural milieu is responsible for producing both cosmopolitan and local attitudes. Making a choice between the two is a matter of ethics and moral judgment, but this judgment should stand independently from our ability to describe the conceptual alternatives.

Acknowledgment

The author would like to thank Susan Paulson, Department of Anthropology, Miami University, and Paul Kennedy, Department of Sociology, Manchester Metropolitan University, for their help in developing the arguments set forth in this chapter.

Notes

1. The word *cosmopolitan* is an English (and French) rendition of the Greek word *kosmo-polite*, a compound noun that literally means "the citizen [*politis*] of the world [*cosmos*]." The term's employment in the eighteenth century maintained its original Greek connotation. See Cheah (1998: 22) and Delanty (2000) for brief reviews of the word's etymology.
2. See the essays in Bohman and Lutz-Bachmann (1997) for Kant's original formulation of the cosmopolitan ideal. See Cheah (1998) for a discussion that traces the evolution of the term's meaning from Kant to Marx. Meinecke's (1909, first German edition; 1970, first English translation) classical study on the connection between nationalism and cosmopolitanism has firmly established the link between the two.

8

Toward a Critical Theory of Globalization: A Habermasian Approach

Darren J. O'Byrne

The Theoretical Discourse on Globalization

Few terms in the social sciences have been as used and abused as *globalization*. This word is now used so frequently that it seems to have taken on an assumed meaning, becoming a "thing-in-itself." That is to say, in its use among journalists, politicians, and academics there would appear to be a common acceptance that it actually means something, like a Durkheimian "social fact." Furthermore, like all social facts, the term comes to signify a singular thing, thus denying the possibility of multiple globalizations. This drift towards essentialism masks a different reality — that there is in fact very little agreement among these commentators as to what it actually means. Furthermore, by treating "globalization" as if it has such essential qualities (there is now a "sociology of globalization" in much the same way as there is a sociology of education, work, religion, or other such social institutions), one can easily forget that the word we are talking about — globalization — signifies not a "thing" but a process, some form of transformation. Just as modernization (an equally controversial word) means the process of becoming modern, *globalization* refers to the process of becoming global.

The problem with such transformative terms, of course, is that we are unlikely to agree on what would constitute the successful completion of the transformation. There is no fixed definition on what constitutes "modern," so necessarily the discourse on modernization is imbued with ideological value judgments. The discourse on globalization would surely have more cohesion if we could agree on how to measure the process of "becoming global." Even here, though, we are faced with different accounts. On the one hand, we can talk about something becoming globalized if it spans the length and breadth of the globe — an expansionist definition. Thus, a capitalist economy that reaches every corner of the planet, a world government that has legitimate authority over the whole planet, or a television show that is seen in every country could serve as examples of economic, political, and cultural globalization using this definition. On the other hand, though, we might think of globalization as a process that can be applied to the inherent properties of a person or thing, so that they relate directly (that is, in an unmediated way) to the globe. Therefore, a marketing campaign by Coca-Cola or Benetton designed to speak to the world as a whole is a form of cultural-economic globalization. The decision of an individual to join an environmental social movement rather than a national political party, and to recycle rather than discard rubbish, represents another form of political globalization.

In either case, though, we might, should we delve beneath the taken-for-granted rhetoric and consider the reality sociologically, come to the not-unreasonable conclusion that there is very little globalization going on. Sklair refers instead to *globalizing* processes and *transnational* realities.[1] In so far as the capitalist economy transcends nation-state borders (and is therefore at least "transnational") and administers a division of labor spanning the globe, then the globalization of the capitalist economy is clearly at a more advanced stage (to talk in terms of unilinear processes) than, say, political or cultural globalization. Indeed, the globalizing processes at work in the cultural sphere are usually discussed not as the "globalization of culture" but as the postnational consequences of the flow of people, capital, and goods across borders. Hence, *hybridization* and *creolization* are more appropriate than *cultural globalization*.[2]

Given such an absence of agreement on the meaning of globalization, it is hardly surprising that attempts to debate its practice have yielded very little fruit. Without at least some shared recognition of the problem of globalization, debates along "traditional" sociological divides (e.g., between Marxist and non-Marxist camps) are meaningless. This tendency to assume rather than debate the apparent meaning of globalization has also given rise to absurd polemics from otherwise intelligent academics, such as the recent division of much literature on the subject into two extreme camps — "skeptics" and "hyperglobalizers" — in order to promote a middle ground or "third way," the way of the "transformationalists," as eminently more sensible.[3] I am not interested in such polemics, because they serve no purpose. I am interested, instead, in looking at the theoretical literature on globalization and examining exactly what the contributors to this literature mean by it.

We can usefully distinguish between three approaches to the study of globalization. These three camps are characterized not by any traditional theoretical borders (e.g., Marxist against "functionalist" accounts) or by value judgments ("pro" or "anti") but by their different understandings of what globalization actually is. The first camp sees globalization as a process, usually a historical and long-term one, which is either synonymous with or simultaneous to modernization. The second camp sees globalization as a significant (and quite recent) transformation within the logic of modernity. The third camp identifies conflicting forms of globalization, and looks at the interplay between these forms as reflecting the contradictions within modernity. I call this the *dialectical* approach. Of course, such distinctions are introduced solely to serve the purpose of analysis, and not to pigeon-hole particular approaches. All the approaches included here are far more complex than this analytical survey might suggest.

Process Accounts

Process theory accounts of globalization grow out of the historical sociology of social change, and can be related to earlier traditions such as modernization theory or historical materialism. Globalization, according to such accounts, is thus a singular, long-term, historical process that operates simultaneously at global and local levels (an unhelpful distinction abandoned by most process theorists), is advanced by a particular dynamic or logic, and which will result in a singular world society — although the constitution of such a society is contested and the process is far from complete.[4]

Within globalization theory, Roland Robertson's work is the best known example of a process account.[5] Robertson sees globalization as a long-term process, beginning in Europe in the early fifteenth century. This process is characterized by the gradual emergence of a global consciousness, an awareness of the world as a single place. Robertson's focus here is (primarily) cultural and his guides are Durkheim (whose *conscience collective* forms the basis for Robertson's global consciousness) and Tonnies (whose *gemeinschaft* and *gesellschaft* provide the blueprints for alternative images of the future global society). Thus, for Robertson, the dynamic or logic that fuels this process is cultural, and the outcome of this process remains uncertain.

An interesting addition to the process theory tradition has been provided by the historian Robbie Robertson.[6] With his interest in the emergence of global consciousness and his interpretation of globalization as an extremely long-term process, there are many similarities between his account and that of his namesake. Robertson actually traces the seeds of globalization almost to the dawn of history, although he focuses primarily on three waves of globalization. The first wave reached its peak in the commercialism of the sixteenth century, and proved to be an extremely destabilizing force. The second wave emerged following the industrial revolution and is connected to European imperialism. The third wave, post–Second World War, bears a distinctly American flavor and is clearly connected to processes of democratization and capitalist expansion.

Although he consciously avoids using the word *globalization*, and his approach does not lend itself to a theory of globalization per se, Immanuel Wallerstein's world-systems analysis can also be defined as a process account.[7] Wallerstein's work is concerned with tracing the historical development of the modern world-system, an integrated capitalist economy that began in Europe in around 1600. Wallerstein thus rethinks Marxist theory and lays down a radical challenge to traditional historical materialism. Although his emphasis remains on the system of nation-states (core-periphery relations) rather than the globe, some of his followers have found his general framework useful for interpreting global transformations, and have in effect produced a theory of globalization from within a world-systems analysis framework.[8] Thus, the evolution of the world capitalist system so meticulously charted by Wallerstein forms part of the process of globalization — the dynamic or logic of which is clearly economic — the final outcome of which will be a single global (as opposed to world) capitalist economy.

Transformative Accounts

Transformative accounts see globalization as an event that creates a rupture or disjuncture in the logic of modernity. This event is relatively recent — usually situated in the second half of the twentieth century. Although there are sharp differences between the theorists included here, these differences tend to refer to the outcomes rather than the nature of the globalization process. Although they agree that globalization has some effect upon modernity and that the result of this is a qualitatively different kind of society, how they describe these outcomes depends largely on how they define the constitution of modernity.

For Anthony Giddens, globalization is a consequence of the logic of modernity itself.[9] Giddens begins with a multidimensional description of modernity, characterized by the interrelationship between capitalism, industrialism, surveillance, and military power. The rise of information and communications technology, together with the postwar globalism, results in a process of globalization (characterized primarily by time–space distanciation and disembedding), which speeds up modernity's logic. Although globalization, in Giddens's account, clearly transforms modernity, it does so within the existing framework (that is to say, it amends rather than replaces the four components of modernity). The result, Giddens claims, is "late" or "reflexive" modernity.

Starting from a different set of assumptions about modernity, David Harvey reaches a similar conclusion.[10] Harvey's components of modernity — drawing primarily on Marx — are capitalism, Fordist production practices, and cultural modernism. A crisis of overaccumulation forces capitalism to adapt toward more fragmented, post-Fordist production practices including flexible accumulation (thus, "late" capitalism). "Postmodernism" is therefore the cultural reflection of these new economic practices. Like Giddens, Harvey is describing a transformation within the existing logic — the internationalization of capitalism supported by the postmodernization of culture.

The most radical transformative account of globalization is provided by Martin Albrow.[11] Albrow argues that globalization does not simply alter the logic of modernity; it signals the end of the "modern age" and the dawn of a new historical epoch, the global age. How does Albrow justify such a claim? First, we need to understand how Albrow defines the modern age. As a disciple of Weber, Albrow suggests that the dominant feature of the modern age has been the pivotal role played by the nation-state. The modern age is thus the age in which the world was mapped, divided into identifiable territories, each administered by a political authority, the centralized means of violence. Necessarily, then, the nation-state is the primary source of identity among individuals, the arena in which social action takes place, and the window that mediates between individuals and the wider world. However, according to Albrow, the contradictions of the modern age have resulted in the decentering of the nation-state as the central unit of analysis. Globalization means individuals and corporations can relate directly to the globe, rendering the nation-state largely redundant. So, if the nation-state has been displaced by the globe, then necessarily the logic of the modern age has also been replaced, by a new logic in which the globe becomes the primary source of identity and the arena for social action.

Dialectical Accounts

Dialectical accounts do not see globalization as a singular process, but as an empty term that gains currency only when it is applied to some concrete aspect of social life. "Globalizations" need not, accordingly, be associated with particular historical junctures, they need not be simultaneous, and they need not form part of a "grand narrative" of historical change. In dialectical accounts, one form of globalization can be countered by another.

The best example of the dialectical approach is provided by Leslie Sklair.[12] Sklair draws on the work of Gramsci to distinguish between capitalism's three forms: the economy, the polity, and culture-ideology. Sklair suggests that the contemporary condition of globalization is best termed *capitalist globalization* and that it is feasible for us to develop an alternative strategy, *socialist globalization*. Culture-ideology is crucial in maintaining the hegemony of the capitalist system. In capitalist globalization, the culture-ideology is consumerism. As a counterhegemonic strategy, Sklair proposes that the culture-ideology of socialist globalization should be human rights.

Not all dialectical theories are Marxist. In their edited volume, *Global Visions*, Jeremy Brecher, John Brown Childs, and Jill Cutler distinguish between "globalization from above" and "globalization from below."[13] The former is the project of the New World Order, a Western project designed to further the interests of capitalism and "liberal democracy," in which extreme economic liberalization results in the polarization of North and South. The latter suggests instead a shift toward a "one-world community," involving democratization at every level from local to global, the recognition of international law, human rights, and environmental justice, and grassroots sustainable development. This approach represents a new transnational activism associated with environmental and human rights movements, a "grassroots surge" of "transnational militancy."[14]

In this chapter and elsewhere, I propose a related model to those of Sklair and Brecher et al., drawing on the work of Jürgen Habermas.[15] I suggest that we can understand alternative and conflicting processes of globalization within Habermas' framework of modernity. Necessarily, though, the boundaries between these three camps are extremely blurred, and any attempt to locate the dynamics of globalization within the theory of modernity proposed by Habermas will have clear affinities with the transformative tradition. My approach, then, attempts to be both dialectic and transformative. It shares with transformative accounts, especially those proposed by Giddens, Albrow, and Harvey, a prior set of assumptions about the key dimensions of "modernity." From such a starting point, it proceeds to explore the extent to which these features have been globalized.

Modernity, System, and Lifeworld

Jürgen Habermas is the contemporary heir to the critical tradition of Kant, Marx, and the Frankfurt School, and the most important among the second generation of critical theorists. Habermas' work covers an enormous range of issues.[16] Over the years he has added his voice to debates over the ideological essence of scientific knowledge, theoretical and methodological issues in the social sciences, the role of universities and of the student movement, capitalist crises, neoconservatism, European integration and citizenship, the reunification of Germany, and the role of religion, among others.[17]

For my purposes here, I am going to concentrate primarily on Habermas' theory of modernity, outlined in *The Theory of Communicative Action* and other works.[18] Habermas challenges the idea — developed fullest by Weber — that modernity involves a singular process of rationalization. Drawing on Horkheimer and Adorno's *Dialectic of Enlightenment*, Habermas suggests that modernity has been a struggle between two competing forms of rationality. One form is *instrumental* or purposive-rational. This informs the projects of capitalist liberalization and nation-state expansion and uses the logic of economics, politics, and science. It is the modernity associated with the rationalization of the economic and political spheres, fueled by the increasing dominance of scientific method based on means–ends calculations. Habermas associates this with the set of structures that make up the "system."

The second form is *abstract* and subjective, extending the Enlightenment project of knowledge, self-discovery, and emancipation, and applies the logic of culture, society, and personality. This form of rationality is articulated through action oriented to the achievement of understanding (in the hermeneutic sense), what Habermas calls *communicative* action. Habermas associates this with the set of structures that make up the "lifeworld."

In Habermas' hands, the terms *system* and *lifeworld* are subjected to a rigorous examination and defy simplification. It would be incorrect, for example, to treat them synonymously with more traditional sociological concepts used to define the constitution of society, such as *structure* and *agency*. At the very least, they constitute distinct fields of social action that manifest themselves in particular logics. So, for our purposes, we can at least identify these distinct "logics of action" that emerge from the two sets of structures. Both of these projects are, Habermas argues, rooted within the logic of modernity and the Enlightenment. Indeed, modernity is characterized by the conflict between them. Systemic rationality has achieved dominance over lifeworld rationality, but lifeworld rationality has persevered in the form of resistance groups and new social movements, such as through the struggle for rights. It is "presupposed in everyday communication and makes its presence felt not only in oppositional, protest movements but also in the inherent instability of repressive social institutions."[19]

The dominance of instrumental rationality has been achieved in part through the marriage of convenience between two distinct projects: the project of capitalism has always been to seek out markets wherever it can find them, whereas the project of nationalism has always been the promotion and legitimation of political boundaries, coupled with territorial expansion. When nation-states have sought to expand their territories, they have done so by promoting a rejection of Otherness. The market, of course, has thrived under conditions of competition and conflict. The dominant economic project of instrumental modernity has been *expansion*, whereas the dominant political project has been one of *division*.

Crucially, the state is a political fiction.[20] The political boundaries that now make up the map of the world are artificial boundaries. Like all dominant myths and fictions, though, they are presented to us as if they are natural entities. Social theories have responded to this challenge in various ways. On one extreme, social contract thinking from Hobbes onward presupposes that society and the state are synonymous. Such theories are self-fulfilling, in so far as they end up justifying the legitimacy of something that is presupposed.[21] Marxist historical materialism, through its concern with consecutive modes of production, suffers from a similar bias. In his attempt to rescue Marxist thought from this dilemma, Wallerstein still finds himself trapped within an analysis of interstate relations. International relations scholars — notably the dominant realists — are equally confined to a state-centric model. On the other end of the spectrum, Robertson tries to construct a more complex model in which nation-states, individual actors, the world-system of states, and humankind in general are dynamically interrelated; he calls this the *global field*. Despite starting from a post-Weberian perspective, Albrow insists that the dominance of the nation-state represented a blip in history rather than a natural continuation. Sklair has also been an outspoken advocate of "decentering" the state.

The Habermasian tradition provides an additional perspective on the role of the nation-state. In particular, it responds to the Kantian dilemma: how to reconcile the individual as a citizen with the individual as a human. "Citizens" are recognized legal subjects within these political fictions; the category of citizenship (at least in the nation-state model) is reliant upon exclusion. The achievement of citizenship rights for some is thus intrinsically connected to the systemic project of achieving territorial legitimacy through division, and is therefore antithetical to the Enlightenment project of humanism, which for Kant is interpreted as cosmopolitanism. This is the paradox that defines modernity, and which forms the basis of Habermas' reworking of critical theory: how to investigate the possibility of a universal ethics based on a common humanity within a world driven by the dynamics of market competition and territorial division.

Habermas has described in detail how the modernity of instrumental rationality has achieved its dominant position over its counterpart. He has shown how resistance to this dominant project has been stifled by the efforts of systemic forces to offer agents some kind of stake in the system itself, thus suppressing their identification with alternative modes of existence and their revolutionary potential.

Globality and Pragmatic Modernity

We can see that early expressions of globality — represented by such identity-claims as *world citizenship* — are clearly embedded in this abstract modernity of the life-world. A sense of belonging to the world could be understood as part of a process wherein an individual, perhaps through interaction with peoples from other nations and cultures, is able to achieve a fuller understanding of the world, and from that attain self-actualization and emancipation. To this Hegelian interpretation we can add a Habermasian distinction between free and distorted communication. That is to say, we can add a dimension of power. Where communication, as an exchange of knowledge, is free and undistorted, the potential arises for an individual's sense of belonging to the world to become actualized. Where this communication is distorted, the result of the exchange or interaction is likely to be nationalism, intolerance, and prejudice. The political manipulation of the nation-state as a source of shared cultural identity, the use of the international political system for war and other forms of territorial or ideological conflict, and the history of imperialism can all be read as ways in which the divisive and oppressive tendencies of instrumental modernity have distorted the sphere of communication, and thus the search for truth and self-actualization.

The Kantian worldview — this orientation towards universal humanity — was never dependent upon the historical particularities of wider social structure. However, such an idealist and universalist account is not fully compatible with the conditions of the late twentieth century and beyond — conditions clearly and accurately described by the various transformative accounts of globalization already discussed. As Habermas states, worldviews develop in historical stages, and reflect a "moral consciousness guided by principles."[22] They reflect, but are not determined by, external conditions. Rooted as he is within a modernist preoccupation with universalism (and evolutionism), Habermas is unable to fully appreciate the extent to which such worldviews and conditions may have changed. What are these conditions, and what impact might they have had on the dual projects of modernity? We can usefully summarize the key transformations under two categories: existential and institutional.

Existential transformations operate in respect of how individuals see the world and their place in it. Surely, one of the most important motors of such transformations would be the advent not of the global age but of the nuclear age, an "age of fatality."[23] The realization of the end of the world as a material (as opposed to theological) possibility (a concern that also drives the environmental agenda) surely has a globalizing effect. That one's death might not be an individual event but might form part of the death of the world does nothing if not establish an unmediated relationship between an individual and the globe![24] An awareness of this kind — awareness of the immediacy of human mortality as well as our capacity for destruction — brings an element of temporality into the globalization discourse.

Institutional transformations operate on the level of law and policymaking. The establishment of the United Nations promised to signal a new era of political power (albeit international, not global, wherein lies many of its contradictions and thus its failures). The emergence of international law and, in particular, the signing of the Universal Declaration of Human Rights in 1948, have surely transformed the legitimacy and validity of claims made under the banner of "rights."[25] Both the existential and institutional transformations have eroded the sovereignty of the nation-state, both as a definitive legal–political institution and as a primary source of identity-formation among individuals. The nation-state faces a crisis of legitimation, its assumed role threatened by both external challenges, such as supranational political institutions or the world market, and internal ones, such as the loyalty of its citizens.[26] Indeed, one of the fundamental characteristics of the contemporary world — at least in so far as it impacts upon identity-formation — has been the separation of nation from state.[27]

The ruptures brought about by these transformations have resulted not in a singular era of globalization, but in the possibility of conflicting globalizations. Institutional transformations have, on the one hand, transformed the dynamics of capitalism. No longer can "the system" be described in terms of the marriage of convenience between the market and the nation-state. Instead, capitalism thrives through its attachment to supranational institutions such as the World Bank. However, on the other hand, international human rights conventions allow for hitherto abstract claims of rights to be validated within a formal framework. Similarly, existential transformations erode essentialist assumptions about identity and release the possibility of multiple identities and identifications,[28] while at the same time giving fuel to the new consumerist dynamic of capitalism. In other words, we can identify transformations within the logic of both instrumental and abstract modernity.

The Global System

The contemporary world capitalist system is the natural evolution of the logic of instrumental modernity. Globality has impacted upon this form of rationality by fracturing the relationship between its two principal forces, capitalism and the nation-state. Capitalism no longer relies upon the nation-state to protect its interests. Thus, the world capitalist system has evolved into a global capitalist system protected by supranational institutions. Its logic, though, remains instrumentalist and purposive-rational. Habermas has outlined, in evolutionary perspective, the forms of transformation inherent in capitalist practices from local to global: transformations in the forms of economic cooperation, from households, through factories, to multinationals; transformations in the scope of the market, from household economies, through national economies, to the world economy; and transformations in the social division of labor, from hunter–gatherers, through crafts, agriculture, industrialism, and, we can add, postindustrialism.[29]

However, another impact of globality at the systemic level has emerged from the realization of the consequences of unrestricted capitalist expansion. The boundaries of capitalism have extended so far as to encounter the outer limits of nature: "ecological balance designates an absolute limit to growth."[30] Thus, capitalist expansion is contained by an awareness of global manufactured risk.[31] This realization of limits to the project of systemic logic is also reflected in the wider distrust of scientific knowledge — a distrust brought about, as Beck, Giddens, and others are at pains to remind us, by the realization that scientific and technological progress, hitherto thought of as benign within the optimism of the Enlightenment, has been a destructive force. In other words, scientific knowledge, driven by the instrumentalist rationality of the systemic logic, has caused so many of the risks and dangers of which we are now so acutely aware.

It is important to note, though, that the global system is not simply synonymous with the global capitalist economy. Capitalism is one manifestation of systemic logic, but not the only one. Especially under globalized conditions, even the logic of capitalism is not reducible solely to financial markets. The global economy is also a cultural economy, an economy of symbols; it is also an information economy or an economy of knowledge, and it is an economy of violence. The global system operates in an increasingly fragmented fashion and is not merely an articulation of capitalism in the traditional sense. However complicated this may appear, it is at least relatively consistent and contained when contrasted with the high level of uncertainty evident in the impact of globality upon the political dimensions of the systemic logic. Increasing bureaucratization at the level of international politics, protectionism and authoritarian populism in democratic states, and the emergence of new nationalisms and ethnic fundamentalisms have all emerged as possible outcomes. If the impact of globality upon the systemic logic that drives capitalism has been to open up new directions for expansion, its impact upon the systemic logic that drives the political system has been to reveal its fragile and unpredictable nature.

The Global Lifeworld

The logic of the alternative project of modernity — abstract modernity — has been transformed under the impact of globality in far more direct and challenging ways. Although it would be wholly against the intentions of the theory of the global lifeworld to suggest that any total transformations have occurred, it would appear at least from an analytical point of view that the component structures of the lifeworld — culture, society, and personality — have undergone significant developments. Hitherto abstract concerns with rights, emancipation, self-discovery, and so on have been transformed into political action in a direct, unmediated, pragmatic way. Social movements exist that act as agents of "life politics" and therefore as expressions of this new, pragmatic globality. The erosion of the role of the nation-state as the monolithic framework within which identity-construction takes place releases the possibility for multiple identities exercised in strategic, pragmatic ways.[32] These are expressions of the transformation from abstract modernity to pragmatic modernity. An example of this transformation is the change from early, abstract models of world citizenship (a universalist notion bound up in abstract ideals divorced from practical realities) to pragmatic models of global citizenship.[33] The global lifeworld is developed through the recognition of the unmediated relationship between the individual and the globe as an arena for action.

The transformation of human rights from abstract ideals to pragmatic social conditions is the most clearly identifiable manifestation of the global lifeworld, but there are others. Some commentators may feel that the revolution in information and communications technology opens up another space in which the global lifeworld can manifest itself. One imagines this would involve the emergence of social relationships without borders. Whether or not such a virtual society actually forms part of the emancipatory project of the lifeworld remains to be seen. Certainly, the new information technology has the potential to ally itself to the project of full democratization, but at present this remains a potential rather than a reality.

Conclusion

We can summarize my application of Habermas' theory of modernity to contemporary global change in diagrammatic form. What has been described by various commentators as an era of intensified globalization — presuming the singularity of such a process — can be better described as the conflict between competing projects that

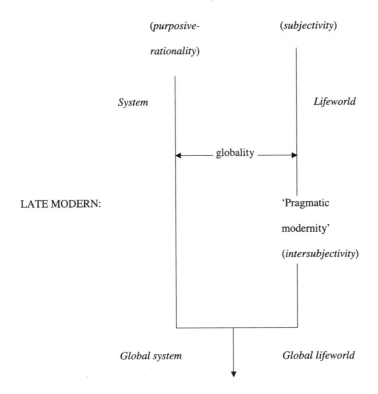

(purposive-   *(subjectivity)*

rationality)

System   Lifeworld

globality

LATE MODERN: 'Pragmatic

modernity'

(intersubjectivity)

Global system   Global lifeworld

END OF MODERNITY?   *full intersubjectivity and communicative rationality*

Figure 8.1. The impact of globality upon the dual projects of modernity.[34] Taken from Darren J. O'Byrne (2003) *The Dimensions of Global Citizenship: Political Identity Beyond the Nation-State*, London: Frank Cass.

equate to Habermas' distinction between system and lifeworld. The global system is characterized by the delinking of the market and the state, by new transnational practices, and by an institutional reflexivity brought about by the awareness of manufactured risk. The global lifeworld involves a shift from an abstract to a pragmatic project of emancipation and self-actualization, itself brought about by a degree of reflexivity related to the interlinking of globality and temporality.

That the systemic and lifeworld projects of modernity are united in a common reflexivity suggests a simultaneous delinking and a tentative recoupling of system and lifeworld. The delinking is apparent at various levels. For example, the separation of nation from state clearly allows for the relative freedom of identities to roam beyond the restrictions of the nation-state; this can surely be understood as a tentative decolonization of lifeworld from system. The combination of existential and institutional reflexivity seems to recouple them in a different way. According to Habermas, the complete reunification of system and lifeworld would signify the end of the modern project. Yet systemic logic still intrudes upon the lifeworld through the reproduction of localist and nationalist worldviews that impede access to the means of globality, while at the same time restricting access to the means of compression (and thus access to the spoils of the market) through more conventional methods of exclusion. Systemic rationality is also reproduced through the culture-ideology of consumerism (the point made by Sklair), and through political apathy, such that in the postpolitical world, "the multinational corporation becomes the model for all conduct."[35] So long as instrumental, systemic rationality remains the dominant project, as it certainly still does albeit in a modified form, modernity remains an unfinished project.

Notes

1. Leslie Sklair (2002) *Globalization: Capitalism and Its Alternatives,* Oxford: Oxford University Press, p. 35.
2. See, among numerous other worthy contributions to the literature: Ulf Hannerz (1996) *Transnational Connections: Culture, People, Places,* London: Routledge, pp. 67–68, p. 167; David Howes (ed.) (1996) *Cross-Cultural Consumption: Global Markets, Local Realities,* London: Routledge, p. 6; John Tomlinson (1999) *Globalization and Culture,* Cambridge: Polity Press, p. 141; Stuart Hall (1992) "The Question of Cultural Identity" in Stuart Hall, David Held and Tony McGrew (eds.) *Modernity and Its Futures,* Cambridge: Polity Press, p. 310.
3. This distinction is advanced by David Held, Anthony McGrew, David Goldblatt, and Jonathan Pearson in *Global Transformations: Politics, Economics and Culture* (Cambridge, Polity Press: 1999), although there are numerous other examples.
4. Stephen Mennell proposes Norbert Elias as an early exponent of what I here call a process account of globalization. The inspiration for this claim comes from his reading of Elias's two volumes of *The Civilizing Process,* volume 1: *The History of Manners* (Oxford: Basil Blackwell, 1978) and especially volume 2: *State Formation and Civilization* (Oxford: Basil Blackwell, 1982). See Mennell (1990) "The Globalization of Human History as a Very Long-term Social Process: Elias's Theory" in *Theory, Culture and Society,* 7, pp. 359–371.
5. Roland Robertson (1992) *Globalization: Social Theory and Global Change,* London: Sage.
6. Robbie Robertson (2003) *The Three Waves of Globalization: A History of a Developing Global Consciousness,* London: Zed Books.
7. Wallerstein's theory is explored in numerous publications, including: Immanuel Wallerstein (1974) *The Modern World-System,* volume 1: *Capitalist Agriculture and the Origins of the European World-Economy in the Sixteenth Century,* New York: Academic Press; *The Modern World System,* Volume 2: *Mercantilism and the Consolidation of the European World Economy 1600–1950,* New York: Academic Press; Wallerstein (1979) *The Capitalist World Economy,* Cambridge: Cambridge University Press; Wallerstein (1980).
8. The clearest example of this is the work of Christopher Chase-Dunn. See Chase-Dunn (1989) *Global Formation: Structures of the World-Economy,* Cambridge, MA: Basil Blackwell; Chase-Dunn (1999) "Globalization: A World-Systems Perspective" in *Journal of World-Systems Research,* 581, May.
9. Anthony Giddens (1990) *The Consequences of Modernity,* Stanford, CA: Stanford University Press.
10. David Harvey (1990) *The Condition of Postmodernity: An Enquiry into the Origins of Cultural Change,* Oxford: Blackwell.
11. Martin Albrow (1996) *The Global Age: State and Society Beyond Modernity,* Cambridge: Polity Press.
12. Leslie Sklair (2002) *Globalization: Capitalism and Its Alternatives* Oxford: Oxford University Press.
13. Jeremy Brecher, John Brown Childs, and Jill Cutler (eds.) (1993) *Global Visions: Beyond the New World Order,* Boston, MA: South End Press.
14. Richard Falk (1993) "The Making of Global Citizenship" in Brecher et al., *Global Visions.*
15. Darren J. O'Byrne (2003) *The Dimensions of Global Citizenship: Political Identity Beyond the Nation-State,* London: Frank Cass. Much of the approach I am about to map out is made in greater detail in this publication.
16. There are numerous introductions and commentaries. One of the best, and clearest, is William Outhwaite (1994) *Habermas: A Critical Introduction,* Cambridge: Polity Press.
17. Jürgen Habermas (1974) *Theory and Practice* London: Heinemann; Habermas (1976) *Legitimation Crisis,* London: Heinemann; Habermas (1987) *Toward a Rational Society: Student Protest, Science and Politics,* Cambridge: Polity Press; Habermas (1987) *Knowledge and Human Interests,* Cambridge: Polity Press; Habermas (1988) *On the Logic of the Social Sciences,* Cambridge: Polity Press; Habermas (1989) *The New Conservatism: Cultural Criticism and the Historians' Debate,* Cambridge: Polity Press; Habermas (1994) *The Past as Future,*

Cambridge: Polity Press; Habermas (1994) "Citizenship and National Identity" in Bart van Steenbergen (ed.) *The Condition of Citizenship*, London: Sage; Habermas (1998) *A Berlin Republic: Writings on Germany*, Cambridge: Polity Press; Habermas (1999) *The Inclusion of the Other: Studies in Political Theory*, Cambridge: Polity Press; Habermas (2001) *The Postnational Constellation: Political Essays*, Cambridge: Polity Press; Habermas (2002) *Religion and Rationality: Essays on Reason, God, and Modernity*, Cambridge: Polity Press.

18. Jürgen Habermas (1984) *The Theory of Communicative Action*, volume 1: *Reason and the Rationalization of Society*, Cambridge: Polity Press; Habermas (1987) *The Theory of Communicative Action*, volume 2: *Lifeworld and System: A Critique of Functionalist Reason*, Cambridge: Polity Press.

19. Larry J. Ray (1993) *Rethinking Critical Theory: Emancipation in an Age of Global Social Movements*, London: Sage, p. vii.

20. On which, see also Andrew Linklater (1990) *Men and Citizens in International Relations*, London: Macmillan; Darren J. O'Byrne (2003) *The Dimensions of Global Citizenship: Political Identity Beyond the Nation-State*, London: Frank Cass.

21. Andrew Linklater (1990) *Men and Citizens in International Relations*, London: Macmillan, p. 77.

22. Jürgen Habermas (1984) *Communication and the Evolution of Society*, Cambridge: Polity Press, p. 103.

23. Darren J. O'Byrne (2003) *The Dimensions of Global Citizenship: Political Identity Beyond the Nation-State*, London: Frank Cass.

24. Anthony Giddens also recognizes the importance of the nuclear age in respect of global transformations, in *Modernity and Self-Identity*, Cambridge: Polity Press, 1991.

25. For more on this, see Darren J. O'Byrne (2002) *Human Rights: An Introduction*, London: Prentice-Hall.

26. Habermas (1976) *Legitimation Crisis*, London: Heinemann.

27. Martin Albrow and Darren J. O'Byrne (2000) "Rethinking State and Citizenship under Globalized Conditions" in Henri Goverde (ed.) *Global and European Polity?: Organizations, Policies, Contexts*, Aldershot, England: Ashgate.

28. On which, see Darren J. O'Byrne (2001) "On the Construction of Political Identity: Negotiations and Strategies Beyond the Nation-State" in Paul Kennedy and Catherine J. Danks (eds.) *Globalization and National Identities: Crisis or Opportunity?*, Basingstoke, England: Palgrave.

29. Jürgen Habermas (1984) *Communication and the Evolution of Society*, Cambridge: Polity Press, p. 49.

30. Habermas (1976) *Legitimation Crisis*, London: Heinemann, p. 41.

31. Ulrich Beck (1992) *Risk Society: Towards a New Modernity*, London: Sage.

32. On which, see John Eade (1994) "Identity, Nation and Religion: Educated Young Bangladeshi Muslims in London's 'East End'" in *International Sociology*, 9, 3, September, pp. 377–394.

33. I discuss this in more detail in Darren J. O'Byrne (2003) *The Dimensions of Global Citizenship: Political Identity Beyond the Nation-State*, London: Frank Cass.

34. Taken from Darren J. O'Byrne (2003) *The Dimensions of Global Citizenship: Political Identity Beyond the Nation-State*, London: Frank Cass.

35. Habermas (1999) *The Inclusion of the Other: Studies in Political Theory*, Cambridge: Polity Press, pp. 125–126.

What Is the Nature of Power and Conflict in the World Today?

9

From Globalization to the New Imperialism

David Harvey

One of the few good things to emerge from the last couple of years of political nightmares is that the seemingly neutral mask of "globalization" has been torn off to reveal the raw imperialism beneath. But imperialisms, like empires, can take many different forms. Our task is to identify more clearly what the capitalist form of imperialism is about in general and what the U.S. form of capitalist imperialism is about in particular, recognizing that there seems to be some momentous shift now occurring as the United States moves from the multilateral neoliberalism that reached its apogee in the mid-1990s to the unilateral militarism and neoconservativism of the current administration.

Territorial vs. Capitalistic Logics of Power

Capitalist imperialism can best be analyzed as a contradictory fusion of a territorial logic derived from the use of state power and a capitalistic logic that derives from market-driven processes of capital accumulation in space and time. The former stresses the political, diplomatic, and military strategies used by a state as it struggles to assert its interests and achieve its goals in the world at large. The latter focuses on the ways in which economic power flows across and through space, toward or away from territories through the daily practices of production, trade, capital flows, money transfers, labor migration, technology transfer, currency speculation, flows of information, cultural impulses, and the like.

These territorial and capitalist logics are not reducible to each other (Arrighi, 1994; Arrighi and Silver, 1999; Harvey, 2003). The motivations and interests of agents differ. Capitalists place money wherever profits can be had and are usually motivated to accumulate more capital. Politicians and statesmen usually seek outcomes that sustain or augment the power of their state vis-à-vis other states. Capitalists seek individual advantage and are responsible to no one except themselves and (to some degree) shareholders, whereas statesmen seek collective advantage and are responsible to citizens or, more often, to an elite group, a class, or some other power structure. Capitalists operate in continuous space and time whereas politicians operate in a territorialized space and, at least in democracies, in the temporality of electoral cycles. Capitalist firms come and go, shift locations, merge, grow phenomenally, or go out of business, whereas states are relatively long-lived entities operating from a fixed territorial base.

The two logics contrast in other ways. State agents arrive at political in the midst of the rough and tumble of a political process where variegated interests clash. Personality conflicts between influential players can sometimes be at the core of decision making. The geographical processes of capital accumulation, on the other hand, are much more molecular and diffuse. Many agents bump into each other in the marketplace, counteracting and at other times reinforcing certain aggregate trends. It is hard to manage these processes except indirectly. The institutional arrangements set up by the state are influential, of course, and there are monetary and fiscal levers (of the sort that Alan Greenspan wields as chairman of the Federal Reserve) as well as a range of fiscal and monetary modes of intervention that position the state as a powerful economic agent. But even in authoritarian or "developmental" states, the molecular processes of capital accumulation often escape control.

Although separate, the two logics intertwine. The literature on imperialism too often assumes, however, an easy accordance between them: that political-economic processes are guided by the strategies of imperial states that always operate out of capitalistic motivations. In practice the logics frequently tug against and sometimes even oppose each other. The relation between them should be seen as problematic, contradictory, and dialectical rather than as functional or one-sided. This sets the stage for a deeper analysis of the nature of capitalist imperialism in general and recent U.S. versions of it in particular.

Imperialistic state practices typically seek to take advantage of the asymmetries that arise out of spatial exchange relations. These asymmetries arise in part because spatial competition is always monopolistic competition and because resources (both naturally occurring and humanly created) are unevenly distributed. The equality condition assumed in perfectly functioning markets is inoperative. The outcome is unfair and unequal exchange, spatially articulated monopoly powers, extortionate practices attached to capital and credit flows and the extraction of monopoly rents. The inequalities that result take on a specific geographical expression with rich regions often growing richer and poor regions often superexploited. One of the state's key tasks is to preserve that pattern of asymmetries in exchange over space in resource endowments that works for its own advantage. If, for example, the United States forces open capital markets around the world through the operations of the International Monetary Fund (IMF) and the World Trade Organization (WTO), it is because specific advantages are thought to accrue to U.S. financial institutions. The state is the political entity, the body politic, that is best able to orchestrate these processes both internally and on the world stage. Failure so to do will likely result in a diminution of the wealth and power of the state. Capitalist imperialism is, then, a property of interstate relations and flows of power within a global system of capital accumulation.

At any given historical–geographical moment, one or other of the logics may dominate the other. The accumulation of control over territory as an end in itself plainly has economic consequences. These may be positive or negative from the standpoint of exaction of tribute, flows of capital, labor power, commodities, and the like. But this looks quite different from a situation in which territorial control (that may or may not entail actual takeover and administration of territory) is intended as a support for the accumulation of capital. But this then poses a crucial question:

how can the territorial logics of power, which tend to be awkwardly fixed in space, respond to the open spatial dynamics of endless capital accumulation? And what does endless capital accumulation imply for the territorial logics of power?

Some light is shed on this problem by way of an acute observation made by Hannah Arendt. "A never-ending accumulation of property," she wrote, "must be based on a never-ending accumulation of power." From this derived "the 'progressive' ideology of the late nineteenth century" that "foreshadowed the rise of imperialism" (Arendt, 1968). If, however, the accumulation of power must necessarily accompany the accumulation of capital, then bourgeois history must be a history of accumulation of ever-greater political power. And this scale-shift is exactly what Arrighi records in his comparative history of the shift from the Italian city states, through the Dutch, the British, and now the U.S. phases of global hegemony (Arrighi, 2003). But if Arendt is right, then any imperial state must endlessly seek to extend and intensify its power. There is, in this, an ever-present danger of overextension. Overreach has again and again proven the Achilles' heel of hegemonic states and empires (Rome, Venice, Holland, Britain) (Kennedy, 1990). Since 1980, the United States has extended its powers and commitments remarkably, both militarily and politically, to the point where the dangers of overreach are palpable. This then raises the further question: If the United States is no longer sufficiently large and resourceful to manage the considerably expanded world economy of the twenty-first century, then what kind of accumulation of political power under what kind of political arrangement will be capable of taking its place, given that the world is heavily committed still to capital accumulation without limit? Some argue that world government is not only desirable but inevitable. Others argue that some collection of states working in collaboration with each other (in much the way that Kautsky suggested in his theory of ultraimperialism and as hinted at in organizations like the G7 — now G8 — meetings) might be able to regulate matters. To this we could add the less optimistic idea that if it proves impossible for some reason to construct this ever vaster accumulation of political power, then endless capital accumulation will likely dissolve into chaos, ending the era of capital not with a revolutionary bang but in tortured anarchy.

The Inner and the Outer Dialectic

In *The Philosophy of Right*, Hegel notes how the inner contradictions of a territorially bounded bourgeois society, registered as an overaccumulation of wealth at one pole and the creation of a rabble of paupers at the other, drive it to seek solutions through external trade and colonial/imperial practices (Hegel, 1967). Lenin quotes Cecil Rhodes as saying that colonialism and imperialism abroad was the only possible way to avoid civil war at home (Lenin, 1965). Class relations and the state of class struggle within a territory clearly affect the drive for imperial solutions. We should, therefore, pay careful attention to the internal circumstances that drive those that command the territorial logic to engage in imperial practices. There are three overlapping impulses behind this drive.

There is, within capitalism, a perpetual tendency to produce crises of overaccumulation, defined as surpluses of capital and labor, side by side, lacking profitable outlets even in the face of many socially urgent tasks to be addressed (Harvey, 1999, 2001, 2003). The Great Depression of the 1930s was a classic case of this. The problem is, then, to find profitable outlets for surplus capital that accumulates within a given territory. The obvious answer is to export capital (in money, commodity, or production capacity forms) to more profitable locations (or, what amounts to the same thing, procure lower-cost inputs through imports of low-wage labor or low-cost raw materials). This requires that markets for both capital and commodities be open across the world so that surplus capital in one territory can easily circulate into other territories where the profits to be had are greater. If markets and resources are not open, then they have sometimes to be forced open by use of economic, political, or military power (as in Iraq). If profits are still to accrue to the home territory, then asymmetrical power relations through the market or other means of domination must be constructed in relation to other territories. Those in charge of the territorial logic must help to find outlets for surplus capital while striving to retain the benefits to be had from foreign trade, export of capital, or import of cheaper inputs. Imperialist practices of this sort can arise wherever capital surpluses begin to pile up. In the 1980s, for example, South Korea and Taiwan began to experience overaccumulation problems and so started to export their business practices (including vicious labor practices) around the world as subcontractors for multinational corporations. Hierarchical structures of imperialism can in this way be orchestrated; for example, Taiwanese subcontractors do the "dirty work" for U.S.-based multinationals. Seeking outlets for surplus capital is the first aspect of imperial practices that arises out of internal conditions within a country.

A second motivation arises because governments in trouble domestically often seek to solve their problems either by foreign adventures or by manufacturing foreign threats to consolidate solidarities at home. The internal condition of the United States during 2002 was, for example, parlous in the extreme. The recession that began early in 2001 (prodded onward by the shock of 9/11) would not go away. Unemployment was rising and the sense of economic insecurity was palpable. Corporate scandals and accounting failures (as well as cases of outright corruption) cascaded over each other, and seemingly solid corporate empires were literally dissolving overnight. Wall Street fell into disrepute and stocks and other asset values were plunging. Pension funds were depleted (if they did not totally disappear as in the case of Enron employees) and the retirement prospects of the middle class took a serious hit. Healthcare was in a mess, federal, state and local government surpluses were evaporating fast and deficits began to loom larger and larger. The current account balance with the rest of the world was going from bad to worse as the United States became the biggest debtor nation of all time. To top it all, the president had been elected by a five to four vote of the Supreme Court rather than by the people. His legitimacy was questioned by at least half the population on the eve of 9/11. The only thing that saved the Republicans from political annihilation was the intense solidarity — verging on a nationalist revival — created around the events of 9/11. The Republicans used the threat of terrorism to launch into a series of foreign ventures beginning with Afghanistan and then switching to Iraq. The diversionary tactic worked. The American public by and large accepted the idea that there was some sort of connection between Al

Qaeda and Saddam. The Republicans were able to consolidate political power through the congressional elections and the President could shed the air of illegitimacy that had hung over his election.

But there is something far deeper than political opportunism at work here. Democracy in the United States has always been chronically unstable. The country sometimes seems impossible to govern except through the corruption of money power. Hannah Arendt observes:

> A community based solely on power must decay in the calm of order and stability; its complete security reveals that it is built on sand. Only by acquiring more power can it guarantee the status quo; only by constantly extending its authority and only through [the] process of power accumulation can it remain stable. Hobbes' Commonwealth is a vacillating structure and must always provide itself with new props from outside; otherwise it would collapse overnight into the aimless, senseless chaos of the private interests from which it sprang .... [The] ever-present possibility of war guarantees the Commonwealth a prospect of permanence because it makes it possible for the state to increase its power at the expense of other states (Arendt, 1968).

During the 1990s there was no clear enemy for the United States. The Cold War was over, and the booming economy should have guaranteed an unparalleled level of contentment and satisfaction throughout all but the most underprivileged and marginalized elements in civil society. Yet, as Arendt might have predicted, the 1990s turned out to be one of the most unpleasant decades in U.S. history. Competition was vicious, scams and fraudulent schemes proliferated, scandals (both real and imagined) were everywhere embraced with gusto, vicious rumors circulated about assassinations plotted in the White House, an attempt was made to impeach the president, Howard Stern and Rush Limbaugh typified a media totally out of control, Los Angeles erupted in riots, Waco and Oklahoma symbolized a penchant for internal violence that had long remained latent, and teenagers shot and killed their classmates in Colombine. Civil society was, in short, far from civil. Society seemed, as Arendt would put it, to be collapsing back into the aimless, senseless chaos of private interests. The engagement with Iraq was a grand opportunity to bring the Commonwealth to heel. Criticism was silenced as unpatriotic. The evil enemy without became the prime force through which to exorcise or tame the devils lurking within. If, as Arendt avers, empire abroad always entails tyranny at home then those, like the neoconservatives, interested in establishing order and dominance at home have every incentive to pursue empire abroad as key to their strategy of internal domination. This is central to the neoconservative form of imperialism now emerging in the U.S.

The third major impulsion behind imperialist practices rests on the dynamics of class relations on the home front. The evidence from the end of the nineteenth century is of interest here. Consider, for example, a figure like Joseph Chamberlain ("Radical Joe," as he was known). Closely allied with the liberal manufacturing interests of Birmingham, Chamberlain was initially resolutely opposed to imperialism (in the Afghan Wars of the 1850s, for example) and devoted much of his time to educational reform and other projects aligned to improving the social and physical infrastructures for production and consumption in his home city of Birmingham, England. This provided, he thought, a productive outlet for surpluses that would be repaid in the long run. An important figure within the liberal conservative movement, he saw the rising tide of class struggle in Britain at first hand and in 1885 made a celebrated speech in which he called for the propertied classes to take cognizance of their responsibilities and obligations to society (i.e., to better the conditions of life of the least well-off and invest in social and physical infrastructures in the national interest) rather than solely to promote their individual rights as property owners. The uproar that followed on the part of the propertied classes forced him to recant and, from that moment on, he became the most ardent advocate for imperialism (ultimately, as colonial secretary, leading Britain into the disaster of the Boer War in South Africa) (Julien et al., 1949).

The turn to a liberal form of imperialism in the late nineteenth century arose not from absolute economic imperatives but from the political unwillingness of the bourgeoisie to give up any of its privileges and thereby absorb overaccumulation through social reform at home. Hobson, for one, identified this as the key problem and sought a social democratic policy that would counter it. Both Roosevelts at a certain point recognized that crises of overaccumulation might be offset by domestic reforms (culminating in the weak attempt to construct a "New Deal" as an answer to the 1930s depression). But for this to go far requires that the rich look to their obligations rather than their rights. The internal state of class relations and of class struggle affect the drive towards imperial solutions. It was internal politics of this sort that forced many European powers to look outwards to solve their problems from 1884 to 1945. Currently in the United States the extraordinary growth in inequality and the pressure of the affluent (backed by a media dominated by right-wing business interests) to gain more in the way of rights rather than to concede anything with respect to their obligations makes resort to imperialism almost inevitable as a way to both mask and avert the consequences of the class war they are waging at home.

These three internal impulsions, the first clearly driven by a capitalist logic but the other two far more contingent upon internal politics exist, we may conclude, in a specific relation to the shaping of imperialist practices by state powers.

Accumulation by Dispossession

Rosa Luxemburg argues that capital accumulation has a dual character:

> One concerns the commodity market and the place where surplus value is produced — the factory, the mine, the agricultural estate. Regarded in this light accumulation is a purely economic process, with its most important phase a transaction between the capitalist and the wage laborer. ... Here, in form at any rate, peace, property, and equality prevail, and the keen dialectics of scientific analysis were required to reveal how the right of ownership changes in the course of accumulation into appropriation of other people's property, how commodity exchange turns into exploitation, and equality becomes class rule. The other aspect of the accumulation of capital concerns the relations between capitalism and the noncapitalist modes of production which start making their appearance on the international stage. Its predominant methods are colonial policy, an international loan system — a policy of spheres of interest — and war. Force, fraud, oppression, and looting are openly displayed without any attempt at concealment, and it requires an effort to discover within this tangle of political violence and contests of power the stern laws of the economic process (Luxemburg, 1968).

These two aspects of accumulation, which I shall term accumulation through expanded reproduction and accumulation by dispossession, are, she argued, "organically linked" and "the historical career of capitalism can only be appreciated by taking them together."

This statement does not fit very well with Marx's general theory of capital accumulation. Marx generally assumes freely functioning competitive markets with institutional arrangements of private property, juridical individualism, freedom of contract and appropriate structures of law and governance guaranteed by a "facilitative" state that secures the integrity of money as a store of value and as a medium of circulation. The roles of the capitalist and laborer are already well-established and "primitive" or "original" accumulation has already occurred. Expanded reproduction (the exploitation of living labor in production) is at the center of the analysis. Such assumptions allow us to see what will happen if the liberal project of the classical political economists or, in our times, the neoliberal project of the economists, is realized. The brilliance of Marx's dialectical method is to show that market liberalization — the credo of the liberals and the neoliberals — will not produce a harmonious state in which everyone is better off. It will, instead, produce greater levels of social inequality (as indeed has been the global trend over the last 30 years). It will also produce chronic crises of overaccumulation, thereby feeding the impulsion to absorb surplus capital by imperialistic expansion or suffer the consequences of crisis and deflation.

The disadvantage of Marx's assumptions is that they relegate accumulation based upon predation, fraud, and violence to an original stage that is considered no longer relevant or, as with Luxemburg, as somehow being outside of the capitalist system. A general reevaluation of the continuous role and persistence of the predatory practices of primitive or original, accumulation is therefore required. Because it seems peculiar to call such an ongoing process primitive or original, I substitute these terms with the concept of *accumulation by dispossession* (Perelman, 2000; Harvey, 2003).

Marx's description of primitive accumulation reveals a wide range of processes that are still with us. These include the commodification and privatization of land; the forceful expulsion of peasant populations; conversion of various forms of property rights (common, collective, etc.) into private property; the suppression of alternative forms of production and consumption; colonial, neocolonial, and imperial processes of appropriation of assets; monetization of exchange and personal taxation; slave trade; and usury, debt, and ultimately the credit system. The state with its monopoly of violence and aura of legality plays a crucial role in both backing and promoting these processes. None of these processes have disappeared and, with respect to privatization and the operation of the credit system, they have arguably moved center stage in the dynamics of capital accuation in recent times. At the same time, wholly new mechanisms of accumulation by dispossession have opened up under the umbrella of neoliberalism. Intellectual property rights and patents preserve monopoly powers and extend corporate rights over genetic materials. Biopiracy is rampant, and the global environmental commons have been degraded in large part through a strategy of privatization. And all manner of fraudulent and predatory practices have sprung up around the stock market, corporate manipulation of accounts, the dispossession of pension rights, and the like.

Neoliberalism — with its dual mantras of privatization and commodification of everything — launched a new wave of enclosure of the commons during the 1980s and 1990s. It used the powers of the credit system backed by state powers to engage in wide-ranging practices of accumulation by dispossession. The financial crises that wracked Mexico (twice), Latin America, Russia, and most of all East and Southeast Asia from 1997 to 1998 facilitated the predation of productive assets by financial powers based in the United States and to a lesser extent Europe and Japan. This was imperialism as accumulation by dispossession. It offered an open field for surplus capitals to play in as assets were released from the public domain into the private realm and as assets already in the private domain were devalued so that they could be bought up at fire-sale prices. The wide swath of resistance to these practices — everything from the Zapatista rebellion to landless peasant movements and protest movements against dam construction, deforestation, and environmental degradation — were largely repressed by state power. The neoliberal state, which largely superseded the social democratic state, withdrew from its social welfare commitments, thus dispossessing populations of their rights even in some of the core capitalist countries. Low-level warfare was waged across the planet as social movements were repressed. A global justice movement arose in response, seeking to reclaim the commons, resist their further degradation, and organize against accumulation by dispossession.

The failure of neoliberalism to deliver on its promises has now produced a crisis within globalization, and it is in that context that we have to interpret the shift towards neoconservative imperialism within the United States (as well as elsewhere, e.g., France, where a president considered illegitimate by many is using his popular stance with respect to the Iraq war to ram through right-wing reforms and build a global coalition favorable to French interests). The United States is currently vulnerable to a capitalistic logic that focuses on international competition. It has lost dominance in most areas of production (with the exception of military, agribusiness, and some fields of advanced technology) and now seems threatened in the realm of finance (its current account deficit with the rest of the world requires over $2 billion a day of capital inflows to be sustained). How can the United States assert its territorial logic to sustain its position in the face of an increasingly unfavorable economic climate? One answer is to use its military superiority to dominate the global economy through control over oil supply. Undoubtedly, it seeks to control OPEC (almost certainly fostering internal discontent in Venezuela and Iran while proclaiming the need to establish democracy in Iraq). That this is yet another form of accumulation by dispossession, but that it has taken a war to accomplish it should be obvious. Oil at $20 a barrel would undoubtedly help revive global capital accumulation while geopolitical control over Middle Eastern oil reserves and oil flow will place the United States in a position to hold competitors (Europe, Japan, Korea, Southeast Asia, and even more important, China) hostage to U.S. control over global oil supplies. Is this what the new U.S. imperialism is about?

From Consent to Coercion

The wave of neoliberal globalization that swept out of the United States during the 1980s and 1990s sought to sustain U.S. hegemony and global capital accumulation through a mixture of multilateral consent backed by coercion. Its center lay in an alliance between the financial powers concentrated primarily on Wall Street (but also in Europe and Japan), the policies of a very activist U.S. Treasury (in alliance with central banker committees in Europe and Japan) and the facilities provided by the IMF, the World Bank, and other multinational institutions (such as the nascent WTO) that were dominated by U.S. interests. Culminating in the Washington Consensus of 1995, neoliberalism set in motion wave after wave of accumulation by dispossession across the globe and forced many states away from any social democratic commitments they may have had towards a politics of dispossession. By forcing capital markets open around the world it sought to open the way to financial predation organized largely for the benefit of the main capitalist powers. Financial tribute flowed into the coffers of the main financial centers in vast waves, spawning a speculative boom within the United States in particular (Gowan, 1999; Brenner, 2002). Neoliberalism masked this imperialistic flow of tribute under the neutral banner of financial globalization. But by the late 1990s this project was in crisis. The devastation wrought in East and Southeast Asia from 1997 to 1998 spread to Russia and Latin America, and a major global crisis was narrowly averted. Stresses began to emerge even within the United States.

Vast swaths of resistance welled up around the world in the form of an articulate though fragmented and sometimes inchoate antiglobalization movement. The conversion of that movement into a global justice movement began to shape a politics that focused increasingly upon resistance to accumulation by dispossession as its nexus of action. This politics is very different from the traditional forms of class struggle mobilized around expanded reproduction. But if Luxemburg is correct, and there is always an organic link between accumulation by expanded reproduction and accumulation by dispossession, then there is also an organic link between the two forms of class struggle. That link needs to be affirmed, strengthened, and built upon as the global justice movement gathers strength (Harvey, 2003).

The answer from within the United States has been to convert the low-level global warfare largely orchestrated by neoliberal state apparatuses around the world into a frontal military assault to gain command over a primary global resource. Command over that resource would assure not only the geopolitical power of the United States vs. its competitors but also, if successful, lower the price of a major input into the processes of capital accumulation. At the same time, an imperial venture of this sort helps to secure the internal position of the wealthiest strata within the United States, to evade class struggle at home by appeal to nationalism, and to realize the neoconservative dream of establishing order within the United States by an expanding accumulation of political power in the hands of a well-organized upper class. The neoconservative state is, however, even more fiercely committed to a politics of accumulation by dispossession, both internally and abroad, as was its neoliberal predecessor. But it is prepared to do so through coercion rather than consent, through unilateralism rather than multilateralism, and through militarism rather than through economic and political diplomacy.

Imperialist projects of this sort rarely last. But they can in the short run prove catastrophic if not suicidal for both the countries and the peoples caught up in the turmoil they generate. In this instance it is not even clear that the exercise of this particular territorial logic of power is in any way consistent with the logic of capital accumulation. The latter points increasingly away from the United States toward some broader configuration of powers, with Europe and above all a renascent China leading the way. The East and Southeast Asian regional power bloc will equal if not surpass U.S. economic power in the not too distant future. It is difficult to see how U.S. militarism can provide an effective answer to this, even if it succeeds in controlling a key global resource like oil. And a danger arises, because fiercer interregional competition between Europe, Asia, and North America could plunge the world into geopolitical confrontations that the United States is unlikely to win even by resort to its superior military power.

In the face of this it is imperative that the global justice movement conjoin with an antiwar movement, bridge the gap in both understanding and in politics between movements around expanded reproduction and movements against accumulation by dispossession, and set out entirely different rules of international engagement such that the logic of capital is contained if not displaced and the territorial logics of power are orchestrated to achieve an equality of well-being and of life-chances that has long been realizable but long been frustrated by class-bound politics. Until the inalienable rights of private property and the profit rate are called into question and controlled, there will be no option except to continue the catastrophic consequences of capitalist imperialism, in no matter what form it occurs.

10

The Crisis of the Globalist Project and the New Economics of George W. Bush

Walden Bello

The Crisis of the Globalist Project

In 1995, the World Trade Organization (WTO) was born. The offspring of 8 years of negotiations, the WTO was hailed in the establishment press as the gem of global economic governance in the era of globalization. The nearly twenty trade agreements that underpinned the WTO were presented as comprising a set of multilateral rules that would eliminate power and coercion from trade relations by subjecting both the powerful and the weak to a common set of rules backed by an effective enforcement apparatus. The WTO was a landmark, declared George Soros, because it was the only supranational body to which the world's most powerful economy, the United States, would submit itself.[1] In the WTO, it was claimed, the powerful United States and lowly Rwanda had exactly the same number of votes: one.

Triumphalism was the note sounded during the First Ministerial of the WTO in Singapore in November 1996, with the WTO, International Monetary Fund (IMF), and the World Bank issuing their famous declaration saying that the task of the future was to make their policies of global trade, finance, and development "coherent" so as to lay the basis for global prosperity.

By the beginning of 2003, the triumphalism was gone and the WTO appeared to be in gridlock. A new agreement on agriculture was nowhere in sight as the United States and the European Union (EU) stoutly defended their multibillion dollar subsidies. Brussels was on the verge of imposing sanctions on Washington for maintaining tax breaks for exporters that have been found to be in violation of WTO rules, whereas Washington threatened to file a case with the WTO against the EU's de facto moratorium against genetically modified foods. Developing countries, some which were once hopeful that the WTO would in fact bring more equity to global trade, unanimously agree that what they have reaped from WTO membership are mostly costs, not benefits. They are dead set against opening their markets any further, and will not do so except under coercion and intimidation. The context for understanding this apparent stalemate at the WTO is the crisis of the globalist project — the main achievement of which was the establishment of the WTO — and the emergence of unilateralism as the main feature of U.S. foreign policy.

But first, some notes on globalization and the globalist project. Globalization is the accelerated integration of capital, production, and markets globally, a process driven by the logic of corporate profitability. Globalization has actually had two phases, the first lasting from the early nineteenth century until the outbreak of the First World War in 1914, and the second from the early 1980s until today. The intervening period was marked by the dominance of national capitalist economies characterized by a significant degree of state intervention and an international economy with strong constraints on trade and capital flows. These domestic and international constraints on the market, which were produced by the dynamics of class conflict internally and intercapitalist competition internationally, were portrayed by the neoliberals as having caused distortions that collectively accounted for the stagnation of the capitalist economies and the global economy in the late 1970s and early 1980s.

As with the first phase of globalization, the second phase was marked by the rise to dominance of the ideology of neoliberalism, which focused on "liberating the market" via accelerated privatization, deregulation, and trade liberalization. There were, broadly, two versions of neoliberal ideology — a "hard" Thatcher–Reagan version and a "soft" Blair–Soros version (globalization with "safety nets"). But underlying both approaches were unleashing market forces and removing or eroding constraints imposed on transnational firms by labor, the state, and society.

Three Moments of the Crisis of Globalization

There have been three moments in the deepening crisis of the globalist project.

The first was the Asian financial crisis of 1997. This event, which laid low the proud "tigers" of East Asia, revealed that one of the key tenets of the globalization — the liberalization of the capital account to promote freer flows of capital, especially finance or speculative capital — could be profoundly destabilizing. The Asian financial crisis was, in fact, shown to be merely the latest of at least eight major financial crises since the liberalization of global financial flows began in the late 1970s.[2] How profoundly destabilizing capital market liberalization could be was shown when, in just a few weeks' time, one million people in Thailand and twenty-one million in Indonesia were pushed below the poverty line.[3]

The Asian financial crisis was the "Stalingrad" of the IMF, the prime global agent of liberalized capital flows. Its record in the ambitious enterprise of subjecting some one hundred developing and transitional economies to "structural adjustment" was revisited, and observations that had been made by such agencies as the United Nations Development Program (UNDP) and United Nations Conference on Trade and Development (UNCTAD) as early as the late 1980s were now validated. Structural adjustment programs designed to accelerate deregulation, trade liberalization, and privatization had almost everywhere institutionalized stagnation, worsened poverty, and increased inequality.

A paradigm is really in crisis when its best practitioners desert it, as Thomas Kuhn pointed out in his classic *The Structure of Scientific Revolutions*, and something akin to what happened during the crisis of the Copernican paradigm in physics occurred in neoclassical economics shortly after the Asian financial crisis, with key intellectuals leaving the fold — among them Jeffrey Sachs, noted earlier for his advocacy of "free market" shock treatment in Eastern Europe in the early 1990s; Joseph Stiglitz, former chief economist of the World Bank; Columbia Professor Jagdish Bhagwati, who called for global controls on capital flows; and financier George Soros, who condemned the lack of controls in the global financial system that had enriched him.

The second moment of the crisis of the globalist project was the collapse of the Third Ministerial of the WTO in Seattle in December 1999. Seattle was the fatal intersection of three streams of discontent and conflict that had been building for sometime:

- Developing countries resented the inequities of the Uruguay Round agreements that they felt compelled to sign in 1995.
- Massive popular opposition to the WTO emerged from myriad sectors of global civil society, including farmers, fisherfolk, labor unionists, and environmentalists. By posing a threat to the well-being of each sector in many of its agreements, the WTO managed to unite global civil society against it.
- There were unresolved trade conflicts between the EU and the United States, especially in agriculture, which had been simply been papered over by the Uruguay Round agreement.

These three volatile elements combined to create the explosion in Seattle, with the developing countries rebelling against the Northern diktat at the Seattle Convention Center, fifty thousand people massing militantly in the streets, and differences preventing the EU and the United States from acting in concert to salvage the ministerial. In a moment of lucidity right after the Seattle debacle, British Secretary of State Stephen Byers captured the essence of the crisis: "[T]he WTO will not be able to continue in its present form. There has to be fundamental and radical change in order for it to meet the needs and aspirations of all 134 of its members."[4]

The third moment of the crisis was the collapse of the stock market and the end of the Clinton boom. This was not just the bursting of the bubble but a rude reassertion of the classical capitalist crisis of overproduction, the main manifestation of which was massive overcapacity. Prior to the crash, corporate profits in the United States had not grown since 1997. This was related to overcapacity in the industrial sector, the most glaring example being the troubled telecommunications sector, where only 2.5 percent of the installed capacity globally was being utilized. The stagnation of the real economy led to capital being shifted to the financial sector, resulting in the dizzying rise in share values. But because profitability in the financial sector cannot deviate too far from the profitability of the real economy, a collapse of stock values was inevitable, and this occurred in March 2001, leading to prolonged stagnation and the onset of deflation.

There is probably a broader structural reason for the length of the current stagnation or deflation and its constant teetering at the edge of recession. This reason may be, as a number of economists have stated, that we are at the tail end of the famous "Kondratieff Cycle." Advanced by the Russian economist Nikolai Kondratieff, this theory suggests that the progress of global capitalism is marked not only by short-term business cycles but also by long-term "supercycles." Kondratieff cycles are roughly 50- to 60-year-long waves. The upward curve of the Kondratieff cycle is marked by the intensive exploitation of new technologies, followed by a crest as technological exploitation matures, then a downward curve as the old technologies produce diminishing returns while new technologies are still in an experimental stage in terms of profitable exploitation, and finally a trough or prolonged deflationary period.

The trough of the last wave was in the 1930s and 1940s, a period marked by the Great Depression and the Second World War. The ascent of the current wave began in the 1950s and the crest was reached in the 1980s and 1990s. The profitable exploitation of the postwar advances in the key energy, automobile, petrochemical, and manufacturing industries ended whereas that of information technology was still at a relatively early stage. From this perspective, the "New Economy" of the late 1990s was not a transcendence of the business cycle, as many economists believed it to be, but the last glorious phase of the current supercycle before the descent into prolonged deflation. In other words, the uniqueness of the current conjuncture lies in the fact that the downward curve of the current short-term cycle coincides with the move into descent of the Kondratieff supercycle. To use the words of another famous economist, Joseph Schumpeter, the global economy appears to be headed for a prolonged period of "creative destruction."

The New Economics of George W. Bush

The intersecting crises of globalization, neoliberalism, overproduction, and capitalist legitimacy provide the context for understanding the economic policies of the Bush administration, notably its unilateralist thrust. The globalist corporate project expressed the common interest of the global capitalist elites in expanding the world economy and their fundamental dependence on one another. However, globalization did not eliminate competition among the national elites. In fact, the ruling elites of the United States and Europe had factions that were more nationalist in character as well as more tied for their survival and prosperity to the state, such as the military-industrial complex (MIC) in the United States. Indeed, since the 1980s there has been a sharp struggle between the more globalist fraction of ruling elites that stressed the common interest of the global capitalist class in a growing world economy and the more nationalist, hegemonist faction that wanted to ensure the supremacy of U.S. corporate interests.

As Robert Brenner has pointed out, the policies of Bill Clinton and his Treasury Secretary Robert Rubin put prime emphasis on the expansion of the world economy as the basis of the prosperity of the global capitalist class. For instance, in the mid-1990s, they pushed a strong-dollar policy meant to stimulate the recovery of the Japanese and German economies, so they could serve as markets for U.S. goods and services. The earlier, more nationalist Reagan administration, on the other hand, had employed a weak-dollar policy to regain competitiveness for the U.S. economy at the expense of the Japanese and German economies.[5] With the Bush administration, we are back to economic policies (including a weak-dollar policy) that are meant to revive the U.S. economy at the expense of the other center economies and push primarily the interests of the U.S. corporate elite instead of that of the global capitalist class operating under conditions of a global downturn.

Several features of this approach are worth stressing:

- Bush's economic team is very wary of a process of globalization that is not managed by a U.S. state which ensures that the process does not diffuse the economic power of the United States. Allowing the market solely to drive globalization could result in key U.S. corporations becoming the victims of globalization and thus compromising U.S. economic interests. Thus, despite the free-market rhetoric, we have a group that is very protectionist when it comes to trade, investment, and the management of government contracts. It seems that the motto of the Bushites is protectionism for the United States and free trade for the rest of us.

- The Bush approach includes strong skepticism about multilateralism as a means of global economic governance because although multilateralism may promote the interests of the global capitalist class in general, it may, in many specific instances, work against U.S. corporate interests. The Bush coterie's growing ambivalence towards the WTO stems from the fact that the United States has lost a number of rulings there, rulings that may hurt U.S. capital but serve the interests of global capitalism as a whole.

- For the Bush people, strategic power is the ultimate modality of power. Economic power is a means to achieve strategic power. This is related to the fact that under Bush, the dominant faction of the ruling elite is the military-industrial establishment that won the Cold War. The conflict between globalists and unilateralists or nationalists along this axis is shown in the approach toward China. The globalist approach put the emphasis on engagement with China, seeing its importance primarily as an investment area and market for U.S. capital. The nationalists, on the other hand, see China mainly as a strategic enemy, and they would rather contain it rather than assist its growth.

- Needless to say, the Bush paradigm has no room for environmental management, seeing this as a problem that others have to worry about, not the United States. There is, in fact, a strong corporate lobby that believes environmental concerns such as those surrounding genetically modified organisms (GMOs) are European conspiracies to deprive the United States of its high-tech edge in global competition.

If these are seen as the premises for action, then the following prominent elements of recent U.S. economic policy make sense:

- Achieving control over Middle East oil — Although this did not exhaust the war aims of the Bush administration in invading Iraq, it was certainly high on the list. With competition from Europe becoming the prime aspect of the trans-Atlantic relationship, this move was clearly aimed partly at Europe. But perhaps the more strategic goal was to preempt the region's resources in order to control access to them by energy-poor China, which is seen as the U.S.' strategic enemy.[6]

- Aggressive protectionism in trade and investment matters — The United States has indulged in one protectionist action after another, one of the most brazen being to hold up any movement at the WTO negotiations. There it defied the Doha Declaration's upholding of public health issues over intellectual property claims by limiting the loosening of patent rights to just three diseases in response to its powerful pharmaceutical lobby. Whereas it seems perfectly willing to see the WTO negotiations unravel, Washington has put most of its efforts in signing up countries into bilateral or multilateral trade deals (such as the Free Trade of the Americas [FTAA]) before the EU gets them into similar deals. Indeed, the term "free-trade agreements" is a misnomer because these are actually preferential trade deals.

- Incorporating strategic considerations into trade agreements — In a recent speech, U.S. Trade Representative Robert Zoellick stated explicitly that "countries that seek free-trade agreements with the United States must pass muster on more than trade and economic criteria in order to be eligible. At a minimum, these countries must cooperate with the United States on its foreign policy and national security goals, as part of 13 criteria that will guide the U.S. selection of potential FTA partners." New Zealand, perhaps one of the governments most doctrinally oriented to free trade, has nevertheless not been offered a free-trade deal because it has a policy that prevents nuclear ship visits, which the United States feels is directed at it.[7]

- Manipulation of the dollar's value to burden rivals among the center economies with the costs of economic crisis and to regain competitiveness for the U.S. economy — A slow depreciation of the dollar vis-à-vis the euro can be interpreted as a market-based adjustment, but the 25 percent fall in value cannot but be seen as, at the least, a policy of benign neglect. Although the Bush administration has issued denials that this is a beggar-thy-neighbor policy, the U.S. business press has seen it for what it is: an effort to revive the U.S. economy at the expense of the EU and other center economies.

- Aggressive manipulation of multilateral agencies to push the interests of U.S. capital — Although this might not be too easy to achieve in the WTO owing to the weight of the EU, it can be more readily done in the World Bank and the IMF, where U.S. dominance is more effectively institutionalized. For instance, despite support for the proposal from many European governments, the U.S. Treasury recently torpedoed the IMF management's proposal for a Sovereign Debt Restructuring Mechanism (SDRM) to enable developing countries to restructure their debt while giving them a measure of protection from creditors. Already a very weak mechanism, the SDRM was vetoed by the U.S. Treasury in the interest of U.S. banks.[8]

- Finally, and especially relevant to our coming discussions, making the other center economies as well as developing countries bear the burden of adjusting to the environmental crisis — Although some of the Bush people do not believe there is an environmental crisis, there are those who know that the current rate of global greenhouse emissions is unsustainable. However, they want other countries to bear the brunt of adjustment because that would mean not only exempting the environmentally inefficient U.S. industry from the costs of adjustment, but also hobbling other economies with even greater costs than if the United States participated in an equitable adjustment process, thus giving the U.S. economy a strong edge in global competition. Raw economic realpolitik, not fundamentalist blindness, lies at the root of Washington's decision not to sign the Kyoto Protocol on Climate Change.

The Economics and Politics of Overextension

Being harnessed very closely to strategic ends, any discussion of the likely outcomes of the Bush administration's economic policies must take into account both the state of the U.S. economy and the global economy and the broader strategic picture. A key basis for successful imperial management is expanding national and global economies — something precluded by the extended period of deflation and stagnation ahead, which is more likely to spur intercapitalist rivalries. Moreover, resources include not only economic and political resources but political and ideological ones as well. For without legitimacy — without what Gramsci called "the consensus" of the dominated that a system of rule is just — imperial management cannot be stable.

Faced with a similar problem of securing the long-term stability of its rule, the ancient Romans came up with the solution that created what was the most far-reaching case of collective mass loyalty ever achieved until then and which prolonged the empire for 700 years. The Roman solution was not just or even principally military in character. The Romans realized that an important component of successful imperial domination was consensus among the dominated of the "rightness" of the Roman order. As sociologist Michael Mann notes in his classic *Sources of Social Power*, the "decisive edge" was not so much military as political. "The Romans," he writes, "gradually stumbled on the invention of extensive territorial citizenship."[9] The extension of Roman citizenship to ruling groups and nonslave peoples throughout the empire was the political breakthrough that produced what "was probably the widest extent of collective commitment yet mobilized." Political citizenship combined with the vision of the empire providing peace and prosperity for all to create that intangible but essential moral element called legitimacy.

Needless to say, extension of citizenship plays no role in the U.S. imperial order. In fact, U.S. citizenship is jealously reserved for a very tiny minority of the world's population, entry into whose territory is tightly controlled. Subordinate populations are not to be integrated but kept in check either by force or the threat of the use of force or by a system of global or regional rules and institutions — the WTO, the Bretton Woods system, NATO — that are increasingly blatantly manipulated to serve the interests of the imperial center.

Though extension of universal citizenship was never a tool in the American imperial arsenal, during its struggle with communism in the post–Second World War period Washington did come up with a political formula to legitimize its global reach. The two elements of this formula were multilateralism as a system of global governance and liberal democracy. In the immediate aftermath of the Cold War, there were, in fact, widespread expectations of a modern-day version of Pax Romana. There was hope in liberal circles that the United States would use its sole superpower status to undergird a multilateral order that would institutionalize its hegemony but assure an Augustan peace globally. That was the path of economic globalization and multilateral governance. That was the path eliminated by George W. Bush's unilateralism.

As Frances Fitzgerald observed in *Fire in the Lake*, the promise of extending liberal democracy was a very powerful ideal that accompanied American arms during the Cold War.[10] Today, however, Washington- or Westminster-type liberal democracy is in trouble throughout the developing world, where it has been reduced to providing a façade for oligarchic rule, as in the Philippines, pre-Musharraf Pakistan, and throughout Latin America. In fact, liberal democracy in the United States has become both less democratic and less liberal. Certainly, few in the developing world see a system fueled and corrupted by corporate money as a model.

Recovery of the moral vision needed to create a consensus in favor of U.S. hegemony will be extremely difficult. Indeed, the thinking in Washington these days is that the most effective consensus builder is the threat of the use of force. Moreover, despite their talk about imposing democracy in the Arab world, the main aim of influential neoconservative writers like Robert Kagan and Charles Krauthammer is transparent: the manipulation of liberal democratic mechanisms to create pluralistic competition that would destroy Arab unity. Bringing democracy to the Arabs is not even an afterthought but a slogan that is uttered tongue in cheek.

The Bush people are not interested in creating a new Pax Romana. What they want is a Pax Americana where most of the subordinate populations like the Arabs are kept in check by a healthy respect for lethal American power, and the loyalty of other groups such as the Philippine government is purchased with the promise of cash. With no moral vision to bind the global majority to the imperial center, this mode of imperial management can only inspire one thing: resistance.

The great problem for unilateralism is overextension, or a mismatch between the goals of the United States and the resources needed to accomplish these goals. Overextension is relative, that is, it is to a great degree a function of resistance. An overextended power may, in fact, be in a worse condition even with a significant increase in its military power if resistance to its power increases by an even greater degree. Among the key indicators of overextension are the following:

- Washington's continuing inability to create a new political order in Iraq that would serve as a secure foundation for colonial rule
- Its failure to consolidate a pro-US regime in Afghanistan outside of Kabul
- The inability of a key ally, Israel, to quell, even with Washington's unrestricted support, the Palestinian people's uprising
- The inflaming of Arab and Muslim sentiment in the Middle East, South Asia, and Southeast Asia, resulting in massive ideological gains for Islamic fundamentalists — which was what Osama bin Laden had been hoping for in the first place
- The collapse of the Cold War Atlantic Alliance and the emergence of a new countervailing alliance, with Germany and France at the center
- The forging of a powerful global civil society movement against U.S. unilateralism, militarism, and economic hegemony, the most recent significant expression being the global antiwar movement
- The coming to power of antineoliberal, anti-U.S. movements in Washington's own backyard — Brazil, Venezuela, and Ecuador — while the Bush administration is preoccupied with the Middle East
- An increasingly negative impact of militarism on the U.S. economy, as military spending becomes dependent on deficit spending, and deficit spending become more and more dependent on financing from foreign sources, creating more stresses and strains within an economy that is already in the throes of stagnation

In conclusion, the globalist project is in crisis. A comeback via a Democratic or liberal Republican presidency should not be ruled out, especially because there are influential globalist voices in the U.S. business community — among them George Soros — that are voicing opposition to the unilateralist thrust of the Bush administration.[11] In our view, however, this is unlikely, and unilateralism will reign for some time to come.

We have, in short, entered a historical maelstrom marked by prolonged economic crisis, the spread of global resistance, the reappearance of the balance of power among center states, and the reemergence of acute interimperialist contradictions. We must have a healthy respect for U.S. power, but neither must we overestimate it. The signs are there that the United States is seriously overextended and what appear to be manifestations of strength might in fact signal strategic weaknesses.

Notes

1. George Soros, *On Globalization* (New York: Public Affairs, 2002), p. 35.
2. See United Nations Conference on Trade and Development, *Trade and Development Report 1998*; and Barry Eichengreen and Donald Mathieson, *Hedge Fund and Financial Markets*, Occasional Paper 166 (Washington, D.C.: International Monetary Fund, 1998).
3. Jacques-chai, Chomthongdi, "The IMF's Asian Legacy," in *Prague 2000: Why We Need to Decommission the IMF and the World Bank* (Bangkok: Focus on the Global South, 2000), pp. 18, 22.
4. Quoted in "Deadline Set for WTO Reforms," *Guardian News Service,* January 10, 2000.
5. See Robert Brenner, *the Boom and the Bubble* (New York: Verso, 2002), pp. 128–133.
6. David Harvey, Speech at Conference on Trends in Globalization, University of California at Santa Barbara, May 1–4, 2003.
7. "Zoellick Says FTA Candidates Must Support US Foreign Policy," *Inside US Trade,* May 16, 2003. This article summarizes a May 8, 2003, speech by Zoellick.
8. For the sharpening conflicts between the U.S. Treasury Department and IMF officials, see Nicola Bullard, "The Puppet Master Shows His Hand," *Focus on Trade,* April 2002 (http://focusweb.prg/popups/articleswindow.php?id=41).
9. Michael Mann, *The Sources of Social Power,* Vol. 1 (Cambridge: Cambridge University Press, 1986), pp. 254.
10. Frances Fitzgerald, *Fire in the Lake* (New York: Random House, 1973), p. 116. "The idea that the mission of the United States was to build democracy around the world had become a convention of American politics in the 1950s. Among certain circles, it was more or less assumed that democracy, that is electoral democracy combined with private ownership and civil liberties, was what the United States had to offer the Third World. Democracy [provided] not only the basis for American opposition to Communism but the practical method to make sure that opposition worked."
11. See George Soros, "America's Role in the World," speech at the Paul H. Nitze School of Advanced International Studies, Washington, D.C., March 7, 2003. Noting that he was for intervention in the Balkans, including a "NATO intervention without UN authorization," Soros denounced the war with Iraq on the grounds that it stems from a fundamentalism that is unsound and wreaking havoc with the U.S.' relations with the rest of the world. The arguments he musters are those heard not only in liberal democratic circles in Washington but also in "pragmatic" Republican party circles and on Wall Street.

11

Globalization and Development Studies

Philip McMichael

Introduction

Globalization and development, arguably, are two sides of the same coin. Both terms — *development* and *globalization* — are fraught with ideological baggage, insofar as they are essentially euphemisms for capitalism in different guises or times. Each, then, needs to be problematized as discursive concepts that capture the imagination of an era. They are neither self-evident terms, nor are they separate terms. To be sure, they have been used to characterize recent periods, where "development" has tended to define the three to four decades following the Second World War, and *globalization* gained currency from the 1980s, defining what some regard as a postdevelopment era. But each term has roots in the world-historical colonial project associated with the rise of capitalism.

Interestingly, debates that dichotomize state-centered vs. transnational analysis, reproduce the ideological separatism of the terminology of development and globalization, obscuring their historical interrelations. World-systems analysis, insofar as it intervened discursively to shift the terms of debate about the project of modernity, identified development as an ideology, subsuming it within its global analytical framework (Wallerstein, 1974). Even so, the state-system hierarchy is represented geographically, and understood, phenomenally, in development terms associated with the monopolization by core states of accumulation opportunities. That is, development, revealed as a systemic ideology, nevertheless remained a powerful *explanandum* (identified with strong states, even though *capitalist* development is global and inherently uneven and contradictory).

Post-world-systems analysis itself tends to reproduce the separatism in seeking to transcend the residual state orientation in world-systems analysis. It suggests that global processes override geopolitical divisions, demanding a transnational framework superseding the conventions of state-centeredness in sociology and political science. This is globalization, and it supersedes development in periodizing the world order from the 1990s. Scholars call for a shift in analytical focus from state-centered to transnational analysis, arguing that globalization reveals the limits of national units of (development) analysis (cf. Castells, 1997; Robinson, 2002; Sklair 2002). A related argument that the "structure of core-periphery becomes a social division, rather than a geographical one" (Hoogvelt, 1997:129), tends to render invisible the role of states in these disembedding market processes and structures. This is a fruitful direction

111

so long as the state remains an important categorical component of transnational or global analysis.

My argument here, however, is that this is not so much an issue of globalization overriding the nation-state in time (and constructing new space); rather, it is an epistemological issue. It requires recognizing that development, globalization, capital, and the state are all (relational) categories integral to the capitalist era, but whose meaning and discursive function change across time and space as that era unfolds.

The question of the mutual relations of state and globalization is rooted in the crisis of sovereignty, captured in Rosenberg's concept of the "empire of civil society" (the duality of public and private political realms across the modern state system). He suggests that the disjuncture of public and private realms (known as globalization) "explains part of the paradox of sovereignty: why it is both more absolute in its 'purely political' prerogatives than other historical forms of rule, and yet highly ambiguous as a measure of actual power" (Rosenberg, 2001:131). This raises a form/content distinction animated by ideologies of sovereignty. In this chapter, I trace the *moments* in recent history of the development/globalization relationship to the ambiguity of sovereignty, arguing this relationship takes various forms, rather than a sequential movement from one to the other.

Global Origins of Development

In the nineteenth century, development was understood, philosophically, as the improvement of humankind. Practically, political elites understood development as social engineering of emerging national societies — formulating government policy to manage the social transformations wrought by the rise of capitalism and industrial technologies (Cowan and Shenton, 1996). Unsurprisingly, this social engineering impulse framed European colonization of the non-European world as colonial administrators assumed the task of developing, or controlling, their subject populations. Development served a legitimating function, where, compared to Europeans, native peoples appeared backward. This apparently natural relation of superiority invited intervention, in the name of development. Forms of colonial subordination differed across time and space, but the overriding object was either to adapt or marginalize colonial subjects to the European presence. That is, development was a relation of power, elaborated nationally and internationally.

Similarly, I would characterize the post–Second World War world order as a construct of power relations using "development" as an enabling and legitimizing discourse. Globalization was ever-present, but was not yet ready for prime time, as development spoke to the colonial condition, the impulse for self-determination during decolonization, and construction of a UN-based system where national sovereignty provided the scaffolding for the international capitalist/socialist order (McMichael 2004a).

The Project of Development

As a conveniently neutral name for a hegemonic form of global capitalism, development was brought about as an international project along the following lines:

First, capitalist development was constructed through the following ideological representations:

1. The hegemonic liberal internationalism of U.S. power, linked with UN principles of equity and dignity for all peoples. Just as colonized subjects had appropriated the democratic discourse of the colonizers in fueling their independence movements, so postcolonial leaders appropriated the idealism of the development era, proclaiming equality as a national and international goal, informed by the UN Universal Declaration of Human Rights (1948).

2. Social-democratic pressures to regulate capitalism *nationally*. This international current stemmed from what Karl Polanyi (1957) has termed "the discovery of society," in the process of the great transformation whereby market fetishism was subordinated to social needs and goals in the welfare or social-democratic state. As Lacher (1999) has shown, market regulation via the welfare state, Fordism, and the Bretton Woods regime, stabilized capitalism and reestablished its international power via the *Pax Americana*.

3. The legitimizing of the notion of the development state via the movement of decolonization. In this sense, development was welfarism writ large (cf. Wallerstein, 1995), and, arguably, expressed a form of racist paternalism in extending the state-system as a form of political and social discipline at the same time as it represented self-determination. Development state ruling elites legitimized themselves through programs of economic nationalism, and the deployment of development initiatives that strengthened patronage systems (Mamdani, 1996) and naturalized poverty and domestic inequality (Ferguson, 1994; Escobar, 1995).

Second, U.S. strategic interests were framed as "free worldism" and "freedom of enterprise" in the construction of an empire of containment as a bulwark against anticapitalist and communist politics (Arrighi, 1982, 1994: 68). This empire was founded on military alliances, disbursements of the dollar (as international reserve currency), and export credits. A global empire of containment was secured through interstate relations.

Third, the Bretton Woods regime of fixed (national) currency exchanges established the World Bank and the International Monetary Fund (IMF) as surrogate institutions of global capitalism via their financial and technical relations with development states (cf. Rich, 1994).

Fourth, as a globally orchestrated form of neocolonialism, the development project incorporated Third World states and their elites into an international market that (1) required national accounting methods standardizing the meaning of development across the states system and reducing the value of productive activity to monetized transactions (thereby devaluing subsistence, household, indigenous cultures), and (2) reconsolidated the international division of labor to sustain First World lifestyles (George, 1977).

The Subordination of Development to Globalization

The ideological function of development was revealed across three decades (1960 to 1990), during which imperial power undressed itself in the exercise of a series of military and financial disciplines visited on the Third World. One might characterize this period as involving a shift from making the world safe for democracy (national development) to making the world safe for capital (globalization). There were four major episodes.

First, was the elimination of economic nationalism. The ideology of economic nationalism stemmed from Raul Prebisch's contributions, through the Economic Commission for Latin America, of the notion of *import-substitution industrialization* as a practical development policy to reverse the effects of the colonial division of labor. It extended, in the process of decolonization, to a general orientation towards reconstructing postcolonial states under the mobilizing theme of economic nationalism. The first assault on this policy actually came in a CIA-sponsored coup in 1953 against Iranian Prime Minister Mossadegh's nationalization of British oil holdings, even as this period consolidated economic nationalism elsewhere in the Third World, spawning the Non-Aligned Movement, which sought to avoid subordination to the empires of the United States and the Soviet Union. A turning point came in 1965, when Indonesian President Sukarno was overthrown in a bloody coup, supported by the CIA and the British Foreign Office, resulting in General Suharto's ascension to power (Kolko, 1988: 81; Pilger, 2002: 25–29).

The elimination of a prominent regime practicing economic nationalism in a strategic region, led to a new discourse of "global development partnership." The war waged in Vietnam by a U.S.-led coalition over the next one-and-a-half decades confirmed this policy, followed by strategic interventions in the 1980s in El Salvador, Nicaragua, and Grenada, and, in the 1990s in Iraq, as well as disbursements of military and economic aid to secure the perimeter of the "free world" and its resource empire for corporate access. Military power was critical to the securing and prying open of the Third World to a project of global development orchestrated by the United States as the dominant power (Kolko, 1988). A further assault on economic nationalism came in the form of the doctrinal policy of economic liberalization. A CIA-sponsored coup in 1973 against recently elected President Allende ushered in the implementation of a comprehensive "structural adjustment" of Chile, even before structural adjustment became fashionable.

Second, there was considerable development agency complicity in the corruption of Third World rulers. General Suharto modeled the capture of between 20 to 30 percent of World Bank loans for his cronies, by the bank's own admission (Pilger, 2002: 20). During the 1970s, when Third World states turned to the private global banks for loans, their disbursements of finance rose by a factor of eleven between 1970 and 1982, from $967 million to $10.4 billion. Much of this money found its way into foreign bank accounts of the political and economic elites. For example, in Latin America, between 1976 and 1984, the rise in public foreign debt equaled, approximately, the parallel outflow of private capital to banks in New York, the Cayman Islands, or other financial centers. Transparency International estimates that 10 to 20 percent of spending financed by export credit agencies is siphoned off as kickbacks (Roodman, 2001: 42, 26).

Third, the lending and borrowing binge of the 1970s laid the groundwork for the debt crisis of the 1980s, following the contraction of credit in 1980 by the Federal

Reserve, as it moved to protect the value of the dollar. The debt regime, when development institutions became debt collection agencies (Bienefeld, 2000), was more than the puncturing of the illusion of development (Arrighi, 1990). It instituted a new technology of financial discipline, under the guise of "good governance," which, through privatization, has intensified the capturing of states and citizens in Latin America and Africa (and, later, Asia) by capital (Patel and McMichael, 2004). "Good governance" informs the politics of the World Trade Organization (WTO) regime (since 1995).

Fourth, in 1986, the First World founders of the GATT Uruguay Round promised, disingenuously, to lower barriers against Third World exports in return for Third World adherence to the rules of the emerging project of globalization (liberalization of agriculture and its trade, of services, and institutionalization of intellectual property rights).

Institutionalizing Globalization as a Project

The institutionalization of globalization as a class-political project has several key features:

First, it is premised on the defeat of economic nationalism, the defeat of the Third World (the New International Economic Order, or NIEO initiative), the role of the debt regime in strengthening the grip of the international financial institutions in managing the global South, the collapse of the Second World as a viable alternative to the capitalist First World, and the universalization via the WTO regime of export fetishism under the reductionist doctrine of "comparative advantage."

Second, it redefined development as "market rule." Development is the reward for joining the global market, managed by the WTO regime. While the World Bank redefined development as "participation in the world economy" in 1980, then-director-general of the WTO, Renato Ruggiero, offered a more comprehensive (in fact, totalizing) view — a legacy of the reductionism of neoliberal economic doctrine:

> More than ever before, trade and the rules of the trading system intersect with a broad array of other policies and issues — from investment and competition policy to environmental, developmental, health, and labor standards ... If we want real coherence in global policymaking and a comprehensive international agenda, then coordination has to come from the top, and it must be driven by elected leaders ... progress in resolving the challenge of the new century will hinge on our ability not just to build a coherent global architecture, but to build a political constituency for globalization ... Without the WTO, we will go back to a world of national barriers, protectionism, economic nationalism, and conflict. (Ruggiero, 2000: xv)

Thus, the WTO director-general articulated the vision of the globalization project: the implementation of the rule of the market via the restructuring of policies and standards across the nation-state system. Trade (two thirds of which is controlled by transnational corporations [TNCs]) is privileged as the motor of development.

Third, the institutional inertia of the WTO regime means that it actually regulates states, not trade. Comprised of member states, the WTO is accountable to them, or at least their competitive relations. Because of this, the inequality among states regularly asserts itself — especially in the double standard whereby the United States and EU states consistently violate multilateralism in the service of their TNCs, not their national citizens. This is most evident in the arena of dumping of agricultural surpluses (McMichael, 2003).

Fourth, the most draconian protocol under consideration in the WTO is GATS 2000. This is represented as a trade agreement: opening U.S. and EU markets for textiles and agricultural products from the global South in return for cross-border corporate provision of services, extending to health, education, water, and "trade in services": such as labor laws, conservation protection, subsidies, licenses, local content provisions, and so on. (Clarke and Barlow, 1997). If implemented, GATS 2000 would accomplish the ultimate replacement of the inclusive social contract between state and citizen with an exclusive private contract between corporation and consumer.

Fifth, the UN global compact with corporations to give "a human face to the global market," consulting with firms about labor, environment, and human rights in return for UN support for liberalization and sponsorship of corporate investment via the leasing of the UN logo and its networks (Borosage, 1999).

Sixth, refining global governance mechanisms (e.g., the World Bank's new loan criteria, linked to "state effectiveness") to stabilize populations impoverished by structural adjustment and continuing debt service, and to relegitimize liberalization by displacing responsibility from the development establishment to the poor (e.g., the World Bank's *Voices of the Poor* project), thereby depoliticizing poverty (Ferguson, 1994).

The Legitimacy Crisis of Development and Globalization

Various scholars have claimed the development project was a confidence trick or an illusion because the world economy has always rested on an exploited periphery (Wallerstein, 1983; Arrighi, 1990), whereas others have argued that it was a success because it was never intended to be universally inclusive (George and Sabelli, 1994: 197).

The development project involved state-managed national economic integration, which was often incomplete. States have differed in their points of departure, degrees of corruption, and resource access. And capitalist development is inherently uneven and unequal. The fixation on industrialization marginalized rural communities. Under the legitimizing mantle of sovereignty, postcolonial regimes routinely exploited weaker communities in their hinterlands (forest dwellers, peasants) in order to build dams, expand mines, plantations, and commercial farms for export revenues, or to relocate other displaced peasants, justifying their actions in the name of national development (cf. Bose, 1997). A considerable portion of the population of the global South remained marginal or experienced dislocation via the development project. Only about one fifth of the world's almost six billion people participate in the cash or consumer credit economy today. Development has been quite limited, unequal, and undemocratic, whatever its successes and however inclusive its ideals. The globalization project intensifies these outcomes via its global assault on the social contract.

The twentieth-century social-democratic trajectory has effectively been reversed as industrial restructuring, offshore investment, public works downsizing, labor demobilization, and rising unemployment have swept across the global North — a veritable countermobilization by capital. On the other side of this process we have seen the incorporation and organization of new labor forces across the global South into global commodity chains, as well as in domestic industrial complexes (Silver, 2003). Peasant contractors, *maquila* workers, child labor, casual female and male labor, sweatshop work, plantation labor, homework, and even slave labor constitute a quite heterogeneous and strategic mix of labor in the global economy (McMichael, 1999). And, with TNC global sourcing and states trimming their national work forces, employment insecurity rises across the world.

Like the development project, the globalization project is an unrealizable ideal from two related angles. First, neither nation-states nor the world community are singularly composed of market-oriented individuals: social divisions of class, gender, race, and ethnicity give texture to the power relationships within which (global) development operates, and power to its growing countermovements for global justice (Starr, 2000). Second, corporate globalization generates its own tensions, expressed in the resistance movements, deep interstate rivalries in the WTO, and intraelite disputes that animate this project (cf. Stiglitz, 2002). The growing fractiousness of the Washington Consensus, the paralysis of the WTO's ministerials (from Seattle to Cancun), and the worldwide suspicion of neoliberal rules (especially in Europe and Latin America) — all reveal a deeply contradictory and contested state of affairs.

The globalization project has not yet had to confront seriously its contradictory effects: it orchestrates the decomposition of the nation-state (from citizen-state to market-state) in realizing its vision but cannot or does not admit to it. One effect alarms the inner circles of global management: the fragility of a deregulated world monetary system. When financial deregulation exerts discipline over states and routinely compels those low on the currency hierarchy to shoulder the cost of market-induced crisis (Cohen, 1998), the system's legitimacy erodes. The United States is the most indebted state in the world but, because those debts are not denominated in other currencies (because trade partners accept dollars), to date it has avoided having to tighten its financial belt under the kinds of debt management conditions laid down by the IMF.

The Bretton Woods Commission stated: "There has been no reliable long-term global approach to coordinating policy, stabilizing market expectations, and preventing extreme volatility and misalignments among the key currencies" (Bacon, 1994: A1). This was prescient, given the 1997 financial crisis in East Asia, fueled by IMF monetary fundamentalism, which left these markets (and subsequently those of Russia and Latin America) exposed to destabilizing withdrawals of short-term money, deepening the crisis and its widespread social impact. The United States may still experience the austerity associated with structural adjustment, imposed through a market "blowback" mechanism rather than by the Bretton Woods institutions. While the United States runs a persistent trade deficit in addition to its net debtor status, Europe runs a trade surplus with the rest of the world, which owes it about $1 trillion, establishing the possibility of substituting euros for dollars, and obliging the United

States to stop assuming that its deficits will continue to be financed because of the dollar's international reserve currency status to date (Thurow, 1999: 22–23).

Meanwhile, the market-induced crisis in Argentina (2001) revealed the legitimacy crisis of the globalization project at the same time as it exposed the ambiguities of sovereignty. Formerly the "blue-eyed boy of Latin American globalization" (Elliott, 2002:10), Argentina's trajectory portends continuing market-induced financial crisis, matched with a disturbing discrediting of democracy by a regime that surrendered sovereignty in its financial policy, and responded to citizen forms of direct democracy with violence (Ferradas, 2003). This is, arguably, the shape of things to come, in political responses to the crisis of globalization — as manifested in both its material failures and resistances.

Increasingly, populations bear witness to the selectivity of corporate globalization as market-induced financial crises discipline states and citizens, and as the IMF lends on conditions of "full cost recovery" in all public utilities, allowing firms to use this edict to cherry-pick lucrative contracts and leaving cash-poor contracts associated with services for the working poor to the devices of local authorities and communities. The latter effect represents a simultaneous downsizing of national budgets to service loans with a loss of public services. The result is a groundswell of resistance, rejection of formal institutions, and the emergence of promising new forms of development — eschewing economic reductionism, respecting diversity, understanding ecology, and building an inclusionary politics (McMichael, 2004b).

Development and Globalization in the Imperial Project

The globalization project's ideology of globalization — its "open world" rhetoric — has always been honored in its breach, especially by its prosecuting Northern states. Within this inconsistent and unequal multilateralism, the traditional unilateralism of the United States has become decidedly more aggressive in response to the competitive relations in a liberal economic order, the need to resolve its ballooning deficit, and in recognition of looming geopolitical changes as China joins the global economy. Anticipating these issues, a think tank, Project for the New American Century (PNAC), was founded in 1997 by conservative interventionists concerned to consolidate a global empire. A PNAC report issued in 2000 stated: "At no time in history has the international security order been as conducive to American interests and ideals. The challenge of this coming century is to preserve and enhance this 'American peace'." At that time, PNAC identified Iran, Iraq, and North Korea as immediate targets, well before President Bush referred to them as the Axis of Evil in 2001 (Pitt, 2003).

The development project was a method of reordering the world in the 1940s, via an ideology of liberal internationalism. This twenty-first century imperial project (*Pax Americana*) also seeks to reorder the world, but without a credible ideology (other than vanquishing the "enemies of freedom") and requiring "constabulary duties" superseding the United Nations (Editors, 2002: 5). The PNAC report advocated expansion of the global U.S. military presence, with a plan for permanent U.S. military and economic domination of every region of the world, unrestricted by international treaty. The project's architects took over the Pentagon, the Defense Department, and the White House under the 2000 Bush Administration. Following September 11, 2001, President Bush elaborated this imperial project in the National Security Strategy of the United States of America (NSSUSA), with its new military doctrine of *preemptive* (or preventive) war, subsequently used against Iraq in 2003, with little or no regard for world opinion, international law, or the sensibilities of the United Nations (Bookman, 2002).

The NSSUSA document observes that the twentieth century produced a "single, sustainable model for national success: freedom, democracy, and free enterprise": values to be protected "across the global and across the ages" (Research Unit for Political Economy, 2003: 68). The document identified multilateral institutions as explicit instruments of U.S. national security, insisting that the World Bank's development assistance is tied to "measurably goals and concrete benchmarks," and "(o)ur long-term objective should be a world in which all countries have investment-grade credit ratings that allow them access to international capital markets and to invest in their future" (ibid: 72–73).

The imperial project is a more explicit use of force to protect U.S. dominance where market rule (the globalization project) falls short. In an era of flawed multilateralism, loss of edge in electronics, biotechnology, and pharmaceuticals, and rising resistance movements across the world, a more powerful U.S. approach to ordering the world was bound to appear — accelerated by the legitimacy gained through the September 11 attacks (even though the PNAC vision was already in motion). Arguably, "regime change" in Afghanistan and Iraq was a first step in the reordering of the power balance in the Middle East, as a precondition for a reordering of the world power balance, as the United States seeks to neutralize (via control of oil) potential rivals in the EU, China, and a reunited Korea (with bomb), and maintain a revenue stream to service its rising imbalance of payments (Arrighi, 2003).

Conclusion

In a neoliberal world, with an increasingly obvious hard edge, development is identified as the outcome of "good governance," that is, market accountability. Whereas the original formula (of the development project) was "development brings democracy," now we have the reverse. In a unipolar world, accountable regimes, imposed perversely by force, are the condition for development, meaning the unevenly distributed spoils of a managed world market. Such ideological representation is driven by power relations, which at the present time are quite centralized (even if quite fragile).

Neoliberalism brings instability, skepticism, and outright disaffection. Unlike "development," it has never achieved international hegemonic status as a universalist ideology, needing to "lock-in" market reforms through free trade agreements to prevent states from backsliding (Panitch, 1998). Although this looks like transnationalism, in subordinating state sovereignty to market rule, it requires the complicity of states in their own ambiguous reinterpretation of sovereignty. In addition, we now see, through the emerging imperial project, a realignment of market rule, where the iron fist of imperialism and its geopolitical imperatives is ungloved. Certainly state-centric analysis alone cannot comprehend such changes, but neither can a transnational perspective unrooted in analysis of the changing coordinates of state sovereignty, in the context of the contradictory machinations of an imperial state.

Arguably, from development through globalization projects to an emerging imperial project, the universal appeal of development has shrunk to a crystallization of its core power relation: that of securing resources and markets to sustain a dominant consumer-state. It is not surprising that the distinguishing feature of this incipient imperial project is its concern with security.

With all imperial ventures, overreach is often highly correlated with mounting resistances, from militarily-occupied populations to states (from Sweden to India) unwilling to participate in global financial or military projects. And February 15, 2003, saw millions of people demonstrating across the world against war in Iraq, many of whom also identify with various strands of the global justice movement. This gathering of peoples has been referred to already as the world's other superpower (Schell, 2003). Alongside of this instant antiwar movement (unlike the long gestation of the antiwar movement during the Vietnam era), new cosmopolitan practices (Held, 1995), strategic diversity, and "self-organization from below" (Hines, 2000; Starr, 2000; Brecher et al., 2000; Houtart and Polet, 2001; Waterman, 2001) are mushrooming in relation, and as alternatives, to the narrowing, or indeed bankruptcy, of global and now imperial forms of development.

12

Globalization and Racism:
At Home and Abroad

Howard Winant

The U.S. Empire and Race

The two Gulf wars have deeply affected the global context in which racial conflict takes place. Although the 1991 war was organized by the United States and undertaken to preserve oil reserves in a U.S. sphere of influence, it was legitimized by the United Nations and carried out by a large bloc of nations. Some noncombatant nations financed the war, and others were subsidized (or bribed) to fight or at least stay neutral. Under these complex conditions the first Gulf War did not yet signal a split in the tacit postimperial consensus. It was a quasi-imperial intervention, which in an earlier time might have been termed "gunboat diplomacy." In 1991 it could still be seen as exceptional. Rather than a harbinger of a new imperial age, it was a "police action." For all the carnage of the first Gulf War, the spanking of Iraq did not extend to occupation; its capital was not seized, and its ruler was allowed to retain his throne.

The second Gulf War, however, has been a very different matter. It was undertaken under the flimsiest of pretexts by the United States, which sought to consolidate its access to petroleum supplies, to shore up the political position of its regional gendarme (Israel), and to increase its quotient of domination in the Middle East. The war commenced without international legitimation, after the blessings of the UN Security Council were sought and refused. The United States invaded Iraq anyway, acting nearly unilaterally, and quickly seized Baghdad. The previous ruling party was outlawed and planning got underway for the creation of a puppet regime. Prolonged occupation will be required. Popular resistance is apparent, although still disorganized.

With imperialism comes colonialism. Although Bush and Company assured the world to the contrary, claiming that U.S. forces would be welcomed as liberators, the country's postinvasion condition was more akin to subjugation than liberation. Self-rule is not around the corner; the domination of Iraq and exploitation of the country's resources are well underway, under the auspices of the U.S. military and favored U.S. corporations. In a few short months a full-scale U.S. imperialist operation has been mounted in the heart of the Middle East, in a core state within the larger Arab nation (Amin, 1978).

With colonialism comes racism. There is nothing very new about this; the notes being struck are familiar. The United States affords itself a civilizing mission in the

Arab world, the Muslim world, much as the British and French did in the past. Although the president and secretary of state sometimes praise Islam as a religion of peace, it is more often seen as a cloak for barbarism and terrorism. Islam has been equated with terror in the West; this is particularly true in the United States after the September 11, 2001, attacks. The flood of periodical ink and broadcast sound bites devoted to the problematic and mysterious essence of Islam — political Islam, fundamentalist Islam, sex and gender under Islam, the putative "backwardness" of Islam in comparison to the enlightened and democratic West, the tutelary role of Christianity and obligation of proselytization in the Islamic world, etc. — signals a regression in the West, and particularly in the United States, to concepts of orientalism at its worst (Said, 1978). It hardly needs repeating that, like the nineteenth-century phenomenon Said analyzed so influentially, twenty-first-century orientalism is also a discursive set of variations on the theme of imperial rule: the tutelary mission of the West is proclaimed — in the values of "freedom," "democracy," "pluralism," "secularism," etc. — while underneath the surface the old agendas advance: most notably political-military power and the capture of natural resources.

The West–East global axis, like the North–South one, is a fundamentally racialized world social structure. West–East was always a key axis of global modernity. Its resurrection in the twenty-first century as an elemental conflict in the global system cries out for interpretation within the cultural and political frameworks of the present.

Historically, the West–East divide was about religion in a different way than the North–South difference was. From roughly the sixteenth century on — and, of course, chiefly from the standpoint of the "lords of humankind" (Kiernan, 1969), the Europe of conquest and nascent empire — the North–South division of the newly encompassed globe was about Europe and "the others": the primitives, the subhumans, the polytheistic, and animistic heathens. The West–East schism, however, predated that by more than half a millennium. It was about Christian Europe vs. the Muslims and the Jews, who were rivals (especially the Muslims) for both sacred and profane dominion, and impediments (especially the Jews) to the millenarian and chiliastic goals of Christianity.

The harnessing of the themes of race, ethnonationality, and religious difference, the menace of "otherness" to the purposes of empire is a very old story. Like the Freudian "return of the repressed," these concepts have found important echoes in the contemporary political panorama: "the clash of civilizations" (of which more below) is perhaps the most prominent of these, but the rise of a theocratic Protestant evangelism in the United States also counts. In fact the politicization of religion all around — in Koran-waving Islam as well as Bible-belting Protestantism and ultraorthodox Judaism, in rising Hindu nationalism and recent battles in the Balkans, in (the former Soviet) Central Asia, in Afghanistan, in the Philippines, in Africa, and elsewhere — represents a major recent shift in global political alignments. Beyond the irredentism still festering in memories of ancient or medieval defeats nurtured over centuries, beyond the literalist readings of sacred texts on the part of fundamentalists of different faiths, there is a disturbingly racist dimension to politicized religion: the "other" is a lesser being, an obstacle to God's will. This racism is as apparent today than it was in 1683.[1]

Global Hegemony and Radical Democracy

Comes now the new imperialism. So is this the "clash of civilizations"? Is it a new Reconquista, a new crusade as radical Islamists would argue, a new Inquisition, a new 1683? Is Islam to be thrown back again, not at the gates of Vienna but at those of Baghdad? Or is the present situation very different from that of the Middle Ages? Is there something problematic about the "clash" thesis?

Good questions, to which only tentative answers can be given. Although the West has made war in the Islamic heartland, there are still limits. There is no prospect for a generalized military assault against the Muslim world — which is what the Crusades were. But there is an effort underway to define the West–East conflict as a new epochal conflict in the manner of the Cold War. In the United States this is called the "war on terror," and in political Islam it is sometimes reviled as a new crusade that must be met with *jihad*. Still, the new imperialism is not a "clash of civilizations," despite the Bushies' tacit (or not so tacit) embrace of that Huntington thesis (1996). It is a clash, all right, but principally a geopolitical one centering on issues of race and class. It is a conflict *within* civilizations or cultures, not among them. The terms and conditions of this new imperial conflict are just now being defined in practice.

From the standpoint of its organizers and theorists in Washington, the new imperialism is an attempt to generate a global hegemonic project for the twenty-first century. It is a bid to reassert quasi-global rule on the part of the imperial U.S. politburo, which finds itself newly beleaguered and deeply threatened not so much by armed resistance as by demands for global redistribution of resources and wealth. Highly militarized but somewhat devoid of political vision, nostalgic for clear-cut conflict on the Cold War pattern, this new initiative repudiates the preceding period's limited but real commitment to sociopolitical reform, reasserts and justifies the metropole's unslakeable thirst for scarce resources and wealth, and dismisses large segments of the world's population as undeserving of economic well-being, political self-rule, or cultural recognition. Its project is principally framed as a national under-taking, in which "all true Americans" participate, and that stigmatizes opponents as outsiders or even traitors. So the new imperialism is nationalistic in a reactionary way, a retro way. Although willing to operate unilaterally outside U.S. borders, the new imperial project nevertheless seeks allies and partners, if for no other reason than utility. A small number of other nations have proved themselves willing to collaborate with the United States — in a strictly subordinate role, let it be noted — in its attempt to reassert a global hegemony. For the present, however, imperial headquarters is confident enough to confront not only the global South and East, but also to tangle with former allies like France and Germany, allies who are unwilling to collaborate.

From the standpoint of its opposition, challenging the new imperialism is a global democratic project. This is an effort to reclaim the traditions of participatory democracy and sociopolitical pluralism in the postcolonial and postsocialist era. Generating this opposition involves building regional alliances and trade agreements (such as MercoSur in South America), and initiating progressive redistribution of resources at the national level where possible — even in the face of IMF-based structural adjustment policies and other pressures for austerity. Most centrally, challenging the new imperialism means organizing and theorizing a popularly based global democracy movement, already visible in some important institutions and mobilizations such as the World Social Forum (2001 to 2003), the UN World Council Against Racism gathering in Durban (2001), and the Seattle (1999) and Genoa (2001) protests against the World Trade Organization (WTO). This movement opposes "free trade" and unequal exchange, environmental depredation, the superexploitation of labor, and perhaps most important, the onerous debt peonage under which the global South staggers year after year (Stiglitz, 2002). It advocates global redistribution of wealth and income, custodianship and protection of the earth's resources, and respect for cultural diversity. It incorporates religious, labor, community, women's, racially-based, and environmentalist organizations from all over the world. And it vindicates participatory democracy as the core political value of our era.

These conflicts have so far been defined primarily as North–South ones and, secondarily, as localized or national conflicts. They still dominate the framework of opposition, for they have been the source of active mobilization for a decade or more now. But in the wake of the 9/11 events, the Afghan and second Gulf Wars, and after the articulation by the Bush regime of an explicit doctrine of preemptive war-making, democratic activists and theorists have begun to turn their attention toward the problem of resurgent imperialism.

It is important to distinguish the counterhegemonic project of participatory democracy from the cloak of democratic advocacy with which the new imperialist project has sought to cover itself. When convenient, the United States has repeatedly sought to frame its interventions — especially in the Middle East and Asia — as undertaken in pursuit of democratic objectives. But after decades of sponsoring or supporting military coups throughout the region (in Iran, Pakistan, Indonesia, and elsewhere); after numerous direct interventions (in Lebanon, Vietnam, Afghanistan, Iraq, and elsewhere); after maintaining cozy alliances with brutal dictatorships in numerous countries in the region (Marcos' Philippines, Rhee's Korea, Suharto's Indonesia, and the Shah's Iran, among others) it hardly becomes the United States to present itself as a tribune of democracy today.

The Challenge of Diaspora and the U.S. Racial Crisis

A global democratic project must assert the rights and help develop the political capacity of those in the global South and global East: people who are excluded from political participation, superexploited, and subjected to institutionalized violence. But any serious challenge to the new imperialism cannot confine itself to the global South and East. It will have to address the parallel conditions and demands of those within the metropole. As in the past, race and racism play a crucial role in challenging the limits of democracy there.

There is a parallel between the post–Second World War dismantling of the old imperialism and the reform of state racial policies in the United States during the same period. Elsewhere I have written extensively about the worldwide racial "break" or rupture set in motion during and after the war (Winant, 2001). In the postwar period antiracist and anticolonial movements interacted extensively (Dudziak, 2002).

Consider Dr. King's denunciation of the Vietnam war in this regard, a position that was seen as controversial at the time. Similarly, postcolonial reform regimes and post–civil rights era racial policies exhibit numerous similarities: both achieved the incorporation of a range of movement demands (generally the more mainstream or moderate ones) in state policy and both also experienced the inclusion (or co-optation) of former insurgents and movement leaders in postcolonial and post–civil rights state apparatuses (in government executives or leaderships, as legislators and officials, etc.).[2]

There are significant consequences of this pattern of "contentious politics" (McAdam, Tarrow, and Tilly, 2001), reform, and incorporation. The price movements pay for winning reforms is demobilization. In addition the more radical demands and sectors of oppositional movements are likely to be marginalized if not repressed after significant reform takes place.

The consequences of the termination of the old empires and the transition to a model of indirect rule after the Second World War is what is generally called global-ization: the north–south patterns already mentioned, the role of the IMF, structural adjustment programs, the WTO, "free trade," etc. But what about the metropolitan side of the parallel? What have been the consequences of movement incorporation and racial reform in the United States? Everyday accounts of race and racism — such as those available from the mainstream media, from political leaders, and even in university settings — tell us that the racial crisis that engulfed the United States a few decades ago has passed. This is the new "common sense": that little remains of the organized black movement that confronted Jim Crow in the South and rose up in anger in the ghetto riots during the mid-1960s; that reforms have been made; that racial attitudes have shifted; that far from espousing white supremacism (which was certainly the norm before the Second World War and far from uncommon even in the 1960s), most whites today call themselves "colorblind." Officially the United States has entered the age of "diversity."

Yet at the same time, by almost every conceivable indicator researchers can bring forward, the same racial inequalities — or shall I say the same "structural racism"? — that existed in the past persist today: modified here and there perhaps, but hardly eliminated and only slightly reduced in scope, especially in terms of black–white disparities. This is not the place to inventory the data, but whether we look at wealth and income equality and inequality, health, access to and returns to education, segregation by residence or occupation, rates of surveillance or punishment by the criminal "justice" system, or many other indicators that compare racial "life-chances," we find patterns strikingly similar to those of the past (Feagin and McKinney, 2002).

So today the parallel between postwar antiimperial movements and antiracist ones continues, as the new imperialism confronts an ongoing demand for greater democ-racy in the global South and East, while post–civil rights racial hegemony confronts an ongoing demand for greater democracy in the U.S. "homeland."

In the era of globalization, however, U.S. racial hegemony faces a formidable new problem in the "homeland": the problem of diaspora. After the Second World War, after CNN, after the Internet, after tidal waves of migration from South to North, from East to West, and from the countryside to the city, globalization is not only the domain of the imperial state and the transnational corporations; it is also a popular domain. As a result the United States, like other national societies of the global North and West — the U.K., France, and Germany — is a lot less homogeneous at the start of the twenty-first century than it was in the heyday of classical imperialism or the era of de jure racism. Despite incessant governmental and civil society–based campaigns on behalf of patriotism and nationalism, the flag, the pledge of allegiance, etc., U.S. national identities are a lot more "diverse" (to use the post–civil rights era parlance once again) than they ever were before.

The United States is a settler nation; it has always been a destination for immigrants. In the post–Second World War period, and especially since the immigration reforms of the 1960s, immigration from Asia, Africa, South Asia, Latin America, and the Middle East — from the global South and East — expanded greatly. This contrasted significantly with earlier patterns, which from the founding of the United States until the later nineteenth century were dominated by less restricted European immigration, and always had a profound nativist and racist dimension. The patterns of immigration to the United States have always reflected the pressures that global political and economic conditions placed on potential migrants, but at the same time U.S. immigration has been organized quite pervasively by national racial policies and practices (Jacobson, 1999; Smith R.M., 1997).

By now there are very substantial migrant communities in the United States, as there are throughout the global North and West. The sociopolitical identities of these groups, as well as the economic and cultural roles they play in their own diasporic/transnational communities, are becoming crucial factors in the developing conflict for global hegemony. Not quite 2 years after the 9/11 attacks, Islamophobia — the current principal form of U.S. nativism — may already have deeply alienated U.S. Muslims. Unconditional U.S. support for the Israeli occupation of the West Bank and Gaza has driven many Muslims in the United States, as it has many throughout Muslim world, to see the United States as an enemy of human and civil rights for Arabs. Mindless terrorism on the part of radical Islamist groups, carried out in various countries, has reinforced the polarization between the U.S. regime and popular democratic aspirations, especially in the Arab lands.[3] Racial profiling of Muslims, of Arabs and Arab-Americans, as well as of South Asians and others, happens in numerous ways: mosques are surveilled, immigration restrictions are stepped up, "voluntary" registration campaigns are mandated, arbitrary and secret detentions occur, and the definition of "terrorism" is expanded to include many activities that for non-Muslims are fully protected forms of political speech or social service. Recall Justin Halperin's account of the raid on the Indian restaurant in New York.

On the other hand, the threat of "terrorist" attacks on civilians is disturbing and real enough after 9/11, even if it is being used for political purposes in Washington. In the enormous and varied diasporic communities in question — Indian, Pakistani, Palestinian, Iraqi, Iranian, etc. — there are millions of people who are highly integrated into U.S. society, who have developed their individual and group identities along the familiar "ethnic" or "hyphenated American" lines, and who do not expect their normal lives to be called into question: at the workplace, in their children's schools, when they travel, or in other ways as well. The vast majority of Muslim

Americans of Middle Eastern or South Asian descent do not accept a radicalized political Islam, remain loyal to the United States, and share the democratic values the country professes (Zaman, 2002). In fact, like other expatriate and postcolonial populations in the United States and elsewhere in the world's North and West, these diasporic minorities represent a tremendous resource for development and democratization, if they can be afforded full citizenship rights, not demonized, harassed, or superexploited. Already private remittances from "developed" countries to poor ones constitute a major source of "foreign aid," surpassing $100 billion in 2001.[4]

So when we ask what civilizations are clashing, we quickly discover that what has been labeled the "clash of civilizations" is as much a series of domestic political conflicts over issues of nationalism, citizenship, nativism, and racism as it is a global conflict: North–South or West–East. Once again in the United States, racial, ethnonational, gender-based, and also class-based issues are politically resurgent. Rather than some epochal "clash" — aka "the war on terrorism" — on the order of the Crusades or Reconquista, today the sociopolitical status of diasporic groups — whether recent immigrants or well-established ethnonational minorities — has become a prominent political issue. Will they receive the protections that the "open society" claims to extend, that the Constitution guarantees, and that the civil-rights era reforms advanced still further? Or will they be subject to the racist harassment of the Patriot Act and its successors? Recall Justin Halperin's account of the raid on the Indian restaurant in New York.

It may be somewhat surprising to hear that "the clash of civilizations" is occurring no less in Washington than in the Middle East! Just as significant democratic, secular, and modernizing tendencies are confronting political Islam in the Middle East and on a world scale, for example (Zaman, 2002), so, too, are powerful theocratic tendencies, notably Protestant evangelical but also Catholic and Jewish ones, gaining significant influence in Washington, despite their antidemocratic and antisecular views. Indeed, the Bush regime is under continuing pressure from these religious–political currents to toughen its stand even more on their key issues: particularly gay rights and abortion rights (Hallow, 2003).

What of overall U.S. racial dynamics in the time of the new imperialism, the post–civil rights era? I have argued that the Bush regime's policies have definite racist dimensions both at home and abroad. Although it is not possible in this chapter to explore these in depth, it seems fitting to complete my discussion of the new imperialism with an overview of this insufficiently recognized problem.

The new imperialism has made a definite turn toward militarism as an instrument of global policy. Yet who does the fighting, and who pays for the war effort? The U.S. armed forces are predominantly composed of working-class youth. They are far more racially diverse than the higher (or even intermediate) reaches of the nation's occupational structure. While the upper-income and wealth-holding strata are doing their best to avoid taxation, they are leaving the burdens of financing military spending to the same working- and lower-middle-class families whose kids do the fighting. Simultaneously the Bush regime is hollowing out the social programs from which working-class and racially defined minorities most benefit: education, healthcare, housing, transportation, and childcare, not to mention welfare.

To the extent that it can be considered a comprehensive social policy, the new imperialism has thus far displayed a tendency toward ferocious antistatism. The one exception to that has been its rampant militarism but, even there, cuts are being made in veterans' benefits. In fact the Bush regime's unprecedented proclivity for regressive redistribution of wealth has been described by one of this policy's chief advocates as predominantly a strategy for drastically reducing the size of government.[5] Defining racism as a practice, then understanding it in terms of its consequences, leads to the inescapable conclusion that the new imperialism is a racist policy not only globally but locally, not only abroad but at home as well. As a comprehensive social policy it has decidedly deleterious effects on the life-chances of racially defined minorities within the United States. It is racially discriminatory.

Although it seems to be riding high at the moment, the Bush regime can also be seen as carrying out a somewhat desperate effort to preserve a moribund social order, both global and national. The new imperialism is the global dimension of the regime's global policy. It is an effort to reassert U.S. global hegemony based largely on military superiority. Domestically, the regime remains dependent in crucial ways on a dying (or at least decadent) form of white racial nationalism, despite its sporadic attempts to portray itself as ecumenically embracing Islam and operating a domestic policy of "compassionate conservatism."

Opposing the somewhat frightening spectacle of an arrogant and clumsy giant — a modern Gulliver trying to subdue by force the growing ranks of the world's alienated Lilliputians — is a developing, counterhegemonic project. At its core is the principle of participatory democracy. Still in its preliminary stages; still limited to largely grassroots and insurgent movements, both in the global South and East and in the northern metropoles; still reeling from the demise of much of the socialist ideal; still trying to regroup after post–Second World War reformism successfully incorporated many progressive movements; and still lacking official support beyond some hopeful preliminary gestures in Latin America (notably in Brazil) and in Europe (in a few "unwilling" EU countries), the movement for participatory democracy nevertheless possesses one great resource: the vast support of millions all around the world. *A luta continua!*

Notes

1. One of many dates that could be selected. On September 12, 1683, Kara Mustapha, commander of a Turkish army of about 150,000 men, was defeated in the Battle of Vienna by a combined Polish and Austrian army commanded by Jan Sobieski. That struggle on the Danube represented the defeat of Islam in Europe. Or did it?

2. As Gramsci noted, incorporation of opposition plays a crucial role not only the the achievement of reform, but also in the maintenance of hegemony (Gramsci, 1971: 182).

3. As ever throughout modern history, terrorism achieves no positive political aims for its practitioners and the causes they support. By what moral or political logic do armed groups attack civilians in cafes, buses, or office buildings?

4. According to World Bank and IMF data (International Monetary Fund, 2002; World Bank, 2002). Data on remittances are notoriously underreported and unreliable. On a related point, Middle Eastern countries have been among the most substantial recipients of remittances from the United States; in 2001 for example, Egypt was the fourth largest national recipient of remittances, receiving a total of $2.91 billion, of which a substantial amount came from the United States. Jordan was the seventh largest recipient, receiving a total of $2.01 billion, nearly 23% of annual GDP. Since 2001, however, these types of financial flows have come under heavy official surveillance and have been seriously curtailed. Data for 2002 were not available as of this writing.

5. Grover Norquist, the right-wing ideologue who has become one of the most powerful men in Washington, once declared: "I don't want to abolish government. I simply want to reduce it to the size where I can drag it into the bathroom and drown it in the bathtub" (Krugman, 2003).

13

Alternative Globalizations:
Toward a Critical Globalization Studies

Peter McLaren and Nathalia E. Jaramillo

Neoliberalism, Capitalist Globalization, and the Crisis of the Educational Left

The central antagonism of the current historical moment is one that we can now unhesitatingly call *empire*. It is most tellingly advanced by the casuistries of those who equate global peace and freedom with the free trade gospel of neoliberalism. But it is also characterized by those who, in taking to the streets of Seattle, Quebec City, Genoa, Prague, and elsewhere, demonstrate their defiant conviction that another world outside the razor-wired precincts of globalized capitalism is possible. As market fundamentalism unleashes its vicious assault against humanity under the auspices of the World Bank, the International Monetary Fund and the Washington Consensus, and as it accords itself the sacerdotal status necessary to divine a future of human dignity, prosperity, and democracy, the transnational ruling elite are being afforded a rite of passage to scourge the earth of its natural resources while besieging the working-class, women, children, and people of color. Faced with a series of draconian policy shifts since 9/11 (such as a proliferation of nuclear weapons, the Bush Administration's Doctrine of Preventative War, the USA Patriot Act, the Homeland Security Act, and a shift from Keynesian state economic and financial policies to Friedmanite neoliberal ones), and a theocratically bent administration filled with "kleptomaniac Contra-funding neo-segregationists associated with Confederate outlets like Southern Partisan magazine and the Council of Conservative Citizens, and Christian fundamentalists who believe themselves to be instruments of God" (Bérubé, 2004), education activists across the globe trenchantly refuse to believe that this is the way things should be, that our collective future is inevitable, that our fate as global citizens is prescored to usher in an apocalyptic destruction of the planet. Critical educators today are struggling assiduously to defend the public sphere from its further integration into the neoliberal and imperialist practices of the state and the behemoth of globalized capitalism (McLaren and Farahmandpur, 2005). Still others are seeking a socialist alternative.

Critical Educators and the Challenge of the Global War State

The drive to obtain "free markets" and to open up investment for U.S. corporations is now accompanied by the most formidable military presence ever known to human-kind, one that is fundamentally unopposed. It is therefore no surprise to see the link between neoliberal globalization and an aggressive U.S. military posture, especially when the military-industrial complex has become such an important economic actor (Gibbs, 2001). Military-Keynesianism is back in vogue. In contrast to its most stead-fast defenders, neoliberal globalization is neither self-correcting nor self-enforcing. As critical educators, we are not convinced that democracy can be sustained in a world ruled by capitalism's law of value — with or without the imposition of empire. If we apply the felicific calculus to the conditions that currently obtain in the United States at the moment, the prospect of democracy looks especially bleak, as the Bush administration puts the country on ideological lockdown (with the help of the ideological state apparatuses such as Fox TV News) in an attempt to return to the halcyon days of the McKinley era when the fat cats of industry ran unimpeded a retrograde financial kingdom that enshrined private property rights and supported the annexation of foreign territories (Greider, 2003). In a social universe pockmarked by the ravages of capitalism's war against the working-class and people of color, there are few places in which to retreat that the global market does not already occupy.

Employing a politics that counts on the stupefaction of a media-primed electorate, the Bush administration has marshaled the corporate media and its blustering cabal of political commentators and talk show popinjays in the service of its foreign policy such that the environment is literally suffused with its neoliberal agenda, with very little space devoid of its ideological cheerleading. Not only has Bush acted like an emperor who has received the laurel wreath (when he should be wearing a wreath of myrtle, signaling in ancient Roman times a hollow victory over an unlawful enemy or one that constituted an inferior force), he has also skillfully used the corporate media to present his foreign policy measures in light of Biblical history. When, on the freshly mopped deck of the carrier *USS Abraham Lincoln*, the U.S. warrior-president emerged in a snug-fitting flight suit from an S-3B Viking aircraft, helmet under his arm, his swagger and grin were greeted by wild cheers from throngs of assembled officers and sailors. Appearing topside before a bold banner that announced "Mission Accomplished" he declared the "battle of Iraq" a "victory" in the ongoing "war on terror." This event was carefully choreographed by Bush's team of seasoned image-makers that included a former ABC producer, a former Fox News producer, and a former NBC cameraman paid for out of an annual budget of $3.7 million that Bush allots for his media coordinators (McLaren and Jaramillo, 2004).

A comparison clearly can be drawn between this example of right-wing showman-ship and Leni Riefenstahl's infamous propaganda film about the 1934 Nazi *Parteitag* in Nuremberg, *Triumph des Willens (Triumph of the Will)* that displayed Adolf Hitler as the world savior.[1] In the German version, Hitler emerges from a Junker 52 aircraft that had been filmed landing at Nuremberg airport to the lofty strains of Wagner. Thousands of Nazi onlookers chant "*Sieg hiel!*" as the musical score builds to a crescendo. And whereas the scene was carefully crafted to suggest that Hitler was a modern manifestation of the ancient Aryan deity Odin (see *The Internationalist*, May 2003), the event on the *USS Abraham Lincoln* was pitching George Bush as a major player in the decidedly Christian drama known as the Second Coming. Bush's speech on the carrier paraphrased Chapter 61 of Isaiah, the very book that Jesus used when proclaiming that Isaiah's prophecies of the Messiah had come true, suggesting perhaps that Bush believes the Second Coming has begun (Pitt, 2003) and that his war on terror is playing an important role in this Biblical prophecy. Leftist commentators have noted that the Pentagon's "Shock and Awe" bombing strategy during the 2003 invasion of Iraq was copied from the Nazi strategy of Blitzkrieg (lightning war) and the Luftwaffe's doctrine of *Schrecklichkeit* aimed at terrorizing a population into surrender, and that the Bush Doctrine of preventative war mirrors the rationale behind Hitler's march into Poland (Hitler had claimed Poland was an immediate threat to safety of the Reich). And while Bush Sr.'s vow to establish a New World Order and Hitler's vow to create a *Neue Ordung* have to be seen in their historical and contextual specificity, the comparison of the Bush dynasty to the Third Reich does extend beyond fascist aesthetics, media spectacle, vatic revelations from Bush Jr., and the police state tactics of the Office of Homeland Security. It can be seen in the machinations of capital and the role of the military-industrial complex in imperialist acts of aggression disguised as "democracy" (McLaren and Jaramillo, 2004).

Under cover of democracy, Bush's carney lingo about saving civilization from the terrorist hordes rings in the air. Although the vast majority of Americans would no doubt recoil in outrage from making a comparison between the present Bush administration and the Nazi regime, celebrated social scientists such as Samir Amin (2003) exercise no such hesitation:

> Today the United States is governed by a junta of war criminals who took power through a kind of coup. That coup may have been preceded by (dubious) elections: but we should never forget that Hitler was also an elected politician. In this analogy, 9/11 fulfills the function of the "burning of the Reichstag," allowing the junta to grant its police force powers similar to those of the Gestapo. They have their own *Mein Kampf* — the National Security Strategy — their own mass associations — the patriot organizations — and their own preachers. It is vital that we have the courage to tell these truths, and stop masking them behind phrases such as "our American friends" that have by now become quite meaningless.

Clearly, this would constitute an egregiously overdrawn — if not patently traitorous — comparison, even among many progressive researchers from the American academy. Yet it is a comparison that is being made more frequently by citizens of countries that have fallen victim to the "full spectrum dominance" of U.S. military and economic policies in the past.

Where classrooms once served as at least potentially one of the few spaces of respite from the ravages of the dominant ideology and a reprieve from the total information control of the state apparatus, they have now been colonized by the corporate logic of privatization and the imperial ideology of the militarized state. Teachers are left suspended across an ideological divide that separates reason and irrationality, consciousness and indoctrination, as they are reminded by their administrators and government officials that to bring "politics" into the classroom is unpatriotic. Consider the case of Bill Nevins, a high school teacher in New Mexico who faced an impromptu paid leave of absence following a student's reading of "Revolution X," a poem that lends a critical eye toward the war in Iraq.

All of this has not gone unnoticed by critical educators. Though they have become used to the academic marginalization that often follows in the wake of reactionary bloviations from conservative educationalists among us, proponents and practitioners of critical pedagogy have long feared being cast into the pit of academic oblivion for being perceived not only as dangerously irreverent to U.S. democracy but also as politically treasonous. At this current historical juncture in U.S. history, when fighting a permanent war against terrorism and expanding the American empire while we are at it, one would think that such a fear is duly warranted. This is partly due to the fact that critical pedagogy earned its early reputation in the 1980s as a fierce critic of U.S. imperialism and capitalist exploitation (McLaren, 2003).

However, times have changed. Today critical pedagogy is no longer the dangerous critic of free-market liberal education that it once was. Rather, it has become so absorbed by the cosmopolitanized liberalism of the postmodernized left that it no longer serves as a trenchant challenge to capital and U.S. economic and military hegemony (McLaren, 2003). Of course, we believe that this can change. There are numerous developments on our campuses related to the antiwar and antiglobalization movements that give us hope that the voices of our youth — and among them, those who will be attending our teacher education programs — will be much more politicized or open to what Freire called "conscientization" than in previous years. There will be pressure on critical educators (in the United States critical educators are mostly liberal, not revolutionary) to respond to the voices of a new generation of politicized student teachers and grassroots activist. But it will not be a simple case of preaching to the converted. There are now more than eighty right-leaning newspapers and magazines circulating on college and university campuses throughout the country. Clearly, there is a concerted effort by conservative organizations to silence progressive voices and to distort historical facts. There is a need for teacher educators to bring a more radical discourse into the educational literature as well as directly into their teacher education programs in order to challenge the distortion of the facts by the right-wing media. Even in the field of critical pedagogy these attempts have been disappointing.[2]

This chapter is meant both as a commentary on the domestication of critical pedagogy, and a challenge for revivifying its political roots and role in the civil societarian left. At this current historical juncture, as the Bush administration sets its sights on abolishing affirmative action, as the right seizes every chance it gets to replace the social wage with the free-market system, and as conservative think tanks game out plans for privatizing what remains of the devastated public sphere, thousands of teachers and teacher educators throughout the country look to the left for guidance and leadership. Clearly this is not the time for pedagogical maundering or for coasting along the eddies of political abulia.

Even so, there still remains a glaring absence within the liberal academy of challenging capital as a social relation. Whereas there is plenty of talk about income redistribution, surprisingly little is said about setting ourselves against the deviances and devices of capital's regime of profit making other than prosecuting a few of the

more disposable CEOs of the latest round of corporate offenders. If, as liberal educators (begrudgingly) and conservative educators (demagogically) insist, there effectively is no alternative to working within an institutionalized market economy, then
admittedly neoliberal policies that champion free-market capitalism and that undermine what is left of the welfare state make sense. And although, surely, the punishment
exacted against the poor can be staggered by parceling out the conditions for mass
poverty in more discreet — yet no less lethal — policies and practices, there remains
the question of how to cope with the havoc that will eventually be wreaked on the poor
and the powerless in the absence of a socialist alternative. It is in this context — of
breadlines, overcrowded hospitals, and unemployment lines longer than those at polling
stations — that the question of organization becomes imperative for the left in a
search for a socialist alternative.

The Politics of Organization[3]

We are beginning to witness new forms of social organization as a part of revolutionary praxis. In addition to the Zapatistas, we have the important example of the
participatory budget of the Workers Party in Brazil. And in Argentina we are seeing
new forms of organized struggle as a result of the recent economic collapse of the
country. We are referring here to the examples of the street protests of the *piqueteros*
(the unemployed) currently underway and which first emerged about 5 years ago in
the impoverished communities in the provinces. More recently, new neighborhood
asambleas (assemblies) have arisen out of local streetcorner protests into an antihi-
erarchical, decentralized, and grassroots movement consisting of both employed and
unemployed workers, mostly women. Canadian activist Naomi Klein (2003) captures
the spirit surrounding the creation of the *asambleas* when she writes:

> In Argentina, many of the young people fighting the neoliberal policies that have bankrupted
> this country are children of leftist activists who were "disappeared" during the military dic-
> tatorship of 1976–1983. They talk openly about their determination to continue their parents'
> political fight for socialism but by different means. Rather than attacking military barracks,
> they squat on abandoned land and build bakeries and homes; rather than planning their
> actions in secret, they hold open assemblies on street corners; rather than insisting on ideo-
> logical purity, they value democratic decision making above all. Plenty of older activists, the
> lucky ones who survived the terror of the '70s, have joined these movements, speaking enthu-
> siastically of learning from people half their age, of feeling freed of the ideological prisons of
> their pasts, of having a second chance to get it right.

At the same time, in this new rise of popular mobilization, as subjectivities become
revolutionized under the assault of capitalism, there needs to occur a programmatic
proposal for a political regroupment of the radical and anticapitalist forces. There
must be more options available for organizers of the revolutionary left. Herrera writes:

> In Mexico, the Zapatista movement could not translate its capacity of mobilization in the
> Consultas and Marches into a political alternative of the left. There was no modification of
> the relationship of forces. The theory of the 'indefinite anti-power' or 'changing the world
> without taking power' has produced neither a process of radical reforms, nor a revolutionary
> process. (2002: 13)

We are more optimistic about the possibilities of the Zapatista movement than Herrera, but we do believe that whatever shape the struggle against imperialism and capitalist globalization will take, it will need to be international. We believe in a multiracial, gender-balanced, internationalist and antiimperialist struggle (McLaren and Jaramillo, 2002, 2004b).

In the struggle against capitalism and its state formations, Alex Callinicos (2003b) discusses two options. One is reformism within the anticapitalist movement. Here, the state is considered to be a vehicle through which social change can be successfully achieved. Callinicos, however, argues that the state simply cannot be used as an instrument of social transformation because it is already too implicated in the social relations of production and the bureaucratic apparatus centered on the means of coercion. "Recent historical experience thus confirms the judgment made long ago by Marx and Lenin that the state can't simply be used as an instrument of social transformation," he states. "It is part of the capitalist system, not a means for changing it. The economic pressures of international capital — reflected particularly in the movements of money across the globe — push states to promote capital accumulation." A second option discussed by Callinicos is the one that is propounded by the autonomist wing of the anticapitalist movement. This position renounces a reliance on the existing state and also eschews the objective of taking power from capital. Callinicos cites Tony Negri and John Holloway as perhaps the best-known exponents of this position. Holloway's "movement of negation" or "anti-power" suggests to Callinicos that any attempt to understand capitalism as a set of objective structures implies the abandonment of Marx's original conception of socialism as self-emancipation. Accordingly, virtually the entire subsequent Marxist tradition is dismissed as "'scientistic' and authoritarian." In the final analysis, Holloway's cry that "we do not struggle as working class, we struggle *against* being working class, against being classified" really amounts to, as Callinicos notes, abolishing capitalist relations of production by pretending that they are not there. If we are really determined to abolish capitalist social relations, it makes less sense to disidentify with working-class struggle than to build more effective forms of working-class struggle and organization. It is to this end that our own Marxist humanist work is directed.

The point here is to cultivate an alternative source of power in capitalist society — what Callinicos describes as "the extraordinary capacities of democratic self-organization possessed by the mass of ordinary people." Although one route for this is trade unionism, such self-organization against capitalism is not the sole preserve of workers' organizations. Other possibilities include anticapitalist, antiwar and anti-imperialist movements. Social movements can serve as points of departure and offer glimmers of hope for an alternative to the governing force of capital. The challenge for us is to translate social movements incubated within national borders into a widespread movement against capital and *for* socialism. The multiplicity of social movements (albeit heterogeneous in composition and diverse in their beliefs on how to combat capital) do identify the same enemy — the transnational capitalist class. They recognize the broad scope of the current crisis, which encompasses a crisis of overproduction, a crisis of legitimacy of democratice governance, and a crisis of overextension that has dangerously depleted the world's material resources. Clearly, we need to work out the dialectics of organization that posits as concretely as possible what humanizing social relations can replace the current capitalist ones.

What needs to be emphasized and struggled for is not only the abolition of private property but also a struggle against alienated labor. The real issue that must not be obscured is the need to abolish the domination of labor by capital. Capital needs to be uprooted through the creation of new human relations that dispense with value production altogether. This does not mean that we stop opposing neoliberalism or privatization. What it does mean is that we should not stop there (Rikowski, 2001). This means working towards a concept of socialism that will meet the needs of those who struggle within the present crisis of global capitalism. We need here to project a second negativity that moves beyond opposition (that is, opposition to the form of property, i.e., private property) — a second or absolute negativity that moves toward the creation of the new. This stipulates not simply embracing new forms of social organization, new social movements, etc., but addressing new theoretical and philosophical questions that are being raised by these new spontaneous movements.[4] We need a new philosophy of revolution, as well as a new pedagogy that emerges out of the dialectic of absolute negation (McLaren, 2003). We have to keep our belief that another world is possible. We need to work out a philosophy of praxis organization-ally, not by providing blueprints *for* the future but by providing a vision *of* the future that speaks to a social universe outside the dehumanized social relations of capital-ism's law of value. A new revolutionary critical pedagogy should enable multiracial and gendered working-class groups to discover not only how capital exploits the use-value of their labor power but also how working class initiative and power can destroy this type of determination and force a recomposition of class relations by directly confronting capital in all of its multifaceted dimensions (Rikowski, 2001). This will require critical pedagogy to reconstruct the object context of class struggle to include school sites. Efforts also must be made to challenge current attempts to corporatize, businessify, and moralize the process of schooling and to resist the endless subordi-nation of life in the social factory so many students call home (Cleaver, 2000; see also Rikowski, 2001).

Toward a Critical Globalization Studies and Pedagogy

As critical social educators, whether we are working inside or outside the academy, we are faced with a new sense of urgency in our fight to create social justice on a global scale, establishing what Karl Marx called a "positive humanism" to replace what Hannah Arendt (1955) called the "negative solidarity" of atomized and displaced individuals. Our feat is not a neutral one; it is a political act based on our interactions with children and families who believe they have no other option than to succumb to the powers that be in education who are resigned to the indicative consciousness of "what is" rather than the subjective consciousness of "what could be" (McLaren, 2003). A critical globalization studies will examine education as a social process embedded within global social relations of production. It will use advancements in technology to foster communication and interaction in order to interrogate critically the racialized nation-state and its insinuation in the new imperialism We are convinced that our society is just one of many possible societies in which to live, and both struggles from below and struggles from above have redefined our thinking about how the floodgates of possibility for the creation of alternative globalizations can be opened. We recognize that "intellectualism" is not confined to the academy, and that to consider the role of intellectuals as a distinct social category is premised upon an elitist misunderstanding of the relationship between knowledge as a social relation and the history of class struggle (Gramsci, 1971). If we are to adopt Gramsci's notion of the organic intellectual, then we accept that all human beings are inherently agents of social transformation and our challenge is therefore to sustain the organic development of new and essential conceptions of the world by connecting material bases of production with intellectual development. The "organic" intellectual is defined as a fundamental element of a particular social class — one who, in essence, directs the ideas and aspirations of the class to which they organically belong, in both an economic sense (through the social relations of production) and a social sense by playing a functional role in sustaining the hegemony ruling class ideology.

In discussing responses to the imperial barbarism and corruption of the empire, Petras (2001) extends Gramsci's notion of organic intellectual by distinguishing *stoics*, *cynics*, *pessimists*, and *critical intellectuals* from what he refers to as *irreverent intellectuals*. The *stoics* are repulsed by the "predatory pillage of the empire" but because they are paralyzed by feelings of political impotence, choose to form small cadres of academics in order to debate theory in as much isolation as possible from both the imperial powers and the oppressed and degraded masses.

The *cynics* condemn both the victims of predatory capitalism and their victimizers as equally afflicted with consumerism; they believe that the oppressed masses seek advantage only to reverse the roles of oppressor and oppressed. The cynics are obsessed with the history of failed revolutions where the exploited eventually become the exploiters. They usually work in universities and specialize in providing testimonials to the perversions of liberation movements.

The *pessimists* are usually leftists or ex-leftists who are also obsessed with the historical defeats of revolutionary social movements, which they have come to see as inevitable and irreversible, but who use these defeats as a pretext for adopting a pragmatic accommodation with the status quo. They have a motivated amnesia for new revolutionary movements now struggling to oppose the empire (i.e., movements by militant farmers and transport workers) and use their pessimism as an alibi for inaction and disengagement. The pessimists are reduced to a liberal politics that can often be co-opted by the ideologists of empire.

Critical intellectuals frequently gain notoriety among the educated classes. Professing indignation at the ravages of empire and neoliberalism and attempting to expose their lies, critical intellectuals appeal to the elite to reform the power structures so that the poor will no longer suffer. This collaborationist approach "vents indignation that resonates with the educated classes without asking them to sacrifice anything" (Petras, 2001: 15).

In contrast to all of the above, the *irreverent intellectual* respects the militants on the front lines of the anticapitalist and antiimperialist struggles. Petras describes them as "self-ironic antiheroes whose work is respected by the people who are actively working for basic transformation" (Petras, 2001: 15). He notes that they are "objectively partisan and partisanly objective" and work together with intellectuals and activists involved in popular struggles:

> They conduct research looking for original sources of data. They create their own indicators and concepts, for example, to identify the real depths of poverty, exploitation and exclusion. They recognise that there are a few intellectuals in prestigious institutions and award recipients who are clearly committed to popular struggles, and they acknowledge that these exceptions should be noted, while recognising the many others who in climbing the academic ladder succumb to the blandishments of bourgeois certification. The irreverent intellectuals admire a Jean-Paul Sartre, who rejected a Nobel Prize in the midst of the Vietnam War. Most of all, the irreverent intellectuals fight against bourgeois hegemony within the left by integrating their writing and teaching with practice, avoiding divided loyalties (Petras, 2001: 15).

The challenge of critical educators over the last several decades has been to humanize the classroom environment and to create pedagogical spaces for linking education to the praxiological dimensions of social justice initiatives (McLaren et al., 2003). To that end we have been enduringly indebted to critical pedagogy. However, approaching social transformation through the optic of a critical globalization pedagogy ratchets up the struggle ahead of us. It urges us in the direction of the irreverent intellectual. It stipulates that we transnationalize our pedagogical project. Critical globalization pedagogy dilates the aperture that critical pedagogy has struggled to provide teachers and students over the last several decades by further opening up the pedagogical encounter so that it can recognize its embeddedness in globalized social relations of exploitation and, conversely, to the revolutionary potential of a transnational, gender-balanced, multiracial, antiimperialist struggle. A critical globalization pedagogy raises another series of questions for consideration by teachers, students, and other cultural workers: What is the circularity that obtains among ideas, individuals, systems of mediation, and modes of production and action? How can we liberate the use-value of human beings from their subordination to exchange-value? How can we convert what is least functional about ourselves as far as the abstract utilitarian logic of capitalist society is concerned — our self-realizing, sensuous, species-being — into our major instrument of self-definition? How can we make critical self-reflexivity a demarcating principle of who we are and critical global citizenship the substance of what we want to become? How can we make and remake our own nature within historically specific conventions of capitalist society such that we can make this self-activity a revolutionary force to dismantle capitalism itself and create the conditions for the development of our full human potential? How can we confront our "producers" (i.e., social relations of production, the corporate media, cultural formations and institutional structures) as an independent power (see McLaren et al., 2004)? How does the generalization of commodity production and the regime of exchange value manufacture internal limits on overconceptions of what is — and what could be — human? What are the ecologies of racism, sexism, and heterosexism that are produced under such constraints?[5]

Answering these questions in the context of developing a critical globalization studies will not be easy. It will require a pedagogy and politics of hope. As we have written elsewhere (McLaren and Jaramillo, 2002), hope is the freeing of possibility, with possibility serving as the dialectical partner of necessity. When hope is strong enough, it can bend the future backward toward the past, where, trapped between the two, the present can escape its orbit of inevitability and break the force of history's hubris, so that what is struggled for no longer remains an inert idea frozen in the hinterland of "what is," but becomes a reality carved out of "what could be." Hope is the oxygen of dreams, and provides the stamina for revolutionary struggle. Revolutionary dreams are those in which the dreamers dream until there are no longer dreamers but only the dreams themselves, shaping our everyday lives from moment to moment, and opening the causeways of possibility where abilities are nourished not for the reaping of profit, but for the satisfaction of needs and the full development of human potential. We are committed to the idea that revolutionary critical pedagogy can play a role in the realization of such a vision. The voices and actions of critical educators will become more crucial in the days ahead. Whatever organizational forms their struggles take, they will need to address a global audience that shares the radical hope in a socialist future (McLaren and Jaramillo, 2002, 2004b). Such a struggle will benefit not only from the unbending efforts of antiglobalization scholars and activists but also from students and teachers in universities and public school settings who are engaging in the ongoing development of a critical globalization pedagogy.

Notes

This chapter is dedicated to Rachel Corrie. It draws from McLaren and Jaramillo, 2002, 2004a, 2004b as well as McLaren et al., 2004 and McLaren, 2003.

1. An expanded discussion of this comparison appears in McLaren and Jaramillo (2004a).
2. This discussion of the domestication of critical pedagogy has been taken from McLaren (2003).
3. This section is greatly expanded in McLaren and Jaramillo (2002 and 2004b).
4. We are indebted to the brilliant work of Peter Hudis for helping us develop our concept of absolute negativity and for his discussions on the philosophy of praxis. See Peter Hudis, "Working out a Philosophically Grounded Vision of the Future." Report to 2004 Convention of News and Letters. Forthcoming in *News and Letters*.
5. This paragraph is taken from McLaren et al. (2004). The article expands on the specific aspects of what it takes to develop a revolutionary critical pedagogy in urban educational contexts.

14

The Military-Industrial Complex in Transnational Class Theory

Jerry Harris

Power grows out of the barrel of a gun.

—Mao Tse-tung

After the Second World War the United States had unquestioned hegemony throughout the capitalist world. But in the early 1970s U.S. power began a long decline, particularly as the economies in Europe and Japan recovered. Nevertheless, the confrontation with the Soviet Union allowed the United States to maintain leadership by providing military security for the West. But the collapse of the USSR also created a crisis for the United States. Its security umbrella was no longer needed, and its economic hegemony had long passed its peak.

Alongside this strategic change was the emerging revolution in information technology. As information capitalism became firmly rooted in all the advanced countries, a system of economic and political globalization rapidly developed. These changing world conditions presented two choices to the U.S. ruling class; either fully integrate into a globalized system of world capitalism or reassert hegemony through military power. Globalization became the choice of consensus, backed by rapidly growing transnational corporations, the immense power of speculative finance, a surge in cross-cultural exchanges and a technological boom that pointed to a new economy. But beneath the new global system remained a powerful nationalist wing within the U.S. capitalist class. These elements retained a solid base of support in the military-industrial complex (MIC), the structural heart of U.S. superpower status.

For most economic and political leaders in the West, the Soviet collapse created the conditions to build a multilateral system of global capital. But U.S. hegemonists held a different viewpoint, that the defeat of the USSR created an opportunity for a unilateral empire. This strategy was laid out in a pivotal policy paper published in 1997 by the neoconservative think tank, Project for the New American Century, and signed onto by Donald Rumsfeld, Paul Wolfowitz, Dick Cheney, and other top White House officials. As the paper reads, "Having led the West to victory, America faces an opportunity and a challenge ... Does the United States have the resolve to shape a new century favorable to American principles and interests? What is required is a military that is strong ... a foreign policy that boldly and purposefully promotes

American principles abroad; and national leadership that accepts the United States' global responsibilities … At present the United States faces no global rival. America's grand strategy should aim to preserve and extend this advantageous position as far into the future as possible." This future rests on "unquestioned U.S. military preeminence [preventing] others an opportunity to shape the world in ways antithetical to American interests" (Donnelly, 1997: i). This vision drives U.S. policy today and is in sharp contrast with the globalist strategy followed throughout the 1990s.

The conflict for power between these two distinct wings within the U.S. capitalist class and the rise of aggressive military ambitions presents transnational capitalist class (TCC) theory with important questions. Previously TCC theory ignored the role of the MIC and instead concentrated on economic and political forces. But because coercive power is fundamental for class rule, the nature of the U.S. MIC must be examined because of its special role in maintaining security for global capitalism. Therefore, we need to review TCC theory in its relationship to the military-industrial base, which in turn necessitates a discussion of strategic policy and the political and economic splits within this arena.

Let me begin by suggesting the capitalist class consists of different networks of power and interests. These would include economic networks of productive and finance capital; political networks that dominate the state apparatus, intellectual circles, and the leading political parties; cultural networks that include media and academic and religious forces; and the MIC. These networks are interconnected and overlap but are also internally divided into various fractions, the most important consisting of globalist and nationalist interests. Fractions in the different networks can link together around common economic, political, cultural, and ideological concerns and coalesce into defined wings of the capitalist class that attempt to build broad-based hegemonic ruling political blocs.

Based upon this approach the MIC exists as a separate and independent network split among a number of different influential fractions. The most important division is between transnational globalists and international hegemonists. The globalists support strategic coordination with global allies in the North and South, humanitarian warfare and nation building to establish stability in countries not fully integrated into the global system, and industrial and technological mergers with allied defense manufacturers. In contrast, international hegemonists promote unilateral world leadership, unquestioned military preeminence, preemptive warfare, a protected industrial base, and a rebuilt military using new information technologies.

TCC Theory

In Leslie Sklair's *The Transnational Capitalist Class*, he divides the globalists into four main class fractions: (1) TNC executive and their local affiliates (the corporate fraction), (2) globalizing bureaucrats and politicians (the state fraction), (3) globalizing professionals (the technical fraction), and (4) merchants and media (the consumerist fraction) (Sklair, 2001: 17). Sklair argues that the TCC has "economic interests, political organizations, and cultural and ideological formations" (2001: 21). Absent is an analysis of the MIC as an independent network codetermining the direction and development of globalization.

William Robinson and I have also theorized about the TCC in an article titled "Towards a Global Ruling Class: Globalization and the Transnational Capitalist Class" (Robinson and Harris, 2000). In this article we define the TCC as "composed of the transnational corporations (TNCs) and financial institutions, the elites that manage the supranational economic planning agencies, major forces in the dominant political parties, media conglomerates, and the technocratic elites and state managers in both the North and South" (2000: 12). As with Sklair, we also ignored the role of the MIC, assuming that it was simply part of the state structure.

Complicating the above approach, the Robinson–Harris thesis also argued that an emerging transnational state has appeared. Although this has no centralized form, we see it as an "emerging network that comprises transformed and externally integrated national states, together with the supranational economic and political forums" (2000: 27) such as the IMF, WTO, and World Bank. But states also have armies to guarantee their security and power. So the question emerges that because the U.S. military is the only global armed force, how does it serve the transnational class and state?

One interpretation argues that when transnational capitalists control the state apparatus, they have effective control over the military and use it to further TCC interests. In fact, this can explain Clinton's military engagements in Haiti, Somalia, and Kosovo, where there were no vital U.S. economic interests. Instead the general interest of global stability were at stake. As General Reimer once put it, the army has become a "rapid reaction force for the global village" (Hasskamp, 1998: 17). Therefore the United States was not seeking sole hegemony but using the military as a global army in the interests of the TCC. The fact that U.S. military involvement often does not coincide with its own economic interests is evident in the charts below:

U.S. Investment in Key Military Allies, 1998

Number of U.S. Owned Affiliates	Assets (in Millions)	Number of Workers (in Thousands)	Compensation (in Millions)	Affiliate Net Income (in Millions)
Taiwan 240	23,611	69.4	1,495	867
S. Korea 235	20,139	57.7	1,553	57
Philippines 147	9,755	70.9	562	633
Turkey 114	6,361	37.7	668	364
Israeli 110	11,483	53.5	1,329	621
Pakistan 34	1,824	8.1	57	114

U.S. Investments in Countries with Minimum U.S. Military Involvement, 1998

Number of U.S. Foreign Affiliates	Assets (in Millions)	Number of Workers (in Thousands)	Compensation (in Millions)	Affiliate Net Income (in Millions)
China (with Hong Kong) 944	83,524	311.9	4,699	3,597
Singapore 484	58,201	112.0	3,052	3,038
Bermuda 329	114,556	4.8	296	8,374
Argentina 325	42,002	106.9	2,751	775
Malaysia 231	20,139	128.1	1,151	12

Source: U.S. Department of Commerce, Bureau of Economic Analysis (BEA) News Release, "International Investment Position in the U.S. 2000."

How do we interpret economic and military concerns that appear at odds with each other? The dichotomy is significantly different from industrial age imperialism when empires maintained both economic and military monopolies over territorial markets. Even after 1945, Cold War containment policies restricted investments in countries with outspoken nationalist governments such as China and Malaysia.

Clearly corporate and financial powers have led the process of globalization. They built banking and tax havens such as Bermuda, pushed integration into China, and entered any world market that offered opportunities to profit. Globalism is most consolidated within this class network. But the MIC is at the opposite end of the scale. It is the class network in which globalism is the least consolidated and still contends with powerful oppositional forces that often elevate national security interests above globalist economics.

Perhaps the best example of this strategic difference is U.S. policy toward China. Whereas globalists continue to invest in China and see it as the biggest twenty-first century market, hegemonists advocate containment, fearing China will become their next great global rival. So while investments continue to accumulate, the U.S. military also continues to ring China with bases in Taiwan, South Korea, and other Asian outposts. As neoconservative writer Robert Kagan has pointed out, "Concern about China was one of the driving forces behind the demand for the technological modernization of the American military … and in a broad sense it has already become an organizing principle of American strategic planning" (Kagan, 2003).

Such continuing differences pose serious questions for TCC theory, which assumes state leadership is the total determinant of military policy. TCC theory argues political leadership operates through a developing transnational state containing globalist fractions from different parts of the world participating, competing, and colluding in supranational institutions such as the WTO and IMF. The national state is part of this political network when transnational capitalists transform their local institutions to serve globalists' aims. But this nation-state transformational process is mainly a local affair between nationalist and globalist wings within each country. Within this context the U.S. military occupies a singular position. As capitalism's only global army it operates under sole U.S. leadership, subject to a variety of powerful national political influences. What TCC theory failed to take into account is that these nationalist forces can use their base inside the MIC network to launch a counterhegemonic project. Such a project would be impossible if the military network lacked an independent character.

Rather than subsuming the military into the state and making it subject to whoever captures the White House, a more nuanced analysis uncovers different fractions within an independent MIC. In fact, the question of how the military serves transnational interests is not just a problem for TCC theory, but an active debate within the military-industrial network that has led MIC globalists to ally with transnationalists both inside and outside the United States. This project did not develop in isolation but was contested by a counterhegemonist strategy that consolidated itself in opposition to globalism and ultimately came to set policy for the Bush White House. In our article Robinson and I stated that the "national/transnational axis cuts across money, commercial, and production capital, such that all three are split internally along the axis." (2000: 25) The MIC should be included in our analysis because it, too, is split along the same axis, with the difference being that MIC globalists have never consolidated their internal leadership and still contend with hegemonists. Leadership in the White House can help promote one or the other MIC fraction, but in turn these fractions influence strategy from their own perspective and position.

Character of the MIC

To understand the MIC, we need to investigate its component parts through which we can examine the globalist–hegemonist split. We can begin with their economic base. The military industry is international not transnational. Transnational corporations manufacture using global assembly lines and supply chains, are engaged in cross-border merger and acquisitions, participate heavily in foreign direct investments, and their foreign-held assets, sales and employment average between 45 to 65 percent of their corporate totals. International corporations have the majority of their investments, production facilities, and employment in their country of origin and mainly access global markets through exports rather than through foreign-owned affiliates. The latter pattern is evident in the defense industry, which has the majority of its assets, employment, and sales inside the United States. Among the big four defense contractors, Lockheed Martin has 939 facilities in 457 cities in 45 states, Northrup Grumman is located in 44 states, Boeing has 61 facilities in 26 states and Raytheon has 79 sites in 26 states. These are the majority of their production facilities. In terms of international sales the majority are exports and run well below the average for TNCs, just 21 percent for Boeing and 25 percent for Lockheed Martin (Harris, 2002).

International corporations also rely on state protectionism. As Robinson and I have pointed out, these corporations are surrounded by a "whole set of traditional national regulatory and protectionist mechanisms"(Robinson and Harris, 2000: 23). This perfectly describes the relationship of the state to the defense industry. For example, in 2001 fully 72 percent of Lockheed Martin's sales came from U.S. government procurements. In fact, a whole set of laws prevent sharing technologies or accepting foreign investments in key military industries. Although international sales are growing, they are mainly national exports overseen by the Departments of Defense, Commerce, and State, all with their own sets of rules and restrictions. Furthermore, the Pentagon processes 75 percent of all U.S. military foreign sales. This means the Department of Defense (DOD) negotiates the terms, collects the funds, and disburses them to U.S. contractors. The main military manufacturers' organization, The National Defense Industrial Association, has 9,000 corporate affiliates and 26,000 individual members with no foreign membership. The association maintains close coordination with the DOD functioning through thirty-four committees, each with direct access to and a working relationship with the military. Divided up among these contractors is the largest single slice of the federal government's budget. Current military spending has hit $383 billion with $62 billion for procurement and $51 billion in research and development.

Within this nationally protected economic base, globalists are at work. Vance Coffman, chairman and CEO of Lockheed Martin, has called for an open and integrated trans-Atlantic market in military production (Coffman, 2000). The powerful Atlantic Council has also advocated military industrial mergers and acquisitions between the EU and the United States, as well as common research and development (Macomber, 1998). Worried about Bush and "growing differences between U.S. and European policies," the Commission of Transatlantic Security and Industrial Cooperation in the Twenty-First Century was recently formed by the Center for Strategic and International Studies. The parent organization is chaired by former Senator Sam Nunn who oversees a $25 million endowment and a staff of 190 researchers. Board members include Henry Kissinger, James Schlesinger, Brent Scowcroft, and Zbigniew Brzezinski. Writing for the International Herald Tribune, the commission's cochairs, French aviation CEO Jean-Paul Bechat and former U.S. ambassador Felix Rohatyn, argued that national defense regulations have been rendered "obsolete and counterproductive by the internationalization of industrial operations." Instead they envision a "trans-Atlantic defense market (in which) any unilateral approach would be unrealistic and unwise." This market should have a "level playing field with equivalent access to each other's markets, the abandonment of 'national champion' industrial policies by governments and cultural norms that amount to 'Buy American' or 'buy European' practices" (Bechat and Rohatan, 2002).

Such calls for global production have fired a debate within the MIC. Hegemonists see a world where "allies come and go," and the need to maintain an industrial base for national security is of "paramount consideration." As argued by Lt. Colonel Wayne Johnson, "U.S. strategy cannot be based solely on economic issues … we can ill afford to export the means of our future defeat" (Johnson, 1998). MIC hegemonists do not want military production entangled with partners they do not fully trust, particularly EU governments filled with globalists, social democrats, greens, and communists.

Military production has been protected from globalization in two important areas. Financing is protected from speculative capital swings because of guaranteed state funding, and the national market is an unchallenged monopoly. For example, Raytheon is financed by more than 4,000 military-funded programs and is included in over 450 major programs in the Defense Appropriations Bill of 2002 (Harris, 2002: 17). With the "War on Terrorism," defense contractors are now adapting military hardware for internal security use, deepening the national character of their market. This market and financing is essentially untouched by global competition. After the demise of the Soviet Union the industry was subject to cutbacks and internal competition that led to large-scale mergers, but this centralization was not driven by global competitive pressure because the industrial base was not subject to transnationalized competition. Immersed in a protected national environment, military manufacturers did not transform themselves as other TNCs. But shrinking defense procurements have driven MIC globalists towards creating a transatlantic market, which aligns with their multilateralist political agenda. This division is an important nationalist–globalist fault line inside the MIC.

Splits over Political/Military Strategy

In terms of the MIC's intellectual life there is a large circle of academics situated in private think tanks, governmental strategic studies institutes, war colleges, and various universities. These circles have vigorous debates and an intellectual life largely separated from other academic networks. They maintain a wide array of journals, web sites, policy papers, seminars, and conferences with a deep pool of researchers and writers. Both globalist and hegemonists are solidly situated among many think tanks. They have significant influence in the National Strategic Studies Institute at the National Defense University, the Strategic Studies Institute at the Army's War College, the Strategic Research Department Center for Naval Warfare Studies, and the Air War College.

Charles Hasskamp of the Air War College articulates the globalist position when he argues "it is now more critical to have the capability to deter war and exercise preventive diplomacy than to have a force unable to react to anything but war. Unfortunately, there are still many who oppose having the military do anything but prepare for total war … Global security now requires efforts on the part of international governmental agencies, private volunteer organizations, private organizations, and other instruments of power from around the world … helping to stabilize the world, promoting social and economic equity, and minimizing or containing the disastrous effects of failed states" (Hasskamp, 1998: 31–32).

Under this policy unilateralism is a dangerous self-isolating strategy. Writing for the National Defense University, Richard Kugler states that "any attempt by the United States to act unilaterally would both overstretch its resources and brand it an unwelcome hegemonic superpower" (Kugler, 2000a). Another study at the Army's War College warns that "Third World perceptions that the United States wants to retain its hegemony by enforcing the status quo at all costs (will encourage) much cynicism about American ideals at home and abroad" (Crane, 2002). Military strategists at both these institutes argued the strongest guarantee for world stability is multilateral civic and military engagement. As Kugler explains, "the best hope for the future is a global partnership between (the EU and U.S.) acting as leaders of the democratic community" (Kugler, 200b).

This globalist strategy was strongly promoted during the Clinton years but never fully supported within the military. Nevertheless hegemonists lacked a strategic rival enemy to focus their thinking and goals. Instead, they opposed nation building as beyond the traditional military role and involved with nonessential global interests. As one military strategist argued, the "armed forces [should] focus exclusively on indisputable military duties" and "not diffuse our energies away from our fundamental responsibilities for war fighting" (Dunlap, 1996). In more blunt terms Samuel Huntington wrote, "A military force is fundamentally antihumanitarian: its purpose is to kill people in the most efficient way possible" (Huntington, 1993). But the hegemonists' opposition had backed itself into a cautious defensive position that called for less foreign intervention limited only to regions of vital interests. Meanwhile globalists put forward a dynamic and proactive engagement policy set inside a new grand strategy for global capitalist penetration and stability.

These policy positions dominated MIC debates until the terrorist attacks on 9/11 provided a new worldwide threat that let hegemonists out of their antiglobalist box and created the long-sought post–Cold War enemy. This made the hegemonists' strategy operational, with the best-articulated position provided by the neoconservatives. They quickly moved to assert a new unilaterialist direction clearly articulated below by Richard Perle: "An alliance today is really not essential … the price you end up paying for an alliance is collective decision making … We're not going to let the discussions … the manner in which we do it [and] the targets we select to be decided by a show of hands from countries whose interests cannot be identical to our own" (Perle, 2001). For hegemonists such policy is a principle of independent political action and a foundation for nation-centric state power.

Donald Rumsfeld puts forward the same doctrine in *Foreign Affairs*. Using terrorism as a political wedge, Rumsfeld states, "Our challenge in this century is … to defend our nation against the unknown, the uncertain, the unseen, and the unexpected … so we can defeat adversaries that have not yet emerged" (Rumsfeld, 2002: 23). This preemptive aggression for an endless war against nonexistent enemies opens the door to unquestioned hegemonist leadership. In his scenario, the role of global allies is to serve policy determined by the United States. Thus "the mission must determine the coalition, the coalition must not determine the mission, or else the mission will be dumbed down to the lowest common denominator" (Rumsfeld, 31).

Conservative geopolitical realists were also quick to argue for a rejection of globalization and a return to hegemonist military traditions. As Harvey Sicherman, president of the Foreign Policy Research Institute points out, "The Clinton administration believed that just as economic globalization would transcend borders, so security could be lifted out of the rut of geopolitics. … This powerful idea needed as its corollary an international military force (but) globalization had begun to falter even before September 11 when the destruction of the World Trade Center ended the era. Today geopolitics is back with a vengeance … American military forces are waging a war today in defense of U.S. national security, not to secure the freedom of Afghanis. Humanitarian warfare is a doctrine come and gone" (Sicherman, 2002).

Common opposition to the globalists' strategy by neoconservatives and geopolitical realists created the foundation for the Bush coalition. But uniting these two ideological currents into a cohesive hegemonist alliance was the aggressive projection of U.S. power solely defined in terms of American interests. Their outlook is based on a common view that sees the world divided into competitive regional blocs driven by nationalist concerns where coalitions are based on temporary self-interests, not long-term mutual goals. In such a Hobbesian world the United States must achieve military preeminence to protect its strategic interests, and therefore the institutional structure for power becomes the MIC. But this alliance needed a broader popular base to consolidate as a ruling political bloc, and so the fear of terrorism, patriotic narratives, and national chauvinism were used to create widespread internal support for their policies.

Although neoconservatives emphasize the importance of ideology, their calculated use of power closely aligns with the primary approach of the geopolitical realists. Such similarities are clear in this statement from the Project for the New American Century: "The United States has for decades sought to play a more permanent role in Gulf regional security. While the unresolved conflict with Iraq provides the immediate justification, the need for a substantial American force presence in the Gulf transcends the issue of the regime of Saddam Hussein. [The need for bases] would endure even should Saddam pass from the scene ... and even should U.S.–Iranian relations improve ... because of longstanding American interests in the region" (Donnelly, 1997). Absent is any concern for spreading democracy and freedom, rather U.S. economic and military interests are paramount just as realists would advocate.

Here it is worthwhile to take a short look at hegemonist strategy for the Middle East because this region occupies such a key position in world affairs. The goal of regime change throughout the Arab world constitutes a key post-Soviet shift away from the European security relationship. Speaking to the Foreign Policy Research Institute, Perle unwraps the strategy: "Those who think Iraq should not be next may want to think about Syria or Iran or Sudan or Yemen or Somalia or North Korea or Lebanon or the Palestinian Authority ... If we do it right with respect to one or two ... we could deliver a short message, a two-word message: 'You're next.'" Continuing on about an U.S. occupation of Iraq, Perle says, "Look at what could be created, what could be organized, what could be made cohesive with the power and authority of the United States" (Perle, 2001).

Thus, domination of the Middle East is the opening battle for what hegemonists see as their endgame, unquestioned U.S. military preeminence in every corner of the world. This policy, which so fundamentally rejects multilateralism, has galvanized international globalist opposition. Within this framework the political struggle over Iraq became the first fully engaged battle between the transnationalist and hegemonist wings of the capitalist class.

Lastly, we can briefly examine the MIC network in the state apparatus and cultural arena. The military's state apparatus surrounds its academic circles and national industrial base. This network includes all branches of the armed services and the largest single bureaucracy in Washington, the Department of Defense. Not taking into account the men and women in uniform, the DOD employs more people than any other part of the federal government. They also write more contracts, buy more goods, and spend more money. Forces abroad account for 200,000 servicemen and women in 70 foreign installations in over 30 countries (Dombrowski, 2000: 22). Other departments in the MIC state apparatus should include NASA, the CIA, NSA, Homeland Security, and the Department of Energy (which oversees nuclear energy).

Military culture also has deep roots and influence. This covers everything from Civil War reenactments, movies, television, music, video games, comics, national mythology, toys, symbols, and dress. Much of this influence is indirect, simply affirming that evil exists in the world and that violence offers the best and quickest solution for security and safety. Other objects such as G.I. Joe action figures have specific and direct influence. Some of these cultural icons are used to quickly respond to political events. For example, Marvel's comic book hero Captain America dresses in red, white, and blue and shortly after 9/11 was fighting terrorists lead by "Al-Tariq." Such mass popular culture helps maintain militarism as an embedded identity in U.S. society and can transform into widespread political support for aggressive policies during periods of crisis.

The hegemonists also give importance to the cultural wars, and here the Christian right plays an important part in their political bloc. The Eurocentric narrative of U.S. history with its Western cultural purity is a key element in defining and defending the nation state. The rejection of multilateralism abroad is tied to the opposition of multiculturalism at home. Hegemonists fear the deconstruction of an Eurocentric narrative will create a "postassimilationist society" that will make "American nationhood obsolete." For hegemonists "transnationalism is the next stage of multiculturalist ideology — it's multiculturalism with a global face (and challenges), traditional American concepts of citizenship, patriotism, assimilation, and at the most basic level, the meaning of democracy itself" (Fonte, 2001). The U.S. Patriot Act, attacks on affirmative action, and a unilateral war on Iraq are component parts of a strategic offensive against external and internal foreign threats. Samuel Huntington's thesis on the "clash of civilizations" provides the theoretical basis that ties cultural wars at home to wars with Islam abroad. Western civilization must be defended within and without, something the hegemonists believe globalists not only fail to do but actively undermine.

Globalists and Hegemonists Compared

Globalist	Hegemonist
Multilateral foreign policy and soft power	Unilateralist foreign policy and hard power
Multicultural national diversity	Eurocentric and Christian nation
Nation building and humanitarian warfare	Preemptive and preventive military warfare
A mutual and stable global empire for world capital	Geopolitical competition, strategic rivals, and regional blocs
Transnational corporate economic base	Military industry complex
Supranational governmental institutions	Nation-centric state

Conclusion

The above four circles of influence — industrial, state, intellectual, and cultural — create a powerful basis for an independent MIC network. Because of its unique private–state symbiotic relationship, the MIC cannot be subsumed solely into commercial or production capital or within the state sector. Furthermore, because of the nationalist nature of its economic production and deeply embedded patriotic culture and ideology, the MIC provides a uniquely solid base for the hegemonist political current. It is around this core that other antiglobalist forces have been able to rally and build a political bloc to challenge the TCC.

John Fonte, a senior fellow at the Hudson Institute, puts the strategic conflict for power between the globalists and hegemonists in clear terms. Hegemonists see the key divide "not between globalist and antiglobalist, but instead over the form Western global engagement should take in the coming decades: Will it be transnational or internationalist?" (Fonte, 2001: 457). Reasserting the nation-state's right to the unilateral use of force and violence, ignoring international law, attacking immigrant rights, and promoting a renewed patriotic cultural narrative are all key elements in a broad counteroffensive against the TCC. Fonte's definition of the social base for "transnational progressivism" closely parallels the class analysis of Sklair, Robinson, and Harris. Fonte includes in this definition corporate executives, Western politicians, the "postnational" intelligentsia, UN bureaucrats, EU administrators, and various NGOs and foundation activists (2001: 457). This is the line of demarcation for hegemonists who see an "intracivilization conflict" for the soul of the nation-state.

Far from a solid hold on power, the hegemonist bloc faces a host of problems. Their unilaterialist strategy is highly contested from within the ruling class and from broad sectors of the world's population. We are at a point in which both the old nation-centric state and the emerging transnational state are faced by considerable contradictions and instability. Both globalist and hegemonist political regimes have developed sharply differing responses to the crisis of world capitalist economic stagnation. Their conflict creates an unstable and dangerous crisis set within a deeper pool of contradictions arising out of economic competition, overproduction, and environmental destruction. Given the economic difficulties faced by the globalists, starting with the 1997 crisis in Asia and leading to the stock market crash in 2001, it is not surprising that a political challenge advocating stability through military force would arise from within the capitalist class. The war on Iraq was but the first contested focal point in a strategic battle for class power. But the implications go beyond the immediate suffering and devastation Iraq has faced. At stake is the nature and rule of the international system.

*New Directions in Globalization
Research and Implications
of Globalization for Scholarship
in the Academy*

15

The Many Scales of the Global: Implications for Theory and for Politics

Saskia Sassen

In this short chapter I want to work on two key features of the many needed to develop critical globalization studies. One of these is the need to destabilize the accepted narratives and explanations of globalization in order to generate new questions for research, questions excluded by dominant narratives. A second feature is the need to develop conceptual architectures that allow us to detect what we might think of as countergeographies of globalization. There are multiple instances of these countergeographies. In this chapter I am particularly interested in types of spaces where we can find resistance to global power and as yet unrecognized forms of participation by actors typically represented as powerless, or victims, or uninvolved with global conditions. Such new narratives and conceptual architectures can help us critically remap the terrain of the global.

These two necessary features for critical globalization studies stem in part from a basic assumption in my own 15 years of research, to wit, that the global is partly endogenous to the national rather than a formation that stands outside and in opposition to the national. Endogeneity can be the result of an originally national condition that becomes reconstructed as global; for example, the fact that what we call global capital is an amalgamation of what often were national capitals. Global capital can then be seen as denationalized national capital. Or endogeneity can result from the partial endogenizing of global dynamics and entities into national institutional orders — for example, the fact that global electronic financial markets are partly embedded in, and dependent on, a network of national financial centers.

Such an approach has theoretical, empirical, and political implications for developing critical globalization studies. The global is not simply defined as that which is outside and in contestation to the national, nor is the global only that which is part of a space of flows that cuts across borders. There are, in my view, components of globalization that we keep coding in national terms, and there are global actors whom we think of as local, who may not move across borders and lack the characteristics of what have become dominant representations of the global. If we understand the global as indeed partly endogenous to or endogenized into the national, we expand the range of actors who are conceivably global. We can then include even those who are immobile, resource-poor, and not able to travel global circuits.

The Subnational: A Site for Globalization

One starting point for me, then, has been to keep on asking the question: What is it we are trying to name with the term *globalization*? In my reading of the evidence, it is actually two distinct sets of dynamics. One of these involves the formation of explicitly global institutions and processes, such as the World Trade Organization, global financial markets, the new cosmopolitanism, and the war crimes tribunals. The practices and organizational forms through which these dynamics operate are constitutive of what is typically thought of as global scales.

But there is a second set of processes that does not necessarily scale at the global level as such, yet, I argue, is part of globalization. These processes take place deep inside territories and institutional domains that have largely been constructed in national terms in much, though by no means all, of the world. What makes these processes part of globalization even though localized in national, indeed subnational, settings is that they involve transboundary networks and formations connecting or articulating multiple local or "national" processes and actors. Among these processes I include cross-border networks of activists engaged in specific localized struggles with an explicit or implicit global agenda, as is the case with many human rights and environmental organizations; particular aspects of the work of states (e.g., certain monetary and fiscal policies critical to the constitution of global markets that are hence being implemented in a growing number of countries); the use of international human rights instruments in national courts; and noncosmopolitan forms of global politics and imaginaries that remain deeply attached or focused on localized issues and struggles, yet are part of global lateral networks containing multiple other such localized efforts.

A focus on such subnationally based processes and dynamics of globalization requires methodologies and theorizations that engage not only global scalings but also subnational scalings as components of global processes, thereby destabilizing older hierarchies of scale and conceptions of nested scalings. Studying global processes and conditions that get constituted subnationally has some advantages over studies of globally scaled dynamics — but it also poses specific challenges. It does make possible the use of longstanding research techniques, from quantitative to qualitative, in the study of globalization. It also gives us a bridge for using the wealth of national and subnational data sets as well as specialized scholarships such as area studies. Both types of studies, however, need to be situated in conceptual architectures that are not quite those held by the researchers who generated these research techniques and data sets, as their efforts mostly had little to do with globalization.

One central task we face is to decode particular aspects of what is still represented or experienced as "national" that may in fact have shifted away from what had historically been considered or constituted as national. In many ways this effort is illustrated by the research and theorization logic developed in global-city studies. But although today we have come around to recognize and code a variety of components in global cities as part of the global, there are many domains where this work has not yet been done.

Three instances serve to illustrate some of the conceptual, methodological, and empirical issues in this type of study. One of these instances concerns the role of place in many of the circuits constitutive of economic and political globalization. A focus on places allows us to unbundle globalization in terms of the multiple specialized cross-border circuits on which different types of places are located. I would include here the emergence of forms of globality centered on localized struggles and actors that are part of cross-border networks; this is a form of global politics that runs not through global institutions but through local ones and constitutes a horizontal, rather than hierarchical, space of globality. Global cities are subnational places where multiple global circuits intersect and thereby these cities are positioned on various structured cross-border geographies, each typically with distinct scopes and constituted in terms of distinct practices and actors. For instance, at least some of the circuits connecting Sao Paulo to global dynamics are different from those of Frankfurt, Johannesburg, or Bombay. Further, distinct sets of overlapping circuits contribute to the constitution of distinctly structured cross-border geographies. We are, for instance, seeing the intensifying of older hegemonic geographies, for example, the increase in transactions among New York, Miami, Mexico City, and Sao Paulo, as well as newly constituted geographies (e.g., the articulation of Shanghai with a rapidly growing number of cross-border circuits). This type of analysis produces a different picture about globalization from one centered on global markets, international trade, or the pertinent supranational institutions.

A second of these instances, partly connected to the first, is the role of the new interactive technologies in repositioning the local, thereby inviting us to a critical examination of how we conceptualize the local. Through these new technologies a financial services firm becomes a microenvironment with continuous global span. But so do resource-poor organizations or households; they can also become microenvironments with global span, as might be the case with activist organizations. These microenvironments can be oriented to other such microenvironments located far away, thereby destabilizing the notion of context which is often imbricated in that of the local and the notion that physical proximity is one of the attributes or markers of the local. A critical reconceptualization of the local along these lines entails an at least partial rejection of the notion that local scales are inevitably part of nested hierarchies of scale running from the local to the regional, the national, and the international.

A third instance concerns a specific set of interactions between global dynamics and particular components of national states. The crucial conditionality here is the partial embeddedness of the global in the national, of which the global city is perhaps emblematic. My main argument here is that insofar as specific structurations of the global inhabit what has historically been constructed and institutionalized as national territory, this engenders a variety of negotiations. One set of outcomes evident today is what I describe as a incipient, highly specialized, and partial denationalization of specific components of national states, notably particular components of the work of ministries of finance, central banks, and regulatory agencies in key sectors such as finance and telecommunications.

In all three instances the question of scaling takes on very specific contents in that these are practices and dynamics that, I argue, pertain to the constituting of the global yet are taking place at what has been historically constructed as the scale of the national. With few exceptions, most prominent among which is a growing scholarship in geography, the social sciences have not had critical distance (i.e., historicized) the scale of the national. The consequence has been a tendency to take it as a fixed scale, reifying it and, more generally, to neutralize the question of scaling, or at best to reduce scaling to a hierarchy of size. Associated with this tendency is also the often uncritical assumption that these scales are mutually exclusive, most pertinently for my argument here, that the scale of the national is mutually exclusive with that of the global.

Finally, the three instances described above go against those assumptions and propositions that are now often described as methodological nationalism. But they do so in a very distinct way. Crucial to the critique of methodological nationalism is the need for transnationalism because the nation as container category is inadequate given the proliferation of transboundary dynamics and formations (e.g., Taylor, 2000; Beck, 2001). What I am focusing on here is a different aspect, although it is yet another reason for supporting the critique of methodological nationalism: the fact of multiple and specific structurations of the global inside what has historically been constructed as national.

The Destabilizing of Older Hierarchies of Scale

Various components of globalization bring with them a destabilizing of older hierarchies of scale — scales and hierarchies constituted through the practices and power projects of past eras, with the national scale eventually emerging as the preeminent one over the last few centuries. Most notable today is what is sometimes seen as a return to older imperial spatialities for the economic operations of the most powerful actors: the formation of a global market for capital, a global trade regime, and the internationalization of manufacturing production. It is, of course, not simply a return to older forms; it is crucial to recognize the specificity of today's practices and the capabilities enabling these practices. This specificity partly consists of the fact that today's transboundary spatialities had to be produced in a context where most territory is encased in a thick and highly formalized national framework marked by the exclusive authority of the national state. This is, in my reading, one of the key features of the current phase of globalization, and it entails the necessary participation of national states in the formation of global systems (Sassen, 1996: chapters 1 and 2).

The global project of powerful firms, the new technical capabilities associated with information and communications technologies, and some components of the work of states have together constituted strategic scales other than the national scale. Most especially among these are subnational scales such as the global city and supranational scales such as global markets. These processes and practices also contain a destabilizing of the scale hierarchies that expressed the power relations and political economy of an earlier period. These were, and to a good extent continue to be, organized in terms of institutional size and territorial scope: from the international down to the national, the regional, the urban, and the local, with the national functioning as the articulator of this particular configuration. That is to say, the crucial practices and institutional arrangements that constituted the system occurred at the national level. Notwithstanding multiple different temporal frames, the history of the modern state can be read as the work of rendering national just about all crucial features of society: authority, identity, territory, security, law, and capital accumulation.

Today's rescaling dynamics cut across institutional size and across the institutional encasements of territory produced by the formation of national states. This does not mean that the old hierarchies disappear but rather that rescalings emerge alongside the old ones, and that the former can often trump the latter. Existing theory is not enough to map today's multiplication of practices and actors constitutive of these rescalings. This includes a variety of nonstate actors and forms of cross-border cooperation and conflict, such as global business networks, the new cosmopolitanism, NGOs, diasporic networks, and spaces such as global cities and transboundary public spheres.

A second feature is the multiscalar character of various globalization processes that do not fit into either older conceptions of hierarchies of scale or conceptions of nested hierarchies. Perhaps most familiar here is, again, the bundle of conditions and dynamics that marks the model of the global city. In its most abstract formulation this is captured in what I see as one of the key organizing hypotheses of the global-city model, to wit, that the more globalized and digitized the operations of firms and markets, the more their central management and specialized servicing functions (and the requisite material structures) become strategic and complex, thereby benefiting from agglomeration economies. To variable extents these agglomeration economies are still delivered through territorial concentrations of multiple resources. This points to multiple scales that cannot be organized as a hierarchy or a nested hierarchy: for example, far-flung networks of affiliates of multinational firms along with the concentration of strategic functions in a single or in a very limited number of locations (e.g., Taylor et al., 2000; GaWC). This is a multiscalar system, operating across scales and not merely scaling upward because of new communication capabilities.

Recovering Place

Including cities in the analysis of economic globalization is not without its analytic consequences. Economic globalization has mostly been conceptualized in terms of the duality national–global where the latter gains at the expense of the former. This conceptualization has largely been in terms of the internationalization of capital, and then only the upper circuits of capital. Introducing cities in this analysis allows us to reconceptualize processes of economic globalization as concrete economic complexes partly situated in specific places (Knox and Taylor, 1995; Abu-Lughod, 2000; Orum and Chen, 2002). This contrasts with the mainstream account about globalization where place is typically seen as neutralized by the capacity for global communications and control. A focus on cities decomposes the nation-state into a variety of subnational components, some profoundly articulated with the global economy and others not (Parnreiter, 2002; Yeung, 2000). It signals the declining significance of the national economy as a unitary category in the global economy.

Why does it matter to recover place in analyses of the global economy, particularly place as constituted in major cities? Because it allows us to see the multiplicity of economies and work cultures in which the global information economy is embedded (Low, 1999; Eade, 1996; Marcuse and Van Kempen, 2000). It also allows us to recover the concrete, localized processes through which much of globalization exists and to argue that much of the multiculturalism in large cities is as constitutive of globalization as is international finance, though in ways that differ sharply from the latter (Sassen, 1998: 1; Cordero-Guzman, Grossfogel, and Smith, 2001; King, 1996; Tardanico and Lungo, 1995). It allows us to see an interesting correspondence between great concentrations of corporate power and large concentrations of "others." Large cities, perhaps especially in the global north, are the terrain where a multiplicity of globalization processes assume concrete, localized forms. A focus on cities makes legible not only the upper but also the lower circuits of globalization.

Finally, focusing on cities allows us to specify a geography of strategic places bound to each other largely by the dynamics of economic globalization and cross-border migrations. I refer to this as a new geography of centrality, at the heart of which is the new worldwide grid of global cities. This is a geography that cuts across national borders and the old North–South divide. But it does so along bounded channels; it is a set of specific and partial rather than all-encompassing dynamics.

It is against this context that I argue that one of the strategic working structures enabling the new empire is the network of global cities, one that might eventually evolve into a grid of imperial and subimperial cities. This network is a strategic infrastructure enabling the production and specialized servicing of components crucial for the constituting of global corporate capital. Second, this network is a key structure for social reproduction, both in a narrow sense (its elites and cadres need to live) and a broader sense (the materializing of global corporate capital as a social force).

The outcome is a new type of geography of centrality and space of power. It is different from earlier imperial structures in that it installs itself in multiple national territories and, in that regard, is not characterized by the types of interimperial rivalries of earlier periods. And, secondly, it constitutes itself institutionally — as distinct from geographically — partly outside the frame of national states and the interstate system. In this regard, my analysis signals the possibility of an empire not centered in a single dominant state. Here I would, then, diverge from much analysis that centers the new empire in the United States.

An emphasis on place and networks of places in a context of global processes makes possible a transnational economic and political opening for the formation of new claims and hence for the constitution of entitlements, notably rights to place. At the limit, this could be an opening for new forms of "citizenship." The city has indeed emerged as a site for new claims: by global capital, which uses the city as an "organizational commodity," but also by disadvantaged sectors of the urban population, frequently as much an internationalized presence in large cities as capital. The denationalizing of urban space and the formation of new claims by transnational actors raise the question, whose city is it?

This is a type of political opening that contains unifying capacities across national boundaries and sharpening conflicts within such boundaries. Global capital and the new immigrant workforce are two major instances of transnationalized actors that have unifying properties internally and find themselves in contestation with each other inside global cities. Global cities are the sites for the overvalorization of corporate capital and the devalorization of disadvantaged workers; but they are also the sites for new types of politics that allow the latter to emerge as political subjects.

A New Geography of Centrality and Marginality

The new economic geography of centrality partly reproduces existing inequalities but also is the outcome of a dynamic specific to the current forms of economic growth. It assumes many forms and operates in many terrains, from the distribution of telecommunications facilities to the structure of the economy and of employment. The most powerful of these new geographies of centrality at the interurban level binds the major international financial and business centers: New York, London, Tokyo, Paris, Frankfurt, Zurich, Amsterdam, Los Angeles, Sydney, and Hong Kong, among others. But this geography now also includes cities such as São Paulo, Shanghai, Bombay, Bangkok, Taipei, and Mexico City. The intensity of transactions among these cities — particularly through the financial markets, transactions in services, and investment — has increased sharply, and so have the orders of magnitude involved. At the same time, there has been a sharpening inequality in the concentration of strategic resources and activities between each of these cities and others in the same country.

The growth of global markets for finance and specialized services, the need for transnational servicing networks due to sharp increases in international investment, the reduced role of the government in the regulation of international economic activity, and the corresponding ascendance of other institutional arenas, notably global markets and corporate headquarters — all these point to the existence of transnational economic processes with multiple locations in more than one country. We can see here the formation, at least incipient, of a transnational urban system. These cities are not simply in a relation of competition to each other; they are part of emergent global divisions of labor (Sassen, 2001: chapters 1, 5, and 7).

Global cities are centers for the servicing and financing of international trade, investment, and headquarter operations. That is to say, the multiplicity of specialized activities present in global cities are crucial in the valorization — indeed, overvalorization — of leading sectors of capital today. And in this sense they are strategic production sites for today's leading economic sectors. This function is reflected in the ascendance of these activities in their economies. Whether at the global or regional level, urban centers — central cities, edge cities — are adequate and often the best production sites for such specialized services. When it comes to the production of services for the leading globalized sectors, the advantages of location in cities are particularly strong.

A focus on the work behind command functions, on the actual production process in the finance and services complex, and on global marketplaces has the effect of incorporating the material facilities underlying globalization and the whole infra-structure of jobs typically not marked as belonging to the corporate sector of the economy. An economic configuration very different from that suggested by the con-cept information economy emerges. We recover the material conditions, production sites, and place-boundedness that are also part of globalization and the information economy.

The Less Visible Localizations of the Global

Cities make legible multiple localizations of a variety of globalization processes that are typically not coded as such in mainstream accounts. The global city is a strategic site for these instantiations of globalization in a double sense. Cities make some of these dynamics more legible than other types of spaces, such as suburbs and rural areas. Second, urban space enables the formation of many of these dynamics, and in this regard is productive space.

Many of these less legible localizations of globalization are embedded in the demo-graphic transition evident in such cities, where a majority of resident workers are today immigrants and women, often women of color. For instance, Ehrenreich and Hochschild (2002) examine the formation of a global supply of maids and nannies in response to the new expanded demand for such workers in global cities (see also Parrenas, 2001; Chang and Abramovitz, 2000). These cities are seeing an expansion of low-wage jobs that do not fit the master images about globalization, yet are part of it. Their embeddedness in the demographic transition evident in all these cities, and their consequent invisibility, contribute to the devalorization of these types of workers and work cultures and to the "legitimacy" of that devalorization.

One of the localizations of the dynamics of globalization is the process of economic restructuring in global cities. The associated socioeconomic polarization has gener-ated a large growth in the demand for low-wage workers and for jobs that offer few advancement possibilities. This, amid an explosion in the wealth and power concen-trated in these cities — that is to say, in conditions where there is also a visible expansion in high-income jobs and high-priced urban space. Women and immigrants emerge as the labor supply that facilitates the imposition of low-wages and power-lessness under conditions of high demand for those workers and the location of those jobs in high-growth sectors. It breaks the historic nexus that would have led to empowering workers and legitimates this break culturally.

Another localization that is rarely associated with globalization, informalization, reintroduces the community and the household as an important economic space in global cities. I see informalization in this setting as the low-cost (and often feminized) equivalent of deregulation at the top of the system. As with deregulation (e.g., as in financial deregulation), informalization introduces flexibility, reduces the "burdens" of regulation, and lowers costs, in this case especially the costs of labor.[1] Informal-ization in major cities of highly developed countries — whether New York, London, Paris, or Berlin — can be seen as a downgrading of a variety of activities for which there is an effective demand in these cities — but also a devaluing and enormous competition, given low entry costs and few alternative forms of employment. Going informal is one way of producing and distributing goods and services at a lower cost and with greater flexibility. This further devalues these types of activities. Immigrants and women are important actors in the new informal economies of these cities. They absorb the costs of informalizing these activities. (See Sassen, 1998: chapter 8). The restructuring of the labor market brings with it a shift of labor-market functions to the household or community. Women and households emerge as sites that should be part of the theorization of the particular forms that these elements in labor-market dynamics assume today.

A Politics of Places on Global Circuits: The Local as Multiscalar

These localizations of the global can, in some cases, actually be constituted at multiple scales. This can be examined through the case of political practices among mostly resource-poor organizations and individuals who are constitutive of a specific type of global politics, one that runs through localities and is not predicated on the existence of global institutions. Because a network is global does not mean that it all has to happen at the global level. Yet there are two specific matters that signal the need for empirical and theoretical work on this dimension. One is that much of the conceptualization of the local in the social sciences has emphasized physical and geographic proximity and thereby a sharply defined territorial boundedness and, usually, closure. The other, partly a consequence of the first, is a strong tendency to conceive of the local as part of a hierarchy of nested scales. To a very large extent these conceptualizations probably express the actual practices and formations likely to constitute most of the local in most of the world. But there are also conditions today that contribute to destabilize these practices and formations and hence invite a reconceptualization of the local, even if it pertains to only a limited range of its features and of its instantiations.

Key among these current conditions are globalization and globality as constitutive not only of cross-border institutional spaces but also of powerful imaginaries enabling aspirations to transboundary political practice. Also important are new computer-centered interactive technologies that facilitate multiscalar transactions. All of this allows local actors to participate in a new type of cross-border politics, one centered in multiple localities yet intensely connected digitally. Adams (1996), among others, shows us how telecommunications create new linkages across space that underline the importance of networks of relations and partly bypass older hierarchies of scale. Activists can develop networks for circulating place-based information (about environmental, housing, political issues, etc.) that can become part of political work and strategies addressing a global condition — the environment, growing poverty and unemployment worldwide, lack of accountability among multinationals, and so on. This is a particular phase in the development of these networks, one when powerful corporate actors and high-performance networks are strengthening the role of private digital space and altering and structure of public-access digital space (Sassen, 2002). Digital space has emerged not simply as a means for communicating, but as a major new theater for capital accumulation and the operations of global capital. But civil society — in all its various incarnations — is also an increasingly energetic presence in cyberspace. (For a variety of angles, see, for example, Rimmer and Morris-Suzuki, 1999; Poster, 1997; Miller and Slater, 2000). The greater the diversity of cultures and groups, the better for this larger political and civic potential of the Internet, and the more effective the resistance to the risk that the corporate world might set the standards. The issue here is not so much the possibility of such political practices; they have long existed even though with other mediums and with other velocities. The issue is rather one of orders of magnitude, scope, and simultaneity. The tech-nologies, the institutions, and the imaginaries that mark the current global digital context inscribe local political practice with new meanings and new potentialities.

Further, an important feature of this type of multiscalar politics of the local is that it is not confined to moving through a set of nested scales from the local to the national to the international, but can directly access other such local actors whether in the same country or across borders. This possibility does not preclude the fact that powerful actors can use the existence of different jurisdictional scales to their advan-tage (Morrill, 1999) and the fact that local resistance is constrained by how the state deploys scaling through jurisdictional, administrative, and regulatory orders (Judd, 1998). On the contrary, it might well be that the conditions analyzed, among others, by Morrill and Judd force the issue, so to speak. Why work through the power relations shaped into state-centered hierarchies of scale? Why not jump ship if this is an option? This combination of conditions and options is well illustrated by research showing how the power of the national government can subvert the legal claims of First Nation people (Howitt, 1998) which has in turn led the latter increas-ingly to seek direct representation in international fora, bypassing the national state (Sassen, 1996: 3).[2] In this sense, then, my effort here is to recover a particular type of multiscalar context, one characterized by direct local-global transactions or by a multiplication of local transactions as part of global networks. Neither type is marked by nested scalings.

There are many examples of such types of cross-border political work. We can distinguish two forms of it, each capturing a specific type of scalar interaction. In one the scale of struggle remains the locality, and the object is to engage local actors — for example, a local housing or environmental agency — but with the knowledge and explicit or tacit invocation of multiple other localities around the world engaged in similar localized struggles with similar local actors. It is this combination of multiplication and self-reflexivity that contributes to constitute a global condition out of these localized practices and rhetorics. It means, in a sense, taking Cox's notion of scaled "spaces of engagement" constitutive of local politics and situating it in a specific type of context, not necessarily the one Cox himself might have had in mind. Beyond the fact of relations between scales as crucial to local politics, it is perhaps the social and political construction itself of scale as social action (Howitt, 1993; Swyngedouw, 1997; Brenner, 1998) that needs emphasizing.

The second form of multiscalar interaction is one where localized struggles are aiming at engaging global actors (e.g., WTO or multinational firms), either at the global scale or in multiple localities. Local initiatives can become part of a global network of activism without losing the focus on specific local struggles. (e.g., Cleaver, 1998; Espinoza, 1999; Ronfeldt et al., 1998; Mele, 1999).[3] This is one of the key forms of critical politics that the Internet can make possible — a politics of the local with a big difference: these are localities that are connected with each other across a region, a country, or the world. From struggles around human rights and the environment to workers strikes and AIDS campaigns against the pharmaceuticals, the Internet has emerged as a powerful medium for non-elites to communicate, support each other's struggles, and create the equivalent of insider groups at scales going from the local to the global. The possibility of doing so transnationally at a time when a growing set of issues are seen as escaping the bounds of nation-states makes this even more significant.

Conclusion

Let me conclude by emphasizing the political dimensions of this type of critical mapping of spaces and actors of globalization. An emphasis on cities and places on global networks makes visible the multiple scales of the global and the work of constructing the geographical scales at which social action can occur. Cyberspace can be a more concrete space for social struggles than that of the national formal political system. It can become a place where nonformal political actors become part of the political scene in a way that is much more difficult in national institutional channels. Nationally, politics needs to run through existing formal systems, whether the electoral political system or the judiciary (taking state agencies to court). Nonformal political actors are rendered invisible in the space of national politics.

The city, especially the global city, also is a more concrete space for politics. In many ways, the claim-making politics evident today in cyberspace resonates with many of the activisms proliferating in large cities: struggles against police brutality and gentrification, struggles for the rights of the homeless and immigrants, struggles for the rights of gays and lesbians. Much of this becomes visible on the street. Much of urban politics is concrete, enacted by people rather than dependent on mass media technologies. Street-level politics makes possible the formation of new types of political subjects that do not have to go through the formal political system in order to practice their politics. Individuals and groups that have historically been excluded from formal political systems and whose struggles can be partly enacted outside those systems, can find in cyberspace and in cities an enabling environment both for their emergence as nonformal political actors and for their struggles.

The types of political practice discussed here are not the cosmopolitan route to the global. They are global through the knowing multiplication of local practices. These are types of sociability and struggle deeply embedded in people's actions and activities. They are also forms of institution-building work with global scope that can come from localities and networks of localities with limited resources and from informal social actors. We see here the potential transformation of actors "confined" to domestic roles into actors in global networks, without having to leave their work and roles in their communities. From being experienced as purely domestic and local, these "domestic" settings are transformed into microenvironments located on global circuits. They do not have to become cosmopolitan in this process; they may well remain domestic and particularistic in their orientation and remain engaged with their households and local community struggles, and yet they are participating in emergent global politics. A community of practice can emerge that creates multiple lateral, horizontal communications, collaborations, solidarities, supports.

Notes

1. For a broader treatment of the informal economy, including a focus on its reemergence with the end of the so-called *Pax Americana*, see Tabak and Chrichlow (2000). For an in-depth examination of how globalization has reorganized the informal economy in the global South, see Beneria and Roldan (1985) and Buchler (2002).
2. Though with other objectives in mind, a similar mix of condtions can also partly explain the growth of transnational economic and political support networks among immigrants (e.g., Smith, 1994; Smith, R.C., 1997; Cordero et al., 2000; Gzesh, 2002).
3. One might distinguish a third type of political practice along these lines, one which turns a single event into a global media event, which then in turn serves to mobilize individuals and organizations around the world — either or both in support of that initial action — or around similar such occurrences elsewhere. Among the most powerful of these actions, and now emblematic of this type of politics, are the Zapatistas' initial, and several subsequent, actions. The possibility of a single human rights abuse case becoming a global media event has been a powerful tool for human rights activists.

16

Globalization, International Migration, and Transnationalism: Some Observations Based on the Central American Experience

Norma Chinchilla

Human history has been characterized by migration since the beginning, but there are few if any parallels to the accelerated growth and scope of international migration in the last decades of the twentieth century. The unprecedented magnitude and wide geographic dispersion of these global population movements since 1945, particularly since the mid-1980s, together with their potential as a force for local and global social transformation, has led Castles and Miller to predict that the closing years of the twentieth century and the beginning of the twenty-first will be "an age of migration" (1998: 3).

Similarly, modern human history, at least that of capitalism, has to some degree always been characterized by spurts in globalization, if by that we mean a tendency toward greater internationalization of capital through conquest, investment, and the reorganization of production, fueled by technological innovations in transportation and communication (Mittelman, 2000; Held and McGrew, 1999). But the rapidity of the changes in global interdependence since the Second World War, and particularly since the 1960s, together with the advances in communications technology that have reduced the importance of physical geography on interaction ("deterritorialization"), have opened up possibilities and introduced challenges that are distinctive to this particular stage of globalization.

Given that globalization and international migration have accelerated in recent decades, have the potential to make a significant impact on the course of human history, and have an increasing number of scholars interested in studying them, it is surprising that there have not been more exchanges among scholars working within the two fields. Traditionally, it would appear that most of the cross-fertilization has been in one direction. That is, the use of a political, economic or macrosociological framework to explain the "pull" on less developed countries' workers to serve as cheap labor in more developed capitalist countries, or the ways in which foreign capital penetration into less developed areas results in disruptions that "free up" labor for migration (e.g., Sassen-Koob, 1978; Cheng and Bonacich, 1984, among others). On the other side, however, surprisingly few scholars working explicitly within a globalization framework give more than a cursory glance to the role of internal and international migration, as a quick review of contemporary texts will affirm. The exceptions are notable (Sassen, 1998; Held and McGrew, 1999; and Mittelman, 2000, for example) but they are the exception rather than the norm.

In the field of immigration studies, scholars interested in understanding the effects of transnationalism, or of transnational links, networks, and social spaces that are constructed by migrants and nonmigrants, have called for a paradigm shift that recognizes the importance of globalization and a critical examination of traditional bipolar dichotomies (such as assimilation vs. ethnic solidarity, sojourner vs. settler, citizen vs. noncitizen, and sending vs. receiving countries). They have called for a more dialectical approach that entertains the possibility of seemingly contradictory processes occurring together and that uncovers the links between immigration and globalization. It is primarily here, in discussions of transnationalism, that some of the most interesting new work on the intersection of globalization and immigration is taking place.

Given the importance of the questions raised by political economists and those scholars working within the newer transnationalism framework, it makes sense that any attempt to develop a critical globalization studies should include questions about the connection between international migration and globalization: How are they interrelated? How and where do they intersect? What substantive findings and analytical strategies are suggested by looking at the case of Central America and should be considered when attempting to integrate an understanding of contemporary international migration into a critical globalization studies agenda?

In the discussion that follows, I focus on Central American, particularly Guatemalan and Salvadoran, migration to the United States to understand some of the ways that globalization stimulates and shapes international migration, on the one hand, and how migrants contribute to and shape global processes on the other. I will also attempt to show how the Central American case provides insight into certain analytical strategy issues that need attention in bringing the literatures on migration, immigration, and globalization together.

The Impact of Globalization on Migration within and from Central America

From the time of the Spanish conquest in the sixteenth century, Central America has been a region strongly shaped by the geopolitical and economic interests of foreign countries and investors. Examples include investments in coffee and banana production through the nineteenth and early twentieth centuries, the occupation of Nicaragua by U.S. Marines in the early 1900s, the 1954 CIA-assisted overthrow of the only democratically elected government Guatemala had up to that time, the U.S. support of de facto military dictatorships in Guatemala, El Salvador, and Honduras, and a decade of attempts to overthrow the Sandinista revolutionary government of Nicaragua in the 1980s.

It has also been a region of resistance movements in response to oppression and economic exploitation by oligarchic elites and foreign intervention. This combination of internal and external forces, which occasioned shifts in access to local resources such as land and jobs and in the demand for labor, resulted in patterns of internal migration within Central America (particularly Guatemala, El Salvador, and Nicaragua) and across national boundaries within the Central American region (particularly from El Salvador to Honduras and from Nicaragua to Costa Rica) long before migration of Central Americans to the United States became an important force in the 1970s and 1980s (see Hamilton and Chinchilla, 2001: 17–35).

Following independence from Spain, for example, Central American countries were definitively drawn into the world economy through the expansion of coffee production for export, which became an important impetus to international migration to and from Central American countries. As in the case of coffee production, banana production, introduced in the early twentieth century, also stimulated the international migration of Central Americans to the United States. By the middle of the twentieth century patterns of internal and cross-border migration were well established in Central America. Although migration to the United States was still minimal, the footprints of a path to several U.S. cities were already visible.

The unprecedented upsurges in Central American immigration to the United States in the 1970s and particularly the 1980s were fueled by the stagnation of economic growth and high unemployment following the global recession of the mid-1970s, by government repression of insurgent movements in El Salvador and Guatemala, carried out with U.S. military, economic, and political assistance in the late 1970s and 1980s, by other forms of U.S. intervention, and by economic dislocations associated with war and insurgency in Guatemala and El Salvador in the 1980s. This large influx followed trajectories established in the past and took advantage of networks that had been established by previous migrants to the United States.

In Central America, the impact of global restructuring became particularly evident in the 1990s. Central American migration received a new impetus with the introduction of the neoliberal model, resulting in the types of disruptions and unemployment that have been seen elsewhere in the world (Sassen, 1998). At the same time, globalization also had a major impact on the conditions that attracted Central Americans to specific locations in the United States. In Los Angeles, for example, the "hourglass" economy that resulted from global restructuring provided numerous opportunities for low-wage, low-skill jobs ranging from housekeepers and private childcare, and elder care workers to factory workers in the garment industry and others, and service-sector workers in such fields as food preparation and office cleaning. Aside from the economic changes, and partly because of them, the number of nonimmigrant women, including those with small children, who worked outside the home expanded rapidly, increasing the demand for childcare and domestic work (Hamilton and Chinchilla, 2001).

Impact of International Migration on Globalization

It is primarily in the discussion of transnationalism or transnational processes and practices, defined broadly here as the multiple ties and interactions — economic, political, social, and cultural — that link people, communities, and institutions across the borders of nation states (Vertovec, 1999: 447) that new ideas and debates about the relationship between globalization and international migration have emerged in contemporary immigration studies. Although the literature is filled with debates, including disagreement about the definition of the term itself, scholars working within this framework generally see transnational links, activities, and spaces as both an effect of globalization and as a force that helps to shape, strengthen, and fuel it. The immigrants and nonimmigrants who create these links and spaces are thus seen as not only as objects upon which globalization acts but as subjects who help to shape its course.

Although most scholars now agree that transnational networks were maintained to a greater degree in earlier waves of immigration than was previously thought (Glick Schiller, 1999), many also believe that transnational links in this current stage of globalization exhibit some important differences in quantity and character. Glick Schiller et al. (1992), Levitt (2001), Portes et al. (1999), and others argue, for example, that transnational ties among recent immigrants are more intense than those of their historical counterparts due to the speed and relatively inexpensive character of travel and communications, and the impact of these ties is increased by the global and national context in which they occur. Furthermore, although the potentially liberating and subversive effect of transnational activities and spaces were undoubtedly over-estimated in early writings (Kearney, 1995; Rouse, 1991; Basch et al., 1994), there is no question that the leveraging potential of many migrants today is greater now than in previous historical periods, both in relation to their states of origin and those in which they currently reside.

In the following discussion, I examine some transnational practices of Central American migrants (and nonmigrants) and their impact on globalization, focusing on four specific aspects: remittances, the creation and expansion of a supporting connective infrastructure, immigrant cross-border organizing, and immigrant-related cross-border initiatives by nonmigrants. In the process, I am guided by two questions: First, how and to what extent do transnational practices of Central American migrants represent an intensification of past immigrant practices vs. something quantitatively or qualitatively new and, second, to what extent do transnational relations undermine or support existing power relations?

Remittances and Their Role in Supporting State Economies

Similar to other immigrants, many Central Americans in the United States send part of their earnings to their families at home on a regular basis; the need to provide family support is in fact often a major incentive for international migration (Massey et al., 1993). Given the poverty of many families left behind in Central America, remittances chiefly support consumption (as opposed to savings and investment), ranging from food and clothing to education and healthcare. They may also be used to construct new houses, import luxury items, and establish small businesses, some-times in combination with savings brought back by returning migrants (Funkhouser, 1995; Orozco, 2002; Landolt et al., 1999). The fact that these financial flows cross borders means that they not only support family consumption (and in some cases investment), but also contribute to the foreign exchange of their respective countries. Awareness of their importance often stimulates national businesses (such as banks and real estate companies) to reorient their investment strategies and governments to seek to establish ties with and influence in migrant communities abroad (Landolt et al., 1999; Landolt Marticorena, 2000; Baker-Cristales, 2004; Hamilton and Chinchilla, 2001).

Remittance flows from Latin American international migrants, including Central Americans, have increased exponentially in recent decades and now constitute more than the region receives from international aid. In 2002, remittances sent by Latin American immigrants to their home countries totaled over $32 billion, nearly 78 percent of them from the United States (International Monetary Fund Report, 2003).

Per capita remittances from El Salvador at nearly $2 billion in 2002 were among the highest in the world according to the International Monetary Fund. Between 1990 and 2002, Salvadoran remittances increased from $322 million to nearly $2 billion, nearly equaling the trade deficit, and constituting 15 percent of the country's GDP. Although per capita remittance rates for other Central American countries are lower than those for El Salvador, remittances from these other countries have also grown dramatically over the last two decades and the percentage of the GDP that they are equivalent to is relatively high (14 percent for Nicaragua, 9 percent for Honduras, and 3 percent for Guatemala in 2001). Ironically, it is the remittances from the export of human beings that neoliberal states have come to depend on, and which, unintentionally, help to mitigate the potential political unrest that might result from these same states' failures to meet basic human needs. Indirectly, then, remittances scraped together by mostly low-wage, exploited Central American workers living and working abroad shore up the very neoliberal economies that failed to provide them with opportunities for work and advancement in the first place, causing them to migrate.

Migrant remittances are also important because of the web of local, national, and transnational connections among human beings, groups, and institutions that they create or reinforce and the social, cultural, and political consequences they engender. Researchers note that remittance-receiving households in Central America begin to orient their consumption, investment, and future migrant-sending decisions to a transnational framework, using information and impressions they have gathered from migrants, returning migrants, and the media. The availability of remittances and goods sent back by migrants may also generate a psychology of dependence and encourage the creation of a U.S.-influenced consumer culture in remittance-receiving households and communities even when the ability to realize it may be severely limited (Landolt et al., 1999; Baker-Cristales, 2004; Funkhouser, 1995; Landolt Marticorena, 2000).

The Growth of Transnational Infrastructures

The unprecedented movement of Central Americans to the United States in the 1980s, and the trips back and forth of those who have papers and are able to travel, has given rise to a connective infrastructure of products and services, formal and informal, licit and illicit, that keep migrants and nonmigrants interconnected and fulfill migrant and nonmigrant needs. These include services associated with the travel and border crossing of migrants without papers (smugglers known as *polleros*, or *coyotes*); travelers (*viajeros*); couriers who transport documents, information, letters, packages, food, medicines, appliances, toys, and other products across borders; and travel agents and airline, telephone, express mail, and import–export companies that cater to the immigrant–nonimmigrant Central American market.

The most essential but dangerous of these transnational infrastructures are those related to the transportation and "accompaniment" of human beings without legal documents across two or more borders. Since 1979 when changes in U.S. policy made it difficult for most Central Americans to migrate legally, many Central Americans, as do many Mexicans, engage the services of often unscrupulous smugglers who guide their journey north. These smugglers, in turn, are connected to an elaborate underground of transportation and "protection" services, safe houses, and rendezvous points in one or more countries and regions. Large quantities of money change hands in the course of smuggling and government officials and others at different levels of the process often receive a cut of the profits generated.

As cooperative efforts between Mexico and the United States to control their borders intensified in the 1990s, the dangers that migrants and their smugglers faced increased, increasing the price of the journey and migrants' dependence on smugglers. A trip that once cost an estimated $1,000 in the early 1990s had risen in price to between $3,000 and $5,000 by the end of the decade. Efforts to intensify U.S.-Mexican border surveillance in some popular crossing places (such as Tijuana) even before the terrorist attacks of September 11, 2001, resulted in migrants and smugglers choosing even more dangerous routes and modes of travel, including trekking through large stretches of desert (where some have been abandoned by the *coyotes* to die of dehydration, heat exposure, or starvation); attempting to swim across rivers with dangerous currents, and accepting transportation in trucks that lack ventilation or are too hot or cold for humans. Despite even more intensified efforts by the United States, Mexico, and Central American countries to police their borders since the 9/11 terrorist attacks on the United States, the interconnective infrastructures associated with human smuggling seem to be in no danger of being dismantled. Indications are that demand for services continues to be high and the smuggling business is thriving.

Transnational contacts between Central American immigrants and their family and friends back home have also resulted in a corresponding growth in transportation and communications infrastructure. In the early 1980s there were only a few direct airline flights between Los Angeles and selected Central American cities; 20 years later there are as many as thirty flights each day to either Guatemala City or San Salvador. By the early 1990s, U.S. telephone companies were offering special packages to Salvadorans who frequently call their families back home, and many businesses in the Pico Union–Westlake area were actively involved in targeting their services and products to a migrant and transnational market (Hamilton and Chinchilla, 2001: 152–179).

By the end of the decade a small but significant number of Central American immigrants and their U.S.-born children were communicating with families and friends in their home countries and in other parts of the United States through e-mail and Internet list-serves such as Chapines on Line (Guatemalan), Guanacos on Line and Guanaqueamos (Salvadoran), and Catrachos on Line (Hondurans). Businesses such as Central American courier and express mail companies, branches of Central American banks, and a community credit union have also arisen to attempt to capture the lucrative remittance transmission market, creating competition for MoneyGram and Western Union, whose direct and indirect costs for transmitting remittances can reach 20 percent.

Immigrant Organizing across Borders

Since the late 1970s, a number of Guatemalan and Salvadoran, and to a lesser extent, Nicaraguan, migrants in the United States have actively promoted and facilitated cross-border organizing of various types for a variety of causes. Relatively well-educated Nicaraguan former students and professionals began the trend by organizing against the Somoza regime in the U.S. during the 1970s and helping to mobilize solidarity and support for the Sandinista government during the 1980s.

The cross-border organizing activities of Salvadorans and Guatemalans in the United States in the 1980s, however, far exceeded these early initiatives in scope and impact. Their activities included organizing affiliates of the major Salvadoran political groups, facilitating the organization of human rights and solidarity organizations such as the Committee in Solidarity with the People of El Salvador (CISPES), the Network in Solidarity with the People of Guatemala (NISGUA), the Guatemala Scholars Network, and the Faculty Committee for Human Rights in Central America (FACHRES), actively participating in religious groups such as the Interfaith Task Force on Central America, and functioning as the motor force behind the establishment and operation of CARECEN and El Rescate, two key multipurpose community organizations that provided a range of services to Central American refugees and immigrants.

Central to these activities were the political ties linking U.S. groups and organizations in the United States to their counterparts in El Salvador, Guatemala, and other Central American countries (for more detailed discussion, see Hamilton and Chinchilla, 2001). Although many of the activists involved in these organizations were U.S. citizens, including those of Central American descent, participating in many of the efforts were a core of Guatemalan and Salvadoran immigrants with previous organizing experience in their home countries. What made these immigrant cross-border organizing activities unusual, if not unprecedented, was that they involved the active participation of a largely undocumented — and therefore vulnerable — immigrant population against the official policy of their host government in an area in which that government was heavily involved. Thus, while the U.S. government was sending advisors, military aid, and economic assistance to support the war effort in El Salvador, the counterrevolutionary insurgency against the Sandinistas in Nicaragua, and the military governments in Honduras (and, less visibly, Guatemala), many Central Americans, including immigrants, and their North American supporters established and expanded their own transnational political networks that linked people opposed to these efforts.

With the peace process in the early 1990s culminating with the signing of peace agreements in Nicaragua in 1990, El Salvador in 1992, and Guatemala in 1996, several organizations primarily oriented to solidarity or antiintervention goals disappeared whereas others, in keeping with the changed situation, reoriented their work toward such new activities as support for workers in the *maquila* industries in Central America and the political and economic empowerment of the newly settled immigrant population, while continuing to address the legal needs of new immigrants and those who were still undocumented.

But as the political work of Central American activists shifted from the transnational to the domestic sphere, new transnational networks were formed. Of particular significance were the hometown associations, community-to-community relations established by Salvadorans and Guatemalans in the United States and in their home countries. These had their origins in the 1980s, particularly among Guatemalans, who formed *fraternidades* linking individuals and families from certain communities to their home communities in Guatemala. These hometown associations grew rapidly in the 1990s, and were primarily oriented to sending back assistance. Hometown associations have sent medicine and medical supplies, fire engines, school buses and ambulances, books and sports equipment to their Central American towns and villages. Some have built clinics, schools or sports arenas, or have provided funds for scholarships, street paving, or potable water. By the end of the 1990s, it was estimated that there were 35 to 50 Salvadoran and 30 to 40 Guatemalan associations, indigenous and nonindigenous, in the Los Angeles region (Baker-Cristales, 2004; Landolt Marticorena, 2000; Popkin, 1999; Hamilton and Chinchilla, 2001).

Cross-Border Initiatives by Nonmigrants

During the 1980s, many U.S. nonmigrant activists responded to the presence of Central American immigrants by supporting campaigns to protect those fleeing war and repression and to end U.S. support of de facto military governments. In the 1990s, nonmigrants in Central America, as well as some in the United States, responded to the presence of large numbers of Central Americans in the United States by engaging in business, political, religious, and charitable initiatives. The impetus for forming hometown associations or adopting certain projects by hometown associations, for example, sometimes came from individuals or groups in migrant-sending communities. Some churches in home countries and communities sent priests temporarily or permanently to emigrant communities to reinforce their ties to their premigration religious traditions and prevent or reduce their vulnerability to recruitment by others (traditional Catholics by charismatic Catholics or evangelicals [see Popkin, 1999]). Politicians from sending countries have campaigned in emigrant communities in the United States with the goal of engendering support and funds, despite the fact that audiences in those communities usually cannot vote in elections back home.

Most unusual of all, has been the recent willingness of a coalition of Central American governments (Guatemala, El Salvador, Honduras, and Nicaragua) to intervene in various ways on behalf of their emigrant communities in the United States, including on behalf of various temporary legal protections and against measures that could lead to massive deportations. Whatever other humanitarian or political reasons they might have for doing so, two important practical considerations obviously motivate this unprecedented (for Central America) activity: massive deportations of Central American immigrant populations from the United States would aggravate the problems of unemployment, underemployment, and poverty confronting home countries and would eliminate a major source of foreign exchange at a time when earnings from production for domestic and export markets have been unstable or declining. U.S. immigration policies have thus proven to be a unifying focus for cross-border organizing and one that, for the first time, gives immigrants avenues for negotiating and bargaining with home as well as receiving countries' governments (i.e., of exercising citizenship independent of their formal status).

Business representatives from El Salvador have also expressed concern that family reunification among immigrants could result in a sharp decline in remittance income, with devastating domestic economic effects. Together with their Guatemalan counterparts, they have organized trade expos, established branches of home country supermarkets and banks in Los Angeles, and promoted the sale of property and houses to emigrants who wish to provide for family members left behind or who dream of eventual return, all in an effort to expand their options for tapping immigrant resources and, in the mid-1990s, began to explore other options for tapping immigrant resources.

Issues and Challenges

Based on this brief review of various aspects of the relationship between globalization and international migration, what can we conclude about the content of this relationship and the analytical strategies used in studying it?

First and foremost, in terms of analytical strategies, globalization and international immigration studies need to be historically grounded. This may seem obvious, but it has not always been the case, leading to exaggerated claims of newness or a failure to clarify distinctions with past patterns and practices.

In the case of transnational ties, it seems clear that such ties were maintained to a greater degree than previously thought by earlier migrants, at the same time that recent innovations in transportation and communication have made possible a density and intensity of links not seen before. This, in turn, makes it possible to live simultaneously in two or more worlds or to create and live in "transnational spaces" to a degree not previously known. Clarifying the context is an essential element of the analytical strategy for understanding what is new and distinctive about contemporary international migration practices and processes.

A second analytical strategy, taking a clue from the transnational migration theorists, is to question seemingly dichotomous and mutually exclusive categories, such as external vs. internal, national vs. international, sending vs. receiving countries, sojourner vs. settler, and citizen vs. noncitizen, and to look for continuities and overlaps between and among them. In attempting to understand how and why international immigration occurs, for example, we have argued that it is important to recognize the continuities between "internal" and "external" migration and the internal impact of foreign economic and political domination. National boundaries have certainly not disappeared as any Central American migrant will testify who is trying to make his or her way across two or more borders and is attempting to live without documentation and undetected by U.S. immigration authorities. However, the undeniable blurring of boundaries in an era of rapid globalization creates many overlaps in social categories and the forces that shape them.

A third analytical strategy, the need to pay attention to the possibility of multiple, dialectical outcomes of international migration in relation to globalization, is closely related to an important substantive question posed by transnational migration scholars, namely, to what extent and in what ways do transnational practices in this stage of globalization increase the autonomy and power of the migrants and nonmigrants engaged in them? In other words, to what extent are transnational ties or spaces liberating? To what extent do they reinforce or challenge existing power structures? In the Central American case, the cross-border political organizing of some migrant activists, particularly Salvadorans and Guatemalans in the 1980s, certainly challenged power structures in both the United States and their home countries. Other practices, such as the efforts of business groups to draw upon Salvadoran and Guatemalan immigrants as investors in their companies, however, could be seen as reinforcing the status quo, although they may offer certain benefits to immigrants as well.

Thus, in some cases, migrant transnational ties and activities unambiguously challenge the status quo. In others, however, the situation is more complex and ambiguous. For instance, remittances from Central America emigrants, as well as the provision of furniture, television sets, compact disk players, and similar items, have undoubtedly benefited many of the most underprivileged Central American families, and probably reduced inequality on the national level. But they also reinforce inequality within recipient communities, which in many cases are divided between those relatively well-off families that receive remittances and those that do not, a situation that is often reinforced by the luxuries consumption of the recipients and returning migrants.

Finally, in attempting to understand the impact of both globalization on international migration and migration on globalization, it is important to acknowledge the importance of agency. The penetration of capitalism into less developed countries and the labor needs of more developed countries may stimulate and shape out-migration flows but the factors that determine the size and composition of these flows are not only economic but political, social, and cultural as well. Furthermore, the forces that stimulate migration operate at various levels, including the household, where decisions about who migrates, where, and when are made — decisions that involve some degree of agency, given the context of costs and benefits. Globalization constructs and imposes certain predictable conditions but it also generates unanticipated responses and even resistance. International migration can be seen as one such unintended response to globalization at the same time that migration and migrants' transnational practices reinforce or challenge elements of globalization. Just as grassroots oppositional groups can take advantage of globalization for counterhegemonic activities (e.g., use of Internet by antiglobalization forces), migrant–nonmigrant transnational activities may contest, resist, and negotiate, as well as reinforce, the hegemonic order. Globalization is not neutral, but neither is it exclusively the domain of the powerful.

17

Globalization and the Making of a Transnational Middle Class: Implications for Class Analysis

Steve Derné

In 1991, the Indian economy opened to foreign investment and trade, leading to an explosion of new media and increased opportunities for those with global connections. A decade later, the orientation of educated Indians with good English-language skills and transnational connections was becoming global. On a fast air-conditioned train to Delhi in 2001, I saw two college women flirt with a young college man. All three wore jeans and Western-style shirts and spoke exclusively in English. They passed copies of *Cosmopolitan* and *Time* magazines back and forth. They joked about abandoning the British "zed" in favor of the American "zee" to refer to the last letter of the English alphabet. One young woman asked the man if he was flirting with her. "Are you pulling my leg?" the young man replied. "What do you want me to pull?" countered the woman provocatively. Later, she asked the man, "Do you have a car? Will you take me for a ride?"

But Indians lacking opportunities in the global economy continue to be oriented to local realities and culture — even as they enjoy foreign media. Unlike the young people on the train, they reject challenges to Indian gender arrangements and temper their enthusiasm for consumerism. Amit, a 22-year-old whom I interviewed in 2001, left his village to study at an urban university. Although he fancies himself a connoisseur of Western fashions and enjoys cable's Arnold Schwarzenegger films and National Basketball Association games, Amit remains attached to distinctively Indian family arrangements and is uneasy about foreign influences. "I want an arranged marriage," Amit says, "but I fear that Fashion Television, MTV, and [music] Channel V are distorting the desires of the younger generation."

Critical globalization studies critiques the lived experience of globalization, but it also pushes critique of our analytical categories. This chapter argues that global dynamics require us to rethink class analysis. Because of globalization, class identities are defined more by transnational contexts than within bounded nations, are based in shared patterns of consumption more than shared positions in the economy, and are increasingly defined by gender relations.

The three young Indians traveling by train are members of a transnational middle class who define their status by cosmopolitan consumption and gender arrangements. Able to hitch their dreams to the new global economy, affluent Indians like those on the train see themselves as middle class on a global stage, between the Indian poor and the consuming classes in Europe and North America. By contrast, Amit is part of a locally oriented middle class, which finds status on a local field. Lacking English-language skills and global connections to take off with the global economy, locally oriented middle-class Indians see themselves squeezed between elite Indians like those on the train and destitute Indians struggling to survive. Locally oriented middle-class Indians distinguish themselves from the poor by purchasing nonnecessities like televisions, while their sober avoidance of wasteful spending opposes the vulgar consumerism of affluent, foreign-influenced Indians. The locally oriented middle class takes particular pride in embracing Indian gender arrangements.

Studying Globalization in India

Until the 1980s, India pursued economic development with limited global entanglements. When the oil price rise associated with the 1991 Gulf War led to a crisis of foreign exchange reserves, the Indian government turned to the IMF for a bailout. In response to IMF demands, the government ended licensing for most industries, reduced restrictions on multinational investment, and devalued the rupee. Within 5 years, imports doubled, exports tripled, and foreign capital investment quintupled.

Cultural globalization followed economic liberalization, as cable television offerings suddenly competed with state-run television and Hollywood films competed with local Hindi films. Fueled by advertisers trying to reach the new Indian market, the number of television channels grew from one state-run channel in 1991 to seventy cable channels in 1999. Access to television increased from less than 10 percent of the urban population in 1990 to nearly 75 percent by 1999. In 1991, cable television reached 300,000 homes; by 1999 it reached 24 million homes. With the easing of foreign-exchange restrictions, previously unavailable Hollywood films were dubbed into Hindi and screened widely, capturing 10 percent of the market.

For Gurcharan Das (2001: 213), a Harvard business school–trained CEO, mid-1991 was a "golden summer" of new opportunities. For ardent advocates of globalization like Das (2001: 213), 1991's economic revolution rivals the importance of 1947's political revolution. During 1991's "golden summer" I was in India interviewing young male Indian filmgoers in the small city of Dehra Dun. Although I mostly interviewed educated men with good jobs or good job prospects, none had access to television beyond the one state-run channel and few had seen even one Hollywood film. To understand how globalization had affected the lives of ordinary Indians like these young men, I returned in 2001 to replicate the study conducted a decade earlier. As in 1991, I interviewed men with good standards of living but who did not speak any (or very much) English. They were professionals or successfully self-employed people (23 percent in 1991; 16 percent in 2001), undergraduate or postgraduate students (41 percent in 1991 and 50 percent in 2001), successful laborers or holders of lower-middle-class jobs such as office clerk (36 percent in 1991; 34 percent in 2001). Their families owned scooters or televisions, but they could barely dream of owning automobiles or traveling abroad. Whereas in 1991 none of the men had seen cable television or Hollywood films, by 2001 about two thirds of the men sought out global media. Although exposed to transnational media, these men did not define themselves through cosmopolitan consumption and were not experimenting with new gender arrangements.

This paper tries to rethink class analysis in a globalizing world by comparing India's transnational middle class that aspires to lifestyles of consuming classes in rich countries with a locally oriented Indian middle class, still limited by local markets for consumption and employment. The transnational middle class is made up of the 3 percent of Indians (10 percent of urban ones) with high incomes (above US$2,150 a year), college degrees, English-language skills, and global connections. They can afford televisions, refrigerators, music systems, and computers, can dine at a Pizza Hut or buy Nike shoes, employ at least one full-time servant, send their children to private English-language schools, and arrange back-up supplies to protect against disruption of water or power. With economic liberalization, they can draw on new high-paying jobs oriented to the international market and can now buy international products, which had previously been restricted by foreign-exchange controls. Locally oriented middle-class Indians, like those I interviewed, often have a college degree and a good job, but lack the English-language skills and global connections that would allow them to take off with the new global economy. Earning US$1,000 to 2,150 annually, ordinary middle-class Indians constitute 16 percent of households India-wide, perhaps 40% of the urban population. They work as clerks, police officers, teachers, government transportation workers, and so on. They may have a television or a scooter, but buy few "global" products, preferring the Rs. 50 restaurant meal to the Rs. 300 Pizza Hut meal, the Rs. 300 Indian-made shoe to the Rs. 3,000 Nike. They see themselves as India's middle class — below the position of the rich jetsetters, but well above the position of the destitute 53 percent of Indians who earn less than US$500 annually. Although embracing some consumer goods, they remain attached to Indianness and especially to family arrangements they see as distinctively Indian.

Understanding Class Transformations in a Globalizing World

Only recently has class analysis begun to address how a globalizing economy is fundamentally altering the class system. Most notably, Sklair (2001) has analyzed the emergence of a transnational capitalist class that works to advance the interests of transnational corporations. Because "those who run the TNCs cannot achieve their ends alone," the class includes "globalizing bureaucrats, politicians, and professionals" who advance TNC interests (Sklair, 2001: 295). While the transnational capitalist class has an interest in promoting open markets and ensuring cheap labor, Sklair (2001: 6) also focuses on this class's interest in promoting the "culture ideology of consumerism." "Global capitalism thrives," he argues, "by persuading us that the meaning and value of our lives are to be found principally in what we possess." Sklair (2001: 11) argues that the main aim of the transnational capitalist class "is to ensure that as many people as possible consume as much as possible by inculcating beliefs about the intrinsic value of consumption as a 'good thing' and the key component of the 'good life.'" The transnational capitalist class wants to especially create the desire of everyone around the world to consume the same products. "Once television is there," one CEO opined, "people of whatever shade, culture or origin want roughly the same things" (Sklair, 2001: 255).

While Sklair emphasized the creation of a transnational capitalist class, there has so far been insufficient attention to how globalization is shaping other classes. But in inciting consumption, the transnational capitalist class ends up creating a transnational middle class, which is oriented to cosmopolitan consumption and which makes up the primary consumers fueling the capitalist system.

This study follows Weber in seeing middle classes as defining themselves in opposition to class others through cultural practices associated with consumption. Liechty's analysis of the development of the middle class in Kathmandu, Nepal, shows the usefulness of Weber's approach. Middle classes, Liechty (2003: 15) emphasizes, construct their identity "in *opposition* to its class others, above and below." Because the middle classes' contributions to production are often hidden, middle classes stake claims to status through discernment, which is often displayed through consumption. For Liechty (2003: 7) "cultures of consumerism" are part of the cultural process "through which an emerging middle class actually creates itself as a sociocultural identity." In the middle-class world, identity is based more on what you have than what you do (Liechty, 2003: 15).

Locating the Middle Classes on a Global Field

Since 1991's economic liberalization, policymakers, the English language press, and academics refer to a growing middle class in India that passionately aspires for consumer goods. With the government's economic liberalization, the cultural focus is on the consuming classes. English-language media focus on groups with money to spend on the scooters and automobiles commonly advertised in English-language outlets. Figures of up to 350 million middle-class Indians are repeated in both academic and nonacademic discourse. The image of India focuses increasingly on the Mercedes-driving, tie-wearing New Delhi-ite and less on the poor man who works and lives on a footpath, where he earns a living using a charcoal-powered iron to press the shirts of the elite. Discourse today describes world-traveling, e-mail-using, consumers of Western lifestyles as India's middle class.

But this so-called middle-class world actually applies to very few Indians. Perhaps 5 percent of Indians speak English well (Page and Crawley, 2001: 77). While estimates of a middle class that aspires for consumer goods reach 350 million, only 200 million people (20 percent of the population) own wristwatches (Gupta, 2000: 7). Just 6 percent of households have a scooter, 9 percent of households have a refrigerator, and 26 percent of households have a cassette recorder (Shurmer-Smith, 2000: 28). The often-used figure of 300 million to refer to the middle class actually refers to the possible market for items like radios, rather than consumer durables (Shurmer-Smith, 2000: 29).

The elite in India sees itself as a "middle" class only by defining itself in opposition to class others on a global field. Affluent Indians whose opportunities for consumption and employment are now shaped by global markets increasingly constitute a transnational middle class that holds the space between the poor in India and the consuming classes in rich countries. Media constantly remind Indians of the lifestyles of consuming classes abroad. Hindi films focus on NRIs (Nonresident Indians) who have become millionaires in London or Hollywood. Advertising for computer training emphasizes life abroad, describing how "two years from now 19-year-old Vijay will be driving his own car … on the other side of the globe" (Shurmer-Smith, 2000: 36). For the Indian reader, the jeans-wearing "Vijay" on a motorcycle in front of his Indian house exists between the Indian poor and the automobile-driving life on offer in "Silicon Valley, California" — the destination trumpeted by the ad.

Even though globalization has allowed elites to pursue consuming lifestyles, affluent Indians are always aware of poor Indians who support affluent Indian's consumer lifestyles. At a macroeconomic level cheap labor is India's comparative advantage. Gupta (2000: 9) points out, moreover, that at a personal level affluent Indians' "rich lifestyle" depends on the support of millions of poor people. A full-time live-in servant costs less per month than a single pizza (Shurmer-Smith, 2000: 32). In rich countries, convenience foods, including packaged flour, ground spices, and frozen dinners help provide a middle-class lifestyle, but in India low-paid servants save the wealthy from the drudgery associated with food preparation (Shurmer-Smith, 2000: 50). In rich countries, clothes washers and driers and dish washers do the work of low-paid servants in India.

Affluent Indians' perception of themselves as a transnational middle class located between the Indian poor and consumers in rich countries is generated by both structural and cultural factors. Since economic liberalization accelerated in 1991, affluent Indians today are more located on a global field. Their jobs are high paying precisely because they produce for a global market. Their lifestyles can aspire to those of consuming classes in rich countries precisely because global goods are more available. The consuming classes in India are responding to governmental policy that focuses now on providing what privileged consumers want. At the cultural level, privileged classes' perception of themselves as middle class is fueled by cable and print advertising that normalizes elite lifestyles and by hit Indian films that increasingly focus on consuming elites (Uberoi, 1998; Inden, 1999).

Despite media and academic discourses that describe consuming elites as India's middle class, people who can afford reasonable housing but can barely imagine themselves jetsetting or e-mailing also see themselves as India's middle class. Research in Madurai (Dickey, 2002: 218) and Hyderabad (Saavala, 2001: 302–303) shows ordinary middle-class people using vernacular Tamil and Telugu to call themselves "middle class" — below the "great people" who drive automobiles but well above those who live in slums, cycle miles to work, and survive day-to-day pulling rickshaws or slogging in sweatshops. The locally oriented middle class' identity is shaped by their own structural realities. Lacking English-language skills or global connections, the locally oriented Indian middle class is, in fact, limited by local markets for employment. Lacking money to buy global goods, they are, in fact, limited by local markets for consumption. Whereas the transnational middle class is oriented to new cosmopolitan worlds of opportunity, national identity remains salient for the locally oriented middle class, who can not, after all, aspire to the consuming lifestyles in rich countries.

Economic possibilities for consumption are conditioned by employment, but middle-class identity in globalizing India is nonetheless rooted in shared consumption patterns. Consumption is one way that affluent Indians advertise new ideas of taste and discernment. The transnational middle class embraces cosmopolitan consumption to identify with consuming elites in rich countries. By consuming Pepsi rather than the local Thumbs Up! or Domino's Pizza rather than roadside samosas (at a cost that might be 35 times higher) elites present themselves as cosmopolitan, transnational movers who are oriented globally rather than locally.

With the end of foreign-exchange restrictions, global goods became increasingly available, and television and advertising that glamorize consumer lifestyles incited affluent Indians' desire to consume. Media researchers Page and Crawley (2001: 150) describe Ahmedabad 17- and 18-year-olds as "openly enthusiastic about TV fashions." One young woman said that she only watches music channels for "the hairstyles, the shoes, the clothes." The dress-shop proprietors Page and Crawley (2001: 160) spoke to indicated soaring demand for fashions shown on cable television. The elite middle-class people whom Fernandes (2000: 614) interviewed saw "new choice of commodities as a central indicator of the benefits of economic liberalization." The people whom she interviewed regarded the new cultural support of consumption as crucial. Referring to the desire for cell phones and holiday homes, a magazine editor told Fernandes (2000: 614) that previously "people would feel a sense of guilt — that in a nation like this, a kind of vulgar exhibition of wealth is contradictory to Indian values. I think now consumerism has become an Indian value." When advertisers are successful, for those who can afford it, consumption is an affect-laden shared identity that supersedes even class- or nation-based affiliations (Matthews, 2000).

Gender and Middle-Class Identities

A key way affluent Indians show their orientation to cosmopolitan worlds is to embrace cosmopolitan gender arrangements and meanings, whereas a key way non-affluent Indians show their orientation to local worlds is by rejecting cosmopolitan gender arrangements. Transnational middle-class Indians show their orientation by advertising cosmopolitan ways of being male and being female. TNCs' efforts to create consumers by inciting desire for fashion and beauty affect affluent Indians. Transnational standards more and more shape affluent Indians' standards of female beauty. Thus, the well-rounded, voluptuous heroines that characterized Hindi films through the 1980s have been replaced by an emphasis on thinness, which can be attained through the purchase of gym memberships and dieting aids (Munshi, 2001). While in earlier eras, English-language fan magazines referred to Sridevi as "thunder thighs" without disapproval, today they routinely praise heroines' weight loss. One English-language fan magazine praised a heroine's workout and dieting regime for turning her "once-upon-a-time pleasantly plump person to the toned-to-almost-perfection personality" (Sai, 2001: 54). A second film magazine praises another heroine for making herself "yummy-licious" by losing "oodles of weight" through an "exercise program and spartan diet" (*Filmfare*, 2001). It is notable that such comments appear largely in English language fan magazines catering to the more affluent Hindi-film viewer.

Susan Parulekar's (n.d.) fieldwork shows that elite Mumbai women increasingly pursue these new standards of beauty through consumption and that women's pursuit of transnational standards of beauty is a key aspect of elite identity. Elite boutiques, beauty parlors, and previously unknown fitness centers are proliferating. Parulekar reports that modeling has become a hobby for affluent Mumbai women who pay US$100 or more for photo shoots. John (1998: 375) describes how advertising that caters to elite Delhi women highlights beauty treatments, weight loss programs, and "'imported services such as bleaches and perms." The affluent woman who tries to achieve a cosmopolitan look by purchasing cosmetics, up-to-date fashion, and health-club memberships uses consumption to confirm not just cosmopolitan standing, but a femininity defined by transnational standards.

For men, too, elite standards of masculinity are rooted in transnational consumption. In the 1980s, advertisements for Bajaj scooters on the back cover of the English-language newsweekly *India Today* celebrated Indianness. Emphasizing "Hamara [*our*] Bajaj," the advertisements featured smiling Sikh children riding on the back of a Bajaj piloted by their turbaned father, and rural men using their Bajaj to carry a string *charpai* (cot) along a dirt track. In 2002, a motorcycle advertisement for Bajaj's "definitely male" Pulsar graces the same privileged spot in *India Today*. There are no images of turbans, dirt tracks, or string cots. Instead, the advertisement focuses on a "design team at Bajaj" that "conceptualized and built the robust-looking Pulsar, which at a glance would have you agreeing it's definitely male." The man who purchases the Pulsar confirms his cosmopolitan status by embracing a masculinity associated with male strength. This intensified image of male strength is furthered in cable television's popular Arnold Schwarzenegger films and WWF wrestling bouts (Derné, 2002, 2004).

Affluent Indians demonstrate cosmopolitan orientation by experimenting with alternative gender arrangements trumpeted in global media. In the 1980s, urban Indian men told me that men, children, or older women did the marketing so that younger women in their teens, twenties, and thirties could be restricted to the home (Derné, 1995). As Mies (1986) argues, capitalism depends on the "housewifization" of women. Capitalists define women as housewives to avoid paying women living wages. In addition, Mies emphasizes, capitalists need housewives to fuel the consumption that is the engine for the economy. As Munshi (2001) argues, the growth of consumerist culture everywhere emphasizes women as active consumers. Thus, John (1998: 379) reports that advertising in India today often addresses women as "active and vital consumers in their own right." Advertising successfully incites women to be consumers of everything from fashion and glamour to music systems and computers.

As affluent women see themselves as consumers and embrace Western fashion, they increasingly reject restrictions to the home, moving freely in elite shopping arcades. Affluent women tell media researchers that *Ally McBeal* episodes "show the way a girl thinks" (Page and Crawley, 2001: 149–150). An MTV VJ who traveled across India says that television has made young college women more free. Even outside the metropoles, she reports, college women are enthusiastic to speak, sometimes snatching the microphone from her (Page and Crawley, 2001: 150). Media researchers report that many young women throughout India desire to participate in the musical talent shows that now run on Zee TV. One principal of a Maharashtra school says that women sometimes join colleges with the desire to appear in musical shows (Page and Crawley, 2001: 143). Although these reports may seem trivial, they do suggest an increased enthusiasm on the part of elite women to participate in events outside the home.

Global media celebrate love as a basis of marriage, and some accounts by social scientists and English-language media suggest a move away from arranged marriages. Articles in the mainstream press describe dating as becoming common for teens (Jain, 1998; Sengupta, 2001). One advertising campaign manager describes Valentine's Day marketing as increasing young people's focus on romantic love (Sengupta, 2001). A Delhi sociologist argues that Valentine's Day celebrations are making "the idea of romance" "more legitimate" (Sengupta, 2001). Sociologist Jyoti Puri (1997: 438) found that of the 101 elite Mumbai college-going female readers of English-language romance novels whom she surveyed, 98 "believed that a girl should marry out of choice" (see also Shurmer-Smith, 2000: 39–41). Although we lack systematic data, these reports show increasing acceptance of love matches among the most affluent. The transnational middle class shows its cosmopolitanism by adopting nonlocal gender arrangements.

Rejecting cosmopolitan gender arrangements, locally oriented middle-class Indians also root class identity in particular gender arrangements. They advertise a local orientation by embracing what they regard as distinctively Indian gender arrangements. By continuing to limit women's movements outside the home and rejecting dating and love marriages, the locally oriented middle class defines itself in opposition to the "big" people whom they see as excessively influenced by foreign lifestyles.

Despite the increased media celebration of love as a basis for marriage, the men whom I interviewed in 2001 remain as committed to arranged marriages as they were before the media onslaught. Virendra, a 22-year-old postgraduate engineering student likes Hindi-film love stories but remains committed to arranged marriages: "In actual life, a love marriage is not possible. I'll marry with my parents' wishes." Another 19-year-old student living in a joint family headed by a father with a professional job likes "love stories" even though they are not "possible in real life." His favorite film features a school teacher encouraging students to pursue love, but the 19-year-old remains certain that "any girl I could find for myself would not be as good as the girl my parents will find for me." Despite a decade of cultural globalization celebrating love and choice, similar percentages of young men say they want an arranged marriage (66 percent in 1991; 68 percent in 2001).

My study's comparison showing little change in ordinary middle-class Indians' attitudes toward marriage is confirmed by a number of other studies. A mid-1990s study found that 68 percent of urban college students wanted to have their parents arrange their marriage (Pathak, 1994). Page and Crawley's (2001: 176) 1998 to 1999 survey of 15-year-olds to 34-year-olds in Delhi, Mumbai, Kanpur, and Lucknow found that 65 percent tried to obey their elders "even if it hurts." Abraham's (2001) 1996 to 1998 study found that a majority of low-income college students in Mumbai thought that love marriages were unsuccessful.

Whereas transnational media have intensified favorable images of independent women who work in the paid economy, locally oriented middle-class men remain attracted to gender arrangements that limit women's public activities and freedom. Men still enjoy cinema halls as a largely male arena in which they can joke, play, and roughhouse, and emphasize how this contrasts with women's home-based lives. Tahsin, a married 25-year-old, describes his compelling attraction to Hindi films as so strong that he used to see at least one movie a day. When I asked him why he did not bring his wife of 7 years to the movies, he proudly relates that she is so "home loving" that "she even objects to seeing movies with her own husband." Other local surveys show ordinary middle-class men's ongoing attachment to gender arrangements that make women primarily responsible for home duties. Abraham's (2001: 142) interviews show most men want women to be simple, home-loving, and compromising.

Claiming status by embracing Indian gender arrangements, locally oriented middle-class men are uneasy with new media that appear to challenge these arrangements. Virendra, the postgraduate engineering student with cable television, is committed to arranged marriages and joint-family living. He likes the "smart dressing" of cosmopolitan heroes but complains that "satellite TV is making younger people too mature." Umesh, a civil draftsmen whose marriage has just been arranged, likes Hollywood movies, cable, and television, yet is disturbed by programming that "gives the message" that "a brother should allow his sister to go with her boyfriend to watch a movie. These are not good things," he says, "so they shouldn't be shown on television." This unease with global media sometimes generates protests against globalization's effect on local gender arrangements. In response to Valentine's Day, protesters attacked couples in restaurants and burned Valentine's Day cards (Sengupta, 2001). Others targeted discotheques for "spoiling the minds of youth" (*India Abroad*, 1999). The 1996 staging of the Miss World pageant in Bangalore was protested against for threatening Indian womanhood (Oza, 2001; Fernandes, 2000: 625).

Middle-class identities in India are, then, increasingly rooted in distinctive gender arrangements. A transnational middle class advertises its cosmopolitan orientation by easing restrictions on women's movements outside the home and experimenting with love marriages, whereas the locally oriented middle class advertises its Indian orientation by keeping to distinctive Indian arrangements. The divergent gender practices of the middle classes in India reflect divergent structural locations within the global economy. For the affluent, challenges to arranged marriages introduced by transnational media make sense because new institutional possibilities allow more young couples to support themselves. But because non-elite middle-class men's institutional possibilities have not similarly changed, locally oriented middle-class Indians remain committed to local gender practices.

Rethinking Class in a Global Economy

With globalization, class identity in India is increasingly defined on a global field and rooted in distinctive gender arrangements and patterns of consumption. Other recent ethnographies in India (Dickey, 2002; Saavala, 2001; Osella and Osella, 2000) and elsewhere (Chin, 1998; Liechty, 2003) confirm that middle classes define themselves in opposition to class others through consumption practices and gender patterns, suggesting that globalization may have a widespread effect on class identities. Significantly, these new insights about class dynamics emerge from ethnographic data, which are not rooted in Marxist categories, but cultural meaning.

In working to spur consumption, the transnational capitalist class creates people who are oriented to consumerism. Because they often want to make women the "agents of consumption" (Mies, 1986: 106), the transnational capitalist class creates housewives who do the "consumption work" (Mies, 1986: 125) that fuels the capitalist economy. Through these processes, the transnational capitalist class creates a transnational middle class with an identity rooted in new consumption patterns and gender arrangements. Bombarded with new media images of unattainable consumption, a locally oriented middle class instead defines itself in opposition to elites, rejecting new gender arrangements and excessive consumerism as foreign.

New global processes, then, show the limitation of understanding class as exclusively grounded in one's position in a productive system. Sklair (2001) shows that TNC executives and globalizing bureaucrats, politicians, and professionals are all part of a transnational capitalist class, which advances TNC interests, despite varying productive positions. My description of middle-class identities in India shows them to be increasingly rooted in transnational contexts rather than bounded nations, based in shared patterns of consumption more than shared positions in a productive system, and defined by particular gender relations. Position in the productive system shapes opportunities for consumption, global movement, and gender arrangements, and, so, remains an important aspect of understanding class. But to fully understand class dynamics today, we must also emphasize how class identities are defined on a global field and rooted in distinctive consumption practices and gender arrangements.

Acknowledgments

The American Institute of Indian Studies supported my 1991 and 2001 research. SUNY–Geneseo provided a sabbatical that allowed me to conduct the 2001 research. The sociology department at Delhi University sponsored both my 1991 and 2001 research. I am especially thankful to my advisors there, Veena Das and Radhika Chopra. A Rockefeller fellowship at the Office of Women's Research at the University of Hawaii in 2002 provided the time to analyze the data and think about the issues I present in this article. I am especially grateful to S. Charusheela for discussions of class analysis. In both 1991 and 2001, Narender Sethi was a capable research assistant who helped me conduct and translate interviews. I am grateful to William Robinson for asking me to present this research at the Critical Globalization Studies conference in Santa Barbara in May 2003, where I learned from responses to my presentation and from others' presentations as well.

18

Critical Globalization Studies and a Network Perspective on Global Civil Society

Barrie Axford

Introduction

Is the concept of global civil society ill suited to contribute much to a critical study of the current phase of globalization? Global civil society (GCS) is a very "now" concept, part of the cosmology that envelopes the world of the new millennium (Keane, 2003: 1). Its appeal to both researchers and activists is understandable in the context of the current world disorder, which — the conceit about "empire" notwith-standing — is somewhere between a realist set and a space of flows. On the one hand, GCS is taken to ameliorate the excesses of markets, while on the other it compensates for the fragility and systemic anarchy of states and the weak performance of the institutions of global governance (Callahan, 1999; Edwards and Gaventa, 2001; Clark, 2003; Johnson and Laxer, 2003).

In some accounts GCS is a consolation for the "rolling back" of welfare nationalism; while as part of a new iconography for the soft Left it offers a chance of redemption, albeit at the price of taking postmaterialist issues and designer activism seriously (Sader, 2002). Even Hardt and Negri's incurably romantic gloss on the "multitude" (2000) and that subset of NGOs that "represents the least among us" (p. 313) is just a cool version of what they describe as "traditional" global civil society. In short, global civil society is all things to all people. On the side of the angels because of its slightly dangerous and antisystemic feel, it also nicely rounds out eminently respect-able and liberal (thin) assumptions about the character or possible demeanor of the global polity and seems to reintroduce agency to the analytical scheme of globaliza-tion studies. Global civil society is a reassuring notion, the human face of globaliza-tion; basically, an idea whose time has come. Or has it?

Inevitably there are cautionary or dissenting voices both from the academy and beyond. Recent attempts to locate organized forms of "antisystemic" zeal in the dynamics of world-system constitution tended to treat these "cultural" phenomena as bit players kicking against the pricks of a systemic global geoculture (Wallerstein, 1991). Even in accounts not infected with theoretical pessimism, globalization from below in the form of transnational social movements is a poor, though strategically necessary, countervailing force to globalization from above. Politics or globalization from below, says Richard Falk (1999), is a strategy for offsetting the tendency for national governments to be co-opted by top–down market forces. As he notes, transnational social forces are playing a part in the development of a global civil society by forging an "innovative and variegated type of politics" that has about it some of the temper of the postmodern and the postnational (1999; Beck, 1999; Axford, 2001a).

On a more polemical note Aziz Choudry (2002) opines, "all this civil society talk takes us nowhere." Such candor is refreshing, although his strictures are aimed primarily at the ideological (read Western) cast of global civil society, rather than against the use of the concept per se. Meanwhile, Johnson and Laxer (2003) are exercised by the ontology, the "thickness," of GCS actors, especially where the effectiveness of collective action across borders relies upon only virtual connections. They write convincingly of the unctuous portrayal of an "heroic" global civil society in the battle against the Multilateral Agreement on Investment (MAI), which featured inventive and subversive use of the Internet by anti-MAI activists. But their attempt to problematize the idea of "bottom–up" globalization is hung up on the chimera of transnational solidarity and the difficulties with meeting conditions likely to promote it. In similar vein, but with less of a normative agenda, Sidney Tarrow (2002: 3) cautions against confusing the "plethora of NGOs, human rights groups, environmental and women's movements, and even public actors acting internationally outside of states," with transnational civil society, which is only one possible outcome of contentious politics.

I want to emphasize that although much of this knockabout is entirely proper and understandable in strategic terms or for hortatory purposes and normative ends, it is less than helpful for a critical study of globalization. While we need to comprehend the vagaries and impacts of transnational action, we should be clearer about whether and how the concept of GCS lends itself to an understanding of global complexity. What we have now is an extant politics in search of a theory of globalization. Of course, the powerful normative gloss on the significance of GCS is not amenable to challenge by pointing to actual features of the globalized world in which we live. But until we have a clearer understanding of the nature and dynamics of globalization we can have no theory of global civil society. At the same time — and here it gets messy — once we have an account of global system construction and dynamics we may also have reached the limits of GCS as an analytical category.

Enacting Globalization: A Structurationist Account with a Little Help from …

Global systems are networks of interaction that transcend both societal and national frames of reference. The images of globalization that do most justice to how the world is configured today are those which conjure neither a picture of global systemness on the brink of closure, nor one slouching to anarchy or dissolution. This world is "intractably disordered" (Gray, 2001) as the ontologies of modern politics and societies are altered through the routine and dramatic imbrication of the personal, the local, and the global, which is the stuff of what we mean by globalization. The disorderliness that often results is a property of dynamic systems, not (or not only) a feature of dysfunctional ones (Axford, 1995).

But how can we depict such systems and the manner of their constitution and transformation? John Urry's intriguing formulation on the nature of global complexity (2003: 98–121) offers a three-part critique of much of the social science of globalization and, by implication, I would suggest, about the concept of global civil society.

- First is its failure to break free of the national, the societal, and the territorial as the basis for social analysis. This complaint has particular relevance for any treatment of GCS, and I will return to it below.
- Second is the tendency for the global "level" to be taken for granted and globalization depicted as the force through which subglobal actors come to identify with the global.
- Finally, because it is taken as an exogenous constraint, globalization becomes a kind of reified "structure," with localities, regions, territorial states and, of course, associational actors seen as "agents." Such a model reinforces a simplistic "domination-resistance" motif of globalization rather the complex enactment of global processes.

Instead Urry argues for globalization as a theory of connections, saying, "There is no agency, no macro, and no micro levels and no system-world and no life-world. This is because each such notion presumes that there are entities with separate and distinct essences that are brought into external juxtaposition with each other … " and "the linear metaphor of scales, such as that stretching from micro to macro level, or from life world to system world … should thus be replaced by the metaphor of connections" (2003: 122; see also, Dicken et al., 2001; Axford, 1995). Phenomena denoted by terms such as "local," "global," "technology," and "identity" have to be rethought "as a constellation of complex, reflexive systems, and self-organizing exchanges and transactions linked to wider systems of power and influence" (Hand and Sandywell, 2002). All this avoids the picture of an integrated and relatively stable global system and its derivative or theoretically subordinate local and networked recipients, where interaction leaves the latter feisty but, at best, relatively powerless and, at worst, as passive and unreflective: consumers, users of technology, viewers, and so on. In the new formulation globalization commutes from being either an overdetermined effect (of capitalist relations, cultural domination, or hegemonic aspiration) or an obvious cause (of GCS) to an "heterogeneous field of world-making practices" (Hand and Sandywell, 2002: 213).

According to Urry (and many complexity theorists) world-making practices have a powerful and necessary emergent quality revealed in the imbrications of local and global, through the interplay of global scapes and contingent glocal actors, and through various "networks, fluids, and governance institutions" (2003: 103; Appadurai, 1990, 1996). Although this still seems rather allusory, it has a number of advantages for the study of global systems.

First, agency remains critical to the account of global dynamics, but not as part of an analytic dualism that reduces questions of relationality to arguments about shades of dominance.

Second, the complaint that the extreme form of contingency found in complexity theory can do no more than caricature the social, is countered by Urry's bold claim that "relationality is brought about through a wide array of networked or circulating relationships that are implicated within increasingly overlapping and convergent material worlds" (2003: 122).

In global systems, the radical autonomy of local systems is modified by the host of formal and informal networks — interdiscursive, economic, political, religious, and so on — that cross the phenomenal and imagined boundaries of localities. In the "construction" of Europe taking place through cross-border networks such as eris@ and TeleCities, localities are no longer just local, although in other ways the distinctiveness of place can be sustained and promoted (Axford and Huggins, 2003; Dai, 2003; Sassen, 2002). Networked individualism, too, is on the increase, breaking with previous forms of social organization. This is a time, says Barry Wellman, "for individuals and their networks, not for groups" (2002: 2).

Third, order and disorder now appear as emergent properties of global systemness rather than as contradictory states vying for the core identity of the system. This reflection underlines the sense that global systems — indeed, all social systems — consist of a surface appearance of stability set in an energy or flux (Axford, 1995). The idea of a system as a flow or an energy rather than an order allows for relationships within it to be generative and degenerative, as the identities of actors and institutions are reproduced through processes of cultural enactment, autopoetic self-reflection, and reflexivity, without loss of systemic energy.

In global systems, agents not only interact with a dominant set of structural and cultural properties, largely based on the foundational principle of territoriality, but by intersecting, overlapping, and sometimes contradictory sets, where institutional scripts and the identities linked to them or dependent upon them — local, national, democratic, gender, welfare, inter- and supranational, and so on — intersect. One of the effects, perhaps the single most important effect of these changes for any discussion of GCS — for agency — is to problematize what constitutes a political sphere or a social and cultural order and who are to be allotted roles as legitimate and competent actors in them.

The labile qualities of globalization as described above point to processes that are reshaping the contours of social action and redefining the space of the political and the identity spaces of individuals and collective actors. This transformative capacity should inform how we interpret both the prospects for world society and how we intimate it through notions such as global civil society and cosmopolitanism. Furthermore, we cannot understand what is clearly a paradigm shift by dusting off old models based on one or another "domestic analogy" (Hardt and Negri, 2000: 8).

Global Civil Society: Use It or Lose It?

Critics of the unreflective use of the concept of global civil society might well consider Sidney Tarrow's cautionary words that it is a teleological construct that assumes what needs to be demonstrated (2002: 1). His critique forces us to look carefully at whether *transnational civil society* is a concept tied to empirical referents or part of a "strong" version of "globalspeak" that "congeals" and confuses the complex relations between nonstate actors, international institutions and norms, transnational activist networks, and transnational social movements. With this stricture in mind, I will address four areas of concern in greater detail. The issues are:

- Practical obstacles to constituting GCS, especially in ideal-typical guise
- The tendency to conflate different kinds of transnational collective action under the banner of GCS
- The question of relationality, especially where this applies to relations between civil society actors and states
- The society focus of much GCS discourse

Claims to discern a fructive GCS or the conditions that can promote it admit a range of criticisms. Johnson and Laxer (2003: 43) portray the anti-MAI and Zapatista struggles as rooted in well-developed and preexisting social movements at the national level. They opine, "How can a global civil society emerge with a unitary vision among multicultured, multitongued peoples, divided by miles of space and oceans of inequality?" (p. 42). Their answer, of course, is that it cannot, because "common feelings about the injustice of globalism are not a sufficient condition for the mobilization of diverse peoples" (p. 43). Now, although this may be intuitively persuasive, it uses a skewed index (transnational solidarity forged through the ideology of antiglobalization) to gauge the extent and intensity of what could be a modal phenomenon (a networked globality). Johnson and Laxer are looking for widespread evidence of particular kinds of "beyond-the-nation solidarity links" (p. 43) before they will even entertain the idea of a global civil society. Broadly speaking, this evidence would have to reveal "deep feelings of identity and solidarity" (p. 43) not usually available, they say, outside national domains and shared local experience.

At the same time they are prepared to admit that, in the case of Zapatismo "solidarity," the (inter)networked basis for uniting actors across time and space is a vibrant example of the attempt to create democratic multinational spaces. This is good social science except for the sense that they have primarily aesthetic objections to the role of the internet in promoting and sustaining transnational, or any, activism. Their reservations about "virtual activism" go beyond necessary caution over the extent to which information and communications technology (ICT) plays a part in initiating action, revealing a more profound concern; namely, that although ICTs disseminate information quickly, they cannot reproduce or even mimic "thick" national or local forms of community or solidarity. Nor are they alone in this belief. Sidney Tarrow (2002) talks rather dismissively of activists catching the Internet "virus," while elsewhere he betrays a deep unease about the very ontology of transnational virtual networks. He worries that such networks cannot deliver the same "crystallization of mutual trust and collective identity" as the interpersonal ties found, for example, among the founders of nineteenth century socialism or Islamic fundamentalism (1996: 14).

But being home alone with the Net is no substitute for "face-to-face-social movement connections" (Johnson and Laxer, 2003: 73). The suspicion is that the Net is a medium through which people construct and reconstruct their individuality rather than a vehicle or context to foster civic association or communities of affect. Aesthetic concerns about virtual connection as the basis for transnational activism have a provenance common to many critiques of the impact of "new" and especially digital media on politics (Axford and Huggins, 2001). The idea of virtual networks, or even networks that use virtual connectivity, sits rather uneasily with any bog-standard model of "thick" identities and cultures. Thick cultures are seen as the basis for cohesive movements and stable communities; they are elemental and binding. By contrast, virtual networks are not real communities or expressions of a true demos. Somewhere (runs the argument) Net exchanges have been robbed of — or else never possessed — sensual qualities and moral weight.

This may be a hard position to maintain. Virtual networks do not banish the world entirely and are seldom free of the problems that plague phenomenal organizations — insider and outsider and powerful and powerless — so why should connectivity remove other characteristics of human interaction? There is no immanent reason why socially desirable attributes like trust must be absent from Net exchanges just because agents are interfaced through a modem and a screen — just ask devotees of eBay. It is also true that research on the use of the Internet in political processes generally is in its infancy (Axford and Huggins, 2001; Rodgers, 1999; Tsagarousianou et al., 1998). Important questions remain unanswered or only partially resolved. Are people likely to become politically engaged through the Internet if they are not so enthused in the phenomenal world? Does Internet activism promote only narrowly focused, issue-oriented political involvement? Is virtual involvement strong enough to initiate action in the "real" world of adversary politics? Can it create and sustain strong identities across borders?

Some research on Internet activism suggests that people are not likely to become politicized through the Net unless they are already politically aware and engaged (Tsagarousianou et al., 1998). But organizations like Friends of the Earth now find that some 80 percent of their online traffic comes from nonmembers, and much of this derives from general searches for environmental issues rather than from deliberate attempts to link to the organization's URL (Rodgers and Gauntlett, 2003). Even this datum raises more questions than it answers. Need an online persona reflect offline identities and interests? Does extensive use of the Internet promote a kind of bespoke individualism over what sites are visited or is it an extension of group tastes and mores? How do different constituencies of activist and nonactivist use the Internet? In particular, can it both subvent what I have called "bespoke individualism" and contribute to the embedding and further networking of group norms and collective network personas?

Elsewhere (Axford, 2001b), I have noted that virtual networks enable diasporic public spheres (Appadurai, 1996); subvent ethnicity by e-mail (Rex, 1998: 83), sustain the activities of a tranche of INGOs and social movements, and provide a degree of information, support, and opportunities for friendship for a host of people ill served by the public services in the "real" civic spaces where they live out their lives. Although this still may not demonstrate that virtuality can constitute identity, maybe we should not worry. The notion of identity draws on imagery of communities and cultures that are rooted in "thick" national experience (Aksoy and Robins, 2002). The upshot is that new forms of transnational modalities are often judged through the lens and with the moral purview of the national imaginary (Aksoy and Robins, 2002: 3), yet the reality is more complex. Writing about transnational communications in the context of diasporic cultures, Aksoy and Robins argue that Turkish migrants who routinely watch transnational satellite television are not simply reproducing "Turkishness" as members of a diasporic audience but enacting new kinds of "transnational mobilities" that redefine the migrant experience and ways of thinking about it. Their research underlines the analytical necessity and the emotional sense of treating new and, especially, digital media as part of a cultural shift in the tenor of life in posthistorical societies under global constraints, rather than as instrumentalities tacked onto a real world of politics and social relations. The results of this shift could be modalities, which may — but may not — reproduce conventionally "thin" or "thick" identities and imaginaries (Kellner, 2001; Dahlgren, 2001; Aksoy and Robins, 2002).

Yet the establishment of transnational connections through "thick web(s) of regular and instantaneous communication" (Portes et al., 1999: 217) does not mean that cross-national collective action (virtual or otherwise) is easy (Klandermans, 1997; McAdam et al., 2001). Neither the existence of "objective" conditions found in the environments of would-be movements and networks nor perceived common cause (imagined community) are of themselves sufficient to build cross-border movements. One of the primary obstacles noted by students of collective action is the alleged difficulty of extending social networks of trust and reciprocity across borders, especially when the issue-attention cycle is in the downturn. As a corollary, the "embeddedness" of identities — in particular, social networks and cultural scripts — also inhibits the creation of "detached" or purposive identities that can traffic across borders, mobilizing and uniting disparate activists (Melucci, 1996; McAdam et al., 2001). Yet skeptics such as Sidney Tarrow are willing to acknowledge the extent to which obstacles have been overcome — for example, in the case of militant Islam — or can be overcome (2002).

Further confusion arises from a tendency to conflate quite different kinds of actors under the umbrella of global civil society, traducing one of the basic rules of good social science: the importance of careful typology. Keck and Sikkink say, rightly, "to understand how change occurs in world politics, we have to address the quite different logics and process among the different categories of transnational actors" (1998: 210). It seems right to distinguish between global or transnational social movements, international nongovernmental organizations, transnational advocacy networks, and epistemic communities. By doing so we can discern differences in aspirations, objectives, resource pools, membership, tactics, political demeanor, and spatial reach.

Which brings me back to the issue of *relationality*, and the relationships between state and nonstate actors. The clearest danger here is to traffic the image of a dynamic global civil society somehow uncoupled from the trammels of history, resources, and statist constraint. States remain ubiquitous actors, and what they do offers at least a context for transnational activism. At most, state action subvents or precipitates transnational action. Tarrow reminds us that Western states especially are "deeply implicated in the funding and promotion of many transnational actors" (2002: 18; Uvin, 2000). State policies trigger action because they are still the "prime targets and fulcra of political exchange" (Tarrow, 2002: 3).

Yet inter-national institutions, formed through cooperation between states, and forms of advanced multilateralism such as the European Union also enable the construction of networks and even identities across borders. For example, the European Parliament and Commission have done much to encourage the setting up of transnational immigrant networks, seeking to provide a common platform through which such actors can treat with the Union and its member states (Kastoryano, 2002). The prospects for transnational activism and governance in the EU are visible, too, in the scope for European publics to emerge around valence issues, and through the networking of localities and "natural" economic zones across borders (Axford and Huggins, 1999; Tarrow, 2002; Dai, 2003). Still, we must avoid jumping to the conclusion that the space of most collective identities has already become de-territorialized due to the "fluidization of regulatory space" (Lipschutz, 2000), to migration, to various kinds of networks across borders and, as a paradigm case, the creation of digital networks.

But the most telling critique of the idea of global civil society is that which questions the appropriateness of the model of liberal civil society to inform analysis of global complexity. In a recent exegesis, John Keane (2003) argues for rejecting the "governmentality" still found in much international relations theory, in favor of a "nongovernmental social sphere that is called global civil society" (2003: 22). The burden of his critique is that we must not place undue emphasis on the old levels of analysis problem. Here that means treating domestic (local) and global "civil societies" as separate zones of identity and action. In such neutered accounts territory is seen as the ultimate foundation of civil society institutions and "the global" appears as "a homeless, extra-territorial phenomenon" (2003: 23; Brenner, 1997). Instead, the simplistic notion of local and global "levels" should commute to what I described earlier as a heterogeneous field of world-making practices. The modern geopolitical imagination, wedded to the isomorphism of people, territory, and culture is ill-equipped to offer a firm analytical purchase on forces such as ICTs that are altering the frame of agency and may be rendering conventional territorialities and subjectivities ambiguous. As David Harvey notes (1990: 240), despatializing processes "so revolutionize the objective qualities of space and time that we are forced to alter … how we represent the world to ourselves."

And it is this matter of representing the world that is crucial in assessing the usefulness of the concept global civil society for an analysis of global complexity. The continued attraction of the "neo-Tocquevillian gaze" (Shapiro, 1997), with its penchant for democratic civil societies organized as territorial states, still blinds us to the need for a critical model of social and political space (Shapiro: 8) and glosses how we evaluate different "spatial and temporal imaginaries" (p. 2).

A Networked Globality?

In a recent paper on the value of conceptual syncretism in the social sciences, Ulf Hannerz (2002) talks about the ways in which "flows, boundaries, and hybrids" now inform the conceptual landscape of the social science of globalization. Networks, especially social networks (because there are cognate terms, which suggest connection but not necessarily agency) fall into the same category. The ubiquity of the concept makes it both attractive for the analysis of global dynamics and promotes a dangerously convenient catchall mentality. In reality, networks have different topologies that produce a variety of networked relationships, some relatively contained by geographical and territorial boundaries, others manifestly global. Attempts to map social movement networks (Diani, 2000) and to assess the importance of social networks on recruitment to social movements (Passy, 2000), reveal complex topologies and network structures. These demonstrate varying intensities of identity with the movement, different patterns of centralization–decentralization, and different spatial scales.

The advantages of the network perspective for the study of globalization are clear.

Hannerz says that the global ecumene is a network of networks where individuals and groups are drawn into a more globalized existence, and the morphology of networks facilitates this shift (1996). Networks can be intra- and interorganizational, as well as transorganizational, and can cut across conventional levels of analysis to link different personal and institutional domains (Axford, 1995: 78–82). Most appropriate to the global setting, networks can structure social relationships without constraint of place or the need for co-presence.

The network perspective foregrounds those increasingly widespread and diverse forms of transnational mobilization, where relationships may be either long-distance or involve a mixture of presence and absence, of coming together and moving apart, of brief encounters on the telephone, of one-to-one or many-to-many exchanges on the Net. The strength of the network metaphor is that it captures the openness of social relationships, which may not involve only economic or market exchanges, and are not just governed by administrative rules, the systematic use of power, or the constraints of place. Network analysis portrays a looseness and diversity, which go some way to capturing the inchoate character of contemporary globalization, and offers a glimpse of the diverse contexts through which a more acute consciousness of the world is occurring for many people.

Final Thoughts

In striving for critical globalization studies we must reflect on the making of a thoroughly, if contentiously, globalized world and subject commonly used and highly plausible concepts to proper scrutiny. Constructing a picture of global complexity, as I have used that idea here, means taking issue with one of the most widely used and normatively potent concepts available in both academic and activist discourses, that of global civil society. I have tried to show that a critical take on contemporary globalization does not require — indeed, is weakened — through use of the concept, rooted as it is in liberal and territorialist assumptions about the nature, spaces, and thickness of association. Instead I have offered a glimpse of a networked globality that allows us to engage with the changed social morphologies of the global on their own terms. By doing so, we retain those key attributes of human social intercourse — civility, community, and democracy — and we gain a better analytical purchase on a world now intractably disordered and likely to remain so.

19

Critical Globalization Studies and International Law under Conditions of Postmodernity and Late Capitalism

A. Claire Cutler

Law is ubiquitous today. Whether one focuses upon the proliferation of subnational, national, regional, or global legal regimes, the conclusion that we are living in an age of legality is inescapable. Nationally and subnationally, the emergence and expansion of the administrative state after the Second World War contributed significantly to the development and expansion of national and local legal systems. Although we have seen considerable retrenchment of the state in some areas of national jurisdiction as neoliberal market discipline replaces welfare states with competition states, in other areas such as administrative, taxation, and immigration laws, we are seeing an intensification of legal discipline. Regionally, there has been a major expansion of law in the European Union (EU) and in other regional economic legal regimes, such as the North-American Free Trade Agreement (NAFTA) and the Canada–U.S. Free Trade Agreement (CUSTA). The creation of international institutions engaged in the progressive development of international law under the auspices of the United Nations (UN) after the Second World War and a growing network of nongovernmental institutions involved in the unification and harmonization of law are forming the foundations for the global rule of law (see Honnold, 1995). In addition, the evolution of the General Agreement on Tariffs and Trade (GATT) into the World Trade Organization (WTO) has contributed significantly to what is often referred to as the "legalization of world politics" (Abbott et al., 2000) and the "globalization of law" (Fried, 1997; Twining, 1996). Furthermore, the emergence of a transnational economic legal regime, the modern law merchant, holds the great promise of a global commercial code and a global business culture and civilization, at least for some (see Cutler, 2003). The intensification of global legal discipline is manifested, as well, in noneconomic areas involving the expansion of constitutional protections for human rights in national, regional, and global legal regimes. These developments are accompanied by a globalization of the judicial world (L'Heureux-Dubé, 1998–1999: 16) and have been aptly characterized as "a world-historical transformation" involving the "rise of world constitutionalism" (Ackerman, 1997: 774, 771).

These developments involve the activities of numerous diverse participants working at a variety of levels, including the subnational, national, and transnational coordination of legal regimes regulating trade, investment, taxation, immigration, crime, and administrative and constitutional standards (see Burley, 1992). Governmental and nongovernmental actors and agencies are involved in these processes, reflecting an interesting mix of private and public authority (see Hall and Biersteker, 2002; Cutler et al., 1999). In fact, nongovernmental actors are increasingly significant in global governance today (see Higgott et al., 2000).

Boaventura de Sousa Santos (1987: 298) identifies similar developments with a postmodern conception of law, observing that "legal life is constituted by the intersection of different legal orders, that is by *interlegality*." Interlegality involves both the globalization of local legal forms and traditions (globalized localism), as well as the localization of global legal forms and traditions (localized globalism) (Santos, 1995). Postmodern law takes on a form specific to conditions of late capitalism, which is defined here in terms of increasingly competitive transnationalized and globalized capital formation and relating patterns of flexible accumulation (see Cutler, 2003). While globalization involves "the intensification of worldwide social relations, which link distant localities in such a way that local happenings are shaped by events occurring miles away and vice versa" (Giddens, 1990: 64), the processes by which local and global events are linked are multiple and complex. They involve more than internationalization, liberalization, universalization, and Westernization, although these processes figure prominently in many current definitions. Scholte (2003, 6–7) argues that a fifth conception of "transplanetary" and "supraterritorial" connections between people that represents globalization as "a shift in the nature of social space" better captures "historically relatively new conditions" in the world. The emphases upon changes in "spatiality" resulting from the increasing extensity and intensity of "supraterritorial relations" and on "globality in the sense of the world as a single social space" delink our understandings of globalization from territorial and statist definitions of political economy and society. Methodologically, the focus on globalization as supraterritoriality better captures transplanetary ecology, global social movements, and transnational capitalism. It is also very useful for sorting out the ways in which law is globalizing and creating a transnationalized legal field. Transnational law produces significant tensions between local and global politico-legal orders, as well as between those identified as the analytical "subjects" and "objects" or "insiders" and "outsiders," respectively, of the emerging transnational legal order.

However, notwithstanding a general recognition of the growing ubiquity and plurality of legal orders involving a multiplicity of different actors and geographical and territorial spaces, law "still seems inherently national" (Slaughter, 1999–2000: 1103). Indeed, since the formation of the European state system, Western law has been regarded as intimately and unavoidably bound up with the state (see Poggi, 1978). Even international law, despite pretensions to universality, has been conceived, at least since the replacement of initially divine and later natural law with positivist origins, as an international legal order.

Indeed, Antony Anghie (1999: 2–3) notes that "the central theoretical debate of the discipline [of international law] over the last century" has been "how can legal order be created among sovereign states?" Anghie here articulates the legal positivist postulate that international law can be no more than exactly that: a law between sovereigns. International law is that law created by the explicit consent (international treaties and conventions) or implicit consent (customary international law) of its subjects, which are states. Law is thus traced to the willing actions of subjects, who are identified as sovereign states. The analytical foundations of international law reflect and, indeed, constitute this statist universe. The doctrine governing international legal personality, or subjects doctrine, identifies states as the "subjects" of the legal order, filtering out nonstate personalities and identities, which are curiously regarded as "objects" of the legal order. Sources doctrine similarly constructs a statist legal universe by limiting the authoritative sources of law to the pronouncements of states (Cutler, 2001a). Analytically and theoretically these doctrines serve to demarcate the international legal universe as an intersovereign domain, excluding from identification as subjects nonsovereign entities, such as individuals, women, non-European, aboriginal, and indigenous peoples, and social movements (Anghie, 1999; Cutler, 2001a). Excluded, as well, are transnational corporations and private business associations, which as private entities lack persona under public international law.

This is not to suggest that states and territoriality no longer matter for law under conditions of postmodernity and late capitalism. Indeed, what is distinctive about the contemporary transnationalization of the legal field is the discontinuous and uneven forms that transnationalized legal relations take. In many cases, law operates dialectically, creating deterritorialized relations, transactions, and agreements, but then reterritorializes them to enable their legal enforcement (see Cutler, 2003: 20). This is the way that transnationalized economic law, human rights law, and the growing corpus of transnationalized administrative, judicial, and constitutional interpretive practices are instantiated as enforceable norms. Transnationalized legal discipline is forced back to territoriality because law enforcement remains a prerogative of the state. However, the processes and norms involved in enforcing transnational legal discipline are increasingly outcomes of private, nonstate actors and private, nonstate law. This reflects an expansion of the private sphere of economy and markets and a contraction, or even a displacement, of the public sphere of polity and governments.

This is a very troubling situation for it suggests that international legal theory, which is premised upon the authority of the territorial state and state law, is at odds with political realities where nonstate actors and nonstate law are increasingly authoritative (see Cutler, 2001b). Moreover, it suggests that the development of a critical understanding of transnational law poses a profound challenge to the analytical and theoretical foundations of statist and territorial international law. Indeed, it is here argued that critical globalization studies in law means the development of a critical understanding of the dialectical relationship between the deterritorialization and reterritorialization of law. This involves understanding the forces that are driving the transnationalization of the legal field, as well as the political, economic, and social interests that are served by it. Critical theory interrogates "who gets what" from the transnationalization of law. This requires developing a political economy of law, both contemporaneously and historically, as the present global political economy contains traces of both the past and the future. A first step involves identifying the material interests served by transnationalized legal rhetoric and the emerging juridical culture of late capitalism. This culture transnationalizes legal disciplines that constitutionalize certain rights to identity, citizenship, and subjectivity in the world and forecloses, marginalizes, and peripheralizes others that are challenging the foundations of international law by seeking recognition as subjects of the legal order.

Challenges to the Foundations of International Law

Conditions of postmodernity and late capitalism provide fertile ground for the emergence of numerous challenges to the statist and territorial foundations of international law. Analytically and theoretically, it is becoming increasingly difficult to account for changing practices concerning both the subjects and sources of international law. Although, in theory, states and to a limited extent international organizations, as determined by member states, are the authoritative subjects of international law, nonstate entities are increasingly functioning authoritatively. Interlegality and transnationlized law are driven by individuals, groups, corporations, and private business associations. In some cases, such as the transnationalization of merchant law, a mix of public and private actors participate in norm creation and dispute resolution. This association forms an elite group or *mercatocracy*, the name derived from the medieval law merchant order (*lex mercatoria*) engaged in the transnationalization of commercial law. The laws governing social relations are also being transnationalized in the modeling of national constitutions on texts developed through multilateral negotiations and in the globalization of the principles guiding national judiciaries. Nonstate actors figure prominently in the development of global standards governing labor relations, human rights and criminality. Moreover, the de facto "subject" status enjoyed by these nonstate entities is mirrored in the increasing authority of nonstate sources of law. Although international treaties and customary law are identified as the main authoritative sources of law, increasingly the pronouncements of international institutions such as General Assembly resolutions, the directives of private business associations and "soft law" form the infrastructure of transnational legal discipline. Soft law may be defined as "guidelines of conduct … which are neither strictly binding norms of law, nor completely irrelevant political maxims, and operate in the grey zone between law and politics" (Malanczuk, 1997: 54). Soft law is becoming increasingly significant in the regulation of the global political economy and global environment. Soft laws may be found in model laws, statements of principle, treaties not yet in force, and in resolutions of international conferences and organizations.

Subjects and Sources of Transnational Law

Challenges to the state-centricity of subject and sources doctrines emanate from a variety of entities, including transnational business corporations, private business associations, individuals, groups, and global social movements. Each will be briefly addressed in turn.

Transnational corporations and private business associations have a rich history in the creation of transnational governance relations in a number of issue areas and sectors, such as maritime transport and trade law, trade and investment laws, intel-lectual property law, commodity trade, telecommunications, electronic commerce, financial standards, and banking (see Cutler et al., 1999). The transnational legal activities of private corporate actors are increasingly significant in an expanding range of areas, including the development of corporate labor, environmental, information technology and privacy standards, and biotechnology (see Haufler, 2001). The ana-lytical, theoretical, and normative significance of private, corporate involvement in the development of transnationalized law cannot be understated. Analytically, these entities are not "subjects" of the international legal order. They are "objects" whose legal personality is filtered through the lens of state sovereignty. This means that they must rely on states to turn their legal unification initiatives into binding international law.

As private entities, business corporations and associations are incapable of creating "hard" international law, but must operate through the agency of national govern-ments to bring their standards into law. However, their standardizing initiatives are very influential as "soft law" and, like General Assembly resolutions that over time acquire the status of customary international law, many of these privatized codes and rules have become law through constant usage over time. What is important to note is that there are different political economies and power relations associated with transnationalization through hard or soft law. Commercial actors from developing states and weaker economies tend to prefer the use of hard law negotiated at a multilateral conference as it is more transparent, inclusive, and potentially more responsive to the protection of the weaker party in international economic relations (see Sempasa, 1992; Abbott and Snidal, 2000). Predictably, developed and more powerful economic actors tend to prefer soft law, which is voluntary, more porous, discretionary, and easier to breach with impunity (Cutler, 1999). Indeed, William Scheuerman (1999 and 2000) argues that the tendency to use soft, porous, and discretionary legal mechanisms in the areas of international trade, banking, business taxation, and dispute resolution constitutes a profound challenge to conventional understandings of the "rule of law." The increasing regularity of unifying corporate law through soft, malleable, and discretionary standards is a dimension of transna-tional legal discipline that requires critical analysis with a view to determining the winners and losers in soft legal regulation.

Paradoxically, the increased presence of corporations and private business associ-ations in the transnationalization of the corporate legal field is spilling over into other areas typically regarded as matters of mandatory national legislation. These include the privatization of dispute settlement concerning competition laws, taxation laws, consumer protection laws, intellectual property, and environmental protection laws. International commercial arbitration in private facilities and according to privatized legal regimes has replaced adjudication in national courts of law (Dezalay and Garth, 1996; Cutler, 1995). This is working a significant privatization of the legal field, an expansion of private power, and the constitutionalization of the rights of corporations as global citizens (see Cutler, 2000). Indeed, under bilateral investment treaties entered into under the auspices of the International Centre for the Settlement of Investment Disputes, an institution created by the World Bank, corporations are granted the right to sue states directly, notwithstanding their legal invisibility as subjects of international law. NAFTA and CUSTA also provide rights of access to binational arbitration panels for nonstate parties (see Cutler, 2000), as too do claims tribunals discussed below.

When we turn to consider the changing status of individuals and groups under international law, an expansion of effective personality that is challenging the analytical and theoretical foundations of international law is also notable. It was mentioned earlier that individuals, as well as groups, lack personality as "subjects" of international law. Like corporations, they are "objects" whose legal existence is determined by states. The subject–object dichotomy thus locates the individual under international law. The individual as an object of international law is incapable of exercising rights or bearing duties as a citizen. The subject–object dichotomy that constitutes the analytical core of the doctrine governing international legal personality places the individual outside or on the periphery of the international legal realm. However, over time and in a variety of fora individuals or groups of individuals and peoples have been accorded increased rights of participation in international law. A growing list of indicators suggests that individuals and people are staking out a place in international law. The examples identified here are the workings of the International Labour Organization, the operations of the Iran–United States Claims Tribunal and United Nations Claims Commission, the increasing caseloads under the European Convention on Human Rights and the First Optional Protocol of the International Covenant on Civil and Political Rights, and the creation of the International Criminal Court.

The International Labour Organization (ILO) is the oldest instance where nonstate participants have been integrated into the development of legal standards and as such is an historical anomaly. From its inception in 1919, the ILO involved individuals and labor relations groups in its operations (see Brownlie, 1998). The ILO regulates labor-related human rights through a series of international conventions and monitoring mechanisms. It establishes minimum standards governing freedom of association, the right to organize, collective bargaining, abolition of forced labor, equality of opportunity and treatment, and other standards relating to the work environment. However, it is important to note that the ILO lacks enforcement capacity, which remains the prerogative of member states.

The Iran–United States Claims Tribunal was created under the Algiers Accords that ended the 1981 hostage crisis at the U.S. Embassy in Iran. It hears cases from U.S. and Iranian nationals, both individual and corporate, as well as interstate claims. The Tribunal has been successful in resolving the majority of filed claims (see Brower, 1998).

The United Nations Claims Commission established as part of the 1991 Gulf War ceasefire also hears individual claims; however, they must be submitted by governments on behalf of the individual as a national. Stateless people or unrepresented parties, such as Palestinians, may, however, make claims (see Artz and Luckashuk, 1998: 168).

The longest experience of individual access to judicial arenas is the Court of Justice for the European Union (EU), to which individuals may in limited circumstances bring claims against the organs of the EU but not against states or other individuals (see Artz and Lukashuk, 1998: 163). However, the increasing caseloads of individual claims under the First Optional Protocol (OP) to the International Covenant on Civil and Political Rights (ICCPR) and the European Convention on Human Rights (ECHR) suggest that they form the major supranational legal avenues open to individuals. The ICCPR is one of two major covenants (the International Covenant on Economic, Social, and Cultural Rights being the other) that push the explicit rights of the individual beyond the basic Universal Declaration of Human Rights.

Another permanent legal avenue open to individuals is provided for under the European Convention on Human Rights. Much like the Optional Protocol, the Convention allows individuals to take their grievances directly to a supranational body. In fact, the increasing caseload under the Convention prompted the establishment of a full-time European Court of Human Rights to deal with the volume of claims. This court replaced the European Commission on Human Rights in 1998, and the latter was dissolved the following year.

Together these international and regional fora for the articulation of human rights claims by individuals effectively illustrate how avenues and space are being opened up to individuals. Although they undoubtedly push up against the boundaries of international law, it is the creation of the International Criminal Court (ICC) that constitutes perhaps the greatest challenge analytically, theoretically, and normatively. The Rome Statute creating the ICC represents a significant transformation of individual duties and responsibilities under international law. Although earlier tribunals established in Nuremberg and Tokyo after the Second World War articulated the principle of individual responsibility, they were always subject to criticism as merely manifestations of the "victors' justice" and attributed little enduring legal effect. The tribunals created to deal with atrocities committed in the former Yugoslavia and Rwanda are subject to limitations deriving from their ad hoc nature as creations of the United Nations Security Council with jurisdictional limitations to egregious crimes committed in those territories. The inadequacies of the international legal order in holding individuals accountable in any regular and predictable way for acts of genocide and other violations of human rights are obvious. The International Court of Justice can only entertain cases involving states, and the traditional means of accountability through the doctrine of state responsibility has allowed individuals to hide behind state borders and claim refuge under the guise of state sovereignty.

The creation of the ICC marks a shift from the traditional view of state sovereign responsibility to individual culpability under international law, reflecting a major change in the normative foundations for dealing with certain kinds of mass violence perpetrated by states.[1] It reflects a marked departure from the attitudes expressed some 40 or 50 years ago that "justice of any sort, in principle as in execution, emanates from the State"[2] and about the impossibility of an international criminal law regime.[3] Although there are significant limitations to the potential practical success of the ICC, the opposition of the United States being a major one (see Wedgewood, 1999), and there is the potential that the court will function merely to contain disorders in the periphery, its theoretical and normative significance cannot be disputed. What is noteworthy about the creation of the ICC is the significant contribution of nongovernmental organizations (NGOs). The Coalition of NGOs for the Establishment of an International Criminal Court assisted in convening the diplomatic conference in

Rome and contributed greatly to raising the awareness among states and peoples of the need for the ICC. The coalition was made up of some 800 organizations and of the 236 NGOs accredited to participate in the conference, only a few were not coalition members. It has been noted that the "fruit of NGO involvement in the process of the establishment of the Court is the Rome Statute which, while not without imperfections, reflects the most fundamental concerns of civil society, and exceeds the expectations of even the most optimistic observers going to the Rome Conference" (Pace and Thieroff, 1999: 391).

NGOs have also been very active in the development of international environmental law and the rights of women and children, suggesting that the state-centric foundations of international law are indeed undergoing transformation (see Clarke et al., 1998). These developments along with those relating to the participation of peoples' movements, which have traditionally been peripheralized by international law, are possibly the most notable aspects of the transnationalization of contemporary international legal order. Although aboriginal and indigenous peoples, for example, still have a long way to go in order to constitute subjects of international law, there are hints of movement afoot to recognize their unique character. It is estimated that from one hundred to two hundred million people in over forty states may be regarded as indigenous people (Malanczuk, 1997: 106). An NGO, the Unrepresented Nations and Peoples Organization (UNPO), has been established at The Hague to promote the rights of indigenous people. The United Nations Commission on Human Rights adopted a Draft UN Declaration on the Rights of Indigenous Peoples in 1994 and in the following year established a Working Group on the Draft Declaration (ibid, and see Anya, 1996). The Rio Declaration on Environment and Development recognizes the unique identity, culture, and interests of indigenous peoples, suggesting a modest beginning for the recognition of identity and subjectivity under international law.

Together, transformations in the subjects and sources of international law are pushing against the analytical and theoretical foundations of international law with significant normative implications. Analyzing the nature of these developments and understanding their significance in terms of determining "who gets what" make contemporary international law a perfect site for critical globalization studies.

Toward Critical Globalization Studies in International Law

Transformations in the subjects and sources of international law go to the very heart of the legal order and confront the analyst with important questions concerning the purposes served by international law. This is because international law confers identity on some, but not on others. Others, like individuals, women, and indigenous people inhabit the periphery of the international legal order, at best as its "objects." Indeed, the denotation of a "subject" requires the existence of an "object" in order to conceptualize "the rest." In this sense, the subjects and objects of international law stand as opposites in their doctrinal treatment, but at the same time they form a mutually constitutive relationship whereby each depends upon the other for its existence. As such, the idea of subject doctrine as constituted by subjects and objects is merely a rhetorical device and a legal fiction that requires critical analysis and eval-uation. Moreover, to the extent that we might analyze the subject and object as constituting a dynamic dialectical relationship that is undergoing transformation, this dimension of the transnationalization of the legal field is not only "ripe" for analytical revision (Twining, 1996: 6), but also fertile ground for emancipatory politics.

Critical globalization studies in international law might begin by studying the analytical foundations of international law, including subject and sources doctrines, the doctrine governing state responsibility, and sovereign immunity with a view to determining whose or what interests are privileged or peripheralized by these legal doctrines. Substantive areas of international law, such as intellectual property law, the laws of war, human rights laws, and international and transnational economic law must be scrutinized to determine how marginalized peoples, women, and others outside or on the legal periphery might be brought into the legal order. Analyzing the potential for integrating elements of global civil society into the international legal system through regularized participation in the United Nations and other law-creating bodies is important as well. Although these moves might appear to be revolutionary for statist international law, it is crucial to recognize that they already are afoot and inherent in the dialectical nature of international law and the resulting conflicts between localizing and delocalizing legal disciplines. Beginning to under-stand the dialectical nature of international law and the tensions between national-izing and transnationalizing forces is a first step to the development of critical glo-balization studies. Further steps require the development of analysis that captures the evolving nature, historical effectivity, and materiality of international law. Finally, and most significantly, critical globalization studies of international law must be emancipatory and focus on principles of inclusion, equity, and justice.

Notes

1. The Rome Statute (Article 5) identifies the following crimes as under its jurisdiction: genocide, crimes against humanity, war crimes, and aggression. See Willmshurst, 1999.
2. President Charles de Gaulle in refusing the request by Jean-Paul Sartre to organize the "Russell Tribunal" to sit in judgment on the U.S. military intervention in Vietnam (see Sartre, 1972: 43–5).
3. Georg Schwarzenberger, 1950.

20

Toward a Sociology of Human Rights: Critical Globalization Studies, International Law, and the Future of War

Lisa Hajjar

At present, there is no such thing as a "sociology of human rights." But there should be because it would foster critical inquiries into the intersections among international law, internationalized violence, state sovereignty, and the rights of human beings in the post-9/11 world, and in this way make a key contribution to a critical globalization studies. A sociology of human rights would be especially useful in providing an analytical framework to contemplate the future of war.

A sociology of human rights would resemble the sociology of law because human rights — similar to any rights — are legal constructs. The sociology of law generally attends to the relations among law, society, and the state. But human rights are, by definition, international because they are constructs of international law. Therefore, a sociology of human rights would liberate sociological inquiries about rights from the conceptual and empirical confines of domestic and national arenas, while at the same time retaining an appreciation for the state because states are (still) the primary makers, arbiters, and enforcers of law — both domestic and international.

To begin, we need a sociological definition of rights. I would define rights as *practices* that are required, prohibited, or otherwise regulated within the context of *relations governed by law*. This emphasis on practices and relations serves (at least) four analytical purposes. First, it draws attention to law as a *social* phenomenon — used, made, changed, fought over, interpreted, and so on, by people. This differs from the kinds of philosophical and legal analyses of rights that ground arguments in abstractions like "nature" or that privilege legal texts and judicial decisions. Second, it foregrounds social consciousness and agency that are inspired and enabled (or impeded and constricted) by law. Rights practices are things people *do*, and the consequences of their (and others') actions inform understandings of the world, whether promoting hegemonic consent (or resignation) or exciting counterhegemonic strategies and forms of resistance to alter the power relations in which they are involved. Third, apprehending rights as *practices* invites inquiries into the interests and claims driving activities and relations among all types of "social actors," be they people acting as individuals, as state agents, as international representatives, as corporate executives, etc. Fourth, as distinct from other domains of sociological inquiry into social practices, law provides a referential frame of value and judgment for practices, while at the same time apprehending that the values and judgments of law are not "given" but "made" and "contested."

To illustrate a way in which this sociological definition of rights might apply to international law and human rights, consider genocide. Prior to the end of the Second World War, there was no law prohibiting the practices that subsequently came to be defined as genocide. In the governance and treatment of human beings, sovereign states were the "highest power" both internationally and domestically. Existing international law (i.e., the laws of nations) governed relations between and among states, and to some extent, the practices of states vis-à-vis "foreign" people (i.e., the subjects of other states), but it did not address the practices of a state toward people within its sovereign domain. Sovereignty was (and still is) the archetype and basis of "states' rights" over populations and territories, manifesting (among other ways) as rights to domestic autonomy and noninterference.

The Nazi Holocaust took this Westphalian logic to a grotesque extreme: in the context of relations between the Nazi state (i.e., agents acting on behalf of the state) and its subjects (citizens and populations of territories occupied by the state), laws were made to authorize practices of racial and other types of extermination. Annihilation was pursued not only as a policy but as a "right" of the state against legally identified categories of people. Indeed, Hermann Goering, one of the architects of the "Final Solution," challenged the legality of treating the extermination of human beings as a crime: "But that was our right! We were a sovereign state and that was strictly our business." And if legal formalism had prevailed, he and his compatriots would not have been prosecuted for this practice.

But the combined consequences of the defeat of Nazi Germany and international abhorrence at the scope and design of state killing generated a counterhegemonic response to the Westphalian logic, cutting into the rights of states by making new laws establishing prohibitions and punishments for such practices. As we well know, genocide did not stop just because it came to be defined as a crime. The Genocide Convention (and the Nuremberg Tribunals that preceded it) set a new legal standard (i.e., value and judgment) of state practice, but lacked the backing of international institutions and agents empowered to enforce it. Hence, although states no longer could claim a sovereign "right" to commit genocide, human beings — the would-be beneficiaries of the right not to be exterminated genocidally — could not claim the concomitant right to no longer fear genocide, in the sense that many millions still were being killed. Thus, there was a gap between law in the books (prohibiting genocide) and law in action (preventing and punishing genocide).

The "gap problem" (of course, not limited to genocide) eventually inspired and motivated forms of activism and organizing that took international law as a reference. This generated a human rights movement that, over time, became globalized. Human rights activism, networking, and advocacy did not close the gap, but did contribute to the visibility of violations, as well as constituting a form of moral and legal pressure on state practices and international relations.[1]

In the early 1990s, the combined consequences of the end of the Cold War, the (relative) visibility and influence of institutional organizations and networks committed to human rights, and the continuation of mass killings produced another counterhegemonic response. This took the form of establishing legal mechanisms to enforce international law by putting (some) perpetrators of genocide (and other crimes) on trial. I will return to the issue of international law enforcement below. To conclude this illustration, I would suggest that a sociological approach is useful to comprehend the interrelations among practices of violence, law making, law violating, and legal activism imbricated in the history of genocide.[2] It should also be stressed that sociological analysis, as distinct from (but not unrelated to) human rights advocacy, would be as attentive to the factors and dynamics — global and local — that constitute obstacles and resistances as to the gains and improvements in the enforceability of law. Whereas the discourse of human rights advocacy tends to be imbued with a teleological logic (i.e., that the world is becoming or should become a "better place"), sociological *analysis* of rights is anti- or counter-teleological.

A sociology of human rights can facilitate critical thought about the role of law in contemporary international politics — what social actors legally can do and should do, and why.[3] Note that I deliberately do not use the rich and suggestive term *global politics* with all its bottom–up implications. The term *international politics* highlights the centrality and importance of the state. International human rights law governs the behavior — that is, the practices — of states vis-à-vis human beings. It also establishes a universal jurisdiction of law to which (at least in principle) everyone in the world is subject. However, as the genocide example illustrates, people only have the rights enshrined in international law if those rights are made available and enforced where they are. Notwithstanding post–Second World War transformations in Westphalianism, we continue to live in a world of states, and therefore enforceability is the purview and responsibility of the state(s).[4]

To explain what a sociology of human rights can contribute, let us elaborate a bit more on the relationship between the history of human rights and scholarship on human rights. Until the 1980s, the study of human rights was dominated almost entirely by international law scholars and political scientists. In the scholarly literature, an idealist–realist dichotomy played out disciplinarily; legal scholars were the idealists and political scientists were the realists, and their respective concerns could be described as the *ought* and the *is* in analyses of the international order. International law scholars were concerned with what ought to happen — what kinds of laws were needed, how existing laws ought to be interpreted, how international organizations like the UN ought to act in order to promote and protect human rights, and so on. Political scientists were concerned centrally with how the world is (or was), and the interests driving and inhibiting states' pursuit of their interests. For the latter, international law was interesting (to the extent that it was) mainly as a rhetorical touchstone to frame judgments about power politics, or as a subject of inquiry about one "language" of power politics.

The idealist–realist dichotomy was, in a sense, a reflection or manifestation of the gap problem. Given that the creation of human rights laws was not accompanied by the establishment of a global government with law enforcement powers, international law functioned (and still, to a large extent, continues to function) like an honor code. Some states willingly complied with some or all of their legal obligations because they perceived it as the correct or appropriate thing to do, not because of a realistic threat of reprisal. Other states paid lip service to human rights principles, but failed or refused to alter their own practices or to legally regulate the practices transpiring within their domain that would constitute violations. There were some exceptions, for example the mounting of international campaigns to put pressure on states to alter unlawful practices, such as the antiapartheid campaign for sanctions against South Africa. For the most part, though, international human rights law functioned as a moral discourse rather than as "law" (i.e., enforceable on its "subjects"). During these decades, international politics was realist: shaped, guided, and governed by states' national interests rather than international laws.

One of the preoccupations, shared by legal idealists and political realists alike, was the question of whether states could be governed by international law.[5] Idealists championed the moral principles enshrined in law and bemoaned the difficulties of bringing those principles to bear in state practices, and realists damned international law as ineluctably utopian because many or most states refused to obey and submit themselves to the legal rules and norms.[6]

Anthropologists, who had traditionally evinced a disciplinary hostility to human rights on the grounds that "universality" was inimical to cultural differences,[7] made a critical break in the 1980s. Specifically, some anthropologists working in "conflict zones" and other areas where rights violations were rampant began doing what could be referred to as "ethnographies of human rights." To their credit, such anthropologists brought to the attention of the academy the ways in which international law was inspiring new forms of social activism and shaping people's legal consciousness about the right to human rights. Thus, anthropologists circumvented the idealist–realist dichotomy prevailing in scholarship, albeit from a bottom–up approach characteristic of anthropological inquiries.[8] Although some sociologists shared with their anthropological colleagues an interest in human rights activism, for the most part sociologists in the Anglo-American academy were strikingly indifferent to human rights until the end of the Cold War, and have remained insufficiently attentive to it since.

One reason I would offer to support the need for a sociology of human rights relates to the changes that have transpired in the international order since the early 1990s, and what sociological inquiry can bring to understanding them. After the end of the Cold War, the realist imperatives of international politics did not dissipate, but the international climate changed to allow for expanded uses of international law. The year 1993 ushered in what appeared to be a new era, when international law started to take on the qualities and powers of law, specifically the powers to do legal violence to (some) law breakers.

This change manifested in the establishment of new types of law enforcement mechanisms (i.e., ad hoc UN tribunals, "mixed" international–national courts, and an International Criminal Court).[9] The uses and development of international criminal law were both a product of and an inspiration for legal entrepreneurialism.[10] Various kinds of social actors (e.g., representatives of states in the UN, human rights advocates, international lawyers) collaborated to transform the role of international law from a moral discourse into an instrument of power, including the power to punish violators. The array of practices associated with human rights expanded from monitoring, reporting, and advocacy to include "accountability" through prosecution (and various nonjudicial alternatives lumped under the term *truth commissions*[11]).

International law enforcement (i.e., prosecution) did not (does not) attend to human rights violations of all sorts (e.g., racial or gender discrimination, religious repression, labor exploitation) — only those forms of *agentic violence* that are defined as international crimes to which individual responsibility (and prosecutability) attaches: genocide, war crimes, crimes against humanity, torture, and terrorism.[12] The development and uses of international law for criminal prosecutions during the 1990s affected the rights of states because some of the people being prosecuted (or sought for prosecution) were state agents.[13] One important characteristic of this prosecutorial turn was a melding of two distinct bodies of law — humanitarian law (also known as laws of war) and human rights law. Ruti Teitel has described this amalgamation as the "new legal humanitarianism" to mark a confluence of the moral principles and the punishing powers of law as a "humanitarian" concern.[14]

In my opinion, the single greatest event in the second half of the twentieth century — for its international legal/political power-reshaping potential — was the indictment and arrest of former Chilean dictator Augusto Pinochet in August 1998.[15] Unlike the ad hoc UN tribunals or the ICC, the Pinochet case signaled the possibility of universal international law enforcement for gross violations. Although the terms *universal* and *international* often are conflated and used interchangeably in discussing international law, when it comes to law enforcement, there is a critical distinction that needs to be appreciated. *International law enforcement* connotes that which transpires under the auspices of the UN, and therefore remains bound to the state-centrism of that organization. In contrast, *universal law enforcement* connotes the global jurisdiction of international law, connected to the state but not necessarily disciplined by the conglomeration of states.[16]

The most exciting progeny of the Pinochet case was the Belgian "universal jurisdiction law" — also referred to as the "antiatrocity law." In 1999, Belgian legislators revised their national law to avail their country's national legal institutions for use in prosecuting people accused of gross violations from anywhere. Belgium became, for a while, a site where justice could be imagined and pursued by individuals with grievances for gross violations they had suffered. The principles enshrined in the Belgian law were not new; the Geneva Conventions, the Torture Convention, and other existing laws clearly defined certain practices as punishable crimes, and contained provisions permitting (encouraging?) states to "prosecute or extradite" violators.[17] Rather, what was new was the opening of an institutional space to put these principles into practice. The seizing of opportunity to bring cases in Belgium from all over the world (e.g., Rwanda, Chad, Lebanon, Israel and Palestine, Cuba, Congo, the United States) was a vivid indication of the problem of impunity, aspirations and demands for legal justice, and the absence of viable alternative venues.

Belgium created a counterhegemonic possibility to pursue international justice "outside" the international system, and this elicited much excitement — and anxiety.[18] Of course, as we now know, politics trumped law in Belgium; the U.S. government mounted a campaign, backed by the threat to relocate NATO headquarters out of

Brussels, to pressure Belgium to roll back its prosecutorial carpet by amending its law, which it did in August 2003.

Now, the advantage or benefit of contemplating these developments *sociologically* is that we do not need to subscribe to the idea that, in the 1990s, the world was becoming more "ideal" (a prominent and clearly teleological presumption of human rights discourse), or that the (impelled) change in Belgium's law (or, for that matter, the ICC "immunity agreements" the United States is forcing dozens of non-NATO countries to sign) are a "step backward" (again, the teleological position prevailing in human rights discourse). Rather, what is sociologically interesting about these developments is why and how they materialized, what effects they have had on the legal consciousness and agency of the vast array of "social actors" affected by them, and the ways they shape the present and future uses of international law.

The potential benefit of a sociology of human rights relates to what sociology can bring to understanding the "why" and "how" of these developments and their con- sequences. For example, to understand why the U.S. government strongly supported the creation of ad hoc UN tribunals but has opposed and sought to derail the Belgian law and the ICC begs further inquiry into the relationship among domestic American (official and popular) "legal consciousness," perceptions and pursuits of "national interests," and foreign policy making, and the ways in which this relationship both plays out domestically (e.g., in electoral politics) and affects the world. By no means would I suggest that these connections have been ignored, but rather that our under- standing of them can be enriched by critically analyzing the linkages.

Like the transnational scope (empirical and theoretical) of the sociology of race or religion (to name but two examples), a sociology of human rights would bring a transnational scope to the study of law in the discipline. And what the discipline can offer to interdisciplinary scholarship on human rights would be transnationalizing inquiries into the relationship among the state(s), society (or societies), and law (domestic and international). Of particular importance is the seriousness that soci- ologists attach to the state in their analyses of the world. Whereas anthropologists certainly take the state seriously, too, they tend to focus more centrally on commu- nities, sub- or transnational groups, and cultures. And although political scientists also take the state very seriously, they tend to under-appreciate the sociality of state power and law. And unlike much legal scholarship, sociology of law apprehends law as *social and political phenomena,* thereby evading the "problem" of idealism (e.g., formalism) without having to forego the relevance, appeal, and contestedness of justice.

Let me now relate these ideas to contemplate the future of war in the post-9/11 world, which relates to and raises questions about the future of human rights and international law in the international order. The multiple, synchronized suicide bombing attacks on the United States on September 11, 2001, were not an act of "war" in the conventional legal sense because, among other reasons, the perpetrators of these attacks did not have legal standing to make war. The hijackings of civilian airplanes were acts of terrorism, and the death and destruction they wrought were "crimes against humanity." However, U.S. officials chose to perceive and treat 9/11 as war and to respond by launching a global "war on terror." Initially, there was strong

international support or acceptance for a military response, bolstered by the acknowledged difficulties of mounting a "law enforcement" campaign to apprehend the
perpetrators (because the Taliban government in Afghanistan where al Qaeda was
primarily based refused to cooperate). But rather quickly international support began
to wither in the face of a continuing and expanding resort to military force that did
not stop at Afghanistan.

The role of international law as a governing framework for war has been intensely
disputed since 9/11, sharpening dramatically with the war in Iraq. Of preeminent
importance — and great dispute — at this juncture is the question of whether a state
like the United States, with unparalleled military (and economic) power, can be
governed by international law. Indeed, American political unilateralism and military
pre-emption would seem to pose very serious challenges to the utility of law and
certainly challenge international consensus on the interpretation and application of
law. Some see the international order after 9/11 as a restoration of unbridled "realism."
Those who embrace this interpretation — especially, but not exclusively, American
neoconservatives — regard the last decade as a dangerously utopian lapse thankfully
and necessarily reversed by a strong self-interested U.S. government. For example,
Richard Perle, at the start of the war in Iraq, published a eulogy for international law.
He wrote:

> What will die is the fantasy of the UN as the foundation of a new world order. As we sift the
> debris, it will be important to preserve, the better to understand, the intellectual wreckage of
> the liberal conceit of safety through international law administered by international institu-
> tions.[19]

Other less cynical but no less skeptical commentators have pondered whether this
era of global war might be "the end of human rights."[20]

Those assessments, I would argue, are *empirically* incorrect. Neither has international law been made irrelevant nor has the possibility of international law enforcement been foreclosed. However, this is a time of great fluidity, and whether a new
hegemonic consensus will emerge is far from certain. For example, since 9/11, there
have been sustained debates over whether the UN Security Council is — or should
be — the final arbiter of war, and whether the Geneva Conventions can apply to a
war on "terror." Thus, war is being waged, in part, on the terrain of international law.

The enduring relevance of international law is apparent in the fact that even the
most anti-international-law unilateralists in the current U.S. administration continue
to seek — because they need — legal legitimation for their actions in going to and
fighting wars. The manner in which this American legitimation is being pursued
could be termed the *Israelization* of international law. By Israelization I am not
referring to the fact that some of the leading American policy makers are neoconservative hawks closely aligned to the Likud Party in Israel. Nor am I talking about the
overlapping of American and Israeli state interests in war-making in the Middle East.
Rather, I am talking about the Israeli-like ways in which American officials are
interpreting international law to frame and wage the "war on terrorism," and the
turning to Israeli models to articulate legal arguments about the legality of American
policies and practices connected to the war.

Israel provides a salient model for several reasons: Israel has been in a continuous state of war since it was established in 1948 and has engaged in military preemption on numerous occasions. But, more important, Israeli officials have always taken international law very seriously. For example, when Israel captured and occupied the West Bank and Gaza in 1967, officials formulated an elaborate legal doctrine establishing the state's rights and duties in those areas.[21] This doctrine does not ignore the Fourth Geneva Convention; on the contrary, it is premised on a highly sophisticated interpretation, albeit one that the international community has never accepted: Israel claimed that the West Bank and Gaza were not technically occupied but, rather, "administered," and therefore that the Fourth Geneva Convention does not apply in a de jure manner. On this basis, Israel could then legally rationalize all kinds of policies that violate the convention, including the settlement of citizens in the territories, the deportation of Palestinian residents, collective punishments, and so on. Moreover, Israel could also claim that it was not bound to adhere to international human rights laws in these areas, even ones to which it was a signatory, because the status of the territories and their Palestinian inhabitants are sui generis and "disputed." Thus, Palestinian statelessness was an important factor in official Israeli legal reasoning and the policies that derived.

This kind of legal reasoning about the limits and inapplicability of the Geneva Conventions when enemies are stateless has been utilized by American officials to wage war on terrorism and to articulate an official U.S. position on the state's rights as conqueror and administrator in Iraq. The legality of practices that contradict international opinion or reinterpret the Geneva Conventions can be disputed, but relying on legal reasoning indicates that the United States, like Israel, is not indifferent to international law.

To understand the sociopolitical and historical origins of official legal reasoning — and the responses to it and consequences of it — begs a sociological perspective. Take the example of assassinations: Israel has engaged in assassinations since the 1970s, but not until November 2000 — 2 months after the start of the second *intifada* — did officials openly acknowledge assassination as policy. Hence, the Israeli state declared its right in accordance with the laws of war to engage in practices that constitute extrajudicial killings — officially termed "targeted killings," "liquidations," and "pre-emptive strikes." The legal rationale for this assassination policy has three components: (1) that Palestinians are "at war" with Israel, (2) that targeted individuals were "ticking bombs" and had to be killed because they could not be arrested, and (3) that the laws of war permit states to kill their enemies. American officials studied and adopted the Israeli legal reasoning to justify the execution of Ali Qaed Sinan al-Harithi and five others (including a U.S. citizen) in Yemen by a pilotless drone.

But Israeli lawyers are contesting the policy of assassinations in the Israeli High Court of Justice on the grounds that those killed — at the time they are killed — do not pose an "imminent threat," that the Israeli state has the power — and the responsibility — to arrest rather than kill them, and that this tactic is "disproportionate" (having caused dozens of bystander deaths along with the killing of "targets"). This litigation is a focused/grounded debate over the rights of states and human beings in war. It raises an array of issues, including the legal definition of war when one side is stateless, the legal definition as well as the rights of *civilians* and *combatants*, the legal parameters of proportionality, and the (il)legality of assassinations.

This litigation draws on a long and rich (and tragic) history of the articulation of violence and law in Israel/Palestine. It involves, directly or indirectly, Israeli political and military officials; Israeli, Palestinian, and international human rights organizations and lawyers; and victims of violence (including Palestinian family members of those assassinated and family members of Israeli victims of suicide bombings, the latter an important factor in the policy of assassination). This litigation also brings to light and focuses public debate about the role and limits of law in a time of war. By litigating tactics and costs of war in court, arguments are sharpened, judgments are judged, and these have rippling effects with international consequences. Thus, the Israelization of international law refers not only to the modeling of Israeli state practices and legal rationales by other states, but also the diverse ways in which people understand and use the law to make, explain, and change a world at war.

In the post-9/11 world, we need to think like sociologists: to look at the state without losing sight of other sites and agents of law, to appreciate the idealism of legal principles that inform (often conflicting) aspirations and mobilizations for rights and justice, while at the same time appreciating the "realities" of power politics that impact upon the interpretations and enforceability of law. Most important, we need to appreciate the global scope of international law and its effects on the social world, which is why, I would argue, we need a sociology of human rights.

Notes

1. Stanley Cohen, *Denial and Acknowledgement: The Impact of Information about Human Rights Violations* (Jerusalem: Center for Human Rights, The Hebrew University, 1995); Margaret Keck and Kathryn Sikkink: *Activists beyond Borders: Advocacy Networks in International Politics* (Ithaca, NY: Cornell University Press, 1998).

2. Leo Kuper, "Theoretical issues relating to genocide: uses and abuses," in *Genocide: Conceptual and Historical Dimensions*, ed. George Andreopoulos (Philadelphia: University of Pennsylvania Press, 1994), 31–46.

3. Susan Silbey, "'Let them eat cake': globalization, postmodern colonialism, and the possibilities of justice," *Law and Society Review* 31 (1997), 207–235.

4. Adamantia Pollis, "Cultural Relativism Revisited: Through a State Prism," *Human Rights Quarterly* 18 (1996), 316–344.

5. John Bolton, "Is There Really 'Law' in International Affairs?" *Transnational Law and Contemporary Problems* 10 (2000), 1–48.

6. Anne-Marie Slaughter, Andrew Tulumello, and Stepan Wood, "International Law and International Relations Theory: A New Generation of Interdisciplinary Scholarship," *American Journal of International Law* 92 (1998), 367–397.

7. Adamantia Pollis and Peter Schwab: "Human rights: a western construct with limited applicability," in Pollis and Schwab, eds., *Human Rights: Cultural and Ideological Perspectives* (New York: Praeger, 1979), 1–17; Allison Dundes Renteln, *Human Rights: Universalism versus Relativism* (Newbury Park, CA: Sage, 1990).

8. Richard Wilson, "Human rights, culture, and context: an introduction," in *Human Rights, Culture, and Context: Anthropological Perspectives*, ed. Wilson (New York: Pluto, 1997), pp. 1–27.

9. Gary Jonathan Bass, *Stay the Hand of Vengeance: The Politics of War Crimes Tribunals* (Princeton: Princeton University Press, 2001); Aryeh Neier, *War Crimes: Brutality, Genocide, Terror, and the Struggle for Justice* (New York: Times Books, Random House, 1998); Geoffrey Robertson, *Crimes against Humanity: The Struggle for Global Justice* (New York: New Press, 2000).

10. Daniel Rothenberg, "'Let Justice Judge': An Interview with Judge Baltasar Garzon and Analysis of His Ideas," *Human Rights Quarterly* 24 (2002), 924–973; David Sugarman, "The Pinochet Precedent and the 'Garzon Effect': On Catalysts, Contestations and Loose Ends," *Amicus Curiae* 42 (2002), 9–15.

11. Priscilla Hayner, *Unspeakable Truths: Confronting State Terror and Atrocity* (New York: Routledge, 2001).

12. Lisa Hajjar, "Sovereign Bodies, Sovereign States and the Problem of Torture," *Studies in Law, Politics and Society* 21 (2000), 101–134.

13. Paul Kahn, "American Hegemony and International Law: Speaking Law to Power: Popular Sovereignty, Human Rights, and the New International Order," *Chicago Journal of International Law* 1 (2000), 1–18.

14. Ruti Teitel, "Humanity's law: rule of law for the new global politics," paper presented at a conference on The Politics and Political Uses of Human Rights Discourse, Columbia University, November 8–9, 2001.

15. William J. Aceves, "Liberalism and International Legal Scholarship: The Pinochet Case and the Move toward a Universal System of Transnational Law Litigation," *Harvard International Law Journal* 41 (2000): 129–184.

16. For example, the U.S. Alien Tort Claims Act (1789) was among the earliest manifestations of the doctrine of "universal jurisdiction," and *Filartega v. Pena* (1980) was a "landmark" case in the universal jurisdiction of the prohibition against torture.

17. Bruce Broomhall, "Towards the Development of an Effective System of Universal Jurisdiction for Crimes under International Law," *New England Law Review* 35 (2001), 399–420.

18. Henry Kissinger, "The Pitfalls of Universal Jurisdiction," *Foreign Affairs* 80 (2001), 86–96.

19. Richard Perle, "Thank God for the Death of the UN," *The Guardian*, March 21, 2003.

20. See Michael Ignatieff, "Are Human Rights Defensible?" *Foreign Affairs* (2001), 102–116; David Luban, "The War on Terrorism and the End of Human Rights," *Philosophy and Public Policy Quarterly* 22 (2002), 9–14; Perry Anderson, "The Special Treatment of Iraq: Are We Sure We Can Get Away with It This Time?" *London Review of Books* (n.d.). See also Michael Neuman, "An Unfounded Rush to Cynicism: A Rebuttal of Perry Anderson," *Counterpunch*, March 10, 2003.

21. See Lisa Hajjar, *Courting Conflict: The Israeli Military Court System in the West Bank and Gaza* (Berkeley: University of California Press, 2005).

21

Reimagining the Governance of Globalization
Richard Falk

Globalization under Stress

In the 1990s it was evident that *globalization*, despite objections about the unsatisfactory nature of the term as misleading or vague, was widely accepted as usefully descriptive and explanatory: namely, that the world order subsequent to the Cold War needed to be interpreted largely from an economic perspective, and that the rise of global market forces was displacing the rivalry among sovereign states as the main preoccupation of world order. This perception was reinforced by the ascendancy of Western-style capitalism, ideologized as *neoliberalism* or as "the Washington consensus," a circumstance reinforced by the collapse of the Soviet Union and the discrediting of a socialist alternative. It seemed more illuminating to think of the 1990s in this light by reference to globalization than to hold in abeyance any designation of world politics by continuing to refer to the historical period as "the post–Cold War." Others spoke convincingly of this being "the information age," highlighting the restructuring of international life that was being brought about by the computer and Internet, but such a label seemed less resonant with the wider currents of emphasis on economic growth on a global scale than did the terminology of *globalization*.

But then came September 11, simultaneously reviving and revolutionizing the modern discourse of world politics, highlighting the severity of security concerns, and war and peace issues, but also giving rise to doctrines and practices that could not be understood by reference to the prior centuries of interaction among territorial sovereign states. The concealed transnational terrorist network that displayed the capability to inflict severe substantive and symbolic harm on the heartland of the dominant state could not be addressed, or even comprehended, by resorting to a traditional war of self-defense. There was no suitable statist adversary that could be defeated once and for all, although this fundamental and disquieting reality was provisionally disguised by the seemingly plausible designation of Afghanistan as responsible for the attacks due to its giving safe haven to al Qaeda. But with the Afghanistan War producing a "victory" in the form of the replacement of the Taliban regime and the destruction of the al Qaeda infrastructure, it became clear that such a campaign was only marginally related to this new type of war. For one thing, most of the al Qaeda leadership and many among the warrior cadre apparently escaped, indicating the absence of any fixed territorial base or meaningful victory, and the U.S. government shifted its focus from the threat of megaterrorism to the quite

different challenge of "Axis of Evil" countries. These moves in world politics drama-
tized the originality of the global setting after September 11, and raised anew the
question of discourse and terminology.

To the extent that globalization is retained as the naming dynamic, its net must
be cast far more broadly. The following section will present this argument by considering the relevance of the September 11 attacks to the reconfiguration of conflict
on a global level, as well as to suggest how the quest for a new framework of regulatory
authority has changed from the 1990s. At the same time, the central contention of
this chapter is that *globalization* retains its relevance as a descriptive label, but that
it needs to be interpreted less economistically since the events of 2001. The final
section will consider approaches to global governance, given this altered understanding of globalization.

The Changing Geopolitical Context of Globalization and Global Governance

To set the stage for this extended view of globalization as incorporating the new
geopolitics of poststatist political conflict, it is necessary to review briefly the evolution
of world politics after the Cold War.

The breakdown of the geopolitical discipline of bipolarity that had managed conflict during the Cold War era generated a security vacuum that could be and was
filled in various ways. The Iraqi conquest of Kuwait in 1991 was an initial expression
of this breakdown. It would have seemed virtually certain that during the Cold War
epoch, without the approval of Moscow and Washington, Iraq would not have
embarked on a path of aggressive warfare against its small neighbor. The American-
led coalition that restored Kuwaiti sovereignty was the mark of a new era being shaped
by American leadership, seemingly a geopolitical debut for unipolarity. The fact that
the UN Security Council endorsed the defensive effort, American operational control
of the Gulf War, and the subsequent ceasefire burdens imposed on Iraq, was far more
expressive of the actuality of unipolarity than it was a sign that Woodrow Wilson's
dream of an institutionalized international community was finally coming true. What
emerged from the Gulf War more than anything else was the extent to which the
Security Council seemed willing to allow itself to be used as a legitimating mechanism
for controversial U.S. foreign policy initiatives.

Another course of action could have been followed, and was even encouraged by
the first President Bush's rhetorical invocation of "a new world order" as a means of
generating public approval at home and international support in the UN for autho-
rizing a collective security response to Iraqi aggression. Such reliance on the procedures of the Security Council to fashion and supervise a response would have been
a genuine expression of the Wilsonian project to shift the locus of authority in war
and peace matters from the level of the state to that of the world community. But
there was no such disposition. Instead, the United States moved to fill the security
vacuum by acting on its own to the extent that it deemed necessary, while seeking
Security Council approval for the sake of a legitimating rationale whenever it would
be forthcoming. The initiation of the Kosovo War under NATO auspices in 1999

made this new American orientation toward law and power clear. With the prospect of a Russian and Chinese veto in the offing, the U.S. government avoided the UN, while organizing "a coalition of the willing" under the formal umbrella of NATO, a deliberate step away from multipolarity of independent policymaking in the Security Council. This departure from the discipline of international law and the UN Charter was widely, although controversially endorsed, throughout Europe and in the United States. It was justified as an exceptional claim necessitated by the perceived imminence of an ethnic-cleansing crisis in Kosovo and against the background of the failure to protects the Bosnian peoples, as epitomized by the 1995 Srebrenica massacre of up to seven thousand Bosnian males while UN peacekeepers stood by as disempowered spectators.

The Iraq crisis was a more revealing and consequential departure from the UN framework of restraint with respect to the use of international force in circumstances other than self-defense. Instead of circumventing the Security Council as in Kosovo, the United States tried hard to enlist the UN in its war plans, and initially succeed in persuading the entire membership of 15 countries to back SC Res. 1441, which implicitly accepted the American position that if Iraqi weapons of mass destruction were not found and destroyed by Baghdad's voluntary action or through the United Nations inspection process, then an American-led war with UN blessings would obtain political backing and international legitimacy. Tensions within the Security Council surrounded mainly the timing and the alleged requirement of an explicit authorization for recourse to war. Evidently concerned that inspection might obviate the case for war, and that the mandate for war might after all not be forthcoming, the United States went ahead on its own in early 2003, inducing a coalition of more or less willing partners to join in the military effort, which produced a quick battlefield victory, but a bloody and inconclusive occupation.

In an important sense President George W. Bush was implementing a vision of a new world order, but not the one that his father appeared to favor from 1990 to 1991 or that Wilson pushed so hard for after the First World War. Unlike the Gulf War where the response, which was endorsed by the United Nations Security Council, was one of collective defense against prior aggression and conquest, or the Kosovo War where the military action appeared necessary and justified as humanitarian intervention, the war against Iraq rested on neither a legal nor moral grounding that was persuasive to most governments in the world; it was opposed by an incensed global public opinion and even seemed politically imprudent from the perspective of meeting the al Qaeda challenge of transnational terrorism. The Bush Doctrine of preemptive war, without a persuasive factual showing of imminent threat, represented a flagrant repudiation of the core international law prohibition of nondefensive force as generally understood and established a precedent that, if followed by other states, could produce a series of wars and undermine the authority of the UN Charter and modern international law. The United States approach filled the security vacuum after the Cold War with the unilateralism and lawlessness of hegemonic prerogatives, and seemed to widen even the claimed right of preemptive defense by resorting to war in the absence of an imminent threat, and possibly in the absence of any threat whatsoever, thereby extending unilateralism and discretionary recourse to war even beyond the expansiveness of so-called preventive war. For the United States to attack Iraq in 2003 — a state by then even weak within its own region and further debilitated by its exhausting stalemate during the 1980s in the Iran/Iraq War — by a devastating defeat in the Gulf War, and by more than a decade of harsh sanctions, was to launch a major war without international or regional backing in a context where there was no credible past, present, or future threat.

And by this audacity on the part of the U.S. government, repeatedly justified by the distinct challenge of megaterrorism made manifest in the attacks of September 11, the United States was also reconstituting world order in three crucial respects: seriously eroding the sovereignty of foreign countries by potentially converting the world as a whole into a battlefield for the conduct of its war against al Qaeda; discarding the restraints associated with international law and collective procedures of the organized world community in the name of antiterrorism; and reestablishing the centrality of the role of war and force in world politics, while dimming the lights that had been illuminating the rise of markets and the primacy of corporate globalization. In effect, the focus on the terminology of globalization and the operations of the world economy were superseded by a novel twenty-first century pattern of geopolitics in which the main adversaries were a concealed transnational network of political extremists and a global state operating without consistent regard for the sovereign rights of normal territorial states. For both of these political actors the territorial framework of diplomacy and restraint that evolved since the Peace of Westphalia in 1648 to regulate political behavior in a world of sovereign states was being treated as obsolete with respect to the resolution of acute transnational conflict. Reliance on the discourse of globalization seems useful to emphasize the extent to which the crucial dimensions of world history are being addressed with a much diminished role for the boundaries of states. These boundaries continue to identify a significant class of political actors on the world stage, but these actors are no longer appropriately treated as the defining forces shaping the history of our times.

Five Globalizations for the Twenty-First Century

Whether this current rupture with the past is an aberration to be corrected shortly or the new framing of global governance is uncertain. The contours and ideological orientation of globalization and governance are almost certain to remain highly contested and fluid, far more so than during the 1990s, and the future of world order will hang in the balance. The old political language of statism will persist in many formal settings, but it will not illuminate the changing structure of world order nearly as effectively as a revamped reliance on the language of globalization.

Five overlapping approaches to governance can be identified as the structural alternatives for the future of world order. These will be briefly depicted, and a few conclusions drawn. The five approaches are corporate globalization, civic globalization, imperial globalization, apocalyptic globalization, and regional globalization. The emerging structure of world order is a complex composite of these interacting elements, varying with conditions of time and space, and therefore incapable of an authoritative "construction." In other words, many constructions vie for plausibility, but none can be prescriptive. The contours and meanings of globalization are embedded in a dialogic process.

Corporate globalization. In the 1990s, with the resolution of the East/West conflict, the center of attention shifted to the ideas, arenas, and practices associated with the functioning of financial markets and world trade, as guided by a privileging of capital formation and efficiency. The role of governments was increasingly seen in relation to this dynamic, and political elites to be "legitimate" had to win the endorsement of private-sector elites. Ideological adjustments were made to upgrade markets, to privatize a wide range of undertakings previously situated within the public sector, and to minimize the role of government in promoting social goals. New arenas of policy formation emerged to reflect this shift in emphasis, giving prominence to the World Economic Forum organized as a gathering of business leaders, but soliciting the participation of the top political figures who came to Davos with the purpose of providing reassurance that they too were championing corporate globalization. Governments and international financial institutions accepted and promoted this economistic agenda, creating arenas designed to facilitate the goals of the private sector, such as the annual economic summit (Group of Seven, then Eight) that brought together the political heads of state of the principal advanced industrial countries in the North.

In the 1990s there seemed to be a rather neat displacement of the territorial and security features of the state system with the capital-driven concerns of the world economy organized according to the ideology of the free market. It appeared that a new nonterritorial diplomacy associated with trade and investment was taking precedence over older concerns with alliances, as well as with friends, enemies, and the security and well-being of the territorial community of citizens. As long as corporate globalization was sustained by impressive growth statistics, even if accompanied by clear indications of persistent massive poverty, widening disparities with respect to income and wealth, and a disturbing neglect of economic stagnancy in sub-Saharan Africa, there was little mainstream questioning directed at the proglobalization consensus. This consensus was seen as a panacea by important champions of globalization, also purportedly contributing to a worldwide trend toward constitutional democracy.[1]

It was only in the wake of the Asian Financial Crisis that began in 1998, and its reverberations in such disparate countries as Argentina, Japan, and Russia, that serious criticism began to produce a controversy as to the future of corporate globalization. In such an atmosphere, the reformist voices of such insiders as George Soros and Joseph Stiglitz began to be heard more widely, lending credibility to the previously ignored leftist critics. And then in late 1999, the Seattle demonstrations directed at an IMF ministerial meeting signaled to the world the birth of a wide and deep antiglobalization movement completely opposed to the basic policies associated with the implementation of neoliberalism. The reaction to Seattle finally generated a debate about the effects of globalization, assessing its benefits and burdens, and focusing especially on whether the poor of the world were being seriously victimized or impressively helped.[2]

In the Bush presidency, despite the focus on global security and the war against mega-terrorism, the U.S. government has dogmatically and unconditionally reinforced its commitment to corporate globalization as the *sole* foundation of legitimate governance at the level of the sovereign state.[3] These policies are being promoted without much fanfare because of the preoccupation with the war/peace agenda, but corporate globalization is being challenged both by the realities of a sharp global recession and by a robust worldwide grassroots movement that has shifted its goals from antiglobalization to alternative globalization.

Civic globalization. As suggested, the effects of corporate globalization have generated a countermovement on the level of ideas and practices, seeking a more equitable and sustainable world economy, although not necessarily opposed to globalization as such. That is, if globalization is understood as the compression of time and space as a result of technological innovation and social and economic integration, if it is considered people-oriented rather than capital-driven, then support for another globalization best describes the identity of the popular movement.[4] Over the years, civic globalization has clarified its dominant tendencies, although diverse constituencies from North and South, from activist groups mainly concerned with human rights, economic well-being, and environmental protection, and from commitments to global democracy, have produced a somewhat incoherent image of what is meant by a people-oriented approach. As suggested, especially through the annual gatherings in Porto Alegre, Brazil, civic globalization has been shedding its negative image of merely being against corporate globalization, and can no longer be accurately described as an antiglobalization movement, despite a continuing repudiation of the main tenets of corporate globalization. In the search for coherence and a positive program, there is an increasing disposition to view civic globalization as essentially a movement dedicated to the achievement of global democracy, which includes a major stress on a more participatory, transparent, and accountable process of shaping and implementing global economic policy.

As might be expected, those concerned with the impact of corporate globalization are also deeply disturbed by the American response to the September 11 attacks, and view resistance to imperial globalization as ranking with, or even more serious and urgent than, opposition to corporate globalization. The mobilization of millions to oppose the Iraq War in early 2003 was mainly a phenomenon in the countries of the North, but it attracted many of the same individuals who had earlier been part of the grassroots campaigns associated with opposition to corporate globalization. There is an uncertainty, at present, as to whether antiwar and antiimperial activism will merge successfully with the struggle for another globalization. It is entirely possible, although not desirable, that two complementary forms of civic globalization will emerge, the one primarily concerned with the democracy and equitable development agenda evolved in reaction to corporate globalization, the other focusing on peace, the United Nations, and the international rule of law in resistance against both imperial and apocalyptic globalization.

Imperial globalization. Even at the high point of corporate globalization in the mid-1990s, there were a variety of assessments that pierced the economistic veil to discern an American project of global domination.[5] It was notable that during the 1990s the United States failed to use its global preeminence to promote nuclear and general disarmament or to create a more robust UN peacekeeping capability or to address the major unresolved conflicts throughout the world. Instead, the U.S. government put its energies into the discovery of new enemies justifying high defense spending, perpetuating a network of military bases and regional naval commands, developing its nuclear arsenal, and embarking on an expensive program for the militarization of space. In retrospect, it seems difficult to deny the charges that U.S. policy, whether or not with full comprehension, was seeking a structure for world order that rested on American imperial authority. True, the apparent priority function of this authority was to make the world safe and profitable for corporate globalization, especially in the face of growing opposition.

September 11 gave an opening to the most ardent advocates of imperial globalization. It converted the undertaking from one of indirection to that of the most vital security imperative in the history of the country. In the immediate aftermath of the attacks it provided the most effective rationale for U.S. global leadership since the Cold War era, and it did so in a setting where the absence of strategic and ideological statist rivalry allowed the U.S. government to project a future world order at peace and enjoying the benefits of a reinvigorated corporate globalization.[6] As suggested earlier, the antiterrorist consensus loomed large at first, giving rise to widespread support for the U.S. decision to wage war against Afghanistan and to dislodge the Taliban regime from control. The move toward war with Iraq disclosed the limits of this consensus as well as the diplomatic limits of American power to induce political support for its project of global dominance. As with Afghanistan, the Iraqi regime was widely deplored as oppressive and militarist, but unlike Afghanistan, Washington's claims of preemption as directed toward Iraq seemed much more connected with geopolitical expansion, especially in the Middle East, than with a response to the continuing threat of the al Qaeda network.

The perception of imperial globalization is a matter of interpretation, as are its probable effects on the governance of political behavior in the world. The advocates of the new imperialism emphasize its benevolent potentialities with reference to the spread of constitutional democracy and human rights, and the provision of peacekeeping capabilities that could allegedly operate far more effectively than what could be achieved by the United Nations.[7] The critics are concerned with arousing a geopolitical backlash in the form of a new strategic rivalry, possibly involving a Sino-European alliance, and about the prospect for a further abandonment of American republicanism at home and abroad under the pretext of responding to the security threats that are present. In this setting, it seems prudent to worry about the emergence of some new oppressive political order that might be most accurately described as "global fascism," a global political fix for disorder that has no historical precedent.[8] Of course, the proponents of imperial globalization resent the frictions associated with civic globalization, and despite the claims of support for "democracy" prefer compliant governmental elites and passive citizenries. Bush rewarded and lavishly praised governments that ignored and overrode the clearly evidenced antiwar sentiments of their citizens, especially Britain, but also Italy and Spain, while punishing those that refused to support fully recourse to aggressive war against Iraq, including France, Turkey, and Germany.

Apocalyptic globalization. There is no entirely satisfactory designation for the sort of political stance associated with Osama Bin Laden's vision of global governance. It does appear dedicated to extreme forms of political violence that challenge by "war" the strongest consolidation of state power in all of human history. Its capability to pose such a challenge was vividly demonstrated on September 11, attacking the United States directly and more effectively than had been done by any state throughout the course of its entire history. Of course, it is arguable that the British attacks during the War of 1812 or Pearl Harbor were more severe threats to survivability of the United States, both mounted by major states at times when the United States was militarily off guard and weak. But the traumatic character of the al Qaeda attacks, their abruptness, and their symbolic as well as substantive challenge at a time when the United States seemed to be the dominant world political actor, has challenged American society more profoundly than these past attacks. The Bin Laden vision also embodies very far reaching goals that if achieved would restructure world order as it is now known: driving the United States from the Islamic world, replacing the state system with an Islamic *umma*, and even ultimately converting the residual infidel world to Islam, thereby globalizing the *umma*. This worldview is here characterized as "apocalyptic" because of its religious embrace of violent finality that radically restructures world order on the basis of a specific religious vision, as well as its seeming willingness to resolve the historical tensions of the present world by engaging in a war of extermination against the "Crusader" mentality of those designated as enemies, including Jews, Christians, and atheists. Bin Laden's extremist turn of mind was disclosed by his oft-quoted assertion to a Pakistani journalist not long after September 11: "We love death. The U.S. loves life. That is the big difference between us." Because the United States as the target and opponent of al Qaeda also expresses its response in the political language of good and evil, but with the moral identities inverted, there seems to exist grounds for the term *apocalyptic globalization*.

Perhaps it confers on al Qaeda an exaggerated prominence to treat its vision as sufficiently relevant to warrant this distinct status as a new species of globalization that approaches the future with its own formula for global governance. At present, the scale of the attacks, as well as the scope of the response, seems to validate this prominence, even though it may seem highly dubious that such an extremist network has any enduring prospect of toppling statism or challenging corporate globalization. As far as civic globalization is concerned, there exists a quiet antagonism, and an even quieter basis for limited collaboration. The antagonism arises because the main support for civic globalization comes from those who regard themselves as secularists, or at least as opponents of extremist readings of any world religion that gives rise to a rationale for holy war. The collaboration possibility, undoubtedly tacit, arises because of certain shared goals, including justice for the Palestinians and opposition to imperial and corporate globalization.

Regional globalization. As with apocalyptic globalization, the terminology is an immediate problem. Does not the postulate of a regionalist world order contradict trends toward globalization? The language may seem to suggest such a tension, but the intention is coherent, to imply the possibility that global governance may in the future be partially or even best conceived by reference to a world of regions. The basic perspective, longer range than the others, is to view European regionalism as an exploratory venture, which if it succeeds, will lead to imitative behavior in other principal regions of the world. What success means is difficult to discern, but undoubtedly includes economic progress, social democracy, conflict resolution in relation to ethnic and territorial disputes, and resistance to, or at least the moderating of, imperial, apocalyptic, and corporate manifestations of globalization. Such region-alizing prospects are highly speculative at this stage, but still worth entertaining, given the dramatic transformations experienced by Europe during the past 50 years, and the difficulties associated with world-order alternatives.

Regionalism is conceptually and ideologically appealing as a feasible synthesis of functional pressures to form enlarged political communities and the rise of identity politics associated with civilizational and religious orientations. Regionalism is geo-politically appealing as augmenting the capabilities of the sovereign state without abandoning its centrality in political life at the national level, especially to allow non-American centers of action to compete economically and to build bulwarks of political resistance to the threats posed by imperial and apocalyptic globalization.

It is also well to acknowledge grounds for skepticism with respect to regional globalization. The United States — as well, possibly, as China, Russia, Japan, Brazil, and India — seems likely to oppose any strong regionalizing moves outside of Europe unless hegemonically controlled, which would hamper, if not altogether defeat their potential role as impediments to humanly detrimental forms of globalization. The disparities in the non-Western regions are so great as to make ambitious experiments in regionalism seem rather utopian for the foreseeable future. Also, the regional frameworks are not entirely congruent with the supposed acknowledgement of civ-ilizational and religious identities. Even in Europe there are large non-Western, non–Judeo-Christian minorities, and in Asia and Africa, the civilizational and reli-gious identities cannot be homogeneously categorized without neglecting the realities of their basic condition of heterogeneity.

A Concluding Observation

The basic argument made here is that it remains useful to retain the descriptive terminology of globalization in addressing the challenge of global governance, but that its provenance should be enlarged to take account of globalizing tendencies other than those associated with the world economy and the antiglobalization movement that formed in reaction. The discourse on globalization to remain useful needs to extend its coverage to the antagonism produced by the encounter between the United States and al Qaeda, acknowledging its borderless character and the degree to which both antagonists sponsor a visionary solution to the problem of global governance, neither of which is consistent with the values associated with human rights and global democracy. Moreover, the European experiment organized many aspects of political community on a regional basis, thereby suggesting an alternative to reliance on statism, (which had been unquestioned at the time the United Nations was established) as well as a potential source of resistance to both imperial and apocalyptic threats.

Such an appreciation of various globalizations is not intended as a funeral rite for the state system that has shaped world order since the mid-seventeenth century or to deride the achievements of territorial sovereignty in promoting tolerance, reason, and a liberal conception of state–society relations. The state may yet stage a comeback, including a normative comeback, providing most of the peoples of the world with their best hope for blunting the sharp edges of corporate, imperial, apocalyptic, and even regional dimensions of globalization.[9] The recovery of a positive world-order role for the state may be further facilitated by collaborative endeavors joining moderate states with the transnational social energies of civic globalization. Such a possibility has already been manifested in impressive moves to support the Kyoto Protocol on Climate Change, the outlawry of antipersonnel landmines, and especially by the movement to establish the International Criminal Court.

The whole project of global governance has been eclipsed by the events of recent years, especially the unleashing of the borderless war and the deliberate Washington effort to sideline the United Nations to the extent that it refuses to implement the policies of imperial globalization. Part of the rationale for reimagining globalization is to encourage a more relevant debate on the needs and possibilities for global governance: that is, suggesting that the world situation is not altogether subject to this vivid clash of dark forces and that constructive possibilities exist, deserving the engagement of citizens and their leaders throughout the world. Of course, it will be maintained by some commentators that such an undertaking is merely rescuing globalization from circumstances that have rendered the discussions of the 1990s irrelevant to present realities and that it is better to deal with the current world by reference to its distinctive, rather unique, characteristics. My concluding view is that despite some merit in this view favoring an entirely fresh language, it is advantageous to retain and revise the globalization discourse, especially in the context of global governance. A different conclusion might well result if the context was an appraisal of political economy or global security.

Notes

1. See, for example, Thomas Friedman, *The Lexus and the Olive Tree* (New York: Anchor, 2000).
2. This debate persists; see *The Economist* for an intelligent recent restatement of the proglobalization spin.
3. Most authoritatively in the White House's *The National Security Strategy of the United States of America* (Washington, D.C.: The White House, September 2002) [available at http://www.whitehouse.gov/nsc/nss.html].
4. See, for example, Richard Falk, *Predatory Globalization: A Critique* (Malden, MA: Blackwell, 1999).
5. For two very different assessments of pre-Bush imperial geopolitics see Michael Hardt and Antonio Negri, *Empire* (Cambridge, MA: Harvard University Press, 2001), and Andrew J. Bacevich, *American Empire: The Realities and Consequences of U.S. Diplomacy* (Cambridge, MA: Harvard University Press, 2002).
6. See President George W. Bush's foreword to *The National Security Strategy of the United States of America*.
7. See Robert Kagan, "The Benevolent Empire," Michael Ignatieff, "The Burden," *New York Times Magazine*, January 1, 2003, 22–27, 50–53.
8. See Falk, "Will the Empire be Fascist?," *Global Dialogue*, forthcoming, 2003; Sheldon S. Wolin, "A Kind of Fascism is Replacing Our Democracy," *Newsday*, July 18, 2003.
9. This possibility is explored in Falk, "State of siege: Will globalization win out?," *Journal of International Affairs* Vol. 75 (January 1997), 123–136.

22

Governing Growth and Inequality: The Continuing Relevance of Strategic Economic Planning

Jeffrey Henderson

Wherever we align ourselves in the debates over globalization, it is hard not to recognize that a key moment of the dynamic that term encapsulates is the pressure to reform economic and welfare policy in line with the prescriptions of neoliberal theory. This has been true not only in the developing world, parts of which have been subject to IMF and World Bank "structural adjustment" programs, but also in the "transitional" and newly industrialized countries, and in the developed world. In the latter, whereas the United States and Britain succumbed to these pressures some years ago, now even the heartlands of the European Union are under threat. In such exemplars of welfare capitalism[1] as Germany and France, for instance, neoliberal reformism threatens to wreak havoc with pension systems and other components of the social wage.

Where economic and welfare projects have already been reconstructed along neoliberal lines, two outcomes (among many others) have been evident: significant increases in inequality and the weakening or abandonment of strategic economic planning (for the latter is the institutional bete noir of neoliberal economic theory). An important question that arises here is whether these consequences are related to one another not merely by virtue of their origins — neoliberal reformism — but are they themselves causally connected? Namely, does the weakening of state planning capacities, in the context of economic globalization, in itself adversely impact the incidence of inequality and poverty? Although there is an emerging body of work that addresses the relationship of globalization, welfare policy, and inequality (see, for instance, Deacon, 1997), there is hardly any literature that broaches what may be the more fundamental question: the relation of economic policy — and thus economic governance — to inequality. It is this issue, however, that concerns us here.

In assessing the relationships between globalization and economic governance, the East Asian economic crisis of the late 1990s has taken on totemic significance. Although state-business corruption or "moral hazard" was ultimately the favored explanation for those influenced by neoliberal theorizing, to more radical commentators it was the deregulation of international finance capital that neoliberal theory had engendered (or, at least, legitimated) which was the principal culprit. Whichever of these positions were seen as necessary to the explanation, however, they were both insufficient. Though "mad money" (Strange, 1998) undoubtedly provided the global context, the onset of the crisis in its national representations was facilitated either by the historical absence of strategic economic planning capacities — as in Thailand or Indonesia — or by the erosion of previously robust ones, as in South Korea (Henderson, 1999). Given that in many cases (though not all — see later) the crisis was accompanied by steep rises in inequality and poverty, the presence or absence of such capacities was no idle matter. On the contrary, the East Asian crisis, together with those (such as Argentina's) that came in its wake, has underlined not merely the question of the appropriate form (or forms) of economic governance in an age of globalization but also the issue of the relation of economic governance to poverty and inequality.

This chapter is especially concerned with the crucial intervening variable in the globalization and inequality–poverty matrix: the role of national economic governance. As we shall see, however, the role of economic governance in this matrix is not clear-cut. Thus, although it yields a story line of general import, it is by no means a simple one. Rather, economic governance and its relation to inequality has been formed and transformed by the "messy" historical specificities of the countries concerned. Although we shall return to this point later, the chapter proceeds by sketching two essential building blocks in the argument: the relation of economic growth to inequality and of economic governance to the growth record. It then turns to an examination of the globalization–governance–inequality/poverty matrix in two of the East Asian countries most affected by the economic crisis of the late 1990s: South Korea and Malaysia. Assessing their contrasting experiences (both historically and in the aftermath of the crisis), the chapter ultimately concludes that, especially in an age of globalization, the maintenance of state capacities for strategic economic planning seems to be essential if economic growth and development is to be achieved and sustained with reasonable levels of social equity.

Growth and Inequality

Whereas concerns with the relation of economic policy to growth go back at least to the dawn of classical political economy in the eighteenth century, concerns with the nature of state institutions and their relation to economic growth are of more recent vintage. While inclinations of these were evident in Austrian political economy of the late nineteenth century (Hodgson, 2001), it was Weber who became the first to systematically elaborate the institutional bases of (what we now refer to as) effective economic governance.

For the best part of a century, then, it has largely been work in the Weberian tradition (albeit given particular specificity by Polanyi, 1957) that has argued that effective public institutions are a cornerstone of economic growth and development. In spite of such a long period of theoretical gestation, however, it is only recently that such arguments have been operationalized for empirical analysis of a growth record. In a widely cited paper, Evans and Rauch (1999; see also Rauch and Evans, 2000) demonstrate that state bureaucracies, measured according to their "Weberianness" (a scale based on meritocratic recruitment to the civil service, making provision for long-term and rewarding civil service careers, etc.) have significant implications for economic growth. On the basis of their analysis of 35 developing and middle-income countries, they show that when controlling for initial levels of economic growth and the skill base, variations in the Weberianness of state bureaucracies captured, for instance, "a key institutional element of the 'high performing' East Asian economies while pointing to an institutional deficit that may help explain low rates of growth in Africa" (Evans and Rauch, 1999: 757).

If there is a strong relationship between bureaucratically competent economic governance and the growth record, as the Evans–Rauch work attests, it is reasonable to hypothesize that there should be a similar relation between such state capabilities and the record on inequality and poverty. Recent econometric analysis of the relation of a state's Weberianness to poverty reduction for a sample of 29 developing and middle income countries does indeed support such a hypothesis (Henderson et al., 2003).[2] The problem with this and the Evans–Rauch work that preceded it, however, is that, inevitably, it works at a level of empirical aggregation that makes it impossible to understand the significance of the historical contexts (nationally and international-ally) in which these relations are forged, and the institutional detail involved in the policy processes (including the politics and political economy of policy formation and implementation). Related work, however, which studied these issues ethnograph-ically in a small sample of countries, allows us to begin to grasp the dynamics in question (for a summary see Henderson and Hulme, 2002).

Although the econometric work referred to above supports the contention that there is a relation between a state's competence for economic governance and its ability to reduce poverty, it provides no sense of the extent to which proactive economic policies were involved in the more successful poverty-reducing countries, nor whether effective economic governance was, at least in part, associated with the state's ability to manage the interface between its domestic economy and the inter-national economy (a combination that I refer to as *strategic economic planning*). Furthermore, this work is unable to enlighten us as to whether explicit antipoverty policies (and, at least implicit, redistributional policies) were part of the story of poverty reduction in the more successful cases. Both of these, however, are very important issues (not least because they go to the heart of neoliberal propositions) and in order to engage with them, we need to introduce explicitly such global and policy dimensions into our considerations; we need to focus, in other words, on how inequality is governed. This we proceed to do by paying specific attention to the cases of South Korea and Malaysia.

From the mid-1970s South Korea (hereafter called Korea) was perceived as not merely an exemplar of rapid industrialization and economic growth but also as a society where substantial reductions in inequality and poverty seemed to have been largely a reflex of economic growth, seemingly providing, in other words, empirical support for the trickle-down hypothesis of increasing human welfare beloved of neoliberal theorists.[3] Although the reasons for Korea's economic development were contested across the ideological and paradigmatic divides,[4] on the basis of the realist tests of empirical adequacy and plausibility (Sayer, 1984), it seems clear that the country hosted what was perhaps the classic developmental state, at least until 1993. With continuing democratization associated with Kim Young Sam's term of office as president, and the beginnings of institutional reform consistent with OECD membership, the apparatus of the developmental state began to be dismantled. In particular the principal agent for strategic planning, the Economic Planning Board (EPB), was absorbed into the ministry of finance. As a consequence, the ministry not only enhanced its role in economic policymaking more generally, but also became the main institutional conduit for the dissemination of neoliberal ideas within government circles. The abandonment of a strategic planning capacity that these developments represented contributed to the deregulation of domestic financial institutions and thus led directly to the economic crisis of the late 1990s and to the growth of inequality and poverty that arrived in its wake (Chang, 1998; Henderson, 1999).

Unlike the Korean case, Malaysia seemed to be one of the very few instances in the history of capitalist economies where antipoverty and redistributional policies enshrined in the New Economic Policy (NEP) and its successor, the New Development Policy (NDP), had been instituted (from 1971) as a central moment of the development project. Although not as impressive as Korea's, Malaysia had achieved a very credible growth record from the mid-1970s and, seemingly as a result of its welfare policy initiatives, had made inroads into poverty and inequality that were far better than any of its Southeast Asian neighbors, with the exception of Singapore. These successes had been achieved — unlike with its counterparts in East Asia — while having a racially diverse population (with the attendant additional tensions and conflicts often associated with such societies).[5] The Malaysian state had evolved, since the late 1960s, with the trappings of the developmental model (in its case, the Economic Planning Unit [EPU] being the rough equivalent of Korea's EPB), but it had never been as effective in guiding and encouraging economic development as had its counterparts in Korea, Taiwan, or, indeed, Singapore. In spite of this, Malaysia's limited strategic planning capacity was not dismantled in the 1990s as was Korea's, and thus although its economy was badly affected by the crisis towards the end of that decade, the Government's new planning agency — the National Economic Action Council (NEAC) — managed to contain the situation by recourse to currency controls and other policy initiatives that ran against the grain of neoliberal prescriptions (Henderson, 1999; Jomo, 2001, 1; Henderson et al., 2002b). Partly as a consequence, and unlike Korea, Malaysia had no need of IMF assistance and the crisis had minimal consequences for the incidence of inequality and poverty.

With Korea and Malaysia we seemingly have two disparate but still related cases of how states that had traditionally attempted to orchestrate economic development (with differing degrees of success) had responded to the increasing globalization of their economies and, particularly, to the challenges posed by the liberalization of international finance capital. Although their approaches to inequality and poverty were seemingly quite different, in what follows we briefly look more closely at their recent development projects so as to uncover their experiential realities and derive from them some of the lessons they might have for how to encourage growth with relative equity.

Governing Growth and Inequality

Recent work in Korea (Henderson et al., 2002; Henderson and Hulme, 2002) has confirmed the broad outlines of the accepted account of that country's dramatic record on reductions in poverty and, seemingly, inequality, also (at least until the late 1990s); namely, these improvements in human welfare were largely a consequence of improvements in economic growth without significant recourse to explicit anti-poverty or redistributional policies. However, what many commentators often fail to recognize is that both the growth record and the reductions in inequality were underpinned by extensive land reform (that is, redistribution to the peasantry), which began under the Japanese occupation in the 1920s and 1930s but was completed by the Korean government in the 1950s. Supplementing the material and social effects of land reform, however, were a series of policies from the late 1960s that, though designed to regulate the power of the *chaebol* (large family-owned conglomerates) in certain domestic markets, had the effect of subsidizing the wage for, at least, urban workers. These included price controls over key foodstuffs and price ceilings on smaller housing units, together with planning and financial controls over the construction of larger units (W.J. Kim, 1997: 147).[6]

Notwithstanding these initiatives, and given that we know that the relation of economic growth to inequality is, in general, ambiguous (see above), if economic growth was the principal factor in the reductions in inequality and poverty in Korea, that still begs the question as to what it was about the nature of economic growth here that made it capable of delivering these improvements in human welfare. Arguably the key issue in Korea is not that of growth per se, but of the economic structure that underpins the growth. We know from cities in the developed world, for instance (the United States and Britain being good examples), that where growth is delivered largely through financial and related services and through low value-adding services such as retailing or tourism, it tends to be associated with significant levels of income and social inequality (Sassen, 1991). Where growth is largely associated with high value-added manufacturing and related services, however, the prospects for material and social equity tend to be better as such activities are usually associated with an increased demand for people with higher manual and technical skills and thus hold the promise of a higher wage economy with more generalized prosperity.

On the basis of this line of argument, the question in the developing world is whether a given country will be able to evolve an approximation to the latter economic structure by a combination of market signals (to domestic and foreign companies) and market facilitating policies (instituted by the state), as typically recommended in neoliberal policy advice. As briefly sketched above and detailed at length in a plethora of publications stretching back nearly 20 years (for instance, Woo, 1991; Chang, 1994; E.M. Kim, 1997; cf. Appelbaum and Henderson, 1992; Amsden, 2001), we know from the implications of the Korean development model (among others) that this is unlikely. Rather, it seems that more proactive state policies, supported by authoritative and bureaucratically competent governance agencies (or, in short, a capacity for strategic planning), is better able to deliver the types of economic structure that, historically, have been more closely related to generalized prosperity.

In Korea, that economic structure was anchored in heavy industries such as steel and shipbuilding, as well as manufacturing industries such as automobiles, consumer electronics, semiconductors and, more recently, telecommunications.[7] That many of these industries were fomented (and subsequently moved into higher value-added production) by state agencies working in particularly close relationships with the private, family-owned conglomerates — the chaebol — is now a matter of historical record. As a result partly of the demands for skilled manual and technical labor that these industries generated as well as the militancy of the trade unions that began to organize their work forces, by the early 1980s significant upward pressure on wages began to be evident (Deyo, 1989). Together with an expansion of the labor markets in these industries that was consistent with the increasing international competitiveness of the principal chaebol, a dynamic towards a relatively high wage economy was set in train, and with it, the possibilities for generalized prosperity.

These developments can be seen in the data for poverty and inequality. In the mid-1960s, for instance, 60 to 70 percent of the Korean population was estimated to be still living in poverty, the vast majority of whom continued to be peasants and agricultural workers. By the mid 1990s, however, absolute poverty had declined to just over 3 percent of the population (undoubtedly consistent with urbanization and proletarianization), giving Korea one of the best poverty records among the OECD membership. In terms of inequality more generally, the Gini data suggests that by 1996 it had fallen to about 0.31 which was, again, a record that was very impressive by any standard — including that of a developed economy (Park, 2001; see Henderson et al., 2002a: 1–6).

Although these spectacular achievements seem to have been largely a product of the nature of the economic structure that had evolved as a consequence of Korea's state-orchestrated form of capitalism, rather than of economic growth in a simple sense or of antipoverty policy, we need to note that the Korean state was not immune to welfare considerations. In addition to the welfare implications of price controls and housing policies indicated above, from the mid-1970s there had been a concern within the EPB about the need for unemployment insurance. It was not until the early 1990s, however, that the EPB — against opposition from some government and business interests — managed to get unemployment provision included in the Seventh Five-Year Economic Plan (Henderson et al., 2002a).[8]

Such expressions of welfare policy were short-lived, however, subsequent to the absorption of the EPB into the ministry of finance in 1993. They were eliminated as the latter's fiscal conservatism became the dominant ethos of Korea's economic governance system, which began to shift from a planning to a more directly market-driven one (and finance-driven also). Consistent with these developments, and as indicated above, the regulatory regime that had underpinned the country's economic stability was weakened. This development became especially problematic with the increase in the numbers of private banks during the 1990s (from a previously state-owned banking system), for it was their relatively unregulated borrowing and corporate-lending activities that were the single most important trigger for the country's economic crisis, which began in 1997 (Chang, 1998).

Among other things, the crisis had profoundly negative consequences for poverty and inequality. In the case of the latter, Gini data suggest that by early 1999 inequality had risen to 0.34; around a 9 percent increase in under 3 years. With regard to poverty, government data suggests that by early 1999, 8.5 percent of the population had become poor. These data, however, were based on earnings only, whereas other data, based on household expenditures, suggest that by early 1998 poverty levels had already risen to 23.5 percent of the population (PSPD/UNDP, 2000; see also Henderson et al., 2002a: 3–4).[9] Either way, however, it seems clear that the Korean economic crisis produced a significant decline in the county's social welfare. As we see below, this was in stark contrast to the situation in Malaysia during similar economic turmoil.

As indicated earlier, Malaysia has been perhaps the only developing country (other than state-socialist ones) to have explicitly pursued antipoverty and redistributional policies as a central component of its development project. Driven by concerns with racial conflict, the New Economic Policy (NEP) of the 1970s and 1980s was designed to irradicate the link between race and class by shifting resources to the *bumiputera*[10] (Malays and other indigenous peoples) majority and to irradicate poverty, irrespective of race. The policy tools deployed to these ends included employment quotas in the private sector, affirmative action (formal and informal) in the public sector, material support for rural development (and hence for the overwhelmingly bumiputera peasantry), and a major expansion of state equity participation in the economy through holding companies involved in manufacturing, petroleum, plantation agriculture, and trading, etc. Underpinning and securing such initiatives were programs to attract foreign investment in manufacturing and related services, especially in electronics, automobiles, and similar industries.

On the face of it, such initiatives have made significant inroads into poverty, although this has been less true for inequality. For instance, whereas over 49 percent of the Malaysian population was poor in 1970, immediately prior to the NEP, by 2000, the poor represented no more than 6 percent of the population. Even rural poverty — always the more intractable in Malaysia — had declined from nearly 59 percent to around 13 percent over the same period (Henderson et al., 2002b; tables 1 and 2:2). Credible reductions in inequality, however, have been less evident. Gini data, for instance, suggests that between 1970 and 1997, the index dropped from 0.50 to 0.46; a reduction of only 8 percent (Roslan, 2001; Henderson et al., 2002b, table 3:3). Although more recent Gini data for Malaysia is unavailable, it is notable that in contrast to the Korean experience, the economic crisis in Malaysia seems to have had only marginal consequences for the incidence of poverty. Between 1997 and 1999 — the period when the crisis was at its zenith — both rural and urban poverty in Malaysia increased by only 1.4 percent (calculated from Henderson et al., 2002b, table 2:2).[11] In terms of the consequences the crisis had for poverty, these data, then, seem point to the relative "superiority" of Malaysia's economic governance system, compared with the system that had been created in Korea (and described above) subsequent to the early 1990s.

Although significant improvements in some aspects of inequality in Malaysia have been made over the past three decades, from the point of view of our current concerns, two questions remain: Can these improvements be attributed largely to the government's antipoverty and redistribution initiatives, and what was the role of economic governance in achieving these ends?

The Malaysian experience of economic governance over the past 30 years under-lines the fact that although, in principle, there seems to be a correspondence between economically proactive states and growth with relative equity, there are significant differences between such states in terms of the coherence, authoritativeness, and competence of their planning agencies (Henderson, 1999; Evans and Rauch, 1999), which have implications for inequality and poverty. Thus, in Malaysia it seems clear that the well-documented corruption within the political elite, coupled with the gradual decline in the quality of the civil service, has resulted in a less impressive record of reducing inequality than would otherwise have been the case. For instance, although the state-holding companies (referred to above) could have been significant tools for the redistribution of wealth, in practice the bulk of their material benefits have flowed to particular individuals and groups close to the prime minister (of over 20 years standing), Mahathir Mohamad, and the leadership of the ruling party, UMNO (Gomez and Jomo, 1997: 3–5), thus restricting the impact they would oth-erwise have had on inequality. Additionally, although from the 1970s to the 1990s, well over 20 percent of the annual development budget (itself around 20 percent of the total state budget) was allocated to poverty reduction, year after year between 19 and 32 percent of the development budget — including funds earmarked for poverty reduction — remained unspent, thus raising questions about the civil service's ability to engage in effective project implementation (Henderson et al., 2002b: 20–28).

If these problems raise questions about the extent to which reductions in poverty and inequality in Malaysia can be attributed to antipoverty and related policies per se, then to what extent can they be attributed to the nature of economic policy — and thus strategic economic planning — in Malaysia?

Although the system of economic governance in Malaysia has achieved some spectacular "own goals"[12] and has continually failed to address significant weaknesses in innovation, the skill base, etc. (Rasiah, 2001), it has still been largely responsible for crafting an economic structure that would have been inconceivable had the Malaysian government, since 1970, adopted an uncritical relationship to neoliberal ideas about trade, investment, and so on. It is this economic structure, with its manufacturing industries on Peninsula Malaysia's west coast (now responsible for about 35 percent of GDP) that has allowed poor peasants (mainly women) to trans-form themselves into a relatively well-paid urban working class. It is in this sense, then, that strategic economic planning in Malaysia (in spite of its institutional weak-nesses relative to Taiwan, Singapore, and Korea prior to the early 1990s; see Hend-erson, 1999) has had a positive impact on poverty and inequality there. Antipoverty and redistributional policies — as enshrined in the NEP and NDP — have, perhaps, in this sense been less significant. Their real achievement seems to have had much more to do with the creation of a *bumiputera* middle class and thus with the delivery of social stability via the avoidance of racial conflict.

Conclusion

I cautioned in the first section that the way a national system of economic governance emerges and develops over time, whether it manages to create and sustain an institutional

apparatus capable of the effective management of the domestic economy and —
crucially, in an age of globalization — of the interface between the domestic and
international economies, depends on an entire series of historical contingencies
(including the particular politics and political economies of development) specific
to the countries in question. Given this reality, it is not surprising that particular
national development projects will have their own gearings to poverty, inequality,
and the means by which they can be reduced. Having said this, the foregoing brief
examination of the somewhat similar, but mainly contrasting, Korean and Malaysian
experiences does allow a number of general conclusions.

The Korean and Malaysian cases both suggest that although robust and sustained
economic growth is a sine qua non for significant reductions in inequality and
poverty, in itself it is insufficient to the task. This does not mean, however, that explicit
antipoverty and redistributional policies are necessarily essential to the process
(though they undoubtedly help) as the Korean case demonstrates by means of their
absence and the Malaysian case, by means of their ineffectiveness.[13] What seems to
be more important is that the economy evolves with a structure that supports industries capable, over time, of delivering higher value-added activities that can underpin
relatively high wages (and that these can be sustained through subsequent movements
into innovation-led growth and development). Almost without exception since the
beginnings of the first industrial revolution through to the present day, the achievement of national economic structures of these sorts has been associated with various
forms of state intervention, as is attested by the work of Chang (2002) on the nascent
stage of practically all the now-developed economies and Amsden (2001) on the "late
industrializers."

The work on which this chapter is based (Henderson et al., 2002a, 2002b) confirms
that forms of national economic governance associated with the maintenance of
institutional capacities for strategic economic planning continues to be vital to the
types of economic structure, and thus the forms of economic growth that are most
conducive to reducing inequality and poverty, and can sustain that downward trajectory during the inevitable periods of recession and even crisis. This conclusion, of
course, runs counter to much neoliberal theorizing and the policy prescriptions that
tend to flow from it. As globalization seems to have brought with it the threat of
increased economic turbulence at national and regional (if not yet world) levels, it
is a conclusion, however, that demands serious attention from national and international agencies and from the development community at large.

Acknowledgment

This chapter draws on research conducted under the auspices of the Department for
International Development (British Government) Research Programme on Globalisation and Poverty (Grant R7861). I wish to thank DFID and the program's director,
John Humphrey, for their support and acknowledge the work of my collaborators in
Korea and Malaysia, Eun Mee Kim, Noorul Ainur, and Jomo K.S. Additionally, the
contributions of my Manchester colleagues, David Hulme and Richard Phillips, have
been invaluable. Many of the ideas and arguments sketched here have developed from

my research and intellectual engagement with them over the past two years. As the immediate provenance of the chapter was a lecture given in March 2003 to the East Asian Policy Forum (School for Policy Studies, University of Bristol), I wish to thank participants in the forum for their comments on that early version. David Hulme and Richard Appelbaum kindly commented on a draft of the chapter when it was at an advanced stage. It goes without saying that none of the aforementioned bears responsibility for what appears in these pages.

Notes

1. There is no consensus on the terminology used to depict national forms of capitalism. For the purposes of this chapter, I adopt Dore's (2000) categorizations.
2. Though arguing from different bases, some of the work collected in Houtzager and Moore (2003) comes to similar conclusions.
3. The empirical basis for the arguments about South Korea and Malaysia, developed in this chapter, can be found in Henderson et al. (2002a, 2002b).
4. Deepak Lal (1983), in his polemic against "development economics," infamously described Korean economic development as a product of "virtually free markets." See Henderson (1998) for a discussion of this and related intellectual constructions of East Asia.
5. Though Singapore is usually assumed to have a multiracial society, in practice it has been dominated — to the tune of 75 percent and rising — by peoples of Chinese origin.
6. Hong Kong and Singapore were the classic examples, however, of how to use such policies — particularly with regard to housing — as development tools (Castells et al., 1990).
7. Additionally it involved "lighter" forms of industrialization associated, for instance, with the footwear manufacture for international brand name companies. For some years in the 1980s and early 1990s, for instance, Korea was the principal producer of sports shoes marketed under the Nike and Reebok brands, among others.
8. Korea, as with Taiwan, used a planning mechanism — the strategic Five Plan — that was more typical of state-socialist societies than it was of capitalist ones.
9. Although there has been an improvement in the incidence of poverty, consistent with economic recovery, as of mid-2002 it had still not dropped to precrisis levels.
10. Meaning, literally, "sons of the soil."
11. From 11.8 to 13.2 percent and from 2.4 to 3.8 percent, respectively (Henderson et al., 2002b, table 2: 2).
12. Largely wasted investments in steel and automobiles and other "flagship" projects, for instance. Arguably these funds would have been better used in stimulating rural industrialization (perhaps along Chinese lines) and in the development and upgrading of small and medium sized firms capable of linking more effectively with the foreign-owned manufacturing companies.
13. Note, however, that redistributional policies are essential for dealing with spatially uneven development. For a general argument on this, see Scott (2002).

23

The International Division of Reproductive Labor: Paid Domestic Work and Globalization[1]

Rhacel Salazar Parreñas[2]

More than 120 million people live in a country other than where they were born. Half of these individuals are women, many of whom have crossed the borders of countries independently of men.[3] In some cases, women even significantly outrepresent men in migratory flows. More than 60 percent of migrant laborers from the Philippines are women, and women constitute approximately 80 percent of Sri Lankan and Indonesian migrant workers.[4] However, theorizations of migration still ignore the particularities of women's migratory experiences, seeing them as an addendum to those of men, based on the belief that "the majority of women who migrate internationally do not do so for work purposes."[5] This argument is said to apply mostly to migratory flows from developing to developed nations.[6]

Yet, in the new economy, the demand for women's work is at a high. No longer do men who seek low-wage jobs in construction and agriculture lead the flow of workers from poorer to richer nations in the new economy. Instead, women are relocating across nation-states and responding to the high demand for low-wage domestic work in richer nations the world over. Consequently, a global South to global North flow of domestic workers has emerged with women from Mexico and Central America entering the homes of working families in the United States,[7] Indonesian women moving to richer nations in Asia and the Middle East,[8] Sri Lankan women to Greece and the Middle East,[9] Polish women to Western Europe, Caribbean women to Canada and the United States,[10] and Filipino women to more than 187 countries and destinations the world over.

In this chapter, I establish the global economy of caring work as a critical platform from which to view unequal relations between men and women and poor and rich nations in globalization. This platform also offers an alternative perspective for understanding the cause of women's migration in globalization, one distinct from the demand for men's migrant labor instead giving emphasis to gender inequalities in the family and economy. With the increasing flow of migrant domestic workers, globalization marks a "new world domestic order," meaning an unequal division of care labor between the global South and global North.[11] No longer are production activities the sole measure of relations of inequality between First and Third World countries but instead reproduction activities are as well. By reproduction activities, I refer to the labor needed to sustain the productive labor force. Such work includes household chores; the care of the elderly, adults, and youth; the socialization of children; and the maintenance of family ties. New regimes of inequalities that are based on social reproduction include the "international division of reproductive labor" or "global care chains" of women purchasing the care of their children from women with lesser resources in the global economy; gender inequalities of social reproduction that encourage the commodification of reproductive labor; the imposition of restrictive laws that limit the social reproduction of migrant workers; and finally the consequent result of transnational mothering for migrant workers. In this chapter, I provide an overview of these unequal global arrangements among women so as to map the organization of social reproduction in globalization and establish the significance of gender in determining global regimes of inequality.

The International Division of Reproductive Labor

At the same time that it remains the work of women, the labor of caring for the family continues to be a private and not a public responsibility.[12] Without adequate social welfare support, this work turns into a burden for women. The international transfer of care work underscores this point. This division of labor refers to the three-tier transfer of care among women in sending and receiving countries of migration. Under this macroprocess, class-privileged women pass down the care of their families to migrant domestic workers as migrant domestic workers simultaneously pass down the care of their own families — most of whom are left behind in the country of origin — to their relatives or sometimes to even poorer women whom they hire as their own domestic workers.

The case of Carmen Ronquillo, a domestic worker in Rome, provides us with a good illustration of the international division of care work. Carmen is simultaneously a domestic worker for a professional woman in Rome and an employer of a domestic worker in the Philippines. Carmen describes her relationship to each one of these women:

> When coming here, I mentally surrendered myself and forced my pride away from me to prepare myself. But I lost a lot of weight. I was not used to the work. You see, I had maids in the Philippines. I have a maid in the Philippines that has worked for me since my daughter was born 24 years ago. She is still with me. I paid her three hundred pesos before, and now I pay her 1000 pesos. I am a little bit luckier than others because I run the entire household. My employer is a divorced woman who is an architect. She does not have time to run her household so I do all the shopping. I am the one budgeting. I am the one cooking. [Laughs.] And I am the one cleaning, too. She has [children] 24- and 26-years old. The older one graduated already and is an electrical engineer. The other one is taking up philosophy. They still live with her … She has been my only employer. I stayed with her because I feel at home with her.

It is quite striking to observe the formation of parallel relationships of loyalty between Carmen (the employer) and her domestic in the Philippines and Carmen (the domestic) and her employer in Italy. Also striking is the fact that Carmen's domestic worker does exactly the same work that Carmen does for her own employer. Yet, more striking is the wide discrepancy in wages between Carmen and her own domestic worker.

Their wage differences illuminate the economic disparity among nations in transnational capitalism. A domestic worker in Italy such as Carmen could receive US$1,000 a month for her labor. As Carmen describes,

> I earn 1,500,000 (US$1,000) and she pays for my benefits. On Sundays, I have a part-time. I clean her office in the morning and she pays me 300,000 lira (US$200). I am very fortunate because she always gives me my holiday pay in August and my thirteenth month pay in December. Plus, she gives me my liquidation pay at the end of the year.

Carmen's wages easily enable her to hire a domestic worker in the Philippines, who on average only earns what is the equivalent of $40 during the time of my interviews. Moreover, the domestic worker in the Philippines, in exchange for her labor, does not receive the additional work benefits that Carmen receives for the same labor.[13]

The international transfer of care refers to a social, political, and economic relationship between women in the global market. Under this division of labor, there is a gradational decline in the worth of care. As sociologist Barbara Rothman poignantly describes, "When performed by mothers, we call this mothering ...; when performed by hired hands, we call it unskilled."[14] Commodified care work is not only low-paid work but declines in market value as it gets passed down the hierarchical chain. As care is made into a commodity, women with greater resources in the global economy can afford the best-quality care for their families. Conversely, the care given to those with fewer resources is usually worth less.

Consequently, the quality of family life progressively declines as care is passed down the international division of care work. Freed of household constraints, those on top can earn more and consequently afford better-quality care than the domestic workers whom they hire. With their wages relatively low, these domestic workers cannot afford to provide the same kind of care for their family. They in turn leave them behind in the country of origin to be cared for by even lesser-paid domestic workers. Relegated to the bottom of the three-tier hierarchy of care work, domestic workers left in the Third World have far fewer material resources to ensure the quality care of their own family.

In the international transfer of care work, migrant domestic workers do not just ease the entrance of other women into the paid labor force but also assist in the economic growth of receiving nations. Patricia Licuanan, in reference to households in Hong Kong and Singapore, explains:

> Households are said to have benefited greatly by the import of domestic workers. Family income has increased because the wife and other women members of working age are freed from domestic chores and are able to join in the labor force. This higher income would normally result in the enlargement of the consumer market and greater demand on production and consequently a growth in the economy (1994: 109).

By spurring economic development, the international transfer of care retains the inequalities of the global market economy. The low wages of migrant domestic workers increase the production activities of the receiving nation, but the economic growth of the Philippine economy is for the most part limited and dependent on the foreign currency provided by their low wages.

A similar observation can be made of the employing families in the international transfer of care. Freed of reproductive labor, the family employing the migrant domestic worker can increase the productive labor generated in their household. The mobility of the migrant domestic worker and her family is for the most part dependent on the greater mobility of the employing family. The same relationship goes for domestic workers in the Third World and the migrant domestic workers who employ them. The international division of care work illustrates social reproduction as a regime of inequality in the global economy. Moreover, the passing down of social reproduction responsibilities between women shows that care still falls largely on women's and not men's shoulders. Equally significant, it also indicates that public accountability for social reproduction remains slim.

The Burdens of Social Reproduction

Gender inequalities of social reproduction promote the formation of the international division of reproductive labor. In the industrialized countries of Asia, the Americas, and Europe, the number of gainfully employed women has climbed dramatically in the last 40 years. Yet, the increase in women's share of labor market participation has not led to drastic changes in the traditional household division of labor. For instance, in France, an additional two million women entered the labor force between 1979 and 1993, a 21 percent increase in the number of working women.[15] In Italy, the downward trend in the labor force participation of women from 1959 to 1972 has also taken a reverse direction.[16] In fact, Italy has witnessed an increasing number of married women in the labor force, but surprisingly a decline in the number of younger single women engaged in paid work.[17] In the United States, women represented 46.5 percent of gainfully employed workers in 1992, a considerable increase over 32.1 percent in 1960.[18] Additionally, mothers are more likely to work. For instance, in the United States, three out of four mothers with school-age children are in the paid labor force, the majority of whom work full-time.[19] Similarly in Italy and Spain, women tend to keep their full-time jobs even when they have young children at home.[20]

Yet, the drastic increase in women's paid employment has not been met with a drastic reduction in women's unpaid work inside the home. Although more fitting of households with a stay-at-home mother and breadwinner father, the work of care — feeding, cleaning, dressing, and watching over young children — is still performed by women much more so than men.[21] According to Arlie Hochschild, in these times of a "stalled revolution," at least in the United States, the vast majority of men do less housework than their gainfully employed partners.[22] A significant number of women have to cope with the double day, or "second shift," because women still perform a disproportionate amount of housework, childcare, and maintain social relations with kin and community. Similarly in Italy, eliminating *doppio lavoro* (literally meaning "double work") has been a recurring agenda in the Italian feminist movement since the early 1970s.[23]

The burden of the double day not only indicates that gender inequalities hamper the family life of women. It also shows that welfare support for the family does not consistently reflect changes brought by the entrance of women, particularly mothers, to the paid labor force. Welfare support in many countries does not address the new demands brought by the increase in women's labor market transformations to the family.[24] This is the case in the United States, as well as various nations in Western Europe. The United States has the least welfare provisions among rich nations in the global economy as families are without access to universal health care, paid maternity and parental leave, government-provided childcare, or family caregiving allowances.[25] The absence of a sense of communal responsibility for care in the United States is, for instance, reflected in the care of the elderly. Studies have shown that family members, usually women, provide approximately 80 to 90 percent of their care without any formal assistance from the government.[26]

Although providing more benefits than that in the United States, the welfare regimes in various European countries also follow a conservative model of the family. The comprehensive publicly funded preschool system in France stabilizes the family life of dual wage earning couples, but feminists have argued that the "strongly entrenched division of labor within the household" still hurts women.[27] This is, for instance, shown by the burden of elderly care falling mainly on women in the family, as the family is not supported with residential care provisions. Other countries such as Greece, Italy, and Spain have relatively low welfare provisions.[28] In contrast, the socially democratic Scandinavian nations provide the most gender-sensitive public benefits for families. Sweden, for instance, promotes gender equality by providing gender-neutral parental leave and universal entitlements in the form of allowances, subsidies, and direct services for the elderly and single-parent households.[29]

Without the benefit of a "public family" system, many overwhelmed working women in various Western countries have had few choices but instead rely on the commodification and consequent economic devaluation of care work. To ease the double day, they have turned to daycare centers and family daycare providers, nursing homes, after-school babysitters, and also privately hired domestic workers. As Joy Manlapit, an elderly care provider in Los Angeles observes:

> Domestics here are able to make a living from the elderly that families abandon. When they are older, the families do not want to take care of them. Some put them in convalescent homes, some put them in retirement homes, and some hire private domestic workers.

Without doubt, women in industrialized countries have come to take advantage of their greater economic resources than women from developing countries: they do this by unloading the care responsibilities in their families to other women, particularly migrant women. Notably, as I address in the next section, limiting the reproduction rights of migrant workers assists in this process.

Partial Citizenship: The Limited Reproduction of Migrant Workers

Despite their economic contributions, migrant domestic workers suffer from their limited incorporation as partial citizens of various receiving nations. By this I mean they face restrictive measures that stunt their political, civil, and social incorporation into host societies. From an economic standpoint, this is not surprising. Receiving nations curb the integration of migrants so as to guarantee their economies a secure source of cheap labor. By containing the costs of reproduction in sending countries, wages of migrant workers can be kept to a minimum; migrants do not have the burden of having to afford the greater costs of reproducing their families in host societies. Moreover, by restricting the incorporation of migrants, receiving nations can secure for their economies a supply of low-wage workers who could easily be repatriated in the event of an economic downturn.

As such, migrants are usually relegated to the status of temporary settlers whose stay is limited to the duration of their labor contracts. Often, they cannot sponsor the migration of their families, including their own children. This is the case in Middle Eastern and Asian receiving nations, which are much more stringent than other countries. For example, in Taiwan, state policies deny entry to the spouses and children of the migrant worker.[30] Singapore even prohibits the marriage or cohabitation of migrant workers with native citizens.[31] Accounting for the nuances engendered by differences in government policies, the restriction of family migration comes in different degrees and levels of exclusion. Temporary residents in Italy have been eligible for family reunification since 1990. Likewise in France and Germany, dependents of migrants were granted the right to work in the 1980s.

However, family reunification remains a challenge to many immigrants in Europe. Despite the more inclusive policies for migrants in Europe than in Asia, European nation-states nonetheless still restrict migrants to the status of "guest workers." With heightened antiimmigrant sentiments in European nations such as Italy, the basis of citizenship is unlikely to become more inclusive and allow permanent settlement for this racially distinct group. As a result, most migrant Filipina workers prefer not to petition for the children whom they have left behind in the Philippines. In France, for instance, they are discouraged by the increase in years of residence to qualify for family reunion as well as the decrease in the age for eligibility as a dependent from 21 to 18 years old.[32] In Germany, children under 16 years of age are required to obtain a visa to visit their legally resident parents. In the U.K., entry conditions for family visits have become stricter with the rising suspicion of the intent of family members to remain indefinitely.[33]

Labor conditions in domestic work also hamper the ability of migrants to reunify their family. Contracts of "guest workers" usually bind them to stay with their sponsoring employer, which again makes them incredibly vulnerable to below-par labor standards. This is especially true of domestic workers because their isolation in private homes aggravates the vulnerability engendered by their legal dependency on their sponsoring employers. For instance, domestic workers in Hong Kong who flee abusive employers automatically face deportation proceedings due to the stringent legislation imposed for foreign domestic workers in 1987.[34]

Eligibility for full citizenship is available in a few receiving nations including Spain, Canada, and the United States. In Spain and Canada, migrant Filipinas are eligible for full citizenship after two years of legal settlement. Despite the seemingly more liberal and inclusive policies in these nations, political and social inequalities, as Abigail Bakan and Daiva Stasiulis (1997a) have pointed out using the case of migrant

Filipina domestic workers in Canada, still mar the full incorporation of migrant workers. In Canada, the Live-in Caregivers Program requires an initial 2 years of live-in service before foreign domestics can become eligible for landed immigrant status. At this time, it restricts these workers to the status of temporary visitors, denies the migration of family, and leaves them vulnerable to facing abusive working conditions. Without the protection of labor laws granted to native workers, migrant domestic workers in Canada — the majority of whom are Filipinos — have fewer rights than full citizens. Filipina domestic workers in the United States, likewise, experience the same vulnerability. Obtaining a green card through employer sponsorship has been described as a "form of state-sanctioned indenture-like exploitation" because "the worker is obligated to stay in the sponsored position until the green card is granted (usually two or more years) (Colen, 1995). During this time, migrant workers are prone to abuse and substandard working conditions.

Without doubt, the imposition of partial citizenship on migrant domestic workers benefits employers. The guest worker status, legal dependency on the "native" employer, ineligibility for family reunification, and the labor-market segmentation of foreign women to domestic work guarantee host societies a secure and affordable pool of care workers at the same time that they maximize the labor provided by these workers and constrain their ability to care for their own family, particularly their own children. This works to the benefit of the employing family, because migrant care workers can give the best possible care when they are free of caregiving responsibilities to their own families. Yet, the experience of partial citizenship for migrant domestic workers points to a central irony in globalization. Migrant domestic workers care for rich families in the North as they are burdened with social, economic, and legal restrictions that deny them the right to nurture their own families. The elimination of these restrictive measures would at the very least grant foreign domestic workers the basic human right of caring for their own family and make transnational mothering an option to be chosen by migrant women instead of a consequence of their restricted social incorporation as partial citizens.

Transnational Mothering

> When the girl that I take care of calls her mother "Mama," my heart jumps all the time because my children also call me "Mama." I feel the gap caused by our physical separation especially in the morning, when I pack (her) lunch, because that's what I used to do for my children … I used to do that very same thing for them. I begin thinking that at this hour I should be taking care of my very own children and not someone else's, someone who is not related to me in any way, shape, or form …. The work that I do here is done for my family, but the problem is they are not close to me but are far away in the Philippines. Sometimes, you feel the separation and you start to cry. Some days, I just start crying while I am sweeping the floor because I am thinking about my children in the Philippines. Sometimes, when I receive a letter from my children telling me that they are sick, I look up out the window and ask the Lord to look after them and make sure they get better even without me around to care after them. [Starts crying.] If I had wings, I would fly home to my children. Just for a moment, to see my children and take care of their needs, help them, then fly back over here to continue my work.

Migrant domestic workers such as Rosemarie Samaniego are overwhelmed by feelings of helplessness: they are trapped in the painful contradiction of feeling "the gap caused by physical separation" and having to give in to the family's dependence on the material rewards granted by this separation. Although they may long to be with their children, they cannot because of their family's dependence on their earnings and the structural constraints that discourage family reunification. In this section, I address the emotional strains of transnational mothering, which include feelings of anxiety, loss, guilt, and loneliness. I do so to emphasize the difficulties imposed by the inequalities of social reproduction in globalization

Transnational mothering involves overwhelming feelings of loss. For missing the growing years of children, many mothers are remorseful and admit to lost intimacy in the transnational family. In general, a surreal timelessness is felt during family separation, and many mothers are suddenly catapulted back to reality the moment they reunite with their children. For example, the widow Ernie Contado describes her homecoming to the Philippines after more than a decade of working continuously as a domestic worker in Rome.

> When I came home, my daughters were teenagers already. [Starts crying.] When I saw my family, I dropped my bag and asked who were my daughters. I did not know who they were, but they just kept on screaming "Inay, Inay!" [Mom, Mom!] I asked them who was which, and they said, "I'm Sally and I'm Sandra." We were crying. I did not know who was which. Imagine! But they were so small when I left, and there they were as teenagers. [Weeps.] They kept on saying, "Inay, Inay."

Maintaining transnational households is quite agonizing for migrant parents. For them, missing their children's adolescence is an insurmountable loss, which sadly turns into a deep-seated regret over the emotional distance it has caused the family. As Ana Vengco, a single mother working in Rome for almost 3 years, explains, missing the small pleasures and familiarities of everyday living is irreplaceable.

> I really, really miss my daughter. I really regret not being able to see my daughter grow up, learn her hang-ups, how she learned to brush her teeth, walk… I left my daughter when she was not even one year old and now she is already three years old.

In transnational households, the absence of daily interactions denies familiarity and becomes an irreparable gap defining parent–child relations.

Transnational mothering also entails loneliness over the denial of intimacy. Migrant mothers often battle with the grief imposed by constant reminders of their children and the emotional distance engendered by unfamiliarity. As the mother Analin Mahusay of Rome states:

> My kids are still very young so they still don't know about my life here …. They often ask my husband where I am and wonder why they have not seen me yet, especially the youngest child of mine, the one who was born here. What I really want is to be able to get papers, because I really want to see my children …. I always think about my children. I always worry about not sending them enough money …. Sometimes when I look at the children that I care for, I feel like crying. I always think about how if we did not need the money, we would all be together, and I would be raising my children myself …. That's what is really hard about life here, being away from one's family. Without your family you are just so much more vulnerable.

Without doubt, family separation aggravates the hardships of migrant life, high-lighting the helplessness brought by the material constraints that force the formation of transnational households.

Conclusion

The hierarchy of womanhood — based on race, class, and nation — establishes a work transfer system of reproductive labor among women: the international transfer of care. It is a distinct form of transnational division of labor that links women in an interdependent relationship. Migrant domestic workers perform the reproductive labor of more privileged women in industrialized countries as they relegate their reproductive labor to poorer women left in the Philippines. The international division of reproductive labor shows us that production is not the sole means by which international divisions of labor operate in the global economy. Local economies are not solely linked by the manufacturing production of goods. In globalization, the transfer of reproductive labor moves beyond territorial borders to connect separate nation-states. The extension of reproductive labor to a transnational terrain is embed-ded in the operation of transnational families and the constant flow of resources from migrant domestic workers to the families that they continue to support in the country of origin. While acting as the primary income earners of their families, migrant domestic workers hire poorer domestic workers to perform the household duties that are traditionally relegated to them as women. In this way, they continue to remain responsible for the reproductive labor in their families but at the same time, as migrant workers, take on the responsibility of productive labor.

The formulation of the international division of reproductive labor treats gender as a central analytic lens for understanding the migration of domestic workers. It shows the movement of migrant domestic workers is embedded in a gendered system of transnational capitalism. While forces of global capitalism spur the labor migration of domestic workers, the demand for their labor also results from gender inequities in receiving nations, specifically the relegation of reproductive labor to women. This transfer of labor strongly suggests that despite their increasing rate of labor market participation, women continue to remain responsible for reproductive labor in both sending and receiving countries. At both ends of the migratory stream, they have not been able to negotiate directly with male counterparts for a fairer division of house-hold work but instead have had to rely on their race and/or class privilege by partic-ipating in the transnational transfer of gender constraints to less-privileged women.

Ironically, women in industrialized (Western) countries are often assumed to be more liberated than women are in developing countries. Yet, many women are able to pursue careers as their male counterparts do because disadvantaged migrant women and other women of color are stepping into their old shoes and doing household work for them. As women transfer their reproductive labor to less and less privileged women, we can see that the traditional division of labor in the patri-archal nuclear household has not been significantly renegotiated in various countries in the world. This is one of the central reasons why there is a heightened need for migrant domestic workers in globalization.

Notes

1. Portions of this chapter are reprinted from Rhacel Salazar Parreñas, *Servants of Globalization: Women, Migration, and Domestic Work* (Stanford, CA: Stanford University Press, 2001) and Rhacel Salazar Parreñas, "Between Women: Migrant Domestic Work and Gender Inequalities in the New Global Economy," *Concilium* 5 (2): 28–39 (2002).

2. Rhacel Salazar Parreñas is Associate Professor of Asian American Studies at the University of California, Davis.

3. Annie Phizacklea, "Migration and Globalization: A Feminist Perspective," pp. 21–38 in *The New Migration in Europe: Social Constructions and Social Realities*, eds. Khalid Koser and Helma Lutz (New York: St. Martin's Press, 1998).

4. Michelle Ruth Gamburd (2000), *The Kitchen Spoon's Handle*, Ithaca, NY: Cornell University Press, p. 35.

5. Hania Zlotnick, "The South to North Migration of Women," *International Migration Review* 29:1(1995): 229–254, p. 230.

6. Hania Zlotnick, "The South to North Migration of Women," *International Migration Review* 29:1(1995): 229–254, p. 230. It is true that historically a greater number of women have crossed borders as dependents of men, following husbands who migrated prior to them or joining grooms to whom they had marriages arranged and brokered in local villages. In the United States, for instance, these options commonly stood for central, eastern, and southern European as well as Asian women at the turn of the last century, until the U.S. Immigration Act of 1924 barred entry to any "alien ineligible for citizenship." This was also the case for later groups of women migrants, including Mexican women who followed husbands who had first relocated to the United States as temporary agricultural field workers under the Bracero Program of the 1950s and 1960s.

7. See Pierrette Hondagneu-Sotelo, *Doméstica* (Berkeley: University of California Press, 2001).

8. See Heyzer, Noeleen, Geertje Lycklama a Nijeholt, and Nedra Weerakoon, eds., *The Trade in Domestic Workers: Causes, Mechanisms, and Consequences of International Labor Migration* (London, Zed Books, 1994).

9. See Gamburd (2000); Nicole Constable, *Maid to Order in Hong Kong* (Ithaca, NY: Cornell University Press, 1997) and Christine Chin, *Of Service and Servitude* (New York: Columbia University Press, 1998).

10. See Abigail Bakan and Daiva Stasiulis, eds., *Not One of the Family: Foreign Domestic Workers in Canada* (Toronto: University of Toronto Press, 1997) for a look at the state incorporation of domestic workers in Canada and Caribbean domestics in New York City and Shellee Colen, "Like a Mother to Them: Stratified Reproduction and West Indian Childcare Workers and Employers in New York," in *Conceiving the New World Order: The Global Politics of Reproduction*, eds. Faye Ginsburg and Rayna Rapp, (Berkeley: University of California Press, 1995), pp. 78-102.

11. Hondagneu-Sotelo (2001).

12. Martin Conroy, *Sustaining the New Economy: Work, Family, and Community in the Information Age* (New York: Russell Sage Foundation Press and Cambridge, MA: Harvard University Press, 2000).

13. Migrant domestic workers usually belong in a higher-class stratum than do domestics left in the Philippines. Often professionals in the Philippines, they use their resources to afford the option of seeking the higher wages offered in more developed nations.

14. Barbara Katz Rothman, *Recreating Motherhood: Ideology and Technology in a Patriarchal Society* (New York and London: W.W. Norton, 1989), p. 43.

15. Conroy (2000), p. 138.

16. Donald Meyer, *The Rise of Women in America, Russia, Sweden, and Italy* (Middletown, CT: Wesleyan University Press, 1987).

17. V.A. Goddard, *Gender, Family, and Work in Naples* (Oxford and Washington, D.C.: Berg, 1996).

18. Parreñas, 2001.

19. Scott Coltrane and Justin Galt, "The History of Men's Caring." In *Care Work: Gender, Labor and the Welfare State*, ed. Madonna Harrington Meyer (New York and London: Routledge, 2000), p. 29.

20. Conroy (2001), p. 137.

21. Coltrane and Galt (2001).

22. Arlie Hochschild (with Anne Machung), *The Second Shift* (New York: Avon, 1989).

23. Lucia Chiavola Birnbaum, *Liberazione della Donne* (Middletown, CT: Wesleyan University Press, 1986).

24. By welfare support, I refer to the government's accountability for the social and material well-being of their citizenry.

25. Francesca Cancian and Stacey Oliker, *Caring and Gender* (Thousand Oaks, CA: Pine Forge Press, 2000), p. 116.

26. Jennifer Mellor, "Filling in the Gaps in Long Term Care Insurance." In *Care Work: Gender, Labor and the Welfare State*, ed. Madonna Harrington Meyer (New York and London: Routledge, 2000), p. 206.

27. Eleonore Koffman, Annie Phizacklea, Parvati Raghuram, and Rosemary Sales, *Gender and International Migration in Europe: Employment, Welfare and Politics* (New York and London: Routledge, 2000), p. 143.

28. Eleonore Koffman, Annie Phizacklea, Parvati Raghuram, and Rosemary Sales, *Gender and International Migration in Europe: Employment, Welfare and Politics* (New York and London: Routledge, 2000), p. 143.
29. Cancian and Oliker (2000), p. 118.
30. Pei-Chia Lan, "Bounded Commodity in a Global Market: Migrant Workers in Taiwan." Paper presented at the 1999 Annual Meeting of the Society for the Study of Social Problems, Chicago, August 6–8.
31. Bakan and Stasiulis (1997).
32. Koffman et al. (2000), p. 68.
33. Koffman et al. (2000), p. 68.
34. Nicole Constable, *Maid to Order in Hong Kong: Stories of Filipina Workers* (Ithaca, NY, and London: Cornell University Press, 1997).

24

Critical Globalization Studies and Gender

Jean L. Pyle

Analysis of the major trends of the most recent period of globalization and their gendered dimensions is important for several reasons. First, such an analysis leads to important insights for the field of gender and development studies and for how we understand the changing labor market and family roles of women and men in so-called industrialized countries.[1] Scholars and activists grounded in many different disciplinary backgrounds are involved in both types of analyses — endeavors that are now seen as clearly interrelated because women's lives have become substantially more interconnected globally. Women in industrialized countries are linked with those in developing or transitional economies. Over the last few decades, we have seen jobs transferred to areas of the world where low-wage women workers are readily available, and more recently we have become aware of streams of female migrants flowing to the industrialized countries as domestic workers or nannies, to work in virtual sweatshops or to become sex workers. Such flows are also widespread throughout the so-called developing world. Sassen (2000) refers to them as alternative circuits for survival.

In addition, and related to this, gendered research on globalization is critical for understanding some of the most important social, economic, political, health, and human rights issues of current times, and it is central to establishing a broad-based, human-centered global justice movement. For example, much domestic labor, low-wage production, or sex work involves considerable risk to the women workers; some of it entails human rights abuses that are now more widely publicized. When women migrate for such work, their family lives are disrupted; the emotional and psychological toll is high (e.g., Constable, 1997; Yeoh and Huang, 2000). The problems of women in low-wage production or export-processing work have long been addressed (e.g., Fernandez-Kelly, 1983; Nash and Fernandez-Kelly, 1983; Beneria and Roldan, 1987; Ward, 1990; Abeywardene et al., 1994; Tiano, 1994; AMRC, 1998). The lack of rights and the abuses women face in sex work or working as maids and nannies have been raised more recently as serious global issues (Kempadoo and Doezema, 1998; Lim, 1998; Heyzer et al., 1994; Parreñas, 2000, 2001; Yeoh et al., 1999; Ehrenreich and Hochschild, 2002). Trafficking for such work is widely discussed as one of the most egregious and widespread of the abuses (Wijers and Lap-Chew, 1997; Raymond et al., 2002). Women have responded in a variety of ways to resist inequities, reduce the risks they face, demand some of their rights, and enhance their own and their families' lives (Basu, 1995; Ward and Pyle, 1995; Naples and Desai, 2002). It is

249

important to understand the reasons for the increasing presence of women in such work. Global justice movements must incorporate and address the issues of such workers and their families.

This chapter also illustrates that a critical globalization studies examining the relationship of globalization to women's lives must look at women's lives in the contexts of their families, communities, nations, regions, and internationally to fully understand the factors involved. Incorporating gender as a central category of analysis and utilizing such a multileveled analysis can lead to a more comprehensive understanding of globalization — of both its effects and the forces in motion to reshape it. It can also shed light on the complex relationships among women from different countries and classes, revealing both the tensions and the similarities.

In this chapter I examine how women's work is influenced by globalization and how gendered global labor networks are established. I focus in particular on understanding the global forces that increasingly draw or push women into informal sector work (such as sex work, domestic labor, or low wage production for export). These sectors span the globe and increasingly involve low pay, substantial health hazards, and higher levels of migration of women and children. This analysis is critical for effectively addressing the abuses women face in such work because the way we ("we" meaning the women involved, activists, academics, and policy-makers) think about the impact of globalization on the gendered division of labor — and what we determine as the causes of the existing problems — are the fundamental bases upon which we develop policies and strategies for change that can reduce gender inequities and promote global justice. It is only by examining these three sectors simultaneously within the context of globalization that we can understand more clearly the causal factors involved and what might be done to address the problems.

Major Trends of the Recent Period of Globalization

The latest wave of globalization began in the late 1960s and early 1970s. Although it created opportunities for some, it caused problems for many others. The political economy of this period of time involved five different components or trends (Pyle, 1999; Pyle and Ward, 2003). Their effects have been distinctly gendered.

First, many more nations have increased the role of markets in the economy and reduced the role of the government. They include not only the formerly socialist countries and many so-called developing countries but also industrialized countries such as the United States and the United Kingdom.

Second, many developing and formerly socialist countries have shifted to production for external trade, an export-oriented development strategy, rather than focusing on producing for their own internal needs, an import-substitution strategy (McMichael, 2003b).

Third, over these past three decades, many corporations in finance and service sectors of the economy have joined manufacturing firms in becoming multinational. These multinational corporations (MNCs) have increased their presence in the global economy by moving into new tiers of countries during this period of time and by establishing extensive networks of subcontractors in many areas (Pyle, 1999). Suppliers of large multinationals have more recently become multinational corporations themselves.

A fourth component of this period of globalization is the structural adjustment policies (SAPs). The International Monetary Fund (IMF) as a condition for obtaining loans, the IMF has been increasingly governed by financial and commercial interests and its function has shifted from stabilizing the global economy to ensuring repayment of loans (Stiglitz, 2002). Countries adopting SAPs must open their economies to trade and financial flows, deregulate, and privatize. This can undermine indigenous sustainable development. It can also result in financial instability as in the Asian Financial Crisis beginning in 1997 (Aslanbeigui and Summerfield, 2000; Stiglitz, 2002). SAPs also call for reduction of government budget deficits via reducing government employment and cutting many social services. Such cuts disproportionately harm the poor, particularly women (Aslanbeigui, Pressman, and Summerfield, 1994; Sparr, 1994; Elson, 1995; Bandarage, 1997; Tauli-Corpuz, 1998; Aslanbeigui and Summerfield, 2000).

Fifth, and overarching this, there has been a shift in the structure of power internationally. There has been an increase in the power of institutions that profess to support market-determined economic outcomes (MNCs, IMF, the World Bank, and the World Trade Organization [WTO]) relative to those that are more people-centered and concerned with human development that is sustainable (the International Labor Organization, many UN agencies, and nongovernment organizations [NGOs]).

It is also important to note that, although the World Bank and IMF now appear to be more interested in alleviating poverty (World Bank, 2001; World Bank, 2004) and in mainstreaming gender concerns (King and Mason, 2001), their current recommendations in this regard will be extremely hard to successfully enact. Earlier WB and IMF policies (such as SAPs) resulted in serious deterioration in the physical and social infrastructures of many countries and severely reduced their capabilities to meet current goals.

I turn now to look at the effects of these global trends in two complementary ways — first at a more macro level and then at a micro level.

Gendered Effects of Globalization

The analysis is more complicated than space allows me to delineate here because the impact of globalization varies by gender and by other attributes such as class, race and ethnicity, and age as well as by sector of the economy and culture of the particular workplace (e.g., Yelvington, 1995; Lee, 1998; Freeman, 2000; Ehrenreich and Hochschild, 2002). It is also important to note that gender is socially constructed. Gender is constituted by societal views of the norms for male and female roles. Major social institutions — economic, political, cultural, and religious — often reinforce them. Women are typically of lower status than men and occupy subordinate and disadvantaged positions in most societies. Globalization can unleash forces that confront and erode existing social constructions of gender. It can also reinforce existing social constructions of gender or instigate backlashes that defend them. As we will see, global organizations such as MNCs and the IMF often use social constructions of gender to their advantage.

Multinational Corporations, Structural Adjustment Policies, and the Informal Sector

There are analytical and causal links between the spread of MNCs into different areas of the world and the use of SAPs, on the one hand, and increases in women's participation in the informal sector on the other hand (Pyle, 1999).

First, regarding MNCs: it is widely known that much production (clothing, shoes, electronics, toys and games, trinkets, and sporting goods) and provision of services (data entry, reservations, customer support, and other call centers) have moved from so-called industrialized countries into many other regions of the world. More recently, higher value-added manufacturing and service work (such as software development and filmmaking) has been moving out of the more industrialized countries.

It has also been widely documented that many multinational corporations (MNCs) in these sectors have preferred female workers who are typically lower paid and whom the corporations perceive as less likely to contest poor working environments than males (an illustration of MNCs using the social construction of gender to their advantage). Many women employed in MNCs perceive these jobs as preferable to the alternatives available to them (Tiano, 1994; Beek, 2001). This perception can vary according to their education level. Nonetheless, as has been well researched, many aspects of the work environment may, however, be oppressive or exploitative (Abeywardene, 1994; AMRC, 1998; Moure-Eraso et al., 1997; Sivalingam, 1994).

Although MNCs have provided jobs for women, when production costs rise (often when workers resist and seek to improve their conditions), MNCs use several different strategies to reduce expenses — all of which push women into employment in the informal sector. They use new technologies or automate or both, they relocate to other developing countries with lower labor costs or fewer regulations, or they establish networks of subcontractors who pay workers less and can terminate them immediately (Pyle, 1999). Women lose jobs when corporations automate or relocate and often have to eke out income in the informal sector. When MNCs foster networks of subcontractors, it is largely women who are the production workers in these informal sector jobs (Beneria and Roldan, 1987; Balakrishnan, 2002) where conditions are even worse than in the MNCs.

SAPs also contribute to the increase of women in informal sector work. SAPs often require governments to reduce government expenditures so that the revenues needed to repay the loans will be available. The IMF encourages reductions in government employment (which is often largely female) and cutbacks in many government social service programs (such as housing, health, education, and food and fuel subsidies). The adverse effects of these policies fall disproportionately on women who try to stem the fall in their families' standard of living (French, 1994; Emeagwali, 1995; Bandarage, 1997). They seek alternative sources of income — often available only in the informal sector. They take on added household responsibilities to make up for the decrease in badly needed social services. They also organize and resist such policies.

In short, as a result of globalization, many women are increasingly pushed into work in the informal economy simply to survive. Increasing numbers become sex workers, maids or domestics, and workers in export-production networks in order to earn incomes in the restructured global economy. Many must migrate domestically or internationally to obtain these types of jobs. Many of these women are trafficked. They are typically deceived into relocating, responding to ads and migrating, they think, for other types of jobs (such as domestic or factory work) that turn out to involve forced sex work or peonage as workers in low-wage production or domestic work (Preliminary Survey Report on Sexual Trafficking in the CIS, 1999). Conditions can be even more exploitative — both financially and in terms of women's physical and mental health and human rights.

Gendered Global Labor Networks — Sex Work, Maids, and Export-Oriented Production

This brings us to the second and more micro way of looking at the effects of globalization on the gendered division of labor. The global trends discussed above have resulted in labor networks that are clearly gendered. The extent to which such networks have developed and the reasons *why* they have happened, however, have not become a central focus of the wide attention given globalization.

Here, we will look simultaneously at three gendered sectors that researchers have previously studied only separately — sex work, domestic labor, and export-oriented production. (See Pyle, 2001 for fuller development of these ideas; Pyle, 2002; Pyle and Ward, 2003.) These are typically lower-income jobs and the majority of workers are women. It is only by analyzing these three sectors together within the context of changes in the world economy that we can more fully understand the causal factors involved.

These industries have expanded throughout the past three decades and span the globe, occurring in ever-widening areas of the developing world as well as throughout the so-called industrialized countries (Heyzer et al., 1994; Wijers and Lap-Chew, 1997; Chen et al., 1999). In spite of their substantial economic importance to their countries, however, women in these sectors are still largely invisible — from national income accounts and from recent discussions by power brokers on the international scene about how to stabilize the international economy and deal with economically troubled nations.

Although the role of women in export-processing industries has long been a focus of researchers, women's roles in the sex industry and as maids or domestics have been more difficult to study because of problems in obtaining accurate data regarding the numbers involved in these sectors (Heyzer et al., 1994; Wijers and Lap-Chew, 1997; Kempadoo and Doezema, 1998; Lim, 1998). This is also true of the women employed, often as home-based workers, in the multilevel subcontracting networks spawned by exporters (Beneria and Roldan, 1987; Ofreneo, 1994; Chen et al., 1999). Governments do not systematically collect information on workers in these sectors and much of the activity takes place in the underground economy.

When we examine work in each of these sectors, we see many similarities although the work is quite different (see Pyle, 2001, and Pyle and Ward, 2003, for elaboration).

Women in these three sectors encounter a wide range of risks. Each sector is typically characterized by low wages, no benefits, long hours, no security, and a lack of rights in their workplaces — all of which add to stress and exhaustion, and can debilitate workers' physical and psychological health (e.g., Moure-Eraso et al., 1997; Lim et al., 2002). Many are subjected to violence — physical, verbal, and sexual (e.g., Miller, 2002). As women in these three sectors are not only "currently" day workers but also reproducers of the next generation of workers, these conditions affect growth possibilities in the future as well as impact on the current economic conditions of households and nations.

Economic and Political Bases: A Multileveled Analysis

This chapter has shown how the global trends identified in the first section have fostered the increase in women's employment in these three specific sectors. The increased reliance on markets globally and the widespread adoption of the export-oriented development strategy provide a very favorable climate for each of these "industries." The policies of MNCs and SAPs can push women into sectors such as these. International institutions such as the IMF and WB have not only mandated that countries adopt structural adjustment policies (which have the effect of pushing women into these sectors); they have also not voiced opposition to injustices and inequities in such work.

The impact of these trends is magnified in times of economic crises and is particularly devastating for households headed by women. Women often shift among these sectors as a survival strategy, particularly when the export-processing jobs are cut back (e.g., Ward et al., forthcoming).

It is within this global context that we can understand why many women and their households "choose" these types of work. It is also within this framework that we can examine the role of national governments in these industries. What interests do the countries of origin have in the existence of such work? Looking at these other levels of "decision-making" in a multi-leveled analysis highlights the reasons women are increasingly working in these sectors, reveals the institutions and groups with vested interests in having them so employed, and lays a foundation upon which strategies to address the problems women face can be developed.

From the point of view of individuals (and households), the decision to become a sex worker, a maid, or an export-production worker is thought to be a reasonable decision, given the options that exist within the world economy. A woman (and her household) may view these types of work (and the migration that is often needed to obtain them) as a necessary income-earning strategy in spite of the risks associated with such jobs (e.g., Yeoh and Huang, 2000). As cited, individuals and families are often deceived about the real nature of the work.

At another level, the government's role in maintaining and supporting these sectors are also related to these dimensions of globalization. Many governments have had to meet the demands of international institutions (such as the IMF or MNCs) while addressing enough of the needs of their citizens to maintain some social stability. They are also propelled by the desires of powerful elites and classes within their society. Many national governments have been pushed into development planning that fosters these three occupations. Attraction of MNCs has been the most-favored growth strategy in the last few decades; this promotes export-processing jobs. Second, the development of a tourism industry has been the second most-favored growth sector in the last decade, often leading to a sex tourist industry. Last, exporting surplus labor to other countries has become an integral part of many countries' development strategy, resulting in many of the emigrating women becoming domestics or sex workers.

Governments take actions that support each of these sectors, regardless of how risky and insecure they are for women, because they provide employment, incomes, and often foreign exchange and because they serve the interests of powerful institutions and classes that national governments have to accommodate. In providing employment and some income for a substantial number of people, they diminish the social unrest that can accompany poverty and undermine or overthrow governments.

In some countries, all three industries have been institutionalized in their development plans. The Philippines and Bangladesh are examples (Rosca, 1993; Ofreneo, 1994; Chin, 1997; Constable, 1997, 2002; Ofreneo and Ofreneo, 1998; Ofreneo et al., 2002; Santos, 2002; Pyle and Ward, 2003; Ward et al., forthcoming). Although governments do not keep official statistics on women's employment in these three sectors, they have clearly built economic development plans on these women's endeavors despite the adverse working conditions they face. When women have organized to improve their work lives, governments have often used their power to suppress their efforts (e.g., Ofreneo, 1994). This knowledge helps us counteract government rhetoric that reliance on work in such informal sectors is short-term or that governments seek to protect the rights of their citizens.

Governments are particularly unlikely to pay attention to the concerns of women workers in the widespread subcontracting networks that have multiplied in the export-oriented industries because governments wish to be hospitable to MNCs and their subcontracting networks. Governments are also unlikely to critically examine sex work or domestic employment. Income from such work is often essential for the survival of poor families and migration may provide a flow of remittances that become the foreign exchange needed to service the debt or buy imports. Therefore, given the nature of the international political economy, the very institution women might seek assistance from in combating the problems of work in these sectors has significant vested interests in the continued existence of these industries.

Conclusions

In conclusion, there are clear analytical linkages between these five dimensions of globalization, women's increased presence in gendered labor networks such as these three sectors, and women's disadvantaged status. Looking at these three sectors together helps us recognize similar issues, problems, and concerns across the sectors and helps us develop a more realistic view about the challenges involved in organizing for change. When we see how important these three sectors are to many countries and how they can be implicitly or explicitly part of a country's development strategy, we are better able to understand the magnitude of the problems and the constraints we face in devising strategies for change.

In light of this broader understanding of the global context within which gendered global labor networks are increasing, and given our understanding of the market forces, ideologies, and institutions involved, we can make some recommendations that can begin to address the problems associated with the global trends identified at the beginning of this chapter:

- We must counter the market ideology and rhetoric, and show that the spread of market processes is really shaped by powerful institutions largely motivated by profits and that these processes have differing effects by gender.
- We must advocate for development policies that foster sustainable indigenous development that incorporates both women and men rather than the widely-advocated export-oriented development that serves the needs of these powerful institutions.
- We need to push MNCs and their subcontracting networks for industrywide global codes of conduct that protect workers' rights.
- We must advocate for SAPs that are designed with human development in mind and incorporate gender perspectives, rather than being designed to ensure repayment of loans to large international lenders. We must amend the new policies of the IMF and WB to include rebuilding of institutions needed for sustainable human development so that women are not pushed disproportionately into these sectors and so that governments are not forced to explicitly or implicitly support such sectors.
- We must strengthen international institutions that have human-based development as their primary focus (UNDP, 1999, 2003) and incorporate gender into data collection, all planning, and all assessment of progress of in attaining development goals such as the Millennium Development Goals (MDG) (e.g., UNIFEM, 2000, 2002).

In addition, juxtaposed to the trends that characterize globalization outlined at the beginning of this chapter, there are many important new approaches, concepts, and methods developed by scholars and activists that are innovative and provide the basis for positive change for gender equality in the future. They include empowering more participants to address the gendered problems associated with globalization (particularly the women involved); challenging existing disciplinary paradigms and establishing multidisciplinary approaches that fundamentally include gender (Beneria, 2003); developing new concepts, gaining acceptance for them, and operationalizing them empirically (e.g., "caring" labor); developing and legitimizing new methodologies (such as gender budgets or gender analysis of government policy); obtaining appropriate and comparable data across countries and across sectors; comprehensively assessing the risks women face and the rights they should have (Summerfield, 2001); creating more extensive indicators of women's progress beyond the UNDP's Gender Sensitive Development Index and Gender Empowerment Index (UNDP, 1995; UNIFEM, 2000); conducting more extensive and comparable case studies (such as Balakrishnan, 2002; see also Beek, 2001); and developing multilevel analyses (such as Parreñas, 2001). Ultimately, demanding accountability from public policies (UNIFEM, 2000, 2002) and crafting alternative policies are critical for positive social change. It may be necessary to fundamentally reconsider the usefulness of current institutions and determine whether they can be transformed or whether new ones are needed. The challenges are serious but these new approaches, concepts, and methods can be powerful in addressing them. A critical globalization studies that incorporates a gender perspective will make a substantial contribution to moving this agenda forward.

Note

1. The various names given to different types of countries are unsatisfactory at best. In full recognition of the oversimplification involved, I use the terms industrialized (to refer to the OECD countries), transitional (to refer to the formerly socialist countries), and developing (to refer to the others, most of which are trying to develop more sustainable economies). I reject the notion that the industrialized countries have achieved a status to which other countries should aspire.

25

Beyond Eurocentrism and Afrocentrism: Globalization, Critical Hybridity, and Postcolonial Blackness

G. Reginald Daniel

Eurocentrism: The Origin of the Master Racial Project

Colonialism and Its Aftermath

Beginning in the late fifteenth and early sixteenth centuries, as they established empires in the New World, Asia, the Pacific, and eventually Africa through colonial expansion, various West European nation-states — specifically Spain, Portugal, Italy, France, Germany, Holland, Denmark, and England —had encounters with populations that were very different culturally and, above all else, phenotypically from themselves. These factors, along with an awareness among the European nation-states of their power to dominate others, laid the foundation for the concept of race. Racial formation had no basis in natural science. It was, rather, the culmination of popular beliefs and assumptions originating in the longer-standing identification of distinctive human groups and their association with differences in physical appearances. Beginning in the middle to late eighteenth century, however, the concept was embraced by naturalists and other learned individuals who gave it legitimacy as a supposed product of scientific investigation. In this intellectual climate, the word *race* increasingly came to designate a biologically defined group. Racial formation not only coincided specifically with the rise of European global domination but also became a way of categorizing what were already conceived as inherently unequal populations. More important, these racial divisions were grounded in exploitive economic relations and served to justify a unique form of slavery involving mainly individuals of African descent. Although expansion, conquest, exploitation, and enslavement had been a part of human history for millennia, none of these phenomena were supported by ideologies or social systems based on race (Smedley, 1993; Omi and Winant, 1994).

A corollary to the rise of European nation-states to global dominion was a Eurocentric worldview. It is a perspective that views Europe as a self-contained entity and as a transcendental nexus of all particular histories by virtue of its unprecedented accomplishments in the realms of materialist rationalism, science, and technology (Sorokin, 1957, 1985). Accordingly, Eurocentrism is integrally linked to the historical period encompassing what is referred to as modernity and has been the master racial project that other racial projects had as a point of reference. Furthermore, Europe became the unquestioned and dominant center of a global civilization from which emanated an encompassing universalism in the form of colonialism and imperialism, directed outward to exploit and dominate the non-Western "Others," as well as force the latter to adopt European norms. Specifically, Eurocentrism is premised on an "either/or" way of thinking that assumes differentiation — racial and otherwise — in terms of dichotomous and hierarchical categories of value, privilege, and experience. This dichotomous hierarchy thus attaches superior status and privileges to whiteness and inferior status and privileges to all racialized Others.

The legitimacy of dichotomous and hierarchical notions of racial (and cultural) difference has been the subject of intense interrogation and deconstruction by proponents of the concept of postcolonial "critical hybridity," which seeks to acknowledge the racial and cultural blending that has been obscured, if not erased, by several hundred years of Eurocentric discourse. Part of this process has involved demystifying the notion of a self-contained Europe, without at the same time embracing the rigid essentialism that underpins radical Afrocentrism and much black nationalist thought. Accordingly, postcolonial critical hybridity opens up new possibilities for understanding not just European history but global history as well. Indeed, to a considerable extent, what is referred to as European civilization is actually a global human heritage "that for historical, political, and geographical reasons" has been bequeathed to the modern world "in the guise of a European or Western synthesis" (Pieterse, 1994: 144).

Globalization and the New World Order

Colonialism was the process by which the European nation-states reached positions of economic, military, political, and cultural domination through conquest, direct settlement, and control of "others" — particularly in terms of occupation of their land — through both the distant control of resources, as well as of direct settlement. In an extended sense, the phenomenon was linked not only to the "First World" capitalist mode of production and mass culture, but also the concomitant destruction of pre- or noncapitalist forms of social organization (Tiffin, 1990; Shohat and Stam, 1994; Williams and Chrisman, 1994). The dismantling of European colonial empires in the twentieth century gave rise to an awareness that West European civilization — and its outposts in Asia, the Pacific, Africa, and the Americas — was no longer "the unquestioned and dominant center of the world" (Slater, 1994: 88). It also raised the hopes of the newly independent countries for the emergence of a truly postcolonial era. Such optimism proved to be short-lived, however. It became apparent that the West had not, in fact, relinquished control, although it had given up colonialism as its primary mechanism of control, which still involved domination, exploitation, and exclusion of subordinate groups in their most explicit and abrasive form. Rather, colonial structures based on domination and exclusion increasingly have been juxtaposed with or replaced by neocolonial structures, characterized by what Italian political theorist and activist Antonio Gramsci describes as "hegemony," which allows dominant groups effectively to maintain control and hierarchy but create the illusion of equality by selectively including its subjects and incorporating its opposition (Omi and Winant, 1994).

The persistence of neocolonial structures and practices is very obvious as compared to the less immediately perceptible emergence of capitalism as a truly global economy. Indeed, the final demise of colonial regimes and subsequent collapse of the Soviet Union removed the barriers to the capitalist world market and opened the way for "an irresistible and seemingly irreversible globalization" of capitalist economic and cultural exchanges (Hardt and Negri, 2000: xi). This has been accompanied by a transformation of the dominant productive process itself. There has been a reduction in the significance of industrial factory labor and an increase in the significance of "communicative, cooperative, and affective labor" (Hardt and Negri, 2000: xiii). These forces in turn have brought about a significant transformation of the modern imperialist geography of the globe. Consequently, the spatial divisions of what have been termed core, semiperipheral, and peripheral regions — or more frequently, "First," "Second," and "Third" Worlds — seem to have become hopelessly commingled (Shohat and Stam, 1994).

Many lament the globalization of capitalist production and exchange as the closing of institutional channels through which workers and citizens can influence or contest the economic forces of exploitation; others celebrate globalization, along with the concomitant frequency and ease with which economic and cultural exchanges move across national boundaries, as the liberation of capitalist economic relations from the restrictions that political forces have imposed on them. Correspondingly, the political sovereignty of the nation-state itself and its ability to regulate production and exchange, money, technology, people, and goods, although still powerful, has progressively declined. Even the most powerful nation-states can no longer be thought of as supreme and sovereign authorities associated with the imperialisms of the modern era. The decline in nation-state sovereignty, however, does not mean that sovereignty itself has declined. Along with the new global market and networks of production, sovereignty itself is taking a new globalized form. It is composed of a series of national and transnational entities united under a single logic of rule that progressively incorporates the spatial totality of the entire global realm within its open, expanding frontiers (Hardt and Negri, 2000).

Many designate the United States as the ultimate authority that rules over the process of globalization. If imperialism in the strict meaning of the term was the domain of Europe, globalization is thus considered the province of the United States, which has become the center of a new global empire. According to this perspective the United States is at worse repeating the practices of old European imperialists; at best it is a more efficient and more benevolent world leader, rectifying the errors of the previous European-dominated imperialist order originating in the modern era (Hardt and Negri, 2000). Both these views are based on the erroneous assumption, however, that the United States has simply donned the mantle of global power that was previously under the authority of European imperial nations. It is true that globalization in some sense originates in the United States and the underpinning of the global world order is, in a sense, Eurocentric. In addition, the United States does occupy a privileged position in the globalization process. Yet, in contrast to imperialism, which consisted of historical regimes originating in conquest, globalization is a social order that has no temporal boundaries and no territorial center of power or spatial limitations to its rule. Consequently, in the emerging global order the United States cannot, and indeed no nation-state can, maintain its position as a world leader in the dominative manner of old European nation-states (Hardt and Negri, 2000). This continuing global Western influence is, rather, maintained through a flexible, yet, complex, interweaving of economic, political, military, ideological, and cultural dynamics and hegemonic power relations, including interventionist politics (Shohat and Stam, 1994).

These power relations not only mask contemporary forms of control, subordination, and exploitation in the manner of neocolonialism but more important, indicate that globalization wields the potential to maintain hegemonic forms of cooptation and rule on an unprecedented scale (Shohat and Stam, 1994; Hardt and Negri, 2000). Yet, globalization also offers new opportunities for the forces of resistance to develop political organization of global flows and exchanges reflective of postcolonial structures and practices aimed toward more egalitarian ends. Indeed, those forces of resistance are themselves not limited to any geographical region. The political task is thus not to resist the forces of globalization per se. Rather, the goal should be to reorganize and redirect them as the basis for an alternative global society based on coexistence, cooperation, and partnership (Eisler, 1988; Arnason, 1990; Featherstone, 1990; Havel, 1994, 1995; Hardt and Negri, 2000; Mittelman, 2000; Robinson, 2002).

Postcolonial Discourse: Decentering Europe and Deconstructing the West Hybridity, Hierarchy, and Hegemony

"While both 'colonialism' and 'neocolonialism' imply oppression and the possibility of resistance, 'postcolonialism' neither posits clear domination nor calls for clear opposition" (Shohat and Stam, 1994: 39). Consequently, the term "postcolonial" obscures the traces of colonialism that exist in the present (Shohat and Stam, 1994). By implying that colonialism has come to an end, the term *postcolonial* lacks a political analysis of contemporary power relations (Shohat and Stam, 1994). *Postcolonial* implies going beyond not only colonialism but also anticolonial nationalist theory — which sought and led to the dismantling of formal political colonial domination — as well as a movement beyond a specific point in history. Postcolonial thought, therefore, stresses deterritorialization and the constructed nature of national borders and nationalism, as well as the obsolescence of anticolonialist discourse (Shohat and Stam, 1994).

Because the *post* in *postcolonial* suggests a stage after the demise of colonialism, it is imbued, quite apart from its users' intentions, with a spatial and temporal ambiguity. *Postcolonial* tends to be associated with Third World countries that gained independence after the Second World War. Yet, it can also refer to the Third World diasporic presence within First World metropolises. The *postcolonial* also collapses diverse chronologies such that the term potentially can be expanded exponentially. It can include processes of liberation originating in all societies affected by colonialism, including areas in North and South America that gained political independence during the late eighteenth and early nineteenth centuries. Yet the majority of countries in Africa and Asia achieved independence during the twentieth century; "some in the 1930s (Iraq), others in the 1940s (India, Lebanon), and still more in the 1960s (Algeria, Senegal, the Congo) and the 1970s (Angola, Mozambique)," among others (Shohat and Stam, 1994: 39).

These ambiguities and contradictions notwithstanding, the term *postcolonial* may be applied to a broader process that involves the dismantling of Eurocentric discourse in the emerging global order (Shohat and Stam, 1994). For example, the concept of *hybridity* in postcolonial discourse calls attention to the complex and multilayered identities generated by geographical displacements. Although racial and cultural hybridity have existed from time immemorial, European colonial expansion accelerated and actively shaped a new world of practices and ideologies of racial and cultural blending. This is particularly the case in the Americas, which have been the site of *syncretism, creolization,* and *mestizaje* involving unprecedented combinations of indigenous peoples, Africans, and Europeans, and later of immigratory diasporas from all over the world (Shohat and Stam, 1994).

On one level, the celebration of hybridity counters the colonialist obsession with racial "purity," which viewed different racial groups as different species created at different times that were therefore forbidden to "interbreed." The hostility to miscegenation — particularly in Anglo-North America — was encapsulated in such pejorative terms as "mongrelization" and "mulattoes" (seen as necessarily infertile) (Young, 1994, 1995). Yet, while rejecting the colonialist obsession with purity, postcolonial hybridity also counterpoises itself against the rigid essentialism that often underpins Third World discourse, including radical Afrocentrism and much black nationalist thought. In addition, the concept of hybridity in postcolonial theory is admirably honed to deal with the complexities and contradictions "generated by the global circulation of peoples and cultural goods in a mediated and interconnected world" (Shohat and Stam, 1994: 42). The hybrid globalized human is confronted with the challenge of moving among the diverse modalities of sharply contrasting cultural and ideological worlds. Consequently, hybrid identities are not reducible to a fixed formula; rather, they form a changing repertory of cultural modalities (Williams and Chrisman, 1994).

As part of the general assault on Eurocentrism, postcolonial discourse not only challenges any notion of racial purity but also interrogates the concept of race. Indeed, given that science has been unable to produce empirical data that would confirm the existence of clearly delineated biophysical racial boundaries, many "deconstructive" postcolonial thinkers present race as a problem, a misconception, a legacy of the past that should be dispensed with altogether. Accordingly, they seek to transcend race in pursuit of a universal humanism as part of an emerging global consciousness (Daniel, 2002). Yet, constructivist postcolonial thinkers argue that any notion of transcending race would be unthinkable until the struggle to achieve equality of racial difference has been won. Indeed, these thinkers challenge the notion that race is something we can or should move beyond. Instead, they posit racial transcendence by acknowledging a more inclusive identity based on a multiplicity of ancestral backgrounds. Many of these "constructive" postcolonial thinkers do agree that the concept of race invokes biologically based human characteristics in the form of racial traits but do not view racial categories and boundaries as being absolutely fixed in biological fact. Racial categories and identities are understood as unstable and decentered complexes of sociocultural meanings that are constantly being created, inhabited, contested, destroyed, and transformed by political struggle. Consequently, racial formation may be thought of not only as an element of social structure but also as a dimension of human cultural representation and signification — rather than an illusion (Omi and Winant, 1994; Daniel, 2002).

However, the impulses behind and implications of the celebration of hybridity are themselves "mixed," it could be said (Shohat and Stam, 1994). The deconstruction of dichotomous notions of purity and celebration of racial and cultural blending per se, if not articulated in the manner of "critical hybridity" — or "radical mestizaje" (Sandoval, 2000: 72) — risks downplaying contemporary forms of neocolonialism that effectively maintain racial hierarchy. Consequently, any discourse on postcolonial hybridity must simultaneously take into consideration questions of hegemony that create the illusion of equality by means of token gestures of inclusion without those in power actually giving up control. For example, national racial and cultural identities in Latin America have often been officially articulated as hybrid, multiracial, and egalitarian (figure 25.1a). Yet, they have been hypocritically integrationist, that is to say, assimilationist ideologies, seeking whitening through racial and cultural blending, which have deliberately obscured subtle hegemonies that reproduce racial hierarchies in a new guise (figure 25.1b).

From Center to Periphery

Despite these caveats, the concept of postcolonial critical hybridity is part of a broader process instrumental to demystifying or deconstructing Europe and acknowledging the specificity of its development by reading its history through multiple racial and cultural lenses. A closer analysis of the celebrated markers in the historical formation of Europe — Greece, Rome, Christianity, the Renaissance, the Enlightenment — indicates that each is a moment of hybridity and integration: Greece, strongly influenced by, if not an actual colony or outpost of, Egyptian, Phoenician, and Asian civilizations; Rome, "strongly indebted" to Greece, Egypt, and Carthage; Christianity, originally a religion of Asian origin, whose link with Byzantium, the Nestorians, and Gnostics at times "loomed larger" than its relationship with European (i.e., Latin Christendom); the Renaissance, "a recovery of Hellenic civilization passed on thorough Arabic civilization and deeply engaged with non-European cultures"; and the Enlightenment, "another period wide open to non-European influences, from China to Egypt" (Pieterse, 1994: 146).

The impetus behind these revisions of Eurocentric history is not, however, necessarily to enhance the role of Africa and individuals of African descent or the non-Western world by linking them with the much-vaunted achievements of Western Europe. Rather, their goal is to point out that many of the philosophies; political principles; forms of knowledge in physics, chemistry, technology, medicine, and metallurgy; and art that have been attributed singularly to Western Europe by virtue of its supposedly inherent superiority have been to a considerable extent multicultural

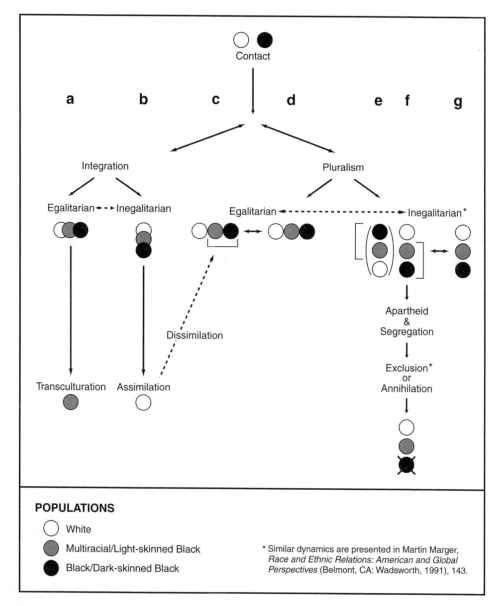

Figure 25.1. Pluralist and integrationist dynamics.

and multiracial, that is to say, plural in origin (figure 25.1d) and transcultural and transracial (or egalitarian integrative) in composition (figure 25.1a). It is significant that the synthesis of these elements is uniquely European. Yet this should not obscure the fact that the sources are plural and intercontinental as well. European civilization becomes more transparent if we look at Europe as part of Eurasia, and Southern Europe as part of a larger Mediterranean continuity encompassing North Africa as well as influences that extend from West Africa. Indeed, the actual borders between the West and the larger non-Western world have been more blurred and porous frontiers than Eurocentric rhetoric and imagery have acknowledged (Shohat and Stam, 1994; Pieterse, 1994).

Radical Afrocentric Discourse and Strategic Essentialism

The Eurocentric paradigm, and its companion pieces, white racism and white supremacy, have had a particularly oppressive impact on individuals of African descent across the globe. It served to justify African enslavement and became the basis for the one-drop rule of hypodescent that designates as black everyone of African descent. Correspondingly, the rule perpetuated a binary racial order that has necessitated individual identification as either black or white. This has obscured and distorted, if not erased, the racial and cultural blending that has taken place since the colonial era. By codifying the dichotomization and hierarchical valuation of whiteness over blackness in the manner of inegalitarian pluralism (figure 25.1f), the rule not only served as part of the strategy for preserving European American cultural and racial "purity" but also as a means of maintaining white privilege.

By drawing boundaries solidifying subordinated racial identity and excluding African Americans from interacting with European Americans as equals, the rule had the unintended consequence of legitimating and forging group identity. The use of the one-drop rule for cultural and political mobilization is most obvious in currents of Afrocentric discourse and in other racial projects that rely on the notion of a primordial African "race" and nation. The rule has been viewed as a form of "strategic essentialism" (Spivak, 1990), which is a necessary, if originally oppressive, means not only of maintaining a distinct, but equal, African American racial and cultural plurality, but more important, mobilizing African-descent individuals in the continuing struggle against white privilege.

The legitimacy of the Afrocentric desire to give voice to the shared global disillusionment and alienation embedded in the African diasporic experience is not in question. Indeed, the strengths of this perspective are undeniable: the fostering of group pride, solidarity, and self-respect among African-descent individuals and an interrogation of the ideology of inegalitarian integration (assimilation) (see figure 25.1b) and the perpetuation of differences in the manner of inegalitarian pluralism (apartheid) (see figure 25.1f) (hooks, 1995; Marable, 1995). But the effectiveness of any organizing principle as the basis for essentialized collectives (viewed as if they were "natural," static, and eternal units), is fraught with irreconcilable contradictions. The exponents of radical Afrocentrism often criticize the validity of the concept of race on the one hand while reinscribing essentialist notions of black identity on the other (Asante, 1980, 1992; Rattansi, 1994; Marable, 1995). They thus rearticulate the notion of "purity" that underpinned nineteenth-century scientific racism. The theorists of the period argued that racial "purity" was a necessary prerequisite for a civilization to be creative. This made it increasingly unacceptable that Greece, as the designated birthplace of the modern West and thus the source of Western rationalism, could have been the result of the blending of indigenous Europeans, African Egyptians, and Semitic Phoenicians, whether in the form of colonization or mere cultural (and racial) exchange resulting from contact through trade, war, etc. However, once the forces of an emergent capitalism were propelled into full drive, Eurocentric theories served as the justification for the enslavement of Africans. Accordingly, Africans were necessarily excluded from any discussion that focused on their contribution to the development of the West and global history by extension (Keita, 1994).

It is imperative to deconstruct the Eurocentric rendering of history (Levine, 1992; Lefkowitz, 1996; Will, 1996). Yet, many radical Afrocentrists apply the term "black" to anyone and anything of African origin, no matter how remote in space or time (Young, 1994; Will, 1996; Lefkowitz, 1996). They rarely explore, and sometimes openly dismiss, the profound dynamics of racial and cultural blending and multiple identities found throughout the African diaspora (Daniel, 1992; West, 1993; Marable, 1995). Radical Afrocentrists thus delineate the contours of blackness and the African diasporic experience from a photographic negative of whiteness (Rattansi, 1994; Marable, 1995). Consequently, the end result of radical Afrocentrism is very similar to the oppressive mechanism of the one-drop rule, which originated in the "either/or" paradigm that has served as the underpinning of modern Eurocentric consciousness. By incorporating to contemporary issues and value the notion of a transhistorical and transgeographical "black" essence, radical Afrocentrists obscure the lived and empirical conditions that are the basis for diverse identities and cultural productions. They thus actually nurture even further the very collective historical amnesia they seek to cure (Daniel, 1992; hooks, 1995).

"Critical Hybridity": The Demise of Eurocentrism or Eurocentrism in a New Guise?

Toward a Postcolonial Blackness

If Afrocentrists wish to dismantle Eurocentrism they must also move beyond the "either/or" thinking that underpins both Eurocentric and radical Afrocentric discourse. The goal should be to embrace a moderate Afrocentrism based on a "both/neither" way of thinking that is compatible with the postcolonial concept of critical hybridity (Collins, 1993; Anderson, 1995; Daniel, 2002). This moderate Afrocentrism is posited on an egalitarian blending of pluralism (figure 25.1d) and integration (figure 25.1a) — integrative pluralism (or pluralistic integration) — in which blackness and whiteness are seen as relative rather than absolute extremes on a continuum of grays. Yet, many radical Afrocentrists view the concept of critical hybridity as tantamount to Eurocentrism in a new guise that would lead to the loss of black distinctiveness and political cohesiveness (figure 25.1c) (Spencer, 1993; Jones, 1994; Lemert, 1996). This criticism, nevertheless, obscures the potential that the concept holds for challenging a myopic and constricting "ontological blackness" (Anderson, 1995). This bias, in turn, precludes acknowledging and exploring new possibilities for the construction of self and community (hooks, 1995), but more important, for critiquing the pathologies of racism that have been sustained by the U.S. binary racial order (Collins, 1993; hooks, 1995).

One factor that divides Afrocentrism — particularly moderate Afrocentrism — from the concept of critical hybridity is that Afrocentrism means different things to different people, and this has obscured its deeper significance. The most common perception is that Afrocentrism seeks to expose individuals — particularly through the education system — to the accomplishments and contributions of individuals of African descent in the manner of egalitarian pluralism (figure 25.1c). Another view is that Afrocentrism is a new form of black nationalism that exposes white racism and promotes racial separatism (or inegalitarian pluralism). In extreme cases, the goal has been to replace white superiority with a new hierarchy premised on the superiority of blackness (figure 25.1e) in response to the perceived failure of civil rights legislation and philosophy to ameliorate the economic, political, social, and psychological oppression that continues to plague African Americans (Schiele, 1991, 1998).

Although Afrocentrism is related to African history and originated in black nationalist thought, it is more appropriately described as a paradigm that places African-descent individuals at the center of their analyses. Accordingly, they become subjects rather than simply objects of history. In addition, Afrocentrism is predicated on traditional African philosophical assumptions. Consequently, it rejects the dichotomization and hierarchical valuation of differences typified by Eurocentric thinking, which divides things into mutually exclusive and unequal categories of value, privilege, and experience (Schiele, 1991, 1998; Asante, 1992; Hochschild, 1995; Kershaw, 1993; Myers, 1998). Whereas Eurocentrism places Europe at the center of everything and dislocates African contributions, Afrocentrism relocates or recenters Africa to its rightful place in human history in terms of human origins and the origins of civilization. Afrocentrism achieves this without ethnocentrism and without making Africa the center of attention. Rather, it posits a cosmovision that happened to originate in Africa, and is centered in an African worldview, simply because Africa is the birthplace of humanity. It acknowledges a global cultural inheritance that has special meaning for people of the African diaspora but is one that all humans share as descendants of the first diaspora out of Africa.

The concept of critical hybridity is thus quintessentially Afrocentric in the deepest meaning of the word. It opens up a long overdue conversation about the shared cultural and ancestral connections that have been obscured, if not erased, by several hundred years of Eurocentrism in the United States and across the globe. In addition, this concept is catalytic in the formation of a "postcolonial blackness" that opposes any reification of the one-drop rule, which has historically represented blackness and whiteness in essentialist and one-dimensional ways to reinforce and sustain white domination and black subordination. Accordingly, the concept of critical hybridity not only serves as the basis for "strategic antiessentialism" (Lipsitz, 2003) in the struggle for black liberation but more important, provides a means through which all individuals can liberate themselves from and move beyond the dichotomous and hierarchical perspectives espoused by both Eurocentric and radical Afrocentric discourse.

26

Globalization and the Grotesque

Lauren Langman and Karen Halnon

Introduction

Neoliberal globalization fosters vast wealth for its elites while majorities face greater inequality, exploitation, alienation, insecurity, declining incomes, and retrenchments of benefits. How and why do majorities "willingly assent" to, if not actively support, this system? We will attempt to argue that globalized "culture industries" serve to entertain, distract, and erase critical reason and render the historically arbitrary nature of neoliberal capital as "natural." Global capital has been able to produce and distribute hegemonic ideologies that secure its reproduction. The most important of these has been the universalization of consumerism as an ideology and set of practices that articulate identities and lifestyles that "willingly assent" to domination (Langman, 1993; Sklair, 2001).

Culture as a "contested terrain" of values, meanings, and identities is a site of struggle, protest, and resistance where alternative, if not transgressive, subcultures contest dominant values and meanings, sometimes retreating to alternative forms of community and identity. As global capital engenders anger and alienation, it produces a market for consumption of commodified forms of cultural resistance that mask the operations of political economy, neutralize political consciousness, and can thwart progressive mobilization. Specifically, we now witness a variety of subcultures and practices that constitute the "carnivalization" of the world (Langman, 1998; Halnon and Langman, 2003). The proliferation of the carnivalesque, the centrality of the grotesque, and transgressive practices in many forms of lifestyle and popular and not so popular culture, stand as critiques of globalization whereas forms of transgression are resistances to domination. But such resistance, at the cultural level, serves to sustain the very system it would critique. As contemporary globalization fosters its own anticultures, it profits and reproduces itself.

Globalization, Domination, and Hegemony

Domination is the extent to which a group has power to secure behavioral and often ideological compliance. Intellectual elites, parts of "historic blocs," fashion cultural beliefs and practices that legitimate elite power and secure willing consent to their authority claims (Gramsci, 1971). For most of history, the hegemony of a church–state elite has been based on religion; leaders were proclaimed gods, god-like, or picked by gods. Following the Enlightenment and the valorization of "Reason," authority claims were made on the basis of "popular sovereignty," the "will of the people." With industrialization, and the ascendance of bourgeois rule as a world-historical fact, nationalism became an integral moment of hegemony. Yet there was resistance in workers' movements, unionization, and socialist revolutions.

In recent decades there have been massive changes in the nature and locations of production, global reorganizations of corporations through conglomeration, down-sizing, mergers, and so forth. With changes in technology, computerization, digita-lization and miniaturization, there have been radical changes in manufacturing, communication, and finance. Anything can be made anywhere — with command and control centers anywhere. Vast amounts of money as profits, investments, and sales circle the globe everyday (Sassen, 1998). Capitalism has become a transnational system, decoupled from the territorial nation-states of their origin, following a neolib-eral logic and dominated by a transnational capitalist class (Sklair, 2001). Yet, as has been widely documented, the claims that capitalism "serves everyone well," and neoliberalization does it even better, increasingly pale against the realities of growing inequality.

Notwithstanding its domination, globalization fosters resistance. But what, then, are the compensatory means by which hegemony is maintained despite growing stagnation and inequality? How is capitalist domination secured at the level of con-sciousness? For a large number of people, consumerism, with its promises of the "goods life," consumer-based, fantastic forms of ideal selfhood, and fandoms (audi-enceship) as communities, provide realms of personal gratification encapsulated from the social that fosters a withdrawal of concerns from social issues to a privatized hedonism and dulling of critical consciousness that sustains hegemony. Carnivaliza-tion, as a genre of consumerism, as the ascendance of a plurality of transgressive subcultures and media expressions, as celebrations of the grotesque and practices of resistance, repudiates the dominant global system yet reproduces it.

Carnival and the Grotesque

The Liminal

Every culture has a normative order, rules, regulations, criteria of evaluation, and standards of desirable conduct. But every social structure generates certain pressures toward deviance. As Durkheim suggested, deviance is necessary in order to defend virtue. Vice must be punished to affirm the dominant values. For Victor Turner (1969), structures foster antistructures, *liminal* times and sites, "in between" places, and moments at the "edges," where typically suppressed and otherwise proscribed forms of deviance are not simply tolerated but made overt and often celebrated. The liminal allows the displacement of tensions and contradictions so that the dominant society may be reproduced. The production of liminality as a commodity serves to reproduce the globalized social order.

Carnival Culture as Liminal   For Bakhtin (1968), the carnival, emergent during the Middle Ages, was a popular celebration that stood opposed to the official feasts and tournaments that celebrated and secured the power of the aristocratic elites. Carnival was a ludic critique of the elites, their cultures, and values. Typical patterns of hierarchy, deference, and demeanor were ignored (Bakhtin, 1968). It was a liminal site of transgression, reversals of the quotidian, inversions of the dominant norms and standards of propriety; restraints of everyday life waned, all forms of the prohibited were valorized. Moral boundaries of "decency" from the political to the erotic were transgressed, especially concerning the body, bodily indulgence, orifices, excreta, the profane, the vulgar, and obscene. Carnivals expressed the Dionysian that Nietzsche claimed was suppressed by restrictive Apollonian domination. Celebrations often involved bodily excreta and secreta; much of the critique of power took scatological forms.

The carnival, as a site of resistance apart from everyday life and subservience to the landowners and clergy, celebrated the disgusting and grotesque. Transgressions, as resistances to elite power, rejected dominant authority and its morals. Typical practices included parody, mocking, satire, and the humiliation and hectoring of kings and queens, priests and bishop. Above all, laughter stood as a rebuke to the elites. But however transgressive carnival may have been, whatever hope and freedom it provided, as a form of cultural resistance, in lieu of political action, it served to sustain the structural arrangements in which land-owning dynasties were legitimated by the clerical elites.

The Grotesque   The grotesque stood in direct opposition to medieval forms of high art and literature. It was a realm of freedom that spoke the truth of the system. The grotesque, often seen in masks or representations of faces with greatly exaggerated and distorted features and shapes, bulging eyes, protruding nose, etc., stands as a critique of the dominant order, whereas forms of resistance as acts of freedom, repudiate elite domination, norms, values, and practices. For Bakhtin (1968), one of the most important aspects of "grotesque realism" is its function of degradation: bringing something or someone down to earth to create something better. "To degrade an object does not imply merely hurling it into the void of nonexistence, into absolute destruction," according to Bakhtin, "but to hurl it down to the reproductive lower stratum, the zone in which conception and a new birth take place. Grotesque realism knows no other lower level; it is the fruitful earth and the womb. It is always conceiving" (1968: 21). In the carnival, the people's laughter was the materialization of the degradation of authority. Thus laughter symbolizes the collective comprehension and shared affirmation of the satire.

Carnival Brazil   Although carnival was brought to Brazil from Venice by modernizing elites, it was quickly appropriated by the masses. It moved from small private celebrations in homes and clubs to massive public festivals in the streets and the parades of the samba schools. Carnival is a spontaneous, spectacular, nocturnal celebration that takes place in the streets and plazas where the boundaries of performer and spectator are blurred. Carnival repudiates the ordinariness of home, work, job, and church where the everyday worlds of dominance, order, and restraint are located. It is a time and place of vibrant play and merrymaking as millions take to the streets to drink, dance, sing, shout, prank, flirt, and sometimes make love (Linger, l992). Carnival demands that the celebrants be in constant immediate physical, often erotic, contact with each other. All who view and participate in Carnival become swept up in its music, passion, and excitement. Revelry abounds, barriers fall, and there are inversions of norms. In the polysemic liminal antistructures of ironic inversion and sensual indulgence, everyone has a good time.

Carnival includes celebrations of the grotesque, and transgressions and degradations against authority and patriarchal gender norms. This is especially evident in the flouting of sexual norms and reversals of gender power. Carnival creates a ludic antistructure of equality that empowers women through erotic agency in a society that is typically repressive. Female modesty and reserve typical of everyday life in the home wane as women wear highly revealing clothing — and often little of that; by contrast, *machoa* men appear timid. Exhibitionism and desire become "normal" as the carnival aesthetic valorizes female sensuality and sexuality through the scanty, erotic. Such inversions empower women by repudiating male standards and thus celebrate the permissible collective eros of carnival (Parker, 1991). Anonymous and indeed egalitarian sexuality is part and parcel of the festival. Liaisons can occur between strangers who wear masks — and frequently little more. For a few days of the year, the poor, the dominated, and exploited women find "encapsulated realms" of agency and dignity.

As a *festa popular*, carnival values life over death, joy over sadness, and the poor over the rich. Carnival provides realms for community, agency, recognition, and dignity, which are rarely found in the daily lives of the impoverished. Here the poor can find microspheres of agency and empowerment, where the janitor may be a great dancer, the maid a fine singer, and the factory worker a songwriter–musician. For a few days the Brazilian poor leave aside their hierarchical, repressive society to live more freely and individually. Indeed, in the context of Carnival, sexuality and aggression as transgressive realms of agency empower selfhood.

Carnival as Commodity

The carnival of Rio has been transformed over the years. First, it was an elite celebration, then a popular festival, and now, in the current age, a commodity in the global tourist circuit of affordable jet travel. Tourism is now one of the major industries of the world. But at the same time — and part and parcel of the process — global tourism has become intertwined with the transgressive that has become a fungible commodity, especially the erotic. This includes the sex tourism of Thailand and the Philippines, singles resorts and the gay festivals of South Africa and Australia. (Carnival Rio also includes a large element of gay, transgendered, and s/m elements). The transgressive moments of partial nudity and liberated eros have now become essential features of a variety of exemplars of carnivalization.

Carnival draws millions of visitors from all over the globe. Many of these visitors join in the popular song, dance, and drink festivities of the street. Many seek out furtive and anonymous sexual encounters. There has developed a small industry for tourists as participants in the carnival and the samba parade. The transgressive eroticism of the carnival has now become one of the widely commodified tour-istscapes ranging from "spring break" for college students to the exhibitionism of Mardi Gras/Bourbon St. "Spring break" in places like Cancùn offers students a week of sun, sex, and drink, not necessarily in that order. Various rituals such as wet T-shirt contests, no T-shirt contests, and various means of consuming great quantities of alcohol encourage anonymous sex, what youth refer to as "hooking up." For the older crowds, visiting New Orleans, a city highly dependent on tourism, Bourbon Street/Mardi Gras has become synonymous with breast baring, mooning, and in some cases, males displaying their accoutrements. There are anecdotal reports that some people actually publicly engage in sex acts. We can clearly see how the sexual freedom that came with modernity and feminism has become a commodified trans-gression. Where as many aspects of carnival appeal to the anger and frustrations of the working classes, the transgressive touristic eroticism provides an encapsulated moment of fun, freedom, and attention in liminal moments apart from school or work, which most often allow people very little of this kind of diversion. Notwith-standing legacies of Puritanism, and/or the extent to which some critics might argue that the participants, especially women, are actively promoting their own subjugation, the participants enjoy these festivals and typically report that transgression is fun.[1]

Varieties of Transgressive Experience

The fundamental model of "carnivalization," the grotesque as critique and a realm of freedom, with transgression, inversion, and humiliation as resistance, can be seen in a plurality of subcultural practices and expressions of mass media that allow the otherwise forbidden in ways that elide political control. Thus such varied practices as breast baring, extreme body modification and decoration, and mass-mediated forms of humiliation and anger allow at the margins what cannot be expressed in the centers, what cannot be allowed to impact the political economy without its profits and neoliberal ideologies being challenged.

Subcultures of the Grotesque

Adolescence is the socially constructed stage in the life cycle that bridges the discon-tinuity between childhood and adulthood as defined by work and economic self-sufficiency. It generally involves differentiation from parents and often rebellion as youth seek to establish autonomy from parents and find their own identities and values. Adolescents typically join identity-granting subcultures of meaning ranging from those that are adult oriented to membership in a variety of oppositional and resistance-based subcultures. Insofar as every generation faces different political-economic realities, there are historically based differences in identities and values mediated through membership in age-based subcultures (Mannheim, 1952).

Subcultures emerge when the larger culture fails to meet people's needs — for example, to provide resources or meanings — so that some people find fault with the culture and form their own identity-granting communities of meanings. Large numbers of young people today have been rendered "surplus" populations with dim economic prospects. Many others find the meanings and values provided by global capital and its culture industries, shallow, empty, vacuous, or dehumanized. Tittley (2000) suggests that some youth-subcultures can be thought of "as a class struggle expressed through the use of style … a rebellion against the dominant culture using shock tactics." Thus, a number of carnivalesque subcultures have emerged that embrace the grotesque as a critique of the dominant order, either withdrawing (e.g., "modern primitives" with extreme body modifications) or developing innovative alternatives, such as Goths or punks, who find encapsulated realms of commodified freedom to transgress and articulate anger and discontent in the spectacles of rock concerts.

Body Modification and the Urban Primitive   Tattoos, piercings, scarifications, and body modifications as adornments of identity, have been widely practiced in primitive societies as markers of transition, identity, etc. In the nineteenth century, a number of Western sailors and whalers, sailing through the South Pacific, subjected themselves to local, traditional tattoo artists. By the early twentieth century, the tattoo had become a working-class urban art form, a marker of difference and distinction clearly denoting class boundaries and celebrations of "real manhood" even if the tattoo proclaimed love to Mom, girlfriend, etc. But in recent decades, the tattoo has crossed class and gender boundaries and has become a marker of differentiation from or repudiation of the dominant society and its norms, values, and lifestyles. Body modifications have been appropriated by a number of groups for a number of different reasons. For example, among young people, a piercing or two — perhaps an earring for a guy, a nose ring, or a tattoo has become a typical fashion statement. Perhaps as many as one third of all students/young people have some form of body modification or ornamentation as a sign of differentiation, if not rebellion, from parents. They are also frequent in various subcultures such as artist communities, bikers, punks, Goths (see below), gays, and s/m–leather crowds as well.

Most such people, but surely not all, use such adornments as an indication of differentiation from the dominant society and membership within an alternative subgroup. Thus, whereas the rational world of global capitalism is seen as cold, sterile, uncaring, and dehumanizing, the transgressive art form — its often grotesque nature — stands as a protest. With its links to traditional, primitive societies, the modification links the person and his or her selfhood to a mythical Shangri-la before contemporary globalization created a universal, if bland sameness. As a rite of transition, it signifies the crossing of an imaginary border from the mainstream to the transgressive.

A large subculture of "urban primitives" embraces extreme body modification, extensive tattoos, and piercing over much of the body. These groups typically reject the values and lifestyles of global capitalism; they often use premodern designs from societies such as the Maori or the Yakuza. Thus, we might find extensive facial tattoos combined with septum rings of horn or bone and perhaps other rings or studs in the face or other parts of the body (Langman and Cangemi, 2003). The ultimate form of grotesque may well be various studs, rings, and chains inserted in the genitals. These are often combined with tattoos of the pubic area ("Cupid's wings"). Such genital decorations, meant for display to others, represent a fundamental inversion and reversal of dominant codes of propriety in which one's privates are meant to be concealed rather than displayed as artworks. In other words, grotesque decoration or modification of the genitals can be read as a "screw you," a critique of globalized modernity by actors who would reclaim a premodern romantic authenticity that inverts current globalization.

Punks[2]   In the late 1970s, as *deindustrialization qua globalization* began to impact the job prospects of youth, tastes in popular music and lifestyles began to differentiate along class lines. It was at this time that rock music, itself seen as transgressive, as for example Elvis' erotic gyrations, the Beatles' psychedelia, Boy George's androgyny, and Pink Floyd's inversions, began differentiating into various genres from heavy metal to bubblegum rock.[3] Whether distinctive genres of music produce subcultures or subcultures create their own musical tastes is an interesting debate, but by the 1980s, with such groups and stars as the Sex Pistols, Dead Kennedys, and Iggy Pop and the Stooges, transgressive violence, sexuality, and obscenity became staples of a nihilistic genre of the grotesque that yet endures. As the Sex Pistols put it, "We're not into music ... we're into chaos," which we now understand as a ludic/transgressive critique of a global economy that provides little economic hope for blue-collar youth — nor does the escapism of mainstream popular culture provide such youth with meaning systems. Instead, they articulated the alienation, nihilism, and rage of the young victims of global capitalism and its neoliberal ideology. The Sex Pistols, more than any other group, created the "look of punk, the way of dressing, behaving, and maybe even thinking."[4] But with the demise of the Sex Pistols, The Clash became the standard bearer of punk and more clearly directed anger and angst toward global inequality and injustice (for example, as seen in their triple CD *Sandinista*).

Today, as more and more blue-collar youth have been marginalized by globalization, punk subcultures are not only found almost everywhere in the "advanced" countries, but punk music and shock rock (see later section) has become a multibillion dollar industry. Moreover, the various fashions, ornamentations, and accoutrements are another significant source of profit, as various aspects of punk fashion come to the edges of the mainstream. Whereas punk fashion emphasizes black, like most forms of "opposition dress" such as fascists, anarchists, bohemians or Goths (see the following section), one of the distinctive features of punk is its attempt to shock in various ways from multicolored, extreme hair styles and body modifications (see above) to wearing various forms of black leather, often studded or spiked, that suggests the wearer is fierce and powerful, although socially marginalized. Like the primitive empowered by wearing a lion mask, wearing a bulldog-like spiked collar not only differentiates the wearer from the larger society, but the grotesque appearance stands as a critique.

Goths: Everyday Is Halloween   If punk can be understood as an expression of working-class anger, Goth can be understood as an expression of the ennui of the more educated — especially various artistic or creative types.[5] Although emergent out of punk music, with groups like Sisters, Bauhaus, and Souxie and the Banshees, Goth emerged as a dark opposite to light and ephemeral disco. Death symbolism is often found, for example, in pale faces and black makeup. As Ice Princess puts it, "The common thread in Goth culture is an appreciation for the dichotomy of life, the contrast between light and dark, good and evil, with an awareness that the two can't exist without each other, and that the traditional value judgments assigned to those opposites are not necessarily true."[6] For our purposes, most Goth is an attempt to "reenchant the world" (Ritzer, 2001). To confront the globalized world of "specialists without feelings," Goths have created a "tribal identity" based on a cultural pastiche of the premodern of Gothic tribes, medieval fantasy, magic, Victorianism, and vampirism (there are subgroups of medieval, Victorian, fairy, and technomodern Goths). Many Goths are new age spiritualists, Wiccans, or occultists into runes, healing stones, and magical practices. Some wear crosses whereas others wear ankhs. Being more educated, they are likely to read Dante, Byron, Tolstoy, Anne Rice, Bram Stoker, and Storm Considine (a Goth writer) and flock to German expressionist films.

Perhaps the most important aspect of Goth is its flamboyant garb, ranging from neomedieval to transgressive latex to fetish. Although black is the dominant color, white shirts, gowns, and peasant blouses are also popular, as are often red and blue. Hair colors are also varied. Fish net nylons, ornamental brassieres, bloomers, bustiers, and so on, that publicly flaunt their oppositional erotic styles are common markers of boundaries of membership designed to shock outsiders. Although exposed flesh is hardly novel today, Goth style emphasizes a transgressive erotic signifier of being more sinful, wicked, and fun. In that most are employed in the dominant economy replete with its bureaucratic codes, Goth subcultures allow the person to both participate in that economy and yet after work, critique its conformity and dehumanization. When they return home, many have created castles, dungeons, or occult havens.[7]

Mass-Mediated Grotesque   The grotesque, as a commodity in the global market and a critique of globalization, has become the basis for a variety of mass-mediated carnivalesque productions of the "culture industries" that articulate alienation, anger, and rage as well as offer highly profitable outlets for its expression that displace political economic frustrations to the cultural where they are politically neutralized. Although there are many variations on the themes, they all share elements of transgression, grotesquerie and, often, humiliation. As the Frankfurt School taught us, those who are stepped on from above need to step on someone below. Those humbled in his or her other roles seek someone from below to see humiliated. *Schadenfrende* (joy in another's misfortune) is alive and well and is itself a profitable commodity.

Professional Wrestling   The growth of professional wrestling, a bizarre form of entertainment, is rooted in the medieval carnival as a tournament with its own pomp and circumstance. "The wrestling match is the giant at the carnival as celebrated by Rabelais. In this hagiography of battle, we see the vulgarizing process as it transforms violent action into symbolic gestures [of] easy to decode rituals of burlesque knights-at-joust and giants tossing each other about" (Twitchell, 1992: 226). Professional wrestling is "theatrical, histrionic, gesticulatory: blue-collar circus" (Twitchell, 1992: 229). It is what Barthes called "spectacle of excess," admittedly staged performances of grandiloquent gestures and feigned violence that quickly resolve moral questions. From the names to the outlandish and grotesque costumes, tattoos, and masks to the highly scripted moves, choreographed pain, and planned outcomes, every detail has been crafted to be outrageous. Oversized, hyperhormonal entertainers, bulked by steroids and fed raw meat, with such names as Macho Man, Hit Man, Cain, Stone Cold, Undertaker, Bulldog, and Hulk enact primitive soap-operatic morality tales replete with fabricated histories of personal grudges, treachery, betrayals, rivalries, and animosities with promises of severe and instant retaliatory justice.

All of the elements of classical carnival are present: the grotesque, the valorized (lower) body, unmodulated affectivity, vulgarity, sexuality, and discharging bodily fluids. In a typical WWE spectacle, the "stars" are likely to point to their genitals, strike those of their opponent, and shout unending profanities. The audience and opponents treated to endless "fuck yous," single-finger salutes, and/or commanded to "suck this." There may be some nudity, mooning, and female breast-baring. There is symbolic, and often not so symbolic, bloodletting, urination, defecation, or spitting. Humiliation, an important aspect of carnival, attempts to debase the self of the Other, from taunting of affairs with his girlfriend to the "stinky face" — putting one's butt in the face of a weakened opponent who is thereby forced to "kiss the ass" of power — an apt metaphor for today. One of the central themes of wrestling as carnival is the disdain of authority. The simulated critique of staged power displaces genuine critique of the actual power of the global capitalist system. Wrestling valorizes a hypermasculinity of those who can dish out as well as take violence "like men." Insofar as the neoliberal economics has eroded the power of blue-collar men as sole bread-winners, mass media supplies a compensatory, symbolic masculinity.

Shock Music   We previously noted the emergence of punk and Goth music and subcultures. For the culture industries, genres are endless variations on the same themes; each "innovation" is a formulaic reproduction of what had been. Thus, there is a direct line of cultural continuity that runs from the shocking, outrageous lyrics, practices, and lifestyles of Sid Vicious and Alice Cooper to current incarnations in Marilyn Manson, Eminem, and Slipknot (Halnon and Langman, 2003). Although each group and artist has its own carnivalesque shtick, the common theme is the valorization of the grotesque and inversions of dominant norms. Perhaps this begins with costumes that are explicitly grotesque, bizarre, and shocking. At times there is nudity, and stage shows include defecation, urination, and vomiting — all markers of the carnival (Bakhtin, 1968). There are even transgressive sexual acts ranging from crotch rubbing and mooning to on-stage oral sex. But it is the lyrics that most clearly differentiate the shock genre, with frequent profanity, allusions to the angst of life (not clearly directed to social factors), rage, anger, alienation, and transgressive sexuality.[8]

Shock TV   Once upon a time, the word *pregnant* could not be used on television. In pursuit of audience share (aka profit) there are no restraints on language or discussions of erotic actions, for example, *Sex in the City*. Given what was previously noted, a number of programs, such as *Howard Stern*, *Man Show*, and *Mancow* (now off air), combine the testosterone levels of a teenaged male with the grotesque and the humiliating. Stern will ask his female guests when they first had oral sex and how they like anal sex. Women will be asked to take off their clothes. Women may come on the program to compete for implants, but must first display what they have to Stern and the television audience — although to home viewers in a pixelated form. But the *Man Show* is even more chauvinistic with endless adolescent discussions that denigrate women, and each show concludes with the Jigglies, a trio of scantily clad women who jump on trampolines to ensure their implants jiggle. Like wrestling, it creates a realm of compensatory phallic masculinity in face of the growing castration and impotence men face in a global political economy. Like wrestling, it is also a critique of the system, articulated as "amusing" humiliation of the Other.

Freak Shows   In his analysis of the Jerry Springer, Jenny Jones, Rikki Lake, and Montel Williams–type talk shows, Gamson (1998) notes that the "guests," typically from the lower stratum, termed *freaks*, are transformed by the culture industries into saleable commodities, entertainments for those who would witness the lifestyles of the poor, the pathetic, and the grotesque. But at the same time, the guests, the "freaks," speak out, seeking to advise the larger world of the problems they face in problematic relationships, in stigmatized identities, in stigmatized relationships, and so on. Thus, tales of incest, infidelity, and deviant sexuality (b/d, s/m, gay/bi sexuality) are told in ways that might start fights between guests on *The Springer Show* or elicit massive disdain from the studio audience of Jones or Lake. Women who turn tricks along with, or pimp for, their daughters might appear one day, men who like to be spanked the next, then female weight lifters, people too fat for skimpy clothes, or shopaholics with their problems.

(Un)reality TV   With the market appeal of humiliation and degradation, a variety of low-cost "reality" shows have appeared, such as *Survivor*, *Fear Factor*, *Bachelor/ette*, *Elimidate*, *Scare Tactics*, and so on. Although each is quite different, the principle is basically the same: "ordinary people" compete with each other for wealth or love. They may be asked to perform difficult, often grotesque feats, like survive in deserts and eat rats or insects or put their heads in a tank of eels. They may be intentionally humiliated. They might have to reveal intimate aspects of self. For example, in each episode of Elimidate, one person begins the "date" with four others, although only one of a group can ever win the prize, the spouse, or the contest; the rest, the losers, face humiliations. How apt a simile and critique of neoliberalism.

Conclusion

Capitalism in its neoliberal global form produces ever greater inequality, immisera-tion, and alienation. But why do we not see mobilizations and political pressures to redress grievances? The ideological control of culture colonizes consciousness in ways that render historically arbitrary forms of class domination natural, normal, and in the best interest of the people who then "assent" to domination. Critiques are labeled immature, pathological, and bizarre. In the feudal era, this was heresy; today, critique is marginalized as the purview of irrelevant academics or misguided malcontents.

For much of the twentieth century, the hegemony of capital was sustained by nationalism and later by consumerism (Sklair, 2001). Consumerism not only secures much of the profits for the global economy, but a loyalty to the system and a withdrawal of concern from social/public issues to the privatized hedonism of consumption (Langman, 1993). But given the growing inequality of neoliberal capital and given the changing income distributions in which people are losing ground, Gramsci's analysis must be supplemented. As we examine the trends of the current culture industry in its global reach, we note a clear trend of what we call the "carnivalization of culture," by which we mean a resurrection of the medieval carnival as commodity in which celebrations of grotesque and transgressive practices serve to critique the dominant system and its elite classes, but at the same time, by encouraging people to let off steam, reproduce that system. This was clear in the medieval carnival (Bakhtin, 1968) and in the latter-day carnival of Rio (Parker, 1991). But in the globalized era, the culture industries have transformed carnival and packaged the grotesque as a commodity to be sold to a variety of niche markets. This can be seen in a number of ways from emergence of subcultures of cultural resistance such as working-class punks and middle-class Goths to touristic erotic transgressions, to the ever more grotesque nature of television's "freak shows," shock jocks, and wrestlers. Our analysis might easily lead to the very cynicism and nihilism that is assuaged by carnivalization. Yet we also see the contradictions of neoliberal globalization fostering a massive alternative globalization movement (Langman, in press). But that is another story for another day.

Notes

1. Katz (1990) has similarly argued that criminal behavior is, indeed, fun and crime is seductive.
2. For a quick history of punk see http://www.fastnbulbous.com/punk.htm.
3. See Weinstien, 2000.
4. http://www.almac.co.uk/personal/brian/sexp.html.
5. For a good history and analysis, see http://www.vamp.org/Gothic/Text/gothic-faq.html#11.
6. http://www.ice-princess.net/academia.html.
7. There is even a website for home furnishings and fashions that bills itself as a Martha Stewart of Goth. http://www.toreadors.com/martha/motifs/index.html.
8. There are other genres and stars that do in fact directly speak to issues of injustice, e.g., Bono of U2, Rage against the Machine, or Anni De Franco.

*Linking Globalization Studies
to Global Resistance Movements:
Marginalized Voices and
Neglected Topics*

27

The Implications of Subaltern Epistemologies for Global Capitalism: Transmodernity, Border Thinking, and Global Coloniality

Ramón Grosfoguel

Can we produce a radical anticapitalist politics beyond identity politics? Is it possible to articulate a critical cosmopolitanism beyond nationalism and colonialism? Can we produce knowledges beyond Eurocentric and Third World fundamentalisms? Can we overcome the traditional dichotomy between political–economy and cultural studies? Can we move beyond economic reductionism and culturalism? How can we overcome the Eurocentric modernity without throwing away the best of modernity as many Third World fundamentalists do? In this paper, I propose that an epistemic perspective from ethnic studies has much to contribute to this debate. It can add to a critical globalization perspective beyond the outlined dichotomies and to a redefinition of capitalism as a world-system.

Epistemological Critique

The first point to be examined is the contribution of ethnic studies to epistemological questions. The hegemonic Eurocentric paradigm that has informed Western philosophy and sciences in the modern–colonial capitalist, patriarchal world-system for the last 500 years assumes a universalistic, neutral, objective point of view. Chicana and black feminist scholars (Moraga and Anzaldua, 1983) as well as Third World scholars inside and outside the United States (Mignolo, 2000) reminded us that we always speak from a particular location in the power structures. Nobody escapes the class, sexual, gender, spiritual, geographical, and racial hierarchies of the modern–colonial capitalist world-system. As feminist scholar Donna Haraways (1988) states, our knowledges are always situated. Black feminist scholars called this perspective *standpoint epistemology* (Collins, 1990), whereas Latin American philosopher of liberation Enrique Dussel called it the "geopolitics of knowledge" (Dussel, 1977).

This is not only a question about social values in knowledge production or the fact that our knowledge is always partial. The main point here is the locus of enunciation, that is, the geopolitical location of the subject that speaks. In Western philosophy and sciences, the subject that speaks is always hidden, concealed, erased from the analysis. Ethnic location and epistemic location are always decoupled. By delinking

283

ethnic location from epistemic location, Western philosophy and sciences are able to produce a myth about universalist knowledge that covers up, that is, conceals who is speaking, as well as the geopolitical location in the structures of power from which the subject speaks. This is what the Colombian philosopher Santiago Castro-Gomez called the "point zero" perspective of Eurocentric philosophies (Castro-Gomez, 2003). The "point zero" is the point of view that hides and conceals itself as being beyond a particular point of view, that is, the point of view that represents itself as being without a point of view. It is this god's-eye view that always hides its local and particular perspective under a universal perspective. Historically, this has allowed Western man (the gendered term is intentionally used here) to represent his knowledge as the only knowledge capable of achieving a universal consciousness, and to dismiss non-Western knowledge as particularistic and, thus, unable to achieve universality.

This strategy has been crucial for Western global designs. By hiding the location of the subject of enunciation, European/Euro-American colonial expansion and domination was able to construct a hierarchy of superior and inferior knowledge and, thus, of superior and inferior people around the world. We went from the sixteenth-century characterization of "people without writing" to the eighteenth- and nineteenth-century characterization of "people without history," then to the twentieth-century characterization of "people without development." We went from the sixteenth-century "rights of people" to the eighteenth-century "rights of man," and to the late-twentieth-century "human rights." All of these are part of global designs articulated to the simultaneous production and reproduction of an international division of labor of core–periphery that overlaps with the global racial–ethnic hierarchy of European and non-European. What is the implication of this epistemological critique to our knowledge production and to our concept of capitalism?

Coloniality of Power as the Power Matrix of the Modern World

Globalization studies, with a few exceptions, have not derived the epistemological and theoretical implications of the epistemic critique coming from subaltern locations in the colonial divide and expressed in academia through ethnic studies and woman studies. We still continue to produce a knowledge from the Western man "point zero" god's-eye view. This has led to important problems in the way we conceptualize global capitalism. The following examples can illustrate this point. If we analyze the European colonial expansion from a Eurocentric point of view, what we get is a picture in which the origins of the capitalist world-system is primarily produced by the interimperial competition in Europe. The primary motive for this expansion was to find shorter routes to the East, which led accidentally to the so-called discovery, and eventual Spanish colonization of the Americas. From this point of view, the capitalist world-system would be primarily an economic system that explains the behavior of the major social whose by the economic logic of making profits as manifested in the extraction of surplus value and the accumulation of capital at a world-scale. Moreover, the concept of capitalism implied in this perspective privileges economic relations over other social relations. Accordingly, the transformation in the relations of production produces a new class structure typical of capitalism as opposed to other social systems and other forms of domination. Class analysis and economic structural transformations are privileged over other power relations.

Without denying the importance of the ceaseless accumulation of capital on a world scale and the existence of a particular class structure in global capitalism, I raise the following epistemic question: What would the capitalist world-system look like if we moved the locus of enunciation from the European man to an indigenous women in the Americas — to, say, Rigoberta Menchu in Guatemala or to Domitila in Bolivia? The first implication of shifting our geopolitics of knowledge is that what arrived in the Americas in the late fifteenth century was not only an economic system of capital and labor for the production of commodities to be sold for a profit in the world market. This was a crucial part but was not the sole element in the package. What arrived in the Americas was a broader and wider system that an economic reductionist perspective of the capitalist world-system is unable to account for. From the perspective of an indigenous woman in the Americas what arrived was a more complex system. A European/capitalist/military/Christian/patriarchal/white/hetero-sexual/male arrived in the Americas and established simultaneously in time and space several entangled global hierarchies:

1. An international division of labor of core and periphery where capital organized labor in the periphery around coerced and authoritarian forms (Wallerstein, 1974).
2. An interstate system of politico-military organizations controlled by European males and institutionalized in colonial administrations (Wallerstein, 1979).
3. A global racial–ethnic hierarchy that privileges European people over non-European people (Quijano, 1993, 2000).
4. A global gender hierarchy that privileges males over females and European patriarchy over other forms of gender relations (Spivak, 1988; Enloe, 1990).
5. A sexual hierarchy that privileges heterosexuals over homosexuals and lesbians. (It is important to remember that indigenous people in the Americas did not consider sexuality among males as pathological and had no homophobic ideology.)
6. A spiritual hierarchy that privileges Christians over non-Christian/non-Western, spirituality institutionalized in the globalization of the Christian (Catholic and later Protestant) church.
7. An epistemic hierarchy that privileges Western knowledge and cosmology over non-Western knowledge and cosmologies, and is institutionalized in the global university system (Mignolo, 1995, 2000; Quijano, 1991).

It is no accident that the conceptualization of the capitalist world-system, from the perspective of the South, will question its hegemonic conceptualization. Following Peruvian sociologist Aníbal Quijano (1991, 1998, 2000), we could conceptualize the present capitalist world-system as a historical-structural heterogeneous totality with a specific pattern of power that he calls a "colonial power matrix." This matrix affects all dimensions of social existence such as sexuality, authority, subjectivity, and labor (Quijano, 2000). The sixteenth century initiates a new global power matrix that by the late nineteenth century came to cover the whole planet. In my reading of Quijano, I conceptualize the coloniality of power as an entanglement of multiple and hetero-geneous hierarchies of sexual, political, epistemic, economic, spiritual, and racial forms of domination and exploitation. What is new in the "coloniality of power" is

how the idea of race and racism becomes the organizing principle that structures all
of the multiple hierarchies of the world-system (Quijano, 1993). For example, the
different forms of labor that are articulated to capitalist accumulation at a world-
scale are assigned according to this racial hierarchy: coercive labor control of non-
European people on the periphery and "free-wage labor" in the core. The idea of race
organizes the world's population into a hierarchical order of superior and inferior
people. Contrary to the Eurocentric perspective, race, gender, sexuality, spirituality,
and epistemology are not additive elements to the economic and political structures
of the capitalist world-system, but an integral and constitutive part of the broad
package called the European modern–colonial capitalist patriarchal world-system
(Grosfoguel, 2002). European patriarchy and European notions of sexuality, epistemology, and spirituality were exported to the rest of the world through colonial
expansion as the hegemonic criteria to racialize, classify, and pathologize the rest of
the world's population in a hierarchy of superior and inferior races.

This conceptualization has enormous implications that I can only briefly mention
here:

1. The old Eurocentric idea that societies develop at the level of the nation-state in
    terms of a linear evolution of modes of production from precapitalist to capitalist
    is overcome. We are all encompassed within a capitalist world-system that articu-
    lates different forms of labor according to the racial classification of the world's
    population (Quijano, 2000; Grosfoguel, 2002).
2. The old Marxist paradigm of infrastructure and superstructure is replaced by a
    historical-heterogeneous structure or a "heterarchy" (Kontopoulos, 1993): that is,
    an articulation of multiple hierarchies, in which subjectivity and the social imagi-
    nary is not derivative but constitutive of the structures of the world-system (Gros-
    foguel, 2002). In this conceptualization, race and racism are not superstructural or
    instrumental to an overarching logic of capitalist accumulation; they are constitu-
    tive of capitalist accumulation at a world-scale. The "colonial power matrix" is an
    organizing principle involving exploitation and domination exercised in multiple
    dimensions of social life, from economic, sexual, or gender relations to political
    organizations, structures of knowledge, state institutions, and households (Quijano,
    2000).
3. The old division between culture and political economy as expressed in postcolonial
    studies and political economy approaches is overcome (Grosfoguel, 2002). Postco-
    lonial studies conceptualize the capitalist world-system as being constituted prima-
    rily by culture, whereas political economy places the primary determination on
    economic relations. In the "coloniality of power" approach, what comes first —
    culture or the economy — is a false chicken–egg dilemma that obscure the com-
    plexity of the capitalist world-system (Grosfoguel, 2002).
4. Coloniality is not equivalent to colonialism. It is not derivative from, or antecedent
    to, modernity. Coloniality and modernity constitute two sides of a single coin. The
    same way as the European industrial revolution was achieved on the shoulders of
    the coerced forms of labor in the periphery, the new identities, rights, laws, and
    institutions of modernity such as nation-states, citizenship and democracy where
    formed in a process of colonial interaction with, and domination–exploitation of,
    non-Western people.

5. Anticapitalist decolonization and liberation cannot be reduced to only one dimension of social life. It requires of a broader transformation of the sexual, gender, spiritual, epistemic, economic, political, and racial hierarchies of the modern world. The "coloniality of power" perspective challenges us to think about social change and social transformation in a nonreductionist way.

From Global Colonialism to Global Coloniality

We cannot think of decolonization in terms of conquering power over the juridical–political boundaries of a nation, that is, by achieving control over a single nation-state (Grosfoguel, 1996). The old national liberation and socialist strategies of taking state power at the level of a nation-state are not sufficient because global coloniality is not reducible to the presence or absence of a colonial administration (Grosfoguel, 2002). One of the most powerful myths of the twentieth century was the notion that the elimination of colonial administrations amounted to the decolonization of the world. This led to the myth of a "postcolonial" world. The heterogeneous and multiple global structures put in place over a period of 450 years did not evaporate with the juridical–political decolonization of the periphery over the past 50 years. We continue to live under the same "colonial power matrix." With juridical–political decolonization we moved from a period of "global colonialism" to the current period of "global coloniality." Although "colonial administrations" have been almost entirely eradicated and the majority of the periphery is politically organized into nation-states, non-European people are still living under crude European/Euro-American exploitation and domination. The old colonial hierarchies of European/non-Europeans remain in place and are entangled with the "international division of labor" and accumulation of capital at a world-scale (Quijano, 2000; Grosfoguel, 2002).

Herein lies the relevance of the distinction between "colonialism" and "coloniality." Coloniality refers to the continuity of colonial forms of domination after the end of colonial administrations, produced by colonial cultures and structures in the modern–colonial capitalist world-system. "Coloniality of power" refers to a crucial structuring process in the modern–colonial world-system that articulates peripheral locations in the international division of labor, subaltern strategies, and Third World migrants' inscription in the racial–ethnic hierarchy of metropolitan global cities. Peripheral nation-states and non-European people live today under the regime of "global coloniality" imposed by the United States through the International Monetary Fund (IMF), the World Bank (WB), the Pentagon, and NATO. Peripheral zones remain in a colonial situation even though are not any longer under a colonial administration.

"Colonial" does not refer only to "classical colonialism" or "internal colonialism," nor can it be reduced to the presence of a "colonial administration." Quijano distinguishes between colonialism and coloniality. I use the word *colonialism* to refer to "colonial situations" enforced by the presence of a colonial administration such as the period of classical colonialism, and, following Quijano (1991, 1993, 1998), I use *coloniality* to address "colonial situations" in the present period in which colonial administrations have almost been eradicated from the capitalist world-system. By *colonial situations* I mean the cultural, political, sexual, and economic oppression and exploitation of subordinate racialized and ethnic groups by dominant racial and ethnic groups, with or without the existence of colonial administrations. Five hundred years of European colonial expansion and domination formed an international division of labor between Europeans and non-Europeans that is reproduced in the present so-called "postcolonial" phase of the capitalist world-system (Wallerstein, 1979, 1995). Today the core zones of the capitalist world economy overlap with predominantly white/European/Euro-American societies such as Western Europe, Canada, Australia, and the United States, whereas peripheral zones overlap with previously colonized non-European people. Japan is the only exception that confirms the rule. Japan was never colonized nor dominated by Europeans and, similar to the West, played an active role in building its own colonial empire. China, although never fully colonized, was peripheralized through the use of colonial entrepôts such as Hong Kong and Macao, and through direct military interventions.

The mythology of the "decolonization of the world" obscures the continuities between the colonial past and current global colonial and racial hierarchies and contributes to the invisibility of "coloniality" today. For the last 50 years, states that had been colonies, following the dominant Eurocentric liberal discourses (Wallerstein, 1995), constructed ideologies of national identity, national development, and national sovereignty that produced an illusion of independence, development, and progress. Yet their economic and political systems were shaped by their subordinate position in a capitalist world-system organized around a hierarchical international division of labor (Wallerstein, 1979, 1984, 1995). The multiple and heterogeneous processes of the world-system, together with the predominance of Eurocentric cultures (Said, 1979; Wallerstein, 1995; Lander, 1998; Quijano, 1998; Mignolo, 2000), constitute a global coloniality between Europeans/Euro-Americans and non-Europeans. Thus, coloniality is entangled with, but is not reducible to, the international division of labor. The global racial–ethnic hierarchy of Europeans and non-Europeans, is an integral part of the development of the capitalist world-system's international division of labor (Wallerstein, 1983; Quijano, 1993; Mignolo, 1995). In these postindependence times the colonial axis between Europeans/Euro-Americans and non-Europeans is inscribed not only in relations of exploitation (between capital and labor) and relations of domination (between metropolitan and peripheral states) but in the production of subjectivities and knowledges. This forces us to examine new utopian alternatives beyond Eurocentrism and fundamentalism.

Border Thinking

So far, the history of the modern–colonial capitalist patriarchal world-system has privileged the culture, knowledge, and epistemology produced by the West (Spivak, 1988; Mignolo, 2000). No culture in the world remained untouched by European modernity. There is no absolute outside to this system. The monologism and monotopic global design of the West relates to other cultures and peoples from a position of superiority and is deaf toward the cosmologies and epistemologies of the non-Western world.

The imposition of Christianity in order to convert the so-called savages and barbarians in the sixteenth century, followed by the imposition of "white man's burden" and "civilizing mission" in the eighteenth and nineteenth century, the imposition of the "developmentalist project" in the twentieth century and, more recently, the imperial project of military interventions under the rhetoric of democracy and human rights in the twenty-first century, have all been imposed by militarism and violence. Two responses to the Eurocentric colonial imposition are Third World nationalisms and fundamentalisms. Nationalism provides Eurocentric solutions to a Eurocentric global problem. It reproduces an internal coloniality of power within each nation-state and reifies the nation-state as the privileged location of social change (Grosfoguel, 1996). Struggles above and below the nation-state are not considered in nationalist political strategies. Moreover, nationalist responses to global capitalism reinforce the nation-state as the political institutional form per excellence of the modern–colonial capitalist patriarchal world-system. In this sense, nationalism is complicit with Eurocentric thinking and political structures. On the other hand, Third World fundamentalisms of different kinds respond with an essentialist "pure outside space" or "absolute exteriority" to modernity. They are antimodern forces that reproduce the binary oppositions of Eurocentric thinking. They respond to the imposition of Eurocentric modernity with an antimodernity that is as hierarchical, authoritarian, and antidemocratic as the former.

A plausible solution to the Eurocentric vs. fundamentalist dilemma is what Walter Mignolo, following Chicana thinkers such as Gloria Anzaldua (1987), calls "critical border thinking" (Mignolo, 2000). Critical border thinking is the epistemic response of the subaltern to the Eurocentric project of modernity. Instead of rejecting the institutions of modernity and retreat into a fundamentalist absolutism, border epistemologies redefines modernity from the cosmologies and epistemologies of the subaltern, located in the oppressed and exploited side of the colonial difference. What border thinking produces is a redefinition of citizenship, democracy, human rights, and humanity, beyond the narrow definitions imposed by European modernity. Border thinking is not antimodern; it is the modern response of the subaltern to Eurocentric modernity.

A good example of this is the Zapatista struggle in Mexico. The Zapatistas are not antimodern. They do not reject democracy and retreat into some form of indigenous fundamentalism. On the contrary, the Zapatistas accept the notion of democracy, but redefine it from a local indigenous practice and cosmology, conceptualizing it as "commanding while obeying" or "we are all equals because we are all different." What seems to be a paradoxical slogan is really a critical redefinition of democracy from the practices, cosmologies, and epistemologies of the subaltern. This leads to the question of how to transcend the imperial monologue established by European-centric modernity.

Transmodernity or Critical Cosmopolitanism as Utopian Projects

An intercultural North–South dialogue cannot be achieved without a decolonization of power relations in the modern world. A horizontal dialogue as opposed to the vertical monologue of the West requires a transformation in global power structures.

We cannot assume a Habermasian consensus or an equal horizontal relationship among cultures and peoples globally divided in the two poles of the colonial difference. However, we could start imagining alternative worlds beyond Eurocentrism and fundamentalism. Transmodernity is the Latin American philosopher of liberation Enrique Dussel's utopian project to transcend the Eurocentric version of modernity (Dussel, 2001). Instead of a single modernity centered in Europe and imposed as a global design on the rest of the world, Dussel argues for a multiplicity of modernities from the subaltern cultures and epistemic location of colonized people around the world. Cultures could provide, as Caribbean cultural critic and writer Edward Glissant would say, a "diversality" of responses to the problems of modernity. Liberation can only come from the critical thinkers of each culture in dialogue with other cultures. Women's liberation, democracy, and civil rights can only come out of the creative responses of local cultures. Western women cannot impose their notion of liberation on Islamic women. Western men cannot impose their notion of democracy on non-Western peoples. This is not a call for a fundamentalist or nationalist solution to the persistence of coloniality. It is a call for border thinking as the strategy or mechanism towards a "transmodernity" that moves beyond Eurocentrism and fundamentalism.

Radicalizing the Levinasian notion of exteriority, Dussel sees a potential in those relatively exterior spaces not fully colonized by the European modernity. These exterior spaces are not pure or absolute. They have been affected and produced by European modernity, but never fully subsumed nor instrumentalized. It is from the geopolitics of knowledge of this relative exteriority, or margins, that critical border thinking emerges as a critique of modernity towards a pluriversal transmodern world of multiple modernities in which a real horizontal dialogue and communication could exist between all the peoples of the world. However, to achieve this utopian project it is fundamental to transform the systems of domination and the exploitation of the colonial power matrix of the modern–colonial capitalist patriarchal world-system.

Anticapitalist Struggles Today

The pernicious influence of coloniality in all of its expressions at different levels (global, national, local) as well as its Eurocentric knowledges have been reflected in antisystemic movements and utopian thinking around the world. Thus, the first task of a renewed leftist project is to confront the Eurocentric colonialities not only of the right but also of the left. For example, many leftist projects in Latin America underestimated the racial and ethnic hierarchies and reproduced White Creole domination over non-European people within their organizations and when in control of the state structures. The Latin American left never radically problematized the racial–ethnic hierarchies built during the European colonial expansion and still present in Latin America's "coloniality of power." The conflicts between the Sandinistas and the Misquitos in Nicaragua emerged as part of the reproduction of the old racial and colonial hierarchies (Vila, 1992). This was not a conflict created by the CIA, as the Sandinistas would have us believe. The Sandinistas reproduced the historical coloniality of power between the Pacific and Atlantic coasts of Nicaragua. The white Creole elites of the Pacific coast hegemonized the political, cultural, and economic relations that subordinated blacks and Indians on the Atlantic coast. The differences between the Somocista dictatorship and the Sandinista regime were not that great when it came to social relations with colonial/racial Others. The CIA utilized for their own benefit the already existing racial conflicts in Nicaragua. Similarly, Cuban white elites hegemonized the power positions in the postrevolutionary period (Moore, 1988). The number of blacks and mulattos in power positions is minimal and does not correspond to the demographic fact that they are the numerical majority. The historical continuities of the coloniality of power in Cuba are greater than the discontinuities. No radical project in Latin America can be successful without dismantling these colonial and racial hierarchies. The underestimation of the problem of coloniality has greatly contributed to the popular disillusionment with leftist projects in Latin America. Democracy (liberal or radical) cannot be fully accomplished if the colonial and racist dynamic keeps a large portion or, in some cases, the majority of the population as second class citizens.

The perspective articulated here is not a defense of "identity politics." Subaltern identities could serve as an epistemic point of departure for a radical critique of Eurocentric paradigms and ways of thinking. However, identity politics is not equivalent to epistemological alterity. The scope of "identity politics" is limited and cannot achieve a radical transformation of the system and its colonial power matrix. Because most modern identities are a construction of the coloniality of power in the modern–colonial world, their defense is not as subversive as it might seem at first sight. Black, Indian, African, or national identities such as Colombian, Kenyan, or French are colonial constructions. Defending these identities could serve some progressive purposes depending on what is at stake in certain contexts. For example, in the struggles against an imperialist invasion or antiracist struggles against white supremacy. But such a politics only addresses the goals of a single group or demands equality within the system rather than developing a radical anticapitalist struggle against the system. The system of exploitation is a crucial space of intervention that requires broader alliances along not only racial, gender, and class lines but also among a diversity of oppressed groups around the notion of social equality. But instead of Eurocentric modernity's limited and formal notion of equality, the idea here is to extend the notion of equality to every relation of oppression such as racial, class, sexual, or gender. The new universe of meaning or new imaginary of liberation needs a common language despite the diversity of cultures and forms of oppression. This common language could be provided by radicalizing the liberatory notions arising from the old colonial pattern of power, such as freedom (press, religion, and speech), individual liberties or social equality, and linking these to the radical democratization of the political and economic power hierarchies.

Quijano's (2000) proposal for a socialization of power as opposed to a statist nationalization of production is crucial here. Instead of state socialist or state capitalist projects centered in the administration of the state and in hierarchical power structures, the strategy of socialization of power in all spheres of social existence privileges global and local struggles for collective forms of public authority.

Communities, enterprises, schools, hospitals, and all of the institutions that currently regulate social life would be self-managed by people under the ideal of extending social equality to all spaces of social life. This is a process of empowerment from below that does not exclude the formation of global institutions that democratize wealth and resources at a world-scale. The socialization of power would also imply the formation of global institutions beyond national or state boundaries to guarantee social equality and justice in production, reproduction, and distribution of world resources. This would imply some form of self-managed, democratic global organization that would work as a collective global authority to guarantee social justice and social equality at a world-scale.

Developmentalist projects that focus on policy changes at the level of the nation-state are obsolete in today's world economy and leads to developmentalist illusions. A system of domination and exploitation that operates at world-scales such as the capitalist world-system cannot have a national solution. A global problem cannot be solved at the nation-state level. It requires global solutions. Thus, the decolonization of the political–economy of the modern–colonial capitalist patriarchal world-system requires the institutionalization of the global redistribution and transfer of wealth from North to South. After centuries of "accumulation by dispossession" (Harvey, 2003), the North has a concentration of wealth and resources inaccessible to the South. Global redistributive mechanisms of wealth from North to South could be implemented by the direct intervention of international organizations and by taxing global capital flows. However, this would require a global struggle that leads to a change in the global balance of power and, eventually, to a transformation of the capitalist world-system. The North is reluctant to share the concentration and accumulation of wealth produced by labor from the South after centuries of exploitation and domination of the latter by the former. Even today, the neoliberal policies represent a continuation of the "accumulation by dispossession" (Harvey, 2003) began by the European colonial expansion with conquest of the Americas in the sixteenth century. Many peripheral countries were robbed of their national wealth and resources during the last 20 years of neoliberalism at a world-scale under the supervision and direct intervention of the International Monetary Fund and the World Bank. These policies have led to the bankruptcy of many countries in the periphery and the transfer of wealth from the South to transnational corporations and financial institutions in the North. The space of maneuver for peripheral regions is very limited given the constraints in the sovereignty of peripheral nation-states. In sum, the solution to global inequalities requires the need to imagine global utopian alternatives beyond colonialist and nationalist, Eurocentric and fundamentalist binary ways of thinking.

28

Neoliberal Globalization and Resistance: A Retrospective Look at the East Asian Crisis

David A. Smith

In the wake of the 9/11 terrorist attacks on the United States, and the U.S. invasions of first Afghanistan and subsequently Iraq, the putative East Asian crisis of the late 1990s may seem like ancient history. The media and the pundits have moved on — and, indeed, the gloomiest visions of the long-term impacts of the crisis probably were overblown because most of the economies of the region have rebounded, at least to some extent. Nevertheless, this East Asian economic crisis was a dramatic event that captured world attention in the closing years of the last century. At the time it appeared that the unfolding events would have far-reaching consequences, with some suggesting that they could shake the very foundations of global capitalism as we entered the new millennium (see, for instance, Wade and Veneroso, 1998).

Surely there is no denying that the stunning reversal of economic fortunes, beginning amid a currency and capital flight crisis in Thailand in mid-1997, led to a Thai government request for International Monetary Fund (IMF) intervention and a major devaluation of the baht in July, and quickly cascaded as panicked foreign investors stampeded out of not just that Southeast Asian country, but the entire region (for an excellent chronology of the East Asian crisis see Kim 1998: preface). A combination of capital flight and attacks on national currencies by foreign speculators spread to the Philippines, Malaysia, Indonesia, and even Hong Kong. By September 1997, South Korea was deeply implicated in the crisis; Korean bank loans and investments in Southeast Asia were going into default at about the same time as the high profile bankruptcies of the *chaebol* (private family conglomerates) were occurring in Seoul (Lee, 1998). As the bad news multiplied, investor confidence plunged and capital pulled out even more rapidly. The result was a major slowdown in economic activity, including declining output, employment, and overnight declines in consumption and standards of living. This economic crisis, in turn, led to increased political volatility throughout the region, with the most notable casualty being Suharto's long-running authoritarian regime in Indonesia. Even Japan, once projected as a possible successor to the United States as world economic hegemon, was sucked into the vortex with a major security house declaring bankruptcy and the stock market swooning.

By early 1998 the talk of the "economic miracle" was replaced by discussions of an East Asian "economic mirage." Data on various economic indicators leave little doubt that East Asian nations were hit by a wave of economic destruction of tsunami force. Although a few commentators claimed that the region's economic problems had been growing for a while (Krugman, 1994), data shows that the four countries hit the hardest (Indonesia, Thailand, South Korea, and Malaysia) had recorded robust real annual GDP growth rates through the 1980s and 1990s, ranging from 6.3 percent to 9.4 percent (World Bank, 2003). But Thailand began to swoon in 1997 when its GDP dropped 1.4 percent; by 1998 all four countries were in economic free fall: South Korea's GDP decline was −6.6 percent; Malaysia's, −9.6 percent; Thailand's, −10.5 percent; and Indonesia's was a whopping −13.1 percent (Economist Intelligence Unit Country Profiles, 2002–2003). Other economies in the region (Hong Kong, Singapore, and the Philippines) also saw declining GDP in 1998 as well, suggesting the regional character of the slump and leading some economists to discuss the East Asian crisis in terms of "contagion." Other indicators tell a similar tale: "The four most badly affected economies — Korea, Thailand, Malaysia, and Indonesia — have undergone import falls of 30 to 40 percent in the past year. The falls reflect deep recessions, which spell debt default, bankruptcies, still lower domestic interest rates, and possibly further 'beggar thy neighbor' currency devaluations" (Wade and Veneroso, 1998: 15). Reports from the International Monetary Fund (1998) and the International Labor Organization (Marx, 1999) said that between ten and twenty million people became unemployed between mid-1997 and the end of 1998 in South Korea, Thailand, and Indonesia alone.

There is no doubt that this "crisis" led to record unemployment in parts of the region and devastated many individuals and families (who may continue to feel the aftereffects for decades). But by 2000 the most impacted East Asian societies were rapidly returning to relative economic health, with improved GDP growth rates for that year: Thailand, −4.6 percent, Indonesia, −4.8 percent, Malaysia, −5.8 percent, and South Korea, −9.2 percent (Economist Intelligence Unit Country Profiles 2002–2003). In 2001 the ILO reported that East Asia "has surprised the pessimists with its fast recovery from the 1997 to 1998 financial crisis" (15) (though noting "the labor market was hit harder than the output market and is recovering more slowly" (32)).

However, this was not anticipated at the time. Instead many Cassandras predicted long-term ruin for the region. This gloomy prognosis prompted a bevy of pundits and scholars — many of whom had previously touted "the Asian model" and searched for the key to the region's success — to join a chorus of critics advancing arguments about inherent flaws in these societies. "After the 1997 bailouts of Thailand and South Korea, influential analysts inveighed against a model of development that had been the apple of Washington's eye since the 1960s" (Cumings 1999: 24). Conveniently ignoring three decades of economic growth, various economic experts in Western countries delivered post hoc analyzes of how tenuous East Asian economies had been all along (predominated by "crony capitalism" and state-led development) and trumpeting the current crisis as an opportunity for economic reform (usually toward U.S.-style neoliberalism). The oft-invoked imagery of the Asian flu suggested that the disease was something societies on the eastern shores of the Pacific Rim had contracted. Echoing the old modernization perspective on development, the problem was ascribed to sick Asian economies. Implicitly, the diagnosis that follows is to urge countries to get healthy by adopting "modern" Western-style capitalism.

Elsewhere (Smith, 1999), I offered my thoughts on the underlying factors that led to the East Asian crisis. My own work has long pointed to the ways that the region's position in the contemporary world-system constrained and limited East Asian economic development (Smith, 1985; Smith and Lee, 1990; Smith, 1996; Smith, 1997). No doubt, the economic meltdown in the late 1990s was also a local manifestation of the "global casino" dynamics of today's international banking and finance system (see Wade and Veneroso, 1998).

My modest goals in this brief chapter are to do some preliminary thinking about the ideological implications of the East Asian economic crisis and its aftermath, as well as grapple with globalization and antiglobalization as dialectical currents manifest in the realm of ideas and social movements, in corporate board rooms, and in people's protests on the streets. The theme is that globalization engenders resistance. After summarizing in capsule form how inadequate the neoliberal imagery is to explain the actual process of state-led "dependent development" that has occurred in the East Asian Newly Industrializing Economies (NIEs) — with special attention to South Korea — the paper discusses how resistance to globalization seems to be making headway both among strategically positioned economic elites and via popular movements.

The Crisis and the Debate on Global Inequality

The sheer magnitude of 10 to 20 million people thrown out of work as a result of the East Asian crisis (and the neoliberal "cures" imposed in subsequent months) created enormous economic pain for many people in the region. Negative growth rates for countries (even if they were relatively short-term) obviously contribute to greater international inequality; the patterns of job losses, bankruptcies, and currency devaluations almost certainly promoted intranational economic polarization as well (for a discussion of this dynamic in postcrisis South Korea, see Lee, 1998). There is little doubt that a proximate result of the economic crisis was some attenuation of global inequality. This further reinforces the overall pattern found by Korzeniewicz and Moran (1997), showing growing gaps in world income distribution over the past three decades.

The Asian economic crisis impacted broad debates about world development. For many people the East Asian "economic miracle" signified to "the Third World" or the "less developed countries" that economic growth — and even growth with a relatively low level of inequality — was possible. The decades of East Asian NIE dynamism were often presented as a crucial case challenging the world-system–global political economy perspective. A number of scholars implied that the experiences of these nations, particularly the leading "four tigers" (Hong Kong, Singapore, South Korea, and Taiwan), provided the crucial evidence to disprove world-system/dependency arguments about uneven development (Barrett and Whyte, 1982; Gold, 1985; for a thorough discussion and critique see Smith and Lee, 1990). Furthermore, as Korzeniewicz and Moran (1997: 1008) argue, "the economic success of East Asia is often presumed to entail a substantial redistribution of world income from wealthy to poor nations."

There was considerable debate among scholars as to the actual "motor" of East Asian growth. Some clung to old culturalist claims about Confucianism (Pye, 1985; also see a 1994 quote from Singapore Prime Minister Lee Kuan Yew, cited in Kim, 1998: 432–433), others focused on developmentalist states (Gold, 1985; Amsden, 1989; Appelbaum and Henderson, 1992; Evans, 1995), whereas still others stressed the ways that East Asian informal networks promoted business (Orru, Biggart, and Hamilton, 1991; Gerlach, 1992; Whitely, 1992). Some economists, judiciously selecting supporting data and using some logical contortions, even went so far as to suggest that the basis of all this growth was "free markets," after all (Balassa, 1981; World Bank, 1993). There were a few who did question the viability of the East Asian development path (notably Bello and Rosenfeld, 1990; also Krugman, 1994; Smith, 1997), and some others stressed the dark side of the economic growth (Deyo, 1989; Smith and Lee, 1990; Harts-Landsberg, 1993). But the works of the skeptics and critics were not taken too seriously — most scholars concurred with the World Bank's famous 1993 report, which officially canonized the regional dynamism as "the East Asian miracle."

What then are we to make of this after 1998? The admiration for the East Asian model quickly was transformed into almost universal scorn. As the economies of the NIEs contracted, the general standard of living fell, and unemployment and socioeconomic inequality rose; these economies were no longer to be emulated — indeed, they were quickly branded as bad examples!

There are three implications of this that seem particularly important. First, we always need to exercise caution in interpreting current events; what turned out to be painful but relatively short-term dislocations in societies like South Korea and Taiwan were read in 1999 as part of an epochal turning point. Second, and more conceptually interesting, the economic crisis and financial turbulence in East Asia should give pause to those who dismissed the world-system perspective on uneven development because this region's experiences supposedly disproved it. Viewed retrospectively from today, countries like Taiwan or South Korea undergoing phenomenal growth in the 1970s and 1980s do look like "deviant cases" — but not in the way that the overly optimistic critics of the world-system and dependency view imagined. At the end of millennium some of the rapid growth, which these scholars saw as an escape from dependency (see Barrett and Whyte, 1982; Gold, 1985), looks much more period-specific and chimerical. This leads to the final point: even though in 2003 we know that some of these East Asian economies rebounded, there is a lesson in the crisis about global power relations. The South Koreans didn't call this "the IMF crisis" without good cause. Even though these nations saw rapid economic growth, growing prosperity, and rising living standards for two or three decades (and may once again), their development path has always been "dependent" rather than "autonomous"; the Korean dreams of growing to join the G7 group of core economic powers was noble but misplaced. Despite the gleaming high-rise office buildings and men in suits and power ties, much of the real power resides not in Jakarta or Seoul or Taipei, but in Washington, New York, London, and (maybe) Tokyo. As Bruce Cumings (1999: 25) succinctly stated after the economic crisis, "(The) apparently autonomous 'Asian tigers,' prospering within an indulgent and hegemonic net for 30 years, find themselves rendered bewildered and dependent by a dimly understood hegemonic mechanism that places their entire society and economy under global jurisdiction." In fact, East Asia has always been enmeshed in a web of dependency relations — now those fibers are just more visible.

Globalization — and Antiglobalization?

Globalization means different things to different people. There is considerable doubt about whether the basic characteristics of today's world order are so new or novel (Cox, 1996; Panitch, 1996); prominent skeptics are dubious that the concept of "globalization" has any real analytical utility (see Arrighi, 1999 or Wallerstein, 1999; for a fuller discussion of these issues see Smith, Solinger, and Topik, 1999). Doubtless, the past two or three decades witnessed a degree of "time-space compression" (Mittelman, 1996; Arrighi, 1999). But perhaps much of the discourse on "globalization" is an ideological argument for neoliberal policies, for which "there is no alternative" (Cox, 1996; Gill, 1996; Panitch, 1996). This view stresses domestic reduction in government economic intervention, deregulation, privatization, and global reductions on tariffs, opening of capital markets, liberalization of foreign investment regimes, etc., in the context of an overall enhanced reliance on market mechanisms.

This rhetoric of neoliberal globalization — to the surprise and dismay of some of us who study the region's recent political economy — framed discussions of the causes and consequences of the East Asian crisis, as well as the search for potential solutions. The dominance of this view, with its dogmatic preference for "free trade" and open investment, eagerness to discount any economically constructive role for governments and states, and insistence that homogenization and standardization of business practices toward current Western norms, seemed particularly bizarre here. The three decades of relative economic success of "the Asian tigers" challenged global neoliberalism's central tenets. The rise of semiperipheral nations in this part of the world was based on controlling capital flows and managing foreign investment, the key role of developmentalist states, and the emergence of distinctive network-based "flexible" business organizations that challenged Western corporate models. Yet, not only scholars and commentators but also East Asian political leaders, fixated on the economic turmoil after 1998, seem eager to discard all the lessons of the past 30 or 40 years.

Bruce Cumings (1999) argues that the metanarrative of the final decade of the twentieth century is the complete triumph of the United States as a "mature hegemonic power" (24). In postcrisis East Asia, this was manifested in the imposition of U.S.-style neoliberalism replacing the former "neomercantilist" developmental states. Although I agree with Cumings about the East Asian crisis on a number of points, my own view is more Polanyian: excessive reliance on markets and liberal ideology, by its very nature, is likely to stimulate countermovements. Emerging evidence suggests that there is a growing dissatisfaction with neoliberal globalization, both at the higher levels of corporate and political leadership, and among the ordinary people who are suffering under market "reforms" and increasingly willing to resist them.

James Mittelman (2000) offers a useful typology for conceptualizing resistance to globalization. In addition to spawning "open countermovements," global neoliberalism also stimulates various less obvious and even "submerged" forms of "everyday resistance." Mittelman presents a challenging research agenda for studying various antiglobalization resistances in all its complexity. I will focus on the much simpler dichotomy of elite and mass discontent.

The View From Above

Some of the most vociferous reactions against the unfettered neoliberalism of contemporary globalization come from the highest echelons of corporate capitalism. Perhaps this is not as surprising as it seems: these people are intimately aware of the types of systemic fragility that developments such as the Asian crisis exposed. Arrighi (1999: 56) reports:

> The effects of the turbulence engendered by the present financial expansion have begun to worry even the promoters and boosters of economic globalization. David Harvey (1995: 8, 12) quotes several of them remarking that globalization is a turning into "a brakeless train wreaking havoc," and worrying about a "mounting backlash" against the effect of such a destructive force ...

Global financier George Soros is one of these outspoken critics, warning of the need to temper the unfetter excesses of unrestrained competition and self-interest. Rodrik (1997) warns that the combination of neoliberalism and antistatism is dangerous because delegitimizing states at the same time that masses of people are experiencing the effects of socioeconomic polarization could lead to political volatility. In turn, this political dynamic could pose a serious threat to the continued viability of the contemporary global economy and the corporate interests that profit from it.

Ironically, the antiglobalization reaction among elites seems to have begun in corporate boardrooms of world cities in the core, and its full implications may not yet be appreciated in East Asian dependencies. Here I will limit my comments to South Korea (about which Wade and Veneroso comment, "Korea is a classic example of how free capital movements in the context of high domestic and foreign debt can destabilize an economy with good 'fundamentals'" (1998: 31)). The enthusiastically "free market liberal" orientation of South Korean President Kim Dae Jung and his government (whose term ended in 2003) was noted above (Cumings (1998: 60) succinctly summarizes, "The IMF's Man in Seoul: Kim Dae Jung").

If my own experiences as a participant at a conference in Seoul on the "East Asian Economy Reconsidered" (November 1998, Yonsei University) are any indicator, President Kim set the ideological tone for his nation's scholars as well. Most of the Korean participants at this event were academic economists and political scientists, though one official from the Bank of Korea served as a discussant. The conference opened with a speech by American economist Lawrence Lindsey (formerly of the U.S. Federal Reserve, more recently the chief economic advisor to President George W. Bush) that, although constituting a clarion call for "free markets" and complete openness to foreign investment, criticized the IMF. Shortly after he finished talking, Lindsey was dramatically whisked away to a meeting with the U.S. ambassador. More than half of the dozen or so papers that followed, including mine, dealt with the regional economic crisis. Even though some of the papers presented trenchant analyses of the causes of the crisis, and a couple critiqued both the IMF and the rapid pace of liberalizing reforms introduced by the Kim government, every paper written by a Korean academic for this conference concluded that neoliberal reforms were progressive, inevitable, and the only way to maintain "international competitiveness." Thirty years of "negotiated dependency" and a "developmental state" (which I took pains to remind them of in my paper!) were now viewed as historical anachronisms with no real relevance to the present. For meaningful resistance to neoliberal globalization to make headway with Korean leaders, this will have to change. My own guess is that these sanguine attitudes toward globalization will change as the pernicious effects of several years of sweeping market reforms begin to show and ordinary Koreans start to feel the pain.

The View from Below

Anyone who watches TV or casually reads the newspaper knows that one result of the East Asian economic disaster was enormous social unrest and political upheaval during the late 1990s. The waves of demonstrations, popular protests, land seizures, destruction of property, and violent rioting in East Asia in 1998 and 1999 make the "food riots" described in response to prior episodes of "structural adjustment" (see Walton and Seddon, 1994) fade into relative insignificance. The size and scope of the popular mobilizations demolish myths, popular in the Western world, of "quiescent Asians." They are indicative of a wellspring of grassroots anger at neoliberal globalization by people whose participation in the contemporary world economy entails paying high costs with very few benefits. If East Asian politicians or social scientists are lagging, these ordinary folks could be at a leading edge of the resistance to globalization.

It's hardly surprising that the most sustained and dramatic protests and upheavals occurred in Indonesia. Even before the economic crisis, this was a highly polarized, notoriously corrupt country. The financial crisis hit Indonesia fast and hard; the government sought and received the first IMF assistance in October 1997, but the rupiah continued its downward plunge well into 1998 (see Kim, 1998). By early summer, rioting, which included rage at the ethnic Chinese business community, that resulted in rapes and murders, was breaking out throughout the archipelago. News stories in the U.S. described massive unemployment and widespread malnutrition as a pretext for nationwide urban unrest and rural mobilizations that included hungry peasants storming golf courses so they could cultivate the arable land. Amid all this upheaval, the long-running Suharto dictatorship, which seemed invincible months before, crumbled.

In South Korea popular mobilization was much less violent, but also more organizationally coherent. Of all the East Asian NIEs, this country has the most robust tradition of confrontation politics, social movement activity, and labor activism (see

Deyo, 1989). Korean students and workers have a long-running reputation for restiveness. The mid- to late-1980s witnessed a surge of popular mobilization (union organizing, strikes, and mass demonstrations) that suggested these movements had some radical potential to threaten state and corporate power (Smith and Lee, 1990). The IMF crisis rekindled popular mobilization. In February 1998, unions organized a massive one-day general strike in Seoul in which 130,000 workers participated (Cumings, 1998: 62). Support for labor goals at a time when so many South Koreans faced hardship and a lack of economic security reached deep into the ranks of white-collar workers. It is likely that these mobilizations from below put something of a brake on President Kim and his advisors as they continued to push neoliberal reforms.

The Real Keys to the "Miracle": Debunking Neoliberal Revisionism

One reason that East Asians are unlikely to surrender easily to neoliberal globalization ideology and policy prescriptions is the irrelevancy of Western style market economics to account for the dramatic "rise of the East" over the past three decades. An alternative sociological explanation is richly grounded in an understanding of world-system dynamics and global political economy. Essentially, there are three key elements of this region's political economy that can be seen as crucial to the decades of rapid growth: (1) the power of states to deal with foreign investment in distinctive ways, (2) the way that corporations and governments negotiated issues of technological dependency and obstacles to local innovation, and (3) the emergence of regional business structures and networks that are particularly conducive to various forms of "flexible production." Laissez faire strategies would have been woefully inadequate to overcome the historical conditions blocking various East Asian "miracles"; similarly, the imposition of Western style "free market capitalism" today would destroy some of the "competitive advantage" East Asian economies developed to confront these critical challenges. Instead, the East Asian NIEs found ways to (1) "negotiate dependency" by selectively regulating and controlling the influx of foreign capital, (2) upgrade their productive capabilities despite continuing "technological dependency" via strategies like "backward engineering," and (3) use informal networks and family relationships to build small and more adaptive and responsive corporate forms that were competitive in the new era of "flexible production" (this is a capsule summary of an argument developed at length in Smith, 1999).

Conclusion

The East Asian economic crisis was a dramatic event that drew enormous attention from scholars, the media, and policymakers. East Asian NIEs played an iconic role in various debates about uneven development and world inequality. Unfortunately, the pundits and politicians probably drew precisely the wrong lessons from this episode! They saw the "crisis" (which, in some of the societies turned out to be rather overblown) as the final, devastating Waterloo of the East Asian model with its developmentalist state. Actually, it makes just as much sense to view the speculative nature of contemporary global capitalism, and even the liberalization process itself, as the cause of the region's financial difficulties. Instead of fitting seamlessly into the meta-narrative of the triumph of Western capitalism and "the end of history," the apparent denouement of these economic success stories in the crisis from 1997 to 1998 is a cautionary tale about how dependent this region really is in the capitalist world-system. East Asian economic vulnerability illustrates how deeply enmeshed the region is on the world-system dynamics creating uneven development and generating global polarization. It also puts neoliberal globalization on center stage. Attempts to impose a neoliberal "solution" in East Asia, with its "one size fits all" approach, engendered strong reactions of resistance, particularly among working people in crisis-affected parts of the region.

Acknowledgment

The author thanks Dennis Downey, Tonya Schuster, and Rich Appelbaum, as well as participants at both conferences, for their useful comments.

29

Historical Dynamics of Globalization, War, and Social Protest

Beverly J. Silver

Introduction

In the 1980s and 1990s the main chord struck in contemporary popular and social scientific discussions on globalization emphasized the disorganizing and weakening impact that globalization processes were having on established social movements. By the turn of the millennium, however, the focus began to shift to an emphasis on the emergence of new types of resistance movements — from Seattle to Genoa — in part generated by the forces of globalization themselves. Yet, in the immediate aftermath of September 11, 2001, with demonstrations and strikes being canceled around the world, questions were raised about the future of movements that had appeared to be on a strong upward trajectory. Then, just 15 months later, on February 15, 2003, with war looming in Iraq, some of the largest demonstrations in world history were held. Even more impressive than the size of any of the individual demonstrations was the global coordination and planning that was in evidence as demonstrations took place simultaneously in hundreds of cities throughout the world.

Whereas the ups and downs in global social protest in the 1980s and 1990s tended to focus the attention of students of globalization on the role of world-economic processes in shaping both the protagonists and terrain on which struggles evolved, the ups and downs of the last few years have refocused attention on the central role played by war and world politics in the dynamics of global social protest. The central importance of world political processes, and the interrelationship among war and social protest, should hardly come as a surprise. Indeed, there is a long established tradition within the social sciences linking wars to revolutions and to social conflict more generally.[1] The "presumed nexus of civil conflict and international conflict," Michael Stohl (1980: 297) suggested, is "one of the most venerable hypotheses in the social science literature"[2]

Drawing on recent empirical research (Silver, 2003; Arrighi and Silver, 1999a), this chapter posits two theses about the relationship between global war and global social unrest. The first is that there has indeed been an intimate link between global war and global social unrest that is traceable back to the late eighteenth-century age of war and revolution in the Atlantic world. More specifically, periods of world-hegemonic transition have been periods marked by a "vicious circle" in which escalating war and social unrest feed off one another. Second, a speeding up of social history is visible from one period of world-hegemonic transition to the next. Not only has the geographical scale and scope of the vicious circle of war and social unrest increased from one hegemonic transition to the next; also the time it has taken for war to trigger massive social unrest has decreased from one hegemonic transition to the next. From these past patterns, I will argue, we can derive important lessons for understanding current dynamics.

I will proceed in three steps. In the next section I will draw on some of my empirical research on the world-historical dynamics of labor unrest (Silver, 2003) to describe the cycle of war and labor unrest (and social unrest more generally) that characterized the first half of the twentieth century. In the second section of the paper, I will draw on recent research comparing the transition from Dutch to British world hegemony in the late eighteenth and early nineteenth century with the transition from British to U.S. world hegemony in the late nineteenth and early twentieth century (Arrighi and Silver, 1999a, especially chapter 3). Lengthening the time horizon of the analysis will allow us to see both the recurrence of a "vicious circle" in both transitions as well as the increased scale, scope, and speed of this cycle from one transition to the next. The final section of the paper will conclude with the implications of these past patterns for understanding the current dynamics of war, world politics, and social conflict.

Labor, War, and World Politics in the Twentieth Century

Figure 29.1 presents a time series of the number of annual newspaper reports about labor unrest worldwide from 1870 to the present. The figure is based on the World Labor Group database, which includes all acts of labor unrest (e.g., strikes, demonstrations) reported in either *The New York Times* or *The Times* (London) from 1870 to 1996.[3]

The most immediately striking feature of figure 29.1 is the interrelationship between world labor unrest and the two world wars — with labor unrest rising on the eves of both world wars, declining precipitously with the outbreak of war, and exploding in the aftermath of the wars. The two highest peaks in overall world labor unrest are the years immediately following the two world wars. The years 1919 and 1920 are the peak years of the series with a total of 2,720 and 2,293 reports, respectively. The next highest peak is 1946 and 1947 with a total of 1,857 and 2,122 reports, respectively.

The early war years themselves are among the low points of the time series. There are only 196 reports in 1915 and only 248 and 279 in 1940 and 1942, respectively. Finally, the years just prior to the outcome of the wars are years of rapidly rising labor unrest leading to local peaks in the time series. Thus, in the decade leading up to the First World War, the total number of mentions of labor unrest increases from 325 in 1905 to 604 in 1909 and 875 in 1913. Likewise, the total number of mentions of labor unrest is rising in the decade leading up to the Second World War (from 859 in 1930 to 1101 in 1934 and 1186 in 1938).[4]

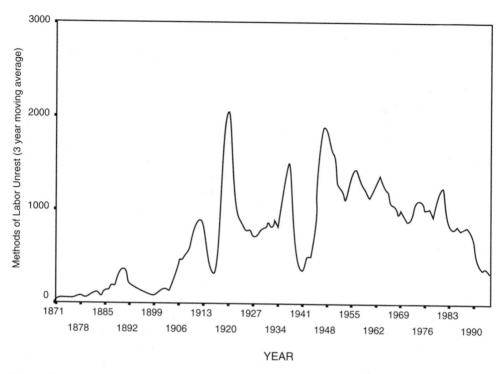

Figure 29.1.

Figure 29.1 thus provides striking prima facie evidence for the existence of a strong link between world wars and world labor unrest. Moreover, given the strong link between labor movements and other key movements of the twentieth century (especially social revolutionary and national liberation movements), figure 29.1 also provides prima facie evidence for the existence of a link between the world wars and broader world social unrest.[5]

In his review of the literature on the international–domestic conflict nexus, Stohl (1980) identified three subvariants of the nexus hypothesis that have been widespread in the scholarly literature:

1. Involvement in war increases social cohesion at the national level and thus brings about internal peace.
2. Involvement in war increases social conflict at the national level and increases the chances of revolution.
3. Social conflict at the national level encourages governments to involve themselves in wars.

Curiously, the patterning of labor unrest in figure 29.1 may be interpreted as providing support for all three hypotheses. Their apparently contradictory nature disappears if we see them as having different temporal relevance. That is, hypothesis 3 (the oft-called scapegoat or diversionary hypothesis) best describes the period leading up to the world wars. Hypothesis 1 (linking war and social cohesion) is most relevant for the early phases of the hostilities, whereas hypothesis 2 (linking war and revolution) is most relevant to the aftermath of the world wars. This combination produced the volatile character of labor (and other social) unrest during the first half of the twentieth century.

The rising and explosive pattern of labor unrest in the first half of the twentieth century (during the period of world-hegemonic crisis and breakdown) gave way to a far less volatile dynamic of labor unrest in the second half of the twentieth century (see figure 29.1). This shift was in part related to the unprecedented concentration of military and economic power in the hands of the United States at the close of the Second World War, which brought an end to the great power rivalries that had fed the vicious circle of war and labor unrest. Of equal importance were deep institutional reforms at the corporate, national, and especially the global levels, which sought to accommodate some of the demands that had been thrown up by the labor, nationalist, and other movements of first half of the twentieth century — movements that had been strengthened and radicalized by decades of war and depression.[6]

As I shall argue in the final section, we can derive insights into the present dynamics from a comparison with those of the late nineteenth and first half of the twentieth century. Yet, as our study of comparative hegemonic transitions has suggested (Arrighi and Silver, 1999a), further insights can be gleaned by lengthening the time horizon to include not only the period of "systemic chaos" and transition to U.S. hegemony in the late nineteenth and first half of the twentieth century but also the period of systemic chaos and transition to British hegemony in late eighteenth and early nineteenth century. It is to a brief description of the similarities and differences in the nature of the link between war and social unrest in these two periods that we now turn in the next section of the chapter.

World-Hegemonic Transitions Compared

In both world-hegemonic transitions strong links between interstate conflict and domestic conflict can be seen. We cannot draw on a database of global unrest similar to that used in the previous section. Nevertheless, a clear pattern emerges from the secondary historical literature. As argued in detail elsewhere (Arrighi and Silver, 1999a, 159–176), the Seven Years' War marked the first step toward a late-eighteenth-century cycle of war and social unrest. The dislocations of the boom–bust cycle caused by the Seven Years' War in North America were important in detonating the American Revolution. The immense costs of France's intervention in the American Revolutionary War, in turn, were crucial in bringing about the final collapse of the French monarchy and the French Revolution. The French Revolution and Napoleonic Wars simultaneously increased social strains and produced the intra-elite rift that opened the space for a full-scale slave insurrection in France's most profitable colony (Saint Domingue — modern-day Haiti), which, in turn, inspired further slave conspiracies and maroon rebellions throughout the Americas, as well as a second wave of abolitionist and reform mobilizations in Europe. The late eighteenth and early nineteenth centuries, like the first half of the twentieth century, was thus an age of "global" war and revolution.

Yet, differences are as important as similarities. My use of the word *global* (and the fact that it is in quotation marks in the preceding paragraph) points to a similarity, but also a first difference between the two periods of hegemonic transition. In the late eighteenth century, globalization processes had advanced to the point where words and deeds in the Americas often had a rapid and resounding impact on Europe (and vice versa). Thus, it would be accurate to characterize the revolutionary ferment of the period as unfolding within the Atlantic world as a whole. Yet, if revolutionary contradictions had largely become diffused within the Atlantic world during the first transition, in the second transition such "contagiousness" had become a truly global affair, interconnecting Africa, Asia, Europe, and the Americas.

A second difference is the fact that interstate and intrastate conflicts were far more deeply intertwined in the second transition. In both transitions, wars produced social unrest. However, in contrast to the transition from British to U.S. hegemony, there is no evidence that the reverse relationship also obtained — that is, neither the Seven Years' War nor the French intervention in the American Revolutionary War seem to have been motivated by efforts to quell social unrest on the home front.

By contrast, not only was class and nationalist agitation escalating on the eve of the First World War, even the colonialist adventures in the late 1890s followed (and attempted to divert) increasing class antagonisms. The Spanish-American War (in the United States) and the South African War (in the U.K.) were seen as examples of "little victorious wars" that could bolster governments. Of course, the danger that lost (or otherwise unpopular) wars represented was also well known — as was taught by the 1905 Russian Revolution, which followed on the heels of Russia's defeat by Japan. In sum, if prior to the nineteenth century, rulers seemed to fight wars with little concern for "public opinion," by the end of the century domestic politics and international politics were intimately intertwined. To put it differently, although all three of Stohl's hypotheses seemed to apply in full force from early on in the second transition, the "scapegoat" hypothesis seems far less relevant, at least in the early phases of the first transition.

Finally, by comparing the dynamics of war and social unrest in the two world-hegemonic transitions, we can detect a "speeding up of social history": over time, war has come to produce mass social unrest far more quickly. As long as old-style armies of paid professionals, mercenaries, and "gentlemen" predominated, wars could drag on without shaking the mass of the population. However, as states came more and more to depend on patriotic mobilization of their citizens in wartime struggles, great power rivalries and social conflict became far more intertwined, and the "vicious circle" of war and social unrest was unleashed far more quickly. With mass conscription and the growing industrialization of warfare in the late nineteenth and early twentieth centuries (McNeill, 1982: chapter 7 and chapter 8), workers became critical cogs in the war machine, not only at the front but also behind the front lines in the factories. Indeed, by the time of the First World War, military strategists were well aware of this close relationship. New military strategies, such as naval blockades aimed at cutting off food supplies and raising the threat of mass starvation among noncombatants, were designed to create domestic instability on the enemies' homefront. Such strategies recognized the importance of retaining popular loyalty (and the danger of losing mass support) for success in war.

By the Second World War, the importance of retaining the loyalty of workers and citizens in the war effort extended beyond the metropolitan countries. Britain's decision to introduce trade unions and conciliation and arbitration mechanisms throughout its empire during the Second World War, in response to major strikes and labor unrest in Africa and Asia, was one sign that colonial workers and subjects had also come to occupy a strategic position within the military-industrial complexes of the belligerent countries as workers supplying raw materials and soldiers were recruited to the front lines.[7]

Into the Twenty-First Century

If the dynamic of war and social unrest has continued to develop in the same directions as discussed in the previous section, then we might expect the following to characterize the crisis and breakdown of U.S. world hegemony.[8] First, the processes linking war and social unrest will play out on an even larger and more interconnected global stage. Second, all three of Stohl's hypotheses will be increasingly relevant, as war and social unrest become increasingly intertwined. Finally, social history will continue to "speed up," with wars producing mass social unrest more quickly.

At first sight, the antiwar movement that emerged in response to the threat of war on Iraq would seem to confirm these predictions, with mass protest preceding the start of the war. To quote Madeleine Bunting's (2003) commentary on the February 15, 2003, worldwide antiwar demonstrations: "Not one bomb has been dropped on Iraq [sic[9]], not one shot fired and already there has been the biggest global protest movement ever seen."

Nevertheless, there are important differences between the nature of warfare today and the nature of warfare in the first half of the twentieth century, and these differences no doubt affect the dynamics of global social unrest. The Vietnam War was a significant turning point. The antiwar movement, the growing refusal of U.S. soldiers to continue fighting,[10] and the "contagion" between the antiwar movement and other social movements demonstrated once again the radicalizing effects of costly and unpopular wars, as well as the propensity of states to deal with the problem by a contradictory effort to expand workers' and citizens' rights. (Here, I have in mind the expansion of the Great Society programs that went hand in hand with the escalation of the Vietnam War.) Yet the intertwined fiscal, military, political, and social crises produced by the stalemate in Vietnam also led the U.S. government to implement a series of major changes in its global economic and military strategy.

The new strategy increased the weight of capital-intensive (as opposed to labor-intensive) warfare. Universal conscription was ended, and the long-term tendency of the United States to rely on high-tech methods of warfare increased still further with the application of "information age" technologies to warfare. Tremendous energies in the research and development sphere have been devoted to the automation of war (i.e., military hardware such as pilotless drones and cruise missiles that allow for the complete removal of the "First World human" from both the risk of being killed and direct contact with the process of mass killing).[11]

The advantages for countries that could afford the high-tech strategy were first made clear by the U.K. in the Falkland/Malvinas War. It was confirmed spectacularly in the 1991 Gulf War and again, less spectacularly, with the Kosovo war. Internal opposition to these wars within First World countries remained low because First World governments (the United States, in particular) went to extreme lengths to keep casualties among their own citizen-soldiers to a minimum (tending toward zero).

This is a very different type of war than the type that radicalized workers and other citizens, and created the explosive pattern of world social unrest in the first half of the twentieth century. Recent wars have inflicted tremendous damage on the generally poor countries on whom the high-tech explosives land — destroying economic infrastructures and hence stable working classes and civil societies — but they have not to paraphrase Durkheim, "violently moved the masses" in the First World. If warfare continues to insulate First World workers (and citizens more generally) from its more horrifying aspects while destroying stable working classes and civil societies elsewhere, it is not likely to produce the kind of powerful and explosive labor and social unrest that characterized the first half of the twentieth century.

At the same time, the more the United States and other First World states move toward the automation of war, the more they emancipate themselves from dependence on their worker-citizens for success in war. As such, the growing bargaining power of workers and citizens vis-à-vis their states — an inadvertent byproduct of the interimperialist and Cold War rivalries of the twentieth century — is being reversed, along with many of the economic and social benefits achieved. It is an open question as to whether the major declines in workers' and citizens' rights in the 1980s and 1990s is causally related to the transformations in the military sphere or is merely coincidental. There is, however, no doubt that the decline in social welfare benefits and the disappearance of union jobs with good wages and benefits, along with rising tuition costs and declining scholarship funds, has made it much easier for the U.S. government to recruit its "all volunteer" army from the ranks of the poor and working class.[12]

With the dismantling of the relatively "labor-friendly" and "development-friendly" international regime in the 1980s and 1990s, the global social-economic context came to share important features with the global social-economic context of the late nineteenth and early twentieth century. In both periods, laissez-faire ideology was embraced, and there was a concerted effort to free up capital from restrictions, facilitating the restructuring of global processes of capital accumulation and the related destruction of existing sources of livelihood and ways of life. In both periods, there were government and employer offensives against labor, and labor movements went into a decline. In the late nineteenth century, the crisis of labor movements was short-lived. Growing grievances and the strengthening structural bargaining power of workers (at the point of production *and on the battlefield*) combined to produce powerful waves of labor and social unrest.

I have argued that in the 1980s and 1990s, the global political-military context contrasted sharply with the global political-military context that produced radicalized and explosive labor and social unrest in the late nineteenth and first half of the twentieth century. However, global transformations, post-September 11, raise the question as to whether the nature and degree of this contrast will remain the same. To what extent has September 11 and the "war on terrorism" begun a process that will fundamentally transform the post-Vietnam global military strategy of the United States? The attack on the World Trade Center appears to have at least partially shattered the isolation that the mass of the population felt from world politics and war. And the more "ambitious" Bush administration plans for redrawing the map of the Middle East (starting with the U.S.-led invasion and occupation of Iraq) cannot be carried out without dramatically increasing the threshold of tolerance for war casualties among First World citizens.[13] The tolerance of "world public opinion" for Iraqi casualties will also have to be extremely high. Indeed, the occupation of Iraq (and the developing military quagmire) is a fundamentally different operation than the routine bombing of Iraq that had been going on since the end of the first Gulf War.

The early signs of demoralization and open protest among U.S. troops in Iraq and their families — protest that has burst into the open at a far earlier stage than it did in the Vietnam War — suggests that the "speeding up of social history" thesis continues to be relevant.[14] Moreover, the passage of an antiwar resolution by the AFL-CIO — a step that breaks with the U.S. labor federation's long-held practice of actively supporting U.S. foreign policy — is a sign that a growing number of labor activists and rank-and-file workers have come to feel that "the war abroad could not be separated from the war on labor at home" (Letwin, 2003).

Thus, we may be seeing "the return of world politics" as a major factor feeding global social protest. But what are the implications of this change? Does it imply a return to a situation that is analogous to 1914 or 1939 or 1944? What impact can the global protest movement have on the evolution of world-economic and political dynamics, including war and peace? These are big questions, and I will only make two points by way of conclusion.

The first point has to do with the effectiveness of global social unrest in influencing the trajectory of earlier periods of hegemonic transition. The protest movements in the first half of the twentieth century were not able to stop the slide into a long period of "systemic chaos" — what we have defined as "a situation of fundamental and seemingly irremediable systemic disorganization" (Arrighi and Silver, 1999a, 1999b). What they were able to do was to affect the nature of the new world order that emerged from the long period of systemic chaos. Moreover, movements from below were far more effective in shaping the newly emergent world order in 1945 than in 1815. At the outset of British world hegemony, France (the main great-power embodiment of the revolutionary challenge of the late eighteenth and nineteenth centuries) had suffered a decisive military defeat, as did the British labor movement domestically. Haiti won its independence, but was ostracized from the international community. Thus, Britain did not face a serious popular revolutionary challenge, and the initial thrust of British domestic and international policy in the immediate aftermath of the Napoleonic Wars was repression at home and the restoration of the *ancien regimes* on the continent. Reform policies only emerged later.

In contrast, at the outset of U.S. hegemony, the Soviet Union (the main great-power embodiment of the revolutionary challenge of the first half of the twentieth century) emerged from the Second World War battered, but much stronger politically and militarily, and was shortly joined by a revolutionary China. Moreover, both labor and nationalist movements emerged from the twentieth-century world wars strengthened and radicalized. The counterrevolutionary challenge of the Axis powers was defeated in the war, while the power and prestige of the revolutionary challenge was enhanced. U.S. hegemony from the start had to incorporate reformist policies designed to respond to the popular demands thrown up from below (Arrighi and Silver, 1999a: 202–203). Thus, in past hegemonic transitions, both the strength and content of popular protest mattered in shaping the long-term outcomes.

This brings us to the second point. As we stand on the eve of a new slide into "systemic chaos," considerations about the eventual impact of popular protest on a future world-hegemonic order may not be particularly comforting. They may not even be relevant for, given the tremendous destructive powers that humans have at their disposal, there is no particular guarantee that most or any of the world's population would survive another long period of systemic chaos. Thus, the problem of avoiding the slide into systemic chaos takes on great urgency. What are the main source(s) of the slide into systemic chaos, and what actors in the global social justice movement might be most effective in helping to stop the slide?

According to David Calleo (1987: 142) the "international system breaks down not only because unbalanced and aggressive new powers seek to dominate their neighbors, but also because declining powers, rather than adjusting and accommodating, try to cement their slipping preeminence into an exploitative hegemony." As we have argued elsewhere (Arrighi and Silver, 1999a, conclusion), a comparison of past hegemonic transitions shows that the role of aggressive new powers in precipitating systemic breakdowns has decreased from transition to transition, whereas the role played by exploitative domination by the declining hegemon has increased. Unlike in past hegemonic transitions, today there are no credible aggressive new military powers that can provoke the breakdown of the U.S.-centered world-system. However, as in past hegemonic transitions, the United States is no longer the center of world capital accumulation. The mushrooming current account deficit of the United States is but one indication that the economic foundations of U.S. world power are shaky, indeed. In this context, the U.S. government has been tempted to try to convert its declining hegemony into an exploitative empire through the use of military force. The intuitive response of the mass social protests around the world seems to be that the United States' effort to do so risks precipitating major worldwide chaos. How effective can these movements be in turning the tide? The analysis carried out here suggests two particular points of strategic bargaining power for movements. First, as in the early twentieth century, transportation workers are still strategic actors, not only for the smooth operation of the world-economy, but also for the smooth operation of the world military-industrial complex. The announcement by railroad and dockworkers in countries around the world that they would refuse to move materials for war on Iraq is important (see Lewtin, 2003). Second, as in conflicts from the First World War to Vietnam, the refusal of soldiers at the front to go on fighting has been key. The signs of growing resistance in America's working-class army and the links being made between social-economic justice issues at home and militarism abroad are thus also important portents. The hope is that these actors, together with less strategically located protestors demonstrating en masse around the globe, will be sufficiently strong not only to get the United States to change course, but also to facilitate a relatively smooth transition from the decaying hegemonic order to a more peaceful and equitable world order.

Notes

1. For extensive reviews of this literature see Levy (1989; 1998) and Stohl (1980).
2. Stohl also points to the extensive debate around the exact form of this nexus, as well as the nexus' spatial-temporal relevance — points to which we shall return.
3. The database only includes the international reports from these two newspaper sources. Thus, reports of labor unrest in the U.K. were excluded from the database created from *The Times* (London) and reports of labor unrest in the United States were excluded from the database created from *The New York Times*. For an extensive discussion of the procedures used to create this database and assessments of its reliability, see Silver (2003, Appendix A).
4. See Silver (2003, especially chapter 4) for a fuller discussion of the labor unrest patterns visible in figure 29.1 and how they can best be interpreted.
5. On the links between labor and national liberation movements in the Third World see Silver (2003, 145–149) On the tendency of the World Labor Group database to "capture" politicized labor unrest, and therefore also be indicative of trends in broader social unrest, see Silver (2003, Appendix A).
6. The various elements of these deep institutional reforms have been referred to as "liberal corporatism," "embedded liberalism," the "globalization of the New Deal," the "welfare-warfare state," and for the Third World, "decolonization" and "development." For a further discussion, see Silver (2003, 149–161).
7. On the central, but contradictory role of "consent" in the late colonial labor policies of Britain and France, see Cooper (1996).
8. Limitations of space and time prevent me from defending the proposition that we are now in a period of crisis and breakdown of United States world hegemony. See Arrighi and Silver (1999a).
9. Of course, technically it is not true that "not one bomb" has been dropped, because U.S. and British warplanes were regularly bombing areas in Iraq prior to the start of "the war."
10. See, among others, Christian Appy (1993).
11. For a discussion of this strategy and of some of the newest weapons in production and development, see Brzezinski (2003).
12. See Halbfinger and Holmes (2003); also Johnson (undated).
13. Alternative (or supplemental) strategies being pursued (with little chance of success) are a return to relying on mass armies from the Third World (harkening back to the role of the Indian Army in the British Empire) and on private armies and private military contractors (harkening back to before the age of nationalism).
14. See Harris and Franklin, (2003). It is possible that unrest in the military ranks had already been building up in response to the high disability rates associated with service in the first Gulf War, combined with cuts in veterans' benefits recently implemented by the U.S. government. Chalmers Johnson (no date) has recently suggested that the U.S. casualties in the 1991 Gulf War are far higher than the wartime battle figures would suggest, given the "potential toxic side effects of the [depleted uranium in the] ammunition now being widely used by [the U.S.] armed forces." He estimates a death and disability rate of 29.3 percent for the first Gulf War, once one includes the deaths and disabilities linked to service-connected exposures during the war.

30

Globalization as a Gender Strategy: Respectability, Masculinity, and Convertibility across the Vietnamese Diaspora

Hung Cam Thai

This chapter addresses the power of status across transnational social fields by high-lighting relations between class and masculinities in globalization (Connell, 2000; Goldring, 1998). I take a critical global approach to the study of masculinities by adopting Arlie Russell Hochschild's (1989) concept of "gender strategy," which Hoch-schild described in her pioneering 1989 work on *The Second Shift* among working parents in the United States. In her exposition of how working husbands and wives deal with the "sharing" of domestic labor, Hochschild explains that a gender strategy

> ... is a plan of action through which a person tries to solve problems at hand, given the cultural notions of gender at play. To pursue a gender strategy, a man draws on beliefs about manhood and womanhood, beliefs that are forged in early childhood and thus anchored in deep emotions. He makes a connection between how he thinks about his manhood, what he feels about it, and what he does .... The term "strategy" refers to his plan of action and to his emotional preparations for pursuing it (p. 15–18).

Why and how do some immigrant men of color use globalization as a gender strategy to "achieve" masculinity? I address this question by engaging with the schol-arly work on the "gendering of transnational spaces" in the new global economy (Constable, 2003: 164), with particular attention to concerns raised by scholars researching transmigration (Hondagneu-Sotelo, 1999; Mahler, 1998; Mahler, 1999; Parrenas, 2001; Pessar, 1999). The central subjects of this chapter are the stories of Tèo ñòan and Tòan Phẩm, two *ViŒt KiŠu,* or Vietnamese migrants living outside of Vietnam. Tèo was a 32-year-old man who worked for his parents at a small sandwich shop in the Silicon Valley, where the second highest concentration of *ViŒt KiŠu* reside. Thirty-year-old Tòan was the afternoon janitor at a public elementary school in urban Los Angeles, the metropolitan area with the highest concentration of *ViŒt KiŠu.* Despite their demographic advantage of living in two heavily-popu-lated Vietnamese metropolitan areas as they both wanted to marry women of Viet-namese-origin, both Tèo and Tòan had recently returned to Vietnam for wives through the arrangements of family and kin throughout the Vietnamese diaspora.

The stories of Tèo ñòan and Tòan Phẩm illuminate how certain historical and structural factors, including the demography of marriage markets in postimmigrant communities, are linked to what Nicole Constable calls "marital subjectivities" in global space. Their narratives show why and how some immigrant men of color, particularly those in low-wage work, utilize globalization as a gender strategy in order to pursue convertibility of social status to claim a sense of self-worth. This convertibility allows them, in turn, to feel, if not become, more marriageable in the global hierarchy of marriage markets. These narratives also reveal how "subaltern men" construct their own masculinity and sense of respectability, given that their lives are placed "at the intersection and interstices of vast systems of power: patriarchy, racism, colonialism, and capitalism, to name a few (Chen, 1999: 589)."

Like Mexicans in the United States whom Luin Goldring (1998) described in her study of transmigrants, Vietnamese immigrant men orient their lives to their place of origin because the "locality of origin provides a unique social and spatial context within transnational communities for making claims to and valorizing social status" (p. 165). The place of origin thus provides an important social space to which "immigrants" can return in order to improve their social position on the basis of material consumptions, which are often translated to symbolic power as purchasing abilities are enormously differentiated between unequal developments of nation-states in the global economy.

At the outset, it is important to point out the distinction between *transnational* and *global* as outlined by Micheal Kearny (1995). "Transnationalism overlaps globalization, but typically has a more limited purview," as Kearney explains. "Whereas global processes are largely decentered from specific national territories, and take place in global space, transnational processes are anchored in and transcend one or more nation-states." By using a critical globalization approach to analyze transpacific marriages among co-ethnics living in different parts of the world, I call attention to the metaphor *anchor* as it permits us to magnify the histories of global inequality between nation-states while seeking to understand the transnational lives of immigrants and the people they care for in their home country. This is because "international migrations are produced, they are patterned, and they are embedded in specific historical phases" (Sassen, 1993: 97).

I confront the questions of how social status is converted across transnational social fields, and more importantly, how this convertibility is gendered across transnational space. In Pierre Bourdieu's view, as a point of reference, social status and distinctions are based not only on economic capital (e.g., income) but are linked to other forms of capital, namely cultural, social, and symbolic. Distinctions of status and boundaries of class for Bourdieu are sites of conflicts because differentiations are made by social groups in order to legitimate symbolic and material power. For scholars of globalization, one of the most insightful and relevant critiques of Bourdieu is the question of convertibility, because for Bourdieu, material and symbolic differences are marked within specific "objective social space" (Hall, 1992: 279).

One of the most striking observations of the question of convertibility has been made by Yen Le Espiritu, who compellingly argued that it is not often possible to use standard measures such as education or occupation to talk about class status among transnational and immigrant populations. As Espiritu (2001) suggested in her study of the Filipino community in San Diego, the class status of most of her informants were both ambiguous and transnational, given the nature of uneven development in the global economy and its implications for transnational populations.

Vietnamese in the United States were initially part of a refugee dispersion that flung them to different parts of the world, which tremendously affected their job prospects when they arrived on Western soil. The Vietnamese, for example, continues to be one of the lowest income-earning groups in Asia America (Yamane, 2001). In my study of international marriages in the Vietnamese diaspora I have found that although most *KiŠu* who return to Vietnam could partake in consumption patterns that they otherwise could not afford in the West, most *ViŒt KiŠu* transpacific husbands, in fact, lived in minimal housing situations, generally could not, in fact, afford properties in Vietnam, and for the most part, had very modest sense of self-worth in their overseas contexts. It is the power of convertibility in globalization at the everyday level of food consumption, small gift-giving activities, and recognitions of differences from the very poor kin members in Third World Vietnam that allow some *ViŒt KiŠu* to recuperate from their loss of self-worth as a result of migration.

The empirical evidence for this chapter is extracted from a larger ethnographic, mainly interview-based research project that I conducted between 1997 and 2001. During 14 months of fieldwork I got to know 69 transpacific marriages. In this distinct and emergent global marriage market, the immigrant Vietnamese men typically go to Vietnam to marry through arrangement and subsequently return to their places of residence in the Vietnamese diaspora (most are from the United States, Canada, France, and Australia) to initiate paperwork to sponsor their wives as immigrants. The couples I got to know in these marriages were, therefore, in a "migration waiting period." That is, they were transnationally separated as the women were waiting to be united with their husbands through migration. I present two life histories in this chapter, and, rather than focusing on decisions around marriage selections, I concentrate on the ways in which men convert their social status across transnational social fields. I echo what Nicole Constable has conveyed about global marriage options: they should not be understood as a "simple unilinear movement from East to West, from underdeveloped 'South' to developed 'North,' from so-called traditional societies to so-called modern ones, or from oppression to liberation" (Constable, 2003: 165).

Gender and Transmigration

There is a chronological paradox to research on gender and transmigration. From the 1950s to the 1970s, scholarship on migration focused almost exclusively on men as the "birds of passage" whereas women, children, and the elderly were seen as following in their paths (Bodnar, Simon, and Weber, 1982; Handlin, 1951; Howe, 1976; Piore, 1979; Simon and Brettell, 1986). This earlier research assumed that males were more inclined and able to take risks and to journey far away in search of better job opportunities, whereas women, if they migrated at all, were depicted as emotional caretakers who accompanied men to ensure family and community stability. This earlier research suppressed women's (and children's) agency in family migration processes and assumed that "children are carried along by their parents, willy-nilly, and wives accompany their husbands though it tears them away from the environment they love" (Lee, 1966: 578).

In the 1970s and 1980s, scholars and policy makers began to focus on women as central actors in the migration process, in part, because of the dramatic growth in feminist scholarship and women's studies programs as well as demographic reports showing that more women than men were migrating to the United States (Hondagneu-Sotelo, 1999; Houstoun, Kramer, and Barrett, 1984; Pessar, 1999). By the late 1990s and early twenty-first century, numerous migration scholars included women in their research. This effort resulted in a collection of important anthologies, articles, and books focusing on women and the migration process (e.g., Brettell and deBerjeois, 1992; Brettell and Simon, 1986; Buijs, 1993; Chant, 1992; Donato, 1992; Gamburd, 2000; Hondagneu-Sotelo, 1994; Hondagneu-Sotelo, 2001; Hondagneu-Sotelo and Avila, 1997; Parrenas, 2001a; Parrenas, 2001b; Pedraza, 1991; Phizacklea, 1983; Romero, 1992; Simon and Brettell, 1986).

The shift to focusing on women, however, for the most part ignored the situation of men in contemporary migration flows and, therefore, of gender as an analytical category. Furthermore, there has been little emphasis on gender in studies on transmigration. Notable exceptions include the works by the few scholars doing research on domestic workers in the new global economy (Ehrenreich and Hochschild, 2002; Gamburd, 2000; Hondagneu-Sotelo and Avila, 1997; Parrenas, 2001b). Sarah Mahler (1999) was one of the first to critique the bipolar approach to understanding gender and transmigration. She argued that the emergence of transnationalism as a "critical optic" mirrors the emergence of gender in migration scholarship (p. 693). "Migration was (and continues to be) gendered long before scholars perceived it as a fundamental axis," Mahler writes, "transnationalism itself is not completely new, yet the predominant doctrine of bipolar migration deterred its detection and investigation."

As global forces shape various immigrant communities by linking migrants and settlers to their home countries, "gender and transnationalism grow in importance as central theoretical principles in migration scholarship" (Mahler, 1999: 694). Despite assertions of employing gender as a key analytical category in migratory and transnational processes by scholars like Pierrette Hondagneu-Sotelo, Patricia Pessar, Rhacel Parrenas, and Sarah Mahler, there is virtually no focus on the meanings of masculinity in globalization among immigrant men of color. This essay is an attempt to remedy in small ways this situation.

Viœt Kišu in the New Global Economy

Vietnamese mass out-migration to the West was part of a specific historical phase in global history dating largely to the political turmoil of the mid-1970s in Southeast Asia, a phase that resulted in the fact that more than two million people have since left Vietnam primarily as political refugees and are now living in more than eighty countries worldwide (Tran, 1997). More than 90 percent of these post-1975 international migrants reside in the core countries of the United States, Canada, Australia, and France (Merli, 1997).

I disembark from the refugee model of Vietnamese migration by paying attention to the emergence of a transpacific marriage market that has been made available to women in Vietnam and Vietnamese men who live overseas. This particular marriage market is gendered because very few overseas women return to Vietnam for husbands as I have discovered in my investigation of case studies and in my confirmation with marriage registration lists at the Vietnamese Department of Justice. The basis of this gendered pattern is that a high male mortality rate during the Vietnam War and the larger number of men than women who emigrated during the last quarter of the twentieth century has produced what demographer Daniel Goodkind (1997) calls the "double marriage squeeze," a situation resulting in a "surplus" of men of marriageable age in Vietnam and a "surplus" of women of marriageable age in Vietnamese overseas communities.

Yet, the recent return of immigrant Vietnamese men to their homeland for wives is not just a matter of an emigration history nor is it simply a matter of demographic skews. It has emerged in the context of global forces and transnational ties that have changed Vietnamese society on many levels, as well as consequences of changing gender relations in postmigrant overseas Vietnamese communities that are partly related to demographic skews (Kibria, 1993). In 1986, after having no contact with the outside world for over a decade, Vietnam adopted a new socio-economic policy called Ç°i m§i[1] (renovation) that, although it did not end state ownership or central planning, moved the country from complete state-sponsored socialism to partial free-market capitalism (Ebashi, 1997; Morley and Nishihara, 1997). Vietnam was admitted to the Association of Southeast Asian Nations (ASEAN) in 1993 and in August 1995, former U.S. President Bill Clinton established full diplomatic relations with the country (Morley and Nishihara, 1997).

The normalization of economic and social ties by 1995 gradually increased the number of individuals from the Vietnamese diaspora who returned as tourists or to visit family members. Incentives provided by the state for the overseas population such as the ability to purchase land and provisions for investment opportunities have created an extraordinarily important Viŵt Kiŝu economy. For instance, remittances grew dramatically from only $35 million in 1991 to more than $2 billion by 2002 (Nguyen, 2002). The Vietnamese government estimates that currently more than one million Viŵt Kiŝu return annually for tourism and to visit relatives, a dramatic increase from the 87,000 who came in 1992, and from 8,000 who visited in 1988. The traffic of Viŵt Kiŝu goods, people, and ideas has manifested itself in profound gendered ways, one of which is the ability of overseas men to convert social status in their pursuit of marriage.

Gender Strategies and the Convertibility of Social Status in Transnational Social Fields

A Vietnamese immigrant man utilizes globalization as a gender strategy when he "performs" transnationalism in order to "achieve" masculinity. He deliberately converts his relatively low status in the West to relatively high status when he goes to Vietnam. In order to do this, a Vietnamese immigrant man engages in small scale conspicuous consumption such as everyday drinking and eating activities and employing simple gift-giving practices (that are often beyond his Western means). This convertibility becomes most — or, sometimes, *only* — meaningful when he establishes and maintains translocal relations that "are constituted within historically and geographically specific points of origin and migration established by transmigrants," and thereby forming a "triadic connection that links transmigrants, the localities to which they migrate, and their locality of origin" (Guarnizo and Smith, 1998: 13). Convertibility benefits a Vietnamese immigrant man by offering him the ability to geographically cross international borders to go from the status of low marriageability to high marriageability.

Just as Hochschild (1989) argues in her study that gender strategies are utilized by women as well as men, I found that both men and women pursue gender strategies based on their gender ideologies. Likewise, men from across social class backgrounds pursue gender strategies. But the interrelated issues of global convertibility, social status, and masculinity are particularly central, salient, and relevant to the lives of low-wage immigrant men, who have found it difficult to find marriage partners in their overseas locations. These men typically earned between $8,000 and not much more than $20,000 annually, and viewed their jobs as highly unrespectable, which they felt also made them unmarriageable in the overseas location.

In the following pages, I supply narratives of Tèo ñòan and Tòan Phẩm to show the following line of argument: first, low-wage Vietnamese-American men are able to convert their "low-income" status of the First World to "high-income" status when they visit Third World Vietnam. Second, material convertibility through small scale conspicuous consumption translates to symbolic status that is used to "trade off" in the Vietnamese transpacific marriage market. Third, convertibility of material and symbolic differences is usually, if not always, anchored in a tangible transnational relation, with people recognizing differential purchasing power between the First and Third Worlds. If the convertibility goes unnoticed, it is often meaningless to the person doing the converting. Finally, convertibility is practical, if not necessary, to valorize self-worth among low-wage Vietnamese immigrant men, but it is costly.

At the Bottom among Men, Top among Nations

Vietnamese American men earn on average 30 percent less than their white counterparts, and they are one of the lowest income-earning ethnic groups in the United States (Yamane, 2001). Yet, they are at the top globally if compared to the men in Vietnam as the United States holds enormous social and economic power in the global economy that makes wage differentials dramatically obvious. Thus, although some of the low-wage men in this study experienced tremendous downward social and economic mobility after migration, their overseas low-wage takes on different economic and social meanings when they return to Vietnam.

Tèo grew up as the middle child in a relatively comfortable home Francisco in the Vietnamese enclave of the Silicon Valley. His parents' lifestyle, as exhibited by the house they lived in and the cars they drove, indicated that they were at least economically middle class. But because his parents, both in their late fifties, owned a simple sandwich shop catering to the mixed-income ethnic community in which they lived, Tèo thought of his parents' work and, by extension, of himself because he also worked at the shop, as part of the working class (tàng lŞp lao Çʃng). Tèo had internalized his style of living in his early adulthood, and particularly when his older brother and younger sister both earned educational credentials to secure office jobs. Because Tèo did not have an office job, as he explained, he had unofficially assumed responsibility for his parents' elderly years in place of his brother who was two years older than he. He assumed this responsibility, in part, because he was also working for his parents at the sandwich shop and still living in their home (which saved him a tremendous amount of money in expensive Silicon Valley).

When Tèo spoke about his brother, he spoke with a sense of discomfort about the fact that his brother and his brother's wife were both professionals. "They are very critical people (*phê bình*)," he said. Tèo said that they were critical about the fact that Tèo had never earned a college degree, and that this would make Tèo unmarriageable. Tèo was moderately confident about his ability to court women in the United States and like many men in this study, he made sure to convey his sense that he did not go to Vietnam to marry because he was simply "*ế*" or "unmarketable," a marker of stigma for those at the marriageable age and yet unmarried. Tèo showed me pictures taken with about half a dozen ex-girlfriends throughout his early adulthood, as if to offer evidence of masculinity. When we spoke at length about the last serious relationship, Tèo explained that it was a very difficult breakup "for her." As I continued in this line of inquiry, I learned that it took Tèo two years to realize that he was "over" [*xong*] the relationship. He met this ex-girlfriend at the community college in the Vietnamese Student Association in 1988 when he was nineteen.

Two years after they started dating, Tèo was, at best, half way through his community college education, while the ex-girlfriend was excelling at her studies, graduated, and was accepted into one of the best University of California campuses. They remained committed to each other when she went to the university, but he felt she lost interest at the point where she was accepted into another UC school to earn her pharmacy degree. He said he always felt comfortable going out with her UC friends, but she did not like to meet or go out with his community college friends — a sign of disrespect to him. According to Tèo, he eventually broke up the relationship, because he felt that she lost interest in him. "She was fine with the break up," Tèo explained, "But I know *she* was in pain." Several more visits with Tèo revealed that he had broken up that serious relationship because he could not envision himself marrying a woman whom he felt had so much more education than he did.

Tèo's ability to court women in his early adulthood did not follow him through his early thirties when people he knew began to earn well in "careers" rather than the sort of job that Tèo took. And the fact that he felt his last ex-girlfriend did not "respect" him because of his lack of high education prompted Tèo to look elsewhere for a marriage partner. "As a man," Tèo said to me with a strong sense of depth, "you have to have a certain kind of status." But as Tèo looked elsewhere in the highly-populated Vietnamese enclave of the Silicon Valley, he found that social status was relatively difficult to achieve regardless of what social circles he entered as he was still a sandwich shop worker, wherever he maneuvered himself. "Vietnamese people here [in the United States] only pay attention to how much money you make or what kind of degrees you have," Tèo said. "The women don't want to marry men who don't have comfortable jobs."

When Tèo began to seriously look for marriage prospects, he moved out of his Silicon Valley cultural corner and, in effect, turned to a transnational space in which he could convert his relatively low social status. Just as virtually all those who desired a transpacific marriage and had relied on transnational networks for marriage arrangements, Tèo sought the help of one best friend, Mảnh, who had a single younger sister still living in Vietnam. Mảnh had been to Vietnam several times and had each time had tried to persuade Tèo to take the trip with him, in part, because Mảnh had wanted to arrange a marriage for Tèo and his younger sister. The two men took the first trip together in 1998, and by early 1999, Tèo had married Mảnh's younger sister. When I asked Tèo to chronicle that first trip back to Vietnam, he immediately raised the issue of convertibility:

> I felt like a different person when I went to Vietnam for the first time, like I had another life in another world. Everything was so cheap, and I could just spend money on luxuries. I didn't have to worry about the cost of anything, like you can take twenty people out to eat a huge feast and it could cost you less than what you would spend on two people in San Jose. It's very luxurious! (*sung sÜ§ng l¡m*)

As someone who barely earned more than $1500 per month in expensive Silicon Valley, Tèo's low-income did not go far in the United States, and this low-income was partly a reflection of his level of education. Both the low-income and the absence of a college degree in the United States meant that Tèo felt he had little opportunity for social mobility in the formal U.S. labor market, and, in Tèo's eyes, to acquire social status, particularly in the Vietnamese–American marriage market. Like many *ViŒt KiŠu* who journey home, Tèo converted his low income to take pleasures in luxuries that he could not otherwise usually afford in the United States like taking "twenty people out to eat a huge feast." The immediate convertibility of money is linked immediately to the convertibility of status and esteem. This process of convertibility allows men like Tèo to participate in a marriage market where they feel they have something to offer and which they, in turn, feel could offer them something.

When men like Tèo talked about consumption and being in Vietnam, it is most often in the context of being under the watchful eyes of family and kin. The anchoring of transnational ties to specific communities of origin means that Tèo had a particular network to validate his social worth. As Tèo explained what seems to be a need for an audience of convertibility:

> When you are a *ViŒt KiŠu,* people in Vietnam watch you. They want to see that you have the ability (*khä næng*) to buy what they cannot. And if you cannot, they will think of you as one of them. And then you are a useless (*vô døng*) *ViŒt KiŠu.* If you love your family, you also want to show them that you can afford what they cannot, that you can take care of them …. But for yourself, you also don't want to have a reputation (*ti‰ong tæm*) of someone who cannot buy the things they cannot.

The Lowest Wage among Low-Wagers

I met Tòan one weekday afternoon in January 2001 at an inner city elementary school in urban Los Angeles where he worked as the after-school janitor. Low-wage men such as Tòan perceived their jobs — jobs that usually paid barely the legal minimum wage and sometimes below it — as sites of degradation. "It is maybe better not to work at all," as Tòan told me, "than to work at a job where you feel humiliated (*nhọc*) to tell people you know." Such feelings of humiliation led Tòan to eventually globalize his marriage options. Prior to leaving Vietnam in 1996, Tòan had a serious relationship with a woman he met when he was in eighth grade from his home village in the province I call Se Long. When Tòan left Vietnam through the sponsorship of his father, he said he did not have intentions of keeping the long distance relationship with this long-term girlfriend. But after being in the United States for only a few months, Tòan soon realized that his prospect for marriage in the United States was low, in a large part because of his low-wage job. Thus after having been in the United States for only two years, Tòan returned to Vietnam to propose marriage, having had kept in touch with his serious girlfriend in Se Long. Like my interviews with most men in this study, I asked Tòan to recount his feelings and experiences with the first visit home:

> We live overseas, we have nothing. We just work. When we go to Vietnam, we have happiness (*có sự sung sÜ§ng*). [Why?] Because we have money when we go to Vietnam. There are people who will look at us, people who will pay attention to us because we have a behavior of a person (*tÜ cách con ngÜ§i*) that is enough for others to have a relation with (*quan hŒ*), we are not an ordinary person (*ngÜ©i tÀm tÜ©ng*) [in Vietnam].

Indeed as a janitor in Los Angeles, Tòan viewed himself as an "ordinary person," someone who was embarrassed to tell people what he did for a wage as in the landscape of urban Los Angeles, Tòan's income of $6.75 per hour translated to the fact that he literally could not afford the sort of lifestyle that he enjoyed whenever he visited Vietnam. As Tòan succinctly confessed his consumption habits, "In the U.S., I often spend a whole day thinking about whether I should go and eat a five dollar bowl of *phª* (beef noodle soup) when I get off work, but in Vietnam, I don't even think twice when I go to a bar or café and pay $2 million Vietnamese dongs (USD$133) for a bottle of Hennessy (cognac)."

How is the convertibility of money, status, and consumption related to marriage choices? If Tèo felt that an absence of a college degree meant that he could not earn respect by marrying the ex-girlfriend who was heading for a pharmacy degree, then Tòan's very low-wage job led him to believe that he was completely unmarriageable in the United States. "If I want to find a wife in the U.S.," Tòan said, "I will have to wait for the next life (*ki‰op sau*)." Both Tèo and Tòan felt marginal in their overseas marriage markets, although in different ways. Whereas Tèo sensed that he deliberately rejected the marriage market in the United States, Tòan felt he was rejected. But their two experiences of rejections were anchored in the same way as they sought to participate in small scale conspicuous consumption in Vietnam: they returned to Vietnam in order to convert their low-income to high-income as a gender strategy to make themselves more marriageable in the Vietnamese global hierarchy of marriage markets. Some men like Tèo and Tòan men are successful at achieving their goals, of upgrading their sense of self-worth, but their use of globalization as a gender strategy comes at a cost that often results in the fact that they must sacrifice at an everyday level in their overseas contexts.

As Le Anh Tu Packard (1999) observes, "Over time, stereotypical images of rich, ostentatious, and arrogant *ViŒt KiŠu* on the one side, and of ignorant, backward, and beggarly 'country bumpkins' on the other, have been replaced by more nuanced views" (p. 82). Indeed, the initial view of Vietnamese nationals was that *Việt Kiều* had an impressive purchasing power because of income differences between Vietnam and the West. Although initial views have not changed entirely, they have been gradually transformed as locals learn that while the high *Việt Kiều* salaries could purchase a luxury life in Vietnam, they in fact could not go far in the West. Thus, men like Tèo and Tòan slowly realized that in order to keep up with their images of *Việt Kiều* who are "ready to play" (*triệu chởi*), they must spend their last cent of savings on the few weeks or months that they visit Vietnam, although they live with very minimal lives in their overseas locations for the rest of the year; they, in effect, reverse their "worlds of consumption." Materially, they live a First World life in Vietnam, and a Third World life in the United States. Tòan told me that in Los Angeles, he ate instant ramen noodles for dinner at least three or four times a week, packed all of his lunches for work, and rarely ate at a restaurant. In contrast, he said in Vietnam, "instant noodles are for the poor," and as a *Việt Kiều*, he needed to demonstrate his ability to pay for expensive food items, like jumbo shrimp or abalone shellfish (two items he said he never consumed in the United States).

Thus, in order to recuperate from their loss of status in their overseas locations as a result of migration, low-wage Vietnamese immigrant men attempt to live up to the expectation that they can afford anything in Vietnam. To live up to this expectation means that these men often deprive themselves of basic necessities in their overseas contexts so that they can accumulate in order to consume "like a *Việt Kiều*" when they are in Vietnam. Kin members in Vietnam also benefit materially from *Việt Kiều* small scale conspicuous consumption patterns, for which the Vietnamese kin members often do not want to undermine. In fact, they go through great lengths to commend *Việt Kiều* for having a "luxurious life in the West," even to the extent of recognizing that *Việt Kiều* can "burn money." On many occasions, transpacific husbands confided to me the burden of consumption when they go to Vietnam. In one story, Tòan told me of a twenty-something female cousin of his wife who, in the presence of over twenty kin members, publicly asked Tòan to buy her a bottle of perfume at a department store that had just opened up in central Saigon. In her public request, Tòan told me she jokingly said, "A $50 bottle of perfume means nothing to you, Tòan. You can burn money when you visit here, right?" As Tòan described to me, while the noisy and attentive audience watched for a reply, Tòan simply said, "Fifty dollars is nothing (*không có gì*)." When I asked what happened afterwards, Tòan said some family members laughed, some clapped their hands at Tòan's reply, and that eventually, but reluctantly, Tòan bought the cousin the bottle of perfume.

"Fifty dollars could buy me several hundreds packages of instant noodles," Tòan explained with laughter, "in Los Angeles."

Note

1. Literally, "changing for the new."

31

The Red, the Green, the Black, and the Purple: Reclaiming Development, Resisting Globalization

Kum-Kum Bhavnani, John Foran, and Molly Talcott

The Crisis of Globalization

Since 1999, ongoing realignments in the cultural and political economies of the world have brought together many previously unconnected constituencies at protests of the G8 economic summits, meetings of the World Trade Organization, and the exclusive World Economic Forum gatherings in Switzerland. In 2003, a massive worldwide peace movement courageously tried to prevent the U.S. invasion of Iraq, and most recently, we have witnessed the glorious collapse of the WTO discussions at Cancún in September 2003.

At the same time, supporters of globalization from above have demonstrated the extent to which they will resort to state violence to ensure that global capitalism continues uninterrupted, while religious fundamentalism rages East to West, environmental degradation continues at an alarming rate, the Bush administration engages in reckless war-making, and global inequality and the feminization of poverty reach ever greater heights. Both security and love are becoming more elusive for many people — especially poor women.

However, there is substantial evidence that all of this is not inevitable. Thai peasants plant organic vegetables on overirrigated golf-courses (Klein, 2002b); indigenous groups of women in India have engaged in far-sighted and sustainable forest regeneration (Rowbotham and Linkogle, 2001); women in Senegal work to eliminate female genital cutting (FGC) in their villages while also taking care of the women whose job is to conduct such cutting (James and Robertson, 2002). North and South, sex work has become a site for discussions about the interconnections of women's work and agency with tourism, militarism, migration, and masculinity (Kempadoo, 2001; Peterson, 2000; Seager, 1999). Women who tap for rubber in western Brazil have created organizations that increase literacy and challenge the domestic violence in their lives (Campbell, 1995). These actions attempt to slow the apparent "juggernaut of globalization" in favor of visions of development as planned social transformation and redistribution. With women at the center, suggest how globalization might be resisted.

As Mahbub ul Huq, creator of the Human Development Index, puts it, "the basic purpose of development is to create an enabling environment for people to enjoy long, healthy, creative lives. This simple but powerful truth is too often forgotten in the pursuit of material and financial wealth" (quoted in UNDP, 1999: 1). In other words, what could make globalization "unnatural" and "not-inevitable" is development. Despite the failures of development, people on the ground everywhere engage with its contradictions, using development to create possibilities for social transformation and the redistribution of wealth and resources.

An emergent paradigm we call "Women, Culture, and Development" (WCD) calls for such a development centered on women, investing culture and human agency with as much significance as political economy (Chua, Bhavnani, and Foran, 2000; Bhavnani, Foran, and Kurian, 2003). A WCD perspective takes into account how practices and discourses of gender, culture, and the South come together in the everyday lives of women in the Third World by integrating production with reproduction and explicitly acknowledging women's agency. Drawing on three modes of enquiry — feminist studies, cultural studies, and Third World and critical development studies — WCD proposes a paradigmatic shift in the relation between women and projects of development at theoretical, political, and policy levels. A WCD approach is able to retain the economic as a key means of grappling with the subordination of poor women in the Third World, yet does not privilege the economic above other aspects of people's everyday lives. Culture must be brought into our discussions because it provides a noneconomistic yet still material way to produce knowledge and to present different strategies for making social change. With its focus on critical pedagogies, practices, and movements for justice, a WCD lens may provide ideas for a politics of transformative development.

The Red, the Green, the Black, and the Purple: Toward Socialist, Ecological, Antiracist, and Feminist Visions of Social Justice

Given that contestation, tension, and contradiction permeate our lives, any viable politics should strive to take account of the unexpected and unpredictable outcomes of globalization. The question we ask is, what forms of politics can move us towards a more just world? Our answer lies in the slightly awkward formulation of a politics based on a socialist, green, antiracist, and feminist vision of social justice.

We know that this vision lies close to an older politics of socialist feminism and are well aware that for many critics socialism is seen as having little credibility as an alternative to globalization. We can have many lively discussions about the erosion of the credibility of socialist critiques, but we wish to invoke the "red" of socialism because the best way to generate new thought and action is to seek out contradictions — for us, a concept central to Marxism. This seeking out of contradictions within development will force notions both of "development" and of "socialism" to shift, and indeed runs parallel with the currently popular terms "social justice" and "global justice."

There has not been enough research and discussion of the fact that corporate globalization, as it is promoted by its elite agents, also signals a moment of profound ecological change. Ariel Salleh writes of the "tele-pharmo-nuclear complex" and describes it as "a colonizing force that literally drives the contradictions of late capitalist patriarchal relations right down to our body cells" (Salleh, 1997: x). The "green" of an environmentally sustainable development is thus indispensable to a project of radical social change today.

We valorize the "black" of racial difference to indicate the centrality of the labors — waged and unwaged, productive and reproductive — of the world's people of color that actualize the profit imperative at the heart of globalization. The lack of international consensus reached at the UN World Conference Against Racism held in Durban, South Africa, in 2001 is just one indicator of the racialized power struggles taking place within the context of the new global order. Racial injustice — expressed across the world through racialized forms of unequal pay and many-sided abuse of immigrant workers, environmental racism, racialized attacks on welfare state policies by those who favor privatization, seizures of indigenous peoples' lands, racialized wars and occupations, forced sterilizations of women of color, and the growth of prison-industrial complexes — has been crucial to corporate globalization. Racial justice advanced by a black politics of resistance is vital to the creation of just forms of development.

We use the "purple" of feminism and sexuality to foreground the idea that production, reproduction, and love are intimately linked in the lives of all people and that this can be seen most clearly in the lives of women. Embracing production and reproduction in the lives of women makes it easier to see how development can be reimagined. The usual move is to engage with the category "woman" as intersected by axes of inequality other than gender — such as race, sexuality, nationality, or wealth — which cut across each other at different angles. A more agentic way to think about inequalities might be with the notion of *configurations*, because to configure connotes movement and fluidity more easily than the somewhat static metaphor of intersection, and because configurations lead to the hard work of forging connections of respect and responsibility demanded by all political work.

As projects of globalization deepen the inequalities of power around the world, some forms of development are starting to suggest the conditions of possibility for resisting the trend toward greater poverty. We propose that a socialist, green, antiracist feminism might allow us to reimagine development. The brief case studies that follow are but two of the many ongoing political projects which run along these lines. They point to the simultaneously ecological, material, and cultural struggles of Third World women for socially just forms of development — and against privatization and trade liberalization. We wish to develop our politics by learning from these examples.

Patent Injustices, Third World Responses

The ecological transformations accompanying global economic restructuring are most striking in the convergence of biotechnology, patenting systems, and trade liberalization. This emerging nexus presents the world with a new set of material conditions linked to the biologizing — and therefore expansion — of the concept of private property. The elite agents of globalization now not only "stoop to pick up the golden apples dropped from the tree of industry" (Marx and Engels, 1988: 107), they also genetically modify and patent them as their own inventions! In this new biopolitical epoch, life forms are patented in the form of "intellectual property." Central to this commodification of life is the private appropriation of knowledge and its production. Even elements of nature that do not require biotechnological shuffling are being designated as commodities, as seen in the World Bank's 1993 elaboration of a water resources management policy that defines water as an "economic good" (World Bank, 1993).

The social and ecological implications of this biopolitical moment can be grasped through the case of the 1995 Trade Related Aspects of Intellectual Property (TRIPS) legislation adopted by the WTO during the Uruguay Round Agreements. The 148 member countries of the WTO must enact domestic legislation to protect patents on cloned or genetically altered plants and animals, and on microorganisms that include human and animal cell lines, genes, and umbilical cord cells. The TRIPS agreement recognizes intellectual property rights (IPRs) only as private rights — not as collective rights linked to socially generated knowledges. Article 27.1 of the TRIPS agreement makes it clear that the protection of IPRs through patents is antithetical to a socially just notion of development, stipulating that knowledges and innovations are entitled to IPRs only when they are capable of generating profits via some "industrial application," not when they merely meet social needs (Shiva, 1997: 10). The significance of patents on life forms (biopatents) is growing: of the six million existing patents, almost 3 million are patents on biological resources and 90 percent of those are controlled by transnational corporations (Delgado, 2002). TRIPS is increasingly central to the intensification of private capital accumulation at the heart of economic globalization.

Numerous examples demonstrate the threat of the TRIPS approach to development. Public health, achieved in part through adequate nutrition and access to needed medicines, is accepted as a cornerstone of humane visions of development, yet is compromised by the TRIPS agreement. India, for example, developed national patent laws that exclude seeds, plants, and other items that have nutritional and medicinal uses to encourage widespread public access. In 2005 the Indian state will be required to change its laws to protect intellectual property rights. Thailand has proposed a law that would allow traditional healers to register medicinal plants with the government to protect them from corporate patenting — and the United States has questioned this law on TRIPS grounds. Despite the dominant discourse of the life-saving promise of biotechnology, patent monopolies undermine the basic needs and human rights of Third World people by increasing the costs of medicinals and seeds, which make them inaccessible to the very communities that depend on them for survival, and have in many cases grown them for generations (Shiva, 2001).

Patents have been obtained by agricultural and pharmaceutical corporations on a variety of biological substances, including corn from North and Central America, the neem tree of India, quinoa in South America, kava from the Pacific, and the potentially cancer-combating compounds found in the Western Australian smokebush, the Kenyan species of *Maytenus buchananni*, and the endod plant, which Ethiopian women have cultivated for centuries (Hawthorne, 2002). But along with exploitation of the "plant sector" is the exploitation of the "animal sector," as described in one OECD document (Field, 1988). U.S. corporations have patented mice engineered to develop cancer, sheep with altered mammary glands, umbilical cord cells, and the so-called "breast cancer" and "obesity" genes (Shiva, 2001). In 1995, as part of the Human Genome Diversity Project, the cell line of a man from the Hagahai people of Papua New Guinea was obtained without his consent and patented by the U.S. government, and the T-cells of a Guaymi Indian woman from Panama were also taken and appropriated (Hawthorne, 2002). In addition, the French corporation, Genset, has an agreement with the Chinese government to collect and patent DNA from peoples living in the country's remote regions (Shiva, 2001). This kind of "animal sector" patenting revives the biological determinism of eugenicist science; it exoticizes the cell lines of indigenous peoples at the same time that "plant sector" patenting attempts to eradicate their non-market-driven cultures and livelihoods.

Such blatant and severe usurpations of human rights (economic, social, and cultural) in favor of corporate rights through TRIPS, IPRs, and the private appropriation of the world's peoples and ecosystems, however, have been met with fierce resistance. Women in the Third World are leading seed-saving practices, passing on knowledges, and collaborating in transnational fora. The 1995 Beijing Declaration of Indigenous Women included the following statement on biopatenting:

> We call for a stop to the patenting of all life forms. This, to us, is the ultimate commodification of life which we hold sacred …. We demand that the Human Genetic Diversity Project be condemned and stopped. Those responsible for this project should be asked to make an accounting of all the genetic collections they have taken from indigenous peoples and have these returned to the owners of these genes. The applications for patents to these genetic materials should be stopped and no applications, thereafter, should be accepted and processed. Indigenous peoples should be invited to participate in the ongoing discussions in UNESCO on the bioethics of the Human Genome (http://www.twnside.org.sg/title/dec-ch.htm).

In India, organizations like the Foundation for the Revitalization of Local Health Practices and Navdanya's Diverse Women for Diversity program also work against the threats to biodiversity, cultural diversity, and public health posed by the privatization and marketing of life forms as exclusive knowledge. In the Lacandón jungle of Chiapas, Mexico, indigenous communities oppose the private appropriation of natural resources being promoted under President Vicente Fox's attempt to open up southern Mexico to the corporate agenda of the Plan Puebla Panama. These kinds of objections to biopatenting are made on both ecological and cultural grounds, and are linked to the material livelihoods — and the very bodies — of indigenous and Third World peoples. Globalizing elites deny the interdependency of the material, ecological, and cultural realms, whereas many indigenous communities of women insist upon them, signaling the idea that globalization is not merely a contested economic project, but also one that faces cultural and ecological challenges from those who contend that "another world is possible."

Feminists have long critiqued the masculinist premises of scientific knowledge, and the socially and ecologically destructive industrial, technocratic approach to development (Sen and Grown, 1987). As environmental concerns became prominent within development agendas, and efforts by feminists and others to promote sustainable development were undertaken, development agencies and local communities acknowledged and drew upon Third World women's knowledges of water maintenance and sustainable forestry, for example, in order to implement such projects. Yet, feminists have only begun to theorize the gender dimensions of emerging trade and IPR legislation in connection with masculinist and increasingly privatized scientific knowledges. Lourdes Benería and Amy Lind (1995) have argued that as the range of patentability extends to biotechnological uses, research must focus on the gender dimensions of patent laws and on women's diverse roles in these processes. The age-old consequences of legal discussion, couched in apparently "gender-neutral" discussions of trade, render women — and their historically and culturally transmitted and lived knowledges — invisible.

Is the recognition of women's knowledges — achieved during discussions of sustainable development — being undermined by the implementation of global trade and patenting agreements? Where will women who live and work to maintain subsistence levels in their households and communities through close interactions with natural resources fit into this new economic paradigm? The political urgency of these questions is also accompanied by the theoretical urgency of examining the gendered ecological transformations connected to the emerging trade and patents regime. Joni Seager has suggested that the gendered nature of ecologically based power structures is often most apparent at moments of ecological change (2003: 966), and the current historical juncture appears to be one such moment. As biopatenting in the Third World by TNCs emerges as a key economic activity, feminists must consider its consequences for Third World women's lived realities, the reconfiguration of North–South power relations, and the ecological sustainability of the planet. In resistance to the dominant, masculinist narrative of globalization that assumes its inevitability, feminists must investigate women's agency in the midst of these changes. Women's voices do not figure prominently into global trade and intellectual property agreements, yet they are central to future analyses of the interface between trade liberalization, the privatized biotechnological appropriation of collective knowledges, and ecological visions for change.

The collapse of the WTO talks in Cancún serves as a reminder of the battles — mainly waged along North–South (or rich countries vs. all others) lines — over international trade practices, economic development, and ecological questions. And yet, behind the alliance of the dissenting G21-plus nations and the declaration of the collapse of WTO negotiations by Kenyan delegate George Ong'wen stand subsistence farmers, herbalists, and health care providers and consumers — mainly women — who are both directly experiencing and resisting the privatizing effects of such trade agreements. Focused analyses of the interface of trade liberalization, ecological change, and women's resistance practices reveal the need for a new kind of development that centers women's empowerment and knowledges, the cultural integrity of peoples who do not abide by the capitalist market system, and ecologically based sustainable livelihoods.

Resistance to Globalization: the Women of Chiapas[1]

Revolutions have everywhere attempted to put in place new forms of development — usually socialist — to solve pressing problems, typically with mixed results. They have many times improved people's lives, including women's, yet everywhere fallen short of the common dreams of their makers: a more inclusive, participatory form of political rule; a more egalitarian, humane economic system; and a cultural atmosphere where individuals and local communities may not only reach full self-creative expression but thereby contribute unexpected solutions to the dilemmas faced by society. This record of failure can be attributed to many things: outside pressures from governments, exemplified by the United States' unspeakably shameful record of intervention in the Third World; the limits of poverty and dependency that continue to exist in revolutionary societies that lack the resources and breathing space to overcome them; and differences among revolutionaries themselves about how to construct a better society — that is, their inevitable flaws as people, and their enmeshment in structures of patriarchy and racism.

If there is to be a better future — and we do believe that the era of radical social change has not closed with the end of the Cold War; indeed it is almost self-evident that the down- and undersides of globalization will spark struggles of all kinds in the future — how might movements for change have better outcomes? We might seek concrete answers in the recent events in Chiapas, where indigenous women have been struggling to claim the right to define the movement alongside men from the beginning.

What are the gender dimensions of this rebellion? We may note the following developments: the direction of the original military occupation of San Cristóbal de las Casas on January 1, 1994, by Major Ana María; the leadership exercised by some indigenous women in the movement, including the charismatic counterpart of Subcomandante Marcos, Comandanta Ramona, who has traveled to Mexico City to represent the Zapatistas; the December 22, 1997, massacre of forty-five peasants, primarily women and children, by government-linked gunmen, showing the depth of the identification of indigenous women with the movement in the government's eye; and the potential links between the rebellion and other forms of organizing throughout Mexico and beyond, including the predominantly female labor force of the border maquiladora industries.

The positive political space created by the practice of women farming together is noted by Comandanta Christina:

> Once we decided to have our own milpa [patch of land], apart from the work we do with the men, everything changed. We laugh, we joke, we never stop talking! It is here where we learn from each other, where the women that have "awakened" talk to those who are still "asleep" and where those that have fears are guided by those that have found their voice. It was in a space similar to this where I first learned about my rights, and learned to lose the fear of my silence in order to speak (quoted by Mora, 1998: 169–70).

The Women's Revolutionary Laws were the outcome of such situations and the internal political struggle of women within the movement. This law was approved in March 1993, before the Zapatistas declared their existence to the world; Subcomandante Marcos commented that the first EZLN uprising "was headed by the women. There were no casualties and they were victorious. Such are things in these lands" (Mora, 1998: 167). Containing ten points, the original law gives women the right to work and own land, to choose their partners and the number of their children, to be educated and to receive health care, and to take positions of revolutionary leadership.

Women's strategies of resistance also shifted creatively as the struggle developed. When the Mexican army first began its heavy onslaught against the areas of rural insurgency, women left their communities and fled with their children to more remote areas. As time went on, they returned to their villages, often sending the men into hiding and becoming the first line of confrontation with the army. As Blanca Flor, a member of the group Kinal Antzetik (Women's Territory) who works with indigenous women in Chiapas, puts it: "Every day the women get madder. And the madder they get, the stronger they get" (quoted in Flinchum, 1998: 31).

The Zapatistas have offered some radically new ways of doing politics to the revolutionaries of the future. Among their core principles are concepts like *mandar obedeciendo* ("to rule, obeying" — that leaders serve at the pleasure of the community and its struggle, not vice versa); *para todos todo, nada para nosotros* ("for everyone, everything, nothing for ourselves"); "walking at a slower pace" (the recognition that change is a long and slow process, not secured with the mere seizure of power or electoral victories); and, indeed, "not aspiring to take political power." As the second declaration of the Lacandón jungle put it in 1994: "In a sense, this revolution will not end in a new class, fraction, or group in power. It will end in a free and democratic space for political struggle" (EZLN, 2002a: 226). But what does this mean and how is it to be done?

Tactics of nonviolence, consensus decision making, and fluid leadership, so effective at the local level in the initial phases of radical mobilization, present complex challenges to building a truly global movement encompassing diverse groups, and these have yet to be fully met. One innovative Zapatista practice is embodied in the phrase *dar su palabra* (literally, "to have one's say"). This refers to a dialogue in which everyone present participates, in which the value of the unique vantage point of each member of a community and the insights this affords is appreciated. It usually means taking far longer to arrive at a collective decision, but it also ensures that decisions have maximum input from the community they will affect, and rest on a stronger consensus that is based on a more open sense of disagreements. As the Zapatistas' Fourth Declaration put it, "In the world we want, many worlds fit" (EZLN, 2002b: 250). Meanwhile, Mexican artist and scholar Manuel de Landa (1997) may have provided the beginnings of an answer to the daunting organizational question, again from observing Zapatista practices: he proposes the term "meshworks" for self-organizing, nonhierarchical and heterogeneous networks, a lead that the global justice movement has been brilliantly pursuing.

Love of life, love of people, love of justice — all play a role in the core values of Zapatismo. These have been expressed in marvelously poetic ways and strikingly beautiful symbolic acts, as well as courageous organizing against state violence and for alternative forms of development. Love is arguably the emotion that most strongly underlies the vital force that impels many ordinary people into extraordinary acts, across time and place. It is the emotion that lies behind much profound personal and social change. The power of love, and visions, and their connection to dreams of breaking the chain of violence, is underlined fictionally in Graciela Limón's novel about the Zapatistas, *Erased Faces* (2001). The weaving of dreams and visions, and the intimation of past lives that we "repeat," link the struggle to past struggles, and make a compelling case that there is a single 500-year-long movement for indigenous autonomy and human liberation in the Americas. It is also a vision of inclusion, as one of the organizers says: "You are part of us. We used to be like stones, like plants along the road. We had no word, no face, no name, no tomorrow. We did not exist. But now we have vision; we know the road on which we are to embark, and we invite you to come and seek, to find yourself, and to find us. We are you, and you are us, and through you the world will come to know the truth" (Límon, 2001: 41).

And what is that vision? Part of it has to do with an ideal society. Articulating an economic alternative to neoliberalism seems less of a fool's quest these days than it did in the 1990s. One principle for such a political economy might be called, simply, the economics of "social justice." Revolutionaries in many places have articulated this goal, always culturally defined yet remarkably consistent in their insistence that this involves the meeting of basic needs for everyone, increasingly coupled with the realization, in North and South, that this also entails ecological sustainability. Social justice has been the foundation of the economic side of revolutionary political cultures the world over, assuming many local expressions: "Land and Liberty" in Mexico in the 1910s; "Bread, Land, and Peace" in 1917 Russia; "Equality," in 1789 France and the 1990s' South Africa, "Socialism with a Human Face" in 1968 Czechoslovakia; and "Fair Trade" and "Democracy" from Seattle to Cancún. The Zapatistas have most concisely expressed their demands as a struggle for "*trabajo, tierra, techo, pan, salud, educación, democracía, paz, independencia, y justicia*" — "work, land, housing, food, healthcare, education, democracy, peace, independence, and justice" (EZLN, 2002 [1994]: 220).

One way forward would be to build on the lessons of the radically democratic revolutions of the past. Though the movements of Mussadiq in Iran and Arbenz in Guatemala in the early 1950s, Lumumba in the Congo in 1960, the French students in May 1968, Allende in Chile and Manley in Jamaica in the 1970s, and in Tienanmen Square in 1989 all experienced defeat, they have given us a form that the radical reformers and revolutionaries of today in Chiapas, Iran, Uruguay, South Africa, El Salvador, Seattle, and beyond are already imaginatively appropriating and trying to deepen. Such democratic revolutionary movements can yield valuable lessons in fighting a *structure*, harder as this is than overthrowing a dictator (we note, too, that the list of leaders is exclusively male). The actions and visions of the revolutionary women and men of Chiapas provide yet another reminder that imagination, coupled with the courage to dream and love, and to transmit these, in many ways, may yet change the world for the better.

The Briefest of Conclusions

These cases, and many others emergent around the world today, express what we mean by the red, the green, the black, and the purple. There is a final reason why we wish to remind ourselves of socialist, green, antiracist feminist visions of social justice; namely, that all human beings have the potential to change — themselves and their social circumstances. Women do make history and, sometimes, in circumstances of our own choosing.

Borrowing from two radicals quoted earlier, globalization "stoops to pick up the golden apples dropped from the tree of industry, and to barter truth, love and honour for traffic in wool, beetroot sugar and potato spirits" (Marx and Engels, 1988 [1848]). Can we bring our politics to bear on how to ensure that truth, love, and honor do not continue to be bartered? Is it possible to reimagine development as a green, feminist, antiracist, and socialist form of social justice? We urgently need to.

Note

1. This section draws on previous work done by John Foran (2001, 2003, 2003a).

32

Transnational Feminism and Globalization: Bringing Third World Women's Voices from the Margin to Center

Ligaya Lindio-McGovern

Introduction

The devastating impact of neoliberal globalization has posed challenges to transnational feminism. Therefore, I propose that transnational feminism in the context of globalization have two projects. One is shaping a transnational feminist scholarship that gives voice to Third World women whose experience has been marginalized in mainstream Western-dominated discourse on globalization. The other project is shaping a transnational feminist activism that creates a counterhegemonic resistance to globalization that puts centrality to the experience of Third World women who, because of their position in the political economy, are most vulnerable to exploitation. The feminist scholar-activist is the bridge that connects these two projects. Forging these two projects has an important role in shaping a global justice movement from below that challenges neoliberal globalization's impact on the Third World. The following discussion elaborates on these two projects. For the first project, I raise substantive and methodological issues relevant to shaping transnational feminism that is sensitive to Third World women's experience of globalization. For the second project, I present vignettes of Filipino women's activism both in their homeland and across national borders that offer theoretical insights about gender, globalization, and transnationalizing resistance. These vignettes are drawn from my broader research project on globalization and labor export in the Philippines and the circuits of resistance against it.

The Transnational Feminist Scholarship Project: Discourse, Power, and Hegemony

Discourse has power and hegemonic dimensions (Mohanty, 2000), and to a certain extent exerts influence in the definition of social reality. But discourse itself can reflect the power structure prevailing in society, because one's location in such power structure will color one's definition of and response to social reality. The globalized body of knowledge produced in such discourse creates an ideational structure that may legitimize or delegitimize existing hegemonies of domination and subordination. Thus, the Western-dominated, Eurocentric mainstream discourse on globalization is a reflection of the prevailing dominant power structure, both in knowledge production and in the globalization process itself. For example, who controls the intellectual establishment? Who controls the press? Who controls the electronic media? Who controls the production process of university presses, journals, and book publishing companies? What is the composition and dominant ideological orientation of reviewers of mainstream journals and books who have the power to give the green light for publication? Answers to these questions shed light as to why the Third World (especially Third World women) is marginalized in the mainstream discourse on globalization. Such continued marginalization limits understanding of how neoliberal globalization is entrenched in micro and macro structures of gender, race, ethnicity, nationality, and class. This in turn limits knowledge on how to forge transnational resistance to globalization.

Where can the corrective measure for this cognitive impasse begin? My proposal lies in forging the transnational feminist scholarship project on globalization. This project has two important dimensions. One dimension is substantive: unraveling the dynamics of globalization that create ties that divide and bind women, ties that divide and bind men and women, and ties that divide and bind families, bringing children into the picture. The second dimension is epistemological: reexamining how we study the dynamics of globalization that will allow us to do the first dimension.

The Substantive Dimension: Unraveling Ties that Divide and Ties that Bind

In unraveling ties that divide and ties that bind women, men, children, and families across the world, transnational feminist scholarship must address or reexamine some critical issues. Among these are (1) imperialism and the imperial army, and the role of the antiwar–antiinterventionist–peace movements, (2) contextualizing analytical categories of women, Third World women, and Third World men, and (3) reconceptualizing the nation-state, especially the Third World nation-state, in the context of neoliberal globalization. These are critical substantive issues that have implications for forging a counterhegemonic transnational feminist activism project that will demarginalize Third World women's experience.

Imperialism, the Imperial Army, and the Antiwar–Antiinterventionist–Peace Movements

Imperialism is one formidable global force that has divided women, men and women, and families. Its violent expansion has been carried on by the imperial army — hence transnational feminism must reexamine whether the imperial army is a place where women should seek integration.[1] The imperial army has become an instrument of world domination and aggression that has wrecked havoc in the lives of women, men, and children in many parts of the world. Cynthia Enloe has raised this issue as well:

"The military is not the place where women should seek equality."[2] By seeking integration in the imperial army, women are allowing themselves to be instruments of imperial expansion that violates the self-determination of nations while it reinforces the hegemonic power that has dominant control of capitalist globalization. It creates an instance where First World women, who while assuming that their entry into the imperial army achieves gender equality in a patriarchal institution, are turned into oppressors of other women (and of men and children as well) in other parts of the world, especially in the Third World, who had been easy targets of imperial expansion, subjugating their national sovereignty or self-determination. Western liberal feminism has given little critical attention to this issue. Thus, Daiva Stasiulis (1999: 183) observes:

> In women's movements in North America, Britain, and Western Europe, white women, who had always [sic] already assumed their status as an oppressed group within patriarchy, initially responded with shock, confusion, and hostility to allegations and analyses by women of color of their role as oppressors within relations of race and colonialism and discourses of Eurocentrism.

Stasiulis argues

> ... that a feminism nurtured within one national sovereignty movement can be oppressive for other groups of women (and men) seeking self-determination as nations or peoples.

The integration of women in the imperial army has also been manipulated by the corporate media in its role in legitimizing imperial expansion. For example, at the start of the invasion of Iraq, the corporate media portrayed an image of women now gaining equality in the military establishment as it showed the first white American woman to be in combat. Such representation, however, has a subtle controlling image as it presents a benign image of the military, camouflaging it as a brutal instrument of imperial violence in the midst of worldwide antiwar protests. On the other hand, the corporate media did not report about the Iraqi women who took to the streets protesting against U.S. imperial aggression.

Transnational feminism does not seek integration into the imperial army. Rather it seeks integration into the global peace movement, the antiwar movement that must be sustained and strengthened. The global peace movement and antiwar movement is a potent transnational space to build connections among women, men, and children across national borders, class, and race. By undermining the human instrument of war, the imperial army, transnational feminism is taking an active resistance for world peace.

Finally, transnational feminism must offer an alternative view of nationalism that does not infringe on the international human rights of other nations for self-determination, especially the Third World whose neocolonial struggles aim at achieving the full exercise of such right. Recognizing that imperialism serves transnational capital for the benefit of a small power elite can be a critical view to begin defining an alternative conceptualization of nationalism that is respectful of Third World nations' sovereignty. Such thinking can begin from the grassroots who feel the negative impact of transnational capital.

The transnational feminist scholarship project in the context of globalization, then, must address imperialism and make visible the many forms it takes. It must unravel the differential ways it impacts grassroots communities, both in the Third and First World, in order to identify transnational spaces of resistance that bind women with other women, women with men, and youth across national borders.

Contextualizing "Women," "Third World Women," and "Third World Men" as Analytical Categories

Here I would like to reiterate Chandra Mohanty's (2000) concerns of the marginalizing effect of decontextualized homogenizing categories and "ethnocentric universalism" (p. 304) in Western feminist discourse and analytical paradigms that "reinforce Western cultural imperialism" (p. 317), which sets "in motion a colonialist discourse which exercises a very specific power in defining, coding, and maintaining existing First/Third World connections."

A transnational feminist scholarship project that will bring gender and women's voice into the mainstream discourse on globalization must be sensitive to how globalization affects women differently when their experience is placed in historical, political, economic, and cultural contexts of their everyday lives. The conceptual category "women" cannot be homogenized when talking about the impact of globalization. Within the First World societies, women of color, migrant women, and poor women may experience the impact of globalization differently from women and men of the wealthy class, as they are the first ones to suffer the negative impact of privatization with consequent cuts in social services (Sassen, 1998), and they are also the ones who are more marginalized and exploited in the split-labor market in the process of capital accumulation.

The category "Third World women" is also nonhomogeneous in their experience of globalization. For instance, there are those who, due to their nations' labor export and structural adjustment policies, are in the economic diaspora as temporary migrant domestic servants and caregivers for wealthier households in richer nations where increasingly privatization of social services also occurs.[3] This phenomenon transnationalizes the household, making it a microcosm where the interplay of gender, race, ethnicity, nationality, and class are articulated, but also contested.

There are also Third World women whose lives get enmeshed in the sex trafficking network and organized prostitution that commoditize, exploiting not only their sexuality, but their whole being.[4] Kevin Bales (1999) includes this phenomenon as one of the forms of modern slavery in the global political economy[5] — which brings into question the Western naming of prostitution as "sex work," a name that makes it sound neutral and insensitive to the complex interplay of structural, economic, social, and development forces that engulf trafficked women's lives. Modern slavery, Bales argues, comprises three major features: vulnerability, gullibility, and deprivation. These features are structurally produced at the bottom of the economic hierarchy that neoliberal globalization creates.

Although there are Third World women who cross national borders to be marginalized in the host societies, there are also those who remain within their national borders but whose everyday lives as landless peasants, workers in multinational assembly lines, service workers, workers in the informal sector, slum dwellers, street vendors, and indigeneous communities embody the microstructures[6] through which macrostructures of globalization get rooted in national economies. Their experience provides clues to sites of resistance to neoliberal globalization that is both localized and transnational.

Dissecting the different experiences of Third World women in different localities (migrants and those who remain within their national borders) and the local and global structures that connect them allow us to see how the process of neoliberal globalization concretely interlocks into preexisting gender and class structures within national economies that are positioned at the more disadvantaged location in the global political economy. This is where the standpoint of transnational feminism must begin. Thus, we can also begin to think of transnational feminism in the context of globalization as occurring not homogeneously but diversely, as women, divided by class, organize collective resistance to neoliberal globalization as they concretely experience it. We, therefore, can conceive transnational feminism as transnational feminisms in which the point of their convergence is a vision and an outcome of that vision: the creation of a more just global system in which the poor (women, men, and children) will begin to claim their fair share of the pie and reclaim their down-trodden political, economic, and cultural rights.

The transnational feminist scholarship project in the context of neoliberal global-ization must also address how Third World men differentially experience neoliberal globalization because of their position in the class and gender structures. In many instances where class is given primacy as a point of unity in national struggles and in national liberation movements, it becomes more important to examine thoroughly how institutional practices intricately and subtly manipulate patriarchal culture in the process of capitalist penetration of national economies. Such unraveling can contribute to the question that is still inadequately answered: How can class and gender inequalities be addressed simultaneously in the process of national liberation and socialist transformations that revolutionary movements in Third World, neocol-onized countries hope to achieve?

The State and Neoliberal Ideology

The Third World nation-state, or what may be called the periphery state within the world-system framework, plays an active and sometimes contradictory role in the context of neoliberal globalization and usually is seen as the instrument for propa-gation of the ideology of neoliberal globalization. But as a peripheral state, it is also constrained by imperial states. The search for how Third World nation-states can be transformed to achieve some autonomy and political will in order to control the dominance of the instruments of neoliberal globalization — such as the IMF, WTO, and GATT — has made the nation-state a contested terrain. The containment of such movements gives rise to the militaristic state that suppresses political rights, such as the right to organize, necessary for the disempowered groups to claim economic rights or for social movements to transform their political economies.

How the state represses, divides, and rules to contain women's activism and other forms of resistance to globalization is an important issue transnational feminism must address. The connection between militarization and counterinsurgency within Third World states and between imperial militarism and expansionism are formidable but important and crucial terrain where First World and Third World women's activism can converge. Discovering, documenting, and analyzing creative ways grassroots women and men (and youth as well) in the villages, in towns, and in cities confront and resist militarization and how transnational connections are forged is a much neglected task. While it is important to know how hegemonies are constructed, it is equally important to understand how counterhegemonies are constructed from below and how they are transforming both social consciousness and social structures.

The Methodological Dimension: Learning from Feminist Research

Arjun Appadurai (2001: 5) in his "Grassroots Globalization and the Research Imagination" began to raise the methodological issue in studying globalization. He points out the importance of "voice, perspective, or location in the study of global capitalism," and advocates an epistemology that does not turn the "more marginal regions of the world" merely into "producers of data for the theory mills of the North." This requires, he argues, a commitment to study the dynamics of "globalization from below" — its institutions, horizons, and vocabularies — as it confronts globalization from above. He thus sees the connection between pedagogy (à la Paulo Freire), activism, and research.

To address this methodological issue, I suggest that the transnational feminist scholarship project in the context of globalization has much to learn from the principles of feminist research in studying empirically the processes of globalization, not only for the purpose of understanding it, but also for the purpose of undermining or resisting it. Some principles or elements of feminist research that could be useful in bringing the voice of Third World women in the transnational feminist scholarship project are: standpoint, reflexivity, positionality, and immersion.[7]

For the feminist standpoint, I think in line with Gita Sen and Caren Grown (1987) who suggest that we begin inquiry from the experience and perspective of poor Third World women who make up the majority of the world's poor and suffer economic, social, and gendered forms of domination. Their lives embody the complex web of micro and macro structures of neoliberal globalization articulated through interlocking forms of gender–race–class stratification.[8]

Reflexivity allows us to see connections between our lives and the people we study. The disjunction or similarities we find are also data for social analysis. Positionality allows us to examine our place in the hierarchy that is part of our inquiry vis-à-vis the position of the women (and men) we study. Reflexivity and positionality allows us to become aware of how the research engagement personally transforms us — allowing ourselves also to be a subject for inquiry as we study other people's lives. Thus, a dimension of intersubjectivity is given to the research process. This too must be reported in the textual presentation of research findings and analysis.

Immersion requires that we be physically present and be able to interact face to face with the people we study, creating occasions to observe the everyday problems of women's lives in various situations. Immersion must inquire both into the "hidden transcripts" [resistance not publicly expressed, nonetheless undermines the dominance of the powerful] (James Scott, 1990) and public collective forms of resistance and to alternatives to globalization from below. This inquiry will present Third World women not only as victims of the brutality of neoliberal globalization but also as agents of alternative world order and social relations. Immersion also means devising ways to have some continuing connections with the communities or people we study, even after we leave the field, such as continuing to participate in or support their struggles in any possible way. Feminist research then has potentials of linking research (often largely confined to academe) and activism for global social justice. Research takes on a political dimension when it gives voice to the muffled, silenced voices of the oppressed and the exploited in defining the injustice created by globalization and in describing or analyzing the process of its deconstruction.

The Activism Project of Transnational Feminism: Vignettes of Filipino Women's Resistance to Globalization

The activism project of transnational feminism in the context of globalization can take different forms, and analysis of their politics and discourse can enlighten mainstream conceptualizations of globalization. The ultimate goal of the activism project of transnational feminism in the context of globalization is to transform society so that it becomes more respectful of the dignity of all people. In the process of resistance, Third World women's politics and discourses imbed theory-making from below, often marginalized in mainstream discourse, but can inform or reinform grand theories on globalization. The task of transnational feminist scholarship is to bring this voice from the margin to the center of analysis that socially constructs or represents reality. In this section I present vignettes of resistance based on my fieldwork in the Philippines and Hong Kong wherein I applied some principles of feminist research.

GABRIELA

Local and Transnational Feminism   GABRIELA is the militant federation of women's organizations in the Philippines that is leading the women's movement there. GABRIELA (named after Gabriela Silang, the woman revolutionary leader who fought against the Spanish colonizers) is a grassroots-based national alliance of approximately 250 organizations (it began with 42 in 1984). Among some of its major member organizations are AMIHAN (a national federation of peasant women that takes up the right of women to own land within a genuine agrarian reform; SAMA-KANA (Association of United and Free Women), a national federation of urban poor; KMK (Women Workers Movement), which organizes women into trade unions that link up with KMU (May First Movement); INNABUYOG, an alliance of indigeneous women's organizations that struggle for their ancestral land rights and against development that harms them; GABRIELA Youth (organization of women students); and KHADIDJA (Moro Islamic Women of Davao United for Self-Determination), an organization of Moro women based in southern Philippines that addresses the issues of the Moro people including their self-determination and Moro women's gender emancipation. Women's organizations under GABRIELA work on issues that may be particular to their sectors and local context, but they are united nationally under GABRIELA's change agenda that includes the struggle for national, economic, and political sovereignty and freedom from all forms of foreign domination: "We believe that the freedom women seek will be brought about by the resolution of the problems of foreign domination, landlessness, and political repression, and in the changing of patriarchal value systems and structures in Philippine society." GABRIELA works "against issues that adversely affect women," such as "landlessness, militarization, the foreign debt crisis and the IMF–WB structural adjustment policies, denial of women's health rights, violence against women and children, prostitution, trafficking in women, and migration."

Every 3 years GABRIELA's National Assembly, its highest policy-making body, convenes to draw up the alliance's general program of action. In between National Assemblies, the National Council, composed of elected officers and sectoral and regional representatives, meets for coordination and periodic assessment of its activities.

GABRIELA's politics goes beyond national borders: it has solidarity networks in the United States, the Canada, Germany, Australia, Japan, Belgium, and the Netherlands. In the United States the network is called GABRIELA Network–USA, with chapters in several states, and has its headquarters in New York. I am a member of the Chicago chapter, of which I was one of the original founders. GABRIELA brings together its international constituents through WISAP (Women's International Solidarity Affair in the Philippines) that is held every 2 years when they analyze global issues and share experiences. For example, WISAP 1998 carried the theme "Building women's unity and solidarity against globalization" and discussed how to "advance the women's movement in the era of globalization."

Through this organizational structure that is locally rooted and globally connected, GABRIELA is able to link local and global issues in a sustained manner. By giving emphasis on organizing grassroots women while creating alliances of women of different occupations, GABRIELA binds women for a common national goal that is transforming the national liberation movement as well as Philippine society.

Critical Themes in GABRIELA's Discourses on Globalization   GABRIELA sees a connection between imperialism and globalization. In its 1998 WISAP, it declared a recommitment to "struggle against imperialist globalization." In its view globalization is not some kind of force propelled by an invisible hand; it is "imperialist countries" that are pushing for neoliberal policies of liberalization, privatization, and deregulation. The term "globalization" sounds neutral for what they consider "brutal" policies.

GABRIELA does not consider the process of globalization neutral. Globalization hurts the poor, the peasants who are displaced by transnational corporations whose interest is served by land conversions, the workers whose wages are made so cheap, and the temporary workers who are made permanent casuals due to labor contractualization.

GABRIELA sees a connection between neoliberal globalization, poverty, and the sex trafficking of women and children. Neoliberal globalization exacerbates poverty in the Philippines, and poor women and children become vulnerable prey for sex trafficking. Labor export, GABRIELA argues, also provides a façade for sex trafficking. The case of women recruited as entertainers in Japan and lured into sexual acts once they are there is an example. Hence, GABRIELA disagrees with some Western feminists (in countries where prostitution is legal) who call prostitution "work." Naming prostitution as "work," GABRIELA argues, condones the commodification of women's bodies — not so much in the moralistic sense, but in the Marxist–Feminist sense. GABRIELA's argument focuses on the profiteering of syndicates, businessmen, pimps, and club owners through the sexual exploitation of women who are vulnerable because of poverty. Instead of calling it "work" GABRIELA calls sex trafficking and prostitution "modern slavery," in line with the thinking of Kevin Bales I mentioned earlier. Hence, GABRIELA resists legalization of prostitution, for how can you legalize slavery? Resistance to legalization of this modern slavery has historical roots in Philippine indigenous culture. GABRIELA propagates the historical knowledge that prostitution was nonexistent in precolonial Philippines — no historical evidence could be found that women sold their bodies. Hence, there was no concept or term for *prostitution* because it was nonexistent. GABRIELA views prostitution as a consequence of colonial domination. Thus, GABRIELA's resistance against prostitution and sex trafficking of women is more indigeneous to its political culture, than the imported Western-originated naming of prostitution as "sex work." Here is a scenario where we see, as I alluded to earlier, that discourse has power, and both the powerful and the powerless use discourse to define reality. A feminist research on globalization that brings the marginalized voice of Third World women to the center of analysis will be sensitive to their experience in naming reality that may have serious implications for the lives of Third World women and children most disadvantaged by globalization.

Through its two decades of political transnational campaign against sex trafficking of women and children, GABRIELA has recently succeeded in having the Philippine government legislate the Anti-Trafficking in Persons Act of 2003.[9] This new law penalizes anyone engaged in the trafficking of persons through mail- and e-mail-order bride syndicates, for military prostitution, operation of sex tours and Internet syndicates that profit from sex trafficking of women and children, and the use of services of trafficked persons for prostitution (those who use prostitutes and those engaged in the organization of prostitution). This new law has officially defined it illegal and a crime to recruit or transport persons for prostitution, slavery, pornography, forced labor, or debt bondage. A stiff penalty (life imprisonment and one million pesos, approximately US$20,000 at an exchange rate of 50 pesos to a dollar) is provided for those who traffic women and children to engage in prostitution with any member of the military, police and law enforcement agencies and for those military, police, and law enforcement personnel who patronize prostitution. This is a departure from the usual crackdown practice where it is mainly the victims of organized prostitution and sex trafficking who are arrested and penalized. GABRIELA has always raised the issue of the sexual exploitation of women around the U.S. military bases both in the Philippines and in other countries, such as in South Korea. Criminalizing the trafficking of women for military prostitution is a radical policy response to what has always been condoned by the imperial army.

GABRIELA's transnational political action that gave birth to the Anti-Trafficking in Persons Act of 2003 is partly made possible by GABRIELA's previous success in gaining a seat in the law-making body of the Philippine government. A coauthor of this new law was GABRIELA's secretary general, Rep. Liza Maza, who had been elected as Bayan Muna Party representative to the House of Representatives where bills are first deliberated before they go to the Senate. The importance that GABRIELA gives to transforming the nation-state in the struggle for women's liberation in the context of globalization negates the argument in the mainstream debate on the diminished role of the state in the process of globalization (Held, McGrew, Goldblatt, and Perrato, 1999: 1–9). For GABRIELA, the nation-state is a site of managing conflict for change and for elevating discourse into law or policy that can counter globalization's negative course. By taking the nation-state as a target of resistance while addressing imperialism, GABRIELA is voicing a conceptualization of a Third World state that must be autonomous in shaping policies that can counter the exploitative tendencies of globalization within its borders and beyond. This has implications for the global social justice movement; antiglobalization movement in the core must challenge imperial states to respect Third World nations' right to self-determination. This will strengthen the ties that bind the periphery in the core and the marginalized in the Third World.

Women on the Move: Resistance across National Borders

Neoliberal globalization must also be conceived in terms of *flow of people*, not only *flow of finance* or *flow of commodities*. Particularly instructive is the example provided by the Philippine labor export policy as a major response to the debt crisis brought about by the IMF's structural adjustment policies.[10] Labor export has resulted in an unprecedented economic diaspora of approximately seven million Filipinos in more than 150 countries. Feminization of Philippine export labor is a rising trend; the majority are women, who are mostly relegated to domestic service work in richer countries.

The feminization of export labor has created transnational spaces for Third World migrant women's resistance. Their resistance provides another lived experience in which theories on globalization process can be reexamined. The collective resistance of Filipino domestic workers in Hong Kong (which has the largest number of Filipino migrant domestic workers in Asia), crystallized in UNIFIL, provides another vignette for such reexamination. I did fieldwork in Hong Kong in the summer of 2000, when I applied some principles of feminist research, conducting in-depth interviews with 35 domestic workers and participated in UNIFIL's political activities. After leaving the field I continued to be in touch with UNIFIL through e-mails and newsletters they send and by responding to their action alerts I receive via e-mails. This connection continues even at the time of this writing.

The United Filipinos in Hong Kong (UNIFIL-HK)

Initiated by Filipino domestic workers and formally launched in May 1985, UNIFIL-HK is the leading organization with a critical perspective on globalization in Hong Kong. A coalition of more than 25 Filipino migrant organizations in Hong Kong, and with an alliance network of more than 80 Filipino migrant groups and individuals there, it has a membership comprised mostly of Filipino domestic workers as they are the majority (approximately 90 percent) of Filipino migrants in Hong Kong.

My analysis of UNIFIL's discourse and politics of resistance reveal themes related to globalization of labor. I will focus on a few themes relevant to the focus of this paper: (1) the politics of naming and the legitimation of dehumanization or exploitation, (2) the commodification of migrant labor, nation-states, and nonstate actors, and (3) the inseparability of migrants' political and economic rights, and human rights based on personhood.

Official discourse on labor export uses what I call a *politics of naming* that neutralizes the dark side of such development policy. For example, Philippine government officials call overseas contract workers *modern-day heroes*. UNIFIL rejects such euphemism for *modern-day slaves* — a term it considers to capture more appropriately the exploitation, human rights violations, and indignities Filipino migrant workers experience. A labor official would refrain from using the term *labor export*, instead refers to it as *international exchange of human resource*, which camouflages the imbalance of power between poor labor-sending countries and richer labor-receiving nations, and the subordinated position of Filipino migrant workers in the global political economy. Although the Hong Kong government calls foreign domestic service work *unskilled labor* to justify low wages, UNIFIL refuses such definition and calls it *skilled labor* because the women who do it are not uneducated.

Labor export, in UNIFIL's consciousness, is viewed as a commodification of migrant labor as it becomes a profiteering trade for the sending and receiving states, and private employment agencies. Thus, one of UNIFIL's stated goals is to "fight the commodification of migrant labor." UNIFIL identifies state and nonstate actors in the process of commodification of migrant labor: the sending and host governments and the employment agencies that profit from labor export. From the experience of Filipino migrant domestic workers the state assumes a contradictory role. Although the Philippine government plays a central role in the labor export process and takes interest in profiting from it, it has little interest in protecting the migrant workers' welfare and human rights that are vulnerably threatened by host governments' desire for cheap labor and the profiteering scheme of employment–recruitment agencies. In its quest for expanding the export labor market, the Philippine government tends to be subservient to the wishes of the labor-receiving states. Thus, embedded in UNIFIL's framing of issues is a demand for an alternative, autonomous concept of a nation-state that can cross borders to protect the human rights of its migrant citizens who are vulnerable to abuse and exploitation. Thus, the call is not for a diminished role of the state, which privatization wants in the process of neoliberal globalization.

During the 1998 Asian economic crisis (and whenever it faces financial crises), the Hong Kong government had attempted to lower the minimum wage of foreign domestic workers by 30 percent, justifying its action by the controlling notion that foreign domestic workers are "family members" of their employers and must share the burden of the national crisis. The Hong Kong government took the side of the Employers' Association who lobbied for such a wage cut. This state action also demonstrates a devaluing of the women's social reproductive work although it plays a significant role in the global city's social economy. In response, UNIFIL organized the Asian Migrant Coordinating Body, an interethnic alliance of Filipino, Indonesian, Sri Lankan, Nepalese, and Thai domestic workers, to conduct a rigorous, militant protest against the proposed wage cut. Their unified voice counteracted the divide-and-rule tactics of the host government, and they succeeded in averting a 30 percent decrease, although the government still managed to impose a 5 percent wage cut as a compromise to the Employers Association's lobbying. Embedded in UNIFIL's discourse and politics is the notion that the exercise of migrants' political rights (such as the right to organize) is crucially linked to claiming and protecting their economic rights. Globalization's labor control regimes attempt to separate these two rights in order to weaken workers' collective power. UNIFIL offers an alternative view of a transnational state that is not simply concerned about making import or migrant labor cheap, but one that will respect migrants' political and economic human rights based on personhood, not just human rights based on citizenship, which tend to be exclusionary.

At the time of this writing (April 2003), AMCB continues to confront the Hong Kong government for its repeated attempt to reduce the foreign domestic workers' minimum wage. In 2001 the Hong Kong government made a second attempt for a wage cut. AMCB's militant transnational protests brought a temporary halt into this attempt. Later, however, the government imposed a 10 percent minimum wage reduction, despite the fact that the Filipino migrant domestic workers have a real wage monthly deficit of more than HK$700.[11] Their discourse in this continuing resistance brings in a new dimension: racial discrimination. They argue that it is a form of racial discrimination, as well as human rights violation, to single out foreign domestic workers for wage cut. In my view, singling out foreign domestic workers for wage reduction during national financial crisis articulates an intersection of racial–ethnic–nationality–gender–class discrimination. The racial–ethnic–nationality dimension is manifested by the fact that it is the foreign domestic workers, not any other, who have been identified to suffer official wage reduction. They are therefore made to suffer the burden of an economic crisis they have not caused. There is the gender dimension because domestic service work is still largely defined as women's work and their wage reduction indicates a devaluing of their work. The class dimension is illustrated by the fact that foreign domestic workers occupy the lowest rank in the occupational hierarchy both in terms of prestige and pay. In Hong Kong, their upward occupational mobility is practically absent as they are not officially allowed to do any other work if they come in as domestic workers, although many of them have college degrees and some even have graduate degrees. Singling them out for wage reduction is also a form of class discrimination that intersects with race, ethnicity, nationality, and gender.

But this intersection is nuanced when contextualized within the dynamics of globalization that is creating the scenario where Filipino women are largely exported as foreign domestic workers (a work that does not only bring them occupational downward mobility but makes them vulnerable to exploitation and sexual and physical abuse) as their country grapples with the debt debacle of the IMF's structural adjustment policies, one of the major instruments of neoliberal globalization. This raises a gendered question that painfully begs being brought from the margin to the center of a critical globalization studies: Who pays the heavier price of neoliberal globalization? Will the woman worker become more visible if the gender–class or gender–race–ethnicity–nationality–class interlock is made integral to the mainstream paradigms that scrutinize the macro–micro structures of globalization? What implications would her analytic visibility bring to the transnational activism project in the context of globalization?

Conclusion

Indeed, the complex dynamics of globalization that has greater detrimental impact on Third World women brings into question the Eurocentric mainstream discourse on globalization that neglects their voices and experience. This poses a challenge to transnational feminism in the context of globalization to consider two important projects: (1) to shape a transnational feminist scholarship that gives voice to Third World women's experience of neoliberal globalization, and (2) to shape a counter-hegemonic transnational activism that gives centrality to the experience of marginalized Third World women. These two projects can inform each other in the process of constructing resistance to globalization as well as in the knowledge production that has a power to legitimize or delegitimize the oppressive nature of neoliberal globalization.

Shaping a transnational feminist scholarship that gives voice to Third World women requires unraveling the ties that divide and bind women, men and women, and families. This would mean addressing substantive issues, such as (1) redefining a concept of nationalism that does not hinder Third World nations' fundamental right to self-determination, (2) questioning the integration of women into the imperial army and strengthening the peace movement, (3) dissecting the differential impact of globalization on women and men, the hierarchy it produces based on their nations' position in the global political economy, and the intersection of gender and class, or gender, race, ethnicity, nationality, and class, and (4) contesting the role of nation-states both in promoting neoliberal ideologies and policies and their prospect of assuming a transformative role in resisting neoliberal globalization.

Shaping a transnational feminist scholarship in the context of globalization has also a methodological dimension. Feminist research offers useful principles that can help bring Third World women's experience of globalization from the margin to the center of analysis: standpoint, reflexivity, positionality, and immersion. Standpoint begins inquiry of globalization from the experience of poor Third World women whose lives embody the gender–race–class interlock. Reflexivity and positionality invite reflection of our own complicity in the unjust course of neoliberal globalization. Immersion engages the researcher into a more personal relationship with the people under study and their struggles.

Feminist research has the potential of bridging academic research with the activism project of transnational feminism in the context of globalization. Third World women's resistance to globalization, their politics, and discourse offer a fertile ground for theory-making from below that can reinform grand theories on globalization. The vignettes of Filipino women's resistance to globalization provide an illustrative example for such theoretical grounding. From their discourse and politics of the militant grassroots-oriented Philippine women's movement led by GABRIELA, we learn that Third World women's experience of colonialism, imperialism, and neoliberal globalization brings into question the universal application of definitions of reality by some Western feminists. They also offer an alternative concept of a nation-state that can exercise autonomy in resisting the negative course of globalization within and across national borders, while transforming gender and class inequalities that ensue from neoliberal globalization.

The women on the move and their resistance to the commodification of migrant labor due to neoliberal globalization, exemplified by the United Filipinos in Hong Kong (UNIFIL-HK) comprising mostly of migrant domestic workers, remind us to think about globalization not only as a disembodied flow of finance or commodities, but also as a flow of people. Beginning the inquiry of globalization from the experience of the marginalized Third World migrant women, pushed out into the periphery in richer nations by the IMF's structural adjustment policies, may illuminate the complex dynamics of gender–class or gender–race–ethnicity–nationality–class interlock that anchors neoliberal globalization. Their discourse and politics imbed theories that challenge the diminished role of the state that serves privatization; an alternative concept of a transnational state that takes interest not in exploiting export–import labor and migrant labor, but in protecting and promoting migrant workers' political, economic, and human rights.

Thus, bringing the theory-making-from-below of those who suffer and resist the dehumanizing injuries of neoliberal globalization, especially Third World women, from the margin to the center of mainstream discourse may change the way we think about globalization, and the way we may resist it on a global scale.

Notes

1. By imperial army, I refer to the armed forces used by imperialist powers to invade, occupy, or colonize another country.
2. Talk at Loyola University, Chicago in 1988 on Women and the Military, sponsored by the Women's Studies Program.
3. This is, for example, the case of the Philippines, Indonesia, Bangladesh, Sri Lanka, and Thailand.
4. The concept of trafficking involves the transport of people for profit with deception, exploitation, and human rights violations.

5. See Kevin Bales's *Disposable People: New Slavery in the Global Political Economy* (1999) for a more detailed discussion of the concept of modern slavery.

6. I quote from Saskia Sassen's talk, "Micro-Structures of Globalization," at the Midwest Sociological Conference, Chicago, April 16–19, 2003.

7. For a more thorough discussion on feminist research see Shulamit Reinharz (1992), *Feminist Methods in Social Research.* New York: Oxford University Press.

8. See for example Ligaya Lindio-McGovern (1997), *Filipino Peasant Women: Exploitation and Resistance.* Philadelphia: University of Pennsylvania Press.

9. Information about this new law is based on the press releases (dated May 5 and 7, 2003) by House Representative Liza Largoza Maza, also the secretary general of GABRIELA — sent to me through e-mail by Migrante International, the international alliance of overseas Filipino workers with main office in Quezon City, Philippines.

10. Other Asian countries devastated by structural adjustment policies have also embarked on labor export, such as Indonesia and Bangladesh.

11. Based on a survey on the Filipino domestic workers' income done by the Mission for Filipino Migrant Workers, a nongovernmental organization in Hong Kong that provide services and advocacy for Filipino migrants and other ethnic groups who may seek its help.

33

Globalization and Transnational Feminist Networks (or How Neoliberalism and Fundamentalism Riled the World's Women)

Valentine M. Moghadam

The capitalist world-system periodically has produced antisystemic movements that cross borders and boundaries, and national-level class conflicts and political contradictions similarly have generated forms of collective action and social protest, including social movements. But a key characteristic of the era of late capitalism, or globalization, is the proliferation of global social movements, including the global women's movement and its organizational expression, the transnational feminist network.

Transnational feminist networks are structures organized above the national level that unite women from three or more countries around a common agenda, such as women's human rights, reproductive health and rights, violence against women, peace and antimilitarism, and feminist economics. They are part of the family of supranational political change organizations that the literature variously describes as global civil society organizations, transnational advocacy networks, and transnational social movement organizations (Smith, Chatfield, and Pagnucco, 1997; Keck and Sikkink, 1998; O'Brien et al., 2000; Khagram, Riker, and Sikkink, 2002; Smith and Johnson, 2002) — and which, along with international nongovernmental organizations, constitute the making of a transnational public sphere (Guidry, Kennedy, and Zald, 2000). Transnational feminist networks work together and with transnational human rights, labor, social justice, and environmental organizations to draw attention to the negative aspects of globalization, to try to influence policymaking, and to insert a feminist perspective in transnational advocacy and activism.

The scholarship on transnational social movements and advocacy networks has expanded our understanding of movement dynamics above and across borders, but much of it fails to conceptually connect such manifestations of "globalization-from-below" to the economic and political aspects of "globalization-from-above." Recent feminist studies have tackled some critical issues facing women's organizations, international feminism, and feminist theorizing (Basu, 1995, 2000; Bulbeck, 1998; Alvarez, 2000; Ling, 2002; Mohanty, 2003). However, much of the feminist literature lacks an explanatory framework for the emergence of transnational feminism in late capitalism–late modernity and does not correlate the emergence of transnational feminism to globalization processes. I will argue in this chapter that apart from the opportunities afforded by the new information and computer technologies, the emergence and spread of transnational feminist networks can best be understood in terms of the neoliberal economic policy shift and its impact on female labor, the decline of the welfarist and developmentalist state, and the fundamentalist threat to women's rights — all of which are key elements of globalization.

Neoliberalism, Fundamentalism, and Transnational Feminism

Scholars have noted that women's groups operated transnationally in the first three decades of the twentieth century, and these included the Women's International League for Peace and Freedom (WILPF), the International Alliance of Women, and the Young Women's Christian Association (Stienstra, 1994; Rupp, 1998; Berkovitch, 1999; Meyer, 1999; Rupp and Taylor, 1999). The Second World War and the rise of Keynesian economics and the welfare state, however, may have shifted women's focus from the international arena to their own national societies. Thus, the women's movement of the second wave, which began in North America and Europe in the 1960s and expanded internationally in the 1970s, consisted of feminist groups that emerged within national borders and addressed themselves to their own nation-states, governments, employers, and male colleagues.

Feminist groups identified with liberal, radical, Marxist, or socialist ideologies, and these political differences constituted one division within feminism. Another took the form of North–South, or First World–Third World differences; many First World feminists saw legal equality and reproductive rights as key feminist demands and goals, whereas many Third World feminists emphasized underdevelopment, colonialism, and imperialism as obstacles to women's advancement. Disagreements over what constituted priority feminist issues came to the fore at the start of the United Nations' Decade for Women, and especially at its first and second world conferences on women in Mexico City in 1975 and Copenhagen in 1980 (Fraser, 1987).

A shift in the nature and orientation of international feminism occurred in the mid-1980s, during preparations for the third UN world conference on women, which was held in Nairobi, Kenya, in 1985. Bridge building and consensus-making across regional and ideological divides took place, and a women's organization of a new type emerged. Three world-systemic developments triggered this change in the women's movement: (1) the transition from Keynesian to neoliberal economics, along with a new international division of labor that relied heavily on (cheap) female labor, (2) the decline of the welfarist and developmentalist state, and (3) the emergence of various forms of fundamentalist movements. These developments led to new thinking and new forms of organizing on the part of activist women in developing and developed countries, including the Latin American *encuentros*, or feminist gatherings, and the emergence of transnational feminist networks devoted to women's economic well-being and their human rights.

The Advent of Neoliberalism: Economic Policy and the State

In the 1980s, global restructuring took the form of Reaganism in the United States, Thatcherism in the U.K., and structural adjustment policies and austerity measures in developing countries. In the 1990s, it took the form of the transition from communism to capitalism in the former Soviet Union and Eastern Europe. One consequence of the post-Keynesian and postcommunist transition to neoliberal capitalism was the feminization of poverty (Chant, 1995; Tanski, 1994; Moghadam, 1997). Meanwhile, cross-national research, including studies by those working in the field of women-in-development or women-and-development (WID/WAD), showed that an ever-growing proportion of the world's women were being incorporated as cheap labor into what was variously called the capitalist world-economy, the new international division of labor, or the global assembly line (e.g., Elson and Pearson, 1981).

Research showed that in the 1970s, women began to gain an increasing share of many kinds of jobs, but the post-Keynesian shift was also characterized by growing unemployment, a decline in the social power of labor, an increase in temporary, part-time, casual, and home-based work, and cutbacks in social services and subsidies. In the 1980s, women began to be disproportionately involved in irregular forms of employment increasingly used to maximize profits; at the same time, they remained responsible for reproductive work. Female labor incorporation did not entail a redistribution of domestic, household, and childcare responsibilities, partly because the welfare services of the state were being cut back. In addition, women remained disadvantaged in terms of wages, training, and occupational segregation in the new labor markets. ILO economist Guy Standing termed this phenomenon the "feminization of labor." He argued that the increasing globalization of production and the pursuit of flexible forms of labor to retain or increase competitiveness, as well as changing job structures in industrial enterprises, favored the feminization of employment in the dual sense of an increase in the numbers of women in the labor force and a deterioration of work conditions, labor standards, income, and employment status (Standing, 1989, 1999). As the function of the state shifted from managing social and economic development to providing a conducive environment for businesses and foreign investors, the economic well-being of women in developing countries became ever more precarious.

Jihad vs. McWorld: The Feminist Encounter with Fundamentalism

The third important development at the level of states, regions, and the world-system that led to the narrowing of the political and ideological divide between First World and Third World feminists and the emergence of transnational feminist activism was the rise of Islamic fundamentalism in Muslim countries and Hindu communalism in India. These movements sought to recuperate traditional norms and codes, including patriarchal laws and family roles for women; they put pressure on states to enforce public morality, increase religious observance, and tighten controls over women — ostensibly to protect the nation or culture from alien influences and conspiracies (see contributions in Moghadam, 1994). In some ways they were responses to the creeping homogenization of economic policies, political practices, cultural symbols, and ideology that are associated with globalization. But they were far from progressive responses. Benjamin Barber has introduced the term *jihad* as shorthand for religious fundamentalism, disintegrative tribalism, ethnic nationalisms, and similar kinds of identity politics carried out by local peoples "to sustain solidarity and tradition against the nation-state's legalistic and pluralistic abstractions as well as against the new commercial imperialism of McWorld" (Barber, 2001: 232). Jihad is in struggle against modernity and cultural imperialism alike, and "answers the complaints of those mired in poverty and despair as a result of unregulated global markets and of capitalism uprooted from the humanizing constraints of the democratic nation-state" (Barber, 2001: i). This is an apt way of contextualizing Islamic fundamentalism.

In the Middle East and North Africa, Islamic fundamentalist movements emerged in the 1970s, expanded during the 1980s, and peaked in the early 1990s. They reflected the contradictions of modernization, the difficult transition to modernity underway in the region, and the conflict between traditional and modern norms, relations, and institutions. Islamic fundamentalist movements emerged as the global economic policy environment shifted from Keynesian to neoliberal, as talks on a new international economic order (NIEO) collapsed, and as world communism went into decline. Islamist movements also emerged as important cultural changes were taking place globally and within countries, including the internationalization of Western popular culture and changes in gender relations, the structure of the family, and the position of women. The Iranian Revolution of 1978–1979, which produced the Islamic Republic of Iran, had a demonstration effect throughout the Muslim world. It appeared to many dissidents that a project for the Islamization of state and society could prevail, and that this would be the solution to economic, political, and cultural crises. It would be a mistake, however, to view Islamist movements as pristine and spontaneous social movements. During the 1970s and 1980s, many were encouraged and financed by external forces — such as Saudi Arabia, Israel, the United States, and various Middle Eastern governments — to undermine and supplant left-wing or communist movements (Hélie-Lucas, 1994: 398; Cooley, 1999). Islamist movements arose in the midst of economic and political crises and have referred to unemployment and deteriorating standards of living as social problems, but they have revealed themselves to be less concerned with economic, military, or foreign policy matters than they are with politics, culture, family, and morality. This preoccupation with identity, morality, and the family placed a heavy burden on women, who were seen as the bearers of tradition, religiosity, and morality, and as the reproducers of the faithful. Such views had profound effects on women's legal status and social positions, especially when fundamentalist views were successfully inscribed in constitutions, family laws, penal codes, and other public policies, as they were in Iran, Egypt, Pakistan, Bangladesh, and elsewhere in the 1980s (Moghadam, 2003: chapter 5).

The emergence of fundamentalist movements in the 1980s alarmed feminists in the peripheral and semiperipheral countries where the movements originated, and they developed innovative strategies to address the problem. One important strategy was to form in 1984 a transnational network of antifundamentalist feminists called

Women Living under Muslim Laws. Similarly, Iranian women living in exile in Europe and the United States established feminist groups opposed to fundamentalism and the Islamization project in Iran. In Britain, Women against Fundamentalism and Southall Black Sisters took public positions against growing fundamentalism among immigrant communities and what they saw as misguided multicultural policies that conceded too much to (often patriarchal) male leaders of immigrant communities. In Algeria, new feminist organizations formed in the late 1980s in response to the growing power of the Islamist movement. In the refugee camps of Pakistan in the 1990s, the Revolutionary Association of Women of Afghanistan (RAWA) railed against the Taliban and the *jehadis* (the former U.S.-backed *mujahideen,* now called the Northern Alliance). The Sisterhood is Global Institute (SIGI), under the direction of an expatriate Iranian feminist, advanced the cause of Muslim women's human rights, and helped to establish a regional branch in Amman, Jordan. And another strategy was that of Islamic feminism, an intellectual movement of believing Muslim women whose reinterpretation of the Koran serves to challenge fundamentalism and orthodoxy (Tohidi, 1997; Badran, 1999; Moghadam, 2002).

The new economic and political realities, therefore, led to a convergence of feminist perspectives across the globe. For many First World feminists, economic issues and development policy became increasingly important, and for many Third World feminists, increased attention was now directed to women's legal status, autonomy, and human rights. Since then, transnational feminist networks have proliferated and although each tends to have a specific focus, they all have adopted the broad global feminist agenda that is critical of neoliberal capitalism and religious fundamentalism and calls for expanded civil, political, and socioeconomic rights for women. That common agenda is inscribed in the 1995 Beijing Declaration and Platform for Action, which was adopted at the close of the UN's Fourth World Conference on Women. But along the way to Beijing, there were other venues where the world's women agreed on issues pertaining to the women's economic well-being and their human rights. These included the UN world conferences of the 1990s: the United Nations Conference on the Environment and Development (UNCED) in Rio de Janeiro in 1992, the Human Rights Conference in Vienna in 1993, the International Conference on Population and Development (ICPD) in Cairo in 1994, and the World Summit for Social Development (the Social Summit) in Copenhagen in 1995. At these conferences, women declared that environmental issues were women's issues, that women's rights were human rights, that governments were expected to guarantee women's reproductive health and rights, and that women's access to productive employment and social protection needed to be expanded.

TFN activities as well as partnerships with other advocacy networks resulted in some successes at the UN conferences of the 1990s. For example, TFN lobbying led to the insertion of important items in the final Vienna Declaration of the 1993 Conference on Human Rights, such as the assertion that violence against women was an abuse of human rights, and attention to the harmful effects of certain traditional or customary practices, cultural prejudice, and religious extremisms. The Declaration also stated that human rights abuses of women in situations of armed conflict — including systematic rape, sexual slavery, and forced pregnancy — were violations of the fundamental principles of international human rights and humanitarian law. This culminated in passage of an international law in 1998 that designated rape a war crime when carried out during civil conflict or war.

Moreover, TFNs succeeded in extracting promises from the World Bank's new director, James Wolfensohn, for institutional changes that would ensure the integration of gender issues in World Bank policies, projects, and lending practices. Indeed, the Beijing Platform for Action contains language calling for gender-sensitive socioeconomic development, an end to structural adjustment policies, the importance of the North's taking a lead with respect to sustainable consumption, and the goals of women's personal autonomy and their political and economic empowerment. Global feminists frequently refer to both the Cairo Plan of Action and the Beijing Platform for Action, as well as the UN's Convention on the Elimination of All Forms of Discrimination against Women, in their national and international campaigns for women's rights. Inasmuch as most of the world's governments have signed on to these documents, they provide a useful legal and discursive tool, and global feminists frequently invoke their moral authority. Certainly these documents have helped to create an international climate more conducive to feminist aspirations and goals.

At the start of the new millennium, the global feminist agenda was expressed in critiques of multinational corporations, the World Bank, the IMF, the WTO, and the policy stances of the U.S. government. Women's groups joined broad coalitions (e.g., the anti-MAI campaign and Jubilee 2000 for Third World debt cancellation) involving labor, religious groups, environmental groups, and human rights groups to challenge corporate capitalism and global inequalities. Like other groups within the global justice movement, TFNs criticized the World Bank and IMF for their corporate bias and for policies that undermine the well-being of workers and the poor; the WTO has been targeted for conducting its deliberations in secret and not subjecting them to rules of transparency and accountability. TFNs and others have argued that the new rules of global free trade undermine existing national laws that protect workers, the environment, and animals; and that WTO intellectual property provisions have allowed large corporations to appropriate (through patents) the knowledge and products of Third World countries and their local communities. Additionally, transnational feminists argued that the employment losses and dislocations brought about by the new international trade agreements have been disproportionately borne by women, that trade liberalization often puts women entrepreneurs and business owners at a disadvantage, and that neoliberal policies and the neoclassical economic theories that inform them are gender-blind. What TFNs contribute to the global justice movement is the call for gender justice as well as economic justice, and for an alternative macroeconomic framework that takes gender relations seriously as a concept and a social fact.

Engaging with States, the Intergovernmental Arena, and the Transnational Public Sphere

What is it that TFNs do? And what are their specific objectives? We can identify three sets of activities and goals. First, TFNs create, activate, or join global networks to mobilize pressure outside states. Examples are WLUML's action alerts and SIGI's e-petition drives pertaining to violations of women's human rights in Muslim countries. TFNs build or take part in coalitions, such as Jubilee 2000, the Coalition to End the Third World Debt, Women's International Coalition for Economic Justice, the Women and Trade Network, 50 Years is Enough, and Women's Eyes on the Bank. Since "the Battle of Seattle" in November 1999, WIDE has become an active player in the global justice movement, taking part in the World Social Forum and working closely with ATTAC, the France-based group that seeks economic justice and redistributive taxation at national and global levels.

Second, TFNs participate in multilateral and intergovernmental political arenas. They observe and address UN departments such as ECOSOC and bodies such as the Commission on the Status of Women (CSW); they consult UN agencies, regional commissions, and the Development Assistance Committee of the OECD; and they participate in the World Bank's External Gender Consultative Group, which was formed after the Beijing Conference. They take part in and submit documents to IGO meetings, such as the UN's Human Rights Conference in Vienna in 1993 and the Financing for Development Conference that took place in Monterrey, Mexico, in 2002; they increase expertise on issues and prepare background papers, briefing papers and reports; and they lobby delegates and cultivate supporters. The purpose of such interaction with IGOs is to raise new issues, such as gender and trade, gender and macroeconomics, and women's human rights, and to influence policy.

Third, TFNs act and agitate within states to enhance public awareness and participation. TFNs work with labor and progressive religious groups, the media, and human rights groups on social policy, humanitarian, development, and militarization issues. For example, WIDE-Austria has been very active in efforts to liberalize immigration policy. In Pakistan, Shirkat Gah, WLUML's branch office in Lahore, has organized protests against patriarchal laws in Pakistan and for Afghan women's rights, while Baobob, the Nigerian-based group that is also associated with WLUML, has protested the Islamization of laws in Nigeria. The AWMR has long worked with WILPF on peace and demilitarization of the Mediterranean, tirelessly passing resolutions and sending petitions to parliaments. Such examples show that TFNs link with local partners, take part in local coalitions, and provoke or take part in public protests. The TFNs that focus on economic policy issues promote social democratic policies, such as the Tobin Tax on financial speculation, the 20/20 compact to devote 20 percent of development assistance and 20 percent of national budgets to the social sectors, ILO labor standards, gender budgets, and valorization of women's unpaid work. In terms of economic analysis and economic policy prescriptions, they are sympathetic to the UNDP's concept of human development.[1] Those that focus on women's human rights monitor governments, offer solidarity, and raise international awareness. For example, WLUML submitted a shadow report on Algeria to the UN's Committee to Eliminate Discrimination against Women (CEDAW) that was critical of both the government and the Islamist groups that terrorized women during the 1990s; others produced reports on countries' implementation of the Beijing Platform for Action.

Whether working at the state, regional, or global levels, TFNs have framed issues and introduced new concepts: "engendering development," "feminization of poverty," "care economy," "women living under Muslim laws," "Women's rights are human rights," and "gender justice and economic justice." Many of these concepts have been adopted by major international organizations, including UN agencies, the World Bank, and the donor agencies of the core countries. A new concept, "reinventing globalization," was the focus of two TFN conferences in 2002: the Association for Women's Rights in Development (AWID) and the Association of Women of the Mediterranean Region (AWMR).

The new information and computer technologies (ICTs) have allowed transnational feminist networks (and other advocacy networks) to retain flexibility, adaptability, and nonhierarchical features while also ensuring more efficiency in their operations. That is, TFNs are now able to perform effectively without having to become formal or bureaucratic organizations. Avoiding bureaucratization is particularly important to feminists. The network form of feminist organizing, which is exemplified by the TFNs that I have been discussing in this paper, suggests a form of organization that may be more conductive to the era of globalization, as well as more consistent with feminist goals of democratic, inclusive, participatory, decentralized, and nonhierarchical structures and processes.

TFNs thus reflect one aspect of the globalization process (opportunities for mobilizing and recruitment through ICTs and ease of travel), while also responding to its dark side (neoliberal capitalism, patriarchal fundamentalism). The claims and demands of "globalizing women" are addressed to states, to institutions of global governance, and to global civil society. They ensure that women's issues remain on the international agenda, and that local activists receive solidarity and support. TFNs reflect the interplay of the local and the global and bridge the divide in an innovative organizational form that eschews nationalist preoccupations and is premised on commonality and solidarity. In our globalizing world, we have not yet seen the formation of a transnational working class or transnational worker organizations. But we do see a global social movement of women and transnational feminist networks that criticize neoliberal capitalism and call for the return of the welfarist, developmentalist state and for the establishment of global Keynesianism. This transnational feminist movement feeds into the larger global justice movement, and offers concrete proposals for an alternative to capitalist globalization that is grounded in human rights.

This is not to say that there are no tensions between the women's movement and other social movements, or tensions within the global women's movement. For example, DAWN has expressed concern that women's reproductive rights could be sidelined in a broad progressive movement that includes religious groups that are against abortion. DAWN also has raised concerns about divisions between feminist groups in the South and the North concerning trade and labor standards. But, increasingly, transnational social movement organizations are recognizing that women's rights are human rights and that the demands, objectives, and methods of the women's movement and of global feminism — encapsulated in the passage below by Peggy Antrobus of DAWN — are essential to the broader project of progressive global change:

> Feminism's tendencies to reject domination and hierarchy and its replacement of the male concept of power (power to dominate and control) with a female concept of power (power

to act, or to empower others), its concern for humanistic values, and its questioning of economistic considerations — all can serve as a brake against the corruption of unchallenged male domination and greed, as expressed in the neglect of human welfare in the interest of capital; the materialism of market liberalization that negates spiritual and cultural values associated with women; and, most importantly, the violence that has emerged with the rise of fundamentalism, often wrapped in the flags of identity politics, which has accompanied the deterioration in the quality of life and the threats of globalization to national identity (Antrobus, 1996: 66–67).

Conclusions

In this chapter I have situated transnational feminist networks in such globalization processes as the neoliberal economic policy shift, the decline of the welfarist and developmentalist state, and the fundamentalist threat. All of these had gender dynamics and implications for women, and were met by organized responses on the part of educated, employed, and politically conscious women with mobility and technological know-how. This chapter also has shown that transnational women's organizations have become major nonstate political actors on the global, regional, and national scenes. They are in a dynamic relationship with states, intergovernmental organizations, and other TSMOs and TANs. They use the global, intergovernmental arena to accomplish national priorities in the areas of women's human rights (such as violence against women and the rights of women in Muslim societies) and economic policies (such as structural adjustment and the new global trade agenda), as well as to influence international norms and conventions. TFNs also refute stereotypical notions that women's organizations are local; or that they are concerned primarily with issues of identity and sexuality; or that they do not engage with economic policy issues. The TFNs that I have described offer a critique of neoliberal capitalism and advocate for the welfare state, for global Keynesianism, and for the establishment of women's human rights no matter what the cultural context.

TFNs contribute several new ideas to current discussions of and collective action around globalization. One idea pertains to understandings and definitions of globalization. Transnational feminists are not, strictly speaking, antiglobalization. They are against neo-liberal capitalism, but they view globalization as a multifaceted phenomenon whose most positive feature is its opportunities for transnational networking and solidarity. They would like to help reinvent globalization and reorient it from a *project of markets* to a *project of peoples*. Their literature is replete with condemnations of the ills of neoliberal capitalism. But their stated solutions and strategies are to remake — democratize and engender — global governance, not to destroy it.

A second idea pertains to the state, currently the subject of much debate among scholars of globalization (see, e.g., Robinson, 1991). For transnational feminists, the state still matters as an institutional actor — even though they eschew nationalist politics in favor of internationalism and transnational solidarity. The state matters to women and to transnational feminists because of the importance of reproductive rights and family law, and because feminists oppose the neoliberal and fundamentalist state and favor the welfarist, developmentalist form of the state that is also woman-friendly.

A third distinctive idea pertains to the transnational feminist call for "gender justice." To be sure, transnational feminists do not want women's rights, including reproductive rights, to be placed on the back burner or postponed until after the triumph of the antiglobalization movement, as has been the case with so many national political movements. But they also believe that global justice is rendered a meaningless, abstract concept without consideration of the gendered (and racial) make-up of working people — or of working families. Without due consideration of the sexual division of labor and the care economy, of the trafficking of women's bodies, of working women's civil rights (i.e., rights to bodily integrity, reproductive rights), and of their social rights (e.g., paid maternity leaves, paternity leaves, and quality childcare), there can be no economic justice for women. As such, the slogan "Gender justice *and* economic justice" may be understood as a variation of the slogan "Women's rights *are* human rights" — both of which are key concepts of global feminism that have been developed and disseminated by transnational feminist networks in an era of globalization.

Note

1. Since 1990 the United Nations Development Programme's Human Development Report Office has produced an annual *Human Development Report*. The concept of human development is meant to be an alternative to the conventional emphasis on economic growth as the principal measure of development; the UNDP argues that the enlargement of people's choices through health, education, income, and women's equality are more adequate measures.

34

Labor and the Global Logistics Revolution[1]
Edna Bonacich

An important aspect of globalization is offshore production. Offshore production by transnational corporations (TNCs) requires global distribution. Production and distribution both involve labor. Much focus has been given to labor in production, namely, the rise of global sweatshops. Much less focus has been given to labor in distribution.

Unlike production, distribution has an implacably local character. A TNC can move production anywhere in the world, but if it plans to import those goods back into the home market, which is typically the case, distribution work must be done in the home country. This is certainly the case for the United States, which serves as a major market for goods produced offshore by U.S.-based corporations. Distribution is therefore one place where we, on the local level, can intervene in the process of globalization–global production. The motto: "Think global, act local" can be implemented through a focus on the local distribution of globally produced commodities.

My focus in this chapter is on labor in distribution. I start with the assumption that organized labor has a critical role to play in countering the power of global capital. Considerable attention has been given to the social movements that are raising a challenge to the neoliberal policies associated with corporate-dominated globalization. Sometimes unions have been part of the protests. Here I want to consider the role that can be played by unions in fighting this form of globalization at the workplace. By putting up a challenge to capital at the point where profit is generated, workers and unions can pose a different kind of threat to capital than the disruptions of mass protests. They can cause capital direct economic damage. Any movement that is serious about changing the current system must include workers and unions as a vital strategic partner in the struggle.

The Meanings of Distribution

Distribution has two distinctive meanings (see figure 34.1). On the one hand, it refers to sales, or the final circuit of capital, in which the initial investment of capital is realized. The circulation of capital begins with financing, moves through production, and ends with distribution in the forms of sales. The process of investment and production is valueless unless the produced goods can be successfully sold for more than the cost of the entire circuit of capital.

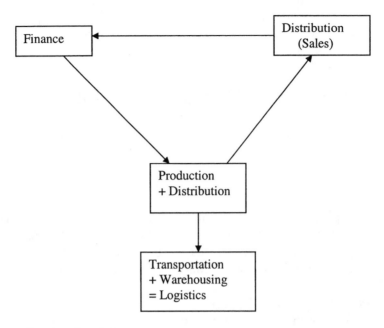

Figure 34.1. Circuits of capital.

On the other hand, distribution can refer to the actual movement and storage of goods, namely freight transportation and warehousing. It is this latter meaning that is referred to as logistics. According to Marxist theory, labor in sales is not productive of surplus value (SV). However, logistics labor is considered by Marx to be part of the production process and is therefore creative of SV. We can thus consider this form of distribution as "distribution in production" (Harvey, 1999). The logistics revolution brings these two meanings of distribution together by linking sales with goods movement.

I am focusing in this chapter on one aspect of logistics, namely, the movement of containerized imports from Asia through the ports of Los Angeles and Long Beach (ports of LA/LB) into the U.S. market. These goods are mainly manufactured consumer items.

The Logistics Revolution

The approach to the movement of goods has been changing dramatically over the last 30 years or so. There has been a paradigm shift, from "push" to "pull" production (see, for example, Abernathy et al., 1999; WERC, 1994). Under the push system, manufacturers would mass produce items, using long production runs to achieve maximum efficiencies and minimize unit costs. They would push the goods out to retailers, who then would sell them as they were able. The system led to the accumulation of excess inventory, as well as shortages of popular goods.

The pull system starts from the other end of the supply chain, by focusing on what consumers are actually purchasing. Point of sale (POS) data are collected electronically using bar coding technology. The information is transmitted back up the supply chain to manufacturers who then produce in response to what is actually selling. This system encourages short-cycle production, and allows for the development of more varied and customized goods (sometimes called mass customization, or flexible production).

The goal of pull production is to minimize the accumulation of inventory all along the supply chain, and to encourage the constant flow of orders up the supply chain, and goods down it. The system ideally operates on just-in-time (JIT) principles. By these means, the twin dangers of excess inventory, which must be marked down to be sold, and stock-outs, when buyers cannot find the goods they are eager to purchase, can be avoided.

Underlying the logistics revolution, which is sometimes referred to as supply chain management (SCM), is an effort to resolve the chronic imbalance between supply and demand that is typical of capitalism. For various reasons, capitalism tends to foster crises of overproduction. Numerous methods have been adopted to try to deal with this issue, including product proliferation, the extension of consumer credit, and branding in order to foster identities linked with particular companies. SCM can be seen as another effort to solve this unsolvable dilemma. To return to figure 34.1, it is an attempt to link distribution in production to distribution via sales.

Dell Computer is considered to be one of the companies that has pioneered the logistics revolution. In Dell's case, the production process is only initiated after an order has been placed. Dell retains no inventory. Of course, this means that suppliers must provide components quickly, and the holding of inventory may be pushed back up the supply chain, rather than eliminated.

In general, the logistics revolution has increased the power of retailers relative to manufacturers. There are some major industry exceptions to this pattern, notably, the automobile industry, which distributes cars through dealerships rather than retailers. However, most consumer goods, including clothing, shoes, furniture, toys, household goods, home improvement products, consumer electronics, etc., are distributed through retailers. We are, in other words, witnessing an increase in the power of commercial capital.

This shift is epitomized by retail industry leader, Wal-Mart Stores, now the world's largest corporation in terms of sales. Wal-Mart is also noted for its excellent logistics system. The fact that a retailer has recently risen to the top Fortune's 500, displacing General Motors, speaks to the shift in power from manufacturers to retailers (see Ortega, 1998).

Wal-Mart is now the largest importer to the United States, as measured by TEUs (20-ft equivalent units, the standardized measure of containers). In 2002, Wal-Mart imported 291,900 TEUs. The next largest importer, at 182,000 TEUs, was Home Depot, and the third was Target Corporation, at 173,100. The top three container importers are all retailers. Moreover, of the 100 largest importers, 32 are retailers, including such companies as Lowe's, Payless ShoeSource, Pier 1 Imports, Kmart, Ikea, and Toys R Us. Wal-Mart imported six times the number of TEUs as the first manufacturer on the list, General Electric (Bonney, 2003).

Retailers now tell their vendors what, when, and where to ship their product. The biggest of them set terms for their suppliers on a take-it-or-leave-it basis and, given the volumes they control, it is hard for a supplier to turn them down. Suppliers must comply with all the retailers' specifications, including the electronic linkages they provide. Meanwhile, producers must go through different hoops for each retailer.

WERC (1994) lists the most demanding service requirements that mass merchants place on their suppliers. These include:

- No backorders
- On-time delivery performance and strict appointment scheduling
- Short lead times (10 days or less in some cases)
- Store-ready packaging
- Advance shipment notification

And there are others.

Impact of Logistics Revolution on Transportation and Warehousing

The logistics revolution has required changes in transportation and warehousing. On the transportation side, the demand has been for cheap, quick, and reliable freight movement. Meanwhile, warehouses have ideally shifted from centers for the storage of inventory, to distribution centers (DCs), where goods flow in one side of the building, get put on conveyor belts for sorting, and exit into waiting trucks on the other side in an uninterrupted flow. This ideal, known as cross-docking, may be rarely found in practice, but it is the goal towards which the system is striving. The overall goal of the logistics system is to have goods in constant motion, since goods that are not moving cease to be capital.

I am focusing in this chapter on ocean transportation, setting aside air freight. Although air freight is growing in importance, and accounts for a significant proportion of the value of shipped goods, it represents only a tiny proportion of the volume of trade. Generally, air is used for the movement of low weight, high value, and time-sensitive commodities. Within ocean transportation, I am also focusing on trans-Pacific shipping, between Asia and the United States, which has the busiest trade lanes in the world today.

Various changes have occurred in this transportation system. First has been the development of intermodalism, made possible by the development of the container. Containers are essentially truck trailers with the wheels removed. They can easily be stacked on ships, double-stacked on trains, and put on chassis to be moved as trucks. The advantage of containers is that they can be filled at the factory and unpacked at the final destination without the necessity of opening them and handling the goods in between. Of course, sometimes some unpacking and reconsolidating is necessary, but in general containerization has made cargo movement much more efficient.

The twin ports of Los Angeles and Long Beach (LA/LB) serve as major container ports for the United States. Los Angeles is the largest container port in the United States; Long Beach, the second largest. Together they comprise the third largest container port in the world, behind Hong Kong and Singapore. They handle about 40 percent of the nation's container cargo, 50 percent of which moves immediately out of the region by rail. Known as "landbridge," the railroads carry Asian manufac-tured products to the rest of the United States.

The containers are carried from Asia to the United States on a regular basis by steamship lines (ocean carriers). Some of the liners used to be U.S. companies, but they have all moved offshore to Asia or Europe. Ocean shipping has been faced with deregulation, and is a highly competitive business. They all feel the pressure to provide global service to their customers, the importers and exporters who are known as shippers. This means that they must enter already saturated markets in order to survive. The steamship lines often take charge of the entire container move, charging a flat rate to shippers for door-to-door moves. They then contract with the railroads and trucking companies for their share of the intermodal move.

The landside transportation modes, namely, the railroads and trucking companies, have both faced major deregulation, starting in the late 1970s, and reaching full strength in the 1980s. As a consequence they have become more competitive. In the case of the railroads, there has been major consolidation, but competition still remains fierce as the remaining giants vie for market share.

Deregulation of transportation has been pushed by shippers (i.e., the beneficial owners of cargo, as opposed to carriers, or transportation providers). The National Industrial Transportation League (NITL), composed of some of the major industrial corporations in the country, played a key role in lobbying for deregulation. The role of the mass retailers in the historical development is less clear to me at this point, but they have certainly been active in the deregulation of international shipping more recently, and continue to push for the minimization of transportation costs.

Southern California Logistics

The Southern California logistics system consists of a complex network of trucking companies, freeways, railroads and rail lines, warehouses, and DCs, linking the ports to both the regional and national economies. In general, if a box (container) gets put on a train, it is headed for a destination east of the Rockies. Containers get loaded on to railroads on dock, but they can also be trucked to rail centers near the ports or in downtown Los Angeles. Moreover, they can be trucked to a warehouse where they are unloaded and repacked into domestic containers or trailers by city of desti-nation, and then put on rail.

The Alameda Corridor was recently opened as a rail line that leads from the ports to downtown Los Angeles and points east. Its purpose was, in part, to alleviate congestion on the roads, and to speed up rail moves out of the region. However, recent news stories are pointing to the fact that it is operating well below capacity because it remains cheaper to move cargo by truck to the downtown railheads.

Meanwhile, the trucking system is causing major problems of congestion and pollution, as the already crowded freeways of Los Angeles face the potential impact of a huge projected rise in imports from Asia. Various proposals are being put forward, from expanding the freeways (a costly enterprise that faces serious community oppo-sition) to keeping the ports open 24 hours a day so that trucks can run at night (a less costly alternative for the public sector, but with additional costs for the steamship lines, some shippers, and some communities).

Warehousing space in the communities near the ports is less and less available, and the result has been a sprouting up of giant warehouses and DCs to the east of Los Angeles County in the "Inland Empire" counties of Riverside and San Bernardino. Land is cheaper and more available there. The area around the city of Ontario, which hosts a growing airport, and serves as a UPS hub, has been most impacted, but DCs continue to move further east and north.

Among the companies that have set up DCs in the area are Wal-Mart, with 2.7 million square feet of warehousing space, Kmart, Pick 'N' Save, Target, Price Costco, and Pier 1 Imports, all with over a million square feet, and various auto parts companies and other retailers and manufacturers. The area has a moonscape quality with one after another of giant, windowless, box-like structures and no people visible except at the times when workers come, go to lunch, and leave at the end of the day.

A major truck route has developed between the ports and Ontario. While there is talk of a rail system along this route, so far the railroads claim it is impractical, and that it only pays to ship by rail beyond a 500-mi radius. Ontario is less than 100 miles from the ports.

Communities in the Inland Empire are also suffering from congestion and pollution, as they face increased truck traffic. The area also suffers from the worst kind of urban sprawl, as communities have pursued a kind of reckless development. Both around the ports, and in the Inland Empire, community activists are rebelling against the local costs that are being borne from the international trade system, and are balking at its seemingly inevitable expansion.

The trade regime also faces post-9/11 hysteria over security. New rules and regulations are being passed and implemented, with implications for all of the actors in the system. However, I shall set this issue aside for the purposes of this chapter, and focus instead on the labor aspects.

Labor and the Logistics Revolution

There is no question that logistics costs have declined. In 1981, logistics costs were 16.2 percent of GDP. They fell throughout the 1980s and more or less stabilized during the 1990s. In 2001 they were valued at 9.5 percent of GDP (Delaney, 2002). This drop is generally attributed to greater efficiency, improved supply chain management through electronically shared information, and by the reduction in inventory levels. No one considers whether squeezing of labor has played a role in these cost reductions. So the question is: How have logistics workers and their unions fared under the logistics revolution?

A number of types of labor are involved in the logistics sector. They include seafarers, longshore workers, port truckers, long-haul truckers, railroad workers, and warehouse/DC workers. I have focused most heavily on longshore, port truckers, and warehouse workers, though would like to collect more information about seafarers and railroad labor. I do not intend to give much attention to long-haul trucking, though inevitably conditions for port truckers are linked to the general state of trucking.

I am interested not only in the state of wages, working conditions, and unionization, but also in race and gender issues in this sector. In addition, I have been investigating the degree of flexibilization that has emerged for logistics workers. In other words, how much have they been impacted by contracting out and other forms of contingent arrangements? Each group of workers has a different story.

Seafarers. For decades steamship lines have moved offshore in search of labor to man their vessels. A system developed called *flags of convenience* (FOCs), in which ships would register in countries like Liberia and Panama, where oversight and regulations were minimal. More recently, the last remaining U.S.-based steamship lines have been bought by foreign companies, so that no major trans-Pacific U.S. carrier remains in operation.

Manning of the ships is often subcontracted to crewing companies, who provide labor from some of the poorest countries of the world. Popular sources include the Philippines, Vietnam, and, increasingly, China. Needless to say, the wages and working conditions of these seafarers are far below the standards that had been attained by U.S. seafaring unions. Sailors suffer from elongated tours of duty, from the absence of shore leave for long stretches of time, and from abandonment in foreign ports.

The manning of vessels has become racialized in the sense that seafarers are almost uniformly people of color who come from countries that have suffered colonial domination and still suffer from forms of neocolonialism.

Longshore workers. Longshore workers on the West Coast are an exception to the pattern of labor degradation that I have been describing. They are organized into a powerful union, the International Longshore and Warehouse Union (ILWU), which, unlike its East Coast counterpart, has a long history of militant, left-wing, democratic unionism. The ILWU is both respected and feared by logistics industry employers.

Constant efforts are made by the industry to curb ILWU power. In 2002 the union faced renegotiation of its contract. The employer, the West Coast steamship lines and terminal operators who are joined together in the Pacific Maritime Association (PMA), were determined to make some fundamental changes that would weaken the union's hold. Supporting this effort was a new organization, the West Coast Waterfront Coalition (WCWC), now renamed the Waterfront Coalition. Composed primarily of giant retailers, including Wal-Mart, the WCWC promised to stand with the PMA in getting tough with the ILWU. The upshot was that the PMA accused the ILWU of a slow-down and locked the union out of ports for 10 days. With the help of the WCWC, the PMA called on the Bush administration to intervene. Some draconian measures were proposed, including bringing the longshore workers under the Railway Labor Act (a more antiunion law than the National Labor Relations Act), or breaking up coastwise bargaining. In the end a contract was reached with the help of a federal mediator, and these options were avoided. A new 6-year contract has been signed, but the possibility of future federal attack lurks in the background.

The ILWU has its own racial character. The workforce remains "American." Whites, blacks, and Chicanos make up the labor force, but concerns about racial discrimination against blacks persist. Women have also made some inroads, but remain a minority in the highest paid jobs. The fact that there are people of color in the relatively high-paying jobs the union has secured may play a role in the attacks against the union by conservative, antiunion forces.

Railroads. The deregulation of the railroads led to a major loss of jobs. In 1973 there were 587,000 railroad workers in the United States. By 1996, the number had dwindled to 282,000. Union membership has remained high, but density has fallen somewhat, from 83 percent in 1973 to 74 percent in 1996. Weekly earnings (measured in 1983–1984 dollars) rose to a high of $507 in 1983, and have fallen since then to $470 in 1996 (Peoples, 1998).

With the decline in the number of workers has come a worsening of working conditions. Railroad workers often face impossible schedules, where they are faced with being called back to work after an 8-hour rest (which may include a commute). Consequently, they suffer from fatigue, raising the chances of accidents. They can be dropped off in the middle of nowhere and must wait in a lonely railroad hotel until a train comes by that can pick them up. As a result, family life suffers among them, as they cannot plan to attend their children's events.

The latest attack on locomotive engineers is the effort to replace them with remote control devices. This a fundamental threat, and the Brotherhood of Locomotive Engineers (BLE) is fighting it, arguing that the technology increases the risk of serious accidents.

Port truckers. Port trucking used to be a unionized job, with the drivers organized by the International Brotherhood of Teamsters (IBT). With deregulation, the union has been broken, as it has throughout the truck-load (TL) sector. The Teamsters continue to hold a strong position in the less-than-truckload (LTL) sector, which includes the movement of small packages by companies like United Parcel Services (UPS).

The effects of deregulation on the U.S. trucking industry as a whole are shown in the following statistics. The workforce has doubled, from 997,000 in 1973 to 1,907,000 in 1996. However, unionization has dropped from 49 percent to 23 percent over the same time period. Concomitantly, weekly earnings in constant 1983–1984 dollars have dropped from $499 to $353 (Peoples, 1998).

Port truckers reflect these changes. Port trucking is part of the TL sector. What has happened is that, instead of being considered as employees, they are treated as independent contractors. They own their own tractors, which they lease to the trucking companies. This arrangement frees the trucking companies of responsibility for many aspects of the business. The port truckers are paid by the move — a form of piece work. For example, if they have to wait in long lines for hours at a terminal gate, the trucker himself must bear the cost.

In reality, most port truckers do, in practice, work as "employees" of the trucking companies. But because that is not their official legal status, their rights to unionize are restricted. If they combine to set a price for their labor, they are viewed by the authorities as violating antitrust law. If the IBT tries to organize them, the union could be faced with massive fines. The result is that port trucking labor has been cheapened.

The switch from unionized workers to independent contractors was accompanied by a shift from native-born to immigrant drivers, mainly from Mexico and El Salvador. Many of the port truckers see themselves as exploited workers, and they have sometimes engaged in militant labor actions, including wildcat strikes. However, their legal designation as independents hurts their chances of achieving any long-term gains.

Nevertheless, the Teamsters have developed a nation-wide port trucker organizing drive, in coalition with the ILWU and the International Longshore Association (ILA) on the East Coast. The campaign has been going on for about 3 years, with some important victories in terms of California legislation that benefit the truckers, but unionization has remained elusive.

Warehouse workers. In examining warehouse and DC workers, I have focused on the Inland Empire, and have not examined those who are employed in warehouses in the ports area. One noteworthy feature of Inland Empire DC employment is a reliance on temporary staffing agencies. Not all DC workers are employed through temp agencies, but a goodly number are, with the implication that they are only employed on a contingent basis.

The use of temp agencies allows DC employers to put a layer between themselves and their employees. This serves two purposes. On the one hand, it allows the ultimate employer to avoid having to deal with the troublesome issue of Workers' Compensation insurance. On the other, it makes unionization much more difficult. Should a union try to organize the steady employees, the employer could outsource the labor to temps. Should the union try to organize the temp agency, the employer could drop that agency and turn to another. Besides, many temp workers are seeking job permanence, and therefore may be especially reluctant to engage in a struggle against an employer with whom they have so fragile a relationship.

The DC labor force is somewhat racialized. The majority of workers are Chicano, i.e., native born Mexican. Part of the attractiveness of the region for DCs is low-cost labor, and the low wages paid these workers undoubtedly reflects their various disadvantages and lack of opportunity in the society at large.

Summary of labor conditions. Throughout the logistics sector that is linked to international trade, with the exception of the longshore workers, there has been deterioration of wages and working conditions. And the longshore exception might not last, as the ILWU has come under attack. Jobs that used to be stable have been outsourced and made contingent, while racialized workers, who suffer from various political disabilities and find it harder to defend themselves, have been employed. Unions have been weakened, and organizing has been made far more difficult, especially with the increase of contingent employment relations like subcontracting, the use of temps, and the turning to independent contractors.

The logistics revolution may have lowered costs by creating greater efficiencies. But a hidden element of its success has been achieved on the backs of logistics workers. One wonders what percentage of the cost savings can be attributed to labor cut-backs. I am not in a position to calculate this at this time, but it seems worth doing.

Possibilities and Challenges

The logistics industry surrounding the port opens up both challenges and opportunities. The rise of contracting, outsourcing, and contingent systems of employment makes organizing much more difficult. The fact that the object of these arrangements is often people of color contributes to the injustice of the whole system. Major strategic thought needs to be put into how this sector might be organized.

The logistics system also affords a couple of major opportunities. On the one hand, its interconnectedness allows for the possibility of inter-union cooperation on a serious level. Already some signs of this are beginning to emerge, with pledges of mutual support between the IBT, ILWU, and ILA. Meanwhile the BLE is merging with the Teamsters, bring rail and trucking workers together. Nevertheless, these efforts are in their infancy, and considerable work would need to be done to build a sectoral campaign.

The second opportunity resides in the incredible strategic importance of the ports and surrounding logistics systems in terms of globalization and world trade. The global economy is made concrete at the ports, and it is through them that most global production must pass. The JIT system and lean inventories mean that corporations cannot withstand serious interruptions in their supply chains. It is for this reason that the battle over the ILWU contract became a national issue. Not only does this make the unions involved vulnerable to pressure. It also affords them the opportunity to use their strategic location for contributing to progressive struggles against corporate-dominated globalization. Local logistics unions could, for example, make a major contribution to the struggles of workers in the global factories that produce for the U.S. market. In addition, logistics unions could use their potential power to join in coalition with others in demanding the rewriting of the rules of globalization — to include a floor for labor and living standards, to protect immigrants' rights, to demand limits on environmental degradation, to push global capitalist institutions like the IMF to change, and to insist on democratizing the decision-making processes.

These may seem like impossible ideals, and the current state of the U.S. labor movement does not give one much cause for optimism. Nevertheless, I believe global production has created its own weaknesses. Labor and other progressive forces have here an opportunity to bring an alternative vision of globalization to reality.

Note

1.   This chapter is part of a larger project on the logistics sector of Southern California.

35

Fighting Sweatshops:
Problems of Enforcing Global Labor Standards

Richard P. Appelbaum

This chapter examines the prospects for labor rights in light of the globalization of production and increasing privatization of regulation. In a world in which the annual sales of transnational corporations approach $5 trillion, representing a third of the world's productive assets, how can labor fight back against oppressive and exploitative conditions?

The Changing Field of Global Organizing

The past 20 years have seen an explosion in the globalization of industry. Between 1980 and 2000, trade in goods as a percentage of goods GDP exploded — a 41 percent increase, from 79 percent to 111 percent for the world as a whole. These trends are even more pronounced for textiles and apparel. Between 1962 and 1999, world exports of textiles and apparel increased fiftyfold. The Multifiber Arrangement (MFA), instituted in 1974, provided for bilateral agreements to regulate trade in apparel and textiles through an elaborate quota system for detailed categories of goods from each trading partner. The quota system became increasingly restrictive as the apparel and textile trade exploded in the 1970s and 1980s, dispersing apparel production throughout the world as core countries sought new sources of production in countries where quotas were unfilled or nonexistent. Under the Uruguay Round of the Agreement on Textiles and Clothing, the quota restrictions of the MFA are scheduled to be phased out by 2005 for all WTO members. The elimination of quotas will allow garment retailers and manufacturers to move their production to those countries offering the lowest labor costs and the most vulnerable workers. Most analysts have concluded that China will be the principal beneficiary (see UNCTAD, 2004, for a detailed discussion of MFA phaseout and its impact on developing countries).

The Growth of Buyer-Driven Commodity Chains: The Rising Power of Retailers

Giant retailers have grown in size to surpass the largest manufacturers in terms of revenues. Among retailers, the United States dominates the world, and Wal-Mart dominates the United States. The four largest U.S. retailers account for about a tenth of total U.S. retail sales. The world's forty largest retailers accounted for nearly $1.3 trillion in revenues in 2001, nearly four percent of the world GDP (derived from Fortune, 2002). Wal-Mart accounts for nearly a fifth of total sales of their combined sales, more than three times those of its nearest competitor, France's Carrefour. In fact, Wal-Mart's revenues of $245 billion made it the world's eighteenth largest economy, roughly tied with Switzerland. In the last few years the giant retailer has surpassed Exxon, General Motors, British Petroleum, and Ford Motors in revenues, signaling the rising power of retailers in the world economy. This suggests an important emerging dynamic in the global economy: the United States and European Union overwhelmingly control the retail end, at a time when retailers in general are exerting increasing control over the global economy.

In terms of labor, the dominance of giant retail transnationals poses a significant challenge to working class organization, as their buyer-driven commodity chains are characterized by extreme post-Fordist production involving networks of global outsourcing and high levels of capital mobility. In the classical global buyer-driven commodity chain formulation, retailers have disproportionate control over the manufacturers who design the goods they sell and the factories where those goods are made (Appelbaum and Gereffi, 1994; Gereffi, 1994, 2001). The Gap, to take one example, sources from four thousand factories in fifty-five countries; Disney, to take another, from thirty thousand factories. Because these giant firms can place their orders anywhere on the planet they choose, their contractors are seen as relatively powerless price-takers, rather than partners and deal-makers. The effects on labor of this arrangement are mixed: one outcome is the "race to the bottom," in which retailers and manufacturers play off competing contractors to force prices (and wages) down and thwart unionization drives. Another outcome, however, is that if large retailers and manufacturers can be made to pressure their suppliers by consumer pressure, gains for labor can also be achieved — as occurred in Mexico's Kukdong (Mexmode) factory and the Dominican Republic's BJ&B cap company (see the following text).

The Rise of Giant Transnational Contractors

This system of retail dominance is being challenged somewhat by the rise of global contractors, mainly from Korea or Taiwan, who typically begin as small local producers in their home countries, using their know-how to go multinational. A handful of these have grown to giant size, and they often have as much power as all but the largest retailers, constituting still another layer of price making and profit taking. Although it may seem that giant factories are in a better position to resist unionization efforts (and consumer pressure) than smaller factories, there is some evidence that the opposite is true: a work stoppage or labor action in factories that employ thousands (and sometimes tens of thousands) of workers can have enormous impact, both on the contractor, who has considerable investment in plant and equipment, and on the retailer or manufacturer, who may rely heavily on the factory for fashion-sensitive items. To the extent that this is the case, work stoppages — particularly if supported by well-organized consumer campaigns — may prove to be effective, as we will see later on in this chapter. Some examples of giant global contractors include:

- Nien Hsing Corporation, a Taiwanese multinational that employs more than 20,000 workers in five Central American factories, as well as thousands of workers in a Mexican factory and two in Lesotho. Founded in 1986, Nien Hsing is currently the world's largest jeans maker, with an output of forty million pairs in 2000, making jeans for Wal-Mart, JCPenney, K-Mart, the Gap, Sears, and Target. It is also the sixth-largest denim maker, producing sixty million yards per year.
- Yupoong, Inc., a Korean multinational, which is the world's second largest cap manufacturer, exporting their "flexfit" hats (motto: "Worn by the world") to some sixty countries. Yupoong (2003) operates the BJ&B hat factory in the Dominican Republic, the scene of the second recently successful labor struggle that we will consider, as well as Dhakarea Ltd. in Bangladesh.
- Boolim, a Korean multinational that was founded in 1994 by Y.S. Lim, who had headed up Macy's in Korea for 14 years. Boolim makes athletic, casual wear, and knitwear in some countries, including China, Indonesia, Sri Lanka, Bangladesh, Saipan, Thailand, Philippines, Malaysia, Myanmar, Guatemala, Mexico, Dominican Republic, Nicaragua, Honduras, El Salvador, and Vietnam. Its clients include Nike, Polo Ralph Lauren, Kenneth Cole, Calvin Klein, and NBA Properties.
- Pou Chen, a Taiwanese multinational, is 50 percent owner of Yue Yen Industrial, a Hong Kong-listed shoe manufacturer that is the world's largest, employing 150,000 to 170,000 workers worldwide. Yue Yen, which makes shoes for Nike (about half of its total production), as well as adidas-Saloman, Reebok, New Balance, Asics Tiger, Converse, Puma, Keds, Timberland, and Rockport, controls 17 percent of the world market. Most of its shoes are made in low-cost factories throughout southern China; its Yue Yen II factory complex in Dongguan, China, employs more than 40,000 workers. The company is Nike's biggest supplier, providing 15 percent of Nike's shoes, with one Indonesian factory turning out a million shoes a month for Nike. The company's Huyen Binh Chanh megafactory in Vietnam will be the largest footwear factory on the planet, employing 65,000 workers (Bailey, 2003; Boje, 2000).

A Framework for Advancing Labor's Interests in the Face of Global Capital

In this section I will examine three approaches to advancing the interests of workers: state-centered enforcement, internationally binding labor laws, and privatized mechanisms. I will argue that the first is being weakened (if not altogether dismantled), at least in the United States; the second is nonexistent; and the third — which is replacing the first — results in a substantial weakening at the level of enforcement.

State-Centered Enforcement: Weakening

When factories are dispersed globally, the enforcement of local labor laws is all but impossible; after all, a principal reason for moving offshore is to avoid regulation and enforcement. Nonetheless, many counties (for example, Mexico) have strong labor laws on the books, which — although seldom enforced — nonetheless create opportunities for successful campaigns. For production that remains in the United States, enforcement — never strong — has been weakened by the Bush administration, which has slashed the budget for the Department of Labor by some 25 percent since taking office and eliminated hundreds of jobs in the area of workers' rights enforcement (NCFLL, 2003).

At the state and local level, a number of governmental bodies have enacted (or are considering) ordinances that require their own purchases to follow minimal labor standards, even when made offshore — requirements that guide purchasing decisions, but which contain no real enforcement mechanisms. In California, the "No More Sweatshops" Advocacy Network succeeded in getting its "no sweat procurement initiative" passed by the state legislature and signed into law in 2003. Similar measures were enacted by the Los Angeles City Council and Unified School District. These measures would apply to police, fire, and other employee uniforms; university, community college, and public school garments; school sports uniforms; athletic equipment such as soccer balls; and pensions that invest in corporations found to be using sweatshop labor. They would ban the purchase of garments and other goods from contractors and subcontractors who do not meet designated labor standards, and require transparency of contracting and subcontracting arrangements, the payment of a living wage, the right to form unions and engage in collective bargaining, and other protections. Similar legislation has been enacted in more than thirty cities, towns and counties throughout the United States, including New York, San Francisco, Pittsburgh, and even Santa Barbara County.

Internationally Binding (and Enforceable) Labor Laws: Nonexistent

There are no internationally binding and enforceable labor laws. The United Nation's International Labor Organization (ILO), which operates on basis of consensus between labor, business, and government, lacks enforcement power. NGOs, which lack legal standing before the ILO, tend to be mistrustful of it. Its conventions to regulate working conditions, to have any force, must be ratified by member states, yet even then, they do not have the force of law, and therefore serve primarily as guidelines. Whereas most of the 182 conventions proposed over the past half century have been ratified by a large majority of the world's countries, the United States has ratified only 13. For the ILO to become an international labor standards enforcement agency, there would have to be a major change in its role (and perhaps, by implication, the role of the United Nations). In fact, in recent years the ILO has committed itself to developing greater coherence among multilateral institutions concerned with labor standards and trade. But it is still a long way away from becoming a global enforcement institution.

For starts, the United States would have to ratify at least the core ILO conventions, not to mention enforce them. The ILO would have to gain status before the WTO (at present, unlike other UN director generals, the head of the ILO is not permitted to speak at WTO ministerial meetings). And were labor standards to be made a part of binding international law, they might well come up against World Trade Organization (WTO) rules that explicitly forbid countries from discriminating against physically similar products on the basis of how they are made.

Other multilateral organizations considering adopting codes of conduct include the World Trade Organization, the World Bank, the United Nations Commission on Sustainable Development, the Organization of Economic Cooperation and Development, and the European Parliament (which has recommended a model code for firms doing business in developing countries). Although it is easy to be cynical about such efforts, in the long term such international institutions could prove to be an important vehicle for establishing and enforcing broad standards, and advocates would do well to work with at least some of these institutions rather than simply write them all off.

At present, the only international organization that is capable of enforcing trade-related rules is the WTO. However, as noted previously, WTO enforcement powers cannot be used to enforce labor standards. It seems highly unlikely that the WTO could become a vehicle for incorporating and enforcing labor standards. The organization was created to favor the interest of transnational corporations in unfettered trade; labor standards are not a part of that concern. Moreover, many developing countries — or at least their probusiness governments — oppose global labor standards on the grounds that however well-intentioned, they will ultimately serve as protection for core country workers by raising the cost of workers in the developing world (but see chapter by Ross in this volume).

Privatized Mechanisms: Do They Really Protect Workers?

There has been a strong movement in recent years towards the privatization of labor law enforcement (Esbenshade, 2003, forthcoming 2004; Sabel, O'Rourke, and Fung, 2000). Increasingly, businesses are seeking to regulate themselves, using private monitors to report on working conditions in their contracted factories. Whereas state regulation focuses on assuring compliance with labor laws at the factory level, the goal of private regulation is typically to certify manufacturers and retailers (more properly understood as branded labels) as compliant by selectively inspecting their contracted factories. Because manufacturers and retailers typically use far-flung networks of such factories — and because those factories themselves are often involved in further layers of subcontracting — critics of this approach argue that it is all but impossible for monitoring and certification programs to encompass all the factories engaged in sewing for a particular label. This has led to a growing concern among labor unions and anti-sweatshop activists that the privatization of enforcement ultimately results in giving a "sweat-free" stamp to branded labels whose production networks include an unknown number of factories with labor abuses (O'Rourke, 2003: 6).

Whereas previously national, state, or local governments would set labor standards and police their enforcement, this is increasingly done today by NGOs, firms, and labor unions, and typically draws on ILO core standards, as well as local laws. Enforcement, rather than relying on state sanctions, is instead ultimately based on consumer vigilance. Bowing to consumer pressure, many businesses have in fact adopted codes of conduct. Nike, for example, established a code of conduct for labor and environmental practices in 1992 for the approximately 900 factories (employing 650,000 workers) that made its shoes and apparel at the time. The company claims a staff of eighty people dedicated to monitoring factory conditions. A point system rewards high scores with potentially lucrative contracts and punishes low scorers with the risk of losing contracts. The Gap, to take a second example, has a "Vendor Compliance Agreement" covering its four thousand factories in fifty-five countries, monitored by a staff of one hundred. Reebok, adidas-Salomon, Levi's, Disney, Wal-Mart, and others have similar codes and self-enforcement mechanisms. In Los Angeles, the leading manufacturers created a "Compliance Alliance," which monitors their standards among local contractors; it is said to cover as much as three quarters of Los Angeles' factories: five thousand to seven thousand factories.

Businesses have developed a variety of codes and monitoring systems they typically use. Most involve certifying factories or brands as "sweat-free" by accrediting external organizations to monitor. The certification programs that are most widely used by U.S. manufacturers and retailers include SA8000, WRAP, and the Fair Labor Association:

- SA8000, a social-accountability standard, was created by the private sector Council on Economic Priorities in 1997. SA8000 standards call for the payment of a living wage (a "basic needs wage"), and also requires firms to "facilitate parallel means of independent and free association and bargaining" in countries like China where there are no independent unions. It certifies factories (not manufacturers or retailers) as compliant with its standards, based on an annual one day audit. SAI audits have been criticized as having a corporate bias, using weak monitors, and being largely ineffective: indeed, as of September 2002, only 150 factories in 27 countries had been certified, including 28 apparel and textile firms (there are an estimated 100,000 factories producing for the U.S. market alone).

- WRAP (Worldwide Responsible Apparel Production) was created by the American Apparel Manufacturers Association (now the American Apparel and Footwear Association) in 1998. Like SA8000, WRAP certifies factories, not brands. It has been criticized as having a strong pro-firm bias. WRAP relies on such major private, for-profit monitoring firms as Cal Safety Compliance and Global Social Compliance (formerly called PriceWaterhouseCooper), which are hired by the manufacturer to whom they will privately report. All audits are preannounced, and are conducted by firms that are paid by the factories being audited. Under such conditions, critics of WRAP place little credence in its certification of compliant factories or on the labels that use them.

- The Fair Labor Association (FLA) is an offshoot of President Clinton's Apparel Industry Partnership. It was set up by a small number of manufacturers, retailers, and NGOs in 1998. As of December 2003, according to its website, the FLA involved 12 footwear and apparel firms, 175 colleges and universities, an NGO Advisory Council (several dozen AC affiliates are listed), and more than 1,100 companies licensed to make logo-ed goods for universities. It is governed by a Board of Directors comprised of fifteen representatives: six manufacturers, six NGOs, and three universities. Its code of conduct is modeled on ILO core standards. Although in response to its critics the FLA has in recent years tightened up its procedures, activists are still concerned that it is dominated by manufacturers.

Given the far-flung nature of outsourcing and the rapid turnover in factories, activists challenge the very notion that any label (as opposed to individual factories) could be reliably certified as "sweat-free." In many cases, workers in factories covered by codes of conduct are not informed by their employers, and as a result are completely unaware, that the codes even exist. Moreover, when manufacturers do adopt codes, they often fail to implement enforcement mechanisms. When such mechanisms are adopted, they typically either involve internal monitoring systems or the hiring of external monitors with expertise in firm auditing. Both of these approaches suffer from the "fox guarding the chicken coop" problem: the monitors are hired and paid by the manufacturers themselves, who obviously have a vested interest in downplaying (or denying outright) any problems that might surface in their contract shops. A substantial and growing body of research documents the ineffectiveness of company-hired monitors (Esbenshade, forthcoming 2004; WWW, 1998, 1999; USDOL, 1996; Varley, 1998; Sajhau, n.d.; Jeffcott and Yanz, 2000; O'Rourke, 1997; NLC, 1999).

A number of studies, as well as informal reports by unions and workers, suggest that the monitoring of codes of conduct have resulted in limited improvements in some factories, and no improvement in others (see the articles in Koepke, Molina, and Quinteros, 2000; WWW, 1998, 1999). In those studies that reported improvements, the most common concrete examples were improvements in the physical conditions in the plants (ergonomically correct equipment, potable water, ventilation, and bathroom access) and correct payment of wages and benefits. There is little evidence that adoption of codes has led to higher wages or respect for the right to organize trade unions. Moreover, one researcher cautions that the costs of physical improvements are borne by the local contractor rather than the manufacturer, and as a result may lead to work speed-up to cover expenses, thereby highlighting some of the difficulties in implementing codes of conduct that are aimed at the top end of the supply chain, but enforced at the bottom. One study shadowed PriceWaterhouse-Cooper monitors as they inspected thirteen factories around the world, where licensed apparel was made for Nike, Champion, JanSport, and adidas-Salomon for sale in five major U.S. universities (O'Rourke et al., 2000). The study, which was conduced for a consortium of universities, reported finding serious health and safety problems, unlawful forced overtime, illegally low pay, verbal abuse, discrimination against women workers, and threats against union organizers — none of which were reported (or indeed even detected) by the PWC monitors.

The privatization of monitoring, in sum, at best provides good public relations for firms, while confusing consumers. At worst, it lulls consumers into complacency as they buy certified "sweat-free" products that are highly unlikely to qualify for that label. O'Rourke (2003) lists a number of other problems as well: the privatization of monitoring undermines governmental regulation by shifting to private enforcement mechanisms that are more easily controlled by firms; it undermines unionization efforts by creating an (ineffective) alternative; it leads firms to eliminate contractors identified as problematic; it costs workers' jobs while displacing the problems elsewhere; it turns independent NGOs from watchdogs into partners with the firms they are supposed to be monitoring; and it has spawned a multibillion-dollar global monitoring industry, adding yet another layer of profit-taking to the cost of production. Finally, with consumer pressures absent (which are always fickle), it is difficult to imagine that most firms would spend the time or resources necessary to try to ferret out problems in their supply chains.

Because of such concerns anti-sweatshop activists — primarily students and labor unions — have adopted a different approach: instead of certifying branded labels as "sweat-free," they have launched a system of compliance that seeks to verify working conditions — at least in the collegiate licensing sector — by following up on worker complaints, and then compelling factories to correct violations.

In 1998, a number of different campus groups formed United Students Against Sweatshops (USAS) to facilitate communication between student anti-sweatshop activists across the country and to plan common strategy and tactics (Featherstone, 2002; Appelbaum and Dreier, 1999). Two years later, USAS, along with the garment workers union UNITE (the Union of Needletrades, Industrial, and Textile Employees), created the nonprofit Workers' Rights Consortium (WRC) as an alternative to the FLA. The WRC's fifteen-member governing board is comprised equally of representatives from member universities, student organizations (including United Students Against Sweatshops), and an advisory council comprised of representatives from NGOs and labor unions, with a few academic experts. Notably absent from the governing board are representatives from industry, a deliberate exclusion that reflects the WRC's desire to distance itself from the industry domination it believes to be the fatal flaw of the FLA. As of October 2003, 117 colleges and universities were members (about two thirds belong to the FLA as well).

The WRC operates on a fundamentally different premise than the FLA: its main approach is not to certify factories as sweat-free, but rather to verify licensee reports about factory conditions, responding to workers' complaints and conducting spot investigations. Among other things, the WRC calls for a living wage (not a minimum or prevailing wage) and strongly emphasizes the right to form unions and engage in collective bargaining. It reasons that universities, through their licensing contracts, have the power to force manufacturers to negotiate with workers, something that will ultimately increase workers' ability to protect themselves, rather than force them to rely on image-conscious firms that are momentarily shamed by conscientious consumers. Worker empowerment is best achieved, the WRC reasons, by supporting workers' efforts at forming independent, effective labor unions. To date, the organization has been involved in four major factory investigations in which it has played a key role in the success of several efforts to form independent unions.

Worker Empowerment

There is evidence that the U.S. labor movement is beginning to take global organizing more seriously, as is evidenced by organized labor's involvement in anti-WTO demonstrations or the Campaign for Global Fairness. UNITE has also supported unionization campaigns in sewing factories in Central America. There are a number of recent examples of successful unionization efforts, in which consumer advocates in the United States, in cooperation with the FLA, the WRC, UNITE, and the AFL-CIO, have played key roles. These include factories owned by Kukdong International in Mexico; BJ&B in the Dominican Republic; Nien Hsing in Nicaragua (the Chentex factory); and PT Dada in Indonesia. Because of space limitations, we will consider only the first two in this section.

Kukdong International (renamed Mexmode) is a Korean-owned factory in Puebla, Mexico, that makes branded apparel under contract with Nike, Reebok, and other suppliers for the U.S. collegiate market. In early January 2001, five workers were fired from the factory, protesting low pay, abusive supervisors, rancid food, and lack of representation by a company union that was imposed on them by factory management. According to one worker, "the food had worms in it …. The meat was spoiled. It was green" (Erlich, 2003). In response, eight hundred (out of nine hundred) workers then went on strike, initiating a protracted (and sometimes violent) struggle that ended the following September with the formation of an independent union (the first in a Mexican garment *maquiladora*) and, in April 2002, a 10 percent wage increase. Early in the strike period, both the WRC and an FLA affiliate (Verité) had conducted independent audits that confirmed the workers' complaints, reports that were made public (by the WRC as a matter of policy; by Verité under public pressure), resulting in demonstrations at Niketown retail outlets and coverage in the mainstream U.S. press. Students, U.S. labor (UNITE and the AFL-CIO), and university administrators put direct pressure on Nike, as well as on the Mexican government, to accept the workers' demands (Esbenshade, 2003, forthcoming 2004). Nike at one point even cancelled its contracts with the factory, reducing its income to a fifth that of previous levels; once the factory agreed to the workers' demands, Nike rewarded it with a new $2.5 million contract (Erlich, 2003). The Kukdong case is evidence of the success that can occur when pressure is brought to bear on the manufacturer, government, and contractor simultaneously — what Esbenshade (2003) calls the "triangle of resistance."

The BJ&B Cap Company is owned by the Korean multinational Yupoong, previously mentioned as the world's second largest cap manufacturer. The company's plant in the Dominican Republic's Villa Altagracia Free Trade Zone made caps for Nike and Reebok under licensing arrangements for a dozen major U.S. universities. Workers began a long-term organizing drive in 1997 because of forced overtime, arbitrary firings, and verbal and physical abuse. Organizing efforts increased in 2001, and twenty workers were eventually fired after signing a petition to form a union. Nike complained to the FLA, which — along with the WRC — launched an investigation that involved unannounced factory visits, offsite interviews with workers, and review of facility payroll, personnel, and timecard records. USAS sent thousands of letters to factory management; university officials and Nike and Reebok executives paid visits to the factory. Although BJ&B management circulated flyers denouncing the unionists as "terrorists," eventually the factory capitulated to public pressure, and workers won independent union representation — the largest factory in a free trade zone anywhere in Mexico, the Caribbean, or Central America to be unionized. The new contract, signed in March 2003, provided for a 10 percent salary increase (to $31 a week) effective January 2004, as well as such benefits as university scholarships for workers and their children, productivity bonuses, protections for unionization rights, the creation of a health and safety committee, and even gift baskets for new mothers (Esbenshade, 2003). In the words of Ignacio Hernandez, the general secretary of the Federation of Free Trade Zone Unions, "I never thought a group of students, thousands of them, could put so much pressure on these brands …. We were determined to win, but without them it would have taken us five more years. And it would have been more traumatic without them because all we would have was the pressure to strike" (as reported in Gonzales, 2003).

Conclusion

In a global production system, especially one that is characterized by powerful retailers and invisible contractors linked together in buyer-driven commodity chains, buyers clearly have an important role to play. But, ultimately, consumer-driven efforts can only be an adjunct of workers organizing, combined with legislative and regulatory remedies. In the long run, only workers themselves can adequately assure that their working conditions are satisfactory. Yet, unionizing in many global industries, particularly labor-intensive ones such as apparel, is presently fraught with problems, ranging from the ever-present threat of capital flight to outright workplace repression (often reinforced by state policy). Building the capacity for unfettered union organizing must necessarily be a long-term strategy for union organizers throughout the world. That is why anti-sweatshop activists and organizations such as the WRC call for independent verification of factory conditions, rather than an exclusive reliance on monitoring and certification, although a combination of both would seem to be the most promising approach. To build an adequate system of monitoring, activists argue, it is necessary to build capacity at the local level, thereby creating a foundation for independent unions.

From the workers' point of view, it would be helpful if consumers the world over, along with human rights advocates, promoted labor standards that would open opportunities for them to organize into unions of their choice. Consumers must be made to realize that they have a strong influence over even the most powerful retailers. The link between workers and consumers lies in promoting policies calling for labor standards and corporate codes of conduct that limit corporate abuse, provide freedom to organize and collectively bargain, and ensure that the public will uphold human rights.

Somewhere between consumer action and unionization lies state action of various sorts. In the United States, that includes legislation aimed at making manufacturers and retailers (the latter in their private label production) legally liable for the goods they design and sell, thereby ending the fiction that contractors are completely independent of the firms that hire them. Joint liability legislation, under which retailers and manufacturers would be held legally liable for violations in their contracted factories, is an important first step. Globally, bilateral trade agreements containing social clauses mandating adequate labor (and environmental) standards and practices would at least initiate some degree of accountability. In the long run, truly global institutions are needed to implement universal standards.

36

Sewing for the Global Economy: Thread of Resistance in Vietnamese Textile and Garment Industries

Angie Ngoc Tran

Introduction

What are various forms of textile and garment workers' response to the global flexible production that takes away their control over the production process and their own labor? How does the relationship between the labor unions and the party-state in Vietnam evolve to address the new conditions of flexible production? How are foreign corporations situated in this context? What is the role of state media in industrial relations and labor disputes?

This chapter examines the workers' justice issues in the Vietnamese textile and garment industries (VTGI) and the ways that the flexible global mode of production affects workers' pay and working conditions. It also examines the role of the Vietnamese labor unions in socialist Vietnam. The evolving role of the labor unions is weakening to some extent in unequal power relations with foreign corporate buyers in flexible production. Yet, labor unions assert their increasingly independent position in an emerging tripartite relationship with the party-state and the managers–owners (state and private) in a market-based economy. In the context of the emerging tripartite relationship, I demonstrate how workers' response to the constraints, primarily triggered by the global flexible production, reflects their historical legacy of self-mobilization which dates back to the French colonial rule. While workers' protests have gained short-term victories, they organized mostly spontaneously, with or without labor unions' assistance. However, there is evidence of higher effectiveness if workers are able to ally with the enterprise labor unions to fight for their legitimate economic equity and decent work conditions.

I include a discussion of gender differentiations throughout the chapter to demonstrate how feminine expectations of flexible production negatively affect workers, especially female workers. With gender sensitivity, I emphasize workers' perspectives on division of labor, training, pay, and their participation in protests. Being of Vietnamese descent, I am extremely grateful that these workers and union representatives trusted me and poured out their grievances and concerns during the interviews in late 1990s, 2001, 2002 and 2003; many took place during peak subcontracting seasons (late summer), so I witnessed firsthand their hideous working conditions and plights.

Flexible Mode of Production, Gender, and Pay

Domestic economic reforms and the changing global politico-economic environment (the collapse of the former Soviet Union and other Eastern European socialist markets in the early 1990s) compelled Vietnam to further integrate into the capitalist world economy. I use the case of the Vietnamese Textile and Garment Industries (VTGI) to bring out the labor issues because it is the only manufacturing industry on the top ten export list (only after oil and gas). It is still the top employer of manufacturing workers, employing about 1.6 million workers, over 80 percent who are women (MPDF, 1999: 44; CRS, June 2002: 5). Most of these workers come from rural areas throughout Vietnam to work in big cities such as Hanoi and Ho Chi Minh City (HCMC).

Similar to the plights of garment workers in other Southeast Asian countries, if only several decades later (Taiwan, South Korea, and Singapore in the 1970s; Malaysia and the Philippines in the 1980s) (Deyo, 1997: 212, 222), the Vietnamese workers do not have real employment alternatives between low paid jobs from the multilevel subcontracting system and underemployment in rural areas. Foreign corporate buyers and middlemen take advantage of expected female roles (such as being docile, dexterous, passive, obedient, flexible, conscientious, and willing to work long hours for on-time deliveries) to demand flexibility from these workers and to raise productivity.

The Vietnamese Labor Code is progressive compared to that of other countries in terms of gender sensitivity and workers' protection in firms with foreign investment.[1] It has stipulations on behalf of female workers,[2] and clauses to request formation of labor unions in the Export Processing Zones (EPZs) and industrial zones.[3] Since 1995, the party-state sanctions the right to strike and requests labor unions' formation within six months of operation of enterprises employing more than ten workers.

The revised Code ratified by Vietnam's Congress on April 12, 2002 stipulates several positive changes for female workers in terms of job security and maternity leave and nursing (*Labor*, (Las Dong newspaper), September 17, 2002; *Vietnam News*, March 25, 2002). However, irrespective of these progressive stipulations, the main problems remain the unequal power relations in piece-work subcontracting system which disproportionately benefits foreign corporations, and the continuing practice of gender imbalances in hiring, paying, and training at the expense of female workers.

Workers get paid by the piece-rate remuneration system. Piece-rate is a part of the total subcontracting price negotiated between foreign corporate buyers–middlemen and the Vietnamese subcontractors. It is kept extremely low by the fragmentation of the production process into hundreds of minute details. On average it is about 0.6 Vietnam Dong (assuming the average exchange rate of 15,000 VND per USD).[4] When the piece rate is that low, workers need to assemble as many pieces as humanly possible to make ends meet, and get paid only after the final products passed quality control.

Moreover, workers face low-skilled, dead-end, and insecure jobs. During peak seasons between May and October, they work over 12 hours per day, 7 days per week, often without overtime pay, but in slow seasons (between November and April), they are underemployed (see Tran, 2001, 2002).

Self-Exploitation and Competition among Workers

Under this piece-rate remuneration system, most workers are compelled to exploit themselves in order to make ends meet. This self-exploitation is the compulsion to perform surplus labor, which ultimately benefits the owners and not the workers themselves (Marx, pp. 769, 1026–1027). The owners of the means of production, the MNCs, reap the lion's share for providing the designs, patterns, and distribution of final products, 80 percent of the total retail value; foreign middlemen receive 15 percent for their fabrics–accessories and supervision; and their Vietnamese counterparts earn less than 4 percent for facilities and labor. Workers at the bottom the subcontracting ladder receive only 2 percent of the total retail value.[5] As foot-loose monopsonists at the top of the subcontracting ladder, the MNCs have the power to shift production to other developing countries, while workers can only compete with similarly placed workers in other developing countries by suppressing wages further, ultimately benefiting the MNCs. The average monthly income of a garment worker was 650,000 VND (about $50); a textile worker earned 801,000 VND (about $62), compared with national industry monthly average income of $53. The service sector earned $55 and the agricultural sector $48. On average, foreign-owned firms tended to pay a bit more: 900,000 VND/month (about $69), although most workers in these firms have no labor union representation (Vu Quoc Huy, September 2001: 49–51).[6] Most men are channeled into higher-skilled positions where they will be trained on the job and then get paid higher than their female counterparts.[7]

As the industrial reserve army swells, workers increasingly compete among themselves for fewer jobs: "Workers do not generally protest if not properly paid, as they are willing to take normal rate in extra-working time. This situation is mainly due to high competition for work" (Vu, September 2001: 51, 54). A recent surge in the export of Vietnamese labor to more affluent neighboring countries (such as Taiwan, Malaysia, Japan, and South Korea) to work low-skilled jobs such as maids and manual laborers confirms this serious lack of work. To facilitate labor export, the state permits local governments to lend each participating family 20 million VND (about US$1,300) and waives the collateral requirement (*Tuoi Tre*, April 23, 2003; *Thoi Bao Kinh Te Vietnam*, April 23, 2003).

Under such fierce competition for jobs, most owners/managers ignore labor stipulations on work hours, minimum wage, and overtime pay. While female workers are entitled to take breaks when they are pregnant, nursing, or menstruating, most skip breaks since they would lose earnings under the piece-rate system or in some cases, even lose their jobs. Also, the piece-rate system renders labor policies on maternity leave ineffective. Most pregnant workers shorten their maternity leave (from 6 to 4 months) and return to work right after delivering their babies in order to feed their families. Hence, suggestions of returning to the 6-month maternity leave with basic salary by well-meaning labor union representatives in some large SOEs turned out to be unrealistic since workers get paid by the piece-rates, and not by the hour or the month.

Evolving Labor Unions' Roles

Labor self-mobilization for the oppressed has been the historical tradition of Vietnamese workers even before the formation of labor unions. In the early 1900s, after waves of factory and mining workers' strikes in factories in Saigon, Hai Phong, Hanoi, and Nam Dinh under the French colonial rule, the Red Trade Union Federation was formed in 1929. This led to the first National Congress of trade unions and the formation of the Vietnam Federation of Trade Union-VFTU (Tong Lien Doan Lao Dong Viet Nam) in 1946 (*Trade Union Movement*, 1988: 7, 9, 48). Moreover, in the capitalist south of Vietnam, labor strikes were also widespread in the 1950s and early 1960s (Beresford, 1998: 66).

Following the consistent market reform in the mid-1980s, the labor unions became more independent, at least in principle. In 1988 Nguyen Van Linh (the then-VFTU president) introduced important structural changes and legalized more independent trade unions. The VTFU became the Vietnamese General Confederation of Labor (VGCL) to reflect a greater separation between labor unions, the party-state, and enterprise management. Also, union representatives no longer need to be Vietnamese Communist Party (VCP) members as long as they are adequately trained at the grassroots level (Norlund, 1996: 90; 1997: 171–172).

In principle, both workers and the management are to contribute to the general workers' funds. The management is to allocate two percent of the total wage funds to union wages, and five percent to social functions such as social security, illness, labor accidents, and childbirth (*Trade Union Movement*, 1988: 20, 23). Workers are to contribute 1 percent of their salary to fund social functions such as weddings, funerals, presents for the sick, and divorce counseling. At present, I found the enterprise unions still provide meaningful social services to workers. Workers in foreign-invested enterprises may earn a bit higher wages, but they do not receive these social services.

Under the centrally planned system prior to the mid 1980s, the state corporatist structure was prevalent when the labor unions were part of the party-state. In the context of a socialist economy (with the absence of privately-employed workers), the relations among state-employed workers, their union representatives, and SOEs' management were conceivably nonadversarial.[8] The unions' role is to protect workers' interests and to enhance the economic management and supervision of state affairs (*Trade Union Movement*, 1988: 19). While strikes have been allowed since 1995, labor union representatives are to arbitrate between workers and management when there is a complaint or dissatisfaction related to pay or working conditions. Workers cannot strike until after such arbitration fails to resolve the conflict.

In firms that established labor unions, the four-member labor union structure (*Bo Tu*) continues to operate. It has a clear presence of the party-state: one on production, manufacturing and technical matters, although non VCP members can also serve this role, (*Chuyen Mon*); one on trade union matters (*Cong Doan*); one on party matters (*Dang*); and one on youth matters (*Doan Thanh Nien*). The leading VCP member in *Bo Tu* casts the decisive vote in the selection of group members.[9] This structure is fluid and is still characterized by personal relationships and connections between the union representatives and the local party-state officials. The elected union representative can negotiate with VCP officials to retain the entire 40 percent of after-tax profits and then redistribute it to workers instead of submitting it to the state budget (Beresford, 1998: 69–71; Norlund, 1996: 86).[10]

The labor union joint-control over the production process with the party-state is lost under the current global production system. Previously under the planning system, this four-member union structure participated in the production process, supplied inputs, and ensured outputs; workers, on the other hand, had access to enterprise resources to improve their personal incomes. Under the flexible mode of production, foreign corporations and middlemen dictate important production decisions. They profit from the flexible small orders and quick turnaround times, while workers have to bear all the fluctuations to ensure such flexibility. MNCs (placing clothing orders with Vietnamese factories) and foreign middlemen (overseeing the production process and supplying most inputs) make all decisions on production and distribution of final products. The resulting wage allocation is based on very low piece-rate agreements between Vietnamese producers and their foreign counterparts.

The economic reality under the flexible mode of production diminishes the power of union representatives and can lead to conflict of interest. Most union representatives are workers themselves. Many work part-time as union representatives and work on the assembly line. Similar to other workers, most rely on piece-rate wages and bonuses to supplement their meager union wages. When the union representatives rely on piece-rate wages for their livelihoods, they are under the control of capitalists (domestic and foreign). Hence, there is a potential conflict of interest and their autonomy to fight effectively for workers' rights is undermined.

A case in point: a labor union representative in a state garment factory in the North of Vietnam explained how his union job was "just on the side" and that he was first and foremost a full-time worker on the assembly line:

> I still had to sew as other workers. The union job was just on the side, and at the same time, I had to make sure to meet productivity and quota levels on the assembly line. Every month, the company paid "tien trach nhiem" (union financial compensation) to four union representatives. Not much to speak of: only about 15,000 dong per month (about $1USD) for each member. Often we spent about one hour total per month to take care of some labor issues (such as competition campaigns for higher productivity, bonuses, and penalties for factory violations). Then I got back to my job on the assembly line, sewing pockets onto men's shirts (interview with union representative H.V.D., 2000).

Tripartite Relationships: The Party-State, the Unions and the Management

There is evidence that the party-state intends to maintain the socialist values in the realm of labor unions even during the flexible mode of production. The VCP leaders assert their influence in the labor union activities and functions. The ninth National

Congress of the VGCL in 2003 received the special attention and participation of all the top VCP leadership, including Party General Secretary Nong Duc Manh, President Tran Duc Luong, Prime Minister Phan Van Khai, and National Assembly Chairman Nguyen Van An, as well as other senior leaders.[11]

State recognition of not only the private sector (since the mid-1980s), but also of the associations that represent private interests (such as the VCCI since 2003) in relations to the state interests and labor interests demonstrate a balancing act of the state in maintaining its presence and influence in the market system. According to Ms. Pham Thu Hang, director of the Small and Medium Enterprise Promotion Center of the Vietnamese Chamber of Commerce and Industry (VCCI), and Rosemarie Greve (the director of the ILO office in Hanoi), the state formally acknowledged VCCI as the most prominent nongovernmental association that represents the interests of the management–owners.[12] Thus a tripartite relationship emerges with three interests, including the party-state (Ministry of Labor, Invalids, and Social Affairs [MOLISA]), the employers' representatives (including the most prominent VCCI, the Vietnamese Textile Associations [VITAS], and Vietnamese Cooperatives Association, VICOOP), and the workers' representative (the VGCL).

Contrary to ideologically-charged and negative expectations about the close relations between the party-state and the labor unions, there is evidence of an increasingly independent VGCL in trying to represent the interests of workers in both state and private sectors.[13] Critical observers and officials from MOLISA, the ILO, and the VGCL supported this viewpoint.[14] They all agreed on the independent labor unions agenda and interests that Ms. Cu Thi Hau (the current VGCL President who is reelected for the second time) brings to the negotiating table of this tripartite relation. According to Nguyen Manh Cuong (Director of Foreign Relations Office, MOLISA), there have been heated debates between MOLISA officials, with Hau staunchly supporting the interests of workers on overtime work, pay, benefits, and retirement age issues.[15]

Revisiting the Independent Trade Union Argument

Ascension of the hegemony of global corporate actors (MNCs and foreign middlemen) in piece-rate subcontracting system calls into question the nonadversarial relationships among workers, labor unions, and the party-state in the corporatist structure. State corporatist structure allowed the labor unions some control over the production process and to take care of workers' concerns, since they all shared common interests in achieving economic targets. With the rise of private interests, especially in firms with foreign investment, workers and labor unions have lost control over the production process and on their own labor (the self-exploitation phenomena). Under the reigning piece-rate subcontracting system, both workers and union representatives (most of whom also rely on piece-rates to make a living) no longer share nor have any control over the economic plans or common interests as under the corporatist relation; instead, they must assemble and deliver apparels to the global market without protests under any circumstances.

Flexible production in a market system can also give rise to an alliance between foreign management and the labor unions, which can lead to conflict of interest. Hoang Thi Lich argued that the lack of independence from foreign management severely compromises "the objectivity and autonomy of trade union representatives when arbitrating labor disputes on the factory floor." She cites cases in which the vice presidents in foreign-invested firms play both the role of management members and of labor union presidents–representatives (Hoang, 1997: 1–6; Greenfield, 1994: 222; *Cong Nghiep Viet Nam*, 2000: 2).

Flexible production regime can reduce labor union representatives to part-timers, as demonstrated in the union representative's case.[16] Most of my interviewees agreed on the fact that given the low fees paid by unions to their representatives and a lack of state subsidy for union activities, most union members depend on their wages as regular workers. Thus, in reality, they end up being part-time union representatives who would not be as effective as full-time ones. Relatedly, Greenfield argued that part-time union members can be more effective because as workers they understand the working conditions better and can effectively fight for workers' rights (Greenfield, 1994: 223). While his argument makes sense in theory, the fatigue of being a worker–union representative in real life negatively affects the performance of the labor unions' role.

The situations get worse when we consider workers' pay, working conditions, and the effectiveness of labor unions. Under the piece-rate flexible subcontracting regime, global actors dictate what and how to produce, supply most inputs and accessories, and distribute the final products. Under this system, labor union representatives receive very low union fees, small (if any) state subsidies, and low pay (under piece-rate system). H.V.D., the union representative, demonstrated this brute reality with his US$1 per month compensation for his union work and the need to also be a full-time worker to make a living. Facing these constraints, the role of union representative is thus severely emasculated since subcontracting work on the assembly line takes up most of their waking hours and significantly curtails their time and energy to carry out union responsibilities.

Hence, the issue is not so much fighting for independent trade unions, which at least in principle are already encouraged and sanctioned since 1988 to allow for greater autonomy from the party-state. The more relevant concern is how to empower the workers and the VGCL, which tries to exist effectively in the market system and has increasingly identified specific workers' interests and fought for them. This empowering effort is necessary to narrow the power differentials between the MNCs and the Vietnamese counterparts. Greenfield's argument on workers' two-pronged struggle, fighting for immediate economic interests and for their democratic participation in making vital decisions on the factory floor, makes sense for a longer term strategy (Greenfield, 1994: 221, 228). In the VTGI context, I argue that the labor unions and workers need to regain the control they had under the corporatist structure and expand it to the growing private sector, including their participation in both production and distribution decision-making, which ultimately affects their remuneration.

Workers' Protests: Labor Unions, the State, and Spontaneous Mobilization

The evolving role of labor union as a structure is still a counterpoint to be reckoned by the management and owners in the growing private sector. Evidence from my fieldwork in Vietnam in 2003 and from other sources (print and multimedia) shows close working relations among different levels of the VGCL (central, provincial, and enterprise),[17] the local MOLISA departments (*So lao dong dia phuong*), and the company management to arbitrate labor strikes. Labor unions at different levels often come down to the strike scenes promptly to serve as liaison between the striking workers and the employers; they often work with the local people's committees to bring all sides to the negotiating table. Increasingly, they also work with the management boards of the EPZs and industrial zones in resolving the disputes in companies with foreign investment. However, in companies that do not yet have enterprise labor unions, they are not in a proactive position to represent workers and negotiate with employers to prevent strikes from happening.

VINATEX, the largest textile and garment state corporation, has its own labor union structure. Playing the role of a bridge, at times it successfully negotiates to get some laid-off workers reinstated in their jobs. According to Nguyen Xuan Con, VINATEX labor union director, their strategy is to preempt labor strikes since these strikes are disruptive and costly to all stakeholders. But if the strikes have already erupted, his office labor representatives must come to those factories to represent the workers and explain to them the situations, as well as to convince the employers to negotiate with the workers.

In monitoring recent labor strikes and disputes, I find that most strikes have had to do with workers' benefits, wages, social security, health insurance, and labor contracts not being upheld by the management. The unions have been able to negotiate and win some short-terms concessions on workers' behalf and to reinstate some laid-off workers so they can go back to work. In January and February 2004, there were three cases in which all sides were brought together with some positive outcomes for the workers; two cases involved 100 percent South Korean–owned companies, and one case with 100 percent Taiwanese-owned company (*Labor Update*, December 2003 to February 2004).

However, the on-going problem remains the short-term nature of these strike resolutions. Since workers cannot sustain themselves for long without work, they can be easily appeased by owners–managers with some short-tem concessions. According to Con, there have been cases in which the company directors have agreed to raise the piece-rates for workers, only to "recuperate" by paying lower piece-rates in subsequent orders.

The Role of State Media

The state media (including print, television, and radio programs) has played a significant role in exposing the labor disputes to the general public and in creating an urgency, as well as credible pressure to bring all sides to the negotiating table. Major central and local newspapers (including *Lao Dong, Nguoi Lao Dong, Nhan Dan, Cong*

Doan, Phap Luat, and *Viet Nam News*) have daily coverage, forums, and analyses about labor issues, rights, and responsibilities. For instance, the journalists from the *Lao Dong* and *Nguoi Lao Dong* newspapers have gone to striking sites as soon as they have received news from the "hotline" (*duong day nong*) about labor strikes. There were cases in which they actively participated in the meetings of three interests in the tripartite relationship. Moreover, there are two weekly television programs on workers and labor unions issues: one focuses on female workers' issues (Nguyen Thi Gai, director of the labor unions television program), and the other covers general labor issues (the Hanoi program).

State media also raises ongoing concerns and suggests ways to overcome the lengthy and unpragmatic procedures to authorize strikes that contribute to the occurrence of wildcat strikes.[18] These are spontaneous strikes in which workers can no longer withstand the injustices done to them on the factory floor and thus decide to organize among themselves to seek immediate relief on pay and work conditions. Nguyen Thi Gai and Vu Van Nhat (international relations department of the VGCL) expressed the same concerns over these lengthy procedures to obtain strike approvals (from the VGCL and local governments). To that end, Gai produced several television programs to shed light on this problem; one of them was aptly entitled *The Labor Court Has Open Door, but without an Entrance.*[19]

Thread of Resistance in State and Nonstate Factories

Labor organizing and collective action in the VTGI began in the 1930s and has persisted to the current market-oriented system. Workers engage in various forms of resistance, with or without labor union help, to demand decent working conditions, pay and bonuses, and benefits. In addition to going through the regular channel consisting of the enterprise labor unions, the local governments (people's committees and MOLISA provincial departments), workers have increasingly utilized the state media (newspapers, television, and radio programs) to expose their hardships in an attempt to alleviate their working conditions.[20] The reliance on labor mobilization and linkages to the state media and local governments is similar to some successful case studies of community mobilization in Vietnam.[21]

Their forms of protests range from spontaneous and self-mobilization (a historical tradition), alliance with spouses, appealing to the state media (such as the labor newspapers, the trade union and labor television programs, and the state radio station), and the state judicial systems (Hanoi People's Oversight Committee, People's Court, and State Investigation Agency).

Historically many strikes took place in both state and nonstate textile factories in HCMC in the late 1980s and early 2000s, demanding not only economic interests (pay and working conditions) but also greater democracy on the factory floor against the authoritarian management system (Greenfield, 1994: 227). At present, workers' protests should be understood in the broader context of piecework subcontracting with the power shifting from the party-state to the MNCs, workers' self-exploitation and part-time labor union work. Even under these real constraints, recent surges in labor disputes and strikes demonstrate labor consciousness among workers in fighting for their economic interests. Although workers initiated most of these strikes, when they can ally with the labor unions and the local governments, the outcomes have been more positive (*Labor Update*, Global Standards, December 2003 to February 2004).

Over 460 nationwide strikes (between January 1995 and March 2003) revolved around vital economic issues, such as labor contracts not often signed, piece-rates lower when announced to workers, salaries and bonuses not paid on time, frequent 12-hour-plus days in peak seasons without any overtime compensation, and job instability resulting in workers overworked for 3 months and underemployed the rest of the year without any health and social insurance (*Vietnam News*, July 31, 2002; *Lao Dong* and *Tuoi Tre*, 2002, 2003). According to state media, over 80 percent of strikes took place in nonstate firms: 55 percent in foreign firms, 30 percent in domestic nonstate firms, and only 15 percent in state firms (VGCL and Vietnam News, May 7, 2002). However, I found cases of workers' protests in some state factories, not just in private enterprises as is often portrayed in the state newspapers and media.

There is evidence of successful strikes in firms with an established labor union structure (*Lao Dong*, March 2003). Labor unions assist workers, directly or indirectly, in negotiations and staging strikes. They divulge timely and important information to workers so they can preempt managers' actions, and negotiate effectively to receive their pay and bonuses on time.

Protests in a garment joint venture owned by Taiwanese and HCMC companies in two consecutive years (2001 and 2002) reflect major labor violations such as pay and work conditions; it also reflects the evolving labor union role, worker–management relations and rural–urban migration in firms with foreign investment. A feisty and friendly 24-year-old single woman from a poor fishing family in Phan Thiet (a coastal province in central Vietnam) recounted two incidents with excitement:

> On April 29, 2001 [Author's note: one day before the April 30 holiday commemorating the fall of Saigon in 1975], the Vietnamese president did not pay us 20% of our wages or our bonus, and we were supposed to work until 8:30 p.m. So many workers who planned to go home in the countryside could not go because they had no money. Therefore we went on strike. It was a very hot day. At around noon, we did not eat lunch nor take a quick nap. Instead, we gathered in front of the president's office and chanted out loud, "Paying wages, paying bonuses." When the labor union, the president and the line leader tried to get us back to work by promising to take care of this, over two thousand of us workers yelled out, "Lying, lying." Can you imagine over 2,000 workers yelling at the top of their lungs?
>
> The management locked the gate to prevent the press and media from coming in to cover this strike.
>
> Then the president spoke over a loudspeaker and asked us, "What do you all want?" We answered resoundingly, "Paying wages, paying bonuses." Under such pressure, in the afternoon, the president gave in and gave each of us 100,000 Vietnamese Dong as a bonus. (Author's note: about US$6.70; interview with T.T.L., August 2002).

This strike scored a small victory for the workers, a small bonus for the holiday. However, the greater significance is that this strike demonstrates the power of labor self-mobilization, even without the union assistance, since the labor union representative in 2001 seemed to be co-opted by the president and the line leader. It also demonstrates the power of the state media; clearly the management was concerned with bad publicity via the state media, and hence capitulated to the small concession.

In 2002, the labor union representatives in this joint venture turned around and mobilized workers to put pressure on the management. They warned the workers about the management plan of giving them each a carton of instant noodle bags (*mi goi*) instead of the more valuable year-end money bonus (just enough for them to go home for a visit). With this information, workers engaged in a preemptive campaign by telling the management that they "would be very embarrassed to receive just 'mi goi' because these are very cheap, especially in comparison to workers in other companies who expect to receive several hundreds of thousands VND as bonus." (Interview with T.T.L., August 2002). The management retorted angrily: "How come you knew about this information when even our office was not yet informed of it?" But fearing that workers might go on strike as in 2001, the management finally capitulated and gave each worker 50,000 VND as a bonus instead of the instant noodle bags. While it was a small victory, for many migrant workers coming from far-flung villages, this small bonus gave them a bus ticket home!

There is no clear gender differentiation in labor organizing and protests. Both male and female workers rise to the occasion to fight for basic decencies and to improve their miserable pay and work conditions in both state and nonstate firms. They mobilize spousal help and expose their plight in the state media. In 1999, many female workers in a state garment company in the north of Vietnam engaged in one-hour work stoppage after not receiving any positive response from the management to their request for an increase in the very low piece-rates. Their husbands protested by writing protest letters to the local television station about their wives being exploited as "*lemons squeezed to the last drop and then thrown away*" (Tran, 2001). These female workers ended up getting a small increase in piece-rates and some bonuses, although back in 1999 they were not allowed to provide inputs to the negotiations between management and their line-leaders.

When the labor union is not responsive or not available on the factory floor, workers mobilize by themselves and utilize both the state media and judicial systems to expose their plights. In 2000, workers from a large state garment firm in the North utilized the state media to stage their resistance. Desperate and distraught by humiliating treatments from their line-leaders who themselves were under tremendous pressure to deliver subcontracting orders on time during peak seasons, many workers signed on protest letters and sent them en masse to be broadcast in the Labor Union Program on the state television station and radio. From another northern state garment factory assembling clothes for export, twenty-six workers signed a poignant letter and sent it to the Hanoi People's Oversight Committee, the People's Court, and the State Investigation Agency. On that collectively signed letter, they revealed the magnitude of their unbearable working conditions, the tremendous pressure they must endure for "flexible production" during peak seasons and the underemployment in slow seasons, as well as various forms of labor repression and humiliation on the factory floor.

In sum, the brute demands of global subcontracting, while sapping workers' energy, does not undermine their collective action to fight for basic economic interests guaranteed in the Labor Code. There is evidence that workers are aware of their common economic interests (class consciousness) and when possible, they ally with the labor unions and the local governments to fight for their basic entitlements (union consciousness). However, their victories are short-term and are not addressing the larger power differentials vis-à-vis the foreign corporate buyers and the middlemen. The challenge is for the labor organizing efforts to move beyond short-term economic interests and to regain control over the production process, division of labor, and access to vital budgetary information for equitable distribution of income. Clearly, this challenge requires conscious efforts from all stakeholders: the workers, the labor unions, the party-state and the management (in state and private sectors).

Conclusion

Workers remain faithful to their historical legacy of self-mobilization to fight for their legitimate economic interests, with or without labor union assistance. They utilize resources at their disposal, spousal and labor union support, and engage in various forms of resistance: work stoppage during critical peak seasons, clever use of the power of state media and state judicial systems to expose their plight and to fight for economic equity and dignity. They expose the exploitative subcontracting piece-rate system, which treats them like a raw and disposable resource.

However, most of these spontaneous strikes and work stoppage only achieve short-term solutions. The longer-term goal is to empower the workers' bargaining power vis-à-vis the MNCs so they have more control over the production process and participate in production and distribution decisions, which ultimately affect their economic interests. Given the emerging tripartite relationships which bring together the interests of three arguably independent entities, the party-state, the labor unions, and the management (state and private), the demand for independent labor unions should entail the strengthening of the role of an increasingly independent VGCL. This more independent VGCL would then be empowered to address the various needs of the segmented labor relations in both state and private sectors.

As Vietnam further integrates into the world-economy, new issues emerge, such as the mixed effects of the Vietnam-U.S. Bilateral Textile Agreement signed in May 2003 on the workers, and the recent popularity of Codes of Conduct posted in many certified big enterprises (state and private) with the intention to show corporate social responsibility of the owners and foreign corporate buyers. However, further research is needed to examine whether these efforts truly empower the workers or if they simply provide lip service and ultimately benefit the MNCs and domestic owners while appeasing the workers and the labor unions.

Finally, cultivating alliances and interacting with external labor organizations such as the ILO and labor unions in neighboring Southeast Asian countries is necessary to exchange information and strategies and to learn from each other in fighting against the domination of flexible piecework subcontracting, in order to empower the workers and the labor unions.

Acknowledgment

I'd like to thank Dr. Nguyen-Vo Thu-Huong for her insightful and constructive feedback on an earlier draft of this work and Dr. Annette March for her helpful comments and editing. This chapter is dedicated to all workers whose perseverance and courage to fight for equity and dignity always inspire my work.

Notes

1. Those Southeast Asian governments had in varying degrees suppressed their labor movements, as most export manufacturing sectors were nonunion, in exchange for political stability to attain export-oriented-industrialization objectives (Deyo 1997: 214; Rasiah, 1993: 3–23; Bonacich, 1994: 9, 11).

2. Those special stipulations include job creation, prioritizing the hiring of women workers if they match the qualifications for a particular position, ensuring healthy and safe working conditions, improving job skills through vocational training, providing good health care coverage, and promoting good remuneration, benefits, and pay raises in order for them to work efficiently and balance responsibilities at work and at home. (Nha Xuat Ban Chinh Tri Quoc Gia Publisher, 1996: 48–51, 163–164).

3. According to Rosemarie Greve, Director, International Labour Organization, ILO Hanoi Office, it is impressive that Vietnam, as one of the few countries in the world, demands this protection for workers in the EPZs. Interview, October 22, 2003.

4. See Tran, 2002, for a detailed explanation on how to calculate piece rates and the average daily income.

5. My 1996 estimates of income/proceeds distribution in the manufacturing and marketing of a boy's dress shirt are supported by a 1998 study on the income distribution of men's shirts (Interview with Pham Quang Ham, 1998).

6. To calculate the USD equivalent, I used the average exchange rate of VND 13,274 for 1998. (Vu Quoc Huy, 2001a: 50–51, and Vu Quoc Huy, September 2001b: 78). But the fact that, on average, garment wages were higher than agricultural wages poses larger structural concerns about causes of underemployment between seasons and land being dispossessed or increasingly concentrated in fewer hands, thus making factory work in urban areas appealing to peasants.

7. Female workers doing exactly the same tasks as male workers earned only about 80 to 90 percent of what a male worker made. For instance, specialized male machine operators earned between 1.6 to 1.7 million VND (about US$107 to 113) per month, compared to only 1.3 million VND (about US$87) per month paid to their female counterparts. Fragmentation of production process blurs the line between female and male workers; at the lowest subcontracting ladder male workers are also subjected to feminine expectations. But this situation is only temporary, since most male workers used this job as a temporary platform to accumulate higher skills and to move up the subcontracting ladder. Ultimately, most change to other jobs that fulfill patriarchal, male expectations and offer better employment security and higher pay. See Tran (2002) for an in-depth analysis of the deskilling process and gender differentiations, and Tran (2004) on male workers' negotiations.

8. Irene Norlund argued this similar point about the possible nonconflictual relations between the working class and the party-state in "The Labor Market in Vietnam: Between State Incorporation and Autonomy," in *Social Change in Southeast Asia*, Johannes Schmidt (ed.), New York: Addison Wesley Longman Limited, 1998. p. 158.

9. Conversation with *Tran Dinh Toan*, vice department head of the training department in Dai Hoc Kinh Te Quoc Dan (National Economics University), July 23, 26, 2001.

10. For instance, workers were able to use state-owned facilities and machinery for their private side businesses or moonlighting.

11. "Workers will remain at the helm of revolution, affirms party leader," *Vietnam News*, October 13, 2003, pp. 1–2.

12. Interviews with Pham Thu Hang and Rosemarie Greve, July 2003. This decision is signed by the prime minister in Decision 123/2003/TTg in June 2003.

13. Interviews with Vo Van Nhat (VGCL), and Nguyen Thi Gai (Labor Union TV), July 2003.

14. Interviews with Nguyen Manh Cuong (director of foreign relations, MOLISA), Rosemarie Greve (ILO), Jan Jung-Min Sunoo (chief technical advisor, ILO), Vo Van Nhat (deputy director, international department, VGCL), July 2003.

15. Interviews with Nguyen Manh Cuong in July 2003.

16. The Trade Union Law (*Luat Cong Doan*) sanctions two types of trade union representatives: (1) full-timers who are paid by the state and partly by union members' fees (which do not amount to a significant share) and

(2) part-timers who are mostly paid by company managers–owners, and some union members' fees. (*Cong Nghiep*, Volume 11, 2001: 37–38).

17. In Vietnamese, they are "Tong lien doan, Lien doan lao dong thanh pho, Cong Doan Co So."

18. Strikes that took place in firms not having labor unions (mostly private firms) or firms having labor unions but without their approvals are considered unauthorized, wildcat, and illegal (*Vietnam News*, November 15, 2002).

19. Norlund also argued this point in her 1997 chapter, p. 179.

20. This is consistent with Lenin's argument that exposure of abuses on the factory floor is a starting point for the awakening of class consciousness, and the beginning of a trade-union struggle (Lenin, 1947: 56–57).

21. O'Rourke provides interesting case studies of community mobilization in which the case of the Taiwanese owned Dona Bochang Textile factory in Dong Nai (south Vietnam) showed that the success of this community in demanding pollution reduction from Dona Bochang comes from strength, organization, persistence of the community, as well as linkages to the state (local and national agencies) and the media. O'Rourke, 2004, pp. 65, 67–68.

37

A Revolution in Kindness

Anita Roddick

Certainly it is possible, as some may argue, for a world trade system that puts basic human rights and the environment at its core. It is possible but it is more than hard, especially when you have the most powerful corporations in the world raging against you. It is definitely enough to make you feel a bit edgy, especially when you also realize, for the first time in our history of humanity, that economic values have now superseded every other human value, and the language of economics is like a gang of thieves breaking and entering our brain and stealing our sense of compassion.

Yes, and yes, again, it is possible for trade justice to thrive if we stop being passive spectators and become actors; better still if we start rewriting the play. We then can become the hope we are looking for.

However, saying all that, I do *not* want to be labeled a consumer or a hungry consumer or a compassionate consumer — even a vigilante one. And neither should you. I am a human merely being and was *not* put on this planet for the sole purpose of keeping the economy vibrant. I will *not* tolerate that. I will *not* be held hostage in a world where nothing is considered sacred, least of all the sense of justice. We are thoughtful and creative individuals just having to coexist at this moment in our history with a mega corporate culture.

Change will *never* come about by our governments. They are economic governments and do *not* measure their greatness by how they treat the weak and the frail. Change will *not* come about by businesses that now are center stage, more creatively richer and organized than any other social institution — and still continue to show no more developed emotion than fear and greed! Change will always come about by moral dissenters and through the persistence of small committed groups of people willing to fail over long periods of time until that rare wonderful moment when the dam of oppression, indifference, and greed finally cracks, and those in power finally accept what the worlds' people have been saying all along that there now has to be a revolution in kindness.

It will be a lifetime's work to clear away all the fatuous fantasies and false promises that have been painted in our minds layer after layer, year after year, on the millions of billboards, in print and electronic ads, in a language of myth and persuasion. And if we still accept what we are told is apparently inevitable — that is, the future the media and our political and economic leaders market to us — then we merely become the audience of our own demise. It is time to declare that trade lacking justice, equity,

393

decency, and compassion is no longer acceptable. Economics, efficiency perceptions, and brutish power calculations no longer suffice; the bottom line has bottomed out.

The most radical act of individualism in which we can engage today is to come here together as students, academics, and activists in order to uncover the biggest secret our media and politicians keep from us — that we are not alone. All over the world people are asking the questions, raising the concerns, and sharing the ambivalences that might illuminate the way to a wiser and more just community.

Make no mistake about it — we are living in heady times. We are experiencing in every country on this planet a global insurgence against much of what we are taught in business as a necessary way of life. "Words create worlds," said Ludwig Wittgenstein, the Austrian philosopher. That thought has always resonated with me, for in these "heady times" there are a number of expressions that leave us such hope — phrases like "civil society" "reclaiming our common space" and "economics as if people matter." Within these remarkable sentiments are a host of social experiments and inventions.

Visit Italy, France, and Spain and experience the hundreds of cities and towns adopting the Slow Food Movement, a glorious antidote to globalization. This movement founded in the hills of Piedmont in Italy chooses to make its stand against big business by preserving and supporting traditional ways of growing, producing, and preparing food. It started as a direct response to the opening of McDonald's on Rome's Spanish Steps. Dubbed as ecogastronomy, it aims to extend the kind of attention that environmentalism has dedicated to endangered species. In the face of agribusiness, ecogastronomy has become a rallying cry for dissent.

Perhaps the real threat to corporate globalization is the irresistible appeal of carnival as a tactic of resistance and dissent. Spontaneity and pleasure are the order of the day. If resistance and rebellion are not fun and do not reflect the world we wish to create, then we will have lost that joyous abandonment and lust for life. Imagine fifty thousand Indian farmers from the state of Karnataka spending an entire day laughing outside the state government offices. (The government collapsed the following week!)

If you look really close you will see a rag-tag line encircling the globe of millions of grass roots initiatives holding together communities, educating the children, protecting the soil, and making their voices heard. At my most optimistic I interpret this as the most creative explosion of social initiatives and solidarity our history has ever seen, made more powerful by the spirit of transformation in which producing new forms of economic cooperation will allow people to work outside the relationship of dependency. To me this feels like a genuine global revolution, a revolution where ideas have wings.

I have traveled during the last few years through the epicenters of resistance, including the Ogoni villages in the Niger Delta in Nigeria. When you see for yourself oil spills, and the oil flares in abundance near villages in Oxonian, the state of the schools where the kids scratch their letters on the walls because they have no access to pen and paper .... When you visit the hospitals and speak to women who have just had Caesareans with no anesthetic .... Or see the human face of slavery in the "free zones" of Nicaragua where a young worker said to me, "All I want to do is move from slavery to poverty." From the farmers in Bolivia defending their water rights to the farmers in India challenging the might of Cargill or Monsanto, it doesn't take much to realize that the economic structure in place is a new form of slavery so that we in the West can protect our standard of living.

I heard this point time and time again. I heard it from the forest dwellers in Brazil and from the Black Family Farmers in Alabama. I heard it in Ghana within the women's cooperatives harvesting shea nuts for The Body Shop. I hear it everywhere: Political freedom without economic freedom is meaningless. This is the shared wisdom and is one of the gathering forces of dissidents, forced into an existence by capitalism more powerful than anything we have ever seen for a century.

The people involved know that freedom isn't just about the right to vote a dozen times during one's life, but the right to decide your economic as well as your political destiny, and that is precisely what economic globalization is stealing from people all over the world.

A British journalist writing in the *New Statesman* put it this way: "It knows that systems must be applied to local needs. But it also believes in global solidarity with its e-mail lists, its social forums, and summit gatherings."

It seems like this is really the new politics for a new century, and this above all else is what keeps me optimistic.

38

Globalization:
A Path to Global Understanding
or Global Plunder?

Njoki Njoroge Njehu

Globalization is a story as old as Marco Polo's voyages. While globalization has taken different forms, the phenomenon of globalization has been with us for a long time. Since the Portuguese voyages around Africa on the way to India and the Spanish claims in the Americas, globalization has always been tied to the search for trading opportunities. The link became clearer, perhaps permanent, in the 1500s and 1600s when corporations (like the Dutch West India Company and the British East India Company) were chartered to develop trade and even to impose and administer law in foreign societies. The trans-Atlantic slave trade is surely the most extreme expression of the "free trade" ideology that goes hand in hand with globalization. By the 1800s, most of the world was conquered or under the protection of European empires, each of which constituted a huge trade network. In the early 1900s, the world economy was by many measures more "globalized" than at any time until just a few years ago.

However, to hear it told by some today, it all started at the failed November 1999 World Trade Organization (WTO) ministerial meeting in Seattle. For centuries people have been part of the process of globalization. A different sort of confrontation took place in Seattle, though in fact it was about the same size as protests against the International Monetary Fund (IMF) and World Bank meetings in West Berlin in 1988. But Seattle did manage to set in motion a new approach to activism on "globalization" issues.

As the World Development Movement (U.K.) has documented in its 2000–2003 "States of Unrest" reports (www.wdm.org.uk, *States of Unrest* reports), opposition to various forms of globalization, in these instances tied to World Bank and IMF mandated austerity programs, is constant and determined in dozens of countries around the world. While the reports only cover IMF–World Bank related protests in client countries of the Global South (Africa, Asia-Pacific, the Caribbean, and Latin America), there is tremendous global opposition to programs, projects, and policies that are hallmarks of corporate globalization — privatization of water, electricity, pensions, etc.; removal of subsidies for basic foods, cooking oil, bread, flour, etc.; price hikes for petrol, heating oil, etc.; increase and/or imposition of school fees from primary education to university levels; salary cuts for teachers, nurses, and doctors, and other civil servants; and labor, trade, investment, and environmental deregulation.

The collapse of the (WTO) ministerial meeting in Cancún, Mexico, in September 2003 was both hailed as a positive development for the economies of developing countries and as a devastating blow for the future of their economies. It is too early to tell, but the most significant development in Cancún was the emergence of the bloc of developing countries, referred to as the G23, that included, importantly, countries such as Nigeria, Argentina, Indonesia, India, Brazil, and China. These countries represented a significant percentage of the world's population and some of the largest emerging-market economies. Perhaps even more important is the fact that the G23 bloc held together and spoke in one voice, in spite of tremendous pressure from the United States and the European Union. To be clear, the collapse of the Cancún WTO talks did not sink or reverse the process of globalization, nor was that the intention of campaigners who had set collapse of the talks as a goal. However, the collapse of the talks in some ways put on the brakes on the WTO negotiations, which are widely viewed, especially in the Global South, as being unfairly skewed against weak and developing countries' economies.

Some refer to globalization as a "project." Indeed, given the coordination and the resources committed to sell a wholesome idea and image of globalization, it is clear that it is a well-planned project. I have been speaking at and participating over the years in numerous and diverse forums having to do in one or another way with globalization, its direction, effects, and implications. These settings have been diverse: the United Nations World Summit on Sustainable Development (WSSD) in Johannesburg, South Africa; the United Methodist Women's National Convention; a classroom at Chulalongkorn University in Bangkok, Thailand; the Visions in Feminism conference at the University of Maryland, College Park; the Afrikafé Networking Series event titled "Africa's Debt: The IMF and World Bank," and the Pax Christi USA National Assembly. I have in these wide-ranging events received similar responses from participants when asked to share images, names, issues, or ideas that come to mind when they hear the word *globalization*. Their varied responses consistently emphasize, among other things, the following institutions, images, policies, claims, demands, and programs:

- Free trade (North American Free Trade Agreement [NAFTA], Free Trade Area of the Americas [FTAA], WTO, Plan Pueblo Panama, etc.)
- Multinational corporations such as Nike, McDonald's, Wal-Mart, Shell, Nestlé, etc.
- The stock market
- Exploitation, colonization, oppression
- International debt, odious debt, stolen wealth
- Profits before people
- Privatization
- New, more efficient technology in transportation and communications
- International financial institutions: the World Bank, the IMF, regional development banks, the Group of 8 (G8) industrialized countries
- Increasing trade between far-flung countries
- Hegemony
- Uneven balance of power and wealth between and within countries

- Hunger, poverty, disease (especially HIV/AIDS, named over and over)
- International solidarity, World Social Forum, antisweatshop campaigning
- Genetically modified foods
- "Free" or deregulated international trade, which works for countries with the most developed industries and markets, but not for others
- Sweatshops, maquiladoras, export processing zones, and many others

Given the billions of dollars spent to sell the "project," it is surprising how little people believe of what the proponents of globalization say. It is also pleasantly surprising how much people know about the assortment of supranational institutions associated with the process (such as the World Bank, the IMF, and the WTO), and that in very rare occasions is the attitude towards these institutions favorable. It may not always have been the case, but it is the case now that people are suspicious, skeptical, and concerned about the many promises and few deliverables from the globalization process. Furthermore, many people are able to sift through the negative images to lift up some positive images, relationships, and experiences of globalization that they have.

It is a short trip to the global economy: the market down the street. The global economy is entering more and more lives — by choice and by design. Costa Rican bananas are available in Washington, D.C., for 69 cents per pound; raspberries are to be enjoyed all year round; mangoes from thousands of miles away cost a dollar for two; designer vegetables are available in and out of season, and Chilean and Australian wine and designer water from major corporations can be found at the local supermarket, perhaps because it is part of a multinational chain of grocery stores. And the desire for the exotic does not end at the grocery store; international goods and services in the form of Laura Ashley clothing, Philip Van Huesen shirts, McDonald's and Wimpy's hamburgers, Dutch tulips and French roses, and Japanese and German cars are available around the world — the list goes on and on. Globalization and "free" trade make it all possible. But it is neither free nor possible to sustain. It comes with the high price of pollution and environmental destruction; the violation of human rights and labor laws; and the exploitation of finite resources, workers, and the communities in which resources are located — for example, those in the Niger Delta where oil drilling is taking place. Corporate control is increasing in the lives of people and communities around the world.

Activists and campaigners of many stripes have raised questions about economic globalization and the institutions that drive, regulate, and champion it. These activists and campaigners are variously vilified and sometimes praised for their statements of opposition and their tactics of expressing it. These activists are mistakenly referred to as "antiglobalization" but in reality are global justice activists. They are clearly in the centrality of solidarity and committed to the solidarity that the campaigning they engage in provides, from the international Jubilee Movement calling for debt cancellation, to the treatment for all HIV/AIDS-affected people, to the campaigns against privatization and an end to policies that limit peoples' access to the basics of life (safe water, food, shelter, education, and health services), and antisweatshop campaigns, etc. These campaigns are not just about opposition, but also about global solidarity, a valued and positive aspect of globalization.

Global campaigns and campaigns that include a multicountry strategy and/or coordinated action are the backbone of one of this positive aspects of globalization — global solidarity. For instance, the impact of economic globalization on women and women's particular experiences of globalization have provided or created key opportunities for articulating and strengthening the global women's movement. The process of economic globalization depends on and exploits productive and reproductive capacities in regard to women's work and women's sexuality, respectively. Looking at economic globalization from women's experiences and perspectives, it is clear that people around the world, and women in particular, are struggling for dignity, for control of their lives and their livelihoods, and for a say in the processes, projects, and programs that impact their lives.

According to the United Nations, women constitute 50 percent of the world's population and contribute to the world economy with 60 percent of the working hours. But women only receive 10 percent of the world's income and own 1 percent of the world's property. As a result three out of five of the world's impoverished are women. But women are not victims of the global economy; they are survivors of the system. They manage under very difficult conditions. They stretch to make ends meet and to provide for their families and their communities, and they stand in the gap when services (water, housing, food subsidies, healthcare, etc.) are removed or fail. And not just in the domestic sphere. Women farmers and agricultural producers from around the world — indigenous women, women farmers in the United States, women peasant farmers in Haiti and the Philippines, the *campesinas* in Nicaragua and Honduras, women among the landless workers in Brazil, rural African women farmers (who, according to the United Nations, produce over 70% of the food consumed on the continent) — all of these women see their livelihoods and their future being determined and undermined by far-away bureaucrats and institutions. Women were a majority at the Small Scale Farmers Convergence at the September 2002 United Nations World Summit on Sustainable Development (WSSD) in Johannesburg. They spoke clearly and strongly against genetic engineering, corporate control of seeds, and affirmed their role and commitment to food security.

According to the United Nations Development Fund for Women (UNIFEM), women are entering the workforce in growing numbers yet their economic situation is deteriorating and the process of globalization intensifies existing inequalities and insecurities to which poor women are already subject. Women constitute over 80 percent of sweatshop workers, most of them young women of school age who are forced into retirement by the age of 30. In dozens of countries, such as Vietnam, China, Indonesia, Mexico, Nicaragua, Honduras, Haiti, Mauritius, Saipan, and many others, women toil for long hours, often under hazardous conditions and for very little pay, producing everything from sneakers to underwear and "fashion" clothing especially for U.S. consumption and for U.S.-based multinational corporations. It is well documented that women working in sweatshops also endure sexual and physical abuse and forced "family planning" and contraception, and enjoy very little to no protection from the law. This reality of women's working conditions and their struggle for dignity and human rights has placed women on the forefront in the building of labor unions and movements around the world.

Women throughout the Global South bear the brunt of economic programs and policies that limit their access to the basics of life, such as water, food security, education, health care, and shelter. Women endure the sharp edge of IMF and World Bank structural adjustment programs (SAPs). They live, toil, and often they die too young under the yoke of SAPs. Life expectancy in a number of African countries is falling due to a combination of impoverishment and the HIV/AIDS pandemic. In some countries life expectancy is as low as 45 years. In Haiti they call SAPs *plan la morte*, the death plan.

For many women, their "slice" of the global economy is in the service sector, where they labor in restaurants and hotels, working as domestics for expatriates and employees of multilateral institutions, in the sex industry, and sold as mail-order brides. Women's human rights and bodily integrity is violated and under attack in the context of the global economy. In November 2002, when terrorists struck at the Paradise Hotel in Mombasa, Kenya, the majority of those killed were young women, some of them in their teens, whose particular slice of the global economy was to perform cultural dances for arriving tourists.

Women confront economic globalization on many fronts everyday. They struggle alongside men in their communities, countries, and in a world where profits are often placed before the rights of people and a healthy planet. Women are helping chart a different future for their families, countries, and for the planet, from the Zapatista women who are central to the fight for autonomy and justice for indigenous peoples in Mexico, to the women of Colombia who struggle for peace and have a strong voice in opposition to the U.S. "Plan Colombia" and the "war on drugs," to the women of the Narmada Valley who have led the fight against the Narmada Dam and the flooding of their homes and communities, to the women in Zambia, Kenya, South Africa, Uganda, and many other African countries, who are leading the charge in ensuring a future for children orphaned by HIV/AIDS, to the many women who led the Jubilee debt cancellation campaigns in many countries and who are now in the forefront of articulating a call for redress and reparations.

At the 1985 United Nations Decade for Women Conference in Nairobi, long before globalization became a buzzword, Lilla Watson, an aboriginal woman from Australia, articulated a clear approach to confronting the oppressive realities of a globalized world. It had to be done *in solidarity*, she insisted. "If you have come to help me, I don't need your help, but if you have come because your liberation is tied to mine, come, let us work together." For activists this is the positive aspect of globalization — global solidarity in the context of understanding that the struggles are the same and need to be fought on many fronts. This understanding is manifest in the World Social Forum process; in the international debt cancellation campaigns under the Jubilee banner; in the World March of Women; in the antiprivatization "Our World Is Not for Sale" coalition, in the international farmers network *Via Campesina*; and in many other ways. Under these and other banners, campaigners and activists develop and articulate clear and precise demands in the struggles for justice and dignity. They demand equality; sustainability and environmental protection; a globalization that puts people before profits, that is, one which meets the needs of people, not the profit margin; peace; debt cancellation so that governments are not required to sacrifice the well being of their citizenry in order to pay the banks; universal access to treatment, especially for HIV/AIDS-affected people; reparations for the harm done by decades-long policies and processes that have not delivered the promised results; respect and defense of human rights and labor rights; asserting the right to self determination and autonomy; globalization that meets the needs of people and the planet; and more.

Global justice activists are not trying to turn back the clock. Rather, we are fighting for a just world. The task is huge, but the very process of globalization and the tools and means it provides make victory possible: workers striking in solidarity with other workers in a country halfway across the world; women activists marching for their rights in dozens of countries around the world; consumers picketing and calling embassies to protest the arrest and/or mistreatment of activists in a faraway African community; 100,000 people participating in the 2003 World Social Forum in Porto Alegre, Brazil; students walking out of their classrooms to demand peace and an end to war; Maasai villagers who respond in empathy by sending fourteen head of cattle to help New Yorkers recover after the attacks of September 11, 2001; and more. Globalization may have its roots in the search for wealth, power, and control, but the search for and commitment to a just and humane process of globalization is being imagined and fought for on many fronts. It is just a matter of time.

Bibliography

Abbott, Kenneth, and Duncan Snidal. 2000. "Hard and Soft Law in International Governance," in the Special Issue on the Legalization of World Politics. *International Organization* 54 (3): 421–456.

Abbott, Kenneth, R. O. Keohane, A. Moravecisk, A. Slaughter, and Duncan Snidal. 2000. "The Concept of Legalization," in the Special Issue on the Legalization of World Politics. *International Organization* 54 (3): 401–420.

Abdul Rahman Embong. 2002. *State-Led Modernization and the New Middle Class in Malaysia.* New York: Palgrave Macmillan.

Abernathy, Frederick H., John T. Dunlop, Janice H. Hammond, and David Weil. 1999. *A Stitch in Time: Lean Retailing and the Transformation of Manufacturing — Lessons from the Apparel and Textile Industries.* New York: Oxford University Press.

Abeywardene, J., R. de Alwis, A. Jayasena, S. Jayaweera, and T. Sanmugam. 1994. *Export Processing Zones in Sri Lanka: Economic Impact and Social Issues.* Geneva: ILO.

Abraham, Leena. 2001. "Redrawing the *Lakshman Rekha*: Gender Differences and Cultural Constructions in Youth Sexuality in Urban India." *South Asia* 24, 133–156.

Ackerman, Bruce. 1997. "The Rise of World Constitutionalism." *Virginia Law Review* 83: 771–797.

Adams, Paul C. 1996. "Protest and the scale politics of telecommunications." *Political Geography* 15 (5): 419–441.

Agnew, John. 1993. "Representing Space: Space, Scale, and Culture in Social Science," in J. Duncan and D. Ley (eds.), *Place/culture/representation.* London and New York: Routledge, 251–271.

Aksoy, A., and Robins, K. 2002. "Banal Transnationalism: The Difference That Television Makes." *ESRC Transnational Communities Programme* WPTC-02-08: Oxford University Press.

Alarcón, Norma. 1983. "Chicana Feminist Literature: A Re-Vision through Malintzín/or Malintzín: Putting Flesh Back on the Object," in Cherríe Moraga and Gloria Anzaldúa, (eds.), *This Bridge Called My Back: Writing by Radical Women of Color.* New York: Kitchen Table/Women of Color, 182–190.

Albrow, Martin, and Darren J. O'Byrne. 2000. "Rethinking State and Citizenship under Globalized Conditions," in Henri Goverde (ed.), *Global and European Polity?: Organizations, Policies, Contexts.* Aldershot: Ashgate.

Albrow, Martin. 1996. *The Global Age: State and Society beyond Modernity.* Cambridge: Polity.

Alexander, M. Jacqui, and Chandra T. Mohanty (eds.), 1997. *Feminist Genealogies, Colonial Legacies, and Democratic Futures.* New York: Routledge.

Ali, T. "Business as Usual." *The Guardian* (May 24, 2003). http://www.guardian.co.uk/Iraq/Story/0,2763,962698,00.html.

Ali, T. 2002. *The Clash of Fundamentalisms: Crusades, Jihads and Modernity.* London: Verso.

Altman, Dennis. 2001. *Global Sex.* Chicago: University of Chicago Press.

Alvarez, Sonia. 2000. "Translating the Global: Effects of Transnational Organizing on Local Feminist Discourses and Practices in Latin America." *Meridians* 1 (1) (autumn): 29–67.

Amin, S. "The American Ideology." *Al-Ahram Weekly* 638 (May 15–21, 2003). http://weekly.ahram.org.eg/2003/638/focus.htm.

Amin, S. 2001. "Imperialism and Globalization." *Monthly Review* 53 (2): 6–24.

Amin, Samir. 1997. *Capitalism in an Age of Globalization.* London: Zed Books.

Amin, Samir. 1978. *The Arab Nation.* Translated by Michael Pallis. London: Zed.

Amin, A., and N. Thrift. 2002. "Spatialities of Globalisation." *Environment and Planning* A 34, 3: 385–399.

Amin, A., and N. Thrift. 1994. *Globalization, Institutions and Regional Development in Europe*. Oxford: Oxford University Press.

Amoore, L. (ed.), "Forthcoming". *The Global Resistance Reader*. London: Routledge.

AMRC, A. M. R. C. 1998. *We in the Zone: Women Workers in Asia's Export Processing Zones*, Hong Kong: Asia Monitor Resource Center.

Amsden, Alice. 2003. "Good-bye Dependency Theory, Hello Dependency Theory." *Studies in Comparative International Development* 38 (1): 32–38.

Amsden, A. H. 2001. *The Rise of "the Rest": Challenges to the West from Late-Industrializing Economies*. New York: Oxford University Press.

Amsden, Alice. 1989. *Asia's Next Giant: South Korea and Late Industrialization*. New York: Oxford University Press.

Anderson, Benedict. 1993. "The New World Disorder." *New Left Review* 193 (May/June): 2–13.

Anderson, Cynthia D., Michael D. Schulman, and Phillip J. Wood. 2001. "Globalization and Uncertainty: The Restructuring of Southern Textiles." *Social Problems* 48 (4): 478–498.

Anderson, Victor. 1995. *Beyond Ontological Blackness: An Essay on African American Religious Criticism*. New York: Continuum.

Anghie, Antony. 1999. "Finding the Peripheries: Sovereignty and Colonialism in Nineteenth Century International Law." *Harvard International Law Journal* 40 (1): 1–80.

Antrobus, Peggy. 1996. "Bringing Grassroots Women's Needs to the International Arena." *Development* 3 (June): 65-67.

Anya, James. 1996. *Indigenous Peoples in International Law*. New York: Oxford University Press.

Anzaldúa, Gloria. 1987. *Borderlands/La Frontera: The New Mestiza*. San Francisco: Spinsters/Aunt Lute.

Appadurai, Arjun. 2001. "Grassroots Globalization and the Research Imagination," in Arjun Appadurai (ed.), *Globalization*. Durham and London: Duke University Press, 1–21.

Appadurai, Arjun. 1996. *Modernity at Large: Cultural Dimensions of Globalization*. Minnesota: University of Minneapolis Press.

Appadurai, Arjun. 1995. "The Production of Locality," in R. Fardon (ed.), *Counterworks: Managing the Diversity of Knowledge*. London and New York: Routledge, 205–225.

Appadurai, A. 1990. "Disjuncture and Difference in the Global Cultural Economy." *Theory, Culture and Society* 7: 295–310.

Appelbaum, Richard P. 1998. "The Future of Law in a Global Economy," *Social & Legal Studies* 7 (2) (June): 171–192.

Appelbaum, Richard P., and Peter Dreier. 1999. "The Campus Anti-Sweatshop Movement," *The American Prospect* (September–October): 71–78.

Appelbaum, Richard P., William L. F. Felstiner, and Volkmar Gessner (eds.), 2001. *Rules and Networks: The Legal Culture of Global Business Transactions*. Oxford: Hart.

Appelbaum, Richard P., and Gary Gereffi. 1994. "Power and Profits in the Apparel Commodity Chain," in Edna Bonacich, Lucie Cheng, Norma Chinchilla, Norma Hamilton, and Paul Ong (eds.), *Global Production: The Apparel Industry in the Pacific Rim*. Philadelphia: Temple University Press.

Appelbaum, R. P., and J. Henderson, (eds.), 1992. *States and Development in the Asian Pacific Rim*. Newbury Park, CA: Sage.

Appy, Christian. 1993. *Working Class War: American Combat Soldiers in Vietnam*. Chapel Hill, NC: University of North Carolina Press.

Arendt, H. 1968. *Imperialism*. New York: Harcourt Brace.

Arendt, H. 1955. *The Origins of Totalitarianism*. London: George Allen and Unwin.

Armbruster-Sandoval, Ralph. 1995. "Cross-National Labor Organizing Strategies." *Critical Sociology* 21 (2): 75–89.

Arnason, Johann P. 1990. "Nationalism, Globalization, and Modernity," in Mike Featherstone (ed.), *Global Culture: Nationalism, Globalization, and Modernity*. Thousand Oaks, CA: Sage, 207–236.

Arrighi, Giovanni. 2003. "Tracking Global Turbulence," *New Left Review* 20: 5–72.

Arrighi, Giovanni. 2001. "Antisystemic Movements and Gramci's 'Piedmontese Function,'" paper presented at the conference The Modern World-System in the *Longue Duree*, Fernand Braudel Center, November 2–3, Binghamton University.

Arrighi, Giovanni. 1999. "Globalization, State Sovereignty, and the 'Endless' Accumulation of Capital," in David Smith, Dorothy Solinger, and Steven Topik (eds.), *States and Sovereignty in the Global Economy*. London: Routledge, 53–73.

Arrighi, Giovanni. 1996. "The Rise of East Asia and the Withering Away of the Interstate System." *Journal of World-System Research* 2 (15). http://csf.colorado.edu/jwsr/archive/vol2/v2_nf.htm.

Arrighi, Giovanni. 1994. *The Long Twentieth Century. Money, Power and the Origins of Our Times*. London: Verso.

Arrighi, Giovanni. 1990. "The Developmentalist Illusion: A Reconceptualization of the Semi-Periphery" in William G. Martin (ed.), *Semiperipheral States in the World-Economy*. Westport, CT: Greenwood.

Arrighi, Giovanni. 1982. "The Crisis of U.S. Hegemony," in Samir Amin, Giovanni Arrighi, Andre Gunder Frank, and Immanuel Wallerstein (eds.), *Dynamics of Global Crisis*. New York: Monthly Review Press.

Arrighi, Giovanni, and Jessica Drangel. 1986. "The Stratification of the World-Economy: An Exploration of the Semiperipheral Zone." *Review* (Fernand Braudel Center) 10 (1): 9–74.

Arrighi, Giovanni, and Beverly J. Silver. 1999a. "Hegemonic Transitions: A Rejoinder," in *Political Power and Social Theory*, Vol. 13.

Arrighi, Giovanni, and Beverly Silver. 1999b. *Chaos and Governance in the Modern World-System: Comparing Hegemonic Transitions*. Minneapolis: University of Minnesota Press.

Arrighi, Giovanni, Takeshi Hamashita, and Mark Selden (eds.), 2003. *The Resurgence of East Asia. 500, 150 and 50 Year Perspectives*. London and New York: Routledge.

Arrighi, Giovanni, Terence K. Hopkins, and Immanuel Wallerstein. 1989. *Antisystemic Movements*. London and New York: Verso.

Arrighi, Giovanni, Po-keung Hui, Ho-fung Hung, and Mark Selden. 2003. "Historical Capitalism East and West," in G. Arrighi, T. Hamashita, and M. Selden (eds.), *The Resurgence of East Asia. 500, 150 and 50 Year Perspectives*. London and New York: Routledge.

Arrighi, Giovanni, Beverly J. Silver, and Benjamin Brewer. 2003. "Industrial Convergence and the Persistence of the North–South Divide." *Studies in Comparative International Development* 38 (1): 3–31.

Arrighi, Giovanni, Beverly J. Silver, and Benjamin Brewer. 2003. "Response." *Studies in Comparative International Development* 38 (1): 39–42.

Artz, Donna, and Ogor Lukashuk. 1998. "Participants in International Legal Relations," in Charlotte Ku and Paul Diehl (eds.), *International Law: Classic and Contemporary Readings*. Boulder, CO: Westview, 155–176.

Asante, Molefi. 1992. *Kemet, Afrocentricity, and Knowledge*. Trenton, NJ: Africa World Press.

Asante, Molefi. 1980. *Afrocentricity: The Theory of Social Change*. Buffalo, NY: Amulefi.

Aschar, G. 2002. *The Clash of Barbarisms: September 11 and the Making of the New World Disorder*. New York: Monthly Review Press.

Aslanbeigui, N., and Summerfield, G. 2000. "The Asian Crisis, Gender, and the International Financial Architecture." *Feminist Economics* 6 (3): 81–103.

Aslanbeigui, N., S. Pressman, and G. Summerfield (eds.), 1994. *Women in the Age of Economic Transformation*. London: Routledge.

Associated Press/El Universal. 2002. En cumplimiento con el Tratado de Libre Comercio quita Estados Unidos restricciones a camiones mexicanos. *Norte* (November 28): B1.

Athreya, Bama. 2000. "We Need Immediate, Practical Solutions." *Chronicle of Higher Education*, Opinion and Arts (April 7).

Authers, J. 2003. *Hopes of Mexican Migrants to U.S. Are Chilled*. Retrieved from *The Financial Times* website http://www.esource.com/login.asp on May 7, 2003.

Axford, B. and Huggins, R. 2003. "Towards a Political Sociology of the Internet and Local Governance." *Telematics and Informatics* 20 (3): 185–194. August Special Issue on The Internet and Local Governance: Some Issues for Democracy.

Axford, B. 2001a. "Enacting Globalization: Transnational Networks and the Deterritorialization of Social Relationships in the Global System." *Protosociology* 15: 119–147.

Axford, B. 2001b. "The Transformation of Politics or Anti-Politics?" in B. Axford and R. Huggins (eds.), *New Media and Politics*. London: Sage.

Axford, B. 1995. *The Global System: Economics, Politics and Culture*. Cambridge: Polity.

Axford, B., and R. Huggins (eds.), 2001. *New Media and Politics*. Sage: London.

Axford B., and Huggins, R., "Towards a Post-National Polity: The Emergence of the Network Society in Europe," in D. Smith and S. Wright (eds.), *Whose Europe? The Turn Towards Democracy*, Oxford: Blackwell, 1999: 173–207.

Bacon, Kenneth M. 1994. "Politics Could Doom a New Currency Plan." *The Wall Street Journal* May 9: A1.

Badran, Margot. 1999. "Toward Islamic Feminisms: A Look at the Middle East," in Asma Afsaruddin, (ed.), *Hermeneutics of Honor; Negotiating Female 'Public' space in Islamicate Societies*, Cambridge, MA: Center for Middle Eastern Studies, Harvard University, 159–188.

Bailey, John. 2003. "S&P Rates HK Yue Yuen's Convertibles BBB-." Standard and Poor's Rating Service (November 28 press release).

Baird, Vanessa. 2001. *The No-Nonsense Guide to Sexual Diversity*. London: New Internationalist.

Bairoch, Paul. 1996. "Globalization Myths and Realities: One Century of External Trade and Foreign Investment," in Robert Boyer and Daniel Drache (eds.), *States against Markets: The Limits of Globalization*. London: Routledge.

Bakan, Abigail and Daiva Stasiulis, editors. 1997. *Not One of the Family: Foreign Domestic Workers in Canada*. Toronto: University of Toronto Press.

Baker-Cristales, Beth. 2004. *Salvadoran Migration to Southern California: Redefining EL Hermans Lejuno (New World Diasporas)*. University of Florida Press.

Bakhtin, Mikhail. 1968. *Rabelais and His World*. Translated by Helen Iswolsky. Cambridge, MA: MIT Press.

Balakrishnan, R. (ed.), 2002. *The Hidden Assembly Line: Gender Dynamics of Subcontracted Work in a Global Economy*. Bloomfield, CT: Kumarian.

Balassa, Bela. 1981. *The Newly Industrializing Countries in the World Economy*. New York: Pergamon.

Bales, Kevin. 1999. *New Slavery in the Global Political Economy*. Berkeley, CA: University of California Press.

Bandarage, A. 1997. *Women, Population and Global Crisis: A Political-Economic Analysis*, London: Zed.

Barber, Benjamin. 1995. *Jihad vs. McWorld*, New York: Times Books.

Barlow, Maude, and Tony Clarke. 2001. *Global Showdown: How the New Activists Are Fighting Global Corporate Rule*. Toronto: Stoddart.

Barrett, Richard, and Martin Whyte. 1982. "Dependency Theory and Taiwan: Analysis of a Deviant Case." *American Journal of Sociology* 87 (5): 1064–1089.

Basch, Linda, Nina Glick Schiller, and Cristina Szanton Blanc. 1994. *Nations Unbound: Transnational Projects, Postcolonial Predicaments, and Deterritorialized Nation-States*. New York: Gordon and Breach.

Bassan, Daniela. 1996. "The Canadian *Charter* and Public International Law: Redefining the State's Powers to Deport Aliens." *Osgoode Hall Law Journal* 34 (3): 583–625.

Basu, Amrita. 2000. "Globalization of the Local/Localization of the Global: Mapping Transnational Women's Movements." *Meridians* 1 (1) (autumn).

Basu, A. (ed.), 1995. *The Challenge of Local Feminisms: Women's Movements in Global Perspective*. Boulder, CO: Westview.

Bechat, Jean-Paul, and Felix Rohatyn. 2002. "Trans-Atlantic Drift Threatens Common Security." *International Herald Tribune* 6–19.

Beck, Ulrich. 2001. "The Cosmopolitan Society and Its Enemies," in Luigi Tomasi (ed.), *New Horizons in Sociological Theory and Research: The Frontiers of Sociology at the Beginning of the 21st Century*. Aldershot: Ashgate. 181–202.

Beck, Ulrich. 2000. *What Is Globalization?* Oxford: Polity.

Beck, Ulrich. 2000. "The Cosmopolitan Perspective: Sociology of the Second Age of Modernity." *British Journal of Sociology* 51 (1): 79–105.

Beck, Ulrich. 1999. *World Risk Society*. Malden, MA: Polity.

Beck, Ulrich. 1992. *Risk Society: Towards a New Modernity*. Translated by M. Ritter. London: Sage.

Beek, K. A. V. 2001. "Maquiladoras: Exploitation or Emancipation? An Overview of the Situation of Maquiladora Workers in Honduras." *World Development* 29 (9): 1553–1567.

Bello, Walden. 2003. *Deglobalization: Ideas for a New World Economy*. London: Zed Books.

Bello, Walden. 2001. *The Future in the Balance: Essays on Globalization and Resistance.* Oakland, CA: Food First Books.

Bello, Walden, and Stephanie Rosenfeld. 1990. *Dragons in Distress: Asia's Miracle Economies in Crisis.* San Francisco: Institute for Food and Development Policy.

Beneria, L. 2003. *Gender, Development, and Globalization: Economics as if All People Mattered.* New York: Routledge.

Benería, Lourdes, and Amy Lind. 1995. "Engendering International Trade: Concepts, Policy, and Action," The Gender, Science, and Development Programme Working Paper Series No. 5 (July).

Beneria, Lourdes and Marta Roldan. 1987. *Crossroads of Class and Gender: Homework, Subcontracting, and Household Dynamics in Mexico City,* University of Chicago Press.

Beresford, Melanie, and Chris Nyland. 1998. "The Labour Movement of Vietnam." *Labour History* 75 (November).

Berger, J. 2003. "Fear Eats the Soul." *The Nation* 276 (18) (May 12): 33–35.

Bergesen, Albert J., and Omar A. Lizardo. 2004. "Terrorism and Hegemonic Decline," in Jonathan Friedman and Christopher Chase-Dunn (eds.), *Hegemonic Declines: Past and Present.* Paradigm.

Berkovitch, Nitza. 1999. *From Motherhood to Citizenship: Women's Rights and International Organizations.* Baltimore, MD: Johns Hopkins University Press.

Bernstein, Eduard. 1961 [1899]. *Evolutionary Socialism: A Criticism and Affirmation.* Translated by Edith C. Harvey. New York: Schocken Books.

Bérubé, Michael. 2004. As retrieved from Michael Bérubé Online: http://www.michaelberube.com/EE/index.php

Beuf, Ann. 1990. *Beauty Is the Beast.* Philadelphia: University of Pennsylvania Press.

Beyer, Peter. 1994. *Religion and Globalization.* London: Sage.

Bhavnani, Kum-Kum. 2000. "Organic Hybridity or Commodification of Hybridity? Comments on *Mississippi Masala.*" *Meridians* 1 (1): 187–203.

Bhavnani, Kum-Kum, John Foran, and Priya A. Kurian. 2003. "An Introduction to Women, Culture and Development," in Kum-Kum Bhavnani, John Foran, and Priya A. Kurian, (eds.), *Feminist Futures: Re-imagining Women, Culture and Development.* London: Zed, 1–21.

Bhavnani, Kum-Kum, John Foran, and Priya Kurian (eds.), 2003. *Feminist Futures: Re-Imagining Women, Culture, and Development.* London: Zed Books.

Bienefeld, Manfred. 2000. "Structural Adjustment: Debt Collection Device or Development Policy?" *Review* 23 (4): 533–582.

Biersteker, Thomas J., Rodney Bruce Hall, and Craig N. Murphy (eds.), 2002. *Private Authority and Global Governance.* Cambridge: Cambridge University Press.

Bixler-Márquez, D. J. 1997. Antecedentes políticos y socioeconómicos de la operación de la patrulla fronteriza, "Hold the Line" paper presented at the Sixth International Congress of Regional History, November 11, Universidad Autónoma de Ciudad Juárez, Chihuahua, México.

Blackburn, Robin (ed.), 1972. *Ideology in Social Science: Readings in Critical Social Theory.* Suffolk, U.K.: Fontana/Collins.

Blackwood, Evelyn, and Saskia E. Wieringo (eds.), 1999. *Female Desires: Same Sex Relations and Transgender Practice across Cultures.* New York: Columbia Univerisity Press.

Bluestone, Barry and Bennett Harrison. 1982. *Deindustrialization of America: Plant Closings, Community Abandonment and the Dismantling of Basic Industry.* New York: Basic Books.

Bodnar, John, Roger Simon, and Michael P. Weber. 1982. *Lives of Their Own: Blacks, Italians, & Poles in Pittsburg, 1900–1960.* University of Illinois Press.

Bohman, J., and M. Lutz-Bachmann (eds.), 1997. *Perpetual Peace: Essays on Kant's Cosmopolitan Ideal.* Cambridge, MA: MIT Press.

Boje, David. 2000. "Pou Chen, Adidas, and Nike." New Mexico State University: College of Business Administration and Economics. http://cbae.nmsu.edu/~dboje/nike/pou_chen_and_nike.htm.

Bonacich, Edna, and Richard Appelbaum. 2000. *Behind the Label: Inequality in the Los Angeles Garment Industry.* Berkeley, CA: University of California Press.

Bonacich, Edna et al. 1994. *Global Production: The Apparel Industry in the Pacific Rim.* Philadelphia: Temple University Press.

Bonilla, Frank, Melendez, Edwin, Morales, Rebecca, and Torres, Maria de los Angeles (eds.), 1998. *Borderless Borders*. Philadelphia: Temple University Press.

Bonney, Joseph. 2003. "Retailers Reign." *Journal of Commerce* Special Report on Top Importers and Exporters. (April 28): 4A-6A, 18A-26A.

Bookman, Jay. 2002. "The President's Real Goal in Iraq," *Atlanta-Journal Constitution* (September 29).

Bornschier, Volker, and Christopher Chase-Dunn (eds.), 2000. *The Future of Global Conflict*. London: Sage.

Borosage, Robert L. 1999. "The Global Turning," *The Nation* (July 19): 19–22.

Borunda, D. 2003. Smuggling on the Rise, Officials Say. *The El Paso Times* (May 17): B3.

Bose, Sugata. 1997. "Instruments and Idioms of Colonial and National Development: India's Historical Experience in Comparative Perspective," in Frederick Cooper and Randall Packard (eds.), *International Development and the Social Sciences*. Berkeley, CA: University of California Press.

Boswell, Terry, and Christopher Chase-Dunn. 2000. *The Spiral of Capitalism and Socialism: Toward Global Democracy*. Boulder, CO: Lynne Rienner.

Bourdieu, Pierre. 1984. *Distinction: A Social Critique of the Judgement of Taste*. Cambridge, MA: Harvard University Press.

Bourguignon, Francois, and Christian Morrisson. 2002. "Inequality among World Citizens: 1820–1992." *The American Economic Review* 92 (4): 727–744.

Bové, José, and François Dufour. 2000. *Le monde n'est pas une merchandise: Des paysans contre la malbouffe*. Paris: Éditions La Découverte.

Braudel, Fernand. 1994. *A History of Civilizations*. Translated by Richard Mayne. New York: Penguin.

Braudel, Fernand. 1990. *Afterthoughts on Material Civilization and Capitalism*. Translated by Patricia Ranum. Baltimore, MD: Johns Hopkins University Press.

Braudel, Fernand. 1984. *Civilization and Capitalism, 15th–18th Century, III: The Perspective of the World*. New York: Harper & Row.

Braudel, Fernand. 1980. *On History*. Translated by Sarah Matthews. Chicago: University of Chicago Press.

Brecher, Jeremy, John Brown Childs, and Jill Cutler (eds.), 1993. *Global Visions: Beyond the New World Order* Boston: South End Press.

Brecher, Jeremy, Tim Costello, and Brendan Smith. 2000. *Globalization From Below. The Power of Solidarity*. Boston: South End Press.

Brenner, Neil. 1998. "Global Cities, Glocal States: Global City Formation and State Territorial Restructuring in Contemporary Europe." *Review of International Political Economy* 5 (2): 1–37.

Brenner, N. 1997. "Global, Fragmented, Hierarchical: Henri Lefebvre's Geographies of Globalization." *Public Culture* 10: 135–168.

Brenner, R. 2002. *The Boom and the Bubble: the U.S. in the World Economy*. London: Verso.

Brennan, Teresa. 2003. *Globalization and Its Terrors: Daily Life in the West*. London and New York: Routledge.

Brettell, Caroline B., and Patricia A. deBerjeois. 1992. "Anthropology and the Study of Immigrant Women" in D. Gabaccia (ed.), *Seeking Common Ground: Multidisciplinary Studies of Immigrant Women in the United States*. Westport, CT: Greenwood, 41–64.

Brettell, Caroline B., and Rita J. Simon. 1986. "Immigrant Women: An Introduction," in R. J. Simon and C. B. Brettell, (eds.), *International Migration: The Female Experience*. New Jersey: Rowman & Allenheld, 3–21.

Broad, Robin. 1988. *Unequal Alliance: The World Bank, the International Monetary Fund & the Philippines*. Berkeley, CA: University of California Press.

Broad, Robin. 2002. *Global Backlash: Citizen Initiatives for a Just World Economy*. Landham, MD: Rowman & Littlefield.

Brown, C. 2001. "Cosmopolitanism, World Citizenship and Global Civil Society." *Critical Review of International Social and Political Philosophy* (3): 7–26.

Brower, Charles. 1998. "The Iran–United States Claims Tribunal: Its Contribution to the Law of State Responsibility." *Emory International Law Review* 12 (3).

Brownlie, Ian. 1998. *Principles of Public International Law*, 5th edition. Oxford: Clarendon.

Brzezinski, Matthew. "The Unmanned Army." *The New York Times* (April 18, 2003).

Buchler, Simone. 2002. "Women in the informal economy of Sao Paulo." Paper prepared for the National Academy of Sciences, forthcoming in *Background Papers. Panel on Cities.* Washington, D.C. National Academy of Sciences.

Buijs, G. 1993. *Migrant Women: Crossing Boundaries and Changing Identities.* Oxford: Berg.

Bulbeck, Chilla. 1998. *Re-Orienting Western Feminisms: Women's Diversity in a Postcolonial World.* Cambridge: Cambridge University Press.

Bunting, Madeleine. "Comment: We Are the people." *The Guardian* (February 17, 2003). http://www.guardian.co.uk.

Burbach, Roger, and William I. Robinson. 1999. "The Fin De Siecle Debate: Globalization as Global Shift." *Science and Society* 63 (1): 10–39.

Burley, Anne-Marie. 1992. "Law among Liberal States: Liberal Internationalism and the Act of State Doctrine." *Columbia Law Review* 92 (8): 1907–1996.

Calabrese, Andrew, and Jean-Claude Burgelman. 1999. *Communication, Citizenship, and Social Policy. Rethinking the Limits of the Welfare State.* Lanham, MD: Rowman & Littlefield.

Callahan, D. 1999. *What is Global Civil Society?*, http://www.civnet/org/journal/vol3no1/ftdcall.htm.

Calleo, David, P. 1987. *Beyond American Hegemony: The Future of the Western Alliance,* New York: Basic Books.

Calleo, David P. 2003. *Rethinking Europe's Future.* Princeton, NJ: Princeton University Press.

Callinicos, A. "War under Attack." *Socialist Review* 273 (April, 2003). http://www.swp.org.uk/SR/273/SR2.HTM.

Callinicos, A. "State of Discontent." *Socialist Review* 272 (March, 2003). http://www.swp.org.uk/SR/272/SR2.HTM.

Campbell, Connie. 1995. "Out on the Front Lines but Still Struggling for Voice: Women in the Rubber Tappers' Defense of the Forest in Xapuri, Acre, Brazil," in Diane Rocheleau, Barbara Thomas-Slayter, and Esther Wangari (eds.), *Feminist Political Ecology: Global Issues and Local Experiences.* London: Routledge, 27–61.

Cantú, Lionel. 2000. "Entre Hombres/between Men: Latino Masculinities and Homosexualities," in P. Nardi (ed.), *Gay Masculinities.* Thousand Oaks, CA: Sage, 224–246.

Caplan, Pat (ed.), 1989. *The Cultural Construction of Sexuality.* London: Routledge.

Capra, F. 2002. *The Hidden Connections: A Science for Sustainable Living.* London: Harper Collins.

Cardoso, Fernando H., and Enzo Faletto. 1979. *Dependency and Development in Latin America.* Berkeley, CA: University of California Press.

Carr, E. H. 1964. *The Twenty Years' Crisis, 1919–1939.* New York: Harper & Row.

Castells, Manuel. 1997. *The Rise of the Network Society.* Oxford: Blackwell.

Castells, M., L. Goh, and R.Y-W. Kwok. 1990. *The Shek Kip Mei Syndrome: Economic Development and Public Housing in Hong Kong and Singapore.* London: Pion.

Castles, Stephen, and Mark J. Miller. 1998. *The Age of Migration: International Population Movements in the Modern World,* 2nd edition. New York and London: Guilford.

Castro, Arachu, and Laure Marchand-Lucas. 2000. "Does Authoritative Knowledge in Infant Nutrition Lead to Successful Breast-Feeding? A Critical Perspective," in L. M. Whiteford and L. Manderson (eds.), *Global Health Policy, Local Realities: The Fallacy of the Level Playing Field.* Boulder, CO: Lynne Rienner, 233–263.

Castro-Gomez, Santiago. 2003. "La Hybris del Punto Cero: Biopolíticas imperiales y colonialidad del poder en la Nueva Granada (1750–1810)." Unpublished manuscript. Bogotá, Colombia: Instituto Pensar, Universidad Javeriana.

Cerny, P.G. 2000. "Structuring the Political Arena: Public Goods, States and Governance in a Globalizing World." in Ronen Palan (ed.), *Global Political Economy: Contemporary Theories.* London: Routledge, 21–35.

Chalmers, Alan, F. 2000. *What is this Thing Called Science?,* 3rd edition. Indianapolis, IN: Hackett.

Chandhoke, N. 2001. "The Limits of Global Civil Society," in H. Anheier et al. (eds.), *Global Civil Society 2001.* Oxford: Oxford University Press.

Chang, Grace and Mimi Abramovitz. 2000. *Disposable Domestics: Immigrant Women Workers in the Global Economy.* Boston: South End Press.

Chang, H-J. 2002. *Kicking Away the Ladder: Development Strategy in Historical Perspective.* London: Anthem Books.

Chang, H-J. 1998. "Korea: The Misunderstood Crisis." *World Development* 26 (8): 1555–1561.

Chang, H-J. 1994. *The Political Economy of Industrial Policy.* London: Macmillan.

Chant, Sylvia. 1995. "Women's Roles in Recession and Economic Restructuring in Mexico and the Philippines," in Alan Gilbert (ed.), *Poverty and Global Adjustment: The Urban Experience.* Oxford: Blackwell.

Chant, Sylvia. 1992. *Gender and Migration in Developing Countries.* London: Behaven.

Chase-Dunn, Christopher. 2002. "Globalization from below: toward a collectively rational and democratic global commonwealth." *Annals of the American Academy of Political and Social Science* Vol. 581 (May).

Chase-Dunn, Christopher. 1999. "Globalization: A World-Systems Perspective," *Journal of World-Systems Research* 5 (2): 187–216 (summer). http://csf.colorado.edu/jwsr/archive/vol5/vol5_number2/html/chase-dunn/index.shtml.

Chase-Dunn, Christopher. 1998. *Global Formation: Structures of the World-Economy,* 2nd edition. Lanham, MD: Rowman & Littlefield.

Chase-Dunn, Christopher, and Peter Grimes. 1995. "World-Systems Analysis." *Annual Review of Sociology* 21, 387–417.

Chase-Dunn, Christopher, and Bruce Podobnik. 1995. "The Next World War: World-System Cycles and Trends." *Journal of World-Systems Research* 1 (6).

Chase-Dunn, Christopher, Rebecca Giem, Andrew Jorgenson, Thomas Reifer, and John Rogers. 2003. "The Trajectory of the United States in the World-System: A Quantitative Reflection." IROWS Working Paper # 8. http://irows.ucr.edu/papers/irows8/irows8.htm.

Chase-Dunn, Christopher, and Thomas D. Hall. 1997. *Rise and Demise: Comparing World Systems.* Boulder, CO: Westview.

Chase-Dunn, Christopher, Yukio Kawano, and Benjamin D. Brewer. 2000. "Trade Globalization Since 1795: Waves of Integration in the World-system." *American Sociological Review* 65 (1): 77–95.

Cheah, Pheng. 1998. "Introduction Part II: The Cosmopolitical — Today," in Pheng Cheah and Bruce Robbins (eds.), *Cosmopolitics: Thinking and Feeling beyond the Nation.* Minneapolis: University of Minnesota Press, 20–44.

Chen, M., Sebstad, J., and O'Connell, L. 1999. "Counting the Invisible Workforce: The Case of Home-based Workers." *World Development* 27 (3): 603–610.

Cheng, Lucie, and Edna Bonacich (eds.), 1984. *Labor Migration under Capitalism: Asian Workers in the United States before World War II.* Berkeley and Los Angeles: University of California Press.

Cheru, Fantu. 2002. *African Renaissance: Roadmaps to the Challenge of Globalization.* London: Zed Books.

Chin, Christine B. N. 1998. *In Service and Servitude: Foreign Female Domestic Workers and the Malaysian "Modernity" Project.* New York: Columbia University Press.

Chin, Christine. B. N. 1997. "Walls of Silence and Late Twentieth Century Representations of the Foreign Female Domestic Worker: The Case of Filipino and Indonesian Female Servants in Malaysia." *International Migration Review* 31 (2): 353–385.

Choudry, A. 2002. "All this Global Civil Society Talk Takes Us Nowhere." http://globalresearch.ca/articles/AZ1202A.html.

Chua, Peter, Kum-Kum Bhavnani, and John Foran. 2000. "Women, Culture, Development: A New Paradigm for Development Studies?" *Ethnic and Racial Studies* 23 (5) (September): 820–841.

Clark, J. 2003. *Worlds Apart: Civil Society and the Battle for Ethical Globalization,* London: Earthscan.

Clarke, Anne Marie, Elisabeth Friedman, and Kathryn Hochstetler. (1998). "The Sovereign Limits of Global Civil Society: A Comparison of NGO Participation in UN Conferences on the Environment, Human Rights, and Women." *World Politics* 51: 1–35.

Clarke, Tony, and Maude Barlow. 1997. *MAI. The Multilateral Agreement on Investment and the Threat to Canadian Sovereignty.* Toronto: Stoddart.

Clean Clothes Campaign. 2002. Update on Mexmode (Kukdong) (April 18). http://www.clean-clothes.org/companies/nike02-04-18.htm.

Cleaver, Harry. 2000. *Reading Capital Politically.* Edinburgh: AK Press; Leeds: Antithesus.

Cleaver, Harry. 1998. "The Zapatista Effect: The Internet and the Rise of an Alternative Political Fabric." *Journal of International Affairs* 51 (2): 621–640.

Cleeland, Nancy. "Garment Makers' Compliance with Labor Laws Slips in L.A." *Los Angeles Times* (September 21, 2000): A-1.

Clinton, William Jefferson. 1999. Telephone Interview with Michael Paulson of the Seattle Post-Intelligencer in San Francisco, November 30, 1999. Public Papers of the Presidents: William J. Clinton — 1999, Vol. 2. U.S. Government Printing Office, Washington, D.C.: 2180–2184. Retrieved from http://www.gpo.gov/nara/pubpaps/srchpaps.html on October 19, 2001.

Coffman, Vance. 2000. "The Defense Industry Today: Implications for Transatlantic Cooperation." The Atlantic Council of the United States (April).

Cohen, Benjamin. 1998. *The Geography of Money*. Ithaca: Cornell University Press.

Colen, Shellee. 1995. "'Like a Mother to Them': Stratified Reproduction and West Indian Childcare Workers and Employers in New York." *Conceiving the New World Order: The Global Politics of Reproduction.* Faye Ginsburg and Rayna Rapp, editors. Berkeley: University of California Press: 78–102.

Collins, Patricia Hill. 1993. "Setting Our Own Agenda." *The Black Scholar* 23 (3, 4): 52–55.

Collins, Patricia Hill. 1990. *Black Feminist Thought: Knowledge, Consciousness and the Politics of Empowerment.* New York: Routledge, Chapman & Hall.

Coltrane, Scott and Justin Galt. 2000. "The History of Men's Caring." *Care Work: Gender, Labour and the Welfare State.* Madonna Harrington Meyer (ed.), New York and London: 15–36.

Connell, Robert W. 2000. *The Men and the Boys*. Berkeley, CA: University of California Press.

Conroy, Martin, 2000. *Sustaining the New Economy: Work, Family, and Community in the Information Age.* New York: Russell Sage Foundation Press and Cambrdige, MA: Harvard University Press.

Constable, Nicole. 2003. "A Transnational Perspective on Divorce and Marriage: Filipina Wives and Workers." *Identities* 10: 163–180.

Constable, Nicole. 2002. "Filipina Workers in Hong Kong Homes: Household Rules and Relations," in Barbara Ehrenreich and Arlie Russell Hochschild (eds.), *Global Woman: Nannies, Maids, and Sex Workers in the New Economy.* New York: Henry Holt, 115–141.

Constable, N. 1997. *Maid to Order in Hong Kong: Stories of Filipina Workers.* Ithaca: Cornell University Press.

Cooley, John. 1999. Unholy Wars: *Afghanistan, America and International Terrorism.* London: Pluto Press.

Cooper, Frederick, and Ann Laura Stoler. 1997. *Tensions of Empire. Colonial Cultures in a Bourgeois World.* Berkeley and Los Angeles: University of California Press.

Cooper, Frederick. 1996. *Decolonization and African Society: The Labor Question in French and British Africa.* Cambridge University Press.

Corbridge, Stuart, Ron Martin, and Nigel Thrift (eds.), 1994. *Money, Power, and Space.* Oxford: Blackwell.

Cowan, M. P., and R. W. Shenton. 1996. *Doctrines of Development*. New York: Routledge.

Cox, Kevin R. 1998. "Spaces of Dependence, Spaces of Engagement and the Politics of Scale, or: Looking for Local Politics." *Political Geography* 17 (1): 1–23.

Cox, Kevin R. (ed.), 1997. *Spaces of Globalization: Reasserting the Power of the Local.* New York: Guilford.

Cox, M. (ed.), 2000. *E. H. Carr: A Critical Appraisal.* London and New York: Palgrave.

Cox, Robert W. 1996. "A Perspective on Globalization," in James Mittelman (ed.), *Globalization: Critical Reflections.* Boulder, CO: Lynne Rienner, 21–30.

Cox, Robert, W. 1995. "Critical Political Economy," in Bjorne Hettne (ed.), *International Political Economy: Understanding Global Disorder.* London: Zed, 31–45.

Cox, Robert W. 1986. "Social Forces, States, and World Orders: Beyond International Relations Theory," in Robert Keohane (ed.), *Neorealism and Its Critics.* New York: Columbia University Press, 204–254.

Cox, Robert W., with Michael G. Schechter. 2002. *The Political Economy of a Plural World: Critical Reflections on Power, Morals and Civilization.* London: Routledge.

Crane, Conrad. 2002. "Controlling Chaos: U.S. National Strategy in a Globalizing World." Strategic Issues. Strategic Studies Institute, U.S. Army War College.

Cruz-Malavé, Arnaldo, and Martin Manalansan, IV (eds.), 2002. *Queer Globalizations: Citizenship and the Afterlife of Colonialism.* New York: New York University Press.

Csordas, Thomas J. 2002. *Body/Meaning/Healing*. New York: Palgrave MacMillan.

Cumings, Bruce. 1999. "The American Ascendancy: The Making and Remaking of Liberal Social Order, 1939–1999," paper presented at the 21st annual World History Conference March, University of California, Irvine, CA.

Cumings, Bruce. 1998. "The Korean Crisis and the End of 'Late' Development." *New Left Review* 231 (September/October): 43–72.

Cutler, A. Claire. 2003. *Private Power and Global Authority: Transnational Merchant Law in the Global Political Economy*. Cambridge: Cambridge University Press.

Cutler, A. Claire. 2001. "Law in the Global Polity," in Richard Higgott and Morten Ougaard (ed.), *Towards a Global Polity*. London: Routledge.

Cutler, A. Claire. 2001. "Critical Reflections on the Westphalian Assumptions of International Law and Organization: a Crisis of Legitimacy." *Review of International Studies* 27: 133–150.

Cutler, A. Claire. 2000. "Globalization, Law and Transnational Corporations: A Deepening of Market Discipline," in T. Cohn, S. McBride, and J. Wiseman (eds.), *Power in the Global Era: Grounding Globalization*. Houndsmills, Bassingstoke, Hampshire: Macmillan and New York: St. Martin's Press, 53–66.

Cutler, A. Claire. 1999. "Public Meets Private: The International Unification and Harmonisation of Private International Trade Law." *Global Society* 13 (1): 25–48.

Cutler, A. Claire. 1995. "Global Capitalism and Liberal Myths: Dispute Resolution in Private International Trade Relations." *Millennium: Journal of International Studies* 24 (3) (winter): 377–397.

Cutler, A. Claire, Virginia Haufler, and Tony Porter (eds.), 1999. *Private Authority in International Affairs*. New York: State University of New York Press.

Dahlgren, P. 2001. "The Transformation of Democracy?," in B. Axford and R. Huggins (eds.), *New Media and Politics*. Sage: London.

Dai, X. 2003. "A New Mode of Governance? Transnationalisation of European Regions and Cities in the Information Age." *Telematics and Informatics* 20 (3): 193–215.

Da Matta, Roberto. 1991. *Carnivals, Rogues and Heroes. An Interpretation of the Brazilian Dilemma*. Notre Dame: University of Notre Dame Press.

Danaher, Kevin, (ed.), 2001. *Democratizing the Global Economy: The Battle against the World Bank and the International Monetary Fund*. Monroe, ME: Common Courage Press.

Danforth, Loring. 2000. "Ecclesiastical Nationalism and the Macedonian Question in the Australian Diaspora," in Victor Roudometof (ed.), *The Macedonian Question: Culture, Historiography, Politics*. Boulder, CO: East European Monographs, distributed by Columbia University Press, 25–54.

Danforth, Loring. 1995. *The Macedonian Conflict: Ethnic Nationalism in a Transnational World*. Princeton, NJ: Princeton University Press.

Daniel, G. Reginald. 2002. *More Than Black? Multiracial Identity and the New Racial Order*. Philadelphia: Temple University Press.

Daniel, G. Reginald. 1992. "Eurocentrism, Afrocentrism, or Holocentrism?" *Interrace Magazine* 3 (2) (1992): 33.

Das, Gurcharan. 2001. *India Unbound: A Personal Account of a Social and Economic Revolution from Independence to the Global Information Age*. New York: Knopf.

Davis, Diana E., (ed.), 1999. "Chaos and Governance." *Political Power and Social Theory,* Vol. 13, Part IV: Scholarly Controversy. Stamford, CT: JAI.

Davis, Mike. 2002. *Late Victorian Holocausts*. London: Verso.

De Angelis, M. "From Movement to Society," in *The Commoner* 4 (May, 2002). http://www.commoner.org.uk/01-3groundzero.htm.

de Landa, Manuel. 1997. *A Thousand Years of Nonlinear History*. New York: Zone Books.

Deacon, B. 1997. *Global Social Policy: International Organisations and the Future of Welfare*. London: Sage.

Del Castillo, G. 2001. "Between Order and Chaos: Management of the Westernmost Border between Mexico and the United States," in Demetrios G. Papademetriou and Deborah Waller Meyers (eds.), *Caught in the Middle: Border Communities in an Era of Globalization*. New York: Carnegie Endowment for International Peace/The Brookings Institute Press, 117–161.

Delaney, Bob. 2002. "13th Annual Cass/ProLogis State of Logistics Report." Cass Information Systems and ProLogis.

Delanty, Gerard. 2000. *Citizenship in a Global Age: Society, Culture, Politics*. Philadelphia: Open University Press.

Delgado, Gian Carlo. 2002. "Biopiracy and Intellectual Property as the Basis for Biotechnological Development: The Case of Mexico." *International Journal of Politics, Culture, and Society* 16 (2): 297–318.

Derbez, L. E. 2003. Keynote address at the Meeting of Mexican Consuls, Secretaría de Relaciones Exteriores. Tucson, AZ: Reported in GALAVISION (March 6).

Derné, Steve. 2004. "Globalizing Gender Culture: Transnational Cultural Flows and the Intensification of Male Dominance in India." pp 1–50 in *Occasional Papers* of the Office of Women's Research, University of Hawaii – Manoa, HI.

Derné, Steve. 2002. "Globalization and the Reconstitution of Local Gender Arrangements." *Men and Masculinities* 5 (2) (October): 144–164.

Derné, Steve. 2000. *Movies, Masculinity, and Modernity: An Ethnography of Men's Filmgoing in India*. Westport, CT: Greenwood.

Derné, Steve. 1995. *Culture in Action: Family Life, Emotion, and Male Dominance in Banaras, India*. Albany, NY: SUNY.

Desjarlais, Robert. 1997. *Shelter Blues*. Philadelphia: University of Pennsylvania Press.

Dewey, J. 1927. "Imperialism Is Easy." *The New Republic* 50 (March 23). http://www.boondocksnet.com/ai/ailtexts/dewey.html, in Jim Zwick (ed.), *Anti-Imperialism in the United States, 1898–1935*. http://www.boondocksnet.com/ai/.

Deyo, Frederic. 1997. "Labour and Industrial Restructuring in South-East Asia," in Garry Rodan, Kevin Hewison, and Richard Robison (eds.), *The Political Economy of South-East Asia: An Introduction*. Melbourne: Oxford University Press.

Deyo, Frederic. 1989. *Beneath the Miracle: Labor Subordination in the New Asian Industrialism*. Berkeley, CA: University of California Press.

Dezalay, Yves, and Bryant Garth. 1996. *Dealing in Virtue: International Commercial Arbitration and the Construction of a Transnational Legal Order*. Chicago and London: University of Chicago Press.

Diani, M. 2000. "Networks and Social Movements: From Metaphor to Theory?," presented to the Conference on Social Movements Analysis: The Network Perspective, June 23–25, Ross Priory, Loch Lomond, Scotland.

Dicken, Peter. 1998. *Global Shift: The Internationalization of Economic Activity*, 3rd edition. New York: Guilford.

Dicken, Peter, Philip F. Kelly, Kris Olds, and Henry Wai-Chung Yeung. 2001. "Chains and Networks, Territories and Scales: Towards a Relational Framework for Analysing the Global Economy." *Global Networks* 1 (2): 89–112.

Dickey, Sara. 2002. "Anjali's Prospects: Class Mobility in Urban India," in Diane P. Mines and Sarah Lamb (eds.), *Everyday Life in South Asia*. Bloomington: Indiana University Press, 214–226.

Dollar, David, and Aart Kraay. 2000. "Growth Is Good for the Poor." Development Research Group, The World Bank.

Dombrowski, Peter. 2000. "Alternative Futures in War and Conflict: Implications for U.S. National Security in the Next Century." Newport, RI: Strategic Research Department Center for Naval Warfare Studies, Naval War College (April).

Dominguez, Virginia. 1998. "Asserting (Trans)Nationalism and the Social Conditions of Its Possibility." *Communal/Plural* (6) 2: 139–156.

Donato, Katharine M. 1992. "Understanding U.S. Immigration: Why Some Countries Send Women and Others Send Men," in D. Gabaccia (ed.), *Seeking Common Ground: Multidisplinary Studies of Immigrant Women in the United States*. Westport, CT: Praeger, 159–184.

Donnelly, Thomas. 1997. "Rebuilding America's Defenses: Strategy, Forces and Resources for a New Century." Washington, D.C., The Project for the New American Century. 4, i.

Dore, R. 2000. *Stock Market Capitalism — Welfare Capitalism: Germany and Japan versus the Anglo-Saxons*. Oxford: Oxford University Press.

Douglas, Mary. 1992. *Risk and Blame: Essays in Cultural Theory*. London and New York: Routledge.

Drucker, Peter (ed.), 2002. *Different Rainbow*. London: Gay Men's Press.

Dudziak, Mary L. 2000. *Cold War Civil Rights: Race and the Image of American Democracy*. Princeton, NJ: Princeton University Press.

Dunlap, Charles, Jr., Colonel. 1996. "Melancholy Reunion. A Report from the Future on the Collapse of Civil-Military Relations in the United States." United States Air Force Institute for National Security Studies, U.S. Air Force Academy, Colorado. (October).

Dussel, Enrique. 2001. *Hacia una Filosofía Política Crítica*. Bilbao, España. Desclée de Brouwer.

Dussel, Enrique. 1977. *Filosofía de Liberación*. México. Edicol.

Eade, John (ed.), 1996. *Living the Global City: Globalization as a Local Process*. London: Routledge.

Eade, John. 1994. "Identity, Nation and Religion: Educated Young Bangladeshi Muslims in London's 'East End,'" in *International Sociology* 9 (3) (September): 377–394.

Ebashi, Masahiko. 1997. "The Economic Take-Off," in J. Morley and M. Nishihara (eds.), *Vietnam Joins the World*. Armonk, NY: M.E. Sharpe, 37–65.

Economist Intelligence Unit Country Profiles. 2002–2003. http://db.eiu.com.

Editorial. "Borders Crucial." *The El Paso Times* (October 29, 2002): 6B.

Editorial. "Security Top Priority: 9/11 Created Many Inconveniences for Border Areas." *The El Paso Times* (September 16, 2002): A2.

Editors, The. 2002. "U.S. Imperial Ambitions and Iraq." *Monthly Review* 54 (7): 1–13.

Edwards, M., and Gaventa, J. (eds.), 2001. *Global Citizen Action*. Boulder, CO: Earthscan.

Ehrenreich, B., and Hochschild, A. R. (eds.), 2003. *Global Woman: Nannies, Maids, and Sex Workers in the New Economy*. New York: Metropolitan Books.

Ehrenreich, Barbara, and Arlie Russell Hochschild. 2002. *Global Woman: Nannies, Maids, and Sex Workers in the New Economy*. New York: Metropolitan Books.

Eisler, Riane. 1988. *The Chalice and the Blade: Our History, Our Future*. San Francisco: Harper & Row.

Elbaum, M. 2002. *Revolution in the Air: Sixties Radicals Turn to Lenin, Mao and Che*, London and New York: Verso.

Elias, Norbert. 1982. *The Civilising Process volume 2: State Formation and Civilisation*. Oxford: Basil Blackwell.

Elias, Norbert. 1978. *The Civilising Process volume 1: The History of Manners*. Oxford: Basil Blackwell.

Elliott, Larry. 2002. "Spare a Tear for Argentina," *Guardian Weekly* (June): 13–19, 10.

Elson, D. 1995. "Male Bias in Macroeconomics: The Case of Structural Adjustment," in D. Elson (ed.), *Male Bias in the Development Process*. Manchester: Manchester University Press, 164–190.

Elson, Diane, and Ruth Pearson. 1981. "Nimble Fingers Make Cheap Workers: An Analysis of Women's Employment in Third World Export Manufacturing." *Feminist Review* (spring): 87–107.

Emeagwali, G. T. (ed.), 1995. *Women Pay the Price: Structural Adjustment in Africa and the Caribbean*. Trenton, NJ: Africa World Press.

Engels, Friedrich. 1895. "Introduction," in Karl Marx, *The Class Struggles in France*. [1850]. *Neue Rheinische Zeitung Revue*. Retrieved from http://www.marxists.org/archive/marx/works/1850/class-struggles-france/intro.htm on April 20, 2003.

Enloe, Cynthia. 1993. *The Morning After: Sexual Politics at the End of the Cold War*. Berkeley, CA: University of California Press.

Enloe, Cythia. 1990. *Banana, Beaches, and Bases: Making Sense of International Politics*. Berkeley, CA: University of California Press.

Epitropoulos, Mike-Frank, and Victor Roudometof (eds.), 1998. *American Culture in Europe: Interdisciplinary Perspectives*. Westport, CT: Praeger.

Erlich, Reese. 2003. "Student Activists and Campus Administrators Join Forces To Fight Against Sweatshops." California Alumni Association Monthly Newsletter (April 20). http://www.alumni.berkeley.edu/Alumni/Cal_Monthly/September_2002/No_sweats.asp.

Esbenshade, Jill. Forthcoming 2004. *Monitoring Sweatshops: Workers, Consumers and the Global Apparel Industry*. Philadelphia: Temple University Press.

Esbenshade, Jill. 2003. "Leveraging Neo-liberal 'Reforms': How Garment Workers Capitalize on Monitoring," paper presented at the PEWS panel on Neo-liberalism at the annual meetings of the American Sociological Association, August 18, Atlanta, GA.

Escobar, Arturo. 1995. *Encountering Development: The Making and Unmaking of the Third World*. Princeton, NJ: Princeton University Press.

Espinoza, V. 1999. "Social Networks among the Poor: Inequality and Integration in a Latin American City," in B. Wellman (ed.), *Networks in the Global Village*. Boulder, CO: Westview.

Espiono, Edith. 1989. "For a Responsible Health Program for Women," in M. J. Mananzan, A. Azcuna, and F. Mangahas (eds.), *Sarilaya: Women in Arts and Media*. Manila, Philippines: St. Scholastica's College Institute of Women's Studies, 221–223.

Espiritu, Yen Le. 2001. "We Don't Sleep Around like White Girls Do: Family, Culture and Gender in Filipina American Lives." *Signs* 415–440.

Evans, Peter. 1995. *Embedded Autonomy: States and Industrial Transformation*. Princeton, NJ: Princeton University Press.

Evans, P., and J. Rauch. 1999. "Bureaucracy and Growth: A Cross-National Analysis of the Effects of 'Weberian' State Structures on Economic Growth." *American Sociological Review* 64 (4): 748–765.

EZLN [The Zapatista National Liberation Army]. 2002b [1996]. "Fourth Declaration from the Lacandón Jungle — 'Today We Say: We Are Here, We Are Rebel Dignity, the Forgotten of the Homeland,'" in Tom Hayden (ed.), *The Zapatista Reader*. New York: Thunder's Mouth Press/The Nation, 239–250.

EZLN [The Zapatista National Liberation Army]. 2002c [1994]. "First Declaration from the Lacandón Jungle: EZLN's Declaration of War — 'Today We Say 'Enough is Enough!' (Ya Basta!),'" in Tom Hayden (ed.), *The Zapatista Reader*. New York: Thunder's Mouth Press/The Nation, 217–220.

EZLN [The Zapatista National Liberation Army]. 2002d [1994]. "Second Declaration from the Lacandón Jungle —'Today We Say: We Will Not Surrender!,'" in Tom Hayden (ed.), *The Zapatista Reader*. New York: Thunder's Mouth Press/The Nation, 221–231.

Falk, Richard. 2003. "Globalization-from-Below: An Innovative Politics of Difference," in Richard Sandbrook (ed.), *Civilizing Globalization: A Survival Guide*. Albany, NY: State University of New York Press, 189–205.

Falk, Richard, et al. 2002. *Reframing the International: Law, Culture, Politics*. New York: Routledge.

Falk, Richard. 2002. *The Great Terror War*. Ithaca, NY: Oliver Branch Press.

Falk, Richard. 1999. *Predatory Globalization: A Critique*. Cambridge: Polity.

Falk, Richard. 1993. "The Making of Global Citizenship," in Jeremy Brecher, John Brown Childs, and Jill Culter (eds.), *Global Visions: Beyond the New World Order*. Boston: South End Press.

Farmer, Paul. 1999. *Infections and Inequalities: The Modern Plagues*. Berkeley, CA: University of California Press.

Farmer, Paul. 1996. "Social Inequalities and Emerging Infectious Diseases." Emerging Infectious Diseases 2 (4): 259–269.

Farmer, Paul. 1992. *AIDS and Accusation: Haiti and the Geography of Blame*. Berkeley, CA: University of California Press.

Feagin, Joe R., and Karyn D. McKinney. 2002. *The Many Costs of Racism*. Lanham, MD: Rowman & Littlefield.

Featherstone, Liza. 2002. *Students against Sweatshops: The Making of a Movement*. New York and London: Verso.

Featherstone, Mike (ed.), 1990. *Global Culture: Nationalism, Globalization and Modernity*. Thousand Oaks, CA: Sage.

Featherstone, Mike. 1990. "Introduction," in Mike Featherstone (ed.), *Global Culture: Nationalism, Globalization and Modernity*. Thousand Oaks, CA: Sage, 1–13.

Ferguson, James. 1994. *The Anti-Politics Machine. "Development," Depoliticization, and Bureaucratic Power in Lesotho*. Minneapolis: University of Minnesota Press.

Ferguson, Yale H., and James N. Rosenau. 2003. "Superpowerdom before and after September 11, 2001: A Postinternational Perspective," paper presented at the annual meeting of the International Studies Association, February, Portland, OR.

Fernandes, Leela. 2000. "Nationalizing 'the Global': Media Images, Cultural Politics and the Middle Class in India." *Media, Culture & Society* 22, 611–628.

Fernandez-Kelly, M. P. 1983. *For We Are Sold, I and My People: Women and Industry in Mexico's Frontier*. Albany, NY: State University of New York Press.

Ferradas, Carmen. 2003. "Argentina and the End of the First World Dream," in Stanley Aronowitz and Heather Gautney (eds.), *Implicating Empire. Globalization and Resistance in the 21st Century World Order*. New York: Basic Books.

Field, Nancy. 1988. "Biotechnology R&D: National Policy Issues and Responses," in *Biotechnology and the Changing Role of Government*, Paris. OECD, 9–64.

Filmfare. 2001. "Raja Rani." (March): 16.

Fingleton, Eamonn. 2001. "Quibble All You Like, Japan Still Looks Like a Strong Winner." *International Herald Tribune* 2 (January), 6.

Finnegan, W. 2003. "The Economics of Empire." *Harper's Magazine* 306 (1836) (May).

Firebaugh, Glen. 2001. "The Trend in Between-Nation Income Inequality." *Annual Review of Sociology* 26: 323–339.

Firebaugh, Glen. 1999. "Empirics of World Income Inequality." *American Journal of Sociology* 104 (6): 1597–1630.

Fisher, William F. 1997. "DOING GOOD? The Politics and Antipolitcs of NGO Practices." *Annual Reviews Anthropology* 26: 439–464.

Flinchum, Robin. 1998. "The Women of Chiapas," *The Progressive* (March): 30–31.

Fonte, John. 2001. "Liberal Democracy vs. Transnational Progressivism: The Ideological War within the West." Foreign Policy Research Institute (October).

Foran, John. 2003a. "Alternatives to Development: Of Love, Dreams, and Revolution," in Kum-Kum Bhavnani, John Foran, and Priya A. Kurian, (eds.), *Feminist Futures: Re-imagining Women, Culture and Development*. London: Zed, 268–274.

Foran, John. 2003b. "Magical Realism: How Might the Revolutions of the Future Have Better End(ing)s?," in John Foran (ed.), *The Future of Revolutions: Re-thinking Radical Change in an Age of Globalization*, London: Zed, 271–283.

Foran, John. 2001. "Studying Revolutions through the Prism of Race, Gender, and Class: Notes toward a Framework." *Race, Gender & Class* 8 (2): 117–141.

Fortune. 2003. "The 2003 Global 500." *Fortune Magazine Fortune.com*. http://www.fortune.com/fortune/global500.

Fortune. 2002. "The 2002 Global 500." *Fortune Magazine Fortune.com*. http://www.fortune.com/fortune/global500.

Fraser, Nancy. 1987. "What's Critical about Critical Theory? The Case of Habermas and Gender," in Seyla Benhabib and Drucilla Cornell (eds.), *Feminism as Critique: On the Politics of Gender*. Minneapolis: University of Minnesota Press, 31–56.

Fray, Brian. 1987. *Critical Social Science*. Cambridge: Polity.

Freeman, C. 2000. *High Tech and High Heels in the Global Economy: Women, Work, and Pink Collar Identities in the Caribbean*. Durham, NC: Duke University Press.

Freire, Paulo. 1998. *Pedagogy of Freedom*. Lanham, MD: Rowman & Littlefield.

French, J. 1994. "Hitting Where It Hurts Most: Jamaican Women's Livelihoods in Crisis," in Pamela Sparr (ed.), *Mortgaging Women's Lives*. London: Zed, 165–182.

Fried, Jonathan. 1997. "Globalization and International Law — Some Thoughts for States and Citizens." *Queen's Law Journal* 23: 259–276.

Friedman, Jonathan. 1994. *Cultural Identity and Global Process*. Thousand Oaks, CA: Sage.

Friedmann, Harriet. 1996. "Prometheus Rebound." *Contemporary Sociology* 35 (3): 319–322.

Fröbel, Folker, Jurgen Heinrichs, and Otto Kreye. 1980. *The New International Division of Labour: Structural Unemployment in Industrialised Countries and Industrialisation in Developing Countries*. Cambridge: Cambridge University Press.

Fukuyama, Francis. 1992. *The End of History and the Last Man*. London: Penguin.

Fullerton, T. P., and Sprinkle, R. L. 2002. *Security Measures, Public Policy, Immigration & Trade with Mexico*. Border Region Modeling Project, The University of Texas at El Paso. (Tech. Report TX03-1).

Funkhouser, Edward. 1995. "Remittances from International Migration: A Comparison of El Salvador and Nicaragua." *Review of Economics and Statistics* 77 (1): 137–146.

GaWC (Globalization and World Cities Study Group and Network). http://www.lboro.ac.uk/departments/gy/research/gawc.html

Galbraith, James. 2002. "A Perfect Crime: Inequality in the Age of Globalization." *Daedalus* (winter): 11–25.

Gamburd, Michele Ruth. 2000. *The Kitchen Spoon's Handle: Transnationalism and Sri Lanka's Migrant Housemaids*. Ithaca, NY: Cornell University Press.

Gamson, Joshua. 1998. *Freaks Talk Back: Tabloid Talk Shows and Sexual Nonconformity*. Chicago: University of Chicago Press.

Garcia, Linda. 2002. "The Architecture of Global Networking Technologies," in S. Sassen (ed.), *Global Networks/Linked Cities*. London and New York: Routledge.

George, Susan, and Fabrizio Sabelli. 1994. *Faith and Credit: the World Bank's Secular Empire*. Boulder, CO: Westview.

George, Susan. 1999. *The Lugano Report*. London: Pluto.

George, Susan. 1997. "Winning the War of Ideas." *Dissent* (summer).

George, Susan. 1977. *How the Other Half Dies. The Real Reason for World Hunger*. Montclair, NJ: Allenheld, Osmun, and Co.

George, Susan. 1976. *How the Other Half Dies*. London: Penguin.

Gereffi, Gary. 1994. "Rethinking Development Theory: Insights from East Asia and Latin America," in A. D. Kinkaid and A. Portes (eds.), *Comparative National Development. Society and Economy in the New Global Order*. Chapel Hill, NC: University of North Carolina Press, 26–56.

Gereffi, Gary. 1994. "The Organization of Buyer-Driven Global Commodity Chains: How U.S. Retailers Shape Overseas Production Networks," in Gary Gereffi and Miguel Korzeniewicz (eds.), *Commodity Chains and Global Capitalism*. Westport, CT: Praeger, 95–122.

Gereffi, Gary. 2001. "Beyond the Producer-Driven/Buyer-Driven Dichotomy: The Evolution of Global Value Chains in the Internet Era." *IDS Bulletin* 32 (3): 30–40.

Gerlach, Michael L. 1992. *Alliance Capitalism: The Social Organization of Japanese Business*. Berkeley, CA. University of California Press.

Gessner, Volkmar, Richard P. Appelbaum, and William L. F. Felstiner. 2001 "Introduction: The Legal Culture of Global Business Transactions," in Richard P. Appelbaum, William L. F. Felstiner, and Volkmar Gessner (eds.), *Rules and Networks: The Legal Culture of Global Business Transactions*. Oxford: Hart, 1–36.

Geuss, Raymond. 1981. *The Idea of a Critical Theory: Habermas and the Frankfurt School*. Cambridge: Cambridge University Press.

Gibbs, N. 2001. "Washington's New Interventionism: U.S. Hegemony and Inter-Imperialist Rivalries." *Monthly Review* 53 (4) (September): 15–37.

Gibson-Graham, J. K. 1998. "Queer(y)ing Globalization," in Heidi J. Nast and Steve Pile (eds.), *Places Through the Body*. London: Routledge, 23–41.

Giddens, Anthony. 2000. *Runaway World: How Globalization is Reshaping Our Lives*. New York: Routledge.

Giddens, Anthony. 1998. *The Third Way: The Renewal of Social Democracy*. Malden, MA: Blackwell.

Giddens, Anthony. 1994. "Living in a Post-Traditional Society," in A. Giddens, U. Beck, and S. Lash (eds.), *Reflexive Modernization: Politics, Tradition, and Aesthetics in the Modern Social Order*. Cambridge: Polity, 56–109.

Giddens, Anthony. 1991. *Modernity and Self-Identity*. Cambridge. Polity.

Giddens, Anthony. 1990. *Sociology*. Oxford: Polity.

Giddens, Anthony. 1990. *The Consequences of Modernity*. Stanford, CA: Stanford University Press.

Giddens, Anthony, Mitchell Duneier, and Richard P. Appelbaum. 2003. *Introduction to Sociology*, 4th edition. New York: W. W. Norton.

Gill, Stephen. 2002. *Power and Resistance in the New World Order*. London: Palgrave.

Gill, Stephen. 2000. "Toward a Postmodern Prince? The Battle in Seattle as a Moment in the New Politics of Globalisation." *Millennium* 29 (1): 131–141.

Gill, Stephen. 1996. "Globalization, Democratization, and the Politics of Indifference," in James Mittelman (ed.), *Globalization: Critical Reflections*. Boulder, CO: Lynne Reinner, 205–228.

Gills, Barry K. (ed.), 2000. *Globalization and the Politics of Resistance*. New York: St. Martin's Press.

Gills, B., J. Rocamora, and R. Wilson (eds.), *Low Intensity Democracy: Political Power in the New World Order*. London: Pluto.

Gilot, L. "Borders Ready for Guard Exit." *The El Paso Times* (May 12, 2003): B1.

Gilpin, Robert. 2000. *The Challenge of Global Capitalism: The World Economy in the 21st Century*. Princeton, NJ: Princeton University Press.

Gindin, S. 2002. "Social Justice and Globalization: Are They Compatible?," *Monthly Review* 54 (2) (June): 1–11.

Glick Schiller, Nina. 1999. "Transmigrants and Nation-States: Something Old and Something New in the U.S. Immigrant Experience," in Charles Hirschman, Philip Kasinitz, and Josh de Wind (eds.), *The Handbook of International Migration: The American Experience*. New York: Russell Sage Foundation, 94–119.

Global Exchange. 2003. "NAFTA Inflames Mexico's Countryside." *The Quarterly Newsletter of the Global Exchange* 54 (spring): 1, 14.

Goesling, Brian. 2001. "Changing Income Inequalities within and between Nations: New Evidence." *American Sociological Review* 66 (5): 745–761.

Gold, Thomas. 1985. *State and Society in the Taiwan Miracle*. Armonk, NY: M. E. Sharpe.

Goldring, Luin. 1998. "The Power of Status in Transnational Social Fields." in M. P. Smith and L. E. Guarnizo (eds.), *Transnationalism from Below*. New Brunswick, NJ: Transaction, 165–195.

Gomez, E. T., and K. S. Jomo. 1997. *Malaysia's Political Economy: Politics, Patronage and Profits*. Cambridge: Cambridge University Press.

Gonzales, David. "Latin Sweatshops Pressed by U.S. Campus Power." *The New York Times* Foreign Desk (April 4, 2003).

González, M. "No planeamos venganza vs México." *El Diario* (April 26, 2003): A6.Good, Byron. 1994. *Medicine, Rationality, and Experience: An Anthropological Perspective*. Cambridge: Cambridge University Press.

Goodkind, Daniel. 1997. "The Vietnamese Double Marriage Squeeze." *International Migration Review* 31: 108–128.

Gowan, P. 1999. *The Global Gamble: Washington's Bid for World Dominance*. London: Verso.

Graeber, David. 2002. The Anthropology of Globalization (with Notes on Neomedievalism, and the End of the Chinese Model of the Nation-State). *American Anthropologist* 104 (4): 1222–1227.

Graham, S., and A. Aurigi. 1997. "Virtual Cities, Social Polarization, and the Crisis in Urban Public Space." *Journal of Urban Technology* 4 (1): 19–52.

Gramsci, A. 1971. *Selections for the Prison Notebooks*. New York: International.

Gramsci, A. 2000. *The Gramsci Reader: Selected Writings 1916–1935*. Edited by D. Forgacs. New York: New York University Press.

Grandin, G. 2003. "What's a Neoliberal To Do?," *The Nation* 276 (9) (March 10): 25–29.

Gray, J. 2001. "The Era of Globalization Is Over." *New Statesman*. (September 24).

Greenfield, Gerard. 1994. "The Development of Capitalism in Vietnam," in Ralph Miliband and Leo Panitch (eds.), *Between Globalism and Nationalism, Socialist Register 1994*. London: The Merlin Press.

Greider, W. 2003. "The Right's Grand Ambition: Rolling Back the 20th Century," *The Nation* 276 (18) (May 12): 11–19.

Grewal, Inderpal, and Caren Kaplan (eds.), 1994. *Scattered Hegemonies: Postmodernity and Transnational Feminist Practices*. Minneapolis: University of Minnesota Press.

Grosfoguel, Ramón. 2002. "Colonial Difference, Geopolitics of Knowledge and Global Coloniality in the Modern/Colonial Capitalist World-System." *Review* 25 (3): 203–224.

Grosfoguel, Ramón. 1996. "From Cepalismo to Neoliberalism: A World-System Approach to Conceptual Shifts in Latin America." *Review* 19 (2): 131–154.

Guarnizo, Luis Eduardo, and Michael Peter Smith. 1998. "The Location of Transnationalism," in M. P. Smith and L. E. Guarnizo (eds.), *Transnationalism from Below*. New Brunswick, NJ: Transaction.

Guidry, John A., Michael D. Kennedy, and Mayer N. Zald (eds.), 2000. *Globalizations and Social Movements: Culture, Power and the Transnational Public Sphere*. Ann Arbor, MI: The University of Michigan Press.

Gupta, Akhil, and James Ferguson. 2002. "Beyond 'Culture': Space, Identity, and the Politics of Difference," in J. Inda and R. Rosaldo (eds.), *The Anthropology of Globalization: A Reader*. Malden, MA: Blackwell, 65–80.

Gupta, Dipankar. 2000. *Mistaken Modernity: India between Worlds*. New Delhi: Harper Collins.

Guttentag, Marcia, and Paul F. Secord. 1983. *Too Many Women?: The Sex Ratio Question*. Beverly Hills: Sage.

Gzesh, S., and R. Espinoza. 2002. "Immigrant Communities Building Cross-Border Civic Networks: The Federation of Michoacan Clubs in Illinois," in A. Annheur and M. Kaldor (eds.), *Global Civil Society Yearbook 2002*. Oxford: Oxford University Press, 226–227.

Habermas, Jürgen. 2002. *Religion and Rationality: Essays on Reason, God, and Modernity*. Cambridge: Polity.

Habermas, Jürgen. 2001. *The Postnational Constellation: Political Essays*. Cambridge: Polity.

Habermas, Jürgen. 1999. *The Inclusion of the Other: Studies in Political Theory*. Cambridge: Polity.

Habermas, Jürgen. 1998. *A Berlin Republic: Writings on Germany*. Cambridge: Polity.

Habermas, Jürgen. 1994. "Citizenship and National Identity," in Bart van Steenbergen (ed.), *The Condition of Citizenship*. London: Sage.

Habermas, Jürgen. 1994. *The Past as Future*. Cambridge: Polity.

Habermas, Jürgen. 1989. *The New Conservatism: Cultural Criticism and the Historians' Debate*. Cambridge: Polity.

Habermas, Jürgen. 1988. *On the Logic of the Social Sciences*. Cambridge: Polity.

Habermas, Jürgen. 1987. *Knowledge and Human Interests*. Cambridge: Polity.

Habermas, Jürgen. 1987. *The Theory of Communicative Action, Volume 2: Lifeworld and System: A Critique of Functionalist Reason*. Cambridge: Polity.

Habermas, Jürgen. 1987. *Toward a Rational Society: Student Protest, Science and Politics*. Cambridge: Polity.

Habermas, Jürgen. 1984. *Communication and the Evolution of Society*. Cambridge: Polity.

Habermas, Jürgen. 1984. *The Theory of Communicative Action, Volume 1: Reason and the Rationalization of Society*. Cambridge: Polity.

Habermas, Jürgen. 1976. *Legitimation Crisis*. London: Heinemann.

Habermas, Jürgen. 1974. *Theory and Practice*. London: Heinemann.

Halbfinger, David M., and Steven A. Holmes. "Military Mirrors Working Class America." *The New York Times* (March 30, 2003).

Hall, John. 1992. "The Capital(s) of Cultures: A Nonholistic Approach to Status, Situations, Class, Gender, and Ethnicity," in M. Lamont and M. Fournier (eds.), *Cultivating Differences: Symbolic Boundaries and the Making of Inequalities*. Chicago: University of Chicago Press, 257–289.

Hall, Rodney, and Thomas Biersteker (eds.), 2002. *The Emergence of Private Authority in Global Governance*. Cambridge: Cambridge University Press.

Hall, Stuart. 1992. "The Question of Cultural Identity," in Stuart Hall, David Held, and Tony McGrew (eds.), *Modernity and Its Futures*. Cambridge: Polity, 310.

Hall, Stuart. 1989 [1996]. "New Ethnicities," in D. Morley and K.-H. Chen (eds.), *Stuart Hall: Critical Dialogues in Cultural Studies*. London: Routledge, 441–449.

Hallow, Ralph Z. "GOP Leaders Warned to Shun Agenda of Gays." *The Washington Times* (May 15, 2003).

Halnon, Karen B., and Lauren Langman. 2003. "Shock Rock and Spectacle," unpublished paper presented at Southern Sociological Association, March 3–5, New Orleans.

Hamilton, Nora, and Norma Stoltz Chinchilla. 2001. *Seeking Community in a Global City: Guatemalans and Salvadorans in Los Angeles*. Philadelphia: Temple University Press.

Hand, M., and Sandywell, B. 2002. "E-topia as Cosmopolis or Citadel: On the Democratising and De-Democratising Logics of the Internet, or, Towards a Critique of the New Technological Fetishism." *Theory, Culture & Society* 19 (1–2).

Handlin, Oscar. 1951. *The Uprooted*. Boston: Little Brown.

Hannerz, Ulf. 2002. "Flows, Boundaries and Hybrids: Keywords in Transnational Anthropology." *ESRC Transnational Communities Programme* WPTC-2K-02. Oxford.

Hannerz, Ulf. 1996. *Transnational Connections: Culture, People, Places*. London: Routledge.

Hannerz, Ulf. 1990. "Cosmopolitans and Locals in World Culture," in Mike Featherstone (ed.), *Global Culture: Nationalism, Globalization, and Modernity*. London: Sage, 237–252.

Haraway, Donna. 1988. "Situated Knowledges: The Science Question in Feminism and the Privilege of Partial Perspective." *Feminist Studies* 14: 575–599.

Harding, Sandra. 1991. *Whose Science? Whose Knowledge? Thinking from Women's Lives*. Ithaca, NY: Cornell University Press.

Hardt, Michael, and Antonio Negri. 2000. *Empire*. Cambridge, MA: Harvard University Press.

Harris, Jerry. 2002. "The U.S. Military in the Era of Globalization." *Race and Class* (October): 1–22.

Harris, Nigel. 1986. *The End of the Third World. Newly Industrializing Countries and the Decline of an Ideology.* Harmondsworth, Middlesex: Penguin.

Harris, Paul, and Jonathan Franklin. 2003. "Bring Us Home: GIs Flood US with War-Weary Emails." *The Observer* (August 10).

Hart-Landsberg, Martin. 1993. *The Rush to Development.* New York: Monthly Review.

Harvey, David. 2003. *The New Imperialism.* New York: Oxford University Press.

Harvey, D. 2001. *Spaces of Capital.* New York: Routledge.

Harvey, David. 1999. *The Limits to Capital,* 2nd edition. London: Verso.

Harvey, David. 1996. *Justice, Nature and the Geography of Difference.* Oxford: Blackwell.

Harvey, David. 1995. "Globalization in Question." *Rethinking Marxism* 8 (4): 1–17.

Harvey, David. 1990. *The Condition of Postmodernity: An Enquiry into the Origins of Cultural Change.* Oxford: Blackwell.

Hasskamp, Charles, Lieutenant Colonel, USAF. 1998. "Operations other than War: Who Says Warriors Don't Do Windows?" Air War College, Air University. Alabama. (March).

Haufler, Virginia. 2001. *A Public Role for the Private Sector: Industry Self-Regulation in a Global Economy.* Washington, D.C.: Carnegie Endowment for International Peace.

Havel, Václav. 1995. "The Search for Meaning in a Global Civilization," in Walter Truett Anderson (ed.), *The Truth about the Truth: De-confusing and Re-constructing the Postmodern World.* New York: G. P. Putman and Sons, 232–238.

Havel, Václav. 1994. "The Need for Transcendence in the Postmodern World," speech presented in Independence Hall, Philadelphia, July 4, 1994.

Hawthorne, Susan. 2002. *Wild Politics: Feminism, Globalisation, Bio/Diversity.* North Melbourne: Spinifex.

Hayden, Tom. 2003. "Seeking a New Globalism in Chiapas." *The Nation* 276 (13) (April 7): 18–23.

Hayden, Tom (ed.), 2002. *The Zapatista Reader.* New York: Thunder's Mouth Press.

Hegel, G.W. 1967. *The Philosophy of Right.* New York: Oxford University Press.

Hekman, Susan. 1997. "Truth and Method: Feminist Standpoint Theory Revisited." *Journal of Women in Culture and Society* 22 (2) (winter): 341–365.

Held, David, Anthony McGrew, David Goldblatt, and Jonathan Perraton. 1999. *Global Transformations.* Stanford, CA: Stanford University Press.

Held, David. 1995. *Democracy and the Global Order: From the Modern State to Cosmopolitan Governance.* Stanford, CA: Stanford University Press.

Hélie-Lucas, Marie-Aimée. 1994. "The Preferential Symbol for Islamic Identity: Women in Muslim Personal Laws," in Moghadam (ed.), *Identity Politics and Women: Cultural Reassertions and Feminisms in International Perspective.* Boulder, CO: Westview, 391–407.

Henderson, J. 1999. "Uneven Crises: Institutional Foundations of East Asian Economic Turmoil." *Economy and Society* 28 (3): 327–368.

Henderson, J. 1998. "Danger and Opportunity in the Asia-Pacific," in G. Thompson (ed.), *Economic Dynamism in the Asia-Pacific.* London: Routledge, 356–384.

Henderson, J., and D. Hulme. 2002a. "Globalisation, National Economic Governance and Poverty Elimination: Insights from East Asia and Eastern Europe." Final Report to the Department for International Development, British Government. http://www.gapresearch.org/governance/DFIDFinalreport3.pdf.

Henderson, J., D. Hulme, R. Phillips, and E. M. Kim. 2002b. "Economic Governance and Poverty Reduction in South Korea." *Working Paper,* 439. Manchester Business School.

Henderson, J., D. Hulme, H. Jalilian, and R. Phillips. 2003. "Bureaucractic Effects: 'Weberian' State Structures and Poverty Reduction." *Chronic Poverty Working Paper 31.* Institute for Development Policy and Management. University of Manchester.

Henige, David P. 1970. *Colonial Governors from the Fifteenth Century to the Present.* Madison, WI: University of Wisconsin Press.

Henshall, S. 2000. "The COMsumer Manifesto: Empowering Communities of Consumers through the Internet." *First Monday* 5.5. http://firstmonday.org/issues5_5/henshall/index.html.

Herrera, E. "Latin America: The Current Situation and the Task of Revolutionaries." *Fourth International Press* 1–16. Retrieved from FI-press—I@mail.comlink.apc.org on July 17, 2002.

Hettne, Björn, and Bertil Odén (eds.), 2002. *Global Governance in the 21st Century: Alternative Perspectives on World Order*. Stockholm: Almqvist and Wiksell International.

Heyman, J. M. 2001. U.S. Ports of Entry in the Mexican Border. *Journal of the Southwest* 43 (4): 681–700.

Heyman, Josiah M. 1994. Changes in House Construction Materials in Border Mexico — 4 Research Propositions about Commoditization. *Human Organization* 53 (2): 132–142.

Heyzer, N., G. Lycklama a Nijeholt, and N. Weerakoon. 1994. *The Trade in Domestic Workers: Causes, Mechanisms and Consequences of International Migration*. London: Zed Books.

Higgott, Richard, Geoffrey Underhill, and Andreas Bieler (eds.), 2000. *Non-State Actors and Authority in the Global System*. London: Routledge.

Hines, Colin. 2000. *Localization. A Global Manifesto*. London: Earthscan.

Hirschman, Charles, Philip Kasinitz, and Josh de Wind (eds.), 1999. *The Handbook of International Migration: The American Experience*. New York: Russell Sage Foundation.

Hirst, Paul, and Grahame Thompson. 1999. *Globalization in Question: The International Economy and the Possibilities of Governance*, 2nd edition. Cambridge: Polity.

Hoad, Neville. 2000. "Arrested Development or the Queerness of Savages: Resisting Evolutionary Narratives of Difference." *Postcolonial Studies* 3 (2): 133–158.

Hoang, Thi Lich. 1997. "Mot vai suy nghi buoc dau ve lao dong nu trong cac xi nghiep co von dau tu nuoc ngoai," in *Khoa Hoc Ve Phu Nu (Journal of Social Science and Gender)*, Hanoi: Trung Tam Nghien Cuu Khoa Hoc ve Gia Dinh va Phu Nu.

Hobsbawm, Eric J. 1990. *Nations and Nationalism Since 1789*. Cambridge: Cambridge University Press.

Hochschild, Jennifer L. 1995. *Facing Up to the American Dream: Race, Class, and the Soul of the Nation*. Princeton, NJ: Princeton University Press.

Hochschild, Arlie, and Anne Machung. 1989. *The Second Shift: Working Parents and the Revolution at Home*. New York: Viking.

Hodgson, G. 2001. *How Economics Forgot History: The Problem of Historical Specificity in Social Science*. London: Routledge.

Holloway, John. 2002. "Twelve Theses on Changing the World without Taking Power." *The Commoner* 4 (May). http://www.commoner.org.uk/04holloway2.pdf.

Hondagneu-Sotelo, Pierrette. 2001. *Domestica: Immigrant Workers Cleaning and Caring in the Shadows of Affluence*. Los Angeles: University of California Press.

Hondagneu-Sotelo, Pierrette. 1999. "Gender and Contemporary U.S. Immigration." *American Behavioral Scientist* 42: 565–576.

Hondagneu-Sotelo, Pierrette. 1994. *Gendered Transitions: Mexican Experiences of Immigration*. Berkeley, CA: University of California Press.

Hondagneu-Sotelo, Pierrette, and Ernestine Avila. 1997. "'I'm Here, but I'm There': The Meanings of Latina Transnational Motherhood." *Gender & Society* 11: 548–571.

Honnold, John. 1995. "International Unification of Private Law," in Oscar Schachter and Christopher Joyner (eds.), *United Nations Legal Order, Volume II*. Cambridge: Grotius, 1025–1056.

Hoogvelt, Ankie. 1997. *Globalisation and the Postcolonial World: The New Political Economy of Development*. London: MacMillan.

hooks, bella. 1995. *Yearning: Race, Gender, and Cultural Politics*. Boston: South End Press.

Horkheimer, Max. 1972. "Traditional and Critical Theory," in Horkheimer, *Critical Theory: Selected Essays*. Translated by Matthew J. O'Connell. Toronto: Herder and Herder, 188–243.

Houstoun, Marion F., Roger G. Kramer, and Joan Mackin Barrett. 1984. "Female Predominance in Immigration to the United States since 1930s: A First Look." *International Migration Review* 18: 908–963.

Houtart, Francois, and Francois Polet. 2001. *The Other Davos. The Globalization of Resistance to the World Economic System*. London: Zed Books.

Houtzager, P., and M. Moore (eds.), 2003. *Changing Paths: International Development and the New Politics of Inclusion*. Ann Arbor: University of Michigan Press.

Howe, I. 1976. *World of Our Fathers*. New York: Simon & Schuster.

Howes, David (ed.), 1996. *Cross-Cultural Consumption: Global Markets, Local Realities.* London: Routledge, 6.

Howitt, Richard. 1998. "Recognition, Reconciliation and Respect: Steps towards Decolonisation?" *Australian Aboriginal Studies* 1998/1: 28–34.

Howitt, Richard. 1993. "A World in a Grain of Sand: Towards a Reconceptualisation of Geographical Scale." *Australian Geographer* 24 (1): 33–44.

Hudis, P. 2003. Presentation for the book, *Philosophy and Revolution*, Chicago, March 23, 2003.

Huntington, Samuel P. 1996. *The Clash of Civilizations and the Remaking of World Order.* New York: Simon & Schuster.

Huntington, Samuel. 1993. "New Contingencies, Old Roles." *Joint Force Quarterly* (autumn): 43.

Huntington, Samuel. 1993. "The Clash of Civilizations?" *Foreign Affairs* 73 (3): 22–49.

Inda, Jonathan, and Renato Rosaldo (eds.), 2002. *The Anthropology of Globalization: A Reader.* Malden, MA: Blackwell.

Inden, Ronald. 1999. "Transnational Class, Erotic Arcadia and Commercial Utopia in Hindi Films," in C. Brosius and M. Butcher (eds.), *Image Journeys: Audio-Visual Media and Cultural Change in India.* New Delhi: Sage, 41–68.

India Abroad. 1999. "Ban Sought on Discotheques." (March 19): 11.

International Confederation of Free Trade Unions (ICFTU). April 6, 2003. "5th Ministerial Conference of the World Trade Organisation (WTO)." Retrieved from http://www.icftu.org/displaydocument. asp?Index=991217396&Language=EN on May 27, 2003.

International Labor Organization (ILO). 2001. *The World Employment Report 2001.* Geneva: ILO.

International Labour Organization (ILO). 1998. "Declaration on Fundamental Principles and Rights at Work." Retrieved from http://ilo.org/public/english/standards/decl/declaration/text/index.htm on May 27, 2003.

International Monetary Fund. 2002. *Balance of Payments Yearbook 2002.* Washington, D.C.: IMF.

International Monetary Fund Staff. 1998. "Mitigating the Social Costs of the Asian Crisis." *Finance & Development: A Quarterly Magazine of the IMF* 35 (3). http://www.imf.org/external/pubs/ft/fandd/ 1998/09/imfstaf2.htm.

International Monetary Fund. 2003. *Balance of Payments Statistics Yearbok 2002.* Washington D.C.: IMF Publications Services.

Isin, Engin F. (ed.), 2000. *Democracy, Citizenship and the Global City.* London and New York: Routledge.

Iyer, Pico. 2000. *The Global Soul: Jet Lag, Shopping Malls, and the Search for Home.* New York: Vintage.

Jacobson, D. 1996. *Rights across Borders: Immigration and the Decline of Citizenship.* Baltimore, MD: Johns Hopkins University Press.

Jacobson, Matthew Frye. 1999. *Whiteness of a Different Color: European Immigrants and the Alchemy of Race.* Cambridge, MA: Harvard University Press.

Jain, Madhu. 1998. "Romance: Move Over, Cupid." *India Today International* (February) 16: 42–43.

James, Stanlie, and Claire Robertson (eds.), 2002. *Genital Cutting and Transnational Sisterhood: Disputing U.S. Polemics.* Urbana and Chicago: University of Illinois Press.

Jeffcott, Bob, and Lynda Yanz. 2000. "Codes of Conduct, Government Regulation and Worker Organizing." Canada: Maquila Solidarity Network.

Jiménez, B. A. "Rechazan negociar Pemex." *El Diario* (May 10, 2003): A2.

John, Mary E. 1998. "Globalisation, Sexuality and the Visual Field: Issues and Non-issues for Cultural Critique," in Mary E. John and Janaki Nair, *A Question of Silence?: The Sexual Economies of Modern India.* New Delhi: Kali for Women, 368–396.

Johnson, Chalmers (no date). "The Real Casualty Rate from America's Iraq War," unpublished manuscript.

Johnson, J., and G. Laxer. 2003. "Solidarity in the Age of Globalization: Lessons from the Anti-MAI and Zapatista Struggles." *Theory and Society* 32: 39–91.

Johnson, Wayne, Lieutenant Colonel, USAF. 1998. "Seller Beware: US International Technology Transfer and Its Impact on National Security." Air War College, Air University. Alabama. (December): 20, 22, 25.

Jomo, K. S. 2001. "From Current Crisis to Recession," in Jomo, K. S. (ed.), *Malaysian Eclipse: Economic Crisis and Recovery.* London: Zed Books, 1–46.

Jonas, Andrew. 1994. "The Scale Politics of Spatiality." *Environment and Planning D: Society and Space* 12 (3): 257–264.

Jones, J. 2002. Plenary Conference, presented at the Environmental Symposium on the Mexico–U.S. Border. University of Texas at El Paso, September 27, 2002.

Jones, Rhett S. 1994. "The End of Africanity?: The Bi-Racial Assault on Blackness." *The Western Journal of Black Studies* 18 (4) (1994): 201–210.

Jonquieres De, Guy. "Clinton Demands Threaten Turmoil at WTO summit: President Outlines Long-Term Goal of Link between Trade and Labor Standards." *The Financial Times* (December 2, 1999): 1.

Judd, Denis R. 1998. "The Case of the Missing Scales: A Commentary on Cox." *Political Geography* 17 (1): 29–34.

Juergensmeyer, Mark. 1993. *The New Cold War? Religious Nationalism Confronts the Secular State.* Berkeley, CA: University of California Press.

Juergensmeyer, Mark. 2001. *Terror in the Mind of God: The Global Rise of Religious Violence.* University of California Press.

Julien, C-A., Bruhat, J., Bourgin, C., Crouzet, M. and Renouvin, P. 1949. *Les Politiques d'Expansion Imperialiste.* Paris: Presses Universitaires de France.

Kaldor, M. 1999. *New and Old Wars: Organized Violence in a Global Era.* Stanford, CA: Stanford University Press.

Kagan, Robert. 2003. *Of Paradise and Power: America and Europe in the New World Order.* New York: Alfred Knopf.

Karim, Karim H. 1998. *From Ethnic Media to Global Media: Transnational Communication Networks Among Diasporic Communities.* http://www.transcomm.ox.ac.uk/working_papers.htm.

Kastoryano, R. 2002. "The Reach of Transnationalism." *Social Science Research Council.* New York.

Katz, Jack. 1990. *Seductions of Crime: Moral and Sensual Attractions in Doing Evil.* New York: Basic Books.

Kautsky, Karl. 1988 [1927]. *The Materialist Conception of History.* Translated and abridged by John H. Kautsky. New Haven, CT: Yale University Press.

Keane, J. 2003. *Global Civil Society?* Cambridge: Cambridge University Press.

Kearney, Michael. 1995. "The Local and the Global: The Anthropology of Globalization and Transnationalism." *Annual Review of Anthropology* 24: 547–565.

Keck, Margaret E., and Kathryn Sikkink. 1998. *Activists beyond Borders: Advocacy Networks in International Politics.* Cornell University Press.

Keita, Mahgan. 1994. "Deconstructing the Classical Age: Africa and the Unity of the Mediterranean World." *Journal of Negro History* 79 (2) (spring): 146–166.

Kellner, D. 2001. *Theorizing Globalization.* http://www.gseis.ucla.edu/faculty/kellner/papers/theory-glob.htm.

Kempadoo, Kamala. 2001. "Women of Color and the Global Sex Trade: Transnational Perspectives." *Meridians: Feminism, Race, Transnationalism* 1 (2) (spring): 28–51.

Kempadoo, K., and Doezema, J. (eds.), 1998. *Global Sex Workers: Rights, Resistance, and Redefinition.* New York: Routledge.

Kennedy, Paul. 2003. "The Role of Socio-Cultural Influences and Interpersonal Relationships in Underpinning the Global Economy: The Case of Transnational Professionals in the Building-Design Service Sector," paper presented at the 2003 Critical Globalization Conference, May 1–4, University of California, Santa Barbara.

Kennedy, Paul. 1993. *Preparing for the Twenty-First Century.* New York: Random House.

Kennedy, P. 1989. The Rise and the Fall of the Great Powers. New York: Random House.

Kennedy, Paul, and Victor Roudometof (eds.), 2002. *Communities across Borders: New Immigrants and Transnational Cultures.* London: Routledge.

Kershaw, Terry. 1993. "Afrocentrism and the Afrocentric Method," in Janice D. Hamlet (ed.), *Afrocentric Visions: Studies in Culture and Communication.* Thousand Oaks, CA: Sage, 27–44.

Khagram, Sanjeev, James V. Riker, and Kathryn Sikkink (eds.), 2002. *Restructuring World Politics: Transnational Social Movements, Networks, and Norms.* Minneapolis: University of Minnesota Press.

Kibria, Nazli. 1993. *Family Tightrope: The Changing Lives of Vietnamese Americans.* Princeton, NJ: Princeton University Press.

Kiernan, Victor. G. 1969. *The Lords of Human Kind: Black Man, Yellow Man, and White Man in an Age of Empire*. Boston: Little Brown.

Kim, Eun-Mee (ed.), 1998. *The Four Asian Tigers: Economic Development and the Global Political Economy*. San Diego, CA: Academic.

Kim, E. M. 1997. *Big Business, Strong State: Collusion and Conflict in South Korean Development, 1960–1990*. Albany, NY: State University of New York Press.

Kim, W. J. 1997. *Economic Growth, Low Income and Housing in South Korea*. London: Macmillan.

King, E., and Mason, A. 2001. *Engendering Development: Through Gender Equality in Rights, Resources, Voice*. Washington, D.C./New York: Oxford University Press/World Bank.

Klandermans, B. 1997. *The Social Psychology of Protest*. Oxford: Blackwell.

Klein, N. "Demonstrated Ideals." *Los Angeles Times* (April 20, 2003). http://www.calendar-live.com/books/bookreview/cl-bk-klein20apr20.story.

Klein, Naomi. "Privatization in Disguise." *The Nation* April 15, 2003. http://www.alter-net.org/story.html?StoryID=15638.

Klein, Naomi. 2002a. *Fences and Windows: Dispatches from the Front Lines of the Globalization Debate*. New York: Picador.

Klein, Naomi. *Guardian Weekly*. (October 17–23, 2002b).

Kleinman, Arthur, Veena Das, and Margaret Lock, (eds.), 1997. *Social Suffering*. Berkeley and Los Angeles: University of California Press.

Kleinman, Arthur. 1992. "Pain and Resistance: The Delegitimation and Relegitimation of Local Worlds," in M-J. D. Good, P. E. Brodwin, B. Good, and A. Kleinman (eds.), *Pain as Human Experience*. Berkeley, CA: University of California Press, 169–197.

Koepke, Ronald, Norma Molina, and Carolina Quinteros (eds.), 2000. *Codigos de Conducta y Monitoreo En La Inustria De Confeccion. Experiencias Internacionales Y Regionales*. El Salvador: Heinrich Böll Foundation.

Koffman, Eleonore, Annie Phizacklea, Parvati Raghuram, and Rosemary Sales, *Gender and International Migration in Europe: Employment, Welfare and Politics*, New York and London: Routledge, 2000.

Kolko, Gabriel. 1988. *Confronting the Third World. United States Foreign Policy 1945–1980*. New York: Pantheon.

Kontopoulos, Kyriakos. 1993. *The Logics of Social Structures*. Cambridge: Cambridge University Press.

Korzeniewicz, Roberto Patricio, and Timothy Patrick Moran. 2000. "Measuring World Income Inequalities." *American Journal of Sociology* 106: 209–214.

Korzeniewicz, Roberto Patricio, and Timothy Patrick Moran. 1997. "World-Economic Trends in the Distribution of Income, 1965–1992." *American Journal of Sociology* 102 (4): 1000–1039.

Krippner, Greta. 2002. "What Is Financialization?," paper presented at the American Sociological Association Meeting, August 16–19, Chicago.

Krugman, Paul. "Duped and Betrayed." *The New York Times* (June 6, 2003).

Krugman, Paul. 1994. "The Myth of Asia's Miracle." *Foreign Affairs* 73 (6): 62–78.

Kugler, Richard. 2000a. "Controlling Chaos: U.S. National Strategy in a Globalizing World." Institute for National Strategic Studies, National Defense University.

Kugler, Richard. 2000b. "Promise and challenge, Europe's role in a globalising world." Institute for National Strategic Studies, National Defense University.

Kuhn, Thomas, S. 1962. *The Structure of Scientific Revolutions*. Chicago: University of Chicago Press.

L'Heureux-Dubé, The Honourable Claire. 1998–1999. "The Importance of Dialogue: Globalization and the International Impact of the Rehnquist Court." *Tulsa Law Journal* 34: 15–40.

Labor (Las Dong Newspaper), September 17, 2002; October 26, 2002.

Lacher, Hannes. 1999. "Embedded Liberalism, Disembedded Markets: Reconceptualising the Pax Americana." *New Political Economy* 4 (3): 343–360.

Lal, D. 1983. *The Poverty of Development Economics*. London: Institute for Economic Affairs.

Lander, Edgardo. 1998. "Eurocentrismo y colonialismo en el pensamiento social latinoamericano," in Roberto Briceño-León and Heinz R. Sonntag (eds.), *Pueblo, época y desarrollo: la sociología de América Latina*. Caracas: Nueva Sociedad, 87–96.

Landolt, Patricia, Lillian Autler, and Sonia Baires. 1999. "From Hermano Lejano to Hermano Mayor: The Dialectics of Salvadoran Transnationalism." *Ethnic and Racial Studies* 22: 2 (March).

Landolt-Marticorena, and Patricia Andre, "The Cause and Consequences of Transnational Migration: Salvadorans in Los Angeles and Washington, D.C.," PhD diss. John Hopkins University, January 2000.

Langman, Lauren. In Press. "From Virtual Public Spheres to Global Justice: A Critical Theory of Inter-networked Social Movements." *Sociological Theory.*

Langman, Lauren. 1998. "Bakhtin the Future," in Devorah Kalekin (ed.), *Designs for Alienation.* Helsinki: SoPhil Press, 341–366.

Langman, Lauren. 1993. "Neon Cages: Shopping for Subjectivity," in Rob Shields (ed.), *Lifestyle Shopping.* London: Routledge, 40–82.

Langman, Lauren, and Katie Cangemi. 2003. "Globalization and the Liminal: Transgression, Identity and the Urban Primitive," in Terry Clark (ed.), *The City as Entertainment, Volume 9 of Research in Urban Policy.* New York: JAI Press/Elsevier, 141–176.

Langman, Lauren, Douglas Morris, and Jackie Zalewski. 2002. "Cyberactivism and Alternative Global-ization Movements," in Wilma A. Dunaway (ed.), *Emerging Issues in the 21st Century World.* Westport, CT: Greenwood, 218–235.

Lapham, L. 2003. "The Demonstration Effect." *Harper's Magazine* (June): 10.

Las Dong Newspaper, September, 2002; October, 2002; March, 2003.

Latina. Caracas: Nueva Sociedad, 139–155.

Lee, Ching Kwan. 1998. *Gender and the South China Miracle: Two Worlds of Factory Women.* Berkeley, CA: University of California Press.

Lee, Everett. 1966. "A Theory of Migration." *Demography* 3: 47–57.

Lee, Su-Hoon. 1998. "Crisis in Korea and the IMF Control," in Eun-Mee Kim (ed.), *The Four Asian Tigers: Economic Development and the Global Political Economy.* San Diego, CA: Academic, 210–228.

Lefkowitz, Mary. 1996. *Not Out of Africa: How Afrocentrism Became an Excuse To Teach Myth as History.* New York: Basic Books.

Lemann, N. "The Next World Order." *The New Yorker* January 4, 2002. http://www.newyorker.com/fact/content/?020401fa_FACT1.

Lemert, Charles. 1996. *Sociology after the Crisis.* Boulder, CO: Westview.

Lemert, Charles. 1993. "Social Theory: Its Uses and Pleasures," in Charles Lemert (ed.), *Social Theory: The Multicultural and Classical Readings.* Boulder, CO: Westview, 1–24.

Lenin, V.I. 1965. "Imperialism: the Highest Stage of Capitalism," in *Selected Works,* Volume 1. Moscow: Progress Publishers.

Lenin, Vladimir Ilyich. 1947. *What Is To Be Done? Burning Questions of Our Movement.* Moscow: Progress.

Lenin, Vladimir Ilyich. 1943. 1971 printing. [1905] *State and Revolution.* New York: International Publishers.

Letwin, Michael. 2003. "Growth of Labor Anti-War Action Tied to Bush's Anti-Worker Moves." Labor Notes (April).

Levine, Molly Myerowitz. 1992. "Review Article: The Use and Abuse of Black Athena." *American Historical Review* (April): 440–464.

Levitt, Peggy. 2001. *The Transnational Villagers.* Berkeley, CA: University of California Press.

Levitt, Peggy. 1999. "The Salvadoran Remittance Business: The Role of Trust in a Transnational Enter-prise," paper given at the American Sociology Association meetings, August, Chicago, IL.

Levy, Jack. 1998. "The Causes of War and the Conditions of Peace," *Annual Review of Political Science* 1: 139–165.

Levy, Jack. 1989. "The Diversionary Theory of War: A Critique," in Manus I. Midlarsky (ed.), *Handbook of War Studies.* London: Allen and Unwin, 258–288.

Licuanan, Patricia. 1994. "The Socio-Economic Impact of Domestic Worker Migration: Individual, Family, Community and Country," in N. Heyzer, G. Lycklama à Nijeholt, and N. Weerakoon (eds.), *The Trade in Domestic Workers: Causes, Mechanisms and Consequences of International Migration.* London: Zed, 103–106.

Liechty, Mark. 2003. *Suitably Modern: Making Middle-Class Culture in a New Consumer Society.* Princeton, NJ: Princeton University Press.

Lim, Hwei-Mian, Chee Heng-Leng, Mirnalini Kandiah, Sharifah Zainiyah Syed Yahya, and Rashidah Shuib. 2002. "Work and Lifestyle Factors Associated with Morbidity of Electronic Women Workers in Selangor, Malaysia." *Asia-Pacific Journal of Public Health* 14 (2): 75–84.

Lim, L. L. (ed.), 1998. *The Sex Sector: The Economic and Social Bases of Prostitution in Southeast Asia.* Geneva: International Labour Office.

Límon, Graciela. 2001. *Erased Faces.* Houston: Arte Publico.

Lind, Amy, and Jessica Share. 2003. "Queering Development: Institutionalized Heterosexuality in Development Theory, Practice and Politics in Latin America," in K.-K. Bhavnani, J. Foran, and P. Kurian (eds.), *Feminist Futures: Re-Imagining Women, Culture and Development.* London: Zed, 55–72.

Ling, L. H. M. 2002. *Postcolonial International Relations: Conquest and Desire between Asia and the West.* U.K.: Palgrave.

Linger, Daniel Touro. l992. *Dangerous Encounters: Meanings of Violence in a Brazilian City.* Stanford: Stanford University Press.

Linklater, Andrew. 1990. *Men and Citizens in the Theory of International Relations.* London: Macmillan.

Lipschutz, Ronnie. 2000. "Regulation for the Rest of Us? Global Civil Society, Social Regulation and National Impacts." Workshop on Human Rights and Globalization, UC-Santa Cruz, December 1–2, 2000.

Lipsitz, George. 2003. "Noise in the Blood: Culture, Conflict, and Mixed Race Identities." *Crossing Lines: Race and Mixed Race across the Geohistorical Divide.* Santa Barbara, CA. Multiethnic Student Outreach in collaboration with the Center of Chicano Studies, University of California, Santa Barbara, 32–35.

Lipsitz, George. 1994. *A Rainbow at Midnight: Labor and Culture in the 1940s.* Urbana: University of Illinois Press.

Lock, Margaret, and Patricia A. Kaufert (eds.), 1998. *Pragmatic Women and Body Politics.* Cambridge: Cambridge University Press.

Lopez-Garza, Marta, and David R. Diaz. 2001. *Asian and Latino Immigrants in a Restructuring Economy: The Metamorphosis of Southern California.* Stanford, CA: Stanford University Press.

Lovink, Geert, and Patrice Riemens. 2002. "Digital City Amsterdam: Local Uses of Global Networks," in Sassen (ed.), *Global Networks/Linked Cities.* New York and London: Routledge.

Low, Setha M. 1999. "Theorizing the City," in Low (ed.) Theorizing the City. New Brunswick, NJ: Rutgers University Press.

Löwy, M. 2002. "Debate: Towards a New International?" *Revista Rebeldia* 2 (December). http://www.revistarebeldia.org.

Luker, Kristin. 1975. *Taking Chances: Abortion and the Decision Not To Contracept.* Berkeley, CA: University of California Press.

Lupton, Deborah. 1999. *Risk.* London: Routledge.

Luxemburg, R. 1968 edition. *The Accumulation of Capital.* New York: Monthly Review Press, 452–453.

MacGregor, Donald G., Paul Slovic, and Torbjorn Malmfors. 1999. "How Exposed is Exposed Enough?" Lay Inferences about Chemical Exposure. *Risk Analysis* 19 (4): 649–659.

Macomber, John, Charles Mathias, Jack Seymour Jr., and Michael E. C. Ely. 1998. "Third Party Arms Transfers: Requirements for the 21st Century." The Atlantic Council of the United States.

Magnusson, Warren. 1996. *The Search for Political Space.* Toronto: University of Toronto Press.

Mahler, Sarah J. 1999. "Engendering Transnational Migration: A Case Study of Salvadorans." *American Behavioral Scientist* 42: 690–719.

Mahler, Sarah J. 1998. *Theoretical and Empirical Contributions toward a Research Agenda for Transnationalism.* New Brunswick: Transaction Press.

Malanczuk, Peter (ed.), 1997. *Akehurst's Modern Introduction to International Law,* 7th revised edition. New York: Routledge.

Mamdani, Mahmood. 1996. *Citizen and Subject. Contemporary Africa and the Legacy of Late Colonialism.* Princeton, NJ: Princeton University Press.

Mann, R. (Director), and Harrelson, W. (Narrator). 1999. *Grass.* Documentary on the history of marijuana in the United States, Canadian.

Mannheim, Karl. 1952. "The Problem of Generations." *Essays in the Sociology of Knowledge.* London: Routledge & Kegan Paul, 276–322.

Marable, Manning. 1995. *Beyond Black and White: Transforming African American Politics*. New York: Verso.

Marchand, Marianne, and Ann Sisson Runyan (eds.), 2000. *Gender and Global Restructuring*. London: Routledge.

Marcos, Subcomandante. 1995. *Shadows of Tender Fury: The Letters and Communiqués of Subcomandante Marcos and the Zapatista Army of National Liberation*. Translated by Frank Bardacke, Leslie López, and the Watsonville, California, Human Rights Committee. New York: Monthly Review Press.

Marcus, George E. 1995. "Ethnography in/of the World System: The Emergence of Multi-Sited Ethnography." *Annual Review of Anthropology* 24: 95–117.

Marcuse, Peter and Ronald van Kempen. 2000. *Globalizing Cities. A New Spatial Order*. Oxford: Blackwell.

Marshall, S. 2003. "Prime Time Payola." *In These Times* 27 (11–12) (May 5): 23–24.

Marx, Karl, *Capital Volume 1*, Penguin Classics, 1990 (reprinted).

Marx, Karl. 1859. "Preface." *A Contribution to the Critique of Political Economy*. Retrieved from http://www.marxists.org/archive/marx/works/1859/critique-pol-economy/preface.htm on April 20, 2003.

Marx, Karl, and Friedrich Engels. 1988 [1848]. *The Communist Manifesto*. Harmondsworth: Penguin.

Marx, Kerstin. "Economic Crisis Causes Massive Unemployment in Asia." *Asia Times Online* (May 25, 1999). http://www.atimes.com/asia-crisis/AE25Db01.html.

Masika, Rachel (ed.), 2002. *Gender, Trafficking and Slavery*. Oxford: Oxfam.

Massey, Doreen. 1993. "Politics and Space/Time" in M. Keith and S. Pile (eds.), *Place and the Politics of Identity*. London and New York: Routledge, 141–161.

Massey, Douglas, Joaquin Arango, Graeme Hugo, Ali Kouaouci, Adela Pellegrino, and J. Edward Taylor. 1993. "Theories of International Migration." *Population and Development Review* 19 (3).

Mathews, Gordon. 2000. *Global Culture/Individual Identity: Searching for Home in the Cultural Supermarket*. London: Routledge.

McAdam, Doug, Sidney Tarrow, and Charles Tilly. 2001. *Dynamics of Contention*. New York: Cambridge University Press.

McLaren, P. and Farahmandpur, R. 2005. Teaching Against Globalization and the New Imperialism: A Critical Pedagogy. Lanham, Maryland: Rowman and Littlefield.

McLaren, P., G. Martin, R. Farahmandpur, and N. Jaramillo. 2004. "Teaching in and against the Empire: Critical Pedagogy as Revolutionary Praxis." *Journal of Teacher Education*. 31 (3) (winter): 131–153.

McLaren, P. 2003. "Critical Pedagogy and Class Struggle in the Age of Neoliberal Globalization." *Democracy and Nature*. 9 (1) (March): 65–90.

McLaren, P. and Jaramillo, N. 2004a. "A Moveable Fascism: Fear and Loathing in the Empire of Sand." Cultural Studies/Critical Methodologies, 4 (2) (May): 223–236.

McLaren P. and Jaramillo, N. 2002. "Critical Pedagogy as Organized Praxis: Challenging the Demise of Civil Society in a Time of Permanent War." *Educational Foundations*, 16 (4) (fall): 5–32.

McLaren P. adn Jaramillo, N. 2004b. "Critical Pedagogy in a Time of Permanent War." In Jeffrey R. DiLeo and Walter R. Jacobs (eds.), If Classrooms Matter: Progressive Visions of Educational Environments. London and New York: Routledge, 75–92.

McMichael, Philip. 2004a. *Development and Social Change. A Global Perspective*. Thousand Oaks: Pine Forge Press. 3rd Edition.

McMichael, Philip. 2004b. "Globalization," in Thomas Janoski, Robert Alford, Alexander M. Hicks, and Mildred A. Schwartz (eds.), *A Handbook of Political Sociology: States, Civil Societies and Globalization*. New York: Cambridge University Press.

McMichael, Philip. 2003a. "Food Security and Social Reproduction: Issues and Contradictions," in Isabella Bakker and Stephen Gill (eds.), *Power, Production and Reproduction*. Hampshire: Palgrave Macmillan, 169–189.

McMichael, Philip. 2003b. *Development and Social Change: A Global Perspective*, 3rd edition. Thousand Oaks, CA: Pine Forge.

McMichael, Philip. 1999. "The Global Crisis of Wage Labour." *Studies in Political Economy* 58: 11–40.

McLaren, P., G. Martin, R. Farahmandpur, and N. Jaramillo. Forthcoming. "Teaching in and against the Empire: Critical Pedagogy as Revolutionary Praxis." *Journal of Teacher Education*.

McNeely, C. L. 1995. Constructing the Nation-State. Westport, CT: Greenwood.

McNeill, William. 1982. *The Pursuit of Power*. Chicago: University of Chicago Press.

Meinecke, Friedrick. 1970 [1909]. *Cosmopolitanism and the National State*. Princeton, NJ: Princeton University Press.

Mele, C. 1999. "Cyberspace and Disadvantaged Communities: The Internet as a Tool for Collective Action," in M. A. Smith and P. Kollock (eds.), *Communities in Cyberspace*. London: Routledge, 264–289.

Melucci, A. 1996. *Challenging Codes: Collective Action in the Information Age*. Cambridge University Press.

Mendonca, M. L. 2003. "New Challenges for Brazilian Grassroots Movements." *Economic Justice News* 6 (1) (April): 3, 14–15.

Menjivar, Cecilia. 2000. *Fragmented Ties: Salvadoran Immigrant Network in America*. Los Angeles, CA: University of California Press.

Mennell, Stephen. 1990. "The Globalization of Human History as a Very Long-term Social Process: Elias's Theory." *Theory, Culture & Society* 7: 359–371.

Merli, Giovanna M. 1997. "Estimation of International Migration for Vietnam 1979–1989." Seattle: University of Washington.

Meyer, John W., John Boli, George M. Thomas, and Francisco O. Ramirez. 1997. "World Society and the Nation-State." *American Journal of Sociology* 103 (1) (July): 144–181.

Meyer, Mary K. 1999. "The Women's International League for Peace and Freedom: Organizing Women for Peace in the War System," in Mary K. Meyer and Elisabeth Prugl (eds.), *Gender Politics in Global Governance*. Lanham, MD: Rowman & Littlefield, 107–121.

Mies, Maria. 1986. *Patriarchy and Accumulation on a World Scale: Women in the International Division of Labor*. London: Zed.

Mignolo, Walter. 2000. *Local Histories/Global Designs: Essays on the Coloniality of Power, Subaltern Knowledges and Border Thinking*. Princeton, NJ: Princeton University Press.

Mignolo, Walter. 1995. *The Darker Side of the Renaissance: Literacy, Territoriality and Colonication*. Ann Arbor: The Univeristy of Michigan Press.

Milanovic, Branko. 1999. "True World Income Distribution, 1988 and 1993." *Policy Research Working Paper 2244*. Washington, D.C.: The World Bank.

Miller, Daniel, and Don Slater. 2000. *The Internet: An Ethnographic Approach*. Oxford: Berg.

Miller, J. 2002. "Violence and Coercion in Sri Lanka's Commercial Sex Industry." *Violence against Women* 8 (9) (September): 1044–1073.

Mills, C. Wright. 1956. *The Power Elite*. New York: Oxford University Press.

Mittelman, James H. 2004. "Globalization Debates: Bringing in Microencounters." *Globalizations* 1 (1) (August): xxx–xxx.

Mittelman, James H. 2004. *Whither Globalization? The Vortex of Knowledge and Ideology*. London: Routledge.

Mittelman, James H. 2002. "Globalization: An Ascendant Paradigm?" *International Studies Perspectives* 3 (1) (February): 1–14.

Mittelman, James H. 2000. *The Globalization Syndrome: Transformation and Resistance*. Princeton, NJ: Princeton University Press.

Mittelman, James H. (ed.), 1996. *Globalization: Critical Reflections*. Boulder, CO: Lynne Reinner.

Moghadam, Valentine M. 2003. *Modernizing Women: Gender and Social Change in the Middle East*, 2nd edition. Boulder, CO: Lynne Rienner.

Moghadam, Valentine M. 2002. "Islamic Feminism and Its Discontents: Toward a Resolution of the Debate," *Signs: Journal of Women in Culture and Society* 27 (4) (summer): 1135–1171.

Moghadam, Valentine M. "The Feminization of Poverty? Notes on a Concept and Trends." Illinois State University Women's Studies Program, Occasional Paper No. 2 (August 1997).

Moghadam, Valentine M. (ed.), 1994. *Identity Politics and Women: Cultural Reassertions and Feminisms in International Perspective*. Boulder, CO: Westview.

Mohanty, Chandra. 2003. *Feminism without Borders: Decolonizing Theory, Practicing Solidarity*. Duke University Press.

Mohanty, Chandra Talpade. 2000. "Under Western Eyes: Feminist Scholarship and Colonial Discourses," in Les Back and John Solomos (ed.), *Theories of Race and Racism*. London and New York: Routledge, 302–323.

Monteiro, A. 2003. "Race and the Racialized State: A Du Boisian Interrogation." *Socialism and Democracy Online* 17 (1). http://www.sdonline.org/33/anthony_monteiro.htm.

Moore, Carlos. 1988. *Castro, the Blacks and Africa*. Los Angeles, CA: Center for Afro-American Studies at University of California.

Mora, Mariana, 1988. "Zapatismo: Gender, Power, and Social Transformation," in Lois Ann Lorentzen and Jennifer Turpin (eds.), *The Women & War Reader*, New York, New York University Press, 164–176.

Moraga, Cherrie, and Gloria Anzaldúa (eds.), 1983. *This Bridge Called My Back: Writing by Radical Women of Color*. New York: Kitchen Table/Women of Color.

Morley, James W., and Masashi Nishihara. 1997. *Vietnam Joins the World*. Armonk, NY: ME Sharpe.

Morrill, Richard. 1999. "Inequalities of Power, Costs and Benefits across Geographic Scales: The Future Uses of the Hanford Reservation." *Political Geography* 18: 1–23.

Moure-Eraso, R., M. Wilcox, L. Punnett, L. MacDonald, and C. Levenstein. 1997. "Back to the Future: Sweatshop Conditions on the Mexico–U.S. Border. II. Occupational Health Impact of Maquiladora Industrial Activity." *American Journal of Industrial Medicine* 31: 587–599.

Munshi, Shoma. 2001. "Marvelous Me: The Beauty Industry and the Construction of the 'Modern' Indian Woman," in S. Munshi (ed.), *Images of the "Modern" Woman in Asia: Global Media, Local Meanings*. Richmond, Surrey: Curzon, 78–93.

Murphy, Craig. 1994. *International Organization and Industrial Change: Global Governance since 1850*. New York: Oxford University Press.

Myers, Linda James. 1998. "The Deep Structure of Culture: Relevance of Traditional African Culture in Contemporary Life," in Janice D. Hamlet (ed.), *Afrocentric Visions: Studies in Culture and Communication*. Thousand Oaks, CA: Sage, 1–14.

Naples, N. A., and M. Desai (eds.), 2002. *Women's Activism and Globalization: Linking Local Struggles and Global Politics*. London: Routledge.

Nash, J., and M. P. Fernandez-Kelly. 1983. *Women, Men and the International Division of Labor*. Albany, NY: State University of New York Press.

NCFLL. 2003. National Council of Field Labor Locals, "2003 Budget Analysis: FY 2003 DOL Budget in Brief Overall." http://www.ncfll.org/2.27.02%20DOL%20Budget.pdf.

Nederveen Pieterse, Jan. 1994. "Unpacking the West: How European Is Europe?," in Ali Ratanssi and Sallie Westwood (ed.), *Racism, Modernity and Identity: On the Western Front*. Cambridge: Polity, 129–150.

Nettime. 1997. Net Critique. Compiled by Geert Lovink and Pit Schultz. Berlin: Edition ID-ARchiv.

Neufeld, Mark. 2002. "Democratic Socialism in a Global(-izing) Context: Towards a Collective Research Programme," paper presented at the 2002 Convention of the International Studies Association in New Orleans, March 23–27.

Nguyen, Hong. 2002. "*Viet Kieu* Remittances Set to Top $2 Billion Target." *Vietnam Investment Review* (December 9).

Nguyen, Van Linh. 1989. "The Trade Unions must renew their activities," in *Vietnam Courier* No. 1.

Nha Xuat Ban Chinh tri Quoc Gia, *Van Ban Huong Dan Thi Hanh Bo Luat Last Dong*. (Documents for the Implementation of the Labor Code). Hanoi: Chinh Tri Quoc Gia Publisher, 1996.

Nissen, Bruce (ed.), 2002. *Unions in a Globalized Environment: Changing Borders, Organizational Boundaries, and Social Roles*. Armonk, NY: M. E. Sharpe.

NLC. 1999. National Labor Committee, "Fired For Crying to the Gringos: The Women in El Salvador Who Sew Liz Clairborne Garments Speak Out Asking for Justice." New York: NLC.

Norlund, Irene. 1997. "The Labour Market in Vietnam: Between State Incorporation and Autonomy," in Johannes Schmidt, Jacques Hersh, and Niels Fold (eds.), *Social change in Southeast Asia*. Harlow, Essex: Longman.

Norlund, Irene. 1996. "Democracy and Trade Unions in Vietnam: Riding a Honda in Low Gear." *The Copenhagen Journal of Asian Studies* (November).

Notes from Nowhere. 2003. *We Are Everywhere: The Irresistible Rise of Global Anticapitalism*. London: Verso.

Nuestra America: una sola patria. 2003. http://www.unasolapatria.org/documento.html.

Nussbaum, Martha C., with Respondents. 1996. *For Love of Country: Debating the Limits of Patriotism*, Edited by Joshua Cohen. Boston: Beacon.

O'Brien, Robert, Anne Marie Goetz, Jan Aart Scholte, and Marc Williams. 2000. *Contesting Global Governance: Multilateral Economic Institutions and Global Social Movements*. Cambridge: Cambridge University Press.

O'Byrne, Darren J. 2003. *The Dimensions of Global Citizenship: Political Identity Beyond the Nation-State*. London: Frank Cass.

O'Byrne, Darren J. 2002. *Human Rights: An Introduction*. London: Prentice-Hall.

O'Byrne, Darren J. 2001. "On the Construction of Political Identity: Negotiations and Strategies Beyond the Nation-State," in Paul Kennedy and Catherine J. Danks (eds.), *Globalization and National Identities: Crisis or Opportunity?* Basingstoke: Palgrave.

Ofreneo, R. P. 1994. "The Philippine Garment Industry," in E. Bonacich, L. Cheng, N. Chinchilla, N. Hamilton, and P. Ong (eds.), *Global Production: The Apparel Industry in the Pacific Rim*. Philadelphia: Temple University Press, 162–179.

Ofreneo, Rene E., and Rosalinda Pineda Ofreneo. 1998. "Prostitution in the Philippines," in Lin Lean Lim (ed.), *The Sex Sector: The Economic and Social Bases of Prostitution in Southeast Asia*. Geneva: ILO, 100–129.

Ofreneo, Rosalinda Pineda, Joseph Y. Lim, and Lourdes Abad Gula. 2002. "The View from Below: Impact of the Financial Crisis on Subcontracted Workers in the Philippines," in Radhika Balakrishnan (ed.), *The Hidden Assembly Line: Gender Dynamics of Subcontracted Work in a Global Economy*, Bloomfield, CT: Kumarian, 87–114.

Olds, Kris, Peter Dicken, Philip F. Kelly, Lily Kong and Henry Wai-Chung Yeung (eds.). 1999. *Globalisation and the Asia-Pacific: Contested Territories*. London: Routledge.

Ollman, Bertell. 1998. "Why Dialectics? Why Now?," *Science and Society* 62 (3): 339–357.

Ollman, Bertell. 1976. *Alienation*, 2nd edition. Cambridge: Cambridge University Press.

Omi, Michael, and Howard Winant. 1994. *Racial Formation in the 1980s and 1990s*. New York: Routledge.

Ong, Aihwa. 1988. "Colonialism and Modernity: Feminist Representations of Women in Non-Western Societies." *Inscriptions* 3/4: 79–93.

Ong, Aihwa. 1987. *Spirits of Resistance and Capitalist Discipline: Factory Women in Malaysia*. Albany, NY: State University of New York Press.

Ong, Aihwa. 1999. *Flexible Citizenship: The Cultural Logics of Transnationality*. Durham, NC: Duke University Press.

O'Rouke, Dara. *Community-Driven Regulation: Balancing Development and the Environment in Vietnam*. Cambridge, MA: MIT Press, 2004.

O'Rourke, Dara. 2003. "Outsourcing Regulation: Analyzing Non-Governmental Systems of Labor Standards and Monitoring." *Policy Studies Journal* 31 (1): 1–29.

O'Rourke, Dara. 2000. "Monitoring the Monitors: A Critique of Pricewaterhouse Cooper's Labor Monitoring," white paper, released September 28, 2000.

O'Rourke, Dara. 1997. "Smoke from a Hired Gun: A Critique of NIKE's Labor and Environmental Auditing." San Francisco: Transnational Resource and Action Center.

O'Rourke et al. 2000. Independent University Initiative: Final Report (September). http://www.acs.ohio-state.edu/osu/newsrel/IUIReport.pdf.

O'Rourke, Kevin H. 2001. "Globalization and Inequality: Historical Trends." *NBER Working Paper Series 8339*. Cambridge, MA: National Bureau of Economic Research.

O'Rourke, Kevin H, and Jeffrey G. Williamson. 2000. *Globalization and History: The Evolution of a 19th Century Atlantic Economy*. Cambridge, MA: MIT Press.

Orozco, Manuel. 2002. "From Family Ties to Transnational Linkages: The Impact of Family Remittances in Latin America." *Latin American Politics and Society* 44 (2) (summer).

Orru, Marco, Nicole Biggart, and Gary Hamilton. 1991. "Organizational Isomorphism in East Asia: Broadening the New Institutionalism," in Walter W. Powell and Paul J. Dimaggior (eds.), *The New Institutionalism in Organizational Analysis*. Chicago: University of Chicago Press, 361–389.

Ortega, Bob. 1998. *In Sam We Trust: The Untold Story of Sam Walton and how Wal-Mart is Devouring America*. New York: Random House.

Orum, Anthony and Xianming Chen. 2002. *Urban Places*. Malden, MA: Blackwell.

Osella, Filippo, and Caroline Osella. 2000. *Social Mobility in Kerala: Modernity and Identity in Conflict.* London: Pluto.

Overbeek, H. 2001. "Transnational Historical Materialism: Theories of Transnational Class Formation and World Order," in R. Palan (ed.), *The New Global Political Economy: Theorizing and Approaches.* London: Routledge, 168–184.

Oza, Rupal. 2001. "Showcasing India: Gender, Geography, and Globalization." *Signs* 26 (4) 1067–1095.

Pace, William, and Mark Thieroff. 1999. "Participation of Non-Governmental Organizations," in Roy Lee (ed.), *The International Criminal Court: The Making of the Rome Statute.* Cambridge, MA: Kluwer Law International, 391–398.

Packard, Le Anh Tu. 1999. "Asian American Economic Engagement: Vietnam Case Study," in E. Hu-Dehart (ed.), *Across the Pacific: Asian Americans and Globalization.* Philadelphia: Temple University Press, 79–108.

Page, David, and William Crawley. 2001. *Satellites over South Asia: Broadcasting, Culture, and the Public Interest.* New Delhi: Sage.

Palan, Ronen. 2000. "New Trends in Global Political Economy," in Palan (ed.), *Global Political Economy: Contemporary Theories.* London and New York: Routledge, 1–18.

Panitch, Leo. 1998. "'The State in a Changing World: Social-Democratizing Global Capitalism?" *Monthly Review* 50 (5): 11–22.

Panitch, Leo. 1996. "Rethinking the Role of the State," in J. Mittelman (ed.), *Globalization: Critical Reflections.* Boulder, CO: Lynne Reinner, 83–113.

Parenti, M. 2003. "To Kill Iraq: The Reasons Why." http://www.michaelparenti.org/IRAQGeorge2.html.

Park, N-H. 2001. "Poverty Rate and Poverty Line in Korea." Conference paper for the Philippine Institute for Development Studies (April).

Parker, Richard. 2001. "Sexuality, Culture, and Power in HIV/AIDS Research." *Annual Review of Anthropology* 30: 163–179.

Parker, Richard. 1991. *Bodies, Pleasures, and Passions: Sexual Culture in Contemporary Brazil.* Boston: Beacon.

Parnreiter, Christoff. 2002. "The Making of a Global City: Mexico City." In Sassen (ed.) Global Networks/ Linked Cities. New York and London: Routledge.

Parreñas, Rhacel Salazar. 2001. *Servants of Globalization: Women, Migration, and Domestic Work.* Stanford, CA: Stanford University Press.

Parreñas, Rhacel Salazar. 2001. "Mothering From a Distance: Emotions, Gender, and Inter-Generational Relations in Filipino Transnational Families." *Feminist Studies* 27: 361–390.

Parreñas, Rhacel Salazar. 2000. "Migrant Filipina Domestic Workers and the International Division of Reproductive Labor." *Gender & Society* 14 (4): 560–580.

Parulekar, Susan. n.d. "Transforming and Imagining Elite Femininity: Globalization and the Elite Female in Bombay India."

Passy, F. 2000. *Socialization, Recruitment and the Structure/Agency Gap. A Specification of the Impact of Networks on Participation in Social Movements.* University of Florence. Mimeo.

Patel, Rajeev, and Philip McMichael. 2004. "Global Fascism versus the Third World: Neo-liberalism and the Regrouping of the Global South." *Third World Quarterly* 25 (1).

Pathak, Rahul. 1994. "The New Generation." *India Today* January 31: 48–60.

Peck, Jamie, and Henry Wai-chung Yeung. 2003. *Remaking the Global Economy: Economic-Geographical Perspectives.* London: Sage.

Pedraza, Silvia. 1991. "Women and Migration: The Social Consequences of Gender." *Annual Review of Sociology* 17: 303–325.

Pels, Dick. 1999. "Privileged Nomads — On the Strangeness of Intellectuals and the Intellectuality of Strangers." *Theory, Culture and Society* 16 (1): 63–86.

Peoples, James. 1998. "Deregulation and the Labor Market." *Journal of Economic Perspectives* 12: 111–130.

Perelman, M. 2000. *The Invention of Capitalism: Classical Political Economy and the Secret History of Primitive Accumulation.* Durham, NC: Duke University Press.

Perle, Ricahrd. 2001. "Next Stop Iraq." http://www.fpri.org/enotes, 11–30.

Peschard-Sverdrup, A. 2003. "México Alert: The Impact of the War in Iraq on México." *CSIS Hemisphere Focus* XI (10).

Pessar, Patricia R. 1999. "Engendering Migration Studies: The Case of Immigrants in the United States." *American Behavioral Scientist* 42: 577–600.

Peterson, V. S. 2003. *A Critical Rewriting of Global Political Economy: Integrating Reproductive, Productive, and Virtual Economies*. London: Routledge.

Peterson, V. Spike. 2000. "Sexing Political Identities/Nationalism as Heterosexism," in Sita Ranchod-Nilsson and Mary Ann Tetreault (eds.), *Women, States and Nationalism: At Home in the Nation*, London: Routledge, 54–80.

Peterson, V. Spike, and Anne Sisson Runyan. 1999. *Global Gender Issues*, 2nd edition. Boulder, CO: Westview.

Petras, J. "Notes toward an Understanding of Revolutionary Politics Today." *Links* 19 (September to December, 2001): 1–21. http://www.dsp.org.au/links/back/issue19/petras.htm.

Petras, J., and Veltmeyer, H. 2001. *Globalization Unmasked: Imperialism in the 21st Century*. Halifax, Canada and London, England: Fernwood and Zed Books.

Pham Quang Ham, Development Strategy Institute Ministry of Planning and Investment, 1998 interview.

Phizacklea, A. 1983. *One Way Ticket: Migration and Female Labour*. London: Routledge & Kegan Paul.

Pilger, John. 2002. *The New Rulers of the World*. London and New York: Verso.

Piñeyro, J. L. 2003. "Mexico's Northern Border, Safe and Smart?" *Visions of Mexico* 62: 10–13.

Piore, Michael J. 1979. *Birds of Passage: Migrant Labor in Industrial Society*. Cambridge: Cambridge University Press.

Pitt, William Rivers. 2003. "Be Afraid." *The Ecologist* 33 (3): 21–22.

Podobnik, Bruce. 2002. "The Globalization Protest Movement: An Analysis of Broad Trends and the Impact of September 11." American Sociological Association Meeting, Chicago.

Podobnik, Bruce. 2003. "Resistance to Globalization: Social Transformations in the Globalization Protest Movement." Paper presented at the annual meeting of the International Studies Association, Portland.

Poggi, Gianfranco. 1978. *The Development of the Modern State: A Sociological Introduction*. Stanford, CA: Stanford University Press.

Polanyi, Karl. 1957. *The Great Transformation: The Political and Economic Origins of Our Times*. Boston: Beacon.

Popkin, Eric. 1999. "Guatemalan Mayan Migration to Los Angeles: Constructing Transnational Linkages in the Context of the Settlement Process." *Ethnic and Racial Studies* 22: 267–289.

Portes, Alejandro. 2000. "Globalization from Below: The Rise of Transnational Communities," in Don Kalb, Marco van der Land, Richard Staring, Bart van Steenbergen, and Nico Wilterdink (eds.), *The Ends of Globalization: Bringing Society Back In*. Boulder and New York: Rowman & Littlefield, 253–270.

Portes, Alejandro, Luis E. Guarnizo, and Patricia Landolt (eds.), 1999. *Transnational Communities. Special Issue of Ethnic and Racial Studies* 22 (2): 217–463.

Portes, Alejandro, Luis Eduardo Guarnizo, and Patricia Landolt. 1999. "The Study of Transnationalism: Pitfalls and Promise of an Emergent Research Field." *Ethnic and Racial Studies* 22 (2): 217–237.

Poster, Mark. 1997. "Cyberdemocracy: Internet and the Public Sphere," in D. Porter (ed.), *Internet Culture*. London: Routledge, 201–218.

Preliminary Survey Report on Sexual Trafficking in the CIS. 1999. MiraMed Institute. http://www.mira-medinstitute.org/pdf/Trafficking%20Survey.PDF.

President of the United States. *The National Security Strategy of the United States of America*. Washington, D.C.: The White House (September 2002). http://www.whitehouse.gov/nsc/nss.pdf.

Project for a New American Century. "Rebuilding America's Defenses: Strategy, Forces, and Resources for a New Century." Washington, D.C.: September 2000. http://www.newamericancentury.org/RebuildingAmericasDefenses.pdf.

PSPD/UNDP. 2000. *Poverty Status and Monitoring of Korea in the Aftermath of the Financial Crisis*. Seoul, People's Solidarity for Participatory Democracy and the United Nations Development Programme.

Puri, Jyoti. 1997. "Reading Romance Novels in Postcolonial India." *Gender & Society* 11, 434–452.

Pye, Lucian W. 1985. *Asian Power and Politics: The Cultural Dimensions of Authority*. Cambridge, MA: Belknap Press of Harvard University Press.

Pyle, J. L. 2002. "Globalization, Public Policy, and the Gendered Division of Labor," keynote address at the Third International Congress on Women, Work and Health. Stockholm, Sweden.

Pyle, J. L. 2001. "Sex, Maids, and Export Processing: Risks and Reasons for Gendered Global Production Networks." *The International Journal of Politics, Culture, and Society* 15 (1): 55–76.

Pyle, J. L. 1999. "Third World Women and Global Restructuring," in J. Chafetz (ed.), *Handbook of the Sociology of Gender*. New York: Kluwer Academic/Plenum, 81–104.

Pyle, J., and Ward, K. 2003. "Recasting Our Understanding of Gender and Work during Global Restructuring." *International Sociology*, special issue on Globalization, Gender, and Social Change in the 21st Century. 18 (3): 461–489.

Quijano, Aníbal. 2000. "Coloniality of Power, Ethnocentrism, and Latin America." *NEPANTLA* 1 (3): 533–580.

Quijano, Aníbal. 1998. "La colonialidad del poder y la experiencia cultural latinoamericana," in Roberto Briceño-León and Heinz R. Sonntag (eds.), *Pueblo, época y desarrollo: la sociología de América Latina*. Caracas: Nueva Sociedad, 139–155.

Quijano, Aníbal. 1993. "'Raza', 'Etnia' y 'Nación' en Mariátegui: Cuestiones Abiertas," in Roland Forgues (ed.), *José Carlos Mariátgui y Europa: El Otro Aspecto del Descubrimiento*. Lima, Perú: Empresa Editora Amauta S. A., 167–187.

Quijano, Aníbal. 1991. "Colonialidad y Modernidad/Racionalidad." *Perú Indígena* 29: 11–21.

Quijano, Aníbal and Immanuel Wallerstein. 1992. "Americanity as a Concept, or the Americas in the Modern World-System." *International Journal of Social Sciences* 134: 583–591.

Ram, K., and M. Jolly (eds.), 1997. *Maternities and Modernities: Colonial and Post Colonial Experiences in Asian and the Pacific*. Cambridge: Cambridge University Press.

Rasiah, R. 2001. "Pre-Crisis Economic Weaknesses and Vulnerabilities," in Jomo, K. S. (ed.), *Malaysian Eclipse: Economic Crisis and Recovery*. London: Zed Books, 47–66.

Rasiah, Rajah. 1993. "Competition and Governance: Work in Malaysia's Textile and Garment Industries." *Journal of Contemporary Asia* 23 (1).

Rattansi, Ali. 1994. "'Western' Racisms, Ethnicities and Identities," in Ali Ratanssi and Sallie Westwood (ed.), *Racism, Modernity and Identity: On the Western Front*. Cambridge: Polity, 15–86.

Rauch, J., and P. Evans. 2000. "Bureaucratic Structure and Bureaucratic Performance in Less Developed Countries." *Journal of Public Economics* 75 (1): 49–71.

Ray, Larry J. 1993. *Rethinking Critical Theory: Emancipation in an Age of Global Social Movements*. London: Sage, 7.

Raymond, J., J. D'Cunha, S. R. Dzuhayatin, H. P. Hynes, Z. R. Rodriguez, and A. Santos. 2002. *A Comparative Study of Women Trafficked in the Migration Process Patterns, Profiles and Health Consequences of Sexual Exploitation in Five Countries (Indonesia, the Philippines, Thailand, Venezuela and the United States)*. Coalition against Trafficking in Women. http://action.web.ca/home/catw/attach/CATW%20Comparative%20Study%202002.pdf.

Reed, Jean-Pierre, and John Foran. 2000. "Political Cultures of Opposition: Exploring Idioms, Ideologies, and Revolutionary Agency in the Case of Nicaragua." *Critical Sociology* 28 (3): 336–370.

Reich, Robert B. 1992. *The Work of Nations: Preparing Ourselves for the Twenty-First Century Capitalism*. New York: Vintage.

Research Unit for Political Economy. 2003. *Behind the Invasion of Iraq*. New York: Monthly Review Press.

Rex, J. 1998. "Transnational Migrant Communities and the Modern Nation-State," in R. Axtmann (ed.), *Globalization and Europe*. London: Pinter.

Rice, J. 2003. "Immigration-Oil Link Stirs Outrage: U.S. Idea to Invest in PEMEX Angers México." (Associated Press), *The El Paso Times* (May 11): A12.

Rich, Bruce. 1994. *Mortgaging the Earth. The World Bank, Environmental Impoverishment and the Crisis of Development*. Boston: Beacon.

Richardson, B. 2003. Keynote Address, presented at the El Paso County Democrats' Biennial Hall-of-Fame Banquet, El Paso, Texas, May 12, 2003.

Ridge, T. 2003. Plenary Conference, presented at the 2003 Legislative Conference of the National Association of Counties. CSPAN1, March 3, 2003, available from CSPAN.ORG.

Rikowski, G. 2001. *The Battle in Seattle: Its Significance for Education*. London: Tufnell.

Rimmer, P. J., and T. Morris-Suzuki. 1999. "The Japanese Internet: Visionaries and Virtual Democracy." *Environment and Planning A* 31 (7): 1189–1206.

Ritzer, George. 2001. *Enchanting a Disenchanted World: Revolutionizing the Means of Consumption.* Thousand Oaks, CA: Pine Forge Press.

Ritzer, George. 2000. *The McDonaldization of Society.* London: Sage.

Robert, Robert J. S., and Kent M. Trachte. 1990. *Global Capitalism: The New Leviathan.* Albany, NY: SUNY.

Robertson, Robbie. 2003. *The Three Waves of Globalization: A History of a Developing Global Consciousness.* London: Zed Books.

Robertson, Roland. 1992. *Globalization: Social Theory and Global Culture.* Newbury Park, CA.

Robertson, Roland, and Kathleen White (eds.), 2003. *Globalization: Critical Concepts.* London: Routledge.

Robinson, William I. Forthcoming. 2004. *A Theory of Global Capitalism: Production, Class, and State in a Transnational World.* Baltimore, MD: Johns Hopkins University Press.

Robinson, William I. 2003. *Transnational Conflicts: Central America, Social Change, and Globalization.* London: Verso.

Robinson, William I. 2002. "Remapping Development in Light of Globalisation: From a Territorial to a Social Cartography." *Third World Quarterly* 23 (6): 1047–1071.

Robinson, William. 2001–2002. "Globalization or Class Society in Transition?" *Science & Society* 65 (4): 492–500.

Robinson, William I. 2001. "Social Theory and Globalization: The Rise of a Transnational State." *Theory and Society* 30 (2): 157–200.

Robinson, William. 2001. "Response to McMichael, Block, and Goldfrank." *Theory and Society* 30, 223–236.

Robinson, William. 1996. *Promoting Polyarchy: Globalization, U.S. Intervention, and Hegemony.* Cambridge, England: Cambridge University Press.

Robinson, William I., and Jerry Harris. 2000. "Toward a Global Ruling Class? Globalization and the Transnational Capitalist Class." *Science & Society* 64 (1): 11–54.

Rodgers, J. 1999. "NGOs, New Communications Technologies and Concepts of Political Community." *Cambridge Review of International Affairs* X11 (spring/summer).

Rodgers, J., and D. Gauntlett. Unpublished 2003. *Teenage Intercultural Communications Online: A Redployment of the Internet Activist Model.* University of Leeds.

Rodríguez, Nestor, and Jacqueline Hagan. 2001. "Transborder Community Relations at the U.S.–Mexico Border: Laredo/Nuevo Laredo and El Paso/Ciudad Juárez," in Demetrios G. Papademetriou and Deborah Waller Meyers (eds.), *Caught in the Middle: Border Communities in an Era of Globalization.* New York: Carnegie Endowment for International Peace/The Brookings Institute, 88–116.

Rodriguez, Robyn M. 2002. "Migrant Heroes: Nationalism, Citizenship and the Politics of Filipino Migrant Labor." *Citizenship Studies* 6: 341–356.

Rodrik, Dani. 1997. *Has Globalization Gone too Far?* Washington, D.C.: Institute for International Economics.

Rogers, George O. 1997. "The Dynamics of Risk Perception: How Does Perceived Risk Respond to Risk Events?" *Risk Analysis* 17 (7): 745–757.

Romero, Mary. 1992. *Maid in the U.S.A.* New York: Routledge.

Ronfeldt, David, John Arquilla, Graham Fuller, and Melissa Fuller. 1998. *The Zapatista Social "Netwar" in Mexico.* Santa Monica, CA: RAND, MR-994-A.

Roodman, David Malin. 2001. *Still Waiting for the Jubilee. Pragmatic Solutions for the Third World Debt Crisis.* Washington, D.C.: Worldwatch Paper 155.

Rosca, Ninotchka. 1995. "The Philippines' Shameful Export." *The Nation* 260 (25) (April 17): 522.

Rosenau, J. N. 2003. *Distant Proximities: Dynamics beyond Globalization.* Princeton, NJ: Princeton University Press.

Rosenau, James N. 1997. *Along the Domestic-Foreign Frontier: Exploring Governance in a Turbulent World.* Cambridge: Cambridge University Press.

Rosenberg, Justin. 2001. *The Empire of Civil Society*, 2nd edition. London and New York: Verso.

Roslan, A. 2001. "Income Inequality, Poverty and Development Policy in Malaysia," paper presented to the Conference on Poverty and Sustainable Development, November, Universite Montesquieu-Bordeaux IV.

Ross, Robert J. S. 2002. "The 'Race to the Bottom' in Imported Clothes." *Dollars and Sense* 239 (January/February): 46–47.

Ross, Robert J. S. 2002. "Author's Update: Race to the Bottom" *Dollars and Sense.* (July/August).

Ross, Robert J. S. 2002c. "Declining Labor Standards in the North American Apparel Industry," in G. Kohler and E. J. Chaves (ed.), in *Globalization: Critical Perspectives.* New York: Nova Science, chap. 10.

Ross, Robert J. S. 1983. "Facing Leviathan: Public Policy and Global Capitalism." *Economic Geography* 59 (2): 144–160.

Ross, Robert, and Kent Trachte. 1990. *Global Capitalism: The New Leviathan.* Albany, NY: State University of New York Press.

Rothstein, Richard. 1995. "The Case for Labor Standards." *Boston Review* 20:6. Retrieved from http://bostonreview.net/BR20.6/Rothstein.nclk on May 5, 2003.

Roudometof, Victor. 2002. *Collective Memory, National Identity and Ethnic Conflict: Greece, Bulgaria, and the Macedonian Question.* Westport, CT: Praeger.

Rouse, Roger. 1991. "Mexican Migrants and the Social Space of Postmodernism." *Diaspora* 1: 8–23.

Rovira, G. 1997. *Mujeres de Maíz.* Mexico: Ediciones Era.

Rowbotham, Sheila, and Stephanie Linkogle (ed.), 2001. *Women Resist Globalization: Mobilizing for Livelihood and Rights.* London: Zed.

Roy, A. 2003. *War Talk.* Boston: South End Press.

Roy, A. "Instant-Mix Imperial Democracy (Buy One Get One Free)." Speech presented at the Riverside Church, May 13, 2003. http://www.cesr.org/roy/royspeech.htm#roy.

Ruggiero, Renato. 2000. "Reflections from Seattle," in Jeffrey Schott (ed.), *The WTO After Seattle.* Washington, D.C.: Institute for International Economics, 13–17.

Rumsfeld, Donald. 2002. "Transforming the Military." *Foreign Affairs* (May/June): 20–32.

Rupert, Mark. 2000. *Ideologies of Globalization: Contending Visions of a New World Order.* London: Routledge.

Rupp, Leila. 1998. *Worlds of Women: The Making of an International Women's Movement.* Princeton, NJ: Princeton University Press.

Rupp, Leila J., and Verta Taylor. 1999. "Forging Feminist Identity in an International Movement: A Collective Identity Approach to Twentieth Century Feminism." *Signs: Journal of Women in Culture and Society* 24 (21): 363–386.

Rutherglen, S. "The Violent Obliteration of Art and Memory." *Yale Daily News* (April 15, 2003). http://www.yaledailynews.com/article.asp?AID=22603.

Rylko-Bauer, Barbara, and Paul Farmer. 2002. Managed Care or Managed Inequality? A Call for Critiques of Market-Based Medicine. *Medical Anthropology Quarterly* 16 (4): 476–502.

Saavala, Minna. 2001. "Low Caste but Middle-Class: Some Religious Strategies for Middle-Class Identification in Hyderabad." *Contributions to Indian Sociology* (n.s.) 35 (3): 293–318.

Sabel, Charles, Dara O'Rourke, and Archon Fung. 2000. "*Ratcheting Labor Standards: Regulation for Continuous Improvement in the Global Workplace.*" Washington, D.C.: The World Bank, Social Protection Discussion Paper No.11.

Sachs, Wolfang (ed.), 1992. *The Development Dictionary.* London: Zed Books.

Sader, E. 2002. "Beyond Civil Society." *New Left Review* 17 (September–October).

Sai, Shiv. 2001. "Don't Crucify Me." *Movie Mag International* (March): 28–34.

Said, Edward W. 1978. *Orientalism.* New York: Pantheon.

Sajhau, Jean-Paul. (n.d.). "Business Ethics in the Textile, Clothing and Footwear (TCF) Industries: Codes of Conduct," (working paper). Geneva: International Labor Organization.

Saldívar, José David. 1997. *Border Matters.* Berkeley, CA: University of California Press.

Salleh, Ariel. 1997. *Ecofeminism as Politics: Nature, Marx, and the Postmodern.* New York: St. Martin's Press.

Sandbrook, Richard (ed.), 2003. *Civilizing Globalization: A Survival Guide.* Albany, NY: State University of New York Press.

Sandoval, Chela. 2000. *Methodology of the Oppressed.* Minneapolis: University of Minnesota Press.

Santos, Aida. 2002. "The Philippines: Interview Findings and Data Analysis: A Survey of Trafficked Women, Women in Prostitution and Mail-Order Brides," in J. Raymond, J. D'Cunha, S. R. Dzu-hayatin, H. P. Hynes, Z. R. Rodriguez, and A. Santos. *A Comparative Study of Women Trafficked in the Migration Process Patterns, Profiles and Health Consequences of Sexual Exploitation in Five Countries (Indonesia, the Philippines, Thailand, Venezuela and the United States).* Coalition against Trafficking in Women. http://action.web.ca/home/catw/attach/CATW%20Comparative%20Study%202002.pdf, 91–123.

Santos, Boaventura de Sousa. 1995. *Towards a New Common Sense: Law, Science and Politics in the Paradigmatic Transition.* London: Routledge.

Santos, Boaventura de Sousa. 1987. "Law: A Map of Misreading. Toward a Postmodern Conception of Law." *Journal of Law and Society* 14 (3): 297–300.

Sartre, Jean-Paul. 1972. *Situations* 8, Paris.

Sassen, Saskia. Under Contract 2004. *Denationalization: Territory, Authority and Rights in a Global Digital Age.* Princeton, NJ: Princeton University Press.

Sassen, Saskia. 2002a. "Towards a Sociology of Information Technology." *Current Sociology* 50 (3): 365–388.

Sassen, Saskia. 2002b. "Digitization: Its Variability as Variable in Shaping Cross-Border Relations." The 2nd Social Study of IT Workshop at the LSE. ICT and Globalization, London, April 22–23, 2002.

Sassen, Saskia. 2001. *The Global City: New York, London, Tokyo,* 2nd edition. Princeton, NJ: Princeton University Press.

Sassen, Saskia. 2000. *Cities in a World Economy,* 2nd edition. Thousand Oaks, CA: Pine Forge Press.

Sassen, Saskia. 2000. "Spatialities and Temporalities of the Global." *Public Culture* 12 (1) (Millenium Issue on Globalization. Re-issued by Duke University Press).

Sassen, Saskia. 2000. "Territory and Territoriality in the Global Economy." *International Sociology* 15 (2): 372–393.

Sassen, Saskia. 2000. "Women's Burden: Counter-Geographies of Globalization and the Feminization of Survival." *Journal of International Affairs* 53 (2): 503–524.

Sassen, Saskia. 1999. "Embedding the Global in the National," in David A. Smith, Dorothy J. Solinger, and Steven C. Topik, *States & Sovereignty in the Global Economy.* London and New York: Routledge, 158–171.

Sassen, Saskia. 1998. *Global City: New York, London, Tokyo.* Princeton, NJ: Princeton University Press.

Sassen, Saskia. 1998. *Globalization and Its Discontents.* New York: The New Press.

Sassen, Saskia. 1996. *Losing Control? Sovereignty in an Age of Globalization.* New York: Columbia University Press.

Sassen, Saskia. 1993. "The Impact of Economic Internalization on Immigration: Comparing the U.S. and Japan." *International Migration Review* 31: 73–99.

Sassen, Saskia. 1991. *Global Cities.* Princeton, NJ: Princeton University Press.

Sassen-Koob, Saskia. "Immigrant and Minority Workers in the Organization of the Labor Process." *Journal of Ethnic Studies* 1: 1–34.

Sassen-Koob, Saskia. 1978. "The International Circulation of Resources and Development: The Case of Migrant Labour." *Development and Change* 9: 509–546.

Sayer, A. 1984. *Method in Social Science.* London: Methuen.

Sayres, Nicole. 2002. "The Vietnam–US Textile Agreement Debate: Trade Patterns, Interests, and Labor Rights." *Congressional Research Service* (June 21).

Schell, Orville. 2003. "The World's Other Superpower." *The Nation* (April 14): 11–12.

Scheuerman, William. 2000. "Global Law in Our High Speed Economy," in Volkmar Gessner et al. (eds.), *The Legal Culture of Global Business Transactions,* Oxford: Hart.

Scheuerman, William. 1999. "Economic Globalization and the Rule of Law." *Constellations: An International Journal of Critical and Democratic Theory* 6 (1) (March 1999): 3.

Schiele, Jerome H. 1998. "Rethinking Organizations from an Afrocentric Viewpoint," in Janice D. Hamlet (ed.), *Afrocentric Visions: Studies in Culture and Communication.* Thousand Oaks, CA: Sage, 73–88.

Schiele, Jerome H. 1991. "Afrocentricity for All." *Black Issues in Higher Education.* (September 26): 27.

Schiffer Ramos, Sueli. 2002. "Sao Paulo: Articulating a Cross-Border Regional Economy," in Saskia Sassen (ed.), *Global Networks/Linked Cities.* New York and London: Routledge.

Schiller, Nina Glick, and Georges E. Fourton. 2001. *Georges Woke Up Laughing: Long Distance Nationalism and the Search for Home.* Durham, NC: Duke University Press.

Schlereth, Thomas. 1977. *The Cosmopolitan Ideal in Enlightenment Thought: Its Form and Function in the Ideas of Franklin, Hume, and Voltaire, 1694–1790.* Notre Dame, IN: University of Notre Dame Press.

Scholte, Jan. 2003. "What is Globalization? The Definitional Issues — Again." Working Paper Series. Institute on Globalization and the Human Condition, McMaster University, Hamilton, Ontario.

Scholte, Jan Aart. 2000. *Globalization: A Critical Introduction.* London: Macmillan.

Schumpeter, Joseph. 1961. *The Theory of Economic Development.* New York: Oxford University Press.

Schumpeter, Joseph. 1954. *Capitalism, Socialism & Democracy.* London: Allen & Unwin.

Scott, A. J. 2002. "Regional Push: Towards a Geography of Development and Growth in Low and Middle-Income Countries." *Third World Quarterly* 23 (1): 137–161.

Scott, James. 1990. *Domination and the Arts of Resistance: Hidden Transcripts.* New Haven and London: Yale University Press.

Seager, Joni. 2003. "Rachel Carson Died of Breast Cancer: The Coming Age of Feminist Environmentalism." *Signs: A Journal of Women in Culture and Society* 28 (3): 945–972.

Seager, Joni. 1999. "Patriarchal Vandalism: Militaries and the Environment," in Jael Silliman and Ynestra King (ed.), *Dangerous Intersections: Feminist Perspectives on Population, Environment and Development.* Cambridge: South End Press, 163–188.

Sempasa, Samson. 1992. "Obstacles to International Commercial Arbitration in African Countries." *International and Comparative Law Quarterly* 41: 387–413.

Sen, Gita, and Caren Grown. 1987. *Development, Crises, and Alternative Visions: Third World Women's Perspectives.* New York: Monthly Review Press.

Sengupta, Hindol. 2001. "Valentine's Day: Time for Expressing Feelings and Making Choices." *India Abroad* (February 16): 51.

Servicio Internacional de Información S. A. de C. V. 2003. "Maquiladora statistics section." *Mexico Now* 1 (2): 58–59.

Shade, Leslie Regan. 1998. "A Gendered Perspective on Access to the Information Infrastructure." *The Information Society* 14: 33–44.

Shapiro, M. J. 1997. *Bowling Blind: Post Liberal Civil Society and the Worlds of Neo-Tocquevillian Social Theory.* Baltimore, MD: Johns Hopkins University Press.

Shenon, P. "Domestic Security: New Devices to Recognize Body Features on U.S. Entry." *The New York Times.* (April 30, 2003): A16.

Shiva, Vandana. 2001. *Protect or Plunder? Understanding Intellectual Property Rights.* London: Zed Books.

Shiva, Vandana. 1997. *Biopiracy: The Plunder of Nature and Knowledge.* Boston: South End Press.

Shohat, Ella, and Stam, Robert. 1994. *Unthinking Eurocentrism: Multiculturalism and the Media.* New York: Routledge.

Shotter, John. 1993. *Cultural Politics of Everyday Life: Social Constructionism, Rhetoric and Knowing of the Third Kind.* Toronto: University of Toronto Press.

Shurmer-Smith, Pamela. 2000. *India: Globalization and Change.* London: Arnold.

Sicherman, Harvey. 2002. "The Revival of Geopolitics." http://www.fpri.org/pubs/articles.html.

Sidney Tarrow. 1996. Fishnet's Internets and Catnets: Globalization and Transnational Collective Action," *Estudios Working Papers 1996/97.*

Silver, Beverly J. 2003. *Forces of Labor. Workers' Movements and Globalization Since 1870.* Cambridge and New York: Cambridge University Press.

Silver, Beverly. 1995. "World-Scale Patterns of Labor-Capital Conflict: Labor Unrest, Long Waves and Cycles of Hegemony." *Review* 18 (1): 53.

Simon, Rita James, and Caroline Brettell. 1986. *International Migration: The Female Experience.* Totowa, NJ: Rowman & Allanheld.

Sivalingam, G. 1994. *The Economic and Social Impact of Export Processing Zones: The Case of Malaysia.* Geneva: ILO.

Sklair, Leslie. 2002. *Globalization: Capitalism and Its Alternatives*, 3rd edition. Oxford: Oxford University Press.

Sklair, Leslie. 2001. *The Transnational Capitalist Class.* Oxford: Blackwell.

Sklair, Leslie. 2000. "The Transnational Capitalist Class and the Discourse of Globalization." *Cambridge Review of International Affairs* 14: 1.

Sklair, Leslie. 1999. "Competing Conceptions of Globalization." *Journal of World-Systems Research* 2: 143–162. http://csf.colorado.edu/wsystems/jwsr/.

Sklair, Leslie. [1991] 1995. *The Sociology of the Global System.* 2nd edition. Baltimore, MD: Johns Hopkins University Press.

Slater, David. 1994. "Exploring Other Zones of the Postmodern: Problems of Ethnocentrism and Difference across the North–South Divide," in Ali Ratanssi and Sallie Westwood (ed.), *Racism, Modernity and Identity: On the Western Front.* Cambridge: Polity, 87–126.

Slaughter, Anne-Marie. 1999–2000. "Judicial Globalization." *Virginia Journal of International Law* 40: 1103–1124.

Slovic, Paul (ed.), 2000. *The Perception of Risk.* London: Earthscan.

Smedley, Audrey. 1993. *Race in North America: Origin and Evolution of a Worldview.* Boulder, CO. Westview.

Smith, David A. 1999. "Lessons of Global Neo-Liberalism? The East Asian Economic Crisis Reconsidered." *Global Economic Review* 27 (3).

Smith, David A. 1997. "Technology, Commodity Chains and Global Inequality: The South Korean Case in the 1990s." *Review of International Political Economy* 4 (4): 734–762.

Smith, David A. 1996. *Third World Cities in Global Perspective: The Political Economy of Urbanization.* Boulder, CO: Westview.

Smith, David A. 1985. "International Dependency and Urbanization in East Asia: Implications for Planning." *Population Research and Policy Review* 4 (3): 203–233.

Smith, David A., and Su-Hoon Lee. 1990. "Limits on a Semiperipheral Success Story? State Dependent Development and the Prospects for South Korean Democratization," in William G. Martin (ed.), *Semiperipheral states in the World-Economy.* Westport, CT: Greenwood, 79–95.

Smith, David A., Dorothy Solinger, and Steven Topik (eds.), 1999. *States and Sovereignty in the Global Economy.* London: Routledge.

Smith, Jackie, and Hank Johnston (eds.), 2002. *Globalization and Resistance: Transnational Dimensions of Social Movements.* Lanham, MD: Rowman & Littlefield.

Smith, Jackie, and Hank Johnston. 1999. "Global Feminization through Flexible Labor: A Theme Revisited." *World Development* 27 (3): 583–602.

Smith, Jackie, Charles Chatfield and Ron Pagnucco (eds.) 1997. Transnational Social Movements and Global Politics. Syracuse University Press.

Smith, Michael Peter. 1994. "Can You Imagine? Transnational Migration and the Globalisation of Grassroots Politics." *Social Text* 39: 15–34.

Smith, Michael Peter, and Luis Eduardo Guarnizo (eds.), 1998. *Transnationalism from Below.* Rutgers, NJ: Transaction.

Smith, Neil. 1993. "Homeless/Global: Scaling Places," in J. Bird, B. Curtis, T. Putnam, G. Robertson, and L. Tickner (eds.), *Mapping the Futures: Local Cultures, Global Change.* London: Routledge, 87–119.

Smith, Robert C. 1997. "Transnational Migration, Assimilation, and Political Community," in Margaret Crahan and Alberto Vourvoulias-Bush (eds.), *The City and the World.* New York: Council of Foreign Relations.

Smith, Rogers M. 1997. *Civic Ideals: Conflicting Visions of Citizenship in US History.* New Haven: Yale University Press.

Smith, T. 2002. "An Assessment of Joseph Stiglitz's *Globalization and Its Discontents.*" Radical Philosophy Association National Convention. Brown University (November 9). http://www.public.iastate.edu/~tonys/Stiglitz.html.

So, Alvin. 1990. *Social Change and Development: Modernization, Dependency, and World-System Theories.* Thousand Oaks, CA: Sage.

Sobo, Elisa J. 1995. *Choosing Unsafe Sex: AIDS-Risk Denial among Disadvantaged Women.* Philadelphia: University of Pennsylvania Press.

Sorokin, Pitirim. 1957/1985. *Social and Cultural Dynamics: The Study of Change in Major Systems of Art, Truth, Ethics, Law and Social Relationships*, Revised and Abridged. Boston: Porter Sargent Books.

Soros, George. 2002. *George Soros on Globalization*. New York: Public Affairs.

Sosa, L. del C. 2003. Desconocen aquí plan de acción para la frontera. *El Diario* (April 26): A4.

Soysal, Y. N. 1994. *The Limits of Citizenship: Migrants and Post-National Membership in Europe*. Chicago: University of Chicago Press.

Sparr, P. (ed.), 1994. *Mortgaging Women's Lives: Feminist Critiques of Structural Adjustment*. London: Zed.

Spencer, John Michael. 1993. "Trends of Opposition to Multiculturalism." *Black Scholar* 23 (1993): 2–5.

Spivak, Gayatari Chakrovorti. 1990. *The Post-colonial Critic: Interviews, Strategies, Dialogues*. New York: Routledge.

Spivak, Gayatri. 1988. *In Other Worlds: Essays in Cultural Politics*. New York: Routledge & Kegan Paul.

Staeheli, Lynn A. 1999. "Globalization and the Scales of Citizenship." *Geography Research Forum* 19: 60–77 (Special Issue *On Geography and the Nation-State*, edited by Dennis Pringle and Oren Yiftachel).

Standing, Guy. 1999. "Global Feminization through Flexible Labor: A Theme Revisited." *World Development*, 27 (3): 583–602.

Standing, Guy. 1989. "Global Feminization through Flexible Labor." *World Development* 17 (7): 1077–1095.

Starr, Amory. 2000. *Naming the Enemy. Anti-Corporate Movements Confront Globalization*. London and New York: Zed Books.

Stasiulis, Daiva. 1999. "Relational Positionalities of Nationalisms, Racisms, and Feminisms," in Caren Kaplan, Norma Alarcon, and Minoo Moallem (eds.), *Between Women and Nation: Nationalisms, Transnational Feminisms, and the State*, Durham and London: Duke University Press, 182–218.

Steger, Manfred B. 2003. *Globalization: A Very Short Introduction*. New York: Oxford University Press.

Steger, Manfred B. 2002. *Globalism: The New Market Ideology*. Lanham, MD: Rowman & Littlefield.

Stevis, Dmitris, and Terry Boswell. 1997. "Labor: From National Resistance to International Politics." *New Political Economy* 2 (1): 93–104.

Stewart, Sharla A. "Revolution from within." *The University of Chicago Magazine* 95: 5 (June 2003). http://magazine.uchicago.edu/0306/features/index-print.shtml.

Stienstra, Deborah. 1994. *Women's Movements and International Organizations*. New York: St. Martin's Press.

Stiglitz, G. 2002. *Globalization and Its Discontents*. New York: Norton.

Stiglitz, J. "The Roaring Nineties." *The Atlantic Monthly* (October, 2002). http://www.theatlantic.com/issues/2002/10/stiglitz.htm.

Stohl, Michael. 1980. "The Nexus of Civil and International Conflict," in Ted Gurr (ed.), *Handbook of Political Conflict: Theory and Research*. New York: The Free Press, 297–330.

Stoller, Paul. 1997. *Sensuous Scholarship*. Philadelphia: University of Pennsylvania Press.

Strange, S. 1998. *Mad Money: A Sequel to "Casino Capitalism."* Manchester: Manchester University Press.

Studer, I. 2003. NAFTA and the Future Integration of North America. Voices of Mexico (63): 23–26.

Su, Julie. 2001. "El Monte Thai Garment Workers: Slave Sweatshops." Sweatshop Watch http://www.sweatshopwatch.org/swatch/campaigns/elmonte.html.

Sum, Ngai-Ling. 1999. "Rethinking Globalisation: Re-Articulating the Spatial Scale and Temporal Horizons of Trans-Border Spaces," in K. Olds et al. (eds.), *Globalization and the Asia-Pacific*. London: Routledge, 129–145.

Summerfield, G. 2001. "Special Issue: Risks and Rights in the 21st Century," *International Journal of Politics, Culture, and Society* 15 (1).

Suter, Christian. 1992. *Debt Cycles in the World Economy: Foreign Loans, Financial Crises and Debt Settlements, 1820–1987*. Boulder, CO: Westview.

Sweatshop Watch (1995). "Slave Conditions in Southern California Garment Shop." Sweatshop Watch 1 (fall):1. http://www.sweatshopwatch.org/swatch/newsletters/1_1.html.

Swyngedouw, Erik. 1997. "Neither Global nor Local: Glocalization and the Politics of Scale," in Cox, K. R. (ed.), *Globalization: Reasserting the Power of the Local*. New York and London: Guilford, 137–166.

Tabak, Faruk and Michaeline A. Chrichlow (eds.) 2000. Informalization: Process and Structure. Baltimore, MD: The Johns Hopkins Press.

Tabb, W. 2001. "Globalization and Education as a Commodity." http://www.psc-cuny.org/jcglobalization.htm.

Tanski, Janet. 1994. "The Impact of Crisis, Stabilization and Structural Adjustment on Women in Lima, Peru." *World Development* 22 (11): 1627–1642.

Tardanico, Richard and Mario Lungo. 1995. "Local Dimensions of Global Restructuring in Urban Costa Rica." *International Journal of Urban and Regional Research* 19 (2): 223–249.

Tarrow, Sidney. 2002. "Beyond Globalization: Why Creating Transnational Social Movements Is so Hard and When is It Most Likely to Happen?" Mimeo.

Tauli-Corpuz, V. 1998. "Asia-Pacific Women Grapple with Financial Crisis and Globalization." Third World Network. http:// www.twnside.org.sg/title/grapple-cn.htm.

Taylor, Peter. 2000. "World Cities and Territorial States under Conditions of Contemporary Globalisation." (1999 Annual Political Geography Lecture). *Political Geography* 19 (1): 5–32.

Taylor, Peter J. 1996. *The Way the Modern World Works: World Hegemony to World Impasse.* New York: Wiley.

Taylor, Peter. 1994. "The State as Container: Territoriality in the Modern World-System." *Progress in Human Geography* 18 (2): 151–162.

Thai, Hung Cam. 2003. "The Vietnamese Double Gender Revolt." *Amerasia Journal* 29: 51–74.

Thai, Hung Cam. 2002. "Clashing Dreams: Highly Educated Overseas Brides and Low-Wage U.S. Husbands," in B. Ehrenreich and A. R. Hochschild (eds.), *Global Woman: Nannies, Maids and Sex Workers in the New Economy.* New York: Metropolitan Books, 230–253.

The Internationalist. May 7, 2003. "Triumph of the Will 2." http://www.internationalist.org/triumph0503.html.

The Research Unit for Political Economy. 2002. "The Real Reason for the US Invasion: The Current Strategic Agenda of the United States." Aspects of India's Economy 33 and 34 (December). http:// www.rupe-india.org/34/reasons.html and http://www.rupe-india.org/34/agenda.html.

The Resident Editorial Board. 2002. *News & Letters* 47 (6) (July): 5–8.

Therborn, Goran. 1985. *Science, Class & Society: On the Formation of Sociology & Historical Materialism.* London: Routledge.

Thurow, Lester. C. 1999. "The Dollar's Day of Reckoning." *The Nation* January 11: 22–24.

Tiano, S. 1994. *Patriarchy on the Line: Labor, Gender, and Ideology in the Mexican Maquila Industry.* Philadelphia: Temple University Press.

Tickner, J. Ann. 2001. *Gendering World Politics: Issues and Approaches in the Post–Cold War Era.* New York: Columbia University Press.

Tiffin, Helen. 1990. "Introduction," in Ian Adam and Helen Tiffin (eds.), *Past the Last Post: Theorizing Post-Colonialism and Post-Modernism.* Calgary, Alberta, Canada: University of Calary Press, 7–16.

Tilly, Charles. 1995. "Globalization Threatens Labor's Rights." *International Labor and Working-Class History* 47: 1–55.

Tilly, Charles. 1992. *Coercion, Capital, and European States, AD 990–1992.* Revised edition. Cambridge, MA: Blackwell.

Tittley, Mark. 2000. "Youth Subcultures and the Commitment Level Model" (Essay). http://www.btc.co.za/model/subcult1.htm.

Tocqueville, Alexis de. 1945. *Democracy in America, Volume I & II.* New York. Vintage Books.

Tohidi, Nayereh. 1997. "'Islamic Feminism': A Democratic Challenge or a Theocratic Reaction?" *Kankash* (13): 106–110 (in Persian).

Toledo Patiño, A. 1999. Globalización, Estado-nación y Espacios Sociales. *Iztapalapa* 19 (46): 35–52.

Tomlinson, John. 1999. *Globalization and Culture.* Chicago: University of Chicago Press.

Torres, A., and J. Martínez. 2003. Condiciona México su respaldo. *El Diario* (April 24).

Torres, Federico A. 1998. *Uso productivo de las remesas en El Salvador, Guatemala, Honduras, and Nicaragua.* Mexico City: Centro Economico Para America Latina (CEPAL), September.

Tran, Ngoc Angie. "What's Woman's Work? Male Negotiations and Gender Reproduction in the Garment Industry." In Lisa Drummond and Helle Rydstrom (eds.), *Gender Practices in Contemporary Vietnam,* Singapore University Press and NIAS Press, 2004.

Tran, Ngoc Angie. 2002. "Gender Expectations of Vietnamese Garment Workers: Viet Nam's Re-Integration into the World Economy," in Jayne Werner and Daniele Belanger (eds.), *Gender, Household, State: Doi Moi in Viet Nam,* Southeast Asia Program Publication Series, Cornell University Press.

Tran, Ngoc Angie. 2001. "Global Subcontracting and Women Workers in Comparative Perspective," in Claes Brundenius and John Weeks (eds.), *Globalization and Third World Socialism: Cuba and Vietnam*. Houndmills, Basingstoke, Hampshire: Palgrave.

Tran, Ngoc Angie. 1996. "Through the Eye of the Needle: Vietnamese Textile and Garment Industries Rejoining the Global Economy," in *Crossroads: An Interdisciplinary Journal of Southeast Asian Studies* 10 (2). Center for Southeast Asian Studies, Northern Illinois University.

Tran, Trong Dang Dan. 1997. *Nguoi Vietnam O Nuoc Ngoai [Vietnamese People Overseas]*. Hanoi, Vietnam: National Political Press.

Trotsky, Leon. 1969. *The Permanent Revolution, and Results and prospects*. New York: Merit.

Tsagarousianou, Roza, Damian Tambini, and Cathy Bryan. (eds.), 1998. *Cyberdemocracy, Technology, Cities and Civic Networks*. London: Routledge.

Tsing, Anna. 2002. "Conclusion: The Global Situation," in. J. Inda and R. Rosaldo (eds.), *The Anthropology of Globalization: A Reader*. Malden, MA: Blackwell, 453–485.

Tuoi Tre Newspaper, September, 2002; October, 2002; March, 2003.

Turner, Victor. 1969. *The Ritual Process: Structure and Anti-Structure*. Chicago: Aldine.

Twining, William. 1996. "Globalization and Legal Theory: Some Local Implications." *Current Legal Problems* 49: 1– 42.

Twitchell, James. 1992. *Carnival Culture: The Trashing of Taste in America*. New York: Columbia University Press.

Uberoi, Patricia. 1998. "The Diaspora Comes Home: Disciplining Desire in DDLJ." *Contributions to Indian Sociology* (n.s.) 32: 305–336.

UNCTAD. 2004. *Impacts of the Agreement on Textiles and Clothing on FDI in and Exports from Developing Countries*. New York and Geneva: United Nations Conference on Trade and Development.

UNDP. 2003. *Human Development Report 2003: Millennium Development Goals: A Compact among Nations to End Human Poverty*. New York: Oxford University Press.

UNDP. 1999. *Human Development Report 1999: Globalization with a Human Face*. New York: Oxford University Press.

UNDP. 1995. *Human Development Report 1995: Gender and Human Security*. New York: Oxford University Press.

UNIFEM. 2002. *Progress of the World's Women 2002: Gender Equality and the Millennium Development Goals*. New York: United Nations Development Fund for Women (UNIFEM).

UNIFEM. 2000. *Progress of the World's Women*. Geneva: United Nations Development Fund for Women (UNIFEM).

Urry, J. 2003. *Global Complexity*. Cambridge: Polity.

USDOL. 1998. "Los Angeles 1998 Compliance Survey" fact sheet. U.S. Department of Labor.

USDOL. 2003. U.S. Department of Labor, "Department of Labor Budget for Fiscal year 2004." (http://www.dol.gov/_sec/Budget2004/).

USDOL. 2003. U.S. Department of Labor, "Budget Overview FY 2004 — Agency Information, ESA Staffing, Budget Authority/Trust Fund Transfers." http://www.dol.gov/_sec/Budget2004/agencies 2004.htm#esa.

USDOL. 1996. U.S. Department of Labor, Bureau of International Labor Affairs. "The Apparel Industry and Codes of Conduct: A Solution to the International Child Labor Problem?" Washington, D.C.: USDOL.

USINS. 2002. *Statistical Yearbook of the Immigration and Naturalization Service, 1999*. Washington, D.C.: U.S. Government Printing Office.

USOTEA. 2003. Office of Trade and Economic Analysis, U.S. International Trade Administration, "U.S. Total Imports from Individual Countries 1996–2002 (Census Basis; General Imports Customs; Millions of Dollars)." http://www.ita.doc.gov/td/industry/otea/usfth/aggregate/H02T07.html.

Uvin, P. 2000. "Rwanda: The Social Roots of Genocide," in E. W. Nafziger, F. Stewart, and R. Vayrynen (eds.), *War, Hunger and Displacement. The Origins of Humanitarian Emergencies*, Vol. 2. Oxford: Oxford University Press.

Vargas, R. E. 2003. "Inútil, que la PGR investigue la venta del padrón electoral a EU. Jorge Camil." *La Jornada* (April 24): 5.

Varley, Pamela (ed.), 1998. The Sweatshop Quandary. Corporate Responsibility on the Global Frontier. Washington, D.C.: Investor Responsibility Research Center.

Väyrynen, R. 2003. "Regionalism: Old and New." *International Studies Review* 5 (1): 25–51.

Vernon, Raymond. 1971. *Sovereignty at Bay: The Multinational Spread of US Enterprises*. Harmondsworth: Penguin.

Vernon, Raymond. 1966. "International Investment and International Trade in the Product Cycle." *Quarterly Journal of Economics* 80 (2): 190–207.

Vertovec, Steven. 1999. "Conceiving and Researching Transnationalism." *Ethnic and Racial Studies* 22 (2): 447–462.

Vidali, H. C. 2003. Binational Economic Partnerships. Paper presented at the Mexico-North Research Network Meeting. San Antonio, TX (February 28–March 1).

Vietnam Federation of Trade Unions. 1988. *The Trade Union Movement in Vietnam*. Hanoi, Vietnam: Foreign Languages Publishing House.

Vietnam News, March 25, 2002; May 7, 2002; July 31, 2002; November 15, 2002; December 13, 2002; October 13, 2003.

Vila, Carlos M. 1992. *La Costa Atlántica de Nicaragua*. Mexico: Fondo de Cultura Económica.

Von Wehrlof, Claudia. 2000. "'Globalization' and the 'permanent' process of 'primitive accumulation': The example of the MAI, the Multilateral Agreement on Investment." *Journal of World-Systems Research* 6 (3): 728–747 (fall/winter).

Vu Quoc Huy. 2001. *Analysis of Competitiveness of Textile and Garment Firms in Viet Nam: A Cost-Based Approach*. Hanoi, Vietnam (September).

Vu Quoc Huy. 2001. *Textile and Garment Industry in Viet Nam*. Institute of Economics — IDRC/CIDA Project "Trade Liberalization and Competitiveness of Selected Industries in Viet Nam," Hanoi (May).

Wade, Robert, and Frank Veneroso. 1998. "The Gathering World Slump and the Battle over Capital Controls." *New Left Review* 231 (September/October): 13–42.

Wade, Robert, and Frank Veneroso. 1998. "The Asian Crisis: The High Debt Model versus the Wall Street-Treasury-IMF Complex." *New Left Review* 28 (March/April): 3–24.

Wagar, W. Warren. 1996. "Toward a praxis of world integration." *Journal of World-Systems Research* 2 (2). http://csf.colorado.edu/wsystems/jwsr.html.

Wagar, W. Warren. 1992. *A Short History of the Future*. Chicago: University of Chicago Press.

Wajcman, Judy. 2002. *Information Technologies and the Social Sciences*. Special Issue of *Current Sociology* (summer).

Wallach, Lori, and Michelle Sforza. 2000. *The WTO: Five Years of Reasons to Resist Corporate Globalization*. New York: Seven Stories.

Waller, Meyers, D. "Security at US Borders: A Move away from Unilateralism. Migration Information Source." Migration Policy Institute. Retrieved from http://www.migrationinformation.org/USfocus/display.cfm?id=149 on August 1, 2003.

Wallerstein, Immanuel. 2001. *Unthinking Social Science: The Limits of Nineteenth-Century Paradigms*, second edition. Philadelphia: Temple University Press.

Wallerstein, Immanuel. 2000. *The Essential Wallerstein*. New York: New Press.

Wallerstein, Immanuel. 1999. "States? Sovereignty? The Dilemmas of Capitalists in an Age of Transition," in David Smith, Dorothy Solinger, and Steven Topik (eds.), *States and Sovereignty in the Global Economy*. London, U.K.: Routledge, 20–33.

Wallerstein, Immanuel. 1998. *Utopistics*. New York: New Press.

Wallerstein, Immanuel. 1996. "The Rise and Future Demise of World-Systems Analysis." *Review* (Fernand Braudel Center) 21 (1): 103–112.

Wallerstein, Immanuel. 1995. *After Liberalism*. New York: Vintage.

Wallerstein, Immanuel. 1992. "The Concept of National Development, 1917–1989: Elegy and Requiem." *American Behavioral Scientist* 35 (4, 5) (March–June): 517–529.

Wallerstein, Immanuel. 1992. "The Collapse of Liberalism," in Ralph Miliband and Leo Panitch (eds.), *The Socialist Register 1991*. London: The Merlin Press, 96–110.

Wallerstein, Immanuel (ed.), 1991. *Geopolitics and Geoculture*. Cambridge: Cambridge University Press.

Wallerstein, Immanuel. 1984. *The Politics of the World-Economy*. Cambridge and Paris: Cambridge University Press and Editions de la Maison des Sciences de l'Homme.

Wallerstein, Immanuel. 1983. *Historical Capitalism*. London: Verso.

Wallerstein, Immanuel. 1979. *The Capitalist World-Economy*. Cambridge and Paris: Cambridge University Press and Editions de la Maison des Sciences de l'Homme.

Wallerstein, Immanuel. 1974. "The Rise and Future Demise of the World Capitalist System: Concepts for Comparative Analysis." *Comparative Studies in Society and History* 16 (4): 387–415.

Wallerstein, Immanuel. 1974. *The Modern World-System*. New York: Academic.

Wallerstein, Michael. 1999. "Wage-Setting Institutions and Pay Inequality in Advanced Industrial Societies." *American Journal of Political Science* 43: 649–680.

Wallerstein, Michael. 1990. "Centralized Bargaining and Wage Restraint." *American Journal of Political Science* 34 (4): 982–1004.

Walton, John, and David Seddon. 1994. *Free Markets and Food Riots: The Politics of Global Adjustment*. Cambridge, MA: Blackwell.

Wapner, Paul. 2002. "Horizontal Politics: Transnational Environmental Activism and Global Cultural Change." *Global Environmental Politics* 2 (2) (May): 37–62.

Ward, K. (ed.), 1990. *Women Workers and Global Restructuring*. Ithaca, NY: ILR.

Ward, K., and J. L. Pyle. 1995. "Gender, Industrialization, Transnational Corporations, and Development: An Overview of Trends," in C. E. Bose and E. Acosta-Belen (eds.), *Women in the Latin American Development Process*. Philadelphia: Temple University Press, 37–64.

Ward, K., F. Rahman, A. S. Islam, R. Akhter, and N. Kamal. "The Effects of Global Economic Restructuring on Urban Women's work and Income-Generating Strategies in Dhaka, Bangladesh." Forthcoming in *Critical Sociology*.

Warehousing Education and Research Council (WERC). 1994. *The Mass Merchant Channel: Challenges and Opportunities*. Oak Brook, IL: WERC.

Warf, B., and J. Grimes. 1997. "Counterhegemonic Discourses and the Internet." *The Geographical Review* 87: 259–274.

Warren, Bill. 1980. *Imperialism, Pioneer of Capitalism*. London: New Left Books.

Waterman, Peter. 2001. *Globalization, Social Movements and the New Internationalisms*. London and New York: Continuum.

Watson, James L (ed.), 1997. *Golden Arches East: McDonald's in East Asia*. Stanford: Stanford University Press.

Weaver, Richard. 1948. *Ideas Have Consequences*. Chicago: University of Chicago Press.

Weber, Max. 1971. *From Max Weber: Essays in Sociology*. Translated and edited by H. H. Gerth and C. W. Mills. New York: Oxford University Press.

Weber, Max. 1949. *The Methodology of the Social Sciences*. Translated and edited by Edward A. Shils and Henry A. Finch. New York: Free Press.

Wedgewood, Ruth. 1999. "The International Criminal Court: An American View." *European Journal of International Law* 10: 93–107.

Weeks, Jeffrey, Janet Holland, and Matthew Waites (eds.), 2003. *Sexualities and Society: A Reader*. Cambridge, U.K.: Polity.

Weinstein, Deena. 2000. *Heavy Metal: A Cultural Sociology*. New York: Da Capo.

Weinstein, Deena. 2000. *Heavy Metal: The Music and Its Culture*. Cambridge, MA: Da Capo Press.

Wellman, B. 2002. "Little Boxes, Glocalization and Networked Individualism." http://www.chass.utoronto.ca/~wellman.

West, Cornel. 1993. *Beyond Eurocentrism and Multiculturalism*, Vol. 1. Monroe, ME: Common Courage.

Whiteford, Linda M., and Lenore Manderson (eds.), 2000. *Global Health Policy, Local Realities: The Fallacy of the Level Playing Field*. Boulder, CO: Lynne Rienner.

Whitely, Richard. 1992. *Business Systems in East Asia: Firms, Markets, and Societies*. Newbury Park, CA: Sage.

Wijers, M., and L. Lap-Chew. 1997. *Trafficking in Women: Forced Labour and Slavery-like Practices in Marriage, Domestic Labour, and Prostitution*. The Netherlands: Foundation against Trafficking in Women.

Will, George. 1996. "Intellectual Segregation: Afrocentrism's Many Myths Constitute Condescension toward African-Americans." *Newsweek* (February 19): 78.

William, Outhwaite. 1994. *Habermas: A Critical Introduction*. Cambridge: Polity.

Williams, Patrick, and Laura Chrisman. 1994. "Colonial Discourse and Post-Colonial Theory: An Introduction," in Patrick Williams and Laura Chrisman (eds.), *Colonial Discourse and Post-Colonial Theory: A Reader*. New York: Columbia University Press, 1–19.

Wilmhurst, Elizabeth. 1999. "Jurisdiction of the Court," in Roy Lee (ed.), *The International Criminal Court: The Making of the Rome Statute*. Cambridge, MA: Kluwer Law International, 127–142.

Winant, Howard. 2001. *The World Is a Ghetto: Race and Democracy Since World War II*. New York: Basic Books.

Wolfensohn, James. 2002. "A Partnership for Development and Peace." *World Bank* (March 6).

Woo, J-E. 1991. *Race to the Swift: State and Finance in Korean Industrialization*. New York: Columbia University Press.

Wood, E. M. 2001. "Contradictions: Only in Capitalism," in L. Panitch and C. Leys (eds.), *A World of Contradictions, Socialist Register*. London: Merlin.

World Bank. 2004. *World Development Report 2004: Making Services Work for Poor People*. Washington, D.C.: World Bank.

World Bank. 2003. "Countries at a Glance" Listings for Indonesia, Korea, Rep., Malaysia, and Thailand. http://www.worldbank.org/data.

World Bank. 2003. World Bank On-Line Publications, WDI Online. https://publications.worldbank.org/.

World Bank. 2002. *World Development Indicators 2002*. Washington, D.C.: World Bank.

World Bank. 2001. *World Development Indicators*. CD-ROM. Washington, D.C.: World Bank.

World Bank. 2001. *World Development Report 2000/2001: Attacking Poverty*. Washington, D.C.: World Bank. http://www.worldbank.org/poverty/wdrpoverty/.

World Bank. 2000. *Voices of the Poor*. New York: Oxford University Press.

World Bank. 1997. *World Development Report 1997: The State in a Changing World*. New York: Oxford University Press.

World Bank. 1993. *The East Asian Miracle: Economic Growth and Public Policy*. New York: Oxford University Press.

World Bank. 1993. *Water Resources Management: A World Bank Policy Study*. Washington, D.C.

World Bank. 1984. *World Tables*, Vol. 1 and Vol. 2. Washington, D.C.: World Bank.

World Information Order. 2002. *World-Information Files. The Politics of the Info Sphere*. Vienna: Institute for New Culture Technologies, and Berlin: Center for Civic Education.

World Party. 1999. http://csf.colorado.edu/wsystems/archive/praxis/wp/index.htm.

World Social Forum International Council. 2003. "Orientations adopted by the International Council of the World Social Forum on its meeting on January 21st and 22nd 2003 in Porto Alegre." http://www.forumsocialmundial.org.br/dinamic.asp?pagina-ci_resolucoes_23jan.

World Trade Organization. 1996. "Singapore Ministerial Declaration, Core Labour Standards." Retrieved from http://www.wto.org/english/thewto_e/minist_e/min96_e/wtodec_e.htm on May 5, 2003.

WWW. 1999. Women Working Worldwide. "Women Workers and Codes of Conduct. Central America Workshop Report." Manchester, U.K.: Women Working Worldwide.

WWW. 1998. Women Working Worldwide. "Women Workers and Codes of Conduct. Asia Workshop Report." Manchester, U.K.: Women Working Worldwide.

Yamane, Linus. 2001. "The Labor Market Status of Foreign Born Vietnamese Americans." Claremont, CA: Pitzer College, Department of Economics.

Yelvington, K. A. 1995. *Producing Power: Ethnicity, Gender, and Class in a Caribbean Workplace*. Philadelphia: Temple University Press.

Yeoh, B. S. A., and S. Huang. 2000. "'Home' and 'Away': Foreign Domestic Workers and Negotiations of Diasporic Identity in Singapore." *Women's Studies International Forum* 23 (4): 413–429.

Yeoh, B. S. A., S. Huang, and J. Gonzalez. 1999. "Migrant Female Domestic Workers: Debating the Economic, Social and Political Impacts in Singapore." *International Migration Review* 33 (1): 114–136.

Yeung, Yue-man. 2000. *Globalization and Networked Societies: Urban-Regional Change in Pacific Asia*. Honolulu, HI: University of Hawaii Press.

Young, Robert J. C. 1995. *Colonial Desire: Hybridity in Theory, Culture, and Race*. New York: Routledge.

Young, Robert J. C. 1994. "Egypt in America: Black Athena, Racism, and Colonial Discourse," in Ali Ratanssi and Sallie Westwood (eds.), *Racism, Modernity and Identity: On the Western Front*. Cambridge: Polity, 150–169.

Yupoong. 2003. "Company Overview." http://www.yupoong.co.kr/company/index.jsp.

Zaman, Muhammad Qasim. 2002. *The Ulama in Contemporary Islam: Custodians of Change*. Princeton, NJ: Princeton University Press.

Zeleza, Paul Tiyambe. 2003. *Rethinking Africa's Globalization, Volume I: The Intellectual Challenges*. Trenton, NJ: Africa World Press.

Contributors

Richard P. Appelbaum is professor of sociology and global and international studies at the University of California at Santa Barbara. He currently serves as director of the Institute for Social, Behavioral, and Economic Research and as codirector of ISBER's Center for Global Studies. He received his B.A. from Columbia University, an M.P.A. from Princeton University's Woodrow Wilson School of Public and International Affairs, and a Ph.D. from the University of Chicago. He has previously served as chair of the Sociology Department, and was founder and Acting Director of the UCSB Global and International Studies Program.

Giovanni Arrighi is professor and chair of the Department of Sociology at The Johns Hopkins University, Baltimore, Maryland. He is the author of *The Long Twentieth Century: Money, Power and the Origins of Our Times* (1994), coauthor with B. J. Silver of *Chaos and Governance in the Modern World System* (1999), and coeditor with T. Hamashita and M. Selden of *The Resurgence of East Asia: 500, 150 and 50 Year Perspectives* (2003). He has twice won the Distinguished Scholarship Award from the Political Economy of the World System Section, American Sociological Association.

Barrie Axford is professor of politics and head of the Department of Politics and International Relations at Oxford Brookes University, U.K. Recent publications include *The Global System: Economics, Politics and Culture* (1996); *Modernity–Postmodernity: From the Personal to the Global* (1996); *Politics: an Introduction* (joint author — 1997 and 2002); *Unity and Diversity in the New Europe* (joint editor, 2000), and *New Media and Politics* (joint editor, 2001). He is an executive committee member of the Global Studies Association and adviser to the Italian ministry of education. He is currently working on three books: *Theorising Globalisation; Globalisation in One Country: Britain in the Global Age;* and *Networks and Borders in the Global System.*

Walden Bello is director of Focus on the Global South in Bangkok, a project of Chulalongkorn University's Social Research Institute, and professor of public administration and sociology at the University of the Philippines. He serves on the programme board of the International Centre for Trade and Sustainable Development in Geneva, which provides NGOs information on the WTO. Bello has regular columns in Philippine and Thai newspapers, *Focus on Trade*, and the *Far Eastern Economic Review*. His most recent books are *Deglobalisation: Ideas for a New World Economy* (Zed, 2002), *Dark Victory: The United States and Global Poverty* (updated second edition; TNI/Food First/Pluto, 1999), and *A Siamese Tragedy: Development and Disintegration in Modern Thailand* (Food First/Zed, 1998).

Kum-Kum Bhavnani's doctorate is from King's College, Cambridge University. She is professor of sociology and women's studies, and chairs a Program in Women, Culture and Development at the University of California at Santa Barbara. Her published work includes writings on antiracism and feminism, youth and politics, incarcerated women, and, most recently, on the women, culture, and development paradigm. From 2000 to 2002 she was the inaugural editor of "Meridians: feminism, race, transnationalism" at Smith College, Northhampton, Massachusetts.

Edna Bonacich is a professor of sociology and ethnic studies at the University of California, Riverside. Her major research interest is the study of class and race, with special emphasis on racial divisions in the working class. She has studied the garment industry, coauthoring *Behind the Label: Inequality in the Los Angeles Apparel Industry* with Richard Appelbaum. She is currently pursuing research on the ports of Los Angeles/Long Beach and the surrounding logistics systems. She tries to link her teaching and research to efforts to produce progressive social change, especially by working with the labor movement.

Christopher Chase-Dunn is distinguished professor of sociology and director of the Institute for Research on World-Systems at the University of California at River-side. His studies of economic and political globalization in the modern world-system over the past 200 years are supported by the National Science Foundation. Chase-Dunn is the founder and coeditor of the electronic *Journal of World-Systems Research*.

Norma Chinchilla is professor of sociology and women's studies and director of the Latin American Certificate Program at California State University, Long Beach. She has published articles on social and economic change in Central America, the impact of feminism on Latin American social movements, and Central American immigration to Los Angeles. Her book of oral histories of several generations of Guatemalan women, *Nuestras Utopias: Mujeres Guatemaltecas del Siglo XX*, was published in Guatemala in 1998 and is currently being translated into English for publication in the United States. She is coauthor with Nora Hamilton of a new book, *Seeking Community in a Global City: Guatemalans and Salvadorans in Los Angeles*, published by Temple University Press.

A. Claire Cutler is an associate professor of international law and relations and graduate advisor in the Political Science Department at the University of Victoria. She is a graduate of the University of British Columbia (B.A.; Ph.D.), the London School of Economics and Political Science (M.Sc.) and McGill University (LL.B.). Cutler specializes in the intersection of international law and international politics and is interested in developing critical theory in international law.

G. Reginald Daniel is associate professor, Department of Sociology, University of California, Santa Barbara. While his research and teaching interests cover a variety of areas, he has been particularly active in the area of race and ethnic relations, as well as cultural analysis. Within these fields, he has examined a wide range of issues including general race and ethnic relations, multiracial identity and interracial relationships, and general cultural analysis. His books entitled *More Than Black?*

Multiracial Identity and the New Racial Order (Temple, 2001) and *Race and Multiraciality in Brazil and the United States: Converging Paths* (Pennsylvania State University Press, in progress) are a culmination of much of his thinking on this topic.

Richard Falk has been the Albert G. Milbank Professor of International Law and Practice at Princeton University since 1965. He obtained a B.S. (economics) at Wharton School, University of Pennsylvania (1952); an LL.B. at Yale Law School (1955); and a J.S.D. at Harvard University (1962). He has been on the editorial boards of about ten journals and magazines, including the *American Journal of International Law* (1961–) and *The Nation* (1978–).

John Foran is professor of sociology at the University of California at Santa Barbara. His areas of interest include the comparative study of revolutions, development, and globalization and Third World cultural studies. His books include *Fragile Resistance: Social Transformation in Iran from 1500 to the Revolution* (Westview, 1993), *A Century of Revolution: Social Movements in Iran* (Minnesota, 1994), *Theorizing Revolutions* (editor, Routledge, 1997), *The Future of Revolutions: Re-thinking Radical Change in an Age of Globalization* (editor, Zed, 2003), and *Feminist Futures: Re-imagining Women, Culture and Development* (coeditor, Zed, 2003). A book titled *The Origins of Revolutions in the Third World: Why a Few Succeed, Why Most Fail* is in progress.

Susan George, American-born and now a French citizen, is associate director of the Transnational Institute, Amsterdam, and vice president of the Attac citizens' movement in France. The most recent of her dozen widely translated books is titled *Another World Is Possible if …* (Verso, London and New York, 2004) in which this chapter also appears.

Ramón Grosfoguel is associate professor in the Department of Ethnic Studies at the University of California at Berkeley and Research Associate of the Maison des Science de l'Homme in Paris. He has published many articles on the political economy of the world-system and on Caribbean migration to Western Europe and the United States. His most recent book is *Colonial Subjects* (University of California Press, 2003).

Lisa Hajjar, associate professor in the Law and Society Program at the University of California at Santa Barbara, is the author of *Courting Conflict: The Israeli Military Court System in the West Bank and Gaza* (University of California Press, forthcoming 2004). She chairs the editorial committee of *Middle East Report*, a publication of the Middle East Research and Information Project.

Karen Halnon is an Assistant Professor of Sociology at Pennsylvania State University at Abington. Her work has been concerned with how capitalism has shaped popular culture in ways that constrain and control alienation. She has published a number of articles and book chapters on shock rock, poverty chic, etc. She is coauthor of a book with Lauren Langman on the Carnivalization of America to be published by Pine Forge Press. She is on the council of the Marxist section of American Sociological Association and on the board of Research Committee 36, Alienation Theory and Research of the International Sociological Association.

Jerry Harris is secretary of the Global Studies Association of North America and is a founding member of cy.Rev, a journal on globalization, technology, and politics (www.cyrev.net). His numerous articles on globalization can also be found in the journals *Race and Class* and *Science & Society*. He is a professor of history at DeVry University, Chicago.

David Harvey is the world's leading senior theorist in the field of urban studies. David Harvey's work has been the single most important, influential, and imaginative contribution to the development of human geography since the Second World War. His reflections on the importance of space and place (and, latterly, "nature") have attracted considerable critical interest across the whole field of the humanities and the social sciences.

Jeffrey Henderson is professor of international economic sociology at the University of Manchester, United Kingdom. He has taught at the Universities of Birmingham and Hong Kong and additionally has held visiting professorships or fellowships at the Universities of California (at Berkeley, Santa Barbara, and Santa Cruz), New England, Melbourne, Lodz, Leeds, Glasgow, and Warwick. Professor Henderson's research interests focus on the dynamics and implications of economic and corporate transformation and their relation to problems of economic governance.

Nathalia E. Jaramillo is a doctoral candidate in the Graduate School of Education at the University of California Los Angeles. She holds a Master's degree in international education policy from Harvard University and has coauthored a number of articles on critical pedagogy. A former elementary school teacher and policy analyst, Nathalia's current academic work primarily centers on the governing rule of capital to understand policy shifts in education and how critical pedagogy, as transformative praxis, can be used to envision a world outside the precincts of capital as a viable and hopeful alternative.

Lauren Langman is a professor of sociology at Loyola University of Chicago. He has long worked in the tradition of the Frankfurt school of critical theory, especially on issues of alienation and relationships between culture, politics, and the psychosocial in the globalized era. His most recent publications include a special issue of *American Behavioral Politics* devoted to the presidency in a television age. He has also published on the alternative globalization movements and on the many forms of identity that emerge in the current age from Islamic fundamentalists to the extremes of body modification; more recently, he has published several book chapters on Islam and fundamentalism. He is working on a book on the *Carnivalization of Society*.

Peter McLaren is a professor in the Graduate School of Education and Information Studies, University of California at Los Angeles. He is the author and editor of over forty books on critical pedagogy, educational theory, and critical sociology of education. McLaren's work has been translated into fifteen languages.

Philip McMichael is professor and chair of development sociology, Cornell University. He is a member of a scientific advisory council in the Nutrition Division of the Food and Agricultural Organization (FAO) of the UN, and of the executive board of the Global Studies Organization. His publication activities include authoring

Settlers and the Agrarian Question (1984) and *Development and Social Change: A Global Perspective* (2004, third edition), and editing *The Global Restructuring of Agro-Food Systems* (1994) and *Food and Agrarian Orders in the World-Economy* (1995). Current research includes global justice movements, and the international food regime.

James H. Mittelman is professor in the School of International Service at American University, Washington, D.C. Previously, he held the Pok Rafeah Chair at the National University of Malaysia and was awarded a fellowship at the Institute for Advanced Study in Princeton, New Jersey. His books include a series of companion volumes on globalization: *Globalization: Critical Reflections* (editor, Lynne Rienner, 1996), *The Globalization Syndrome: Transformation and Resistance* (Princeton University Press, 2000), *Capturing Globalization* (coeditor, Routledge, 2001), and *Whither Globalization? The Vortex of Knowledge and Ideology* (Routledge, 2004).

Valentine M. Moghadam is director of women's studies and associate professor of sociology at Illinois State University. Born in Tehran, Iran, Moghadam received her higher education in Canada and the United States. After obtaining her Ph.D. in sociology from American University in Washington, D.C., in 1986, she taught the sociology of development and women in development at New York University. Moghadam has written two books, *Modernizing Women: Gender and Social Change in the Middle East* (first published in 1993; updated second edition, 2003) and *Women, Work and Economic Reform in the Middle East and North Africa* (1998). Her third book, *Globalizing Women: Gender, Globalization, and Transnational Feminist Networks*, is to be published by The Johns Hopkins University Press. Her current areas of research are globalization, transnational feminist networks, civil society and citizenship in the Middle East, and women in Afghanistan. She lectures and publishes widely and consults with several international organizations.

Njoki Njoroge Njehu is a Kenyan national who worked with women's groups and the Greenbelt Movement in Kenya for over a decade. She grew up learning from the work of Kenyan women, especially her mother, Lilian Njehû, a grassroots and community activist. Before joining the 50 Years Is Enough Network she worked at Greenpeace International for 3 years, focusing on the international toxic trade and on biodiversity and oceans issues. She joined the 50 Years Is Enough Network in July 1996 and was named director in October 1998. She has testified before the U.S. Congress on African debt, the IMF's Enhanced Structural Adjustment Facility (ESAF) which until 1999 administered the IMF/World Bank structural adjustment programs, and on the role of the African Development Bank in addressing debt, HIV/AIDS, and other crises facing Africa. She is a founding member of the International Coordinating Council of the World Social Forum and the Africa Social Forum.

Darren J. O'Byrne is senior lecturer in sociology and human rights at the University of Surrey, Roehampton, United Kingdom, where he convenes the undergraduate program in human rights, as well as teaching classes on globalization and social theory. He is the author of *Human Rights: An Introduction* (London: Longman, 2002) and *The Dimensions of Global Citizenship: Political Identity Beyond the Nation-State* (London: Frank Cass, 2003), and coeditor of *Global Ethics and Civil Society* (Burlington, Vermont: Ashgate, 2004). He is also the chair of the Global Studies Association.

Rhacel Salazar Parreñas is associate professor of Asian American Studies at the University of California, Davis. She is the author of *Servants of Globalization: Women, Migration, and Domestic Work* (2003) and the forthcoming *Children of Global Migration: Transnational Families and Gendered Woes*.

Jean L. Pyle is a senior associate at the Center for Women and Work and a professor emerita in the Department of Regional Economic and Social Development at the University of Massachusetts, Lowell. An economist, she specializes in the overlapping areas of labor, economic development, and policy, with particular attention to gender and diversity issues. Her recent work shows how the major trends characterizing the recent period of globalization have contributed to the rise of several types of work (sex work, domestic service, and production in subcontracting networks for export) that are distinctly gendered, span the globe, and increasingly involve the migration or trafficking of women. She is the author of *The State and Women in the Economy: Lessons from Sex Discrimination in the Republic of Ireland* (SUNY Press) and she recently coedited *Globalization, Universities, and Issues of Sustainable Human Development* (Edward Elgar) and *Approaches to Sustainable Development: The Public University in the Regional Economy* (University of Massachusetts Press).

William I. Robinson is professor of sociology, global and international studies, and Latin American and Iberian studies at the University of California at Santa Barbara, and is on the executive board of the Global Studies Association. He has lectured broadly in recent years at universities and in public forums in North and Latin America, Africa, East Asia, and Europe on globalization, international affairs, development, the global crisis and social change. His most recent books are: *A Theory of Global Capitalism: Production, Class, and State in a Transnational World* (Baltimore, 2004); *Transnational Conflicts; Central America, Social Change, and Globalization* (London, 2003); and *Promoting Polyarchy: Globalization, U.S. Intervention, and Hegemony* (Cambridge, 1996), which won the Distinguished Scholarship Award from the Political Economy of the World System Section, American Sociological Association.

Anita Roddick started The Body Shop in 1976 in Brighton, England. Twenty-eight years later, The Body Shop — one of the most widely recognized and respected brands in the world — has 2000 stores in 51 different countries. Roddick is a key pioneer of socially responsible business, proving that commerce with a conscience is not merely a moral imperative. She was named a Dame of the Order of the British Empire in 2003. Roddick has written several books, including the autobiographical *Body & Soul* and *Business as Unusual*, and was editor of the popular 2001 title *Take It Personally: How To Make Conscious Choices to Change the World*. Her new publishing company, Anita Roddick Books, published two titles in 2003: *A Revolution in Kindness* and *Brave Hearts, Rebel Spirits: A Spiritual Activists Handbook*. Her website is www.AnitaRoddick.com.

Victor Roudometof is assistant professor with the Department of Social and Political Sciences at the University of Cyprus. He has edited several volumes and authored two books and numerous articles on ethnic conflict, transnationalism, globalization, and post-1989 European politics, Americanization, and religion. Among his latest publications are a special issue of the *Journal of Political and Military Sociology* on the "Politics of Collective Memory" (Vol. 31, No. 2, 2003) and the article "Transnationalism, Cosmopolitanism and Glocalization" (*Current Sociology*, forthcoming). Currently, he is editing a volume on the relationship between Eastern Orthodoxy and globalization.

Saskia Sassen is the Ralph Lewis Professor of Sociology at the University of Chicago, and Centennial Visiting Professor at the London School of Economics. She is currently completing her forthcoming book *Denationalization: Economy and Polity in a Global Digital Age* (Princeton University Press, 2003) based on her 5-year project on governance and accountability in a global economy. Her most recent books are *Guests and Aliens* (New York: New Press, 1999) and her edited book *Global Networks/Linked Cities* (New York and London: Routledge, 2002). *The Global City* came out in a new fully updated edition in 2001. Her books have been translated into ten languages.

Beverly J. Silver is a professor in the Department of Sociology at The Johns Hopkins University. Her research focuses on problems of development, labor, and social conflict, using comparative and world-historical methods of analysis. She is the author of *Forces of Labor: Workers' Movements and Globalization Since 1870* (Cambridge University Press, 2003) and coauthor of *Chaos and Governance in the Modern World System*, University of Minnesota Press, 1999 (winner of the 2001 Distinguished Scholarship Award from the American Sociological Association PEWS Section).

Leslie Sklair is professor of sociology and director of the doctoral program in sociology at the London School of Economics and Political Science. He was the Hans Speier Distinguished Visiting Professor at the Graduate Faculty, New School for Social Research, New York, in Spring 2002. He is author of *The Transnational Capitalist Class* (2001; Chinese edition, 2002; German edition forthcoming). His *Sociology of the Global System* (1991; second edition, revised and updated, 1995) has been translated into Japanese, Portuguese, Persian, Korean, and Spanish. A new version was published by Oxford University Press in 2002 under the title *Globalization: Capitalism and its Alternatives* (Chinese and Portuguese editions forthcoming). He is on the executive committee of the Global Studies Association and on the editorial boards of the journals *Review of International Political Economy* and *Global Networks*.

David A. Smith is a professor of sociology and director of labor studies at the University of California at Irvine. He is the author of *Third World Cities in Global Perspective* (Westview, 1996) and numerous journal articles, and a coeditor of *States and Sovereignty in the Global Economy* (Routledge, 1999) and *Labor, Race and Empire* (Routledge, 2004). His research focuses on urbanization and development, East Asian political economy, global commodity chains, international trade and labor relations, and the world city system. He is a former editor of the journal *Social Problems*.

Molly Talcott is a doctoral candidate in sociology at the University of California at Santa Barbara. Her dissertation research explores gendered struggles with plant bioprospecting, development policies, and intellectual property rights in the context of globalization processes. She is also a community media producer–activist and can be reached at mtalcott@umail.ucsb.edu.

Hung Cam Thai is assistant professor of sociology at the University of California at Santa Barbara. He is currently completing a book with Rutgers University Press titled *For Better or for Worse: Marriage and Migration in the New Global Economy.*

Angie Ngoc Tran is associate professor of political economy, Social and Behavioral Sciences Department, Pacific Rim Studies Institute, California State University, Monterey Bay.

Howard Winant is professor of sociology at the University of California at Santa Barbara. His work focuses on the historical and contemporary importance of race in shaping economic, political, and cultural life, both in the United States and globally. He is the author of *The World Is a Ghetto: Race and Democracy Since World War II* (Basic Books, 2001); *Racial Conditions: Politics, Theory, Comparisons* (University of Minnesota Press, 1994), and *Racial Formation in the United States: From the 1960s to the 1990s* (Routledge, 1994), coauthored with Michael Omi; *The New Politics of Race: Globalism, Difference, Justice,* (University of Minnesota Press in 2004).

Index